Hate Groups and Extremist Organizations in America

Hate Groups and Extremist Organizations in America

An Encyclopedia

Barry J. Balleck

ABC-CLIO™

An Imprint of ABC-CLIO, LLC

Santa Barbara, California • Denver, Colorado

Copyright © 2019 by ABC-CLIO, LLC

Library of Congress Cataloging-in-Publication Data

Names: Balleck, Barry J., author.
Title: Hate groups and extremist organizations in America : an encyclopedia /
    Barry J. Balleck.
Description: Santa Barbara, California : ABC-CLIO, [2019] | Includes
    bibliographical references and index.
Identifiers: LCCN 2019003789| ISBN 9781440857508 (alk. paper) | ISBN
    9781440857515 (ebook)
Subjects: LCSH: Radicalism—United States—Encyclopedias. | Hate
    crimes—United States—Encyclopedias. | Extremists—United
    States—Encyclopedias.
Classification: LCC HN90.R3 B3328 2019 | DDC 303.48/403—dc23
LC record available at https://lccn.loc.gov/2019003789

ISBN: 978-1-4408-5750-8 (print)
        978-1-4408-5751-5 (ebook)

23 22 21 20 19   1 2 3 4 5

This book is also available as an eBook.

ABC-CLIO
An Imprint of ABC-CLIO, LLC

ABC-CLIO, LLC
147 Castilian Drive
Santa Barbara, California 93117
www.abc-clio.com

This book is printed on acid-free paper ∞
Manufactured in the United States of America

Contents

S

T

U

V

W

Preface

This encyclopedia includes a selection of some 200 hate groups and extremist organizations that have been identified by three organizations that are widely recognized for their expertise in the identification and tracking of hate groups. The first, and perhaps most important, organization is the Southern Poverty Law Center (SPLC). Founded in 1971 as a civil rights law firm, the SPLC has maintained information on hate groups and other extremists since the early 1980s. Today, the SPLC tracks more than 1,600 extremist groups in the United States, informing the public through the publication of investigative reports, offering expert analysis to the media, training law enforcement officers, and sharing key intelligence with U.S. law enforcement agencies (Southern Poverty Law Center, Fighting Hate). The second group, the Anti-Defamation League (ADL), was founded in 1913 "to stop the defamation of the Jewish people, and to secure justice and fair treatment to all" (Anti-Defamation League, Our Mission). The ADL maintains files on groups that "threaten our very democracy," tracking incidents of hate, "including cyberhate, bullying, bias in schools and in the criminal justice system, coercion of religious minorities, and contempt for anyone who is different" (Anti-Defamation League, What We Do). Finally, the U.S. Federal Bureau of Investigation (FBI) is the premier "intelligence-driven and threat-focused national security organization" in the United States (Federal Bureau of Investigation, About). One of the FBI's highest priorities is the protection of civil rights, "not only because of the devastating impact they [the violation of civil rights] have on families and communities, but also because groups that preach hatred and intolerance can plant the seed of terrorism here in our country" (Federal Bureau of Investigation, Hate Crimes). The FBI investigates hate crimes, and the individuals and groups that may commit such crimes, when the crimes are "based on a bias against the victim's race, color, religion, or national origin" (Federal Bureau of Investigation, Hate Crimes). Thus, these three organizations—the SPLC, ADL, and FBI— together provide the parameters for the groups covered in these pages.

Although these three organizations may not be the only ones that track hate groups, they are the most noted and respected. While the FBI is an organ of the federal government, there is nevertheless selective bias as to which groups the FBI wishes to report upon. This is certainly true as well in the case of the SPLC and the ADL, both of which use subjective criteria to identify hate groups from what may be admittedly a "left side of the political spectrum" basis. However, this bias is largely unavoidable, as there are no recognized, respectable groups from the "right side" that report such activities. Moreover, this book includes not only groups but movements that may subsume groups within their ideologies. For instance, the white supremacist movement and white nationalism groups may include a variety of organizations that adhere to their ideologies (e.g., Neo-Nazis, KKK groups, and Proud Boys). By the same token, Black Muslims are generally subsumed into the category of black nationalism, which is generally characterized as "broadly anti-Semitic, anti-white and usually anti-LGBT" (Al Jazeera).

A note on language: In the pages that follow, direct quotations retain their original wording. Some of this language may be uncomfortable for the reader. Nonetheless, in order to preserve the hateful language in its original, unvarnished form, the language will appear in its original form in quotations. To omit potentially uncomfortable language is to deny the reader the chance to understand more deeply the nature of these hate groups.

FURTHER READING

Al Jazeera. February 21, 2018. "Hate Groups in US Grow for Third Straight Year: SPLC." Al Jazeera. https://www.aljazeera.com/news/2018/02/hate-groups-grow-straight -year-splc-180221192119355.html. (Accessed December 1, 2018.)

Anti-Defamation League. "Our Mission." Anti-Defamation League. https://www.adl.org /who-we-are/our-mission. (Accessed October 13, 2018.)

Anti-Defamation League. "What We Do." Anti-Defamation League. https://www.adl.org /what-we-do. (Accessed October 13, 2018.)

Federal Bureau of Investigation. "About." Federal Bureau of Investigation. https://www .fbi.gov/about. (Accessed October 13, 2018.)

Federal Bureau of Investigation. "Hate Crimes." Federal Bureau of Investigation. https:// www.fbi.gov/investigate/civil-rights/hate-crimes. (Accessed October 13, 2018.)

Southern Poverty Law Center. "Fighting Hate." Southern Poverty Law Center. https:// www.splcenter.org/fighting-hate. (Accessed October 13, 2018.)

Introduction

In 2017 (the last year for which complete statistics are available), the Southern Poverty Law Center (SPLC), the premier organization for monitoring and tracking hate groups and their activities in the United States, identified 954 hate groups in the country, a 4 percent increase from the 917 groups in 2016 but a 20 percent increase from the number of groups present in 2014. According to the SPLC, "2017 was the third straight year to witness a rise in the number of hate groups. It was also the first year since 2009 that hate groups were documented in all 50 states." Yet even 954 hate groups "likely understates the real level of hate in America because a growing number of extremists, particularly those who identify with the alt-right, operate mainly online and may not be formally affiliated with a hate group" (Southern Poverty Law Center, February 21, 2018).

Like hate groups, hate crimes in the United States rose correspondingly in 2017. The number of hate crimes "topped a previous high, with law enforcement reporting 7,175 incidents—an uptick of 17 percent over the five-year high reached in 2016" (Barrouquere). Yet the number of hate crime incidents reported in 2017 did not include two of the highest profile hate crimes perpetrated that year: the murder of two men in Portland, Oregon, in May 2017 while they were defending Muslim women against a racist, Islamophobic rant and the killing of Heather Heyer in Charlottesville, Virginia, in August 2017 when she was run down by a white supremacist while she was peacefully protesting the "Unite the Right" rally in the city. Why were these crimes not reported as hate crimes? The fact is,

> the vast majority of hate crimes don't get counted. The Bureau of Justice Statistics estimates there are about 250,000 each year. There are several reasons for the vast discrepancy. First, studies show that only about half of all hate crimes get reported to the police. Second, the FBI relies on some 18,000 local enforcement agencies to forward their data to the federal government. Since the system is voluntary, many don't do it. And many that do provide the data simply don't properly identify hate crimes in the first place. In addition, the definition of a hate crime varies from state to state. (Southern Poverty Law Center, November 16, 2018).

The rise in the number of hate groups and amount of hate crime activity in the United States has been buoyed by the administration of President Donald Trump. According to Heidi Beirich, director of SPLC's Intelligence Project, Trump has "stoked the flames of white supremacy and anti-immigrant xenophobia." Beirich notes, "President Trump in 2017 reflected what white supremacist groups want to see: a country where racism is sanctioned by the highest office, immigrants are given the boot and Muslims [are] banned" (Al Jazeera). Critics note that President Trump's rhetoric acts as a sort of dog whistle for white supremacist groups, emboldening those who, until Trump's election, spewed their particular brand of racism in Internet chat rooms and on white supremacist websites. Now, however, these individuals and groups that once lurked in the shadows believe that they have an ally in the White House.

This latest rise in hate group activity has been reported across several categories of groups, including those associated with white supremacist, white nationalist, anti-LGBT, anti-Muslim, anti-Semitic, and black nationalist hate organizations. According to the SPLC, the rise in the number of black nationalist groups is not surprising, given that "the ranks of black nationalist hate groups . . . always rise as a reaction to a rise in white racism" (Southern Poverty Law Center, February 21, 2018). The SPLC is quick to note, however, that unlike white supremacist and white nationalist groups, black nationalist groups "have virtually no supporters or influence in mainstream politics, much less in the White House" (Southern Poverty Law Center, February 21, 2018).

The Anti-Defamation League (ADL), another organization that tracks hate group activity—particularly as it relates to anti-Semitic incidents—"recorded 457 anti-Jewish incidents in *elementary and secondary schools* [emphasis added] in 2017, a 94 percent increase from the 234 in the year prior." Jonathan Greenblatt, chief executive officer of the ADL, has called such increases—documented in the formative years of a child's education—"deeply troubling" (Smith).

The only groups that demonstrated a marked decline in 2017 were the various Ku Klux Klan (KKK) groups, an "indication that the new generation of white supremacists is rejecting the Klan's hoods and robes for the hipper image of the more loosely organized alt-right movement" (Southern Poverty Law Center, February 21, 2018).

WHAT IS "HATE"?

In order to better understand the phenomenon of the rising number of hate groups and hate crimes in the United States today, it is necessary to examine the very definition of "hate" itself. Hate can be considered either as a noun or as a verb. As a noun, hate is an "intense hostility and aversion, usually deriving from fear, anger, or a sense of injury." It is "extreme dislike, or disgust," or, most appropriate to this work, it is "a systematic and especially politically exploited expression of hatred" (*Merriam-Webster*). When paired with another noun, hate becomes a noun adjunct, or an attributive noun—such as in the case of "hate mail," "hate crime," or "hate group" (*Merriam-Webster*). The use of "hate" as an attributive noun makes the resulting compound noun leap off the page, as a term that is immediately intensified and rife with ominous overtones. Finally, as a verb, hate is an action—"to feel extreme enmity toward" someone or something; "to regard with active hostility"; or "to have a strong aversion" to someone or something (*Merriam-Webster*).

The point here is that hate is visceral. It is a basic emotion within the experience of every human being, and all human beings can describe someone or something that they hate or have hated. Yet hate has many subtle shades and meanings. Jose Navarro, a researcher in the Department of Psychology at the University of Cadiz, Spain, describes hate as a "commitment" that is "characterized by ideas of devaluation and reduction of the human characteristics of an individual or group" (Navarro, et al.). As such, hate can be differentiated into seven nominal categories:

1. Accepted hatred. Denial of intimacy only. The hater hates the other, but does not want to act against him/her.

2. Hot hatred. Only passion (anger, fear). Extreme feelings of hatred toward someone who is seen as threatening; the reaction may be to attack or escape. A traffic incident can be an example of this hot hatred.

3. Cold hatred. Only feelings of devaluation or commitment. Something is wrong with the members of the hated group. We have been indoctrinated to characterize this group as the axis of evil, or the evil empire, as the USSR was called.

4. Burning hatred. There is commitment and passion. Characteristic of the hatred towards a group. They are seen as sub human or inhuman and threatening, and something must be done to reduce that threat. The hated group may change from time to time.

5. Simmering hatred. There is denial of intimacy and devaluation of commitment. The individual is seen as unpleasant and always will be. Premeditated killings are sometimes a result of this hatred.

6. Furious hatred. There is passion and devaluation of commitment. There is a feeling of revenge towards the person. These people have always been a threat and always will be. Mass violence often has this feature.

7. All-embracing hatred. There is denial of intimacy, devaluation of commitment and passion. The result is the need to annihilate the other.

As noted by Navarro and his colleagues, hate can be an individual experience, a collective experience, or a combination of both. Understanding the reasons that we hate, then, is perhaps more perplexing than understanding the emotion itself. To this end, extensive research has been conducted regarding the basis for human emotions (see Ortony and Turner). Intuitively, our own experiences with hate come largely from our associations with people we know. In fact, as pointed out by one observer, "the main reasons we hate people include betrayal—including infidelity but also broken promises of other sorts—and intense aversion to others' personalities" (Herbert). We are most likely to "hate" those that we love, or have loved. People generally express their greatest hatred "toward those they are closest to on a daily basis—acquaintances, friends, family, exes. Even within the family, the 'nearest and dearest' arouse the most hatred—fathers especially, followed by mothers, in-laws, sibs [siblings]. Curiously, very few hate their own significant others—just 1 in 100—but far more hate a friend's boyfriend or girl-friend" (Herbert).

But when we ask the question of why we would hate those that we don't know, have never met, have never been acquainted with, or have never associated with, the reasons for hate become more complex. One behavioral researcher, Patrick Wanis, has suggested that hatred of others, either individuals or groups, can be explained by the "in-group out-group theory," which posits

> that when we feel threatened by perceived outsiders, we instinctively turn toward our in-group—those with whom we identify—as a survival mechanism. Wanis explains, "Hatred is driven by two key emotions of love and aggression: One, love for the in-group—the group that is favored; and two, aggression for the out-group—the group that has been deemed as being different, dangerous, and a threat to the in-group." (Abrams)

The "fear of others" can also be coupled with "fear of ourselves." Clinical psychologist Dana Harron has suggested that

> the things people hate about others are the things that they fear within themselves. She suggests thinking about the targeted group or person as a movie screen onto which we project unwanted parts of the self. The idea is, "I'm not terrible; you are."
>
> This phenomenon is known as projection, a term coined by Freud to describe our tendency to reject what we don't like about ourselves. Psychologist Brad Reedy further describes projection as our need to be good, which causes us to project "badness" outward and attack it: "We developed this method to survive, for any 'badness' in us put us at risk for being rejected and alone. So we repressed the things that we thought were bad (what others told us or suggested to us that was unlovable and morally reprehensible)—and we employ hate and judgment towards others. We think that is how one rids oneself of undesirable traits, but this method only perpetuates repression which leads to many mental health issues."(Abrams)

Explanations of the hate toward others can also be found, not only in a basic lack of self-compassion or empathy toward others, but also in societal and cultural factors. According to Silvia Dutchevici, president and founder of the Critical Therapy Center, the answer as to why we hate

> lies not only in our psychological makeup or family history, but also in our cultural and political history. "We live in a war culture that promotes violence, in which competition is a way of life," she says. "We fear connecting because it requires us to reveal something about ourselves. We are taught to hate the enemy—meaning anyone different than us—which leaves little room for vulnerability and an exploration of hate through empathic discourse and understanding. In our current society, one is more ready to fight than to resolve conflict. Peace is seldom the option." (Abrams)

And last, and perhaps most important for the purposes of this work, we hate those whom we don't know because "it fills a void." According to psychologist Bernard Golden,

> Acts of hate are attempts to distract oneself from feelings such as helplessness, powerlessness, injustice, inadequacy and shame. Hate is grounded in some sense of perceived threat. It is an attitude that can give rise to hostility and aggression toward individuals or groups. Like much of anger, it is a reaction to and distraction from some form of inner pain. The individual consumed by hate may believe that the

only way to regain some sense of power over his or her pain is to preemptively strike out at others. In this context, each moment of hate is a temporary reprieve from inner suffering. (Abrams)

As will be evident from the entries in this book, many of those who choose to hate—and it should be clear that it is a conscious choice that many are making to hate individuals or groups whom they have never met—do so out of feelings of "powerlessness, injustice, inadequacy and shame" and that the only way they believe that they can regain their power "is to preemptively strike out at others" (Abrams). As many of the entries in this encyclopedia will attest, those in the United States who have felt that recent social, demographic, and political changes in the country have contributed to their feelings of powerlessness are far more likely to associate with hate groups than do those who are more comfortable with such change.

A cursory overview of the entries contained within this text will demonstrate that the vast majority of "participants" in hate group activity tend to be whites, and particularly white males. This is not to suggest that there are not dozens of hate groups that are made up by a majority of African Americans, Hispanics, Asians, Muslims—or any other combination of a number of racial, ethnic, or religious ties. But in the United States today, whites, and particularly white males, feel "outnumbered." As noted by Michele Norris of *National Geographic*:

Outnumbered is a word that came up often when I talked with white residents of this eastern Pennsylvania town [Hazelton]. Outnumbered in the waiting room at the doctor's office. Outnumbered at the bank. Outnumbered at the Kmart, where the cashier merrily chitchats in Spanish with Hazelton's newer residents. (Norris)

Norris notes that Hazelton's experience

offers a glimpse into the future as white Americans confront the end of their majority status, which often has meant that their story, their traditions, their tastes, and their cultural aesthetic were seen as being quintessentially American. This is a conversation already exploding across the country as some white Americans, in online forums and protests over the removal of Confederate monuments, react anxiously and angrily to a sense that their way of life is under threat. Those are the stories that grab headlines and trigger social media showdowns. But the shift in status—or what some are calling "the altitude adjustment"—is also playing out in much more subtle ways in classrooms, break rooms, factory floors, and shopping malls, where the future has arrived ahead of schedule. Since 2000, the minority population has grown to outnumber the population of whites who aren't Hispanic in such counties as Suffolk in Massachusetts, Montgomery in Maryland, Mecklenburg in North Carolina, as well as counties in California, Colorado, Florida, Georgia, New Jersey, and Texas. (Norris)

Norris notes ominously that

there is growing evidence that race is no longer a spectator sport for white Americans: The growth of whiteness studies courses on college campuses. Battles over immigration and affirmative action. A rising death rate for middle-aged white Americans with no more than a high-school diploma from drugs, alcohol, and suicide in what economists are calling "deaths of despair." The increasingly racially polarized electorate. The popularity of a television show called Dear White People that satirizes "post-racial" America. The debate over the history and symbols of the Confederacy. The aggression and appeal of white nationalism, with its newest menacing chant: "You will not replace us." (Norris)

Thus, hate arises "as an essential survival strategy." Indeed, as human beings our basic reaction is to "assign blame for misfortune," "protect our self-esteem," protect and strengthen our community, and "alleviate our fears" (Beaumont). According to Leland R. Beaumont—the creator and webmaster of the websites "Emotional Competency" and "Wise Path"—our "ability to quickly separate friend from foe" is essential to our survival. Moreover, "[b]ecause mistaking an enemy for a friend can be deadly, mental processes are biased toward doubt, caution, mistrust, and dismissal in evaluating others" (Beaumont). Fortunately,

> an unbiased consideration of the evidence, correct thinking, thoughtful dialogue, and empathy can overcome the primitive urges of hatred and the cognitive errors that sustain it. Today many threats are psychological rather than physical, but the same primitive impulse to destroy the offender often takes hold. (Beaumont)

As pointed out by Beaumont, hate is a "biased" mental process that arises from ignorance, mistrust, lack of information, and lack of empathy. Yet these deficiencies can be overcome by "unbiased" observations, "correct" thinking, thoughtful dialogue, and an increased capacity for empathy—all things that are rarely exhibited when someone is steeped in hate.

WHAT DEFINES A "HATE GROUP"?

The SPLC defines a hate group as "an organization that—based on its official statements or principles, the statements of its leaders, or its activities—has beliefs or practices that attack or malign an entire class of people, typically for their immutable characteristics" (Southern Poverty Law Center, Frequently Asked Questions). According to the SPLC, the organizations that they identify as hate groups "vilify others because of their race, religion, ethnicity, sexual orientation or gender identity—prejudices that strike at the heart of our democratic values and fracture society along its most fragile fault lines" (Southern Poverty Law Center, Frequently Asked Questions). The FBI uses similar criteria when defining a hate crime: "[A] criminal offense against a person or property motivated in whole or in part by an offender's bias against a race, religion, disability, sexual orientation, ethnicity, gender, or gender identity" (Federal Bureau of Investigation, Hate Crimes).

The SPLC further defines a group

> as an entity that has a process through which followers identify themselves as being part of the group. This may involve donating, paying membership dues or participating in activities such as meetings and rallies. Individual chapters of a larger organization are each counted separately, because the number indicates reach and organizing activity. (Southern Poverty Law Center, Frequently Asked Questions)

Of course very few groups will self-identify as hate groups, and virtually all of the organizations covered within this text would probably claim that they do not hate anyone. Their defenders will mimic this mantra. For instance, in August 2018, then U.S. Attorney General Jeff Sessions told one SPLC-designated hate group that they were, in fact, "not a hate group," claiming "that the term is simply a 'weapon [wielded] against conservative organizations that refuse to accept their orthodoxy and choose instead to speak their conscience'" (Jarrett). The group Sessions was defending—the Alliance Defending Freedom (ADF)—is a "far-right Christian group" that "has a long history of homophobia and transphobia, including pushing to legalize so-called 'conversion therapy' of gay people, and backing the forced sterilization of transgender people in Europe" (Schwartz). For Sessions, such views are perfectly acceptable, and he insisted that "groups like yours [the ADF] fight for the religious freedom, the civil rights, and the constitutional rights of others" (Schwartz). In criticizing the SPLC's designation of the ADF as a hate group, Sessions stated: "They [the SPLC] use it [the designation as a hate group] to intimidate groups like yours, which fight for religious freedom, which is indeed the civil rights, the constitutional rights of American people" (Resnick).

But the ADF is not the only group that takes exception to the "hate group" designation placed on it by the Southern Poverty Law Center. Another SPLC-designated hate group—the Family Research Council (FRC)—is widely recognized as "one of the country's largest and most established Christian advocacy groups" (Schreckinger). Yet the FRC, citing research, has claimed that "homosexuality is harmful to children and families," a claim that the group contends does not constitute "hate" (Mellinger). Yet the SPLC has responded to such claims by pointing out that "[t]he FRC often makes false claims about the LGBT community based on discredited research and junk science" (Schreckinger).

Designation of an organization as a hate group is "'invariably going to be controversial,' said Brian Levin, director of the Center for the Study of Hate and Extremism at California State University at San Bernardino and a former Southern Poverty Law Center employee" (Stiffman). To assemble their hate group list, the SPLC

> fields tips and scours websites, message boards and news reports to compile its directory of 917 mostly ring-wing hate groups. But finding and defining hate groups is not exactly a science, leaving the process open to criticism even under the best of circumstances. (Schreckinger)

J. M. Berger, "a researcher on extremism and a fellow with the International Centre for Counter-Terrorism at The Hague," says that

> defining a hate or extremist group is notoriously problematic when using extensive, technical criteria, and that the problem becomes greater in the case of the SPLC, which reserves discretion in how and when it applies those labels. "There's no consensus academic definition of extremism, and the SPLC's methodology for making that call isn't clear," he says. "So it's very subjective even within academia, and even more so for a motivated organization." (Schreckinger)

While calling the SPLC's hate group list "principled," Brian Levin states that the list is "incomplete—leaving out, for example, groups viewed as far left" (Stiffman). Heidi Beirich, director of the SPLC's Intelligence Report, notes that the SPLC "does include in its hate group list several left-wing organizations" but "concedes that the SPLC prioritizes the other end of the political spectrum. 'We are focused, whether people like it or not, on the radical right. . . . We believe that it's uniquely threatening to democracy'" (Schreckinger). Such selectiveness, according to J. M. Berger, creates a problem in that "the organization [SPLC] wears two hats, as both an activist group and a source of information" (Schreckinger).

Though selective bias is no doubt a reason that many groups object to finding themselves on a list accusing them of hate, another, more powerful reason may be that many of the groups that find themselves labeled as hate groups by the SPLC, ADL, or FBI are designated by the U.S. federal government as nonprofit organizations. Thus, admitting to impropriety would be expensive. Groups can be granted tax-exempt status for a variety of reasons, including purposes that are "most commonly educational, charitable, or religious." However, an organization can only be considered tax-exempt "if it produces materials that are factually supported and which allow people to make up their mind about a particular viewpoint. Distorting facts, providing only unsupported opinions, or using inflammatory or disparaging terms based on emotions rather than facts may influence the IRS determination" (Stiffman).

The federal government has "granted tax-exempt status to more than 60 controversial nonprofits branded by critics as 'hate groups,' including anti-immigrant and anti-gay-rights organizations, white nationalists, and Holocaust deniers" (Stiffman). Yet the IRS "must balance First Amendment rights against concerns that it is essentially granting government subsidies to groups holding views that millions of Americans may find abhorrent" (Stiffman). Critics claim that the SPLC is a tool of the left, and criticize the IRS for having "discriminated against conservative political organizations." The federal government, therefore, must be "careful about what we're [the IRS] requiring the public to subsidize through tax exemption and at the same time we want not to inhibit speech too much" (Stiffman).

But some organizations are "increasingly pushing the boundaries of how far they can go and still meet the standard for tax exemption" (Stiffman). Take, for instance, the National Policy Institute (NPI), headed by Richard Spencer, who became infamous for hailing "President-elect [Donald] Trump's victory with a Nazi-style salute" at a December 2016 meeting of the NPI (Stiffman). During Trump's campaign, Spencer warned white Americans that they were increasingly under siege in their own country and "doomed to be a hated minority as people of color grow ever more numerous and politically powerful" (Marans). The NPI's senior fellows include Wayne Lutton, an author on the extreme right; Jared Taylor, editor of *American Renaissance*, which promotes pseudoscientific studies and research that purports to show the inferiority of blacks to whites; and Kevin Lamb, a noted racist (Southern Poverty Law Center, Groups). The NPI realizes that whether it is due to economic stagnation, a culture of xenophobia and fear, a growing distrust for the government and traditional institutions, or a myriad of other causes, "people's loyalties are up for grabs" (Ellis). Spencer has reinforced this notion by stating:

> America as it is currently constituted—and I don't just mean the government; I mean America as constituted spiritually and ideologically—is the fundamental problem. I don't support and agree with much of anything America is doing in the world. (Wines and Saul)

Ironically, the NPI lost its tax-exempt status in March 2017 for failing to file tax returns for three years, a move Spencer believed was "retaliatory." However, the group regained its status in October 2018 (Jones). Spencer, who popularized the term "alt-right," called the status change a "nice, small victory" but noted that NPI's "deplatforming" by online payment processors (such as PayPal and Stripe) in the aftermath of the Charlottesville "Unite the Right" rally in August 2017 was an even bigger blow to the group, as "losing access to those services has been a bigger obstacle to fundraising than losing tax-exempt status" (CBS News).

Though NPI's designation as a hate group may admittedly be subjective, there is little doubt that many of those who claim membership in such organizations exhibit the passions from which hate arises—in other words, the desire to assign blame to others for misfortune; to protect self-esteem; to protect and strengthen community; to alleviate fears; and to distance oneself from those deemed harmful (Beaumont).

In the aftermath of the Charlottesville, Virginia, "Unite the Right" rally in August 2017, in which hundreds of young white males marched while chanting the words "You will not replace us" and the Nazi slogan "Blood and Soil," there were "a lot of people [who] were disturbed and surprised to see that these white nationalists were mostly young, male, and dressed like suburban dads in tan khakis and golf shirts, not white hoods or studded black leather" (Pazzanese).

Bart Banikowski, associate professor in Harvard's Sociology Department and a faculty affiliate at the Center for European Studies and the Weatherhead Center for International Affairs, noted that the participants at Charlottesville were a new type of white supremacist:

> The fact that many of these people were middle-class white men is not surprising at all. White supremacist groups have long had support among middle-class Americans and not just the poor and uneducated. That's been the case throughout U.S. history. It also shows that the kind of racial resentment that Trump draws on cannot be fully attributed to economic anxiety. For some supporters it is, but not overwhelmingly and not exclusively. These are people who lead reasonably comfortable lives, but what they perceive as a threat is a change to the demographic and cultural makeup of the country. They have a strong sense of subjective status loss and white victimization. These are long-standing narratives. So the fact that they're middle class is not surprising. On the other hand, the fact that they're not wearing masks, that they're willing to show their faces, suggests that they're emboldened, and they think that their ideology is seen as legitimate by at least some people, including presumably the administration. This is clearly an effort to demonstrate mainstream appeal. (Pazzanese)

Hate groups have always existed, and there is no reason to assume that they will disappear any time soon, given the natural human propensity to see others as enemies. As noted above, such bias against others can only be overcome by "unbiased consideration," "correct thinking," "thoughtful dialogue," and "empathy." Unfortunately, such "unbiased" traits seem in short supply. Though the threats that many individuals and groups perceive that cause them to hate are "psychological and not physical," the "same primitive impulse to destroy the offender often takes hold" (Beaumont). Until societies can find ways to temper their distrust of those different from themselves, hate will continue its march through our collective experience.

FURTHER READING

Abrams, Allison. March 9, 2017. "The Psychology of Hate." *Psychology Today*. https://www.psychologytoday.com/us/blog/nurturing-self-compassion/201703/the-psychology-hate. (Accessed October 13, 2018.)

Al Jazeera. February 21, 2018. "Hate Groups in US Grow for Third Straight Year: SPLC." Al Jazeera. https://www.aljazeera.com/news/2018/02/hate-groups-grow-straight-year-splc-180221192119355.html. (Accessed December 1, 2018.)

Anti-Defamation League. "Our Mission." Anti-Defamation League. https://www.adl.org/who-we-are/our-mission. (Accessed October 13, 2018.)

Anti-Defamation League. "What We Do." Anti-Defamation League. https://www.adl.org/what-we-do. (Accessed October 13, 2018.)

Barrouquere, Brett. November 16, 2018. "FBI: Hate Crime Numbers Soar to 7,106 in 2017; Third Worst Year Since Start of Data Collection." Southern Poverty Law Center: Hatewatch. https://www.splcenter.org/hatewatch/2018/11/16/fbi-hate-crime-numbers-soar-7106-2017-third-worst-year-start-data-collection. (Accessed December 1, 2018.)

Beaumont, Leland R. 2009. "Hate." Emotional Competency. http://www.emotionalcompetency.com/hate.htm. (Accessed October 20, 2018.)

Berg, Sven. August 19, 2017. "Why Is a Church on List of Idaho Hate Groups with KKK, Neo-Nazis?" *Idaho Statesman*. https://www.idahostatesman.com/news/northwest/idaho/article168227847.html. (Accessed October 20, 2018.)

Berg, Sven. April 22, 2018. "The Churches Are 'Hate Groups,' a Watchdog Says. But What's Really Behind That Label?" *Idaho Statesman*. https://www.idahostatesman.com/news/northwest/idaho/article209568694.html. (Accessed October 20, 2018.)

CBS News. October 4, 2018. "Richard Spencer's Alt-Right Group Regains Tax-Exempt Status." CBS News. https://www.cbsnews.com/news/richard-spencer-national-policy-institute-alt-right-regains-tax-exempt-status/. (Accessed October 20, 2018.)

Ellis, Emma Grey. October 9, 2016. "How the Alt-Right Grew from an Obscure Racist Cabal." *Wired*. https://www.wired.com/2016/10/alt-right-grew-obscure-racist-cabal/. (Accessed October 20, 2018.)

Federal Bureau of Investigation. "About." Federal Bureau of Investigation. https://www.fbi.gov/about. (Accessed October 13, 2018.)

Federal Bureau of Investigation. "Hate Crimes." Federal Bureau of Investigation. https://www.fbi.gov/investigate/civil-rights/hate-crimes. (Accessed October 13, 2018.)

Heim, Joe. February 21, 2018. "Hate Groups in the U.S. Remain on the Rise, According to New Study." *Washington Post*. https://www.washingtonpost.com/local/hate-groups-in-the-us-remain-on-the-rise-according-to-new-study/2018/02/21/6d28cbe0-1695-11e8-8b08-027a6ccb38eb_story.html. (Accessed December 1, 2018.)

Herbert, Wray. May 23, 2014. "The Anatomy of Everyday Hatred." Huffpost. https://www.huffingtonpost.com/wray-herbert/the-anatomy-of-everyday-h_b_5380440.html. (Accessed October 13, 2018.)

Jarrett, Laura. August 8, 2018. "Sessions: Group That Backed Baker Who Turned Away Gay Couple Not a 'Hate Group.'" CNN. https://www.cnn.com/2018/08/08/politics/jeff-sessions-adf/index.html. (Accessed December 6, 2018.)

Jones, Alexandra. October 5, 2018. "Tax-Exempt Status Restored for White Nationalist Group." Courthouse News Service. https://www.courthousenews.com/tax -exempt-status-restored-for-white-nationalist-group/. (Accessed October 20, 2018.)

Link, Taylor. March 14, 2017. "Richard Spencer's Nonprofit, Pro-Hate National Policy Institute Lost Its Tax-Exempt Status." Salon. http://www.salon.com/2017/03/14 /richard-spencers-nonprofit-pro-hate-national-policy-institute-lost-its-tax -exempt-status/. (Accessed October 20, 2018.)

Marans, Daniel. March 7, 2016. "How Trump Is Inspiring a New Generation of White Nationalists." Huffington Post. http://www.huffingtonpost.com/entry/trump -white-nationalists_us_56dd99c2e4b0ffe6f8e9ee7c. (Accessed October 20, 2018.)

Mellinger, Mark. "The Debate over 'Hate.'" Focus on the Family. https://www.focuson thefamily.com/socialissues/citizen-magazine/the-debate-over-hate. (Accessed October 20, 2018.)

Merriam-Webster. "Definition of Hate." *Merriam-Webster.* https://www.merriam-web ster.com/dictionary/hate. (Accessed October 13, 2018.)

Navarro, Jose I., Esperanza Marchena, and Immaculada Menacho. 2013. *The Open Criminology Journal.* Issue 6. https://benthamopen.com/contents/pdf/TOCRIJ/TOCRIJ -6-10.pdf. (Accessed October 13, 2018.)

Norris, Michele. April 2018. "As America Changes, Some Anxious Whites Feel Left Behind." *National Geographic.* https://www.nationalgeographic.com/magazine /2018/04/race-rising-anxiety-white-america/?user.testname=none. (Accessed October 20, 2018.)

Ortony, A., and T. J. Turner. 1990. "What's Basic about Basic Emotions?" *Psychological Review.* Vol. 97 (3). https://www.researchgate.net/publication/21485724_What's _Basic_About_Basic_Emotions. (Accessed October 20, 2018.)

Pazzanese, Christina. August 15, 2017. "The Focal Point: White Supremacy." *Harvard Gazette.* https://news.harvard.edu/gazette/story/2017/08/charlottesville-violence -gives-white-supremacist-movement-the-attention-it-wanted-professor-says/. (Accessed October 20, 2018.)

Resnick, Sofia. August 9, 2018. "Sessions Defends Controversial Organization against Hate Group Designation." Rewire News. https://rewire.news/article/2018/08/09 /sessions-defends-controversial-organization-against-hate-group-designation/. (Accessed December 6, 2018.)

Schreckinger, Ben. July–August 2017. "Has a Civil Rights Stalwart Lost Its Way?" Politico. https://www.politico.com/magazine/story/2017/06/28/morris-dees-splc-trump -southern-poverty-law-center-215312. (Accessed October 20, 2018.)

Schwartz, Rafi. August 8, 2018. "Jeff Sessions Assures Anti-LGBTQ Hate Group They're Okie-Dokie." Splinter News. https://splinternews.com/jeff-sessions-assures-anti -lgbtq-hate-group-theyre-okie-1828221520. (Accessed October 13, 2018.)

Smith, Kate. November 13, 2018. "Acts of Hate Rise among American Teens." CBS News. https://www.cbsnews.com/news/acts-of-hate-rise-among-american-teens-anti -defamation-league-report-and-fbi-hate-crimes-statistics-suggest/. (Accessed December 1, 2018.)

Southern Poverty Law Center. "Fighting Hate." Southern Poverty Law Center. https:// www.splcenter.org/fighting-hate. (Accessed October 13, 2018.)

Southern Poverty Law Center. "Frequently Asked Questions about Hate Groups." Southern Poverty Law Center. https://www.splcenter.org/20171004/frequently-asked -questions-about-hate-groups#hate%20group. (Accessed October 13, 2018.)

Southern Poverty Law Center. "The Groups." Southern Poverty Law Center: Intelligence Report. https://www.splcenter.org/fighting-hate/intelligence-report/2015/groups. (Accessed October 20, 2018.)

Southern Poverty Law Center. February 21, 2018. "The Year in Hate: Trump Buoyed White Supremacists in 2017, Sparking Backlash among Black Nationalist Groups." https://www.splcenter.org/news/2018/02/21/year-hate-trump-buoyed-white -supremacists-2017-sparking-backlash-among-black-nationalist. (Accessed December 1, 2018.)

Southern Poverty Law Center. November 16, 2018. "Weekend Read: The FBI Is Massively Undercounting Hate Crimes." Southern Poverty Law Center. https://www .splcenter.org/news/2018/11/16/weekend-read-fbi-massively-undercounting-hate -crimes. (Accessed December 1, 2018.)

Stiffman, Eden. December 22, 2016. "Dozens of 'Hate Groups' Have Charity Status, Chronicle Study Finds." *Chronicle of Philanthropy.* https://www.philanthropy .com/article/Dozens-of-Hate-Groups-/238748. (Accessed October 20, 2018.)

Wines, Michael, and Stephanie Saul. July 5, 2015. "White Supremacists Extend Their Reach through Websites." *New York Times.* https://www.nytimes.com/2015/07/06 /us/white-supremacists-extend-their-reach-through-websites.html?_r=1. (Accessed October 20, 2018.)

Hate Groups and Extremist Organizations in America

A

ACT for America

ACT for America is "characterized by the Southern Poverty Law Center (SPLC) as an anti-Muslim hate group." According to the SPLC:

> all anti-Muslim hate groups exhibit extreme hostility toward Muslims. The organizations portray those who worship Islam as fundamentally alien and attribute to its followers an inherent set of negative traits. Muslims are depicted as irrational, intolerant and violent, and their faith is frequently depicted as sanctioning pedophilia, coupled with intolerance for homosexuals and women.
>
> These groups also typically hold conspiratorial views regarding the inherent danger to America posed by its Muslim-American community. Muslims are viewed as a fifth column intent on undermining and eventually replacing American democracy and Western civilization with Islamic despotism, a conspiracy theory known as "civilization jihad." Anti-Muslim hate groups allege that Muslims are trying to subvert the rule of law by imposing on Americans their own Islamic legal system, Shariah law. (Southern Poverty Law Center, Anti-Muslim)

Calling itself the "NRA [National Rifle Association] of national security," ACT for America claims to be the "nation's largest and most influential national security grassroots advocacy" (ACT for America, About ACT). Claiming "more than 750,000 members and over 1,000 local chapters," ACT for America is dedicated to "protecting the United States of America and the Western values upon which our nation was built" as well as "supporting Israel" (Act for America, About ACT).

ACT For America "was founded in 2007 by Brigitte Gabriel, born Hanan Qahwaji" and was "launched as a response to the 9/11 attacks and educates citizens and elected officials to impact policy involving national security and defeating terrorism" (Southern Poverty Law Center, ACT for America). Gabriel is a Lebanese Christian who has published two controversial books that portray Islam as an imminent threat to the United States. In public statements, Gabriel has referred to Arabs as "barbarians" (Southern Poverty Law Center, ACT for America). The *"New York Times Magazine* has described her as a 'radical Islamophobe' " (Lenz). Gabriel wrote her books as a call to action to America for what she calls the "truth behind Islam that she says she learned as a child during the civil war in Lebanon" (Lenz). She has told the *New York Times* that "America has been infiltrated on all levels by radicals who wish to harm America. They have infiltrated us at the CIA, at the FBI, at the Pentagon, at the State Department" (Lenz). Gabriel has claimed that "any Muslim that follows the explicit tenets of Islam cannot be a loyal citizen of the United States" (Lenz).

According to the SPLC, ACT has "stayed true to its mission by working to advance anti-Muslim legislation at the local and federal level while flooding the

American public with hate speech demonizing Muslims" (Southern Poverty Law Center, ACT for America). ACT's agenda has been to lobby state governments in favor of laws banning sharia (Islamic) law. Legal experts

> call such anti-Sharia measures superfluous because there is no mechanism by which any foreign criminal or civil code can trump U.S. laws. By the summer of 2013, however, anti-foreign law measures had passed in Texas, Oklahoma, Alabama, Arizona, Tennessee, South Dakota, North Carolina, Louisiana and Kansas. Since 2010, there have been at least 201 anti-Sharia laws introduced in 43 states. (Southern Poverty Law Center, ACT for America)

ACT for America has also ventured into anti-LGBT territory, as Gabriel "has been a regular guest on the radio shows of anti-LGBT figures" and has addressed the Family Research Council's "'Watchman at the Wall Conference,' an event that routinely attracts some of the most prominent anti-LGBT figures" (Southern Poverty Law Center, ACT for America).

ACT openly supported Donald Trump's presidential campaign and celebrated when Trump captured the presidency, "knowing that the group would have a direct line to the president" (Southern Poverty Law Center, ACT for America). Trump's appointment of two key ACT allies, Gen. Mike Flynn as a key adviser and Mike Pompeo as CIA director, have elevated the public profile of the organization. In the past, Flynn has characterized Islam as "a cancer," and Pompeo "addressed ACT's national conference in 2013 and 2015" (Southern Poverty Law Center, ACT for America).

So-called patriot groups, "such as Oath Keepers and the Three Percenters," have embraced the philosophies of ACT for America. The group has also been "embraced by other, more mainstream groups, such as evangelical Christian conservatives, hard-line defenders of Israel (both Jews and Christians), and 'Tea Party' Republicans" (Goodstein). Though the group intends to "shroud its character with several agenda items that seem more palatable to a broader swath of Americans," its antiterrorism message seems to be paramount. In 2011, a *New York Times* article, speaking of the group and particularly of Gabriel, stated that "[she] presents a portrait of Islam so thoroughly bent on destruction and domination that it is unrecognizable to those who study or practice the religion" (Elliott).

In 2018, in an attempt to expand its reach to college campuses, ACT for America "launched a new project called 'Campus Hate Watch' to 'expose and challenge college or university employees who discriminate against student's (sic) First Amendment rights and spread hateful propaganda inside the classroom'" (Hatewatch staff). ACT "claims it will be monitoring faculty who are supposedly spewing 'anti-Americanism' rhetoric and 'anti-Semitism,'" though it "makes no mention of those who might be challenging anti-Muslim hate" (Hatewatch staff).

See also: Bureau on American Islamic Relations; Center for Security Policy; Family Research Council; Family Security Matters; Oath Keepers; Three Percenters

FURTHER READING

ACT for America. "About ACT." ACT for America. http://www.actforamerica.org/aboutact. (Accessed June 27, 2018.)

ACT for America. "Official Policy Statement." ACT for America. http://www.actfora merica.org/policy. (Accessed June 27, 2018.)

Elliott, Andrea. July 30, 2011. "The Man behind the Anti-Shariah Movement." *New York Times*. https://www.nytimes.com/2011/07/31/us/31shariah.html. (Accessed June 27, 2018.)

Goodstein, Laurie. March 7, 2011. "Drawing U.S. Crowds with Anti-Islam Message." *New York Times*. https://www.nytimes.com/2011/03/08/us/08gabriel.html. (Accessed June 27, 2018.)

Hatewatch Staff. June 22, 2018. "Anti-Muslim Round-Up: 6/22/18." Southern Poverty Law Center: Hatewatch. https://www.splcenter.org/hatewatch/2018/06/22/anti -muslim-round-62218. (Accessed June 27, 2018.)

Lenz, Ryan. August 24, 2011. "Acting Out." Southern Poverty Law Center: Intelligence Report. https://www.splcenter.org/fighting-hate/intelligence-report/2015/acting-out. (Accessed June 27, 2018.)

Piggot, Stephen. October 2, 2017. "Despite Major Setbacks, Anti-Muslim Hate Group ACT for America Kicks Off Its Annual Conference Today in Virginia." Southern Poverty Law Center: Hatewatch. https://www.splcenter.org/hatewatch/2017/10/02 /despite-major-setbacks-anti-muslim-hate-group-act-america-kicks-its-annual -conference-today. (Accessed June 27, 2018.)

Southern Poverty Law Center. "ACT for America." Southern Poverty Law Center. https://www.splcenter.org/fighting-hate/extremist-files/group/act-america. (Accessed June 27, 2018.)

Southern Poverty Law Center. "Anti-Muslim." Southern Poverty Law Center. https:// www.splcenter.org/fighting-hate/extremist-files/ideology/anti-muslim. (Accessed June 27, 2018.)

Southern Poverty Law Center. "#Counteracthate: Call Out ACT for America's Hate." Southern Poverty Law Center. https://www.splcenter.org/counteracthate-call-out -act-americas-hate. (Accessed June 27, 2018.)

ACTBAC NC

The Alamance County Taking Back Alamance County (ACTBAC NC) organization, which was founded in 2015, is "a fledgling neo-Confederate group based in North Carolina" (Hatewatch staff). According to the Southern Poverty Law Center (SPLC), ACTBAC NC is a neo-Confederate hate group. Groups designated as neo-Confederacy groups are dedicated "to a reactionary, revisionist predilection for symbols of the Confederate States of America (CSA), typically paired with a strong belief in the validity of the failed doctrines of nullification and secession— in the specific context of the antebellum South—which rose to prominence in the late 20th and early 21st centuries." Neo-Confederacy "also incorporates advocacy of traditional gender roles, is hostile toward democracy, strongly opposes homosexuality and exhibits an understanding of race that favors segregation and suggests white supremacy" (Southern Poverty Law Center, Neo-Confederate). According to ACTBAC NC's "story":

> In the past few years, months, weeks, and most importantly DAYS, our rights as Americans have been taking away and and [sic] most Importantly [sic] to me, OUR SOUTHERN RIGHTS!! This is not just to support our precious Confederate Flag but to support our rights as American Citizens and at any point and time our Religion, our morals, our Heritage, our well being as a Country is taken away, we need

to stand up and at some point take matters into our own hands!! There are a few that are willing and wanting and I hope we can grow to make it possible that if we cant [sic] change the world at least we can protect our small piece of ground we call home!! Alamance County!! Maybe if we start to take small issues into our own hands as the people we can have others follow and make a solid stand. (ACTBAC NC, 2018)

ACTBAC NC was founded in 2015, the same year in which Dylann Roof "killed nine black parishioners at an historic black church in Charleston, South Carolina" (Burton Wire). Roof's Facebook page—which was littered with images of the Confederate flag and with references to the inspiration he drew from white supremacist organizations, such as the Council of Conservative Citizens (CCC)—prompted a backlash against the Confederate flag around the country. In South Carolina's capital city, Columbia, the Confederate flag was ceremoniously retired from the capitol grounds, where it had flown for more than 50 years (HuffPost). On its website, Southern Heritage Preservation, ACTBAC NC provides greater insights into its mission to preserve the heritage of the Confederacy:

> Founded right in the heart of Alamance County, NC. by Gary Williamson, ACT-BAC started as a group that is willing and wanting to preserve our Southern rights and grow to show our support for not only our county but our state as a whole when faced with issues against our Confederate history. We hope to broaden our efforts by addressing more pressing issues related to the Constitution of the United States that directly affects us all. ACTBAC has successfully organized numerous support rallies to gain recognition and support for our Confederate monuments and their history that we greatly value and cherish. We aim to preserve the southern history that we know and love and hope to one day have everyone come together and uphold not only our southern roots, but our constitutional rights as Americans as well. (ACTBAC NC, About)

In 2017, the SPLC designated ACTBAC NC as a neo-Confederate hate group. ACTBAC's founder, Gary Williamson, called the designation "basically blasphemy" and stated, "There's no reason whatsoever we should even be on there. We have no reason to be on there. There is nothing we've ever done that expresses racism or hate. . . . The reason we made it on there is strictly because we hold Confederate rallies" (Janicello). In 2018, the group was again listed as a hate group by the SPLC, specifically because an Identity Evropa banner had been strung at one of its rallies (Identity Evropa is a white supremacist group that focuses on the preservation of "white American culture") and because SPLC claimed that ACTBAC had posted "anti-Muslim material online" (Croxton). Williamson stated that the Identity Evropa banner had been hoisted without the group's knowledge ("At the time, I didn't even know who Evropa was") and that the anti-Muslim material had been removed from its Facebook page (Croxton). Nevertheless, the SPLC claimed that "ACTBAC's pro-Confederate flag mantra" put it in a relationship with one of the most virulent neo-Confederate hate groups on the SPLC's list: the League of the South (LOS).

In March 2018, ACTBAC announced "plans to raise multiple Confederate flags along highways across North Carolina . . . primarily on four sites in the Orange County region, including areas along U.S. 70 in Hillsborough, NC-54 outside of

Chapel Hill and Interstates 40 and 85" (Tate). ACTBAC undertook the action with the full knowledge that "Orange County banned the Confederate flag and 'other divisive symbols' in its school dress code in the wake of deadly violence by white supremacists in Charlottesville, Va., over the [2017] summer" (Chamberlain). An Orange County commissioner noted that "a large number of people . . . use the Confederate flag to signal their racial hatred, and because of that, it leads the onlooker guessing what its [sic] for. . . . People are very, very upset about this. They don't want their county to be known as hate county. Those flags are just hateful—that's all there is to it—they are just hateful" (Tate).

But an ACTBAC spokesperson noted that

> [a] property owner has the right to fly whatever flag on his own property as he pleases. There are no flag pole height restrictions in the Orange County code of ordinance. Specifically related to flag poles or flags. If the flag is up, it's flying, it's on private property, legal permit, and we followed all rules and regulations.
>   Simple as that. (Tate)

See also: Council of Conservative Citizens; League of the South; Neo-Confederates; White Nationalism; White Supremacist Movement

FURTHER READING

ACTBAC NC. "About." Southern Heritage Preservation. http://southernheritagepreserva tion.org/about.html. (Accessed July 31, 2018.)

ACTBAC NC. February 14, 2018. "Our Story." Facebook.com. https://www.facebook .com/pg/ALAMANCEOURS/about/. (Accessed July 31, 2018.)

Burton Wire. January 4, 2016. "Trump: Why Do So Many Agree with Him?" http://the burtonwire.com/2016/01/04/politics/trump-why-do-so-many-agree-with-him/. (Accessed November 24, 2018.)

Chamberlain, Samuel. April 30, 2018. "Controversy after Confederate Battle Flag Raised over Liberal North Carolina County." Fox News. http://www.foxnews.com /us/2018/04/30/controversy-after-confederate-battle-flag-raised-over-north-caro lina-county.html. (Accessed July 31, 2018.)

Croxton, Kate. February 23, 2018. "SPLC Lists ACTBAC for Second Year as 'Hate Group.'" Times News. http://www.thetimesnews.com/news/20180222/splc-lists-ac tbac-for-second-year-as-hate-group. (Accessed July 31, 2018.)

Hatewatch Staff. May 23, 2017. "ACTBAC NC Joins Neo-Confederates Rallying around Lost Cause Icons." Southern Poverty Law Center: Hatewatch. https://www.splcen ter.org/hatewatch/2017/05/23/actbac-nc-joins-neo-confederates-rallying-around -lost-cause-icons. (Accessed July 31, 2018.)

HuffPost. July 10, 2015. "Confederate Flag Removed from South Carolina Capitol Grounds." HuffPost. https://www.huffingtonpost.com/2015/07/10/confederate-flag -removal_n_7769300.html. (Accessed July 31, 2018.)

Janicello, Natalie Allison. February 16, 2017. "'Basically Blasphemy': SPLC Label Rankles ACTBAC." Times News. http://www.thetimesnews.com/news/20170216/ba sically-blasphemy-splc-label-rankles-actbac. (Accessed July 31, 2018.)

Southern Poverty Law Center. "Neo-Confederate." Southern Poverty Law Center. https:// www.splcenter.org/fighting-hate/extremist-files/ideology/neo-confederate. (Accessed July 31, 2018.)

Tate, Karlton. March 8, 2018. "Some Groups Want More Confederate Flags in N.C.—Here's How Orange County Is Reacting." Dailytarheel.com. http://www.dailytarheel.com/article/2018/03/confederate-flag-0308. (Accessed July 31, 2018.)

Advanced White Society

The Advanced White Society (AWS) was a small white supremacist group formed in New Jersey around 2010 by Jason Hiecke. The AWS, according to information from the site ZoomInfo, was a "legal, social and political organization, composed of racially aware White people." The AWS's goal was to "bring together like-minded individuals to preserve and protect the white race" (ZoomInfo). According to the Anti-Defamation League (ADL), Hiecke was a "defector from the neo-Nazi National Socialist Movement" (Anti-Defamation League). In 2015, when the Southern Poverty Law Center (SPLC) designated AWS as a hate group, Hiecke referred to the SPLC as "the largest hate organization in the United States" and retorted that "they [the SPLC] portray anybody that does not fall under their beliefs, or conform to them, as a hate group. Why should we be considered a hate organization because we want to look out for the advancement of our own race?" (Flammia). Hiecke stated that his group believes that "every race should have the right to prosper without outside influence of other races" (Flammia).

As of this writing, it is unclear as to whether AWS is still active. The SPLC listed the group as an "active white nationalist group" in 2015, but the group does not appear on its 2018 list (Southern Poverty Law Center, 2015; Hate Map). Nor is the group's website (www.theadvancedwhitesociety.org) currently active.

The disappearance of AWS from the hate group scene may have something to do with observations posted on Stormfront soon after the group's founding. Stormfront is widely regarded as the web's most prominent racial hate site, though it has been experiencing financial stress of late (Weill). Two observations about AWS, posted by an individual self-identified as "Defend our Homeland," are indicative of the future of lesser-known white supremacist groups:

> I don't wish to rain on anyone's parade but the Advanced White Society is a newer Nationalist organization and as I have posted before White Nationalists need to refrain from starting any new groups as we have too many already. Consolidation is the key to success along with joining the better organizations already in place. David Duke's EURO is the best Nationalist group and the Council of Conservative Citizens is the best Confederate style group and these are the ones I think Nationalist thinking pro White Whites should join. A political party is a big deal and has to be done right, only certain key people are qualified to be in charge of something of this magnitude.

The second post by "Defend our Homeland" was even more critical:

> In the 1960's about the only Nationalist group around was the American Nazi Party. Since the dissolution of that group in the early 1970's we now have nearly 1,000 Nationalist organizations. One of the problems with having that many groups is sooner or later some of these units are bound to evolve into something resembling gangs and as a matter of fact that is exactly what is happening. Europeans who are Nationalists have no problems coming together and I fail to see why that shouldn't

be the case in America. That should actually be the core mission of Stormfront but despite being a well-designed and operating WN / NS chat room no real organizing has taken place here. It's too bad William Pierce couldn't last another 15 years or so because if he had I think there would be a lot more productive behavior but even when he was around there were those who just had to hang out and party rather than do something to make a positive difference. (Stormfront)

Soon after the posts by "Defend our Homeland," Jason Hiecke, founder of AWS, identifying himself as "Matthias," posted, "Although we have only a few states that have met our criteria to have authorized active chapters at this time, we as a proud white organization continue to grow with good solid members and supporters" (Stormfront).

See also: Stormfront

FURTHER READING

Anti-Defamation League. "Advanced White Society." Anti-Defamation League. https://www.adl.org/education/references/hate-symbols/advanced-white-society. (Accessed May 25, 2018.)

Flammia, Dino. March 25, 2015. "'Hate Groups' in NJ Respond to New Report—Actually, They Hate It." New Jersey 101.5. http://nj1015.com/hate-groups-blast-new-report/. (Accessed May 25, 2018.)

Southern Poverty Law Center. "Hate Map." Southern Poverty Law Center. https://www.splcenter.org/hate-map. (Accessed May 25, 2018.)

Southern Poverty Law Center. March 2, 2015. "Active White Nationalist Groups." Southern Poverty Law Center: Intelligence Report. https://www.splcenter.org/fighting-hate/intelligence-report/2015/active-white-nationalist-groups. (Accessed May 25, 2018.)

Stormfront. 2013. "Re: A.W.S. Advanced White Society." Stormfront. https://www.stormfront.org/forum/t1004650/. (Accessed May 25, 2018.)

Weill, Kelly. April 10, 2018. "Stormfront, the Internet's Oldest White Supremacist Site, Says It's Going Broke." Daily Beast. https://www.thedailybeast.com/stormfront-the-internets-oldest-white-supremacist-site-says-its-going-broke. (Accessed May 25, 2018.)

ZoomInfo. "The Advanced White Society." ZoomInfo. https://www.stormfront.org/forum/t1004650/. (Accessed May 25, 2018.)

Alliance Defending Freedom

The Alliance Defending Freedom (ADF) is an American conservative Christian organization cofounded in 1994 by Alan Sears, "former executive director of the U.S. Attorney General's Commission on Pornography," and James Dobson, "founder of Focus on the Family" (Southern Poverty Law Center). The ADF was founded to thwart what many conservative Christians viewed as a deterioration of traditional Judeo-Christian values in American social, cultural, and political life, as well as threats posed by the American Civil Liberties Union (Eckholm). ADF believes that "Christians are being punished for living by their convictions" and that the U.S. legal system, "which was built on a moral and Christian foundation, ha[s] been steadily moving against religious freedom, the sanctity of life, and marriage and family" (Alliance Defending Freedom). In 2016, the Southern Poverty Law Center (SPLC) added ADF to its list of anti-LGBT hate groups for its

> demonization of LGBT people, its support of criminalization of gay sex in the U.S. and abroad and its continued attempts to create state and local policies and legislation (so-called "religious liberty" laws) that allow Christians to deny goods and services to LGBT people in the public sphere and marginalize LGBT students in schools. (Hatewatch staff)

As noted by the SPLC, ADF was not named as a hate group "simply for having biblical objections to homosexuality or for opposing same-sex marriage." Rather, ADF has been labeled a hate group because of its "legal advocacy and training that has supported the recriminalization of homosexuality in the U.S. and criminalization abroad; has defended state-sanctioned sterilization of trans people abroad; [and] has linked homosexuality to pedophilia and claims that a 'homosexual agenda' will destroy Christianity and society" (Southern Poverty Law Center). ADF has stated that it seeks to recover "the robust Christendomic theology of the 3rd, 4th, and 5th centuries, which is catholic, universal orthodoxy and is desperately crucial for cultural renewal" (Southern Poverty Law Center).

In 2017, Alan Sears, president and CEO of ADF, was replaced by "longtime theocratic right-wing activist, attorney, and Baptist minister" Michael Farris (Southern Poverty Law Center). Farris's history with the religious right dated "to the 1970s when he opposed the Equal Rights Amendment" and became part of Jerry Falwell's Moral Majority organization. Farris also signed the 1986 Coalition on Revival (COR) Manifesto, which was a "commitment to worldwide revival, renewal, and reformation in the Church and society, that will practically implement the Biblical and Christian Worldview" (Reformation.net). Among the COR's positions was this dictum: "We deny that anyone, Jew or Gentile, believer or unbeliever, private person or public person is exempt from the moral and juridical obligation before God to submit to Christ's Lordship over every aspect of his life in thought, word and deed" (Southern Poverty Law Center).

The ADF's long-standing battle against LGBT people has been most prominently manifested in the promotion of its idea of a "homosexual agenda." According to the interpretation of the ADF, "the homosexual agenda" is

> a nefarious scheme to destroy Christianity and, eventually, civilization through LGBT people's efforts to secure equality under the law. To those who believe in this conspiracy theory, LGBT people are not really seeking equality; rather, they are actually seeking to destroy such things as Christianity, the family and culture. (Southern Poverty Law Center)

The ADF continually warns people "about homosexuality, to support the pseudoscientific and dangerous practice of so-called 'ex-gay' therapy," and continues "to falsely link homosexuality to pedophilia, and claim[s] that schools are 'indoctrinating children' into homosexuality" (Southern Poverty Law Center). In 2018, ADF became incensed when Amazon, the world's largest online retailer, "would not allow customers to make donations to the group through the AmazonSmile program, which gives a small percentage from the purchase price of eligible products to a customer's chosen charity" (Ford). Amazon, which had traditionally excluded hate groups from the AmazonSmile program, noted ADF's continued support of positions that were "homophobic, transphobic, and derogatory" (Ford). A spokesperson for ADF noted, "Amazon needs to realize it's marginalizing not just those of the Christian faith, but those of the Jewish, Islamic faiths who share similar beliefs. We stand for the fundamental freedoms of all Americans, even those we disagree with and those from all walks of life" (Ford).

See also: Focus on the Family

FURTHER READING

Alliance Defending Freedom. "Who We Are." Alliance Defending Freedom. https://adfle gal.org/about-us. (Accessed May 28, 2018.)

Eckholm, Erik. May 11, 2014. "Legal Alliance Gains Host of Court Victories for Conservative Christian Movement." https://www.nytimes.com/2014/05/12/us/legal-alli ance-gains-host-of-court-victories-for-conservative-christian-movement.html. (Accessed May 28, 2018.)

Ford, Zack. May 4, 2018. "Anti-LGBTQ Group Freaks Out after Amazon Blocks It from Using Donation System to Raise Money." ThinkProgress. https://thinkprogress .org/alliance-defending-freedom-amazon-0468719394a6/. (Accessed May 28, 2018.)

Hatewatch Staff. July 24, 2017. "Alliance Defending Freedom through the Years." Southern Poverty Law Center. https://www.splcenter.org/hatewatch/2017/07/24/alliance -defending-freedom-through-years. (Accessed May 28, 2018.)

Reformation.net. "Welcome to Coalition on Revival." Reformation.net. http://www.refor mation.net/. (Accessed May 28, 2018.)

Southern Poverty Law Center. "Alliance Defending Freedom." Southern Poverty Law Center. https://www.splcenter.org/fighting-hate/extremist-files/group/alliance-defen ding-freedom. (Accessed May 28, 2018.)

Alt-Right Movement

The alternative right (alt-right) movement has been described by the Southern Poverty Law Center (SPLC) as

> a set of far-right ideologies, groups and individuals whose core belief is that "white identity" is under attack by multicultural forces using "political correctness" and "social justice" to undermine white people and "their" civilization. Characterized by heavy use of social media and online memes, Alt-Righters eschew "establishment" conservatism, skew young, and embrace white ethno-nationalism as a fundamental value. (Southern Poverty Law Center)

Besides bending toward white nationalism, racism, and neo-Nazism, the alt-right movement has also been described as embracing anti-Semitism, nativism, Islamophobia, antifeminism, and homophobia (Krieg). At the heart of the alt-right ideology is a break with mainstream conservatism and large portions of the Republican Party (GOP), since the nomination of Barry Goldwater for president in 1964. This mainstream brand of conservatism emphasized liberty, freedom, free markets, and capitalism, which those in the alt-right movement consider to be "anti-ideals" and the reasons that the movement wants to define a new kind of conservatism (Southern Poverty Law Center).

Richard Spencer is credited with coining the term "alt-right" in 2010 when he created the website AlternativeRight.com. Spencer describes alt-right adherents as "younger people, often recent college graduates, who recognize the 'uselessness of mainstream conservatism' in what he describes as a 'hyper-racialized' world" (Southern Poverty Law Center). As such, alt-right has opposed the immigration and resettlement of Syrian refugees in America and has been a major proponent of U.S. president Donald Trump's plan to crack down on illegal immigration, particularly that which comes from across the United States' southern border with Mexico. The alt-right movement has been associated with American identitarianism, an iteration of a European ideology that emphasizes cultural and racial homogeneity within different countries. Like their European counterparts, alt-right members believe that older conservatives within their countries have sold out the younger generations in support of worn-out and dated conservative values (Southern Poverty Law Center).

Social media has been instrumental in the growth of the alt-right movement. As noted by the SPLC, "Legions of anonymous Twitter users have used the hashtag #AltRight to proliferate their ideas, sometimes successfully pushing them into the political mainstream." One example of this proliferation of ideas is the popularization of the term "cuckservative." This term is a combination of the terms "cuckold" and "conservative," and it designates mainstream conservative (mostly Republican) politicians who are seen as traitors to the American people inasmuch as they are willing to sell out their traditional ideals in order to support programs and policies related to globalism and certain liberal ideals (Southern Poverty Law Center). The phrase is racist in its overtones, as the term "cuckold" implies that establishment conservatives are like white men who allow black men to sleep with their wives.

The presidential campaign of Donald Trump attracted great attention from the alt-right movement. During the Republican primaries, Donald Trump was the only male Republican candidate to whom the term "cuckservative" was not applied. Reportedly, alt-right adherents are drawn to Trump, who eschews "political correctness" and regularly rails against Muslims, immigrants, Mexicans, Chinese people, and others (Southern Poverty Law Center).

The alt-right movement is hardly monolithic; it attracts some diverse characters. Milo Yiannopoulos, whose Jewish roots have put him at odds with some in the neo-Nazi and white supremacist movements, has become a noted alt-right apologist. Yiannopoulos was once a senior editor at Breitbart News but was fired after he was banned from Twitter in 2016 for "inciting or engaging in the targeted abuse or harassment of others" (Isaac). In an article written for Breitbart News in March 2016, before his firing, Yiannopoulos wrote that the alt-right movement is "fundamentally about youthful provocation and subversion, rather than simply another vehicle for the worst dregs of human society: anti-Semites, white supremacists, and other members of the Stormfront set" (Bokhari and Yiannopoulos). In the final analysis, as pointed out by the SPLC, "coat-and-tie racists like Richard Spencer and Jared Taylor [a neo-Nazi who runs the white supremacist publication *American Renaissance*], and oddball figures like Yiannopoulos have more in common, in terms of sharing a vision of society as fundamentally determined by race, than they disagree about" (Southern Poverty Law Center).

See also: *American Renaissance*; Neo-Nazis; White Nationalism; White Supremacist Movement

FURTHER READING

Bokhari, Allum, and Milo Yiannopoulos. March 29, 2016. "An Establishment Conserva- tive's Guide to the Alt-Right." Breitbart News. http://www.breitbart.com /tech/2016/03/29/an-establishment-conservatives-guide-to-the-alt-right/. (Accessed March 15, 2018.)

Caldwell, Christopher. December 2, 2016. "What the Alt-Right Really Means." *New York Times*. https://www.nytimes.com/2016/12/02/opinion/sunday/what-the-alt-right-re ally-means.html. (Accessed March 15, 2018.)

Isaac, Mike. July 20, 2016. "Twitter Bars Milo Yiannopoulos in Wake of Leslie Jones's Reports of Abuse." *New York Times*. https://www.nytimes.com/2016/07/20/tech nology/twitter-bars-milo-yiannopoulos-in-crackdown-on-abusive-comments .html. (Accessed March 15, 2018.)

Krieg, Gregory. August 25, 2016. "Clinton Is Attacking the 'Alt-Right'—What Is It?" CNN. http://www.cnn.com/2016/08/25/politics/alt-right-explained-hillary-clinton -donald-trump/. (Accessed March 15, 2018.)

Southern Poverty Law Center. "Alt-Right." Southern Poverty Law Center. https:// www.splcenter.org/fighting-hate/extremist-files/ideology/alternative-right. (Accessed March 15, 2018.)

Wallace-Wells, Benjamin. May 5, 2016. "Is the Alt-Right for Real?" *New Yorker*. http:// www.newyorker.com/news/benjamin-wallace-wells/is-the-alt-right-for-real. (Accessed March 15, 2018.)

America First Committee

The America First Committee (AFC) has been designated as "a neo-Nazi hate group by the Southern Poverty Law Center (SPLC)." According to the SPLC, neo-Nazi hate groups

> share a hatred for Jews and an admiration for Adolf Hitler and Nazi Germany. While they also hate other minorities, homosexuals, and even sometimes Chris- tians, they perceive "the Jew" as their cardinal enemy and trace social problems to a Jewish conspiracy that supposedly controls governments, financial institutions, and the media. (Southern Poverty Law Center, 2017)

AFC, "which was founded in 1940, opposed any U.S. involvement in World War II, and was harshly critical of the Roosevelt administration, which it accused of pressing the U.S. toward war. At its peak, it had 800,000 members across the country, included socialists, conservatives, and some of the most prominent Americans from some of the most prominent families" (Calamur). However, one of the hallmarks of the AFC was anti-Semitism:

> It had to remove from its executive committee not only the notoriously anti-Semitic Henry Ford but also Avery Brundage, the former chairman of the U.S. Olympic Committee who had prevented two Jewish runners from the American track team in Berlin in 1936 from running in the finals of the 4x100 relay. (Calamur)

But it was celebrated aviator Charles Lindbergh who gave one of the most infamous speeches associated with AFC. A mere three months before Pearl Harbor, "Lindbergh expressed sympathy for the persecution Jews faced in Germany, but suggested Jews were advocating the U.S. to enter a war that was not in the national interest." Lindbergh stated:

> Instead of agitating for war, the Jewish groups in this country should be opposing it in every possible way for they will be among the first to feel its consequences. Tolerance is a virtue that depends upon peace and strength. History shows that it cannot survive war and devastations. A few far-sighted Jewish people realize this and stand opposed to intervention. But the majority still do not.
> Their greatest danger to this country lies in their large ownership and influence in our motion pictures, our press, our radio and our government. (Calamur)

While AFC largely disintegrated when the United States entered World War II, feverish nationalism and anti-Semitic sentiments have seen the group become consequential once again. In April 2016, as then-candidate Donald Trump campaigned using the phrase "America First as a slogan describing his approach to foreign affairs," the "Anti-Defamation League (ADL) urged Trump to jettison the phrase":

> The undercurrents of anti-Semitism and bigotry that characterized the America First movement—including the assumption that Jews who opposed the movement had their own agenda and were not acting in America's best interest—is fortunately not a major concern today. However, for many Americans, the term 'America First' will always be associated with and tainted by this history. In a political season that already has prompted a national conversation about civility and tolerance, choosing a call to action historically associated with incivility and intolerance seems ill-advised. (Anti-Defamation League, 2016)

Despite the ADL's urging, on January 20, 2017, at President Trump's inaugural address, he stated, "From this day forward, it's going to be only America first. America first" (Calamur).

President Trump's presidency, and his "America First" rhetoric, has emboldened those on the extreme right wing of American politics to come into the light. Art Jones, for instance, who is a member of the America First Committee (see Viets), is a longtime neo-Nazi who emerged in February 2018 as the "likely Republican nominee for U.S. Representative in Illinois' 3rd Congressional district" (Anti-Defamation League, 2018). Incidentally, the AFC's headquarters are located in Lyons, Illinois (Southern Poverty Law Center, Neo-Nazi). In his campaign information, Jones has paired "'America First' language with outright Holocaust denial, including a 'Holocaust Racket' diatribe that blames 'Organized World Jewry' for perpetrating 'the biggest, blackest lie in history'" (Anti-Defamation League, 2018). Jones has "called the Holocaust nothing more than an international extortion racket by the Jews" (Anti-Defamation League, 2018).

See also: Holocaust Denial; Neo-Nazis; White Nationalism; White Supremacist Movement

FURTHER READING

Anti-Defamation League. April 28, 2016. "ADL Urges Donald Trump to Reconsider 'America First' in Foreign Policy Approach." https://www.adl.org/news/press-releases/adl-urges-donald-trump-to-reconsider-america-first-in-foreign-policy-approach. (Accessed July 31, 2018.)

Anti-Defamation League. February 9, 2018. "Arthur Jones." Anti-Defamation League. https://www.adl.org/news/article/arthur-jones. (Accessed July 31, 2018.)

Calamur, Krishnadev. January 21, 2017. "A Short History of 'America First.'" *Atlantic.* https://www.theatlantic.com/politics/archive/2017/01/trump-america-first/514037/. (Accessed July 31, 2018.)

Holocaust Online. "America First Committee." Holocaust Online. http://holocaustonline.org/america-first-party/. (Accessed July 31, 2018.)

Lenz, Ryan, and Booth Gunter. April 27, 2017. "100 Days in Trump's America." Southern Poverty Law Center. https://www.splcenter.org/20170427/100-days-trumps-america. (Accessed July 31, 2018.)

Southern Poverty Law Center. "Neo-Nazi." Southern Poverty Law Center. https://www.splcenter.org/fighting-hate/extremist-files/ideology/neo-nazi. (Accessed July 31, 2018.)

Southern Poverty Law Center. February 15, 2017. "Active Hate Groups 2016." Southern Poverty Law Center: Intelligence Report. https://www.splcenter.org/fighting-hate/intelligence-report/2017/active-hate-groups-2016. (Accessed July 31, 2018.)

Viets, Sarah. July 21, 2016. "Meet the Aryan National Alliance—A Racist Hodgepodge Doomed to Fail." Southern Poverty Law Center: Hatewatch. https://www.splcenter.org/hatewatch/2016/07/21/meet-aryan-nationalist-alliance-%E2%80%93-racist-hodgepodge-doomed-fail. (Accessed July 31, 2018.)

American Border Patrol/American Patrol

Sometimes called "Voice of Citizens Together," the American Border Patrol (also known as American Patrol) is an anti-immigration group largely based in Arizona. Its founder, Glenn Spencer, has called Mexican immigration a "cultural cancer" in the United States, and the group often rails against what it calls the Mexican plan to reconquer the parts of the American southwest that used to be Mexican territory.

The conspiratorial theories of a Mexican attempt to retake the American southwest now permeate other groups of the radical right. On the group's website, an article purported that President Obama had concluded a secret deal with the Mexican government to cede back to Mexico the Gadsden Purchase, a nearly 30,000 square mile portion of southern Arizona and New Mexico that once belonged to Mexico before being purchased by the United States in 1854 (American Patrol).

In 2002, Spencer founded American Border Patrol (ABT) as a "shadow" border patrol to augment the efforts of the American government's border patrol. However, "according to the Southern Poverty Law Center," which views the ABT as a "virulent anti-immigration group," the group's activities were actually meant to "embarrass the federal government into fully militarizing the border by capturing images of undocumented workers on film and uploading them to the American Border Patrol website for all to see" (Southern Poverty Law Center).

In 2016, the group initially embraced Donald Trump's campaign and the attention it brought to the border issue with Mexico. However, because of Trump's focus on the issue, money flowed away from the group and toward more mainstream sources that supported the Trump presidential campaign.

See also: Center for Immigration Studies; Federation for American Immigration Reform

FURTHER READING

American Border Patrol. http://americanborderpatrol.com/.

American Patrol. October 24, 2016. "Obama to Rescind Gadsden Purchase?" http://ameri canborderpatrol.com/2013-2014/161115.html. (Accessed October 25, 2017.)

Southern Poverty Law Center. "American Border Patrol." Southern Poverty Law Center. https://www.splcenter.org/fighting-hate/extremist-files/group/american-border -patrolamerican-patrol. (Accessed March 9, 2018.)

Spencer, Glenn. "Trust but Verify." American Border Patrol. https://americanborderpa trol.com/17-FEATURES/170309/170309-Feature.html. (Accessed March 9, 2018.)

Weigel, David. May 6, 2013. "The Fence Junkies." Slate. http://www.slate.com/articles /news_and_politics/politics/2013/05/glenn_spencers_american_border_patrol_is _waging_a_high_tech_campaign_to.html. (Accessed March 9, 2018.)

American Christian Dixie Knights of the Ku Klux Klan

The American Christian Dixie Knights (ACDK) is a Ku Klux Klan (KKK) hate group based mostly in Alabama (Southern Poverty Law Center). The ACDK, however, claims to have active "Klaverns," or chapters, in Alabama, Mississippi, Florida, Georgia, Tennessee, Kentucky, North Carolina, Missouri, Michigan, Connecticut, Pennsylvania, Utah, and California (American Christian Dixie Knights, Home/Welcome). According to its website, the ACDK

> was made up from 2 separate groups, the Midwest Dixie Knights in Missouri and American Christian Knights of Mississippi. Both groups had been around for years and with combined efforts and mutual respect we decided the merge was a must. So in July 2014 on Klan Hill the marriage was compete and have been ACDK ever since. We have recently combined and absorbed the remaining members of the Mid West Dixie Knights and the White Knights of the Wasatch Front making 1 extremely large, well organized and far reaching Klan. (American Christian Dixie Knights, Home/Welcome)

The ACDK claims that it is a "traditional order" of the KKK and that they follow "the ways of old and the original Ku Klux Klan." According to ACDK:

> We stand behind our convictions and promote God, Race, Nation and Family. We love America the way it used to be and believe in protecting the Constitution the way it was originally written. We are proud white Christian Patriots that work tirelessly for white rights and the advancement of our beautiful race. We want to ensure a future for our white families while living through God. (American Christian Dixie Knights, Home/Welcome)

The ACDK emphatically states that it will not take any "Jews, homosexuals, anti-Christians, or anti-white" members. "WE ARE A 100% WHITE ORGANIZATION

ONLY!!! [emphasis in original]" (American Christian Dixie Knights, Home/ Welcome).

The ideology of the ACDK is consistent with most KKK, white nationalist, and white supremacist groups. The ACDK claims that "America is in distress" and that, as a "true klan," they are working for "the advancement of the white race working arm and arm with our brothers and sisters" (American Christian Dixie Knights, Home/Welcome). The ACDK also spews many of the same ideas that can be found among many hate groups:

We believe in fighting for our rights that are quickly being stripped from us on a regular basis due to the anti-American Muslim terrorist in office, and the Jew controlled media that loves to stir the cultural pot making America a cess pool.

America needs help! Right now this country is turning anti-American right under your noses. Our children are no longer allowed to say Merry Christmas or recite the pledge of allegiance in school because it may offend someone. Our military is no longer allowed to openly practice Christianity punishable by law. This is unacceptable and the people need a voice.

It is not illegal to be white, yet. However if you are proud of your heritage and not ashamed of being white, you are a biggot! The homosexuals can demonstrate and that's OK with society. If the blacks say they are black and proud and work as a network, they are considered brave and are backed by cowards such as the NAACP, ADL, SPLC and countless others to make sure they get their way. The Mexicans have la razza and the Jews own almost all media outlets to abolish the white race. (Which is their ultimate goal).

It is now more socially acceptable to mix races and taint the blood line of the Caucasian than it is to preserve them.

Blacks make up a mere 17.5% of the American population and yet contribute to 87.2% of all violent crime. These are not made up numbers. these are solid statistics. Black on white violent crimes have skyrocketed, and these are not viewed as hate crimes.

In the last few years, the new era of the Black Panthers have been recruiting again and making their menacing presence known. Going as far as to be at voting stations to intimidate white people during the last presidential election. Obama ordered the release of an original member of the black panthers found guilty of murdering a white police officer and gave him a job on his security detail.

These are just a few examples of the crumbling of America and the disintegration of the white race as we know it. (American Christian Dixie Knights, Home/ Welcome)

Yet the ACDK claims that there is "good news." The KKK is "rapidly growing and fighting back," and there are "Klans starting to surface and resurface, and we are all growing strong once again" (American Christian Dixie Knights, Home/ Welcome).

In recent years, the ACDK has taken to posting neighborhood flyers dealing with issues of the extermination of the white race, the control of the media by Jews, and the "abomination" of homosexuality. Indeed, in one such flyer, the ACDK says, "You cannot save your race by being homosexual" (American Christian Dixie Knights, Fliers).

See also: Ku Klux Klan; White Nationalism; White Supremacist Movement

FURTHER READING

American Christian Dixie Knights. "Frequently Asked Questions." American Christian Dixie Knights. http://ackkknights.com/faq-s.html. (Accessed June 30, 2018.)

American Christian Dixie Knights. "Home/Welcome." American Christian Dixie Knights. https://sites.google.com/site/ackkukluxklan/. (Accessed June 30, 2018.)

Southern Poverty Law Center. "Ku Klux Klan." Southern Poverty Law Center. https://www.splcenter.org/fighting-hate/extremist-files/ideology/ku-klux-klan. (Accessed June 30, 2018.)

American College of Pediatricians

The American College of Pediatricians (ACPeds), despite its official-sounding name, is designated by the "Southern Poverty Law Center (SPLC) as an anti-LGBT hate group" (Southern Poverty Law Center). According to the SPLC, "ACPeds opposes adoption by LGBT couples, links homosexuality to pedophilia, endorses so-called reparative or sexual orientation conversion therapy for homosexual youth, believes transgender people have a mental illness and has called transgender health care for youth child abuse" (Southern Poverty Law Center). ACPeds was founded in 2002 and "consists of about 200 members." The group started

> because a small group of anti-LGBT physicians and other healthcare professionals broke away from the 60,000 member American Academy of Pediatrics (AAP), composed of leaders in the professional field, to form its own group after the AAP issued a new policy statement in 2002 in support of adoption and foster parenting by same-sex couples. (Hatewatch staff)

ACPeds also contends that "LGBT people are more promiscuous than heterosexuals" and that "LGBT people are a danger to children" (Hatewatch staff). The founder of ACPeds, Joseph Zanga, "described what he hoped the group would become: essentially a Judeo-Christian, traditional-values organization . . . open to membership for pediatric medical professionals of all religions who hold our core beliefs . . . that life begins at conception and that the traditional family unit, headed by an opposite-sex couple, poses far fewer risk factors" (Lenz).

ACPeds continually appeals to "junk science" to justify its claims and has distorted or misused the information of credible scientists. In 2010, for instance, ACPeds printed a pamphlet, "Facts about Youth," that directly contradicted the findings of both the American Academy of Pediatrics and the American Psychological Association (Lenz). Francis Collins, then director of the National Institutes of Health (NIH), said the ACPeds pamphlet misrepresented the findings of the NIH. "It is disturbing to me to see special interest groups distort my scientific observations to make a point against homosexuality," Collins said. "The information they present is misleading and incorrect" (Lenz). Also in 2010, ACPeds distorted the work of Gary Remafedi, professor at the Medical School at the University of Minnesota. Upon learning of the distortions of his work that ACPeds was using to justify its anti-LGBT position, Remafedi commented: "What was so troubling was that these were fellow doctors, fellow pediatricians. They knew better, and they have the same ethical responsibilities to their patients that I do, but they deliberately distorted my research for malicious purposes" (Pinto).

In 2015, "the president of ACPeds, Dr. Michelle Cretella, described the U.S. Supreme Court's decision in *Obergefell v. Hodges*, which legalized gay marriage in the United States," as "a tragic day for America's children." Later that year, ACPeds

> filed an amicus brief with the Alabama Supreme Court on November 6, 2015, urging the state court to defy the U.S. Supreme Court's earlier decision legalizing same-sex marriage in the United States. The brief cited discredited anti-LGBT research while attacking legitimate research by professional organizations like the American Psychological Association. (Southern Poverty Law Center)

On its website, ACPeds states:

> The American College of Pediatricians has position statements on topics ranging from the importance of eating together as a family to the dangers of marijuana upon the adolescent brain. The College has also presented the evidence-based position that non-heterosexual attractions and gender confusion develop from the interaction of both nature and nurture, that these feelings often change spontaneously (especially during adolescence), and that non-heterosexual lifestyles carry significant health risks. *These scientific facts, and they are facts* [emphasis added], run counter to the agenda of identity politics, and this is what the SPLC finds egregious. (American College of Pediatricians, 2017)

When asked about the veracity of ACPeds and its claims, Scott Leibowitz, "medical director of the THRIVE program at Nationwide Children's Hospital and chair of the sexual orientation and gender identity issues committee for the American Academy of Child & Adolescent Psychiatry," did not hesitate to express his disdain of the group. Leibowitz stated: "It can hardly be a credible medical organization when it consistently chooses to ignore science and the growing evidence base that clearly demonstrates the benefits of affirmative care with LGBT youth across all ages" (Turban).

See also: Alliance Defending Freedom; American Family Association; Family Research Council; Family Watch International; Pacific Justice Institute; Ruth Institute; Traditional Values Coalition; Westboro Baptist Church; World Congress of Families

FURTHER READING

American College of Pediatricians. "About Us." American College of Pediatricians. https://www.acpeds.org/about-us. (Accessed June 23, 2018.)

American College of Pediatricians. August 21, 2017. "Decrying the Politics of Hate." American College of Pediatricians. https://www.acpeds.org/decrying-the-politics-of-hate. (Accessed June 23, 2018.)

Hatewatch Staff. November 13, 2015. "Meet the Anti-LGBT Hate Group That Filed an Amicus Brief with the Alabama Supreme Court." Southern Poverty Law Center: Hatewatch. https://www.splcenter.org/hatewatch/2015/11/13/meet-anti-lgbt-hate-group-filed-amicus-brief-alabama-supreme-court. (Accessed June 23, 2018.)

Lenz, Ryan. March 1, 2012. "American College of Pediatricians Defames Gays and Lesbians in the Name of Protecting Children." Southern Poverty Law

Center: Intelligence Report. https://www.splcenter.org/fighting-hate/intelligence
-report/2012/american-college-pediatricians-defames-gays-and-lesbians-name
-protecting-children. (Accessed June 23, 2018.)

Media Bias/Fact Check. "American College of Pediatricians." Media Bias/Fact Check.
https://mediabiasfactcheck.com/american-college-of-pediatricians/. (Accessed June
23, 2018.)

Pinto, Nick. May 26, 2010. "University of Minnesota Professor's Research Hijacked."
City Pages. http://www.citypages.com/news/university-of-minnesota-professors
-research-hijacked-6725473. (Accessed June 23, 2018.)

Southern Poverty Law Center. "American College of Pediatricians." Southern Poverty
Law Center. https://www.splcenter.org/fighting-hate/extremist-files/group/ameri
can-college-pediatricians. (Accessed June 23, 2018.)

Turban, Jack. May 8, 2017. "The American College of Pediatricians Is an Anti-LGBT
Group." *Psychology Today.* https://www.psychologytoday.com/us/blog/political
-minds/201705/the-american-college-pediatricians-is-anti-lgbt-group. (Accessed June
23, 2018.)

American Eagle Party

The American Eagle Party is a white nationalist hate group located in Gatlinburg, Tennessee (Southern Poverty Law Center, 2017). According to the Southern Poverty Law Center (SPLC):

> Adherents of white nationalist groups believe that white identity should be the organizing principle of the countries that make up Western civilization. White nationalists advocate for policies to reverse changing demographics and the loss of an absolute, white majority. Ending non-white immigration, both legal and illegal, is an urgent priority—frequently elevated over other racist projects, such as ending multiculturalism and miscegenation—for white nationalists seeking to preserve white, racial hegemony. (Southern Poverty Law Center, White Nationalist)

According to an article by Red Phillips of the *Independent Political Report*, the American Eagle Party was formed from the remains of the American Third Position Party (A3P) and the American Freedom Party. According to Phillips:

> the American Third Position party was a pro-white third party that formed a few years back. I said at the time that that was a really bad choice for a name for a rightist American party and that it wouldn't thrive. Third Positionism is primarily a European concept, and it doesn't fit well into the political milieu of America or the political consciousness of the American right. Third Positionism and the overt anti-capitalism that inspires it is an idea that is held dear by some white nationalist intellectual types, but it doesn't resonate with the American right base or accord with American political history. (Phillips)

Phillips states that "the primary focus of the A3P/Freedom Party was always protecting the interests of American whites, not freedom as an abstract concept" (Phillips). The American Eagle Party, on the other hand, says it stands for: "(1) ending U.S. involvement in wars around the world; (2) curtailing immigration; (3) reclaiming constitutional rights for citizens; (4) improving the national economy" (Winger). But Phillips notes:

> Notice there is no explicit mention of white interests. This statement makes it seem like an essentially paleoconservative party. I'm sure some will call this a cave.

Some will call it a necessary concession to political reality. What I don't know is if there is any back story about conflict among AFP leadership that brought this split about. (Phillips)

In 2016, lawyer Glenn Keith Allen was fired by the city of Baltimore, Maryland, after it came to light that Allen had contributed money to the neo-Nazi National Alliance organization and the American Eagle Party. In fact, Allen was the vice chairperson of the party, though he insisted that the American Eagle Party "has nothing to do with race though it is critical of Israel" (Weiss).

See also: American Freedom Party; National Alliance; White Nationalism; White Supremacist Movement

FURTHER READING

Phillips, Red. February 2015. "American Eagle Party Forms from the Remnants (?) of the A3P/American Freedom Party." Independent Political Report. http://independent politicalreport.com/2015/02/red-phillips-article-on-new-american-eagle-party/. (Accessed June 27, 2018.)

Southern Poverty Law Center. "White Nationalist." Southern Poverty Law Center. https://www.splcenter.org/fighting-hate/extremist-files/ideology/white-nationalist. (Accessed June 27, 2018.)

Southern Poverty Law Center. February 15, 2017. "Active Hate Groups 2016." Southern Poverty Law Center: Intelligence Report. https://www.splcenter.org/fighting-hate /intelligence-report/2017/active-hate-groups-2016. (Accessed June 27, 2018.)

Weiss, Debra Cassens. August 22, 2016. "Ex-DLA Lawyer Says He's Not a White Supremacist after Baltimore Fires Him for Alleged Neo-Nazi Ties." *ABA Journal*. http://www.abajournal.com/news/article/ex_dla_lawyer_says_hes_not_a_white _supremacist_after_baltimore_fires_him_fo/. (Accessed June 27, 2018.)

Winger, Richard. February 8, 2015. "Merlin Miller, 2012 Presidential Nominee of American Third Position, Forms American Eagle Party." Ballot Access News. http://ballot-access.org/2015/02/08/merlin-miller-2012-presidential-nominee-of-ameri can-third-position-forms-american-eagle-party/. (Accessed June 27, 2018.)

American Family Association

The American Family Association (AFA) "was founded in 1977 as the National Federation for Decency" (Southern Poverty Law Center). Originally, the group was established "to combat what it considered indecent television programming and the spread of pornography in American media" (Southern Poverty Law Center). In 1988, the group changed its name to the American Family Association to emphasize its core value: "the protection of the American family." The AFA has defined itself as "a Christian organization promoting the biblical ethic of decency in American society with primary emphasis on television and other media," emphasizing "moral issues that impact the family" (American Civil Liberties Union).

The AFA's founder, Donald Wildmon, "was appointed to former Attorney General Ed Meese's Commission on Pornography" in 1985 (Southern Poverty Law Center). In his position, "Wildmon successfully orchestrated the removal of *Playboy* and *Penthouse* magazines from some 17,000 convenience stores" (Southern Poverty Law Center). During his time on the commission, Wildmon ramped up the group's anti-LGBT activities by lobbying major corporations to pull their ads from television shows that portrayed gay scenes or romances. According to Wildmon and the AFA, "the primary goal of the homosexual movement was to abolish the traditional, Judeo-Christian view of human sexuality, marriage, and the family" (Southern Poverty Law Center).

The AFA has lobbied Congress on several occasions to eliminate funding for the National Endowment for the Arts (NEA), particularly in regard to projects that it finds objectionable. The AFA is particularly interested in fighting against the "homosexual agenda" portrayed in the media, stating that the Bible "declares that homosexuality is unnatural and sinful" (American Family Association, 2016). AFA's founder, Donald Wildmon, has reportedly stated that he believes that Hollywood "is heavily influenced by Jews, and that television network executives and advertisers have a 'genuine hostility' toward Christians" (Institute for First Amendment Studies). Upon the "election of the first Muslim to the United States Congress in 2006," the AFA requested that its members "write their Congressional representatives to create a law making the Bible the book used in the swearing-in ceremony of representatives and senators" (American Family Association, 2006).

In 2010, "the AFA was designated an anti-gay hate group by the Southern Poverty Law Center" (Southern Poverty Law Center). It continues to orchestrate boycotts against companies, organizations, places, and individuals that it believes promote anti-family and anti-Christian values (Right Wing Watch).

See also: Alliance Defending Freedom; American College of Pediatricians; Family Research Council; Family Watch International; Liberty Counsel; Pacific Justice Institute; Traditional Values Coalition

FURTHER READING

American Civil Liberties Union. June 1, 1995. "The Religious Right in Washington." American Civil Liberties Union. https://web.archive.org/web/20070403192146 /http://www.aclu-wa.org/detail.cfm?id=149. (Accessed January 3, 2018.)

American Family Association. "Does AFA Hate Homosexuals?" American Family Association. https://web.archive.org/web/20100812033322/http://www.afa.net/FAQ.aspx? id=2147483677. (Accessed January 3, 2018.)

American Family Association. November 28, 2006. "A First for America: The Koran Replaces the Bible at Swearing-In Oath." American Family Association. Found at https://web.archive.org/web/20070522063621/http://www.afa.net/aa112806_2.asp. (Accessed January 3, 2018.)

American Family Association. August 26, 2016. "Romans I and Unnatural Sexuality." American Family Association. https://afa.net/the-stand/culture/2016/08/romans -1-and-unnatural-sexuality/. (Accessed February 8, 2019.)

Institute for First Amendment Studies. May 21, 1989. "Religious Leaders Denounce Wildmon's Anti-Semitism." Institute for First Amendment Studies. http://www .publiceye.org/ifas/fw/8906/wildmon.html. (Accessed January 3, 2018.)

Right Wing Watch. "American Family Association." Right Wing Watch. http://www.right wingwatch.org/organizations/american-family-association/. (Accessed January 3, 2017.)

Southern Poverty Law Center. "American Family Association." Southern Poverty Law Center. https://www.splcenter.org/fighting-hate/extremist-files/group/american-family-association. (Accessed January 3, 2017.)

American Freedom Defense Initiative

The American Freedom Defense Initiative (AFDI) is "an anti-Muslim hate group co-founded by anti-Islamists Pamela Geller and Robert Spencer" (Southern Poverty Law Center). The AFDI claims as its central tenets "a commitment to freedom of speech, as opposed to the Islamic prohibitions of 'blasphemy' and 'slander,' which quash open dialogue about jihad and Islamic supremacism; freedom of conscience, as opposed to the 'Islamic death penalty for apostasy;' and equal rights of all people, as opposed to institutionalized discrimination against women and non-Muslims in Sharia law, or strict Islamic law" (Yan). The "Southern Poverty Law Center (SPLC) has designated the AFDI as an anti-Muslim hate group" because of its "extreme hostility toward Muslims," and their broad defamation of Islam, "which [it] tends to treat as a monolithic and evil religion" (Southern Poverty Law Center). These anti-Muslim groups "generally hold that Islam has no values in common with other cultures, is inferior to the West and is a violent political ideology rather than a religion" (Yan).

As cofounder and advocate for the AFDI, Pamela Geller has a long history of anti-Islamic activity. Her Islamophobic stance came to the public's attention when she publicly stated her opposition to an Islamic community center that was "proposed to be built near the former site of the World Trade Center" (Southern Poverty Law Center). In May 2015, AFDI helped sponsor the "Draw the Prophet cartoon contest in Garland, Texas," which drew an attack by two Islamic extremists. The "Islamic State of Iraq and the Levant (ISIL) claimed responsibility for the attack," though U.S. officials could only say that the attacks were "inspired" by ISIL, not necessarily directed by that organization (Southern Poverty Law Center). Geller consistently blogs about "creeping Sharia" in the United States, a reference to Islamic sharia law, which Geller and other anti-Islamic groups claim Muslims want to impose in the United States. The Southern Poverty Law Center (SPLC) characterizes Geller as "relentlessly shrill and coarse in her broad-brush denunciations of Islam" (Southern Poverty Law Center).

Geller stated that "she was profoundly affected by the 9/11 attacks" (Southern Poverty Law Center). After the attacks, she contributed several essays to various outlets, in which she examined Muslim militancy (Howard). Eventually, she would begin her own blog, Atlas Shrugs, which consisted of "unvarnished anti-Muslim stridency" that won her many followers (Southern Poverty Law Center).

Geller's "evolution from blogger to activist began in 2007 when she joined 'Stop the Maddrassa,' an initiative meant to stop the opening of a secular public Arabic-English school in Brooklyn, New York" (Southern Poverty Law Center). In December 2009, Geller became more widely known when she blogged about the Park51 project, "a proposal by a New York City imam to renovate an abandoned building in lower Manhattan into a 13-story mosque and community center, not far from the site of the former World Trade Center" (Southern Poverty Law Center).

In 2010, Geller teamed up with "radical Muslim alarmist" Robert Spencer and took over the Stop Islamization of America (SIOA) organization, also known as the American Freedom Defense Initiative (AFDI). One of AFDI's first projects was to oppose the Park51 project. The demonstration "drew thousands of demonstrators and Geller and Spencer depicted the project's planners as radical extremists" (Southern Poverty Law Center). AFDI even described the project as an "Islamic victory mosque" to celebrate the 9/11 attacks, though no Muslim had ever used the term in any public way. After the scuttling of the Park51 project, Geller became a media darling, particularly for outlets on the conservative right. Indeed, for months afterward, Geller became a fixture on Fox News, where she propagated her claims that Muslims intended to impose sharia law throughout the United States.

In 2012, "AFDI launched an ad campaign in the Washington, D.C. subway system which read, 'In any war between the civilized man and the savage, support the civilized man. Support Israel. Defeat Jihad'" (Yan). Geller defended the AFDI's ad campaign by stating, "We don't think it's controversial. It's truth. Telling the truth now is equated with 'hate' and 'bigotry' in an attempt to silence and demonize the truth-tellers. That makes my ads all the more important" (Yan).

Through her website,

> Geller has promulgated some of the most bizarre conspiracy theories found on the extreme right, including claims that President Obama is the love child of Malcolm X, that Obama was once involved with a "crack whore," that his birth certificate is a forgery, that his late mother posed nude for pornographic photos, and that he was a Muslim in his youth who never renounced Islam. She has described Obama as beholden to his "Islamic overlords" and said that he wants jihad to be victorious in America. (Southern Poverty Law Center)

Geller has been willing to "ally with any individual or movement that expresses anti-Muslim sentiments" (Southern Poverty Law Center). Thus, she has found confederates among neo-Nazis and white nationalists on the extreme right—"a rather remarkable feat, considering she is Jewish" (Southern Poverty Law Center). Geller "has been the subject of several positive postings on racist websites such as Stormfront, VDARE, *American Renaissance*, and the League of the South" (Southern Poverty Law Center). Geller's anti-Muslim activity was among several references that "Norwegian terrorist Anders Breivik cited in his manifesto, posted online before he killed 77 people, mostly teenagers," who were attending a left-wing youth camp in 2011. She and her SIOA partner, Richard Spencer, were cited by Breivik 64 times (Southern Poverty Law Center).

Though Geller "makes no pretense about being learned in Islamic studies," she nevertheless has garnered many followers through her beliefs that Muslims are infiltrating every level of the U.S. government (Southern Poverty Law Center). In 2013, she was forbidden to appear at the Conservative Political Action Conference (CPAC) because she accused "CPAC board members Grover Norquist and Suhail Khan of being 'members of the Muslim Brotherhood and secret Islamist agents'" (Seitz-Wald).

In 2015, Geller was the object of an assassination plot by an individual who had been radicalized by ISIL. The individual had planned to assassinate Geller by beheading for her role in the "Draw the Prophet" cartoon contest (Perez and Prokupecz).

See also: *American Renaissance*; League of the South; Stormfront; VDARE

FURTHER READING

Bernard, Anne, and Alan Feuer. October 8, 2012. "Outraged, and Outrageous." *New York Times*. http://www.nytimes.com/2010/10/10/nyregion/10geller.html. (Accessed March 25, 2017.)

Howard, Greg. November 28, 2012. "Pamela Geller's War." *Village Voice*. http://www.villagevoice.com/news/pamela-gellers-war-6436870. (Accessed March 25, 2017.)

Perez, Evan, and Shimon Prokupecz. June 3, 2015. "Boston Shooting: Suspect Plotted to Behead Pamela Geller, Sources Say." CNN. http://www.cnn.com/2015/06/03/us/boston-police-shooting/index.html. (Accessed March 25, 2017.)

Seitz-Wald, Alex. March 16, 2013. "Pam Geller: CPAC Board Member Is 'Worse' Than Anwar al-Awlaki." Salon. http://www.salon.com/2013/03/16/pam_geller_cpac_board_member_is_worse_than_anwar_al_awlaki/. (Accessed March 25, 2017.)

Southern Poverty Law Center. "Pamela Geller." Southern Poverty Law Center. https://www.splcenter.org/fighting-hate/extremist-files/individual/pamela-geller. (Accessed March 25, 2017.)

Steinback, Robert. May 5, 2011. "Muslim-Basher Pamela Geller Pushes Another Obama Fairy Tale, Proudly." Southern Poverty Law Center: Hatewatch. https://www.splcenter.org/hatewatch/2011/05/05/muslim-basher-pamela-geller-pushes-another-obama-fairy-tale-proudly. (Accessed March 25, 2017.)

Steinback, Robert. June 17, 2011. "The Anti-Muslim Inner Circle." Southern Poverty Law Center: Intelligence Report. https://www.splcenter.org/fighting-hate/intelligence-report/2011/anti-muslim-inner-circle. (Accessed March 25, 2017.)

Yan, Holly. May 4, 2015. "Garland Shooting: What Is the American Freedom Defense Initiative?" CNN. https://www.cnn.com/2015/05/04/us/what-is-american-freedom-defense-initiative/index.html. (Accessed May 28, 2018.)

American Freedom Party

Founded in 2009 as the American Third Position, or A3P, the American Freedom Party is a group of white nationalists that portends to represent the interests of white Americans, particularly as they relate to the immigration of non-Europeans. Like many white nationalist groups, the American Freedom Party has a noticeably racist element, believing that the current demographic makeup of the United States is no longer "recognizable" and puts white Americans in an inferior position.

In 2013 the A3P was renamed to the American Freedom Party, and the group has dedicated itself to raising awareness and funds in support of its causes. The group has attempted to court both Tea Party Republicans and Libertarians. In an Internet broadcast in 2010, a member of the group stated, "There's a great overlap in Patriot activities and Patriot causes, and we have, we will have a big effect on this much larger movement, the Ron Paul Revolution, that has millions of people engaged . . . we'll be pulling them from the right" (Southern Poverty Law Center).

Like many right-wing extremist groups, the American Freedom Party appeals to Americans who believe that the "white essence" of American political and social life is being eroded by governmental policies and the continuing influx of immigration from nonwhite countries. The tagline of the group's website proclaims, "Liberty, Sovereignty, Identity" (American Freedom Party). These code words are familiar to most patriot and other extremist groups, as they symbolize the disaffection that many white Americans feel in their own country. The group has used such statements as "We . . . embrace principles that will secure the existence of our people and a future for our children," which is very similar to "the 14 Words that are from a passage in Hitler's *Mein Kampf*" that have served as inspiration for neo-Nazis and other white supremacists: "We must secure the existence of our people and a future for white children" (Southern Poverty Law Center).

The group takes issue with both Republicans and Democrats, seeing independents and Libertarians as the base from which to draw new members. Pronouncements have stated that the party will rally to the banner of any group that best represents the "interests of white Americans" (American Freedom Party).

See also: White Nationalism; White Supremacist Movement

FURTHER READING

American Freedom Party. http://american3rdposition.com/. (Accessed August 12, 2017.)
Southern Poverty Law Center. "American Freedom Party." Southern Poverty Law Center. https://www.splcenter.org/fighting-hate/extremist-files/group/american-freedom-party. (Accessed August 12, 2017.)

American Freedom Union

The American Freedom Union (AFU), founded in 1995, is designated "by the Southern Poverty Law Center (SPLC) as a white nationalist hate group." According to the SPLC:

> White nationalist groups espouse white supremacist or white separatist ideologies, often focusing on the alleged inferiority of nonwhites. Groups listed in a variety of other categories—Ku Klux Klan, neo-Confederate, neo-Nazi, racist skinhead, and Christian Identity—could also be fairly described as white nationalist.
>
> Adherents of white nationalist groups believe that white identity should be the organizing principle of the countries that make up Western civilization. White nationalists advocate for policies to reverse changing demographics and the loss of an absolute, white majority. Ending non-white immigration, both legal and illegal, is an urgent priority—frequently elevated over other racist projects, such as ending multiculturalism and miscegenation—for white nationalists seeking to preserve white, racial hegemony. (Southern Poverty Law Center)

The AFU claims to be "the largest nationalist political organization in the United States. We are always pro-American in outlook; we believe in taking care of America and Americans first" (American Freedom Union). The AFU publishes the *Nationalist Times* newspaper, which "educates Americans about the systematic plundering of their way of life by giving them the best news and views available. . . . The Nationalist Times exposes the problems plaguing America and gives the needed solutions to those with eyes to see and ears to hear" (American Freedom Union). In typical white nationalist form, AFU claims to speak for the "dispossessed majority" (i.e., white people) in the United States:

> It's time to end the fracturing of America's dispossessed majority into hundreds of splinter groups. A united bloc of Americans can elect a government which will serve the great Middle American core which built America and which still sustains it, but which finds itself today without political representation. Join the American Freedom Union today! (American Freedom Union)

According to the SPLC, AFU's headquarters are located in Hampton Township, Pennsylvania (Southern Poverty Law Center).

See also: America First Committee; White Nationalism; White Supremacist Movement

FURTHER READING

American Freedom Union. "About." American Freedom Union. http://www.american freedomunion.com/about/. (Accessed July 31, 2018.)

Southern Poverty Law Center. "White Nationalist." Southern Poverty Law Center. https://www.splcenter.org/fighting-hate/extremist-files/ideology/white-nationalist. (Accessed July 31, 2018.)

American Nationalist Association

The American Nationalist Association (ANA) is considered a white nationalist hate group (Southern Poverty Law Center). According to the Black Talk Radio Network (BTRN), "The ANA is a white nationalist organization that is interested in protecting the so-called dignity and honor of racists, white supremacists, human slave traders, land thieves and mass murderers" (Southern Poverty Law Center). The Southern Poverty Law Center (SPLC) states:

> White nationalist groups espouse white supremacist or white separatist ideologies, often focusing on the alleged inferiority of nonwhites. Groups listed in a variety of other categories—Ku Klux Klan, neo-Confederate, neo-Nazi, racist skinhead, and Christian Identity—could also be fairly described as white nationalist.
>
> Adherents of white nationalist groups believe that white identity should be the organizing principle of the countries that make up Western civilization. White nationalists advocate for policies to reverse changing demographics and the loss of an absolute, white majority. Ending non-white immigration, both legal and illegal, is an urgent priority—frequently elevated over other racist projects, such as ending multiculturalism and miscegenation—for white nationalists seeking to preserve white, racial hegemony. (Southern Poverty Law Center)

The BTRN reports that, on a now-defunct website (www.ana-ann.com), ANA had posted a "Statement of Objectives," which read, in part:

> To unite all honorable, dedicated, courageous and selfless men and women of European-American decent; proud of their European blood, culture, traditions,

language, and ideals. Dedicated to our proud and respectable American National Community to advance the interests of our people and protect the dignity and honor of our ancestors. (Black Talk Radio Network)

BTRN also notes that the ANA is "very concerned about the genetic survival of white people and charts the growth of the Hispanic populations across America" (Black Talk Radio Network).

According to a website that claims to be the ANA's official site, the ANA is dedicated to the following propositions:

Native Americans are all those born here, regardless of whether our ancestors came more or less remotely from Africa, Asia, or Europe.

Immigration is good for the immigrants, but not for native Americans: it ought to be stopped.

English is the common language of all Americans, and should be officially recognized as such.

All encroachments on America's national sovereignty should be stopped and reversed: we must get out of the UN and NAFTA.

The proper goal of foreign policy is "to provide for the common defense" of the USA—not to solve foreigners' problems or settle their disputes

America should have no foreign possessions: Puerto Rico, the Virgin Islands, Eastern Samoa, Guam and the Northern Mariana Islands should be given their independence as quickly as possible.

The Moon belongs to America, because we got there first. (American Nationalist Association, Index)

In what appears to be a personal statement by ANA's founder(s) (presumably Rodney Martin and John Friend) (Stormfront), the group's activities are further articulated:

Its activities would be centered on meetings, rallies, and demonstrations, with enough ritual and pageantry to stir the soul and promote a sense of unity. I envision four ongoing subsidiary enterprises: a Publication Office providing a website, newsletter, pamphlets and books; a National-Syndicalist Organization, working through and alongside trade unions, organizing American workers and lobbying for their interests; Action Squads to provide an outlet for youthful energy and high spirits—non-violent, to be sure, but defensive and retaliatory, if necessary: citizens' arrests of illegal aliens, surveillance of mosques and jihadist organizations, security for the association's events, playing pranks on the disloyal opposition, etc.; a Liaison Office to co-ordinate with foreign nationalist movements—especially in Canada to promote Quebec's independence and the re-unification of British North America, and globally to promote an Anti-Jihad Front. (American Nationalist Association, "American Nationalist Association")

According to the white supremacist Internet forum Stormfront, ANA touts itself as a "White civil rights organization" (Stormfront).

See also: Stormfront; White Nationalism; White Supremacist Movement

FURTHER READING

American Nationalist Association. "American Nationalist Association." http://karljahn .tripod.com/tan/ANA.html. (Accessed July 31, 2018.)

American Nationalist Association. "Index." http://karljahn.tripod.com/tan/index.htm. (Accessed July 31, 2018.)

ANA-ANN. http://www.ana-ann.com/membership.html. (Website appears defunct. Could not access on July 31, 2018.)

Black Talk Radio Network. October 20, 2014. "White Supremacist Says Dead Press TV Reporter Fell Victim to 'CIA Black Op.'" BlackTalkRadioNetwork.com. http://www.blacktalkradionetwork.com/2014/10/20/white-supremacist-says-dead-press-tv-reporter-fell-victim-to-cia-black-op/. (Accessed July 31, 2018.)

Southern Poverty Law Center. "White Nationalist." Southern Poverty Law Center. https://www.splcenter.org/fighting-hate/extremist-files/ideology/white-nationalist. (Accessed July 31, 2018.)

Stormfront. April 13, 2013. "A New White Nationalist Organization Called American Nationalist Association." Stormfront. https://www.stormfront.org/forum/t960483/. (Accessed July 31, 2018.)

American Nazi Party

Founded by George Lincoln Rockwell in 1959, the American Nazi Party exists to foster the goals of national socialism in the United States. The group claims to be guided by the so-called 14 Words: "We must secure the existence of our people and a future for white children" (American Nazi Party, The Fourteen Words).

Like other national socialists, the American Nazi Party believes in the supremacy of the white race over all other races and holds that the American national system of government has been corrupted by Jewish influences. Their beliefs look much like those of other right-wing extremist groups. Though these beliefs appear benign in their expression, they become vitriolic in practice. The American Nazi Party professes the following principles: (1) Race—calling for the union of all Aryans in North America; (2) Citizenship—only those of Aryan blood can be citizens of the state; (3) Aryan Community—the demand that society be organized into racial communities that will fully recognize, and embrace, Aryanism as a separate race; (4) The Family Farm—demands for protection of the family farm and stable market and fair prices for the farmer's goods; (5) Motherhood and Family—a demand that the family be recognized as indispensable to Aryan society and that motherhood be elevated from a position of "low esteem" to one that is universally recognized as the "noblest position to which any Aryan woman can aspire"; (6) A New Educational System—the demand for a new educational system that will emphasize the physical and moral development of young people; (7) An Honest Economy—a demand for the creation of an honest and debt-free economy based on the productive capacity of the Aryan worker; (8) Energy and Environment—a goal to be totally self-sufficient in energy; (9) Culture and Science—a demand that the state promote every form of Aryan cultural expression and that "alien" influences be removed from the cultural life of the community (i.e., "modern art" and "modern music"); (10) Foreign Policy and Defense—a demand based on the long-term interests of the Aryan race; (11) White Self Defense—the absolute right to keep and bear arms; (12) A Better Race—a demand for the state to use eugenics to propagate the highest racial elements of the Aryan race, while demanding that the state halt the spread of hereditary defects and "racially impure blood"; and (13) A Spiritual Rebirth—a demand that the state take an active part in the spiritual life of the community and turn citizens away from "materialism, cynicism, and egoism" (American Nazi Party, What We Stand For).

In 2016, the American Nazi Party endorsed the candidacy of Donald Trump by stating:

> Trump has had the balls or the gall, to REACH OUT to the true feelings of most of what is left of White America, and "say the things they have longed to hear for decades"—he has brought them out from under the stones where they have been HIDING, and given them a VOICE to vent one last, long call of despair before they are subsumed in a sea of non-White creatures from every corner of planet earth, who are intent on TAKING from the hands of the pathetic Mighty Whiteys who shamble along like the Walking Dead Zombies, who have LOST their heritage/history of being willing to FIGHT, both tooth and nail to PRESERVE what is THEIRS! (American Nazi Party, News)

See also: National Socialist Movement

FURTHER READING

American Nazi Party. "The Fourteen Words." http://www.americannaziparty.com /14wordscards.pdf. (Accessed October 26, 2017.)

American Nazi Party. "News." http://www.americannaziparty.com/full-width__trashed /news/ (Accessed October 26, 2017.)

American Nazi Party. "What We Stand For." http://www.americannaziparty.com/what -we-stand-for/. (Accessed February 8, 2019.)

American Patriot Party

The American Patriot Party (APP) is a loose collection of individuals and groups that attempts to educate members about the "inalienable" rights of American citizens, as well as the virtues of states' rights and local control (American Patriot Party). The APP was founded in 2011, at the height of the Tea Party movement, and its fundamental goal is to deemphasize federal control in favor of state and local control. The APP's official motto is "Inalienable Rights, States Rights, Local Control" (American Patriot Party). The APP has been designated as an active patriot and anti-government group by the Southern Poverty Law Center (SPLC) (Southern Poverty Law Center, 2017). The platform of the APP is very much in line with those of other patriot and anti-government groups that have organized themselves to resist perceived government overreach into local matters of social and political importance. The fundamental belief of the APP is that the "United States Government and appointed officials need to respect the Constitution." The APP believes in upholding the rights of the states and individuals over those of the federal government (Patriot Party). The APP's platform is to:

> [p]rotect, defend and implement the intents set forth in the Originating Founders Letters which includes "The Absolute Rights of the Colonists of 1772" and the

Declaration of Independence, the documents which define Freedom. This Platform may be amended as needed through the literal understanding of these documents that define and establish freedom and a free country. (American Patriot Party)

The APP's goal is to have the federal government tie all of its platform statements into the standard interpretation of the Declaration of Independence, the U.S. Constitution, and other founding documents. The APP has divided its platform into ten distinct subjects:

1. Origin of Government
2. Limited Federal Government
3. Rights of the Individual
4. Rights of the States
5. Responsibilities of the Federal Government
6. Rights of Local Communities over State, County, Federal Governments, Entities, and Outside Intervention.
7. Roles and Duties within the Federal Government: The Executive Branch
8. Roles and Duties within the Federal Government: The Judicial Branch
9. Roles and Duties within the Federal Government: The Legislative Branch
10. Campaigns and Elections

Much of what the APP articulates can be found in groups that have preceded it. For instance, the APP's emphasis on the rights of individuals and local communities over any state, county, or federal structure is very similar to the thought of the sovereign citizens movement and the Posse Comitatus. These groups, also seen as anti-government in nature, believe that the federal government has usurped power and has gone far beyond the limited power that was ceded to it at the founding. Patriot and other anti-government groups seek to reduce the power of the federal government and bring it back in line with a more idealized version of limited government that most adherents of this view believe is epitomized by the U.S. Constitution as it was originally constructed.

Today, the American Patriot Party has chapters in 27 states (Southern Poverty Law Center, Active Antigovernment Groups).

See also: Three Percenters

FURTHER READING

American Patriot Party. "American Patriot Party National Platform." American Patriot Party. http://www.americanpatriotparty.cc/platform/. (Accessed May 15, 2017.)

Balleck, Barry J. 2015. *Allegiance to Liberty: The Changing Face of Patriots, Militias, and Political Violence in America*. Praeger.

Patriot Party. http://thepatriotparty.org/. (Accessed May 15, 2017.)

Southern Poverty Law Center. "Active Antigovernment Groups in the United States." Southern Poverty Law Center. https://www.splcenter.org/active-antigovernment -groups-united-states. (Accessed May 15, 2017.)

Southern Poverty Law Center. February 15, 2017. "Active Patriot Groups in the US in 2016." Southern Poverty Law Center: Intelligence Report. https://www.splcenter .org/fighting-hate/intelligence-report/2017/active-patriot-groups-us-2016. (Accessed May 15, 2017.)

American Renaissance

American Renaissance is a magazine published by the New Century Foundation. It puts forth questionable scientific studies that attempt to demonstrate what the organization claims is the supremacy of the white race over all other races. The magazine was published as a monthly periodical from October 1990 through January 2012. However, since its last print issue in 2012, the magazine is found in an online version only (American Renaissance, Who We Are).

American Renaissance, founded by noted white supremacist Jared Taylor in 1990, conveys to readers "that race is an important aspect of the individual and group identity" (American Renaissance, What We Believe). Of the many issues that can be characterized as fault lines that punctuate the divisions in society, *American Renaissance* asserts that the issue of race is the most important and the most divisive.

The Southern Poverty Law Center (SPLC) contends that *American Renaissance* is a front for the New Century Foundation. The New Century Foundation is a white supremacist organization that hosts "suit-and-tie affairs" in order to attract a number of extremist groups to its conferences, including "neo-Nazis, white supremacists, Ku Klux Klan members, Holocaust deniers and eugenicists" (Southern Poverty Law Center). However, unlike many other right-wing extremists, founder Jared Taylor is known for displaying a less virulent brand of anti-Semitism and for encouraging Jews to participate in his events. In an interview with Phil Donahue on MSNBC-TV in 2003, Taylor said Jews "are fine by me" and "look white to me" (Southern Poverty Law Center). This attitude has put Taylor and *American Renaissance* at odds with other white supremacist groups and has led to conflict within the movement, particularly in terms of funding. In recent years, Taylor has taken up the cause of a "whites only" homeland somewhere in the United States. Believing that whites will soon be a minority in the country, Taylor believes that the American government has been a traitor to its own people. He also points out that the desire among whites for a national homeland automatically labels them as "haters" of all other peoples.

See also: New Century Foundation

FURTHER READING

American Renaissance. "What We Believe." American Renaissance. http://www.amren .com/about/. (Accessed October 7, 2017.)

American Renaissance. "Who We Are." http://www.amren.com/about/. (Accessed October 7, 2017.)

Southern Poverty Law Center. "American Renaissance." Southern Poverty Law Center. https://www.splcenter.org/fighting-hate/extremist-files/group/american-renais sance. (Accessed October 7, 2017.)

American Vikings

American Vikings is a racist skinhead group located in Danville, Indiana. The group was founded by veteran neo-Nazi Brien James. In 2003, James, along with Eric Fairburn, cofounded the Vinlanders Social Club, a loose coalition of racist skinhead groups in several states. Before founding the Vinlanders, James had been a member of the Outlaw Hammerskins, a group that directly challenged the authority of Hammerskin Nation, the largest and best-organized skinhead group in the United States. In 2000, "James allegedly punched and stomped a man to the point of death at a party in Indianapolis, Indiana" when the partygoer refused to "seig heil." James would later brag that his "JTTF (Joint Terrorism Task Force) file is a mile long" (Southern Poverty Law Center, Brien James). James was often described by contemporaries as "nuts and violent" (Southern Poverty Law Center, 2006).

In 2013, James organized yet another skinhead group, the American Vikings, which chose as its logo the hammer of the Norse god Thor. James stated that American Vikings would be "dedicated to creating entertaining and meaningful discussion about issues affecting patriotic, constitutional libertarian leaning, working class Americans" (Morlin). James touted the new group as a project "created by long-time former members of the American White Nationalist movement in the hopes that we can create a realistic and constructive dialog amongst several different types of patriots" (Morlin).

After founding American Vikings, James proclaimed on his website that the American Vikings group "is a new movement. We intend to offend racists and anti-racists alike. Liberals and conservatives. We have nothing to lose and nothing to fear" (Morlin).

As part of the launch of American Vikings, James created American Viking Clothing, which advertises T-shirts with sayings such as "F—Antifa" and "If you don't love the United States, you can always return to your s—hole country" (American Vikings). To drum up interest in American Vikings, James offered a free American Viking patch "for everyone who [bought] a T-shirt—once he personally check[ed] out the authenticity of the applicant" (Morlin).

See also: Hammerskin Nation; Neo-Nazis; Racist Skinheads; Vinlanders Social Club; White Nationalism; White Supremacist Movement

FURTHER READING

American Viking Clothing. https://www.facebook.com/americanvikingsclothing/. (Accessed May 31, 2018.)

American Vikings. "Welcome to American Vikings." American Vikings. https://shop .americanvikings.com/. (Accessed May 31, 2018.)

Morlin, Bill. May 17, 2013. "Veteran Skinhead Forms New Racist Club, Peddles T-Shirts on Internet." Southern Poverty Law Center: Hatewatch. https://www.splcenter .org/hatewatch/2013/05/17/veteran-skinhead-forms-new-racist-club-peddles -t-shirts-internet. (Accessed May 31, 2018.)

Southern Poverty Law Center. "Brien James." Southern Poverty Law Center. https:// www.splcenter.org/fighting-hate/extremist-files/individual/brien-james. (Accessed May 31, 2018.)

Southern Poverty Law Center. "Hate Map by State." Southern Poverty Law Center. https://www.splcenter.org/hate-map/by-state. (Accessed May 31, 2018.)

Southern Poverty Law Center. October 16, 2006. "Profiles of 10 Racist Skinheads." Southern Poverty Law Center: Intelligence Report. https://www.splcenter .org/fighting-hate/intelligence-report/2006/profiles-10-racist-skinheads. (Accessed May 31, 2018.)

America's Promise Ministries

Founded in 1967 by an "adherent of Christian Identity, Sheldon Emry, America's Promise Ministries" gained notoriety in the late 1980s when Emry's successor, "his son-in-law, Dave Barley, moved the organization to the northern Idaho town of Sandpoint" (Make America Safer Today). In this location, America's Promise Ministries found itself among other Christian Identity groups, as well as local networks of neo-Nazi and Ku Klux Klan groups. Richard Butler, the founder of Aryan Nations, and Louis Beam, a former leader in the Ku Klux Klan, were frequent speakers at America's Promise gatherings. America's Promise Ministries believes in a literal interpretation of the Bible and insists that Jesus Christ was white. Indeed, America's Promise holds that "all greatness achieved in the United States is attributed to the work of the white race and none other" (Humanist.com).

When Vincent Bertollini, a former Silicon Valley entrepreneur, moved to northern Idaho to help create a whites-only homeland, he donated large sums of money to America's Promise Ministries to "aid in the publication and distribution of the group's Christian Identity pamphlets" (Southern Poverty Law Center). Adherents of America's Promise Ministries have been linked to several violent attacks. In 1996, "three individuals who had attended America's Promise meetings detonated pipe bombs at an abortion clinic and a newspaper outlet in Washington state, and committed a string of bank robberies that totaled over $100,000" (Southern Poverty Law Center). The "leader of the criminal group was a protégé of Dave Barley," the leader of America's Promise Ministries (Southern Poverty Law Center). Three years later, in 1999, another member of Barley's congregation went on a shooting rampage in a "Jewish Community Center in Los Angeles, wounding three children, before killing a Filipino-American" mail carrier (Southern Poverty Law Center). Barley "has denied any link between the Christian Identity theology" preached at America's Promise Ministries and these acts of violence and terrorism (Southern Poverty Law Center).

As noted by the Southern Poverty Law Center, "America's Promise Ministries is now one of the few remaining outposts of white supremacy in the Idaho Panhandle. . . . America's Promise Ministries continues to have a widespread impact in the Identity world through its publishing business [and] its summertime family retreats . . . draw pastors and adherents from throughout the United States" (Southern Poverty Law Center).

See also: Aryan Nations; Christian Identity; Ku Klux Klan

FURTHER READING

Humanist.com. March 5, 2014. "5 Dangerous 'Christian Hate' Groups." Humanist.com. https://thehumanist.com/news/religion/5-dangerous-christian-hate-groups. (Accessed January 3, 2018.)

Make America Safer Today. http://www.makeamericasafertoday.org/. (Accessed November 24, 2018.)

Southern Poverty Law Center. "America's Promise Ministries." Southern Poverty Law Center. https://www.splcenter.org/fighting-hate/extremist-files/group/americas-promise-ministries. (Accessed January 3, 2018.)

Army of God

The Army of God (AOG) is a Christian terrorist organization that perpetrates attacks on abortion clinics and abortion providers. The U.S. Department of Justice defines the group as an underground terrorist organization with no definable structure or leadership. Individuals who have perpetrated attacks on abortion providers have claimed to act on behalf of the Army of God. A website that purports to be part of the Army of God is full of biblical scriptures and graphic pictures of aborted fetuses. The website also celebrates the acts of several individuals who have perpetrated acts of violence, including murder, against doctors who perform abortions, abortion clinics, and the patrons of abortion or family planning clinics.

The first known violent act claimed in the name of the Army of God was perpetrated in 1982 when a doctor who performed abortions and his wife were kidnapped and held captive for eight days. Subsequent individuals either succeeded in killing their targets or severely injured those whom they attacked. Eric Robert Rudolph, the bomber of the Atlanta Olympics, who also bombed two Atlanta abortion clinics and a lesbian nightclub, is held in high esteem by members of the Army of God. The AOG claimed credit for Rudolph's actions and, after his arrest, encouraged others to take up his cause. On November 27, 2015, Robert Lewis Dear Jr. killed three individuals, "including a University of Colorado at Colorado Springs police officer, in an attack on a Planned Parenthood clinic in Colorado Springs, Colorado" (Johnson). Claiming that he was engaged in "God's work," Dear praised the activities of AOG and claimed that he was "killing the killers." In addition to killing three individuals at the Planned Parenthood clinic, Dear wounded nine other individuals, including five police officers, in the standoff that followed the initial killings. Dear used a semiautomatic rifle and possessed hundreds of rounds of ammunition. Because of his actions, Robert Lewis Dear Jr. maintains a prominent position on the website dedicated to the Army of God.

See also: Family Research Council

FURTHER READING

Army of God. http://www.armyofgod.com/. (Accessed July 14, 2018.)

Johnson, Daryl. September 25, 2017. "Hate in God's Name." Southern Poverty Law Center. https://www.splcenter.org/20170925/hate-god%E2%80%99s-name. (Accessed July 14, 2018.)

Aryan Brotherhood

According to the Southern Poverty Law Center (SPLC), the Aryan Brotherhood (AB),

> also known as The Brand, Alice Baker, AB or One-Two, is the nation's oldest major white supremacist prison gang and a national crime syndicate. Founded in 1964 by Irish bikers as a form of protection for white inmates in newly desegregated prisons, the AB is today the largest and deadliest prison gang in the United States, with an estimated 20,000 members inside prisons and on the streets. (Southern Poverty Law Center, Aryan Brotherhood)

AB began in the California prison system during the 1960s as a result of desegregation. When American society began to desegregate during the civil rights era, so did the prison system of the United States. Thus, during the 1960s, when "black and white inmates were thrown up against each other in many cases for the first time," the result was often violent conflict between the racial groups (Southern Poverty Law Center, Aryan Brotherhood). AB "was formed at the San Quentin State Prison in California in 1964, organizing defensively against a violent black prison gang, the Black Guerilla Family, and becoming the first major white supremacist prison gang in the country in the process" (Southern Poverty Law Center, Aryan Brotherhood). Many "other prison gangs now use the 'Aryan Brotherhood' name (such as the Aryan Brotherhood of Texas), but they are independent and unrelated to the 'original' Aryan Brotherhood" (Anti-Defamation League).

White supremacy is at the core of AB's ideology. From its inception, AB was "explicitly racist" and new recruits (called "progeny") were "drilled" with white supremacist ideology (Stockton). The group's constitution,

> which members are supposed to memorize and only write out for new members to memorize, explicitly calls for exclusive loyalty and respect on the basis of a shared white heritage.
>
> For the first 10 years of its existence, the gang took this blood oath very seriously and kept its members far away from other races. AB . . . was so serious about race and ethnicity in the early days that members would sometimes turn white prospects away if they weren't at least part Irish [the group's founding members were mostly Irish inmates]. (Stockton)

AB "operates both inside and outside prisons, and although it clearly has a white supremacist ideology, it is above all a criminal enterprise. Given the choice between making money and showing their racism, members virtually always go for the cash, meaning the gang has often worked with Latino and other gangs for profit" (Southern Poverty Law Center, Aryan Brotherhood). As "a crime syndicate, the AB . . ."

> participates in drug trafficking, male prostitution rings, gambling, and extortion inside prison walls. On the streets, the AB is involved in practically every kind of

criminal enterprise, including murder-for-hire, armed robbery, gun running, meth-amphetamine manufacturing, heroin sales, counterfeiting and identity theft. (Southern Poverty Law Center, Aryan Brotherhood)

In 1985, AB reorganized itself, an act that briefly split the gang into a California prison wing and a federal prison wing. The new structure "made an already-dangerous gang even more dangerous. From its first days, AB distinguished itself by the extreme brutality of its attacks and the complete lack of tolerance it showed to disloyalty, disrespect, or to potential threats from outside" (Stockton). A former "AB commissioner" summed up AB's "policy toward prison murder":

> For the Aryan Brotherhood, murder is a way to make a social statement. If blacks attack whites, we send a message. We go pick one of their shot callers. We catch them walking across the yard under guard escort in handcuffs. It don't matter. We're going to butcher him in front of God and everybody at high noon in the middle of the yard. And it's not just going to be a few clean stab marks. It's going to be a vicious, brutal killing. Because that's how brothers take care of business, and a brother's work is never done. (Stockton)

AB's ability to influence criminal activities outside of prison walls "received a huge boost when Italian-American Mafia boss John Gotti was sentenced to life in prison without parole and transferred to the Marion [Ohio] facility in 1992." According to the SPLC:

> Gotti hired the AB to protect him, but went on to organize a business partnership between his associates and AB members on the outside. The move gave the AB unprecedented power on the streets, where the group had been operating in major cities since the 1980s, with an appointed leader in each city or, in the case of more sparsely populated areas, each region. (Southern Poverty Law Center, Aryan Brotherhood)

Charles Manson had also tried to enlist AB's protection, but he was "refused membership because he declined to kill other inmates because of their skin color." Nevertheless, AB used Manson's "coterie of female fans to smuggle drugs and weapons into San Quentin" (Southern Poverty Law Center, Aryan Brotherhood).

Today, AB members make up "less than one percent of the U.S. prison population but [are] responsible for 21 percent of the murders across the system" (Stockton). The AB may have as many as 20,000 members both inside and outside of prison. Many adherents "belong to the group for the identity and purpose it provides" (Anonymous). The group's motto, "Blood In/Blood Out," indicates how members both enter and leave the organization: in other words, "killing a black or a Hispanic prisoner" and remaining in the organization until you die—"Quitting isn't an option. There's only death" (Anonymous).

See also: White Supremacist Movement

FURTHER READING

Anonymous. April 1, 2013. "Why I Fear the Aryan Brotherhood—and You Should, Too." Daily Beast. https://www.thedailybeast.com/why-i-fear-the-aryan-brotherhoodand -you-should-too. (Accessed August 3, 2018.)

Anti-Defamation League. "Aryan Brotherhood." Anti-Defamation League. https://www
.adl.org/education/references/hate-symbols/aryan-brotherhood. (Accessed August 3,
2018.)

Barroquere, Brett. June 7, 2018. "I Told You It Was Going to Happen." Southern Poverty
Law Center: Hatewatch. https://www.splcenter.org/hatewatch/2018/06/07/i-told
-you-it-was-going-happen. (Accessed August 3, 2018.)

Federal Bureau of Investigation (FBI). "Aryan Brotherhood." FBI.gov. https://vault.fbi
.gov/Aryan%20Brotherhood%20. (Accessed August 3, 2018.)

Morlin, Bill. July 11, 2018. "One of the Founders of the Aryan Brotherhood Dies in Federal Prison." Southern Poverty Law Center: Hatewatch. https://www.splcenter
.org/hatewatch/2018/07/11/one-founders-aryan-brotherhood-dies-federal-prison.
(Accessed August 3, 2018.)

Pelisek, Christine. April 3, 2013. "What's So Scary about the Texas Aryan Brotherhood?
Take a Look at the Indictments." Daily Beast. https://www.thedailybeast.com
/whats-so-scary-about-the-texas-aryan-brotherhood-take-a-look-at-the-indict
ments. (Accessed August 3, 2018.)

Southern Poverty Law Center. "Aryan Brotherhood." Southern Poverty Law Center.
https://www.splcenter.org/fighting-hate/extremist-files/group/aryan-brotherhood.
(Accessed August 3, 2018.)

Southern Poverty Law Center. "Aryan Brotherhood of Texas." Southern Poverty Law
Center. https://www.splcenter.org/fighting-hate/extremist-files/group/aryan-brother
hood-texas. (Accessed August 3, 2018.)

Stockton, Richard. May 9, 2018. "Inside the Aryan Brotherhood, One of the World's Most
Dangerous Prison Gangs." AllThatsInteresting.com. https://allthatsinteresting
.com/aryan-brotherhood-gang. (Accessed August 3, 2018.)

Wood, Graeme. October 2014. "How Gangs Took Over Prisons." *Atlantic.* https://www
.theatlantic.com/magazine/archive/2014/10/how-gangs-took-over-prisons/379330/.
(Accessed August 3, 2018.)

Aryan Nationalist Alliance

The Aryan Nationalist Alliance (ANA) was organized in April 2016 in an attempt
to "unify the unruly and questionable characters that populate the ranks of the
white supremacist world under a new banner" (Viets). The ANA was formed after
a rally in Rome, Georgia, in which "racist skinheads, and avowed white nationalist groups vowed to create an 'ethnostate' where each racial group could govern
themselves according to their culture and ethnic self-interest" (Viets). People of
color, "Jews and other groups who have light skin . . . should have their own
homes, separate from ours" (Viets). The rally in Rome, Georgia, was punctuated
by familiar hate tropes, such as burning crosses and prominent displays of the
Nazi swastika, together with chants of "White Power." At one point, one of
the attendees shouted, "For God! For Race! For Nation!" Gathered members were
then instructed to "[a]pproach your symbol [the cross]. Do not turn your back
on the symbol" (Vocativ). In August 2016, ANA helped organize a White Lives
Matter protest "that targeted the Houston offices of the NAACP" (Mayo). The
protest was organized a month after five Houston police officers died at a Black
Lives Matter rally. The perpetrator in the attack, a black man, had stated that
he was angry about police shootings of black men and had made it known that he
wanted to kill white people.

According to one commentator, the formation of ANA was a reaction to changing social, economic, and political conditions in the United States:

White nationalists see a litany of significant problems that draw people to their ranks, including lax border security and President Barack Obama's executive actions to give U.S. citizenship to millions of undocumented immigrants. Then there's the federal government's plan to allow Syrian refugees into the country, not to mention the removal of the Confederate battle flag from statehouses across the South after Dylann Roof, a self-made white supremacist inspired by white-pride rhetoric, allegedly killed nine people at a predominantly black church in South Carolina. Add to that the candidacy of Donald Trump, who has certainly helped fan the flames of white supremacy with his anti-immigrant rhetoric. The success of the Black Lives Matter movement threw additional fuel on the fire. (Vocativ)

Jeff Schoep, longtime leader of the National Socialist Movement, stated that the formation of the ANA was "making history. We are putting together all the white organizations. . . . There is no more time for division" (Vocativ). Another white nationalist, Matthew Heimbach, founder of the white supremacist organization Youth for Western Civilization (YWC), stated upon the founding of ANA:

We have the potential to be able to work with so many of these millions of families to be able to then move them in our direction. Donald Trump is a gateway drug . . . we can then move them from civic nationalism and populism to nationalism for us—and these people are ready for our message. (Vocativ)

When ANA members are asked if they advocate violence, they will answer no. Yet at the Rome rally, people recited such chants as "Death to the ungodly! Death to the Jews!" (Vocativ). And in one particularly disturbing chant, ANA adherents were heard to ask, "How many Jews can you fit in a Volkswagen? However many you can fit in the ashtray!" (Vocativ).

See also: National Socialist Movement; Neo-Nazis; Racist Skinheads; White Lives Matter; White Nationalism; White Supremacist Movement

FURTHER READING

Mayo, Marilyn. August 23, 2016. "White Supremacist Group behind Houston 'White Lives Matter' Protest." Anti-Defamation League. https://www.adl.org/blog/white-suprem acist-group-behind-houston-white-lives-matter-protest. (Accessed May 31, 2018.)

Viets, Sarah. July 21, 2016. "Meet the Aryan Nationalist Alliance—A Racist Hodgepodge Doomed to Fail." Southern Poverty Law Center: Hatewatch. https://www.splcen ter.org/hatewatch/2016/07/21/meet-aryan-nationalist-alliance-%E2%80%93-rac ist-hodgepodge-doomed-fail. (Accessed May 31, 2018.)

Vocativ, James King. October 25, 2016. "Rival White Supremacist Groups Unite to Fight 'Race War.'" Huffpost. https://www.huffingtonpost.com/entry/white-supremacist -groups_us_5722407ce4b01a5ebde4ca74. (Accessed May 31, 2018.)

Aryan Nations

Aryan Nations (AN) is a white supremacist organization originally based in Hayden Lake, Idaho. It was founded in 1977 by Richard Butler, who was an adherent of Christian Identity, which preached a virulently racist and anti-Semitic message. During the 1980s and 1990s, AN was the most powerful organizing force for white supremacists in the United States, and it attracted neo-Nazis, racist skinheads, Ku Klux Klan (KKK) members, and white nationalists. The organization also spawned other organizations, such as the Order, that became even more violent than itself. In 2000, AN began to disintegrate after losing a civil rights lawsuit brought by the Southern Poverty Law Center (SPLC). The group had to sell its compound and assets in Idaho to satisfy the damages that were assessed to AN in the judgment. In the aftermath of the defeat, AN fractured and then lost all cohesion when founder Richard Butler died in 2004. Today, Aryan Nations still exists as an entity, but it has all but faded from the white supremacists' scene, with only a few dozen adherents scattered across the United States (Morlin).

Though Richard Butler founded Aryan Nations (AN), the roots of the organization are found in the "theology" of Christian Identity, an anti-Semitic and white supremacy organization that teaches that white people are God's chosen people and that Jews are the spawn of a union between Eve and Satan. Butler was introduced to Christian Identity by Wesley Swift, who founded a Christian Identity church—the Church of Jesus Christ Christian—in California in the 1940s. One of Swift's associates was William Potter Gale, a retired army colonel who had been on the staff of Gen. Douglas MacArthur. After World War II, Gale became a leading figure in various anti-tax and paramilitary movements before founding the anti-government and anti-Semitic organization Posse Comitatus ("force of the county") in the 1960s. Gale introduced Butler to Posse Comitatus, and Butler began attending Christian Identity meetings and sermons. Around 1965, Butler became an ordained Christian Identity minister (Southern Poverty Law Center).

Butler had long expressed his admiration for Adolf Hitler and longed for a whites-only homeland in the Pacific Northwest, the only portion of the country where blacks and minorities were not found in large numbers. Butler retired as an aeronautical engineer in 1973, and the next year, he moved to Hayden Lake, Idaho, where he bought 20 acres of land and an old farmhouse and formed his own "Christian Posse Comitatus" group. In 1977, Butler opened a congregation of the Church of Jesus Christ Christian on his property and organized Aryan Nations as the congregation's political arm.

In 1981, Butler's church was bombed, causing more than $80,000 in damage. Butler then fortified his land with a two-story guard tower, and he posted armed guards all around the land (Southern Poverty Law Center). For the next 20 years, Butler would host gatherings of racists, white nationalists, white supremacists, anti-Semites, KKK members, and other extremists at the annual Aryan World Congress gatherings on his property. During the 1980s, Aryan Nations became the most powerful voice in the white supremacist movement, and its influence was felt across the breadth of the United States.

An acolyte of Butler's, Bob Mathews, believed that the white race was on the verge of extinction because of immigration and higher birth rates among minority groups. Mathews had attended several AN meetings and had made many friends within the organization. In 1982, Mathews made an effort to attract white families—what he called the "White American Bastion"—to settle in the Pacific

Northwest in order to create a "whites-only homeland." In a speech at a National Alliance convention the next year, Mathews called upon "yeoman farmers and independent truckers" to join his "White American Bastion" group (Martinez and Guinther). At the time, the National Alliance was the leading neo-Nazi organization in the United States. As inspiration for his movement, Mathews drew upon the published material of William Pierce, the founder of the National Alliance. In *The Turner Diaries*, Pierce had imagined a future world in the United States where politicians, academics, and "race traitors" (the "System") are exterminated in a race war led by militants calling themselves the Order. Thus, "the Order" became Mathews's new organization. The group would go on to become one of the most notorious terror groups in the United States, purloining over $3.6 million in funds from armored car heists and assassinating Jewish talk show host Alan Berg in Denver, Colorado, in 1984. Mathews would die in a shoot-out with the FBI in December 1984.

Aside from Mathews, other AN members committed violent crimes, including the murder of a state trooper in Missouri in 1985 and conspiracy to commit murder of federal agents. In 1987, Butler and 13 others were charged as the "godfathers" of a conspiracy hatched at the 1983 Aryan World Congress to commit a variety of crimes and violent acts across the country. After a trial, the defendants were all acquitted (Southern Poverty Law Center).

In 1989, Butler celebrated Adolf Hitler's 100th birthday by inviting racist skinheads and other extremist groups to the AN compound for a celebration that included musical performances by white power skinhead bands. This event was the beginning of Butler's attempts to recruit younger members into AN.

By 1997, AN had lost half of its membership, and Butler was seeking to appoint a successor. Butler appointed a fellow Christian Identity pastor, Neuman Britton, but he died before taking the reins of the organization. Eventually, Butler named Ray Redfeairn to replace him, even though Redfeairn would leave AN, return, and then leave again before eventually returning to take over the organization upon Butler's death.

In 1998, a former Aryan Nations guard fired more than 70 rounds with a submachine gun at a Jewish community center in Los Angeles, California. He would confess that he perpetrated the attack because of his hatred for Jews. The same year, AN security guards chased down a woman and her son who had been traveling in the area of the AN compound when their car backfired. Thinking that the vehicle was firing upon the compound, the AN guards ran down the car and forced it into a ditch. The mother and son were brutally assaulted before being released.

In 2000, the Southern Poverty Law Center (SPLC) brought a civil rights lawsuit against Aryan Nations in behalf of Victoria and Jason Keenan, whom the AN guards had assaulted. Claiming that the assault was the result of the virulent hatred preached by Aryan Nations, a jury eventually awarded a $6.3 million judgment against AN, of which Butler was responsible for $4.8 million. In February 2001, Aryan Nation's Hayden Lake compound and intellectual property, including the names "Aryan Nations" and "Church of Jesus Christ Christian" were transferred to the Keenans, who sold the property to an Idaho philanthropist (Keenan v. Aryan Nations). Both the guard tower and the church on the property were burned down during firefighting drills. Butler remained in the Hayden Lake area after a wealthy supporter bought him a house (Southern Poverty Law Center).

Butler died in September 2004. Aryan Nations then split into two factions, one located in Pennsylvania and the other in Georgia. After several attempts to revive the organization, the last self-proclaimed leader of Aryan Nations, Morris Gulett, announced on November 15, 2015, that he was disbanding the organization. In announcing the move, Gulett said:

> I will never lose respect for the noble and honorable organization that Pastor Butler created 40 years ago, but our Holy White Race has evidently lost the will to live. Because of the degeneration of our people, the noble and honorable organization Aryan Nations no longer exists with the veracity that it once had. Therefore, it deserves to be respectfully laid to rest. No doubt some will continue to haul Aryan Nations through the mud by attaching its Christian standard to their filthy unwashed lives. (Morlin)

Today, there is a movement afoot to resurrect Aryan Nations in the Hayden Lake, Idaho, area, spurred by those who were influenced by the "indelible ideological marks" that AN left on the region (Day). Their numbers are small, however, and it is not apparent that the rejuvenation will last long.

See also: National Alliance; Neo-Nazis; The Order; White Nationalism; White Supremacist Movement

FURTHER READING

Anti-Defamation League. "Aryan Nations/Church of Jesus Christ Christian." Anti-Defamation League. https://www.adl.org/education/resources/profiles/aryan-nations. (Accessed May 19, 2017.)

Day, Meagan. November 4, 2016. "Welcome to Hayden Lake, Where the White Supremacists Tried to Build Their Homeland." Timeline.com. https://timeline.com/white-supremacist-rural-paradise-fb62b74b29e0. (Accessed May 19, 2017.)

Keenan v. Aryan Nations. Case Number: CV-99-441. Southern Poverty Law Center. https://www.splcenter.org/seeking-justice/case-docket/keenan-v-aryan-nations. (Accessed May 19, 2017.)

Macdonald, Andrew (a.k.a. William Pierce). 1999. *The Turner Diaries*. 2nd ed. National Vanguard Books.

Martinez, Thomas, and John Guinther. 1999. *Brotherhood of Murder*. iUniverse.

Morlin, Bill. December 17, 2015. "Aryan Nations Quickly Fading into Racist History." Southern Poverty Law Center: Hatewatch. https://www.splcenter.org/hatewatch/2015/12/17/aryan-nations-quickly-fading-racist-history. (Accessed May 19, 2017.)

Southern Poverty Law Center. "Aryan Nations." Southern Poverty Law Center. https://www.splcenter.org/fighting-hate/extremist-files/group/aryan-nations. (Accessed May 19, 2017.)

Aryan Nations Worldwide

Aryan Nations Worldwide is an organization created from the remnants of Aryan Nations (Louisiana), a group founded by the one-time self-proclaimed leader of Aryan Nations—Morris Gulett. Aryan Nations is based in Villa Rica, Georgia, and is "designated by the Southern Poverty Law Center (SPLC) as a neo-Nazi hate group" (Southern Poverty Law Center). According to the SPLC, "Neo-Nazi groups share a hatred for Jews and a love for Adolf Hitler and Nazi Germany. While they also hate other minorities, gays and lesbians and even sometimes Christians, they perceive 'the Jew' as their cardinal enemy" (Southern Poverty Law Center). Like various other Aryan Nations offshoots, Aryan Nations Worldwide professes the doctrine of Christian Identity, an ideology that believes that "white Europeans are the 'lost tribes' of Israel and God's true chosen people. It also teaches that other races are inferior or even subhuman" (Joyner, June 24, 2016). Aryan Nations Worldwide is currently led by Randall Wiley Smith, who has "a long history in the white supremacist movement." Smith "used to be active with the Southern White Knights of the Ku Klux Klan and in 1986 accepted a plea deal for attacking a Black teenager in Cedartown, GA. Smith is now part of the Aryan Nations Worldwide 'leadership council' " (Anonymous).

Though the membership in Aryan Nations Worldwide is small, they are "extremely anti-Semitic and racist" (Joyner, June 24, 2016). The group "endorsed the mass shooting in Orlando at a gay nightclub, which claimed 49 lives. The Pulse nightclub massacre was 'the Lord's work,' " one member noted. He attributed "the high death toll to God's own hand on the trigger. That was nothing more than a Sodom and Gomorrah in that club" (Joyner, June 23, 2016). In March 2017, members of Aryan Nations Worldwide gathered at the Douglas County Courthouse in Douglasville, Georgia, to protest "the sentencing of Jose Torres and Kayla Norton for terrorizing an 8-year old boy's birthday party with Confederate flags and brandished guns" (Atlanta Antifascists). The racist rampage perpetrated by Torres and Norton "included shouting racial slurs, making armed threats and waving Confederate battle flags" (Chappell).

During the 2016 U.S. presidential campaign, Aryan Nations Worldwide members—who, as part of their Christian Identity ideology, "believe that the Apocalypse is close at hand"—hoped that Democratic Hillary Clinton would be elected. As one member stated, "In all honesty, I really think it would help the movement if Hillary Clinton wins. Our country's knees are bent. If she wins, our knees will be on the ground" (Joyner, June 23, 2016). Imagining the "country's presumed total collapse" because of a Clinton presidency, Aryan Nations Worldwide

> described a vision of America where racial segregation and white rule is re-established under the banner of the Christian church. Given a Clinton-induced revolution . . . "race mixing" and homosexuality would no longer be tolerated and whites would rule. Oh, and it will be white men at the helm. (Joyner, June 23, 2016)

Though Aryan Nations Worldwide is based in Villa Rica, Georgia, they insist that their movement is worldwide. "We are seeing the downfall of civilization," one Aryan Nations Worldwide member said. "Thank god for the internet" (Joyner, June 23, 2016). As noted by one journalist:

> The internet has helped create a homogenized, international hatred of non-whites, immigrants, and LGBT communities that transcend organizational boundaries. That unity is oxygen for a movement that has suffered from decades of imprisoned leadership, costly court battles and fractious internal politics. (Joyner, June 23, 2016)

See also: Aryan Nations; Christian Identity; Neo-Nazis; White Supremacist Movement

FURTHER READING

Anonymous. October 3, 2016. "Anti-Racists Flyer Woodstock, Georgia Neighborhood to Oppose Aryan Nations." It's Going Down. https://itsgoingdown.org/anti-racists -flyer-woodstock-georgia-neighborhood-oppose-aryan-nations/. (Accessed June 8, 2018.)

Atlanta Antifascists. April 9, 2017. "Documentation: No-Show from North Mississippi White Knights, Assorted Racists Stay Low Key, Douglassville GA March 5, 2017." Atlanta Antifascists. https://afainatl.wordpress.com/2017/04/09/documenta tion-no-show-from-north-mississippi-white-knights-assorted-racists-stay-low -key-douglasville-ga-march-5-2017/#more-1389. (Accessed June 8, 2018.)

Chappell, Bill. February 28, 2017. "Racist Assault at a Child's Birthday Party Yields Long Prison Terms in Georgia." National Public Radio. https://www.npr.org/sections /thetwo-way/2017/02/28/517688757/racist-assault-on-a-childs-birthday-party -yields-long-prison-terms-in-georgia. (Accessed June 8, 2018.)

Joyner, Chris. June 23, 2016. "The Hater Next Door: My Interview with Our Local Aryan Nations." Atlanta Journal-Constitution. https://www.myajc.com/news/the-hater -next-door-interview-with-our-local-aryan-nations/SvlOWGnXCvLAEPf7 y9cvCO/. (Accessed June 8, 2018.)

Joyner, Chris. June 24, 2016. "The Aryan Nations: 5 Things to Know." Atlanta Journal-Constitution. https://www.myajc.com/blog/investigations/the-aryan-nations-things -know/8czBuVfIWJ7foxzXvygygI/. (Accessed June 8, 2018.)

Morlin, Bill. February 17, 2016. "Aryan Deflations." Southern Poverty Law Center: Intelligence Report. https://www.splcenter.org/fighting-hate/intelligence-report/2016 /aryan-deflations-0. (Accessed June 8, 2018.)

Southern Poverty Law Center. "Neo-Nazi." Southern Poverty Law Center. https://www .splcenter.org/fighting-hate/extremist-files/ideology/neo-nazi. (Accessed June 8, 2018.)

Aryan Renaissance Society

The Aryan Renaissance Society (ARS) has been labeled "a neo-Nazi hate group by the Southern Poverty Law Center" (SPLC) (Southern Poverty Law Center, Neo Nazi). According to the SPLC, "Neo-Nazi groups share a hatred for Jews and a love for Adolf Hitler and Nazi Germany. While they also hate other minorities, gays and lesbians and even sometimes Christians, they perceive 'the Jew' as their cardinal enemy" (Southern Poverty Law Center, Neo-Nazi). The Anti-Defamation League notes that ARS is "a small but long-lived white supremacist group that has resembled both a racist skinhead group and a prison clique at times. It has had members from a variety of places, but many came from Texas and New Jersey" (Anti-Defamation League). The "About" section of the ARS website is largely an advertisement for recruitment, but within the rhetoric lies the cores of ARS's philosophy:

> The Preservation, Progression and Proliferation of the Aryan Race.
> At this time, the ARS is embarking on a significant period of recruitment and expansion to meet the strong need for racial and cultural awareness in our communities. Recruits should desire providing strategic and innovative leadership to the development, articulation, and implementation of both substantive and operational aspects of White Separatism. These men and women should set the direction for

medium and long term strategy, ensuring that their priorities reflect collective interests, vision and mission in the context of achievement of racial and cultural goals, and in alignment with the strategic objectives of key planning of the Aryan Renaissance Society. (Aryan Renaissance Society)

ARS was founded in 2011, and since that time it has been trying to increase its membership and visibility. Requirements to be part of the ARS "team" include "extensive racial awareness and leadership skills and experience at the field level (local chapters)" and "fluency and the ability to convey organizational ideology clearly" (Aryan Renaissance Society). In early 2016, ARS joined the fledgling United Aryan Front, a "hodgepodge of racist skinheads, neo-Nazis, Christian Identity adherents and Ku Klux Klan members" (Viets, February 2016). The United Aryan Front was formed to "create an internationally-oriented network of dedicated White Separatists diligently striving to impart a New Racial Consciousness to Aryankind" (Viets, February 2016).

ARS has also been a leading force behind the White Lives Matter (WLM) movement. One of ARS's members, Rebecca Barnette (who has since left ARS in favor of another neo-Nazi organization), has been credited with being one of the "key leaders" of WLM (Viets, August 2016). Barnette, "who describes herself as a 'revolutionist' [and] who is working to 'create a new world' for white people' " is deeply involved in the social media presence of WLM (Viets, August 2016). The WLM website, which Barnette runs, "describes the movement as dedicated to promotion of the white race and taking positive action as a united voice against issues facing our race." Barnette has also stated that "Jews and Muslims have formed an alliance 'to commit genocide of epic proportions' of the white race. Now is the time . . . for the blood of our enemies [to] soak our soil to form new mortar to rebuild our landmasses" (Viets, August 2016).

In 2017, an ARS member, Horace Scott Lacy, was found distributing WLM material in western New York in order to recruit new members. Lacy claimed to be a former member of the Aryan Circle prison gang and presumably was an organizer "of an August 2016 protest of the NAACP headquarters in Houston [Texas] . . . [and] he was also present an October [2016] armed protest at the Anti-Defamation League" (Anonymous).

ARS, which appears to be most prominent in Texas, "promotes and publicizes White Lives Matter (WLM) as 'a movement dedicated to [the] promotion of the white race' " (Blumenfeld).

See also: Neo-Nazis; United Aryan Front; White Lives Matter; White Nationalism; White Supremacist Movement

FURTHER READING

Anonymous. March 30, 2017. "Neo-Nazi Horace Scott Lacy Recruiting in Western New York." It's Going Down. https://itsgoingdown.org/neo-nazi-horace-scott-lacy -recruiting-western-new-york/. (Accessed June 29, 2018.)

Anti-Defamation League. "Aryan Renaissance Society." Anti-Defamation League. https://www.adl.org/education/references/hate-symbols/aryan-renaissance-soci ety. (Accessed June 29, 2018.)

Aryan Renaissance Society. "About." Aryan Renaissance Society. https://www.causes
.com/causes/642201-aryan-renaissance-society/about. (Accessed June 29, 2018.)

Blumenfeld, Warren. July 20, 2016. "'White Lives Matter' so Whites Can Live without
Fear." Good Men Project. https://goodmenproject.com/featured-content/white
-lives-matter-so-whites-can-live-without-fear-wcz/. (Accessed June 29, 2017.)

Southern Poverty Law Center. "Neo-Nazi." Southern Poverty Law Center. https://www
.splcenter.org/fighting-hate/extremist-files/ideology/neo-nazi. (Accessed June 29,
2018.)

Southern Poverty Law Center. February 15, 2017. "Active Hate Groups 2016." Southern
Poverty Law Center: Intelligence Report. https://www.splcenter.org/fighting-hate
/intelligence-report/2017/active-hate-groups-2016. (Accessed June 29, 2018.)

Viets, Sarah. February 11, 2016. "American and International Racists Create 'United
Aryan Front' Coalition." Southern Poverty Law Center: Hatewatch. https://www
.splcenter.org/hatewatch/2016/02/11/american-and-international-racists-create
-united-aryan-front-coalition. (Accessed June 29, 2018.)

Viets, Sarah. August 3, 2016. "White Lives Matter." Southern Poverty Law Center: Intelligence Report. https://www.splcenter.org/fighting-hate/intelligence-report/2016
/white-lives-matter. (Accessed June 29, 2018.)

Aryan Strikeforce

Aryan Strikeforce "is labeled a racist skinhead hate group by the Southern Poverty Law Center" (SPLC) (Southern Poverty Law Center, Racist Skinhead).
According to the SPLC, "Racist Skinheads form a particularly violent element of
the white supremacist movement, and have often been referred to as the 'shock
troops' of the hoped-for revolution. The classic Skinhead look is a shaved head,
black Doc Martens boots, jeans with suspenders and an array of typically racist
tattoos" (Southern Poverty Law Center, Racist Skinhead). Aryan Strikeforce
describes itself in the following manner:

> The Aryan Strikeforce is a white nationalist organization that is reputable as a
> defense league with several main purposes as a foundation that shall never be com-
> promised under any conditions or circumstances. Our goal is to protect the honour
> of our women, children, and the future of our race and nation. The Aryan Strike-
> force's main goal is to provide today's adolescence, an alternative to this failed State
> of a Zionist eroded government We will educate our youth about their culture and
> heritage. As well as teach our race to feel pride for who they are. We will educate
> the masses about the preservation of our race, heritage, and our way of life. We will
> show them real life examples about how Zionism has slowly eroded our bloodline,
> morals, and values. By organizing our race and strengthening our selves physically
> and mentally we will Not tolerate Red trends imposing upon on lineage and nations
> we are the few who are qualified and prepared for when the time comes to regain
> our once great, but now fallen, nation. (Aryan Strikeforce)

Aryan Strikeforce "was founded in 2013 by New Jersey racist skinhead Josh
'Hatchet' Steever, who has a long, violent criminal history" (Anti-Defamation
League). According to the Anti-Defamation League (ADL), Steever established
Aryan Strikeforce after being kicked out of another racist skinhead group that he
had created. Aryan Strikeforce has become infamous for the violence of its mem-
bers. In June 2017, a racist named Cameron "Twisted Lonewolf" Anthony of

Arlington, Massachusetts, "was arrested after allegedly using a baseball bat to threaten a Latino man, while simultaneously brandishing a knife and shouting 'white power.' Anthony, who was charged with assault with a dangerous weapon and civil rights violations, has been connected to the Aryan Strikeforce crew since 2014" (Anti-Defamation League). In early March 2018,

> federal prosecutors revealed that members of Aryan Strikeforce talked about committing a suicide bombing attack on counter-protestors at a November 2016 white supremacist rally in Harrisburg, PA. The attack would have been perpetrated by a terminally ill member of the group, who planned to hide the bomb in his portable oxygen tank. There is no indication that the plan, which displayed a type of delusional thinking that's typical among white supremacist groups, ever advanced beyond the discussion phase. (Anti-Defamation League)

Within an eight-month span from late 2016 until the middle of 2017, eight members of Aryan Strikeforce were arrested and indicted on charges of "conspiracy to defraud the U.S., racketeering, money laundering, dealing with unregistered interstate commerce, transfer of machine gun parts and firearms by convicted felons, and two counts of conspiracy to distribute a controlled substance [methamphetamine]" (Novak). The U.S. Federal Bureau of Investigation (FBI) had infiltrated the group under "court approved action" as "part of an ongoing investigation" (Novak). Most of the Aryan Strikeforce members indicted as a result of the investigation "face a minimum of 10 years in federal prison and at least five years of supervised release after getting out" (Barrouquere, May 9, 2018).

According to the SPLC, Aryan Strikeforce has chapters in Arizona, California, Colorado, Florida, Iowa, Illinois, Indiana, Kentucky, Massachusetts, Minnesota, Missouri, New Jersey, New York, Ohio, Oklahoma, Pennsylvania, Texas, Virginia, and Vermont (Southern Poverty Law Center, 2015).

See also: Racist Skinheads; United Aryan Front; White Nationalism; White Supremacist Movement

FURTHER READING

Anti-Defamation League. June 30, 2017. "For Racist Skinhead Crew Aryan Strikeforce, 88 Stands for 8 Arrests in 8 Months." Anti-Defamation League. https://www.adl.org/blog/for-racist-skinhead-crew-aryan-strikeforce-88-stands-for-8-arrests-in-8-months. (Accessed June 30, 2018.)

Aryan Strikeforce. "Aryan Strikeforce/Combat 18 International." https://vk.com/as318. (Accessed June 30, 2018.)

Barrouquere, Brett. April 19, 2018. "Two Aryan Strikeforce Members Set to Plead Guilty in Federal Drug Case." Southern Poverty Law Center: Hatewatch. https://www.splcenter.org/hatewatch/2018/04/19/two-aryan-strikeforce-members-set-plead-guilty-federal-drug-case-0. (Accessed June 30, 2018.)

Barrouquere, Brett. May 9, 2018. "A Member of Aryan Strikeforce Pleads Guilty to Federal Drug Charge." Southern Poverty Law Center: Hatewatch. https://www.splcenter.org/hatewatch/2018/05/09/member-aryan-strikeforce-pleads-guilty-federal-drug-charge-2. (Accessed June 30, 2018.)

Morlin, Bill. May 1, 2017. "Serious Federal Charges Filed against 'Aryan Strikeforce.'" Southern Poverty Law Center: Hatewatch. https://www.splcenter.org/hate

watch/2017/05/01/serious-federal-charges-filed-against-%E2%80%9Caryan
-strikeforce. (Accessed June 30, 2018.)

Novak, Steve. April 29, 2017. "The White Supremacists Next Door: How Feds Infiltrated Aryan Strikeforce." Lehigh Valley Live. https://www.lehighvalleylive.com/warren -county/index.ssf/2017/04/white_supremacist_phillipsburg.html. (Accessed June 30, 2018.)

Southern Poverty Law Center. "Racist Skinhead." Southern Poverty Law Center. https:// www.splcenter.org/fighting-hate/extremist-files/ideology/racist-skinhead. (Accessed June 30, 2018.)

Southern Poverty Law Center. March 2, 2015. "Active Racist Skinhead Groups." Southern Poverty Law Center: Intelligence Report. https://www.splcenter.org/fighting -hate/intelligence-report/2015/active-racist-skinhead-groups. (Accessed June 30, 2018.)

Aryan Terror Brigade

The Aryan Terror Brigade (ATB) is a racist skinhead group "formed in 2009 that today has members in the United States, South America and Europe" (Anti-Defamation League). Though the group's activities take place largely on the Internet, members of the group have been linked to violent, racist activity mostly in the northeastern part of the United States. A website maintained with the name "Aryan Terror Brigade/Combat 18" states:

> The Aryan Terror Brigade is a pro white organization that is reputable as a defense league with several main purposes as a foundation that shall never be compromised under any conditions or circumstances. Our goal is to protect the honour of our women, children, and the future of our race and nation. The ATB's main goal is to provide today's adolescence with an alternative to this failed social experiment known as the "melting-pot" of multiculturalism. We will educate our youth about their culture and heritage. As well as teach our race to feel pride and not "white guilt" for who they are. We will educate the masses about the preservation of our race, heritage, and our way of life. We will show them real life examples about how Marxism has slowly eroded our bloodline, morals, and values. By organizing our race and strengthening our selves physically and mentally we will be prepared for when the time comes to regain our once great, but now fallen, nation. (Vk.com)

Josh Steever, an ATB member who served time "both for beating a man with an axe handle and for threatening to stab two black high school students," is perhaps the most infamous member of ATB. Steever is easily recognizable "by his tattoos as he has the word 'racist' and 'a swastika' tattooed on his face" (Southern Poverty Law Center, 2013). In 2013, Steever was in jail in Middlesex County, New Jersey, on charges of making terroristic threats (Philly Antifa). However, in an article published by Philly Antifa, an anti-fascist blog, there were accusations made that ATB members, who had been arrested after randomly attacking Arab residents of a housing community, had been "snitched on" by a fellow ATB member because, in actuality, Steever was a "police informant," and that "Aryan Terror Brigade might have been created with the express purpose of attracting some of the more reckless and unstable elements of the White Power scene in the US" (Philly Antifa). As noted by Philly Antifa,

Police informants and undercover agents are no new phenomenon in Neo-Nazi/Far Right circles. Powerhouses in their movement such as The Order, the World Church of the Creator and the certain incarnations of the KKK have been destroyed by state infiltration and snitches. (Philly Antifa)

Whether or not the charges made against Steever were true has never been established. Nevertheless, "according to the Southern Poverty Law Center (SPLC)," ATB remains an active racist skinhead group in 16 states: "Arkansas, California, Florida, Kentucky, Louisiana, Massachusetts, Missouri, Nebraska, Nevada, New York, Ohio, Oklahoma, Oregon, Pennsylvania, Virginia, and West Virginia" (Southern Poverty Law Center, 2015).

See also: Creativity Movement; Neo-Nazis; Racist Skinheads; The Order; White Nationalism; White Supremacist Movement

FURTHER READING

Anti-Defamation League. "Aryan Terror Brigade." Anti-Defamation League. https://www.adl.org/education/references/hate-symbols/aryan-terror-brigade. (Accessed May 31, 2018.)

Philly Antifa. February 8, 2013. "More NJ Boneheads in Legal Trouble: A Snitch to Blame?" Philly Antifa. https://phillyantifa.org/tag/aryan-terror-brigade/. (Accessed May 31, 2018.)

Southern Poverty Law Center. February 27, 2013. "Neo-Nazi Website Targets Enemies, Lists Personal Information." Southern Poverty Law Center: Intelligence Report. https://www.splcenter.org/fighting-hate/intelligence-report/2013/neo-nazi-website-targets-enemies-lists-personal-information. (Accessed May 31, 2018.)

Southern Poverty Law Center. March 2, 2015. "Active Racist Skinhead Groups." Southern Poverty Law Center: Intelligence Report. https://www.splcenter.org/fighting-hate/intelligence-report/2015/active-racist-skinhead-groups. (Accessed May 31, 2018.)

Terrorism Research and Analysis Consortium. "Aryan Terror Brigade." Terrorism Research and Analysis Consortium. https://www.trackingterrorism.org/group/aryan-terror-brigade-atb. (Accessed May 31, 2018.)

Vk.com. "Aryan Terror Brigade/Combat 18." Vk.com. https://vk.com/atb318. (Accessed May 31, 2018.)

Atomwaffen Division

The Atomwaffen Division (AWD) ("Atomwaffen" meaning "Atomic Weapons" in German) is a "virulently neo-racist, racist organization that in its short existence has become one of the most violent hate groups in the United States" (Myre). Though other hate groups have been around much longer than AWD and have exhibited spates of violence from time to time, members of AWD have been responsible for the deaths of five people in its short three years of existence (Myre). AWD is organized like many terror groups, being divided into a series of cells that operate independently from one another. Estimates are that AWD may have anywhere between 40 and 100 members in the United States, organized into perhaps 20 cells across several states (Thompson, et al., May 3, 2018; Weill). Amazingly, several members of AWD are allegedly active-duty members of the U.S. military (Thompson, et al., May 3, 2018), while others claim to be Satanists (Weill). AWD "embraces Third Reich ideology and preaches hatred of minorities, gays and Jews" (Thompson, et al., February 23, 2018). The Southern Poverty Law Center (SPLC) characterizes the group as "accelerationists" who believe that "violence, depravity and degeneracy are the only sure way to establish order in their dystopian and apocalyptic vision of the world" (Southern Poverty Law Center). The chief ideological influences on AWD are "James Mason, a member of the American Nazi Party"; Charles Mason, who advocated racial war through Helter Skelter; Joseph Tommasi, an American neo-Nazi who founded the National Socialist Liberation Front; and "William Pierce, founder of the National Alliance and author of the notorious dystopian novel, *The Turner Diaries*, which is a favorite among neo-Nazis and white supremacists" (Southern Poverty Law Center). AWD members also have expressed their admiration for mass murderers "such as Adolf Hitler, Osama bin Laden, Dylann Roof, Anders Breivik, Ted Kaczynski, and Timothy McVeigh" (Southern Poverty Law Center; Anti-Defamation League). Brandon Russell, considered a leader in AWD, stated that the group is a

> very fanatical, ideological band of comrades who do both activism and militant training. Hand to hand, arms training, and various other forms of training. As for activism, we spread awareness in the real world through unconventional means. [keyboard warriorism is nothing to do with what we are.]
>
> Joining us means serious dedication not only to the Atomwaffen Division and its members, but to the goal of ultimate uncompromising victory. With this means only those willing to get out on the streets, in the woods, or where ever we maybe in the world and work together in the physical realm. As started earlier, no keyboard warriorism, (we do however do a lot [sic] of hacking, you won't hear about this though) if you don't want to meet up and get things done don't bother. (Southern Poverty Law Center)

AWD is considered so extreme that "they cause a ton of controversy within the radical right" (Bromwich). Much of this controversy has to do with the extreme violence that has been perpetrated by the group, but more critical is the contention that the organization serves as a "gateway organization for a satanic cult" (Weill). Whereas many white nationalists and white supremacists express their disdain for many of the same groups as AWD, at the heart of much of their ideology is a fealty to white Christianity. AWD, however, flies in the face of these beliefs. Several members of AWD have expressed an affinity for the Order of the Nine Angels, "a satanic group that encourages members to infiltrate extremist political movements, whose members might be susceptible to conversion" (Weill). In 2017, a chat log demonstrating the AWD's satanic ties was exposed by an ex-AWD member when he linked "audio of a call, purportedly between Atomwaffen members arguing about satanism" (Weill). In one exchange, an Atomwaffen member reportedly says:

> Have you read the Satanic Principles? The f—ing baseline ideas of what Satanism stands for? You cannot honestly read that and tell me it reflects none of what national socialism teaches. You guys can get all moralistic if you want about Satanism . . . but when the f—in' race war comes, morals aren't going to do anything but get you f—in' killed. (Weill)

Aside from its alleged ties to satanism, another contention between AWD and other hate groups is the level of violence that the group has exhibited in its short history. In May 2017, "a Florida teenager, Devon Arthurs, told the police he had killed two of his neo-Nazi roommates for disrespecting his Muslim faith. (He had recently converted)" (Bromwich). An investigation revealed that Arthurs was a member of AWD, as were both of his slain roommates. A fourth roommate, Brandon Russell, believed to be a major leader within AWD, was later arrested after investigators discovered

> a cache of weapons, detonators and volatile chemical compounds in his home, including a cooler full of HMTD, a powerful explosive often used by bomb-makers, and ammonium nitrate, the substance used by Timothy McVeigh in the Oklahoma City attack. Russell was also in possession of two radioactive isotopes, americium and thorium. (Thompson, et al., May 3, 2018)

In December 2017, "a husband and wife were shot to death in their Reston, Virginia home" after forbidding their daughter from continuing to see a boy she was dating. The parents believed that the young man, Nicholas Giampa, was a neo-Nazi. Before his arrest, Giampa attempted to commit suicide by shooting himself in the head. He survived, and subsequent investigations established his links to Atomwaffen (Myre). Indeed, his "Twitter account housed a litany of calls for a race war and the execution of Jewish persons" (Southern Poverty Law Center).

Finally, "on January 9, 2018, the body of Blaze Bernstein," who had been missing for a week, was discovered "in the Foothills Ranch community of Orange County, California." Bernstein, who was Jewish and openly gay, was discovered in a shallow grave with at least 20 stab wounds in his body (Southern Poverty Law Center). Within two weeks, 20-year-old Samuel Woodward, "a former high school classmate of Bernstein's, was arrested and charged with Bernstein's murder" (Southern Poverty Law Center). The subsequent police investigation revealed that Woodward was a member of AWD. In fact, he was "described as a key member of the organization's emerging California cell—a role he assumed after attending 'a three-day training camp' in Texas that involved 'instruction in firearms, hand-to-hand combat, camping and survival skills'" (Southern Poverty Law Center).

Because of their virulent messages of hate, many forums associated with AWD have been shut down in recent years. The group's Internet forum, Iron March (IM), once carried the slogan "Gas The Kikes! Race War Now! 1488! Boots on the Ground!" (Southern Poverty Law Center). Moreover, before it was suspended, the group's website—https://atomwaffendvision.org—enunciated the group's ideology:

> The rest of the world is collapsing beneath us as we speak. The system is beginning to suffer the consequences of its corruption. The failure of democracy and capitalism has given way to the Jewish oligarchies and the globalist bankers resulting in the racial and cultural displacement of the white race. We have absolutely no room for moderates and cowards. We wish to appeal to the radical in this struggle, as it is the radical that etches their place into history. There is nothing that can be fixed in a system so inherently flawed, National Socialism is the only solution to reclaim dominion over what belong to us. The west cannot be saved, but it can be rebuilt and even stronger without the burdens of the past. (Atomwaffen Division)

Members of Atomwaffen were at the "Unite the Right" rally in Charlottesville, Virginia, in August 2017, though characteristically, as per their penchant to keep their faces hidden and to maintain the secrecy of their cells, they were masked behind a black skull-and-crossbones handkerchief. In online chats leading up to Charlottesville, one AWD member reported that he was "encouraged to be vicious with any counterprotestors, maybe even sodomize someone with a knife. He'd responded by saying he was prepared to kill someone" (Thompson, et al., May 3, 2018). AWD causes a great deal of concern today because of its active recruitment strategies on college campuses. When asked, an FBI spokesperson would not comment directly on any active investigations into AWD's activities. The spokesperson did say,

> The F.B.I. does not and will not police ideology, but has been investigating the criminal activities of white supremacy extremists for nearly a century. When an individual takes violent action based on belief or ideology and breaks the law, the F.B.I. will enforce the rule of law. (Bromwich)

A former deputy assistant director of the FBI, Danny Coulson, stated that once a group has engaged in violence, it is easier "to wiretap them and to place informers in their midst." Coulson speculated on the types of individuals that gravitate toward a group like AWD:

> [P]articipants in such groups [demonstrate] inadequate personalities [and] choose to hate others because of their own insecurities. We all have our own insecurities. There's always something we'd like to be better at. To be stronger, a better shot, a better dad. But these [acts of hatred] are things that are more like chronic inadequacies, stating that the quality that unites white supremacists is that they "never succeeded at anything." (Bromwich)

See also: National Alliance; National Socialist Liberation Front; Neo-Nazis; White Nationalism; White Supremacist Movement

FURTHER READING

Anti-Defamation League. "Atomwaffen Division (AWD)." Anti-Defamation League. https://www.adl.org/resources/backgrounders/atomwaffen-division-awd. (Accessed May 31, 2018.)

Atomwaffen Division. https://atomwaffendivison.org. (Accessed January 10, 2018.)

Bromwich, Jonah Engel. February 12, 2018. "What Is Atomwaffen? A Neo-Nazi Group, Linked to Multiple Murders." *New York Times*. https://www.nytimes.com/2018/02/12/us/what-is-atomwaffen.html. (Accessed May 31, 2018.)

Myre, Greg. "Deadly Connection: Neo-Nazi Group Linked to 3 Accused Killers." NPR. https://www.npr.org/2018/03/06/590292705/5-killings-3-states-and-1-common-neo-nazi-link. (Accessed May 31, 2018.)

Southern Poverty Law Center. "Atomwaffen Division." Southern Poverty Law Center. https://www.splcenter.org/fighting-hate/extremist-files/group/atomwaffen-division. (Accessed May 31, 2018.)

Thompson, A. C., Ali Winston, and Jake Hanrahan. February 23, 2018. "Inside Atomwaffen as It Celebrates a Member for Allegedly Killing a Gay Jewish College

Student." ProPublica. https://www.propublica.org/article/atomwaffen-division -inside-white-hate-group. (Accessed May 31, 2018.)

Thompson, A. C., Ali Winston, and Jake Hanrahan. May 3, 2018. "Ranks of Notorious Hate Group Include Active-Duty Military." ProPublica. https://www.propublica .org/article/atomwaffen-division-hate-group-active-duty-military. (Accessed May 31, 2018.)

Weill, Kelly. March 21, 2018. "Satanism Drama Is Tearing Apart the Murderous Neo-Nazi Group Atomwaffen." Daily Beast. https://www.thedailybeast.com /satanism-drama-is-tearing-apart-the-murderous-neo-nazi-group-atomwaffen. (Accessed May 31, 2018.)

B

The Barnes Review

According to the Southern Poverty Law Center (SPLC), "The Barnes Review (TBR) is one of the most virulent anti-Semitic organizations around. . . . The Barnes Review and its website, Barnesreview.org, are dedicated to historical revisionism and Holocaust denial" (Southern Poverty Law Center, Barnes Review). TBR is classified by the SPLC as a "Holocaust Denial" hate group located in Upper Marlboro, Maryland (Southern Poverty Law Center, 2017). TBR was founded by Willis Carto in 1994 (Anti-Defamation League). Willis Carto was a far-right-wing individual in American politics who used lobbying and publishing to foster his anti-Semitic views and racist attitudes toward other minorities. He also led the U.S. movement of individuals and groups that collectively became known as "Holocaust deniers"—those who held that the Holocaust was a fabrication and that there never was a systematic effort by Adolf Hitler and the Nazis to exterminate the Jewish race. TBR is named after Harry Elmer Barnes, "a prominent 20th-century anti-Semite and Holocaust denier" (Southern Poverty Law Center, Barnes Review). Claiming that its mission "is to tell the whole truth about history,"

> TBR really practices an extremist form of revisionist history that includes defending the Nazi regime, denying the Holocaust, discounting the evils of slavery, and promoting white nationalism. The Barnes Review magazine has published articles entitled "Adolf Hitler—An Overlooked Candidate for the Nobel Prize?," "Treblinka Was No Death Camp," "Is There a Negro Race?" "'Reconquista': The Mexican Plan to Take the Southwest," and "David Duke: An Awakening." (Southern Poverty Law Center, Barnes Review)

On its website, Barnesreview.org, the tagline of TBR is "Home of TBR revisionist history magazine & bookstore: dedicate to bringing history into accord with the facts" (Barnes Review). Besides peddling its own books that perpetuate theories that the Holocaust never occurred, TBR also has a section entitled "Banned by Amazon." These books include titles such as *The Six Million: Fact or Fiction*; *White World Awake! Stopping the Planned Extermination of Our Volk*; and *Auschwitz Crematorium I: The Alleged Homicidal Gassings* (Barnes Review).

A review of one particular issue of TBR, conducted by "JHate: A Blog about Anti-Semitism," notes that the issue references books that document a "nefarious plot to control the world that was formulated way back in Biblical times and proceeds unabated to the present" (Tuchman). The issue intimates who the "perps" of the plot are, being "Jews, of course, and warns that their sole business is to pursue, against any and all odds, their goal of world conquest which they have been plotting since ancient times" (Tuchman).

TBR holds annual conferences that invite various white nationalist and white supremacist speakers. The publication has also posted articles in support of Christian Identity, "a radical theology that claims that Jews are the literal descendants of Satan" (Southern Poverty Law Center, Barnes Review). TBR praised Christian Identity theology, stating, "[T]he [Christian] Identity message holds out the hope for survival—not only spiritual and cultural survival—but racial survival" (Southern Poverty Law Center, Barnes Review).

See also: Christian Identity; Holocaust Denial; Institute for Historical Review; Liberty Lobby; White Nationalism; White Supremacist Movement

FURTHER READING

Anti-Defamation League. "Willis Carto." Anti-Defamation League. https://www.adl.org /sites/default/files/documents/assets/pdf/combating-hate/Willis-Carto-Extremism -in-America.pdf. (Accessed June 27, 2018.)

Barnes Review. https://barnesreview.org/. (Accessed June 27, 2018.)

Southern Poverty Law Center. "Barnes Review/Foundation for Economic Liberty, Inc." Southern Poverty Law Center. https://www.splcenter.org/fighting-hate/extremist -files/group/barnes-reviewfoundation-economic-liberty-inc. (Accessed June 26, 2018.)

Southern Poverty Law Center. "Willis Carto." Southern Poverty Law Center. https:// www.splcenter.org/fighting-hate/extremist-files/individual/willis-carto. (Accessed June 26, 2018.)

Southern Poverty Law Center. February 15, 2017. "Active Hate Groups 2016." Southern Poverty Law Center: Intelligence Report. https://www.splcenter.org/fighting-hate /intelligence-report/2017/active-hate-groups-2016. (Accessed June 26, 2018.)

Tuchman, Aryeh. March 25, 2011. "Let's Read 'The Barnes Review' (March/April 2011)." JHate. https://jhate.wordpress.com/2011/03/25/lets-read-the-barnes-review-marchapril -2011/. (Accessed June 27, 2018.)

Black Hebrew Israelites

Black Hebrew Israelites (BHI) consists of individuals, groups, and organizations that believe that African Americans and other people of color (e.g., Hispanics, Latinos, and Native Americans) "are descendants of a lost tribe of ancient Israelites" (Carter). BHI, considered to be "on the extremist fringe of the black nationalist movement," embraces a "theology that dates back to the 19th century" (Southern Poverty Law Center). Its doctrine asserts that African Americans are "God's true chosen people because they, not the people known to the world today as Jews, are the real descendants of the Hebrews of the Bible" (Southern Poverty Law Center). BHI adherents "believe that Jews are devilish impostors and . . . openly condemn whites as evil personified, deserving only death or slavery" (Southern Poverty Law Center). BHI believe that blacks and other people of color are "empowered by God with superiority" and are willing to engage in violence "as long as it helps rid the world of evil" (Johnson). BHI members can often be found "at busy intersections, parks, bus terminals and subway stations in major cities in the U.S. BHI street preachers are often aggressive and very intimidating to onlookers, because they use racial epithets and shout at people" (Johnson). The "notorious white supremacist leader Tom Metzger" once stated that BHI members "are the black counterparts of us [white supremacists]" (Southern Poverty Law Center). In fact, the belief system of BHI members

> is basically the reversed-color mirror image of the Christian Identity theology embraced by many white supremacists, which holds that mainstream Jews are the descendants of Satan and that white people are the chosen ones, divinely endowed by God with superior status over "mud people," believers' term for non-white individuals. (Southern Poverty Law Center)

BHI adherents hold religious beliefs that "differ from those of modern Jewish communities in Israel" (Jaynes). BHI members "permit polygamy and forbid birth control," while practicing vegetarianism, "avoiding the consumption of meat, dairy, eggs, and sugar. Members adopt Hebrew names to replace names they believe could be derived from slavery" (Jaynes). BHI members "keep the Jewish Sabbath and many other Jewish customs including circumcision, dietary laws, and the observance of certain Jewish holidays and festivals like Yom Kippur and Passover" (Turner). They "use the Old and New Testament to support their teachings, especially the five books of Moses (Genesis to Deuteronomy)," but "[t]hey do not consider themselves to be Jews in the modern sense of the term as associated with Orthodox, Reformed, Conservative, or Hasidic Judaism" (Turner). Nevertheless, a substantial number of BHI members attempted to immigrate into Israel in the 1970s because of Israel's law offering citizenship to all Jews, regardless of their previous citizenship. Because Black Hebrew Israelites "could produce no evidence to substantiate their Jewish heritage . . . the Chief Rabbinate of Israel decided that the Black Hebrew Israelites were not really Jewish and were not entitled to citizenship" (Jaynes).

BHI adherents identify as "Hebrew Israelites," thereby being "modern descendants of ancient Israelites," whereas a "Jew is a person who practices the religion of Judaism" and, as such, is not a "true descendant of Hebrew Israelites" (Carter). However, adherents

> do not consider all people of color to be part of the lost tribe either. As one BHI website explains, "Israel is just one black nation that exist among many. The Egyptians, Canaanites, Ethiopians, babyloians etc [sic] were black skinned but they were not Israelites. . . . To say all black skinned people are Israelites is like saying all Asians are Chinese, or All Europeans are French." [Israelite Heritage]. BHIs also believe that the trans-Atlantic slave trade was prophesied in Deuteronomy 28:68 (. . . which accounts for why so many "Hebrew Israelites" are found in America). (Carter)

Many hard-line BHI adherents look forward to "an imminent and bloody demise for whites and other enemies at the hands of a vengeful returning Christ" (Southern Poverty Law Center). In a BHI-produced documentary, an extremist BHI preacher "delivers a sermon with his foot planted on the back of a white man laying flat on the sidewalk, arms splayed at his sides." He warns, "White boy, you're next," and adds, "All you white people get ready for war. We're coming for you, white boys. Negroes are the real Jews. Get ready for war!" (Southern Poverty Law Center).

See also: Black Muslims; Black Nationalism; Black Separatists; Christian Identity; Israelite Church of God in Jesus Christ; Sicarii 1715; White Supremacist Movement

FURTHER READING

Carter, Joe. May 19, 2017. "9 Things You Should Know about Black Hebrew Israelites." Gospel Coalition. https://www.thegospelcoalition.org/article/9-things-you-should-know-about-black-hebrew-israelites/. (Accessed June 22, 2018.)

Israelite Heritage. June 22, 2018. "Frequently Asked Questions." Israelite Heritage. https://web.archive.org/web/20080211213509/http://www.hebrewisraelites.org:80/faq.htm#WHAT%20IS%20A%20HEBREW?. (Accessed June 22, 2018.)

Jaynes, Gerald D. "Black Hebrew Israelites." *Encyclopedia Britannica.* https://www.britannica.com/topic/Black-Hebrew-Israelites. (Accessed June 22, 2018.)

Johnson, Daryl. August 8, 2017. "Return of the Violent Black Nationalist." Southern Poverty Law Center: Intelligence Report. https://www.splcenter.org/fighting-hate/intelligence-report/2017/return-violent-black-nationalist. (Accessed June 22, 2018.)

Jude 3 Project. October 17, 2017. "10 Things to Study before Engaging Black Hebrew Israelites." Jude 3 Project. http://www.jude3project.com/blog/10thingstostudybhi. (Accessed June 22, 2018.)

Southern Poverty Law Center. August 29, 2008. "Racist Black Hebrew Israelites Becoming More Militant." Southern Poverty Law Center: Intelligence Report. https://www.splcenter.org/fighting-hate/intelligence-report/2008/racist-black-hebrew-israelites-becoming-more-militant. (Accessed June 22, 2018.)

Turner, Ryan. Edited by Matt Slick. "Black Hebrew Israelites." Christian Apologetics & Research Ministry. https://carm.org/black-hebrew-israelites. (Accessed June 22, 2018.)

Black Muslims

In the United States, Black Muslims historically were among the first African Americans to call for a movement that advocated black separatism and black nationalism. Since the late 1970s, Black Muslims have largely split into two groups: the American Society of Muslims and the Nation of Islam. Though a renewed African American religious movement that centered on Islam began in the United States in the 1930s, by the 1950s and 1960s the Nation of Islam dominated the political and social landscape that had been created by the Black Muslims. The Nation of Islam had only numbered about 8,000 when Elijah Muhammad assumed control of the group in 1934. With the ascension of Malcolm X, however, membership grew to include tens of thousands of Black Muslims. Malcolm X's charisma and powerful speaking style attracted many adherents who believe in the message that Black Muslims were preaching: that whites were a race of "devils" and black people were God's original people. As Elijah Muhammad had stated,

> The Blackman is the original man. From him came all brown, yellow, red, and white people. By using a special method of birth control law, the Blackman was able

to produce the white race. This method of birth control was developed by a Black scientist known as Yakub, who envisioned making and teaching a nation of people who would be diametrically opposed to the Original People. A Race of people who would one day rule the original people and the earth for a period of 6,000 years. Yakub promised his followers that he would graft a nation from his own people, and he would teach them how to rule his people, through a system of tricks and lies whereby they use deceit to divide and conquer, and break the unity of the darker people, put one brother against another, and then act as mediators and rule both sides. (Blake)

A break between Elijah Muhammad and Malcolm X weakened the Black Muslim movement for a time, and the movement would suffer a severe blow when Malcolm X was assassinated in 1965. When Elijah Muhammad's son, Warith (W.) Deen Mohammed, took over from his father in 1976, he preached a less inflammatory and more accommodating version of Black Islam than had his father. The younger Mohammed "aligned the organization with the international Islamic community, moving toward Sunni Islamic practice, and opened the group (renamed the World Community of al-Islam in the West, then the American Muslim Mission, and later the American Society of Muslims) to individuals of all races" (Encyclopedia.com).

In 1977, a disaffected member of the organization—Louis Farrakhan—split off from W. Deen Mohammed's organization and took dozens of Black Muslims with him. Farrakhan broke with W. Deen Mohammed because of his "integrationist ideals and lack of allegiance to his father's brand of Islam" (Encyclopedia.com). The splinter group assumed the Nation of Islam name and sought to emulate the thoughts and teachings of Elijah Muhammad. In 1995, the Nation of Islam organized the Million Man March in Washington, D.C., to promote African American unity and family values. Under Farrakhan's leadership, the Nation of Islam tried to redefine the "black male stereotype" of individuals plagued by drug-related crimes and gang violence. Since assuming control of the Nation of Islam, Farrakhan has promoted social reform within African American communities and challenged African Americans to foster traditional forms of self-reliance and economic independence that focus on the family and not the government (Nation of Islam).

Farrakhan has continued preaching a message of black nationalism and black separatism. On April 13, 1997, Farrakhan was a guest on NBC's *Meet the Press*, where he was interviewed by Tim Russert and David Broder. During the interview, Russert asked Farrakhan to clarify the Nation of Islam's teachings on race. Farrakhan replied:

You know, it's not unreal to believe that white people—who genetically cannot produce yellow, brown or black—had a Black origin. The scholars and scientists of this world agree that the origin of man and humankind started in Africa and that the first parent of the world was black. The Qur'an says that God created Adam out of black mud and fashioned him into shape. So if white people came from the original people, the Black people, what is the process by which you came to life? That is not a silly question. That is a scientific question with a scientific answer. It doesn't suggest that we are superior or that you are inferior. It suggests, however, that your birth or your origin is from the black people of this earth: superiority and inferiority is determined by our righteousness and not by our color. (Final Call)

When Russert asked Farrakhan if he agreed with Elijah Muhammad's teaching that whites are "blue-eyed devils," Farrakhan responded:

> Well, you have not been saints in the way you have acted toward the darker peoples of the world and toward even your own people. But, in truth, Mr. Russert, any human being who gives themself over to the doing of evil could be considered a devil. In the Bible, in the "Book of Revelation," it talks about the fall of Babylon. It says Babylon is fallen because she has become the habitation of devils. We believe that ancient Babylon is a symbol of a modern Babylon, which is America. (Final Call)

In the late 1990s, the Nation of Islam began moving away from its overt message of racism to embrace more traditional Islamic practices. In 2000, Farrakhan and W. Deen Mohammed publicly declared an end to the rivalry between their two groups. In 2003, W. Deen Mohammed resigned as head of the American Society of Muslims (Encyclopedia.com).

Today, many black Muslims struggle not only with the stereotypes sometimes associated with black people but also the hostilities and resentments that have been leveled at Muslims since 9/11. Black American Muslims are under intense scrutiny by law enforcement and are vilified by the media. As one author has noted, "efforts of anti-Islamophobia activism in Muslim communities seemed more about regaining the privilege of proximity to whiteness that Arab and South Asians enjoyed before 9/11, rather than about justice" (Hill).

See also: Black Nationalism; Black Separatists; Nation of Islam

FURTHER READING

Blake, Dorothy. 1991. *Yakub and the Origins of White Supremacy: Message to the White Man and White Woman in America.* 1st ed. Conquering Books.

Encyclopedia.com. "Black Muslims." Encyclopedia.com. http://www.encyclopedia.com /philosophy-and-religion/islam/islam/black-muslims. (Accessed June 12, 2018.)

Final Call. June 13, 2008. "Tim Russert's Interview with Minister Louis Farrakhan." *Final Call.* http://www.finalcall.com/artman/publish/Perspectives_1/Tim_Russert_s _interview_with_Minister_Louis_Farrak_4842.shtml. (Accessed June 12, 2018.)

Hill, Margari. December 15, 2016. "Islamophobia and Black American Muslims." Huffington Post. http://www.huffingtonpost.com/margari-hill/islamophobia-and-black -am_b_8785814.html. (Accessed June 12, 2018.)

Nation of Islam. "Honorable Minister Louis Farrakhan." Nation of Islam. https://www .noi.org/hon-minister-farrakhan/. (Accessed June 12, 2018.)

Southern Poverty Law Center. "Black Separatists." Southern Poverty Law Center. https:// www.splcenter.org/fighting-hate/extremist-files/ideology/black-separatist. (Accessed June 12, 2018.)

Black Nationalism

Black nationalism was a political and social movement that arose in the United States during the 1960s and early 1970s. Many adherents to black nationalism hoped that the culmination of the movement would be the creation of a separate black nation populated by African Americans. The core of the black nationalism movement was a desire among blacks to maintain and promote their separate identity as people with black ancestry, as opposed to being assimilated into an American nation that was predominantly white. With such slogans as "black power" and "black is beautiful," the black nationalism movement and its adherents sought to instill a sense of pride among blacks in the United States at a time when the civil rights movement was seeking equal rights for blacks (*Encyclopedia Britannica*). Through black nationalist groups such as the Nation of Islam and charismatic individuals like Malcolm X, "proponents of black nationalism advocated economic self-sufficiency, race pride for African Americans, and black separatism" (King Encyclopedia). In the 1960s, black nationalists criticized the nonviolent, interracial activism advocated by Martin Luther King Jr. King once described himself as "standing between the forces of complacency and the hatred and despair of the black nationalist" (King Encyclopedia). There are many in the United States today who believe that the black nationalism of the 1960s has been resurrected in the form of the Black Lives Matter movement that has emerged in the last few years (Williams).

The roots of black nationalism date to the 19th century, when Booker T. Washington and his adherents emphasized a message of "racial solidarity, economic self-sufficiency, and black self-help" (Digital History). After World War I, such black leaders as Martin Delaney believed that blacks would never be able to achieve true equality in the United States given the social and political impediments that black people faced. Therefore, Delaney advocated for the repatriation of blacks back to Africa, "where they would settle and assist native Africans in nation-building" (King Encyclopedia).

The rise of black nationalism was revitalized during the economic depression of the 1930s when Farad Muhammad founded the Nation of Islam (NOI), which sought "to develop an intentionally separate and economically self-sufficient black community governed by a revised version of the Muslim faith" (King Encyclopedia). NOI's cause was later taken up by Farad Muhammad's successor, Elijah Muhammad, who became NOI's leader. Elijah Muhammad took up the cause of black separatism and black supremacism when he declared that "whites were doomed to destruction." Elijah Muhammad declared:

> The white devil's day is over. He was given six thousand years to rule . . . He's already used up most trapping and murdering the black nations by the hundreds of thousands. Now he's worried, worried about the black man getting his revenge. Unless whites accede to the Muslim demand for a separate territory for themselves, your entire race will be destroyed and removed from this earth by Almighty God. And those black men who are still trying to integrate will inevitably be destroyed along with the whites. (Digital History)

The Nation of Islam and Black Muslims preached a message that encouraged blacks to lift themselves up and engage in actions of self-help. The Black Muslim movement called upon black Americans to "wake up, clean up, and stand up in order to achieve true freedom and independence" (Digital History). To counteract the behaviors that they believed reinforced racist stereotypes, the Black Muslims "forbade eating pork and cornbread, drinking alcohol, and smoking cigarettes" (Gprep.org). They also encouraged black entrepreneurship by supporting the creation of black businesses.

By the late 1950s, Malcolm X was recognized as the most eloquent spokesperson for the Nation of Islam and the cause of black nationalism. Malcolm X had been born Malcolm Little. But after a stint in prison in the early 1950s, he adopted the name Malcolm X to replace "the white slave-master name which had been imposed upon my paternal forebears by some blue-eyed devil" (Digital History). Malcolm X denounced alcohol, tobacco, and premarital sex. He rapidly became the face and voice of the black nationalist cause. However, Malcolm X's rhetoric and tactics ran afoul of the larger civil rights movement that was then being led by the Reverend Martin Luther King Jr. Whereas King preached nonviolent resistance to the segregationist policies found around the United States, Malcolm X declared, "If ballots won't work, bullets will" (Digital History). Malcolm X attacked King on several occasions, calling him a "chum" and an "Uncle Tom." He also directly challenged King's leadership of the cause for black civil rights when he stated, "If you're afraid of Black nationalism, you're afraid of revolution. And if you love revolution, you love black nationalism" (King Encyclopedia). After King's 1964 "I Have a Dream" speech, Malcolm X stated, "While King was having a dream, the rest of us Negroes are having a nightmare" (Cone).

Malcolm X left the Nation of Islam in 1964 and established his own organization for the betterment of African Americans. Malcolm X was assassinated by Nation of Islam members in 1965. By that time, many black activists had become skeptical of the power of nonviolent resistance, as preached by Martin Luther King Jr., to positively influence the white power structure in the United States. The death of student activists during the Freedom Summer in 1964 and the marginalization of the Mississippi Freedom Democratic Party at the Democratic National Convention that same year convinced many black activists that nonviolence was not working and would not further the black nationalist cause.

In 1966, two black civil rights organizations—the Student Nonviolent Coordinating Committee (SNCC) and the Congress on Racial Equality (CORE)—embraced the tenets of black nationalism. Stokely Carmichael, who would eventually become an activist in the black power movement, was elected chairperson of SNCC, and he proceeded to move away from a strategy of nonviolence to an all-black organization committed to black power. Carmichael stated, "Integration is irrelevant. Political and economic power is what the black people have to have" (Digital History). Carmichael began using the ideal of black power to promote "racial self-respect and increased power for blacks in economic and political realms." He asserted that "the concern for black power addresses itself directly to . . . the necessity to reclaim our history and our identity from the cultural terrorism and depredation of self-justifying white guilt" (Carmichael). In his statements, Carmichael reiterated the sentiments of the fallen Malcolm X, who had declared that "[t]he worst crime the white man has committed has been to teach us to hate ourselves" (Digital History).

Of all the groups that advocated for racial separatism and black power, none was more influential than the Black Panther Party (BPP). The BPP was founded by Huey P. Newton and Bobby Seale in October 1966 as "an armed revolutionary socialist organization advocating self-determination for black ghettoes" (Digital History). As one member of the BPP declared, "Black men . . . must unite to over-throw their white oppressors, becoming 'like panthers—smiling, cunning, scien-tific, striking by night and sparing no one!" (Digital History). Members of the BPP showed up armed at a California State Assembly Committee Hearing in May 1967. Later that same month, the BPP would publish the "Ten Point Program," also known as "What We Want," which was a set of guidelines established by the BPP to direct their ideals and ways of operation.

By the early 1970s, the rhetoric of black nationalism had receded. But the advo-cacy of black nationalism had

> exerted a powerful and positive influence upon the Civil Rights Movement. In addi-tion to giving birth to a host of community self-help organizations, supporters of black power spurred the creation of black studies programs in universities and encouraged black Americans to take pride in their racial background and to recog-nize that "black is beautiful." A growing number of black Americans began to wear "Afro" hairstyles and take African or Islamic surnames. Singer James Brown cap-tured the new spirit: "Say it loud—I'm black and I'm proud." (Digital History)

In 2013, the Black Lives Matter movement was birthed after the acquittal of George Zimmerman in the shooting death of African American Trayvon Martin. Black Lives Matter demonstrations were held around the United States following the death of other African Americans in 2014. Because of their increased numbers and advocacy for black rights, the Black Lives Matter movement was criticized by those on the political right. At the 2016 Republican National Convention, the theme of "Make America Safe Again" was at least partly aimed at the Black Lives Matter movement, which right-wing citizens and politicians alike were blaming for the shooting deaths of police officers in Dallas, Texas, and New Orleans, Loui-siana. Author Yohuru Williams stated:

> All of this rhetoric is part of a rising chorus after the Texas and Louisiana killings, an effort to define a new category in the war on extremism—so-called black-nation-alist terrorism. Proponents struggle to manufacture a domestic equivalent for Al Qaeda. Efforts to link the violence against law enforcement to some mythical, larger black separatist movement, which has made retaliatory violence against police one of its chief aims, is weak at best and irresponsible at worst. (Williams)

Williams would note that, like the black nationalism movement of the 1960s and 1970s, the Black Lives Matter movement engages in activities of self-defense in order "to create a sense of security and belonging for people of color under oppres-sive circumstances—not retaliatory violence or unprovoked attacks against whites or police, as it is often erroneously portrayed" (Williams).

See also: Black Muslims; Israel United in Christ; Israelite Church of God in Jesus Christ; Israelite School of Universal Practical Knowledge; Nation of Islam; New Black Panther Party; Nuwaubian Nation of Moors; Sicarii 1715

FURTHER READING

Carmichael, Stokely. 1966. *Toward Black Liberation*. Student Nonviolent Coordinating Committee.

Cone, James H. 2012. *Martin and Malcolm: A Dream or a Nightmare*. Orbis Books.

Digital History. "Black Nationalism and Black Power." Digital History. http://www.digit alhistory.uh.edu/disp_textbook.cfm?smtid=2&psid=3331. (Accessed May 5, 2017.)

Encyclopedia Britannica. "Black Nationalism." Britannica.com. https://www.britannica .com/event/black-nationalism. (Accessed May 5, 2017.)

Gprep.org. "America in Ferment: The Tumultuous 1960s." Digital History. http://claver .gprep.org/sjochs/black%20power%20and%20Black%20Nationalism.htm. (Accessed February 8, 2019.)

King Encyclopedia. "Black Nationalism." King Encyclopedia at Stanford University. http://kingencyclopedia.stanford.edu/encyclopedia/encyclopedia/enc_black _nationalism.1.html. (Accessed May 5, 2017.)

Southern Poverty Law Center. "Black Nationalist." Southern Poverty Law Center. https:// www.splcenter.org/fighting-hate/extremist-files/ideology/black-nationalist. (Accessed August 18, 2018.)

Williams, Yohuru. July 20, 2016. "The Coming War on 'Black Nationalists.'" *Nation*. https://www.thenation.com/article/the-coming-war-on-black-nationalists/. (Accessed May 5, 2017.)

Black Riders Liberation Party

The Black Riders Liberation Party (BLRP) labels itself "as the successor to the Black Panther Party (BPP) of the 1960s-1970s" (Southern Poverty Law Center, Black Nationalist). The BPP was a black socialist revolutionary organization founded at the height of the civil rights movement in the United States. The Southern Poverty Law Center (SPLC) has designated BRLP as a black nationalist hate group (Southern Poverty Law Center, Black Nationalist). According the SPLC, the black nationalist movement

> is a reaction to centuries of institutionalized white supremacy in America. Black nationalists believe the answer to white racism is to form separate institutions—or even a separate nation—for black people. Most forms of black nationalism are strongly anti-white and anti-Semitic. Some religious versions assert that black people are the biblical "chosen people" of God. (Southern Poverty Law Center, Black Nationalist)

According to BLRP's website:

> The Black Riders Liberation Party is the new generation of the Black Panther Party for Self Defense. The BRLP began in a Y.T.S. gang prison in California when general T.A.C.O. (Taking All Capitalists Out) and other Bloods and Crips began learning about their history of how they were created as up and coming soldiers of the Black Panther Party and the black liberation movement. Once the leadership of the BPP was killed or imprisoned the youth began to take a self destructive turn. When they learned of this and how the racist United Snakkkes [i.e., United States] government has been murdering and using black people since the first Afrikan [sic] slaves were brought here, they decided to stop committing [sic] genocide against each other and to stand up against white supremacy and kkkapitalist oppression. Molding our organization after the first black revolutionary vanguard in the U.S. the Black Panther Party for Self Defense. (Black Riders Liberation Party, Who Are We?)

The group was founded in 1996 "to educate the masses of Afrikan [sic] people in this country and all throughout the diaspora to stop begging the system for freedom and just take it!!!!" (Black Riders Liberation Party, Who Are We?). BLRP has called for the implementation of the BPP's 10-Point Platform and Program. The program became the guiding manifesto by which all Black Panther Party members were encouraged to live. The Ten-Point Program comprised two sections entitled "What We Want Now!" and "What We Believe." The program was a statement about what the Black Panthers believed was the inherent right of every black American. Two points of particular note were the notion of monetary reparations for the centuries of slavery under which black Americans had been forced to labor (point 3) and the end of conscription for black soldiers who, as the program noted, are "forced to fight in the military service to defend a racist government that does not protect us" (point 6) (History of the Black Panther Party).

The BLRP have called the U.S. government "fascist" and regularly refer to it as a "kkkcapitalist government," using the letters "KKK" to signify the white oppression that is heaped upon black people by the government (Kambon). It also notes the high number of blacks incarcerated by the U.S. government, asserting that the government is engaged in a "Prison Industrial Complex" (Kambon). Like the BPP's 10-Point Program, the BLRP demands "that every single person that lives in America of African descent be released from incarceration" (Dubois). BLRP has also dedicated itself to emulating the BPP's

> Police Patrols that were organized against police brutality in the Afrikan [sic] community; as it was the Panther Party's belief that "armed citizen patrols and the arming of the citizenry as guaranteed by the Constitution were the most effective deterrents to excessive use of police force." (Kambon)

The SPLC reports that there are chapters of the BLRP in California, Nevada, New York, Oregon, and Texas (Southern Poverty Law Center, Hate Map by State).

See also: Black Nationalism; Black Separatists; New Black Panther Party

FURTHER READING

Black Riders Liberation Party. "About." https://www.facebook.com/pg/Black-Riders-Liberation-Party-552621838086002/about/. (Accessed June 22, 2018.)

Black Riders Liberation Party. "Who Are We?" http://2servethapeople.wixsite.com/brlp. (Accessed June 22, 2018.)

Dubois, Jake. August 13, 2016. "Black Riders Liberation Party: People Ready for Anything." BlackMattersUS. https://blackmattersus.com/13490-black-riders-liberation-party-people-ready-for-anything/. (Accessed June 22, 2018.)

4Struggle. May 2, 2013. "The US Government War against the Black Riders." 4StruggleMag. https://4strugglemag.org/2013/05/02/the-us-government-war-against-the-black-riders/. (Accessed June 22, 2018.)

Hatewatch Staff. January 12, 2017. "Black Separatist Groups Find Fertile Ground for Recruitment after Election." Southern Poverty Law Center: Hatewatch. https://www.splcenter.org/hatewatch/2017/01/12/black-separatist-groups-find-fertile-ground-recruitment-after-election. (Accessed June 22, 2018.)

Hatewatch Staff. May 3, 2017. "New Black Panther for Self Defense Member Committee Suicided after Shooting Three People and Killing One." Southern Poverty Law Center: Hatewatch. https://www.splcenter.org/hatewatch/2017/05/03/new-black

-panther-self-defense-member-committed-suicide-after-shooting-three-people
-and. (Accessed June 22, 2018.)

History of the Black Panther Party. "Black Panther Party Platform and Program: What
We Want, What We Believe." Stanford University. https://web.stanford.edu/group
/blackpanthers/history.shtml. (Accessed June 22, 2018.)

Kambon, Malaika. September 20, 2013. "To Serve the People: Black Riders Liberation
Party, New Generation Black Panther Party for Self-Defense." San Francisco
Bay View. http://sfbayview.com/2013/09/to-serve-the-people-black-riders-libera
tion-party-new-generation-black-panther-party-for-self-defense/. (Accessed June
22, 2018.)

Southern Poverty Law Center. "Black Nationalist." Southern Poverty Law Center. https://
www.splcenter.org/fighting-hate/extremist-files/ideology/black-nationalist.
(Accessed June 22, 2018.)

Southern Poverty Law Center. "Hate Map by State." Southern Poverty Law Center.
https://www.splcenter.org/hate-map/by-state. (Accessed June 22, 2018.)

Black Separatists

Black separatists are a separatist political movement in the United States that
seeks to separate those of African descent into distinct economic, political, and
cultural units. Black separatism is generally recognized as a subcategory of black
nationalism. Black separatists "typically oppose integration policies and disdain
interracial marriage" (Southern Poverty Law Center). Most black separatists want
a separate nation for blacks, apart from whites and other minority groups. Most
black separatists "are virulently anti-white and anti-Semitic, and groups with a
religious bent assert that blacks are God's chosen people" (Southern Poverty Law
Center). Black separatism teaches that blacks should seek their original cultural
homeland because blacks are hindered in their advancement by a society that is
dominated by a white majority (Hall). The Southern Poverty Law Center (SPLC)
"recognizes that black racism in America is, at least in part, a reaction to white
racism" and dominance over blacks for several centuries. However, it "notes that
white groups espousing beliefs similar to those of black separatists would be considered racist" and that it would designate them as hate groups. Therefore, "[t]he
same criterion should be applied to all groups regardless of their color" (Southern
Poverty Law Center).

According to the SPLC, a prime example of black separatism can be seen in the
teachings of the Nation of Islam (NOI) and its current leader, Louis Farrakhan.
One of NOI's early leaders, Elijah Mohammed, regularly expressed "anti-white,
anti-Semitic, anti-Catholic, and anti-gay views" (Southern Poverty Law Center).
According to NOI beliefs articulated by Elijah Mohammed, an evil black scientist,
Yacub, created whites as "blue-eyed devils." Because of the evil nature by which
they came forth, whites are inherently evil and ungodly. After Elijah Mohammed's death, his successor, Louis Farrakhan, took up his mantra, and he has
decried the abuses heaped on black people by whites, particularly blaming Jews
for their complicity in aiding and abetting the slave trade that brought black people
to the United States. When a subordinate of Farrakhan's called for the slaughter-
ing of white South Africans, Farrakhan regretted the "tone" of the comments but

agreed with the message and renewed NOI's call for racial separatism and the denouncement of the evils of interracial relationships.

In July 2016, Micah Xavier Johnson was identified "as the man who shot 14 law enforcement officers during protests in Dallas, Texas" (Beirich and Lenz). According to the Dallas police chief, "Johnson was upset about a rash of police shootings in which white police had killed black, sometimes unarmed, citizens." Because of these shootings, "[t]he suspect said he was upset at white people. The suspect stated he wanted to kill white people, especially white officers" (Beirich and Lenz). Johnson killed five police officers and injured nine others. After the shootings, he fled and was eventually cornered inside a building where, after a standoff with police, he was killed by a bomb attached to a bomb-disposal robot. After Johnson's death, a police investigation showed that Johnson had liked several Facebook groups of black separatist movements, "including the Nation of Islam (NOI), the Black Riders Liberation Party, and the New Black Panther Party (NBPP)," all designated as hate groups by the SPLC. In 1996, the NBPP held a protest in which its leader, Malik Zulu Shabazz, led the crowd in chants of "Fifty Shots! Fifty Cops! Kill the pigs who kill our kids!" (Beirich and Lenz). Johnson had also liked the page for NOI "prophet" Elijah Mohammed.

See also: Nation of Islam; New Black Panther Party

FURTHER READING

Beirich, Heidi, and Ryan Lenz. July 8, 2016. "Dallas Sniper Connected to Black Separatist Hate Groups on Facebook." Southern Poverty Law Center: Hatewatch. https://www.splcenter.org/hatewatch/2016/07/08/dallas-sniper-connected-black-separatist-hate-groups-facebook. (Accessed March 18, 2017.)

Hall, Raymond. 1978. *Black Separatism in the United States*. Dartmouth.

Southern Poverty Law Center. "Black Separatist." Southern Poverty Law Center. https://www.splcenter.org/fighting-hate/extremist-files/ideology/black-separatist. (Accessed March 18, 2017.)

Blood & Honour

Blood & Honour is an "international coalition of racist skinhead gangs that operates in the United Kingdom" (Southern Poverty Law Center). In the United States, "two rival groups claim to have affiliation with the parent organization—Blood & Honour America Division and Blood & Honour Council USA" (Southern Poverty Law Center). Blood & Honour was founded in 1987 by Ian Stuart Donaldson, the lead singer of the hate-rock band Skrewdriver (Donaldson later shortened his name to Ian Stuart). Stuart intended Blood & Honour—named in homage to a slogan of the Hitler youth movement—to bring racist music groups together in protest of what was perceived as "growing racial tolerance" of the far-right National Front, which had previously served as the skinhead "home" in the United Kingdom (Southern Poverty Law Center). When the group splintered after Stuart's death in 1993, two factions arose that eventually made their way to the United

States. Both U.S. factions claimed to be the legitimate successor to Stuart's dream of a unified skinhead movement.

Stuart's original intention was to bring skinheads and other racist groups together through hate music. When Stuart died, some in the movement believed that the organization began to profit from the music, as opposed to the music expressing the angst of the white power movement. The first U.S. successor, Blood & Honour America Division, counted various Christian Identity skinhead groups as well as neo-Nazi skinhead groups in its ranks. Collectively, these groups were known as Hammerskin Nation, and Blood & Honour America Division intended to carry out what they saw as Stuart's driving vision: to promote the white power movement through its music.

The Blood & Honour America Division was opposed by Blood & Honour USA, which advocated a more militant approach to white power. Blood & Honor USA consisted of anti-Hammerskin groups and included different coalitions "of skinheads, neo-Nazis, and Ku Klux Klan (KKK) members" (Southern Poverty Law Center). The group called itself the "Blood & Honour Council, or Council 28, since 28 represents the positions of 'B' and 'H' in the alphabet" (Southern Poverty Law Center). Council 28 eventually "joined forces with the National Alliance in order to exploit the neo-Nazi ties of the group." The council proposed adopting "more mainstream lyrics, in addition to blatantly racist ones," in order to make money off public concerts and use the funds to promote white power causes (Southern Poverty Law Center).

After conducting several summer festivals between 2005 and 2009, Council 28 stopped using the Blood & Honour name. In 2009, members of the two American Blood & Honour offshoots called a truce. A spokesperson for the groups said, "We will just not participate in, or carry on, a conflict that started overseas" (Southern Poverty Law Center).

See also: Ku Klux Klan; National Alliance; Neo-Nazis

FURTHER READING

Southern Poverty Law Center. "Blood & Honour." Southern Poverty Law Center. https://www.splcenter.org/fighting-hate/extremist-files/group/blood-honour. (Accessed January 10, 2018.)

Brotherhood of Klans

The Brotherhood of Klans (BOK) has been described as "one of the largest and most widespread Ku Klux Klan organizations in the United States. It's also the only KKK faction to establish chapters outside the U.S., with a sizable presence in Canada" (Southern Poverty Law Center, Brotherhood of Klans). The Southern Poverty Law Center (SPLC) describes the BOK as a throwback to KKK groups of the past. Whereas present-day Klan groups like to "splash their activities across the media on their websites and online forums," the Brotherhood of Klans seems to be much more "secretive" about their activities, "offering scant details of its actions online and conducting serious background checks of prospective members" (Southern Poverty Law Center, Brotherhood of Klans). Like its contemporary equivalents, however, the Brotherhood of Klans forgo wearing white robes in public in favor of appearing in paramilitary uniforms. Its "leadership networks with many non-Klan white supremacist groups, most notably racist skinheads and outlaw biker gangs" (Southern Poverty Law Center, Brotherhood of Klans).

The "Brotherhood of Klans was founded by Dale Fox in 1996." Fox was "an old-school Southern Klansman who vowed to bring the Klan back to its roots in Pulaski, Tennessee," though he never was able to establish a chapter in that city (Southern Poverty Law Center, Brotherhood of Klans). Under Fox's leadership, "the Brotherhood of the Klans became one of the largest KKK groups in the United States." Fox's visibility increased when his biggest rival, Ron Edwards, the imperial wizard of the Imperial Klans of America, stepped down after "coming under intense scrutiny from federal law enforcement" (Southern Poverty Law Center, Brotherhood of Klans). Edwards appointed Fox as his successor, but Edwards reclaimed his position only a year later, although not before Fox "took a number of Imperial Klan chapters with him" (Southern Poverty Law Center, Brotherhood of Klans).

Fox "died of heart attack in November 2006 and was succeeded by Jeremy Parker, a former skinhead," who expanded the Brotherhood of Klans into Canada (Southern Poverty Law Center, Brotherhood of Klans). The BOK's expansion to Canada makes it the only KKK faction to establish chapters outside of the United States (Southern Poverty Law Center, Brotherhood of Klans). In 2010, Parker "left the KKK for Aryan Nations and took 38 chapters of the Brotherhood of the Klan with him" (Palmer).

Those who track Klan activity point out that KKK groups today are hard pressed to maintain their membership rolls in the face of the growth of other racist hate groups (Anti-Defamation League). As noted by Brian Palmer of *Slate*:

> Young racists tend to think of the Klan as their grandfathers' hate group, and of its members as rural, uneducated, and technologically unsophisticated. The Klan doesn't seem to have used the web and social media as well as its competitors. The group's failure to effectively deploy technology is a bit of an irony, since one of those newfangled motion pictures, *The Birth of a Nation*, launched the KKK's second era in 1915. (Palmer)

See also: Ku Klux Klan; Racist Skinheads; White Nationalism; White Supremacist Movement

FURTHER READING

Anti-Defamation League. "Despite Internal Turmoil, Klan Groups Persist." Anti-Defamation League. https://www.adl.org/resources/reports/despite-internal-turmoil-klan-groups-persist. (Accessed June 30, 2018.)

Counter Extremism Project. "Ku Klux Klan (KKK)." Counter Extremism Project. https://www.counterextremism.com/threat/ku-klux-klan. (Accessed June 30, 2018.)

Palmer, Brian. March 8, 2012. "Ku Klux Kontraction." Slate. http://www.slate.com/articles/news_and_politics/politics/2012/03/ku_klux_klan_in_decline_why_did_the_kkk_lose_so_many_chapters_in_2010_.html. (Accessed June 30, 2018.)

Southern Poverty Law Center. "Brotherhood of Klans." Southern Poverty Law Center.
    https://www.splcenter.org/fighting-hate/extremist-files/group/brotherhood-klans.
    (Accessed June 30, 2018.)
Southern Poverty Law Center. "Hate Map by Ideology." Southern Poverty Law Center.
    https://www.splcenter.org/hate-map/by-ideology. (Accessed June 30, 2018.)
Southern Poverty Law Center. "Ku Klux Klan." Southern Poverty Law Center. https://
    www.splcenter.org/fighting-hate/extremist-files/ideology/ku-klux-klan. (Accessed
    June 30, 2018.)

Bureau on American Islamic Relations

The Bureau on American Islamic Relations (BAIR) is "classified by the Southern Poverty Law Center (SPLC) as an Anti-Muslim hate group." According to the SPLC:

> All anti-Muslim hate groups exhibit extreme hostility toward Muslims. The organizations portray those who worship Islam as fundamentally alien and attribute to its followers an inherent set of negative traits. Muslims are depicted as irrational, intolerant and violent, and their faith is frequently depicted as sanctioning pedophilia, coupled with intolerance for homosexuals and women.
>
> These groups also typically hold conspiratorial views regarding the inherent danger to America posed by its Muslim-American community. Muslims are viewed as a fifth column intent on undermining and eventually replacing American democracy and Western civilization with Islamic despotism, a conspiracy theory known as "civilization jihad." Anti-Muslim hate groups allege that Muslims are trying to subvert the rule of law by imposing on Americans their own Islamic legal system, Shariah law. (Southern Poverty Law Center)

BAIR is "a loosely-formed anti-Islamic organization" that formed in Irving, Texas, "in the wake of the [2015] Paris terror attacks" (Badash). BAIR's Facebook page states that it is "an organization that stands in opposition(on all levels) of C.A.I.R. (and other Islamic organizations)" (BAIR). CAIR stands for the Council on American-Islamic Relations, which is a group whose mission "is to enhance understanding of Islam, protect civil rights, promote justice, and empower American Muslims" (CAIR).

Though it is unclear who founded BAIR or when exactly it was founded, a primary spokesperson for the group is David Wright, who is also a member of the "so-called III Percenters, a national movement of gun-toting, antigovernment 'Patriots' that takes its name from the discredited myth that only 3% of colonists fought against the English in the American Revolution" (Nelson). At the November 2015 protest in Dallas, Texas, of an Islamic mosque, Wright led several armed protesters who gathered to express their concerns about the immigration of Syrian refugees into the United States and the potential for "Islamisation" of American political and social values (Burr). Wright stated that "his decision to bring a 12-gauge hunting rifle to the peaceful suburban scene" was based on a notion of self-defense. "I'm not going to lie. We do want to show force. . . . It would be ridiculous to protest Islam without defending ourselves" (Nelson).

Though Nelson claimed that protesters carried guns at an Islamic mosque for "self-defense," others believe his aim was to "savage Islam" (Piggott). "That's what my group [BAIR] does," Wright wrote in 2016. "We monitor them and their activity, we show up in their neighborhoods armed and let them know they're being watched and if they f— up my guys will take em [sic] out. That's exactly what needs to happen" (Piggot).

In February 2016, BAIR "published the names and addresses of more than 60 Muslims and 'Muslim sympathizers' " on the group's Facebook page (Chasmar). The post was meant to target those "who spoke or signed up to express an opinion at an Irving [Texas] city council meeting . . . where the council voted to endorse a planned state bill emphasizing the already enshrined primacy of domestic laws above foreign laws" (Burr). One of the targets of the posting stated, "We have a right to disagree, but we do not have the right to target and cause . . . harm just because we differ in our beliefs. That is the goal of this post: to put a bulls-eye on the back of all the people that stood up against the so-called anti-Shariah law bill" (Chasmar).

See also: ACT for America; Center for Security Policy; Family Security Matters; Three Percenters

FURTHER READING

Badash, David. December 3, 2015. "Anti-Islamic Group Clashes with KKK over Gays and Guns." New Civil Rights Movement. https://www.thenewcivilrightsmovement.com/2015/12/anti_islam_group_says_it_s_too_gay_friendly_to_partner_with_kkk/. (Accessed June 27, 2018.)

BAIR (Bureau on American Islamic Relations). "About." BAIR: Facebook. https://www.facebook.com/pg/BAIR-909810615766870/about/. (Accessed June 27, 2018.)

Beirich, Heidi. April 24, 2018. "Trump's Anti-Muslim Words and Policies Have Consequences." Southern Poverty Law Center: News. https://www.splcenter.org/news/2018/04/24/trumps-anti-muslim-words-and-policies-have-consequences. (Accessed June 27, 2018.)

Burr, Edmondo. November 26, 2015. "Bureau of American Islamic Relations Posts Names of Texas 'Muslims.' " YourNewsWire.com. https://yournewswire.com/bureau-of-american-islamic-relations-posts-names-of-texan-muslims/. (Accessed June 27, 2018.)

CAIR (Council on American-Islamic Relations). "About Us." Council on American-Islamic Relations. https://www.cair.com/about_us. (Accessed June 27, 2018.)

Chasmar, Jessica. November 27, 2015. "Texas Anti-Islam Group Publishes Addresses of Muslims, 'Muslim Sympathizers.' " *Washington Times*. www.washingtontimes.com/news/2015/nov/27/texas-anti-islam-group-publishes-addresses-of-musl/. (Accessed June 27, 2018.)

Levin, Brian. July 21, 2017. "Islamophobia in America: Rise in Hate Crime against Muslims Shows That What Politicians Say Matters." *Newsweek*. http://www.newsweek.com/islamophobia-america-rise-hate-crimes-against-muslims-proves-what-politicians-640184. (Accessed June 27, 2018.)

Nelson, Leah. February 17, 2016. "Backlash." Southern Poverty Law Center: Intelligence Report. https://www.splcenter.org/fighting-hate/intelligence-report/2016/backlash. (Accessed June 27, 2018.)

Piggot, Stephen. February 10, 2017. "One More Enemy." Southern Poverty Law Center: Intelligence Report. https://www.splcenter.org/fighting-hate/intelligence-report/2017/one-more-enemy. (Accessed June 27, 2018.)

Southern Poverty Law Center. "Anti-Muslim." Southern Poverty Law Center. https://www.splcenter.org/fighting-hate/extremist-files/ideology/anti-muslim. (Accessed June 27, 2018.)

C

Center for Immigration Studies

In February 2017, for the first time, the Southern Poverty Law Center (SPLC) "designated the Center for Immigration Studies (CIS) as a hate group" (Southern Poverty Law Center). According to the SPLC, CIS "is a nativist think tank that churns out a constant stream of fear-mongering misinformation about Latino immigrants" (Beirich, 2009). In 1985, the group was founded as one of a network of anti-immigration groups by John Tanton, "an activist with white nationalist leanings and a fondness for extreme 'population control' measures" (Right Wing Watch). The SPLC has dubbed Tanton as the "racist architect of the modern anti-immigrant movement" (Southern Poverty Law Center). Predictably, the executive director of CIS, Mark Krikorian, condemned the designation, complaining that it lumps the organization in with groups such as the KKK and that it was made simply because SPLC does not share CIS's beliefs. But the SPLC has stated that:

> Hate has gone mainstream. Today, the purveyors of hate don't always burn crosses or use racial slurs. They might wear suits and ties. They might have sophisticated public relations operations. They might even testify before Congress.
>
> They're also more likely to be animated by a nativist or white nationalist ideology that sees the "white race" as being under siege by immigrants of color across the Western world. Reflecting this trend, our annual list of hate groups has evolved to include more groups closely linked to white nationalism. (Beirich, 2017)

The CIS has been criticized for periodically publishing reports deemed misleading and for using poor or questionable methodology when reporting statistics on immigration. Though such reports have from time to time found their way into the mainstream media, they have been criticized as being misleading and skewing the argument to the CIS's point of view (Sherman). The CIS regularly circulates pieces on its website (cis.org) that have been authored "by white nationalists, Holocaust deniers, and other material from explicitly racist websites" (Piggott). In the past, CIS has circulated pieces from the white nationalist website *American Renaissance* (AmRen), which is run by Jared Taylor, "one of America's most prominent and outspoken racists" (Piggott). Taylor has stated that "[b]lacks and whites are different. When blacks are left entirely to their own devices, Western civilization—any kind of civilization—disappears" (Piggott). In October 2016, AmRen published an article about a CIS event that featured Charles Murray, author of the controversial text *The Bell Curve*, which "uses racist pseudoscience and misleading statistics to argue that social inequality is caused by the genetic inferiority of black and Latino communities" (Piggott). CIS has also circulated links to the anti-immigrant and nationalist hate site VDARE. Run by white nationalist Peter Brimelow, who has argued that America is a historically white-dominated society and should remain that way, VDARE "is a hub for white nationalist and anti-Semitic authors" (Beirich, 2009).

Though one commentator has stated that the designation of CIS as a hate group is based more on "its associations rather than its current work" (Sherman), the director of SPLC's Intelligence Project articulated why CIS landed on SPLC's "hate radar":

> CIS has a long history of bigotry, starting with its founder, white nationalist John Tanton, but in 2016, the group hit a new low. CIS commissioned Jason Richwine, a man who's [sic] Ph.D. dissertation endorses the idea of IQ differences between the races, to write multiple reports and blog pieces for the organization. The group also continued to circulate racist and anti-Semitic authors to its supporters, and finally, staffer John Miano attended the white nationalist group VDARE's Christmas party in December. (Sherman)

SPLC has stated that CIS also "circulates a weekly email listserv with dozens of links to articles about immigration" (Southern Poverty Law Center). These e-mails highlight articles

> by "white nationalists" such as Paul Weston, a Holocaust denier, and articles by American Renaissance, run by Jared Taylor, who has made racist statements about blacks. One article entitled "Voting for Hillary equals more Muslim killings of Americans" claimed that Clinton's assistant "works fervently for Sharia law in America" and that Trump would give the United States a chance to "survive this immigration invasion." (Sherman)

In March 2017, CIS executive director Mark Krikorian wrote an opinion piece in the *Washington Post* in which he complained of the "poison of the blacklist" that accompanies the "hate designation" affixed to CIS by the SPLC (Krikorian). While Krikorian did not articulate exactly what CIS believes, he did state that the organization's views regarding immigration are "held by a large share of the American public" (Letters to the Editor). Heidi Beirich of the SPLC retorted: "So? At one time a 'large share' of the American public thought slavery was okay. Today, a large share of Americans believe white people are superior to others and that any religion besides Christianity is evil. Just because a large share of people believe something doesn't make it right or moral" (Letters to the Editor). Beirich concluded that CIS certainly is not an organization that "promotes love and acceptance" (Beirich, 2017).

See also: American Renaissance; Federation for American Immigration Reform; Holocaust Denial; Occidental Quarterly; VDARE; White Nationalism; White Supremacist Movement

FURTHER READING

Beirich, Heidi. January 31, 2009. "The Nativist Lobby: Three Faces of Intolerance." Southern Poverty Law Center. https://www.splcenter.org/20090201/nativist-lobby-three-faces-intolerance. (Accessed May 22, 2018.)

Beirich, Heidi. March 23, 2017. "Hate Groups like Center for Immigration Studies Want You to Believe They're Mainstream." Southern Poverty Law Center: Hatewatch.

https://www.splcenter.org/hatewatch/2017/03/23/hate-groups-center-immigra tion-studies-want-you-believe-they're-mainstream. (Accessed May 22, 2018.)

Krikorian, Mark. March 17, 2017. "How Labeling My Organization a Hate Group Shuts Down Public Debate." *Washington Post*. https://www.washingtonpost.com/opin ions/how-labeling-my-organization-a-hate-group-shuts-down-public-debate/2017 /03/17/656ab9c8-0812-11e7-93dc-00f9bdd74ed1_story.html. (Accessed May 22, 2018.)

Letters to the Editor. "Does the Center for Immigration Studies Deserve to Be Labeled a 'Hate Group'?" *Washington Post*. https://www.washingtonpost.com/opinions /does-the-center-for-immigration-studies-deserve-to-be-labeled-a-hate-group/201 7/03/24/89ab4cda-0f38-11e7-aa57-2ca1b05c41b8_story.html. (Accessed May 22, 2018.)

Piggott, Stephen. November 7, 2016. "Anti-Immigrant Center for Immigration Studies Continues to Promote White Nationalists." Southern Poverty Law Center: Hate-watch. https://www.splcenter.org/hatewatch/2016/11/07/anti-immigrant-center-immi gration-studies-continues-promote-white-nationalists. (Accessed May 22, 2018.)

Right Wing Watch. "Center for Immigration Studies." Right Wing Watch. http://www .rightwingwatch.org/organizations/center-for-immigration-studies/. (Accessed May 22, 2018.)

Sherman, Amy. March 22, 2017. "Is the Center for Immigration Studies a Hate Group, as the Southern Poverty Law Center Says?" PolitiFact.com. http://www.politifact .com/florida/article/2017/mar/22/center-immigration-studies-hate-group-south ern-pov/. (Accessed May 22, 2018.)

Southern Poverty Law Center. "John Tanton." Southern Poverty Law Center. https:// www.splcenter.org/fighting-hate/extremist-files/individual/john-tanton. (Accessed May 22, 2018.)

Center for Security Policy

The Center for Security Policy (CSP) was founded by Frank Gaffney Jr., a neo-conservative who had served as a government official in the Ronald Reagan administration. The CSP was founded as a think tank, "[t]o identify challenges and opportunities likely to affect American security, broadly defined, and to act promptly and creatively to ensure that they are the subject of focused national examination and effective action" (Center for Security Policy). From its founding through the mid-2000s, CSP was seen as a mainstream, though hawkish, organi-zation that followed the neoconservative ideal of "peace through strength." Like many neoconservative organizations, however, CSP struggled to justify its exis-tence after the end of the Cold War. Communism had been defeated, and the United States was the lone remaining superpower. With 9/11 and subsequent U.S. wars in Iraq and Afghanistan, CSP was able to shift its focus from fighting com-munism to fighting Islam. When the anti-Muslim movement ratcheted into high gear in the late 2000s, CSP was ready, and it had extensive Washington roots to draw upon.

CSP focuses on claims that American Muslims are engaging in a vast conspir-acy to overthrow the U.S. government from within. Much of what CSP publicizes is conspiratorial in nature, like the notion that Muslims intend to establish sharia law under the guise of constitutional protections regarding freedom of religion.

CSP has called the imposition of sharia law the "preeminent totalitarian threat of our time: the legal-political-military doctrine known within Islam as shariah" (Southern Poverty Law Center). Much of what CSP publishes intends to show that prominent Muslim organizations in the United States are actually fronts for the Muslim Brotherhood, an organization that has the stated goal to instill the Koran (holy book of Islam) and Sunnah (teachings and sayings of Muhammad) as the "sole reference point for . . . ordering the life of the Muslim family, individual, community . . . and state" (Kull).

In 2010, CSP produced a report about the Muslim threat in America in which it called for a halt to all government outreach-related efforts to Muslim communities, warnings to imams that they would be charged with sedition if they spoke of imposing sharia law in the United States, and the dismantling of so-called "no-go zones," neighborhoods that law enforcement is unable to police because they are so overwhelmingly Muslim. In 2015, Donald Trump, who was then running for president, picked up on this CSP claim and used it in campaign material (Gunter). A prominent member of CSP, retired Lt. Gen. Jerry Boykin, a former U.S. deputy undersecretary of defense for intelligence under President George W. Bush, stated in 2010 that "[Islam] should not be protected under the First Amendment, particularly given that those following the dictates of the Quran are under an obligation to destroy our Constitution and replace it with sharia law" (Southern Poverty Law Center).

In 2015, CSP devoted itself to creating in the United States a climate of fear around Syrian refugees entering the country. In stoking the anti-immigrant and anti-Muslim fires, CSP's founder, Frank Gaffney, invited Jared Taylor, the white nationalist who founded the virulently racist website American Renaissance, onto CSP's radio show. During the interview, Gaffney called American Renaissance "wonderful" and tried depict the flow of Syrian refugees into Europe as hastening the "death" of that continent.

CSP teamed up with Donald Trump and Ted Cruz for an anti-Iran rally in Washington, D.C., in September 2015. In December 2015, Donald Trump issued a press release that urged the U.S. government to ban Muslims from entering the United States. Trump cited statistics from a CSP poll that indicated that "25% of those polled agreed that violence against Americans here in the United States is justified as a part of the global jihad." However, as was later noted, the poll was an opt-in online survey that "cannot be considered representative of the intended population, which was, in this case, Muslims" (Southern Poverty Law Center).

See also: ACT For America; American Renaissance; White Nationalism; White Supremacist Movement

FURTHER READING

Center for Security Policy. "About Us." Center for Security Policy. http://www.center forsecuritypolicy.org/about-us/. (Accessed January 13, 2018.)

Gunter, Joel. December 8, 2015. "Trump's 'Muslim Lockdown': What Is the Center for Security Policy?" BBC News. http://www.bbc.com/news/world-us-canada -35037943. (Accessed January 13, 2018.)

Kull, Steven. 2011. *Feeling Betrayed: The Roots of Muslim Anger at America*. Brookings Institution Press.

Southern Poverty Law Center. "Center for Security Policy." Southern Poverty Law Center. https://www.splcenter.org/fighting-hate/extremist-files/group/center-security -policy. (Accessed January 13, 2018.)

Christian Defense League

The Christian Defense League (CDL) is a Christian Identity–affiliated organization that professes a neo-Nazi ideology. According to the Southern Poverty Law Center (SPLC):

> [N]eo-Nazi groups share a hatred for Jews and an admiration for Adolf Hitler and Nazi Germany. While they also hate other minorities, homosexuals, and even sometimes Christians, the perceive "the Jew" as their cardinal enemy and trace social problems to a Jewish conspiracy that supposedly controls governments, financial institutions, and the media. (Southern Poverty Law Center, 2016)

The SPLC identifies the Christian Defense League as an active hate group, with its primary membership headquartered in Villa Rica, Georgia (Southern Poverty Law Center, 2016). The group was founded in the 1960s by James K. Warner, a leading proponent of Christian Identity. Christian Identity is a theology/ideology practiced by many white nationalist and white supremacist groups in the United States. The tenets of Christian Identity follow:

> Anglo-Saxon-Celtic peoples (whites) are God's real "chosen people," and descend in an unbroken line from Adam and Eve. They are by nature a superior race.
>
> Jews derive from Cain, himself the product of a sexual liaison between Eve and the Serpent (the original sin) in Eden, and so are biologically evil, the "synagogue of Satan."
>
> Non-whites are "pre-Adamic" beings, soulless and akin to the Biblical "beasts of the field." Cain mated with these peoples to produce today's Jews.
>
> Jews are part of a Satanic plot to unite the world under a single government, to be taken over ultimately by the Devil himself. The plot is thousands of years old.
>
> Whites in America (the true "House of Israel") must battle bloodily to usher in a period of Godly rule prior to the Second Coming. That means a race war. (Southern Poverty Law Center, 1998)

Currently, the CDL rails against "political correctness" and asks the question, "What will we answer future generations when words like 'Merry Christmas' are banned and everyone is forced to use new phrases like 'Happy Holidays'? What will history say about us?" (Christian Defence League, Why CDL?). The organization also states:

> Evil is on the rise. The gay community has hijacked and stolen the rainbow of God's promise to now use as a symbol of their own.
>
> Muslim communities continue to grow and dominate many landscapes around the globe. They are allowed to spew any type of speech they deem is important to their cause, yet cry racist and whine they are misunderstood or attacked for no reason. Why, when they claim they are a peaceful religion? Many believers today have become blinded and buy into a "sanitized" and therefore inaccurate view of Islam.

They don't even realize it was shaped by the needs of Islamic policy-makers and those that choose to align themselves with this group, rather understand what is truly going on. (Christian Defence League, Why CDL?)

The CDL commits itself to sharing the "good news" with all those "who are blinding others by corruption, by false religions, by living ungodly lifestyles." As the organization notes:

> We owe it to our country to stop the onslaught that by lies, deception or force that seeks to lead our country further into a land ruled by those with agendas that seek to control, enslave and demand we live according to what they say—no matter how corrupt or vile it is. . . .
>   We will stand with others of like mind who want to stop the further degradation of our county's values. (Christian Defence League, Why CDL?)

See also: Christian Identity; Neo-Nazis; White Nationalism; White Supremacist Movement

FURTHER READING

Christian Defence League. "Who We Are." Christian Defence League. http://www.chris tiandefenceleague.com/pdf/Who%20-%20new%20red%20logo%20 (1).pdf. (Accessed June 30, 2018.)

Christian Defence League. "Why a Christian Defence League?" Christian Defence League. http://www.christiandefenceleague.com/why.php. (Accessed June 30, 2018.)

Christian Defence League—United States. https://www.facebook.com/Christian-Defence -League-United-States-1421124121473964/. (Accessed June 30, 2018.)

History Commons. "Profile: Christian Defense League (CDL)." History Commons. http:// www.historycommons.org/entity.jsp?entity=christian_defense_league_1. (Accessed June 30, 2018.)

Southern Poverty Law Center. March 15, 1998. "How the Christian Identity Movement Began." Southern Poverty Law Center: Intelligence Report. https://www.splcen ter.org/fighting-hate/intelligence-report/1998/how-christian-identity-movement -began. (Accessed June 30, 2018.)

Southern Poverty Law Center. February 17, 2016. "Active Hate Groups in the United States in 2015." Southern Poverty Law Center: Intelligence Report. https://www .splcenter.org/fighting-hate/intelligence-report/2016/active-hate-groups-united -states-2015. (Accessed June 30, 2018.)

Christian Identity

Christian Identity is an anti-Semitic and racist pseudo-theology that rose in prominence among adherents of the racist right in the 1980s and 1990s. Christian Identity teaches that all nonwhite peoples will eventually be exterminated or compelled to serve the master white race in a heavenly kingdom that will be ruled over by Jesus Christ himself. Christian Identity has spawned some of the most virulently racist extremist groups and individuals in the United States, but its influence has extended to other countries as well (Southern Poverty Law Center, Christian

Identity). Christian Identity is estimated to have perhaps as many as 25,000 adherents (Anti-Defamation League).

Christian Identity espouses a white supremacist philosophy, justifying the beliefs on specific interpretations of the Bible and influences from elsewhere. Some adherents of Christian Identity (e.g., Aryan Nations) couple a strongly held anti-government sentiment with their theological beliefs. Christian Identity "theology" consists of several tenets: (1) Adam and Eve were the progenitors of the white race and all other races are pre-Adamic or beasts that evolved into human form; (2) contemporary Jews are not the true descendants of the tribe of Judah but are descendants of Esau, Isaac's oldest son, who sold his birthright; (3) there will be an "End Times" and the epic battle of Armageddon, which will herald the Second Coming of Jesus Christ; (4) interracial marriage, homosexuality, and any "deviant" behavior is not of God and is, therefore, beastly and deserving of eradication; and (5) a general suspicion of the federal government and, in particular, anything pertaining to a "New World Order" (Balleck).

Christian Identity posits what is known as "two-house theology," which asserts that the ancient kingdom of Israel was split into two houses—Israel and Judah—about 931 BCE. Approximately 722 BCE, most of those living in the northern portion of what had been the Kingdom of Israel were taken into captivity and scattered about after having been conquered by the Assyrians. The southern part of the kingdom, including Judah, largely survived to constitute modern-day Jews. However, whereas British Israelism held that Jews were descended from the tribe of Judah, Christian Identity in its American "bastardization" believes that the true descendants of Judah (and Israel) are instead white Europeans. These were members of the original Lost Ten Tribes, which had been scattered but which had settled in Scotland, Germany, and other European countries. These "true Israelites" are "Anglo-Saxon, Celtic, Germanic, Nordic, and kindred peoples" (Roberts).

In the theology of Christian Identity, contemporary Jews are the descendants of Esau (son of Isaac), who sold his God-given birthright for a bowl of pottage (Genesis 25:29–34). Jacob, his younger brother who would become Israel (and would have 12 sons), thus became the recipient of the promises made to Abraham and his posterity. The "dual seedliner" strain of Christian Identity thought holds that the Jews are actually the spawn of Satan through Adam and Eve's son, Cain. In this belief, Satan seduced Eve, and she gave birth to Cain, while Abel, whom Cain would slay, was the "pure" progeny of Adam and Eve. This line of reasoning was originally fostered by a 1900 book by Charles Carroll, entitled *The Negro: A Beast or in the Image of God?* In his treatise, Carroll concluded that only the white race was the true offspring of Adam and Eve, "while Negros are pre-Adamite beasts and could not possibly have been made in God's image and likeness because they are beastlike, immoral and ugly" (Carroll). Carroll insisted that blacks did not have souls and that the mixing of the races led to the blasphemous ideas of atheism and evolutionism (Carroll). Variants on these themes have led many Christian Identity adherents to fiercely defend such policies as the separation of the races, while other Christian Identity adherents go so far as to suggest that the mixing of the races is a defilement of the white race and that the penalties for this and other "beastly" behaviors (e.g., homosexuality) should be death (Ago).

In addition to racism, Christian Identity teaches that there will be an end of times and that the biblically foretold battle of Armageddon, in which the forces of good will battle the forces of evil, will be fought. This end-times scenario makes Christian Identity members extremist in their interpretation of events. For instance, adherents view the United Nations as an organization controlled by a Jewish-backed conspiracy that aims at overthrowing the United States of America (Kaplan). Jews also play prominently in their control of the world banking system and their control of the "root of all evil" (i.e., paper money). As noted by author James Alfred Ago, "The creation of the Federal Reserve System in 1913 shifted control of money from Congress to private institutions and violated the Constitution. The money system encourages the Federal Reserve to take out loans, creating trillions of dollars of government debt and allowing international bankers to control America" (Ago). Christian identity preacher Sheldon Eery similarly claims that "[m]ost of the owners of the largest banks in America are of Eastern European (Jewish) ancestry and connected with the (Jewish) Rothschild European banks." Thus, in the doctrine of Christian Identity, "the global banking conspiracy is led and controlled by Jewish interests" (Ago).

A leading figure in the cause of Christian Identity was William Potter Gale, a former aide to Gen. Douglas MacArthur. Gale was anti-tax during the 1970s and 1980s and was a leading figure in the paramilitary and militia movements of the same time, including the Posse Comitatus (History Commons). Several past and current patriot/militia groups identify with Christian Identity ideas, including "[t]he Covenant, Sword, and the Arm of the Lord; the Faience Priesthood; the Aryan Republican Army; the Church of Jesus Christ, Christian; Church of Israel; and, Kingdom Identity Ministries" (Southern Poverty Law Center, Christian Identity).

Perhaps the most successful of the groups associated with Christian Identity theology is Aryan Nations. Aryan Nations adheres to most of the regular tenets of Christian Identity, but they differ in the zeal with which they profess anti-government sentiments. The ultimate goal of Aryan Nations is to establish a "whites only homeland in five northwestern states—Oregon, Idaho, Wyoming, Washington, and Montana" (Southern Poverty Law Center, Christian Identity). If relinquished by their governments, these states would become the base of the white power movement and would be known as the "Northwest Territorial Imperative." The headquarters of Aryan Nations was Hayden Lake, Idaho, from the late 1970s until the early 2000s. The group was founded by Richard Butler, who had been inspired by William Potter Gale's association with the Posse Comitatus movement. Butler was a great admirer of Adolf Hitler, and he strove to establish a "whites-only homeland in the Pacific Northwest" (Southern Poverty Law Center, Aryan Nations). In 1981, Butler held the first Aryan World Conference at his Hayden Lake compound. These "confabs" would attract

> almost every nationally significant racist leader around. Among them: Tom Metzger, former Klansman and leader of White Aryan Resistance; Louis Beam, another onetime Klansman who promoted the concept of leaderless resistance; Don Black, the former Klansman who created Stormfront, the oldest and largest white nationalist forum on the Web; and Kirk Lyons, a lawyer who has represented

several extremists and who was married on the compound by Butler. (Southern Poverty Law Center, Aryan Nations)

William Butler died in September 2004, but by that time his legacy had already become bloodied. Butler's most loyal and committed follower was Robert J. ("Bob") Mathews, who founded the Order. Mathews and his organization would go on to be dubbed by the Federal Bureau of Investigation (FBI) one of the most dangerous domestic terror groups in the United States. Today, Christian Identity continues to provide the ideological foundation for dozens of extremist groups.

See also: Aryan Nations; The Order; Stormfront; White Nationalism; White Supremacist Movement

FURTHER READING

Ago, James Alfred. 1995. *The Politics of Righteousness: Idaho Christian Patriotism*. University of Washington Press.

Anti-Defamation League. "Christian Identity." Anti-Defamation League. https://www.adl.org/education/resources/backgrounders/christian-identity. (Accessed March 27, 2018.)

Balleck, Barry J. 2015. *Allegiance to Liberty: The Changing Face of Patriots, Militias, and Political Violence in America*. Praeger.

Barkun, Michael. 1996. *Religion and the Racist Right: The Origins of the Christian Identity Movement*. University of North Carolina Press.

Carroll, Charles. 1900. *The Negro a Beast . . . or . . . In the Image of God*. American Book and Bible House. https://moorishamericannationalrepublic.com/course-materials/A%20NEGRO%20THE%20BEAST%20OR%20IMAGE%20OF%20GOD%20BOOK.pdf. (Accessed February 8, 2019.)

History Commons. "Profile: William Potter Gale." History Commons. http://www.historycommons.org/entity.jsp?entity=william_potter_gale_1. (Accessed March 27, 2018.)

Kaplan, Jeffrey. 2002. *Millennial Violence: Past, Present, and Future*. Routledge.

Quarles, Chester L. 2004. *Christian Identity: The Aryan American Bloodline Religion*. McFarland & Company.

Roberts, Charles H. 2003. *Race over Grace*: *The Racialist Religion of the Christian Identity Movement*. iUniverse Press.

Southern Poverty Law Center. "Aryan Nations." Southern Poverty Law Center. https://www.splcenter.org/fighting-hate/extremist-files/group/aryan-nations. (Accessed March 27, 2018.)

Southern Poverty Law Center. "Christian Identity." Southern Poverty Law Center. https://www.splcenter.org/fighting-hate/extremist-files/ideology/christian-identity. (Accessed March 27, 2018.)

Confederate Hammerskins

The Confederate Hammerskins are a regional variation of what is known as "Hammerskin Nation" (HSN), an organization that the Anti-Defamation League (ADL) characterizes as "the most violent and best-organized neo-Nazi skinhead group in the United States" (Anti-Defamation League, The Hammerskin Nation). The Southern Poverty Law Center (SPLC) lists the Confederate Hammerskins and Hammerskin Nation as racist skinhead groups, stating that "racist skinheads form a particularly violent element of the white supremacist movement, and have often been referred to as the 'shock troops' of the hoped-for revolution. The classic Skinhead look is a shaved head, black Doc Martens boots, jeans with suspenders and an array of typically racist tattoos" (Southern Poverty Law Center, Racist Skinhead). Because Hammerskin Nation was founded in Dallas, Texas, in 1987, Confederate Hammerskins consider themselves the "first and founding chapter of the HSN representing the United States from Texas to Florida" (Hammerskin Nation, Confederate Hammerskins).

According to the Anti-Defamation League, Confederate Hammerskins generally add the Confederate flag to all of their materials, and many members can be found with tattoos of the Confederate flag. Generally, however, the

> name and symbol of the Hammerskin Nation came from The Wall, a 1979 album by the rock group Pink Floyd that was made into a film in 1982. The Wall tells the story of Pink, a rock singer who becomes a drug addict, loses his grip on reality and turns to fascism. Pink performs a song in which he expresses a desire to line all of the "queers," "Jews," and "coons" in his audience "up against the wall" and shoot them. In obvious references to the Holocaust, he sings of the "final solution" and "waiting to turn on the showers and fire the ovens." The swastika is replaced by Pink's symbol: two crossed hammers, which he boasts will "batter down" the doors behind which frightened minorities hide from his fascist supporters. Though Pink Floyd does not support fascism, the Hammerskin Nation has made real the gruesome fantasy depicted in the band's film: racist rock music and racially motivated violence under a banner bearing two red, white and black crossed hammers. (Anti-Defamation League, Hammerskin Nation)

Red, white, and black, of course, are also the colors of the Nazi flag. And much of the ideology of both Confederate Hammerskins and Hammerskin Nation aligns closely with the white supremacist values of Nazism and neo-Nazis in the United States. Confederate Hammerskins "desire to have 'their own state,' which consists of only white people," and "believe they are in a race war and list any of their members who are in jail or prison as POWs" (Hall). In addition, Confederate Hammerskins, like others in Hammerskin Nation, ascribe great significance to the numbers 14 and 88. The number 14, which stands for the "14 Words" and was penned by now-deceased white supremacist David Lane, refers to the ideology of Western Hammerskins and other white supremacist groups: "We must secure the existence of our people and a future for white children" (Hall). The number 88 refers to "Heil Hitler because H is the eighth letter in the alphabet" (Hall).

Confederate Hammerskins "operate as a street-level bonehead (racist skinhead) crew, generally organizing through the white power music scene as well as maintaining links with sectors of the broader racist movement" (Atlanta Anarchist Black Cross). Confederate Hammerskins have existed in the state of Georgia for over a quarter of a century, and they can host national gatherings of white supremacist groups—such as "Hammerfest," a concert event that features music from hate-rock groups and other white supremacist bands—"because they can utilize resources from other parts of white power movement in [the southern] region, and also because they have the support of the Hammerskin Nation as a whole when hosting the crew's annual national gathering" (Atlanta Anarchist Black Cross).

See also: Hammerskin Nation; Neo-Nazis; Racist Skinheads; White Nationalism; White Supremacist Movement

FURTHER READING

Anti-Defamation League. "The Hammerskin Nation." Anti-Defamation League. https:// www.adl.org/education/resources/profiles/hammerskin-nation. (Accessed June 26, 2018.)

Anti-Defamation League. "Hammerskins." Anti-Defamation League. https://www.adl .org/education/references/hate-symbols/hammerskins. (Accessed June 26, 2018.)

Atlanta Anarchist Black Cross. August 24, 2016. "Neo-Nazi 'Hammerfest' Gathering Planned for Georgia, October 1st." It's Going Down. https://itsgoingdown.org /neo-nazi-hammerfest-gathering-planned-georgia-october-1st/. (Accessed June 26, 2018.)

Hall, John. October 26, 2001. "Suspects Linked to Gang." *San Diego Union-Tribune*. http://www.sandiegouniontribune.com/sdut-suspects-linked-to-gang-2001oct26 -story.html. (Accessed June 26, 2018.)

Hammerskin Nation. http://www.hammerskins.net/. (Accessed June 26, 2018.)

Hammerskin Nation. "Confederate Hammerskins." Hammerskin Nation. http://hammer skins.net/chs/index.html. (Accessed June 26, 2018.)

Reynolds, Michael. December 15, 1999. "Hammerskin Nation Emerges from Small Dallas Group." Southern Poverty Law Center: Intelligence Report. https://www .splcenter.org/fighting-hate/intelligence-report/1999/hammerskin-nation -emerges-small-dallas-group. (Accessed June 26, 2018.)

Southern Poverty Law Center. "Racist Skinhead." Southern Poverty Law Center. https:// www.splcenter.org/fighting-hate/extremist-files/ideology/racist-skinhead. (Accessed June 26, 2018.)

Southern Poverty Law Center. March 2, 2015. "Active Racist Skinhead Groups." Southern Poverty Law Center: Intelligence Report. https://www.splcenter.org/fighting -hate/intelligence-report/2015/active-racist-skinhead-groups. (Accessed June 26, 2018.)

White Prison Gangs. "Hammerskins." http://whiteprisongangs.blogspot.com/2009/05 /hammerskins_02.html. (Accessed June 26, 2018.)

Confederate White Knights of the Ku Klux Klan

The Confederate White Knights of the Ku Klux Klan (CWK) is one of "just over 40 active Klan groups that currently exist in the United States" (Anti-Defamation League). According to the Anti-Defamation League (ADL):

> The organized Ku Klux Klan movement continues to struggle due to several factors, including infighting, the perception among adherents that current Klan groups (or their leaders) are not authentic, as well as competition for membership from other white supremacist movements. These include the surging "Alternative right" and a rising number of white supremacist prison gangs. (Anti-Defamation League)

The ADL states that "one of the clearest signs of the declining state of Ku Klux Klan groups is their inability to demonstrate stability or continuity," as evidenced by the fact that "more than half of the currently active Klan groups were formed or re-started in the last three years" (Anti-Defamation League). Lamenting such chaos, one Pennsylvania Klansman noted "that there were more Imperial Wizards [of the KKK] on Facebook than at Hogwarts Academy" (Anti-Defamation League).

The CWK is categorized as a Ku Klux Klan (KKK) hate group by the Southern Poverty Law Center (SPLC). According to the SPLC, "The Ku Klux Klan, with its long history of violence, is the most infamous—and oldest—of American hate groups. Although black Americans have typically been the Klan's primary target, it also has attacked Jews, immigrants, gays and lesbians and, until recently, Catholics" (Southern Poverty Law Center, Ku Klux Klan). The CWK is "part of the Knights of the Ku Klux Klan (KKKK), an organization founded by David Duke in 1975" that attempted to "put a 'kinder, gentler' face on the Klan, courting media attention and attempting to portray itself as a modern 'white civil rights' organization" (Southern Poverty Law Center, Knights of the Ku Klux Klan).

The CWK organized one of the largest Klan events in 2016, when "approximately 10 members and associates of the Confederate White Knights (CWK) rallied at Fireman's Park in Madison, Indiana" (Anti-Defamation League). During the event, "CWK leaders Imperial Wizard Richard Preston and Indiana Grand Dragon Anthony 'Tony' Berry delivered speeches that addressed government tyranny, bullying, and stopping drug abuse (with violence if necessary). They also denounced the Black Lives Matter movement" (Anti-Defamation League).

In 2017, the CWK was one of a handful of KKK groups that distributed flyers throughout the country focusing on

> perceived threats to the white race, including the Black Lives Matter movement, Islam and the building of mosques, the LGBT community (particularly transgender restrooms), "black on white crime," immigration (particularly Mexican), and the threatened removal of Confederate symbols from public spaces such as government buildings, parks, and schools. (Anti-Defamation League)

But according to the ADL, "the distribution of racist, anti-Semitic, homophobic and Islamophobic fliers remains the most consistent Klan activity" (Anti-Defamation League).

According to CBS News, the CWK operate in Arkansas, Indiana, Kentucky, Louisiana, Maryland, Missouri, New Jersey, North Carolina, South Carolina, and Virginia (CBS News).

See also: Knights of the Ku Klux Klan; Ku Klux Klan; White Supremacist Movement

FURTHER READING

Anti-Defamation League. "Despite Internal Turmoil, Klan Groups Persist." Anti-Defamation League. https://www.adl.org/resources/reports/despite-internal-turmoil-klan-groups-persist. (Accessed June 30, 2018.)

CBS News. "Hate Groups in America: Confederate White Knights of the Ku Klux Klan." CBS News. https://www.cbsnews.com/pictures/hate-groups-in-america/4/. (Accessed June 30, 2018.)

Counter Extremism Project. "Ku Klux Klan (KKK)." Counter Extremism Project. https://www.counterextremism.com/threat/ku-klux-klan. (Accessed June 30, 2018.)

Southern Poverty Law Center. "Hate Map by Ideology." Southern Poverty Law Center. https://www.splcenter.org/hate-map/by-ideology. (Accessed June 30, 2018.)

Southern Poverty Law Center. "Knights of the Ku Klux Klan." Southern Poverty Law Center. https://www.splcenter.org/fighting-hate/extremist-files/group/knights-ku-klux-klan. (Accessed June 30, 2018.)

Southern Poverty Law Center. "Ku Klux Klan." Southern Poverty Law Center. https://www.splcenter.org/fighting-hate/extremist-files/ideology/ku-klux-klan. (Accessed June 30, 2018.)

Council of Conservative Citizens

The Council of Conservative Citizens (CCC) "is an American far-right organization that opposes all efforts to mix the races" and publicly "supports causes related to white nationalism, white supremacism, and white separatism." (Southern Poverty Law Center). The roots of the CCC lay in the original "Citizens' Councils of America (CCA) (originally configured as White Citizens' Councils) which was an overtly racist organization formed in the 1950s in opposition to the U.S. Supreme Court's decision in *Brown v. Board of Education* that outlawed public school segregation" (Southern Poverty Law Center). The CCA celebrated the "Southern way of life," and the group "used a traditionalist rhetoric that appealed to better-mannered, more discreet racists; while the Klan burned crosses, the CCA relied on political and economic pressure" (Anti-Defamation League). By the 1970s, when the CCA had lost the cultural struggle of segregation, the group faded from public view, though many former members retained their racist views—a fact that would lead to the group's rebirth in the 1980s and its influence into the 21st century.

Rising from the ashes of the CCA, the CCC was founded in 1985 by Gordon Baum, a former CCA field organizer in the Midwest. Baum and 29 others gathered in Atlanta, Georgia, because of their collective frustration "with government "giveaway programs, special preferences and quotas, crack-related crime and single mothers and third generation welfare mothers dependent on government checks and food stamps" (Anti-Defamation League). Using old CCA mailing lists, the CCC was established, with Baum appointed as the chief executive of the new organization. The group rapidly gained members, and by 1999, the CCC had 15,000 members in more than 20 states, with the majority of adherents located in just three states: Mississippi, Alabama, and Georgia (Anti-Defamation League).

The beliefs of the CCC reflected those of the CCA, but the CCC played on the collective fears of its new membership by focusing on issues like "interracial marriage, black-on-white violence, and the demise of white Southern pride and culture—best exemplified by the debate over the display of the Confederate battle flag" (Anti-Defamation League). In addition, the CCC picked up on themes of anti-government distrust by its inflammatory rhetoric regarding the New World Order and its contention that states' rights were being subverted by the federal government. By illuminating these issues, the CCC found many sympathizers among those in the patriot and militia movements who expressed the same angst about the power of the federal government.

Most Americans became aware of the CCC in 1998 "when a scandal erupted after it became public knowledge" that several prominent southern politicians had intimate ties with the group. In 1998, "former Congressman Bob Barr (R-GA) had given the keynote address at the CCC's national convention, and it was later revealed that then-Senate majority leader Trent Lott (R-MS) had spoken to the group five times" (Southern Poverty Law Center). Both Barr and Lott claimed ignorance of the CCC's racist agenda, though an *Intelligence Report* published by the Southern Poverty Law Center (SPLC) and "publicized by national television and newspaper reports, definitely demonstrated that the CCC was, in fact, a hate group . . . that routinely denigrated blacks as 'genetically inferior,' complained about 'Jewish power brokers,' called LGBT people 'perverted sodomites,' accused immigrants of turning America into a 'slimy brown mass of glop,' and named Lester Maddox, the now-deceased, ax-handle-wielding, arch-segregationist former governor of Georgia, 'Patriot of the Century'" (Southern Poverty Law Center).

However, Barr and Lott were only the most visible supporters of the CCC. After the SPLC's report, it became public knowledge that former governors of both Mississippi and Alabama had ties with the group, as did 34 members of the Mississippi state legislature (Anti-Defamation League). Also in Mississippi, "all five members of the Lamar County Supervisors Board attended a meeting of the CCC in which the ongoing battle to save our beloved state flag" was discussed (the Mississippi flag displays the Confederate battle flag as part of its design) (Anti-Defamation League). Other prominent state and national figures included former politicians from Tennessee, South Carolina, and Arkansas.

In January 1999, a resolution was introduced into Congress "that condemned the racism and bigotry espoused by the Council of Conservative Citizens." The resolution "was modeled after a 1994 House resolution that had passed which criticized former Nation of Islam member Khalid Muhammad for racist and anti-Semitic remarks, while also condemning any manifestations or expressions of racial and religious intolerance, wherever they were found" (Anti-Defamation League). But whereas "the resolution against Muhammad passed through both houses of Congress in 20 days, the criticism of the CCC never even made it to the floor, due largely to the reluctance of Republicans to accept what amounted to an indirect censure of their leadership" (Anti-Defamation League).

The public exposure of politicians and their connections to the CCC did not end with the revelations that came to light in 1998. In 2004, an *Intelligence Report* published by the SPLC noted that no fewer than 38 southern politicians "from the federal, state, and local areas of government had attended CCC events between 2000 and 2004, most of them giving speeches to local chapters of the organization" (Southern Poverty Law Center). Right Wing Watch also reported that "a number of figures on the religious right have spoken before CCC conventions or defended them in the press, a signal of uneasy and often hidden alliances between the Religious Right and racist groups" (Right Wing Watch). Among those singled out by Right Wing Watch were Mike Huckabee, former governor of Arkansas; Tony Perkins, president of the Family Research Council; Roy Moore, the Alabama chief justice who defied federal orders to remove a monument to the Ten Commandments; John Eidsmoe, "the intellectual godfather of a strain of Christian nationalism that takes to an extreme the idea that 'God's law' must always be put before 'man's law' "; and Ann Coulter, the anti-immigrant pundit for Fox News (Right Wing Watch).

The danger of "race mixing" continues to be a major theme for the CCC. On the CCC's website in 2001, a story appeared that declared, "God is the author of racism. God is the One who divided mankind into different types. . . . Mixing the races is rebelliousness against God" (Southern Poverty Law Center). The CCC's publication, the *Citizens Informer*, "has also published numerous stories detailing 'scientific' evidence for the superiority of whites over any other race" (Southern Poverty Law Center). In a 2004 article that discussed how striking down public school segregation still left America "short of racial equality," a *Citizens Informer* contributor stated that the lack of progress "should surprise no one, because racial inequality is genetic and cannot be changed by social programs. . . . Blacks are on average probably less intelligent than Whites and more aggressive, impulsive and prone to psychopathologies" (Southern Poverty Law Center). To emphasize this point, "another article in the *Citizens Informer* in the aftermath of Hurricane Katrina described accounts of little children—girls and boys—being gang raped, rescue vans and copters being repeatedly fired upon by mobs of violent blacks, anarchy, chaos, confusion, looting even by black police officers" (Southern Poverty Law Center).

As illegal immigration came to the forefront in American politics, the CCC was there to prime the pump of hysteria regarding the issue. The CCC has prominently "supported the rhetoric of major nativist group leaders, such as Barbara Coe and Glenn Spencer, both of whom worked to pass the anti-immigration California Proposition 187" (Southern Poverty Law Center). The CCC has also invited prominent racist leaders, including Jared Taylor and Don Black, to its annual conferences. Both Taylor and Black are leaders in the white supremacist communities.

Long-time leader Gordon Baum died in March 2015, just prior to the CCC bursting on the national scene once more when Dylann Roof—a 21-year-old white supremacist—entered the historic Emanuel African American Episcopal Church in downtown Charleston, South Carolina, and shot twelve parishioners, killing nine. After the massacre, it was discovered that Dylann Roof had been inspired by the CCC's messages of "black-on-white" crime:

> The event that truly awakened me was the Trayvon Martin case. I kept hearing and seeing his name, and eventually I decided to look him up. I read the Wikipedia article and right away I was unable to understand what the big deal was. It was obvious that Zimmerman was in the right. But more importantly this prompted me to type in the words "black on White crime" into Google, and I have never been the same since that day. The first website I came to was the Council of Conservative Citizens. There were pages upon pages of these brutal black on White murders. I was in disbelief. At this moment I realized that something was very wrong. How could the news be blowing up the Trayvon Martin case while hundreds of these black on White murders got ignored? (NPR)

In the aftermath of Roof's revelations about the CCC's influence on him, the CCC issued a statement defending Roof, stating that he had "legitimate grievances." In the statement, the CCC "condemned Roof's murderous actions" but warned that our society's silence about [such] crimes—despite enormous amounts of attention to "racially tinged" acts by whites—only increase the anger of people like Dylann Roof. This double standard *only makes acts of murderous frustration more likely* [emphasis by the council]. In his manifesto, Roof outlines other grievances felt by many whites. Again, we utterly condemn Roof's despicable killings, but they do not detract in the slightest from the legitimacy of some of the positions he has expressed. (Gross)

As the investigation into the Charleston shooting progressed, Roof was found to have photographed himself several times with the Confederate battle flag, while also displaying many other white supremacist symbols. The CCC's president, Earl Holt III, pointed out that he had donated money to the campaigns of several GOP politicians, "including Ted Cruz, Rick Santorum, Mitt Romney, and Rand Paul." A spokesman for Ted Cruz's presidential campaign later reported that it had returned the CCC's money (Gross).

See also: League of the South; Neo-Confederates; White Nationalism; White Supremacist Movement

FURTHER READING

Anti-Defamation League. "Council of Conservative Citizens." Anti-Defamation League. https://www.adl.org/sites/default/files/documents/assets/pdf/combating-hate /Council-of-Conservative-Citizens-Extremism-in-America.pdf. (Accessed May 27, 2018.)

Blue, Miranda. June 24, 2015. "The Religious Right's Council of Conservative Citizens Connection." Right Wing Watch. http://www.rightwingwatch.org/post/the-reli gious-rights-council-of-conservative-citizens-connection/. (Accessed May 27, 2018.)

Counter Extremism Project. "Council of Conservative Citizens." Counter Extremism Project. https://www.counterextremism.com/threat/council-conservative-citizens. (Accessed May 27, 2018.)

Graham, David A. June 22, 2015. "The White Supremacist Group That Inspired a Racist Manifesto." *Atlantic*. https://www.theatlantic.com/politics/archive/2015/06/coun cil-of-conservative-citizens-dylann-roof/396467/. (Accessed May 27, 2018.)

Gross, Allie. June 21, 2015. "White Nationalist Group Defends Dylann Roof's 'Legitimate Grievances.'" *Mother Jones*. http://www.motherjones.com/politics/2015/06 /council-conservative-citizens-dylann-roof. (Accessed May 27, 2018.)

NPR. January 10, 2017. "What Happened When Dylann Roof Asked Google for Information about Race?" NPR. http://www.npr.org/sections/thetwo-way/2017/01/10/508363607 /what-happened-when-dylann-roof-asked-google-for-information-about-race. (Accessed May 27, 2018.)

Southern Poverty Law Center. "Council of Conservative Citizens." Southern Poverty Law Center. https://www.splcenter.org/fighting-hate/extremist-files/group/council -conservative-citizens. (Accessed May 27, 2018.)

Counter-Currents Publishing

The founder of Counter-Currents Publishing, Greg Johnson, has called the publishing house the "flag-bearer of the North American New Right" (Southern Poverty Law Center). Counter-Currents is the repository for published material that advocates for a white "ethnostate," or a state where whites control all aspects of political, cultural, and social life. To date, Counter-Currents has published around 40 books, most focusing on the notion of the "ethnostate" and the desire to correct the "crimes, mistakes, and misfortunes of the Old Right" (Southern Poverty Law Center). Counter-Currents "is the creation of Greg Johnson, a white nationalist who is notoriously reclusive compared to other white nationalists in the public eye" (Southern Poverty Law Center). Johnson, who holds a PhD in philosophy, takes pains to emphasize that "white nationalism is not white supremacy because it is not our preference to rule over other groups. Although if *forced* [emphasis in original] to live under multicultural systems, we are going to take our own side and try to make sure that our values reign supreme" (Southern Poverty Law Center). Johnson takes great care to temper his explanations of white nationalism to make the sentiments more palatable to the general public. In Johnson's words:

> Counter-Currents operates from the assumption that white nationalism is not palatable to the mainstream because "it offends the values of the electorate . . . our people think our goals are immoral . . . incoherent and impractical . . . because our enemies control academia, the school system, publishing, the arts, the news and entertainment media, and they have remade the American mind to their liking. My aim is to change people's sense of what is politically desirable and right, and their sense of what is politically conceivable and possible. (Southern Poverty Law Center)

Johnson founded Counter-Currents in 2010 to promote the notion of the "North American Right, inspired by the French New Right" (Southern Poverty Law Center). The publishing house "reaches into various global white nationalist communities by translating books and articles from various European white nationalists into English, and translates many English articles to European languages" (Southern Poverty Law Center). According to Johnson and the materials published by Counter-Currents, "the North American New Right's point of departure" from other views of white nationalism/white supremacy is the notion of "white genocide." As Johnson wrote:

> [T]he white race is threatened with simple biological extinction, compared to which all other political issues are trivial distractions. . . . The nature of this ethnic cleansing or white genocide is packed in euphemisms like "diversity" and "multiculturalism." This "identity politics for white people" positions itself as the answer, and sees its goal as an ethnostate removed of all non-whites. (Southern Poverty Law Center)

While some of Johnson's positions put him directly at odds with many ideas promoted by white nationalists—for instance, Johnson has published material by openly gay authors—the majority of Johnson's ideas, as reflected in Counter-Currents' publications, fall squarely within ideals championed by those in white nationalist, white supremacy, and alternative right (alt-right) circles. For instance, Johnson has stated:

> Blacks don't find white civilization comfortable. It is like demanding they wear shoes that are two sizes too small when we impose our standards of punctuality and time preferences, demand that they follow our age-of-consent laws, or foist the bourgeois nuclear family upon them. These things don't come naturally to Africans.

White standards like walking on the sidewalk, not down the middle of the street, are oppressive to blacks. Such standards are imposed by the hated 'white supremacy' system. But if we don't impose white standards upon them, we have chaos. We have great cities like Detroit transformed into wastelands. (Southern Poverty Law Center)

Johnson has also stated, "America would be improved by fewer Blacks, Asians, and Mestizos, not more of them. America would be improved by fewer Muslims, not more of them" (Southern Poverty Law Center). Johnson has lamented that "[w]hite America is a mixture of people from all over Europe, slowly being submerged in a rising tide of mud" (Southern Poverty Law Center).

As much disdain as Johnson holds for blacks, Asians, and Hispanics, he reserves his greatest vitriol for Jews. Johnson admits that "White Nationalism is inescapably anti-Semitic," and he fully subscribes to "the familiar conspiracy theory that Jews own and manipulate most of Western society, and their control of society and of Hollywood will lead to the extinction of the white race" (Southern Poverty Law Center). He has written that "the organized Jewish community is the *principal* enemy—not the sole enemy, but the principal enemy—of every attempt to halt and reverse white extinction. One cannot defeat an enemy one will not name" (Southern Poverty Law Center). Writing in Counter-Currents under his pseudonym, T. C. Lynch, in 2013 Johnson wrote in a piece entitled "To Cleanse America: Some Practical Proposals":

As for the Jews . . . At the very least, all their property should be confiscated. At the very least. There are two reasons for this. First, we should consider it reparations. Second, if they were allowed to keep their wealth, they would immediately use it to stir up trouble against us. Just look at what happened when Adolf Hitler, with the typical excess of kindness that was his greatest flaw, allowed the Jews of Germany to emigrate with their fortunes. (Southern Poverty Law Center)

During the 2016 U.S. presidential campaign, Johnson intimated that then-candidate Donald Trump "could lead to the salvation for the white race in North America" (Eyes on the Right). Johnson contended that "America could be fixed" and that he could "conceive of ways in which it can be fixed."

But, you know, at a certain point, you know, if your house is riddled with termites, you have a choice. Do you try and tweeze every little bit of vermin out of the woodwork? Or do you just torch it and build something next door? Right? Something new. And I've become increasingly, you know, leaning toward the second thing. (Eyes on the Right)

Counter-Currents remains "a small but functioning publishing house" (Southern Poverty Law Center). It has upward of "197,000 unique visitors a month . . . compared to 6,000 when it first started" (Southern Poverty Law Center). Counter-Currents relies heavily upon donations for its day-to-day operations, raising around $40,000 per year (Southern Poverty Law Center). Like many extremist groups, Counter-Currents took advantage of the "Amazon affiliates program," which allowed it to "receive a 7% commission on all purchases made on Amazon by donors" (Southern Poverty Law Center). In the aftermath of the violence at Charlottesville, Virginia, in August 2017, Amazon, along with "companies like

Facebook and PayPal, decided to curtail the usage of their platforms by white nationalists" (Southern Poverty Law Center). The Charlottesville "Unite the Right" rally, which was supported by several white nationalist/white supremacy groups affiliated with the alt-right movement, caused the death of three individuals and thereby prompted several corporations to take direct action against white nationalist groups. Counter-Currents, for instance, had "its Facebook page deleted, as well as its PayPal account." Greg Johnson stated that "the worst blow was from PayPal, since this put us in a cash crunch" (Southern Poverty Law Center).

Counter-Currents survived the shutdowns, however. After Charlottesville, "thousands and thousands of dollars in donations" poured in to Counter-Currents, enabling Johnson to amass a "war chest" (Southern Poverty Law Center). Counter-Currents also started accepting donations in Bitcoin and planned to publish a tutorial on how potential donors could utilize digital currencies.

See also: Alt-Right Movement; White Nationalism; White Supremacist Movement

FURTHER READING

Anti-Fascist News. April 3, 2017. "Meet the Exterminationist Wing of the Alt Right Who Is Open about Wanting to Kill Jews and Non-Whites." Anti-Fascist News. https:// antifascistnews.net/tag/counter-currents/. (Accessed June 4, 2018.)

Beirich, Heidi. February 25, 2014. "Financing Hate." Southern Poverty Law Center: Intelligence Report. https://www.splcenter.org/fighting-hate/intelligence-report/2014 /financing-hate. (Accessed June 4, 2018.)

Counter-Currents Publishing. "About." Counter-Currents Publishing. https://www.counter -currents.com/. (Accessed June 4, 2018.)

Daileda, Colin. August 27, 2016. "Meet the Pillars of the White Nationalist Alt-Right Movement." Mashable. https://mashable.com/2016/08/27/alt-right-white-men-pil lars-of-movement/#RvCAf7XSOSqt. (Accessed June 4, 2018.)

Eyes on the Right. May 26, 2016. "Greg Johnson Says Donald Trump Could Lead to the 'Salvation of the White Race' in North America." Angry White Men. https:// angrywhitemen.org/2016/05/26/greg-johnson-says-donald-trump-could-lead-to -the-salvation-of-the-white-race-in-north-america/#more-11514. (Accessed June 4, 2018.)

Hankes, Keegan. January 7, 2015. "Swimming Upstream: Counter-Currents Accuses American Renaissance of Futility." Southern Poverty Law Center: Hatewatch. https://www.splcenter.org/hatewatch/2015/01/07/swimming-upstream-counter -currents-accuses-american-renaissance-futility. (Accessed June 4, 2018.)

Southern Poverty Law Center. "Greg Johnson." Southern Poverty Law Center. https:// www.splcenter.org/fighting-hate/extremist-files/individual/greg-johnson. (Accessed June 4, 2018.)

The Covenant, the Sword, and the Arm of the Lord

The Covenant, the Sword, and the Arm of the Lord (CSA) "was a white supremacist paramilitary group based in Arkansas in the late 1970s and 1980s" (History Commons). CSA "was connected with a number of crimes and terror plots, including a plot to bomb the Alfred P. Murrah Federal Building in Oklahoma City,

Oklahoma" (Encyclopedia of Arkansas History and Culture). The group dissolved after federal agents besieged its compound for four days in 1985 (Egan).

The CSA "was founded near Elijah, Missouri by Texas minister James Ellison in 1970. In 1976, Ellison purchased a 220-acre farm near Bull Shoals Lake in Marion County, Arkansas, approximately seven miles southwest of Pontiac, Missouri" (Encyclopedia of Arkansas History and Culture). Ellison originally named the group Zarephath-Horeb. According to the Encyclopedia of Arkansas History and Culture:

> The CSA was true to its ideological rhetoric when selecting the name of their compound: Mount Horeb was the mountain to which Moses moved the Hebrews during the Exodus from Egypt, and Zarephath is listed in the Bible as the city to which God ordered Elijah to move in order to undergo a crucible for his faith. This isolated portion of the state was suitable for Ellison's intentions because it is demographically concentrated with a predominantly white population, is secluded in rural terrain that makes monitoring by law enforcement agencies difficult, and is positioned on the border between two states, complicating jurisdictional responsibilities. (Encyclopedia of Arkansas History and Culture)

Until 1979, racism was not a major tenet of CSA's ideology. However, in that year Ellison adopted the beliefs of Christian Identity, a white supremacist ideology that espouses that the white race is God's chosen people and that Jews are the offspring of a union between Eve and Satan. Under Ellison, CSA became an organization that believed that doomsday was inevitable and that an armed confrontation between the forces of good (CSA) and evil (the federal government) would soon come to pass. Members of CSA believed in the tenet of the Zionist Occupation Government (ZOG), a belief that the government of the United States was under the control of Jewish interests intent on controlling the world. For that reason, Ellison "intensified paramilitary training at his compound and changed the name of the group to the Covenant, the Sword, and the Arm of the Lord (CSA) to reflect the group's new militant outlook" (Encyclopedia of Arkansas History and Culture). Ellison explained that CSA was establishing an "Ark for God's people" for the coming race war (Encyclopedia of Arkansas History and Culture). As CSA gained prominence, members of other white supremacist groups, including Aryan Nations and the Order, began to visit CSA's compound to engage in paramilitary training (Egan).

CSA members "sold weapons, distributed literature and engaged in other criminal activity. The group began to construct terror plots after the death of Gordon Kahl, a white supremacist who had killed two U.S. marshals and was later killed in a federal raid, making him a martyr for the extreme right" (Egan). CSA members had plans to assassinate government officials who had prosecuted Kahl before his death, "including a judge, an FBI agent, and a U.S. attorney" (Egan). The planned assassinations were never carried out, though a CSA member, Richard Snell, did mistakenly kill an individual he believed to be a Jew as well as an African American state trooper.

Beginning on April 19, 1985, more than 300 federal agents from the Federal Bureau of Investigation (FBI) and the Bureau of Alcohol, Tobacco, and Firearms (ATF), as well as state and local law enforcement officials, surrounded the

Zarephath-Horeb compound. "After a four-day standoff, law enforcement officials entered the compound," without shots being fired, and seized "weapons, ammunition, explosives, gold, and thirty gallons of potassium cyanide," which was intended to poison the water supply of several major cities in an effort to expedite the Second Coming of the Messiah (Encyclopedia of Arkansas History and Culture). James Ellison, along with other key members of the CSA, were indicted on charges of "conspiring to overthrow the U.S. government." Neither Ellison nor any of his compatriots were convicted on this charge, but they were convicted on "various weapons charges as well as for violations related to the Racketeer Influence and Corrupt Organizations (RICO) statute" (Egan). Ellison faced a maximum sentence of 20 years in prison, but he was released after agreeing to testify against senior members of the Aryan Nations (Encyclopedia of Arkansas History and Culture). After his release, the CSA disbanded, and Ellison moved to Elohim City ("City of God"), Oklahoma, where founder Robert Millar had established a community that had rejected mainstream American life (Southern Poverty Law Center). Several years after the CSA dissolution, it was revealed that members of the group may have plotted to "blow up the Alfred P. Murrah Federal Building in Oklahoma City, Oklahoma in 1983" (Thomas).

See also: Aryan Nations; Christian Identity; The Order; White Nationalism; White Supremacist Movement

FURTHER READING

Egan, Nancy. May 29, 2016. "The Covenant, the Sword, and the Arm of the Lord." *Encyclopedia Britannica*. https://www.britannica.com/topic/The-Covenant-the-Sword-and-the-Arm-of-the-Lord. (Accessed March 14, 2018.)

Encyclopedia of Arkansas History and Culture. "Covenant, the Sword and the Arm of the Lord." *Encyclopedia of Arkansas History and Culture*. http://www.encyclopediaofarkansas.net/encyclopedia/entry-detail.aspx?entryID=4031. (Accessed March 14, 2018.)

History Commons. "Profile: Covenant, Sword, and Arm of the Lord (CSA)." History Commons. http://www.historycommons.org/entity.jsp?entity=covenant_sword_and_arm_of_the_Lord_1. (Accessed March 14, 2018.)

Southern Poverty Law Center. August 29, 2001. "Changing of the Guard." Southern Poverty Law Center: Intelligence Report. https://www.splcenter.org/fighting-hate/intelligence-report/2001/changing-guard. (Accessed March 14, 2018.)

Thomas, Jo. May 20, 1995. "Oklahoma City Building Was Target of Plot as Early as '83, Official Says." *New York Times*. http://www.nytimes.com/1995/05/20/us/oklahoma-city-building-was-target-of-plot-as-early-as-83-official-says.html. (Accessed March 14, 2018.)

Creativity Movement

The Creativity Movement is a white separatist religious movement that was founded in 1973 by Ben Klassen. A virulent racist, Klassen founded the movement "under the name of the Church of the Creator (COTC)." Adherents of the Creativity Movement "believe that race, not religion, is the embodiment of absolute truth and that the white race is the highest expression of culture and civilization" (Southern Poverty Law Center). Jews and nonwhites "are viewed as mud races who conspire to subjugate whites and destroy their culture and civilization" (Southern Poverty Law Center). Creators, as members of the Creativity Movement have sometimes called themselves, advocate RAHOWA, or "racial holy war," and "some have been arrested and imprisoned for violent, race-based crimes" (Southern Poverty Law Center). After Klassen's death in 1993, Matt Hale joined COTC and seized control of the group and began recruiting Neo-Nazis and racist skinheads to the organization. Hale's actions "resurrected the group and he subsequently changed COTC's name to the World Church of the Creator (WCOTC) and declaring himself to be the Pontifex Maximus," or "great high priest" (Southern Poverty Law Center). Under Hale's leadership, the WCOTC attracted hard-core neo-Nazis and racist skinheads and grew from 14 chapters in 1996 to 88 by 2002 (Southern Poverty Law Center). After soliciting an undercover federal agent to kill a federal judge in 2004, Hale was convicted and sentenced to a 40-year federal prison sentence. As a result of Hale's conviction, membership in the WCOTC fell from 88 chapters to just five. Though attempts were made to revive the organization, such attempts were never able to replicate the success that had been achieved under Hale.

Members of the Creativity Movement "do not believe in God, heaven, hell or eternal life." To "creators," "[r]ace is everything: the white race is 'nature's highest creation,' 'white people are the creators of all worthwhile culture and civilization,' 'every issue, whether religious, political or racial . . . [should be] viewed through the eyes of the White Man and exclusively from the point of view of the White race as a whole'" (Anti-Defamation League). Ultimately the Creativity Movement

> hopes to organize white people to achieve world domination, "free from alien control and free from pollution of alien races. . . . Only on the basis of recognizing our enemies, destroying and/or excluding them and practicing racial teamwork can a stable lasting government be built." (Anti-Defamation League)

While still under the control of Klassen, Creativity "reverend" George Loeb "was convicted of the racially-motivated killing of a black sailor and Gulf War veteran"—Harold Mansfield. In 1993, "eight individuals with ties to the COTC were arrested for plotting to bomb a black church in Los Angeles, California, as well as assassinate Rodney King, whose videotaped beating by L.A. police officers in 1991 had sparked the L.A. riots in 1992" (Southern Poverty Law Center).

In "anticipation of a civil rights lawsuit being brought by the Southern Poverty Law Center (SPLC) against COTC for the Mansfield murder," Klassen sold most of the assets associated with COTC to the neo-Nazi National Alliance, headed by William Pierce. After selling his assets, Klassen committed suicide. The SPLC did bring a lawsuit against the COTC on behalf of the Mansfield estate, but Klassen's successor failed to defend the COTC against the charges, resulting in a default judgment of $1 million. The assets sold to the National Alliance had been resold by Pierce at a profit of $85,000. The SPLC later sued Pierce "for engaging in a scheme to defraud Mansfield's estate and Pierce was forced to give up the profit he had made on the resale of Klassen's assets" (Southern Poverty Law Center).

In 1999, WCOTC came into the national spotlight when "creator" Ben Smith went on a three-day rampage in Illinois and Indiana "that left two non-whites dead and nine wounded. Smith had undertaken the killing spree after the Illinois Bar Association had refused to grant Hale a law license." In the fall of 2002, another of Hale's followers was convicted "of a plot to blow up landmarks on the East Coast" (Southern Poverty Law Center).

Hale's downfall began when the TE-TA-MA Truth Foundation, a peace-loving multicultural church in Oregon, sued WCOTC over the name "Church of the Creator." In 1987, the U.S. Patent and Trademark Office "had accepted the foundation's request to copyright the name." (Southern Poverty Law Center). After the violence associated with WCOTC hit national headlines, the Truth Foundation sued WCOTC for copyright infringement, demanding that the racist and neo-Nazi organization cease using the copyrighted name. Hale initially won the suit when a U.S. District Court judge ruled in his favor. However, "an appeals court reversed the decision and sent the case back to the District judge—Joan Humphrey Lefkow—for reconsideration" (Southern Poverty Law Center). Abiding by the appeals court decision, Lefkow ruled against Hale and ordered WCOTC to give up all use of the "Church of the Creator" moniker (Southern Poverty Law Center).

Outraged by the ruling, Hale attempted to solicit the murder of Judge Lefkow, confiding his plan to an individual who turned out to be an undercover federal agent. In 2004, "Hale was found guilty of one count of solicitation of murder and three counts of obstruction of justice." A year later, he was sentenced to a federal prison for the maximum sentence allowed: 40 years (Southern Poverty Law Center). In Hale's absence, WCOTC collapsed, losing nearly 90 percent of its membership.

After Hale's departure, the Creativity Movement "was racked with schisms and the lack of a centralized leadership" (Morlin). In 2011, the Creativity Movement showed signs of life when Allen Goff, an 18-year-old neo-Nazi from Montana with a criminal record, began to attract new followers. The resurgence coincided with other white supremacist and neo-Nazi activity in Montana at the time (Keller). In 2017, the FBI arrested a Georgia man with ties to the Creativity Movement after he sought medical attention for exposure to the deadly poison ricin. The FBI launched a formal investigation into the matter after finding that the individual's car tested positive for ricin (Morlin).

See also: National Alliance; Neo-Nazis; White Nationalism; White Supremacist Movement

FURTHER READING

Anti-Defamation League. "Creativity Movement (Formerly World Church of the Creator)." Anti-Defamation League. https://www.adl.org/education/resources/profiles /creativity-movement. (Accessed May 22, 2017.)

Keller, Larry. February 27, 2011. "Neo-Nazi Creativity Movement Is Back." Southern Poverty Law Center: Intelligence Report. https://www.splcenter.org/fighting-hate/intelligence-report/2015/neo-nazi-creativity-movement-back. (Accessed May 22, 2017.)

Morlin, Bill. February 9, 2017. "FBI Investigates White Supremacist for Deadly Poison." Southern Poverty Law Center: Hatewatch. https://www.splcenter.org/hatewatch/2017/02/09/fbi-investigates-white-supremacist-deadly-poison. (Accessed May 22, 2017.)

Southern Poverty Law Center. "Creativity Movement." Southern Poverty Law Center. https://www.splcenter.org/fighting-hate/extremist-files/group/creativity-movement-0. (Accessed May 22, 2017.)

Crew 38

Crew 38 has been "designated by the Southern Poverty Law Center (SPLC) as a racist skinhead hate group" (Southern Poverty Law Center). Crew 38 is a "support group for Hammerskin Nation, which the Anti-Defamation League (ADL) calls the most violent and best-organized neo-Nazi skinhead group in the United States" (Anti-Defamation League, The Hammerskin Nation). Hammerskin Nation is best known for its promotion and production of white power hate-rock music. Crew 38 consists mostly of "female associates of [Hammerskin Nation] as well as males interested in becoming members" (Anti-Defamation League, 38). A Crew 38 website "says the group is for people who are interested in the (Hammerskins) and wish to be a Hammer Skin one day or because of work, family, distance or that they appreciate and support the (Hammerskins) and do not want membership, to show support to the Nation and have some part in the brotherhood" (Terrorism Research & Analysis Consortium).

Crew 38 takes its name from the white nationalist/white supremacist penchant for finding symbolism in numbers. Much like Werewolf 88 takes its name from "Heil Hitler" (H being the eighth letter in the alphabet), Crew 38 stands for "CH or 'Crossed Hammers,' a reference to the crossed hammers of the group's logo" (Anti-Defamation League, 38).

See also: Hammerskin Nation; Racist Skinheads; Werewolf 88; White Nationalism; White Supremacist Movement

FURTHER READING

Anti-Defamation League. "38." Anti-Defamation League. https://www.adl.org/education/references/hate-symbols/38. (Accessed June 2, 2018.)

Anti-Defamation League. "The Hammerskin Nation." Anti-Defamation League. https://www.adl.org/education/resources/profiles/hammerskin-nation?xpicked=3&item=15. (Accessed June 2, 2018.)

Atlanta Antifascists. August 24, 2016. "Crew 38." Atlanta Antifascists. https://afainatl.wordpress.com/tag/crew-38/. (Accessed June 2, 2018.)

Forum 38. "The Hammerskins Forum at Crew38.com." Forum 38. http://www.crew38.com/forum38/content.php. (Accessed June 2, 2018.)

Southern Poverty Law Center. "Hate Map by State." Southern Poverty Law Center. https://www.splcenter.org/hate-map/by-state. (Accessed June 2, 2018.)

Terrorism Research & Analysis Consortium. "Hammerskin Nation." Terrorism Research & Analysis Consortium. https://www.trackingterrorism.org/group/hammerskin -nation. (Accessed June 2, 2018.)

WPTV. August 17, 2017. "Southern Poverty Law Center Lists Active Hate Groups by State." WPTV.com. https://www.wptv.com/news/national/southern-poverty-law -center-lists-active-hate-groups-by-state. (Accessed June 2, 2018.)

D

Die Auserwahlten

Die Auserwahlten is a racist skinhead group that operates mostly out of Louisiana (Southern Poverty Law Center). The name "Die Auserwahlten" means "chosen few." The group is also known by the name "Crew 41," the number being a common tactic used by neo-Nazis and racist skinheads to identify themselves by associated letters of the alphabet (much like the neo-Nazi group Werewolf 88). Thus, "41" corresponds to the fourth and first letters of the alphabet: *D* and *A*. Die Auserwahlten is most notorious for a crime spree among a few members during 2013. In one case, a Die Auserwahlten member "attacked a 27-year-old man in Nebraska, kicking in his skull." In another incident, a married couple that adhered to the tenets of Die Auserwahlten killed a middle-aged couple in their home in South Carolina.

Die Auserwahlten was founded sometime in 2012 (Terry, July 2013). According to Don Terry of the Southern Poverty Law Center (SPLC), the group was essentially "created and organized as a 'pop-up' gang" (Terry, November 2013). It originally claimed to have chapters in Nebraska, Utah, and South Carolina (Terry, July 2013). The first president of Die Auserwahlten was Brandon Hoffpauir from Pride, Louisiana. When interviewed by the SPLC, Hoffpauir claimed that the group was "more than a flash in the pan, insisting we are not Internet Nazis" or "keyboard warriors" (Terry, November 2013). Hoffpauir went on to articulate the ideology of Die Auserwahlten: "We're American National Socialists. Which means, we are standing up for America. What true America used to be. What it was. What it can be without the filth" (Terry, November 2013).

The founder of Die Auserwahlten, Johnathan "Monster" Schmidt, once wrote to his followers: "I suggest yiu [sic] make your body and mind your primary weapon . . . be in shape and be prepared to dine in Valhalla 841!!!!" (Terry, November 2013). In Norse mythology, Valhalla is home to the brave warriors who died in combat.

In July 2013 in Kearney, Nebraska, Johnathan Schmidt was arrested for "dragging a man out of his car . . . and kicking him so hard in the head that the man's skull was fractured" (Terry, November 2013). Schmidt's accuser picked him out of lineup, which was not difficult given Schmidt's distinctive appearance—"covered in tattoos from the top of his shaven head to his face to his stomach inked with a large swastika" (Terry, April 2014). Schmidt faced a 50-year prison sentence in the assault but was later arrested and charged for assault with a deadly weapon in a separate incident in April 2014 (Terry, April 2014).

Unfortunately, Schmidt's violent activities were not the only ones undertaken in the name of Die Auserwahlten. About the same time as Schmidt's first assault charge in Nebraska in July 2013, a couple—Jeremy Moody and his wife, Christine—shot and stabbed to death a husband and wife in their Union County, South Carolina, home on July 21, 2013. Jeremy Moody, who had stated, "I've been a skinhead for 16 years, and am completely dedicated and interested in furthering Crew 41 and its foundation," told "authorities that he killed Charles Parker after finding Parker's name on a list of registered sex offenders" (Terry, November 2013). As to why Parker's wife, Gretchen, was also killed, "Moody claimed she was 'simply a casualty of war'" (Terry, November 2013). In May 2014, both Moody and his wife were given life sentences for their crimes (McLaughlin and Baldacci).

Though Die Auserwahlten remains on the list of hate groups designated by the SPLC, in 2017 its activities appeared to be largely contained to the state of Louisiana (Southern Poverty Law Center).

See also: Neo-Nazis; Racist Skinheads; Werewolf 88

FURTHER READING

McLaughlin, Eliott C., and Marlena Baldacci. May 8, 2014. "Neo-Nazis Feign Remorse, Taunt Family of Murdered Sex Offender." CNN. https://www.cnn.com/2014/05/07 /justice/south-carolina-neo-nazis-murder-sex-offender/index.html. (Accessed May 31, 2018.)

Southern Poverty Law Center. "Racist Skinhead." Southern Poverty Law Center. https:// www.splcenter.org/fighting-hate/extremist-files/ideology/racist-skinhead. (Accessed May 31, 2018.)

Terry, Don. July 24, 2013. "Members of New Skinhead Gang Accused in Two States." Southern Poverty Law Center: Hatewatch. https://www.splcenter.org/hatewatch /2013/07/24/members-new-skinhead-gang-accused-two-states. (Accessed May 31, 2018.)

Terry, Don. November 19, 2013. "First Blood." Southern Poverty Law Center: Intelligence Report. https://www.splcenter.org/fighting-hate/intelligence-report/2013/first-blood. (Accessed May 31, 2018.)

Terry, Don. April 17, 2014. "Crew 41 Founder Johnathan 'Monster' Schmidt Arrested for Assault with Deadly Weapon." Southern Poverty Law Center: Hatewatch. https:// www.splcenter.org/hatewatch/2014/04/17/crew-41-founder-johnathan-%E2%80% 9Cmonster%E2%80%9D-schmidt-arrested-assault-deadly-weapon. (Accessed May 31, 2018.)

E

East Coast Knights of the True Invisible Empire

The East Coast Knights of the True Invisible Empire ("East Coast Knights") is designated by the Southern Poverty Law Center (SPLC) as a Ku Klux Klan (KKK) hate group. According to the SPLC, KKK groups have a "long history of violence, [and are] the most infamous—and oldest—of American hate groups. Although black Americans have typically been the Klan's primary target, it also has attacked Jews, immigrants, gays and lesbians and, until recently, Catholics" (Southern Poverty Law Center, Ku Klux Klan).

In typical KKK fashion, the East Coast Knights do not believe themselves to be racists or haters of other peoples. On their website, they state: "We're the patriotic, God fearing, family oriented working men & women of the East Coast Knights of the Ku Klux Klan, and we're fighting for the same values your family lives & breathes every day. We do not preach hate & at no time would we react hatefully to any man, woman or child" (East Coast Knights of the True Invisible Empire). The East Coast Knights even claim that they live by the motto of the KKK—"Non Silba, Sed Anthar"—which means "not for self, but for others" (East Coast Knights of the True Invisible Empire).

The East Coast Knights are not shy, however, about expressing their true purpose: the preservation of the white race. As they state:

> We do wish to preserve the White Christian ways. The same way other races wish to preserve their race and beliefs. The East Coast Knights wish to take back only the right of free speech, and right to say that we are White and Proud! We see people of all races walking with their heads held high, proud to be of whatever race or religion never to be persecuted or questioned as to their motives. Except for the Whites!
>
> How long will the White Race have to continue persecution? We will not let this continue! We know that there are those out there who strongly agree, but do not wish to stand up for your rights. The rights of your children, grandchildren and the future for those to come.
>
> Think about your loved ones. Those once considered minority races are flourishing recieving [sic] welfare handouts. Meanwhile, all the hard working people can't get a break. Our own government is taking jobs away sending them overseas, putting hard working Americans out of jobs. Taking food off the table, prices of gas are going up, bills are to much to think about. We can go on and on, but it's up to you America! (East Coast Knights of the True Invisible Empire)

In December 2017, the East Coast Knights distributed "fliers and peppermints to North Carolina residents on Christmas Eve" (Dupuy). The flyers, meant to recruit new members, were also distributed in other states. They questioned, "[W]hy is the KKK seen as racist?" and asked, "Why can't pro-white rights organizations exist without being labeled racist?" The flyer read, "White pride doesn't mean hate! It's OK, you can say it! I'm proud to be white! There is no need to feel guilty because of the past!" (Dupuy).

According to the Anti-Defamation League (ADL),

[T]he fliers are an out-dated method the Klan uses to stay relevant. . . . [T]he Klan is falling apart compared to a younger white nationalist movement grabbing headlines. But Klan members say they don't want to be a part of the younger movement known as the alt-right, which gained national attention following the violent riots that broke out in Charlottesville in August, 2017. (Dupuy)

According to the "fliers distributed in North Carolina," the East Coast Knights message is part of the "Klan's strategy to normalize white supremacy" (Dupuy):

Klan members say that fellow members no longer wear their distinct white robes and hoods, and that they do not associate themselves with violence, despite the years of violence the group waged against black Americans who were bombed and lynched. Now, members want to be able to express their white pride without being branded white supremacists—members prefer the term white separatists. They want a place where they can be with people like them.

The SPLC notes that the East Coast Knights have chapters in Delaware, Maryland, North Carolina, Pennsylvania, and Texas (Southern Poverty Law Center, 2017).

See also: Ku Klux Klan; White Nationalism; White Supremacist Movement

FURTHER READING

Dupuy, Beatrice. December 29, 2017. "KKK Says Pro-White Message Isn't Racist, Celebrates White Pride." *Newsweek*. http://www.newsweek.com/kkk-north-caro lina-racist-racism-white-pride-ku-klux-klan-765473. (Accessed July 14, 2018.)

East Coast Knights of the True Invisible Empire. http://www.eastcoastknightsofthetruein visibleempire.com/. (Accessed July 14, 2018.)

Simmons, Taj. December 26, 2017. "KKK Flyers Found in Garner Neighborhood." Spectrum News. http://spectrumlocalnews.com/nc/triangle-sandhills/news/2017/12/27/ ku-klux-klan-flyers-found-in-garner-neighborhood. (Accessed July 14, 2018.)

Southern Poverty Law Center. "Ku Klux Klan." Southern Poverty Law Center. https:// www.splcenter.org/fighting-hate/extremist-files/ideology/ku-klux-klan. (Accessed July 14, 2018.)

Southern Poverty Law Center. February 15, 2017. "Active Hate Groups 2016." Southern Poverty Law Center: Intelligence Report. https://www.splcenter.org/fighting-hate /intelligence-report/2017/active-hate-groups-2016. (Accessed July 14, 2018.)

Eastern Hammerskins

The Eastern Hammerskins is a chapter of the larger Hammerskin Nation "on the east coast of the United States" (Eastern Hammerskins). According to the parent organization, Hammerskin Nation "is a leaderless group of men and women who have adopted the White Power Skinhead lifestyle. We are blue collar workers, white collar professionals, college students, entrepreneurs, fathers and mothers" (Hammerskin Nation). Eastern Hammerskins, along with all other chapters of Hammerskin Nation, ascribe to the ideology of the "14 Words," a phrase created by white supremacist and neo-Nazi David Lane of the infamous terror group the Order. The fourteen words—"We must secure the existence of our people and a future for White Children"—articulate the goals of the Hammerskin Nation (Hammerskin Nation). The Anti-Defamation League (ADL) "has labeled Hammerskin Nation and its affiliates as the most violent and best-organized neo-Nazi skinhead group in the United States" (Anti-Defamation League). The Southern Poverty Law Center (SPLC) "characterizes the Eastern Hammerskins as a racist skinhead hate group with chapters in New Hampshire and Pennsylvania" (Southern Poverty Law Center, Racist Skinhead). According to the SPLC, racist skinheads "form a particularly violent element of the white supremacist movement, and have often been referred to as the 'shock troops' of the hoped-for revolution. The classic Skinhead look is a shaved head, black Doc Martens boots, jeans with suspenders and an array of typically racist tattoos" (Southern Poverty Law Center, Racist Skinhead).

Like its parent organization, Hammerskin Nation, the Eastern Hammerskins draw their inspiration from the 1979 rock album *The Wall*, by the group Pink Floyd. According to the ADL:

> The Wall tells the story of Pink, a rock singer who becomes a drug addict, loses his grip on reality and turns to fascism. Pink performs a song in which he expresses a desire to line all of the "queers," "Jews," and "coons" in his audience "up against the wall" and shoot them. In obvious references to the Holocaust, he sings of the "final solution" and "waiting to turn on the showers and fire the ovens." The swastika is replaced by Pink's symbol: two crossed hammers, which he boasts will "batter down" the doors behind which frightened minorities hide from his fascist supporters. (Anti-Defamation League)

The Hammerskins "first appeared in the late '80s as the Dallas-based Confederate Hammerskins and spread to Georgia, Tennessee and Florida. More namesakes followed: the Northern Hammerskins in the Great Lakes region, the Eastern Hammerskins in Pennsylvania and New Jersey, and the Western Hammerskins in Arizona and California" (Reynolds).

According to the SPLC, all chapters of Hammerskin Nation, including the Eastern Hammerskins, "are among the most dangerous radical-right threats facing law enforcement today" (Southern Poverty Law Center, 2012). The Hammerskins are

> products of a frequently violent and criminal subculture, these men and women, typically imbued with neo-Nazi beliefs about Jews, blacks, LGBT people and others, are also notoriously difficult to track. Organized into small, mobile "crews" or acting individually, skinheads tend to move around frequently and often without warning, even as they network and organize across regions. For law enforcement, this poses a particular problem in responding to crimes and conspiracies crossing multiple jurisdictions. (Southern Poverty Law Center, 2015)

The SPLC notes that new media platforms—such as Facebook, Instagram, Twitter, and Snapchat—"are being used by racist skinhead groups to recruit and expose others to their views" (Southern Poverty Law Center, 2015). According to the ADL, the Eastern Hammerskins are responsible for the "well-designed" Hammerskin Nation website, which "features concert reviews, chapter listings and information about upcoming events" (Anti-Defamation League). More sinister, however, is the fact that the site also includes a "Cyber-Terrorist" page, "which contains viruses, password-stealing programs, e-mail 'bombers' and other downloadable hacking tools" (Anti-Defamation League).

See also: Crew 38; Hammerskin Nation; Neo-Nazis; The Order; Racist Skinheads; Western Hammerskins; White Nationalism; White Supremacist Movement

FURTHER READING

Anti-Defamation League. "The Hammerskin Nation." Anti-Defamation League. https://www.adl.org/education/resources/profiles/hammerskin-nation. (Accessed July 14, 2018.)

Eastern Hammerskins. https://hammerskins.net/ehs/index.html. (Accessed July 14, 2018.)

Hammerskin Nation. "Who We Are." Hammerskins.net. http://www.hammerskins.net/. (Accessed July 14, 2018.)

Reynolds, Michael. December 15, 1999. "Hammerskin Nation Emerges from Small Dallas Group." Southern Poverty Law Center: Intelligence Report. https://www.splcenter.org/fighting-hate/intelligence-report/1999/hammerskin-nation-emerges-small-dallas-group. (Accessed July 14, 2018.)

Southern Poverty Law Center. "Racist Skinhead." Southern Poverty Law Center. https://www.splcenter.org/fighting-hate/extremist-files/ideology/racist-skinhead. (Accessed July 14, 2018.)

Southern Poverty Law Center. June 25, 2012. "Racist Skinheads: Understanding the Threat." Southern Poverty Law Center. https://www.splcenter.org/20120625/racist-skinheads-understanding-threat. (Accessed July 14, 2018.)

Southern Poverty Law Center. March 2, 2015. "Active Racist Skinhead Groups." Southern Poverty Law Center: Intelligence Report. https://www.splcenter.org/fighting-hate/intelligence-report/2015/active-racist-skinhead-groups. (Accessed July 14, 2018.)

Endangered Souls RC/Crew 519

Endangered Souls Racist Club (RC) and Crew 519 is a "pro-white racial club dedicated to the advancement and preservation of our [white] race" (Endangered Souls/Crew 519). According to the Southern Poverty Law Center (SPLC), Endangered Souls RC/Crew 519 is a neo-Nazi group with chapters in Florida, Georgia, and Idaho (Southern Poverty Law Center). Neo-Nazi groups "share a hatred for Jews and a love for Adolf Hitler and Nazi Germany. While they also hate other minorities, gays and lesbians and even sometimes Christians, they perceive 'the Jew' as their cardinal enemy" (Southern Poverty Law Center). Endangered Souls RC/Crew 519 states on its website:

> We are proud of our heritage and the accomplishments of our ancestors. Our club was formed with the belief "WE MUST SECURE THE EXISTENCE OF OUR PEOPLE AND A FUTURE FOR WHITE CHILDREN" [emphasis in original] (14 words). We are a separatist club geared toward education and support for those that have a like mind-set. We believe in the Constitution of the United States and the Bill of Rights. We are against out-sourcing of American jobs and goods, employers

that hire illegal aliens, government abuse of power and all of its bulls—. We do not tolerate any double standard that discriminates against whites. If the white race is to survive, we must rule our own destiny and protect our culture. Without action now, our history will not live on. (Endangered Souls RC/Crew 519)

The group's fealty to the "14 Words" is "typical of most neo-Nazi and white supremacist groups." The words—"We must secure the existence of our people and a future for white children"—were "coined by David Lane, former member of The Order, a neo-Nazi and white supremacist organization that was active for a brief period of time in the mid-1980s" (Southern Poverty Law Center). Lane was convicted and sentenced to life in prison for the assassination of Alan Berg in 1984. Berg was a Jewish radio talk show host in Denver, Colorado. Lane's 14 Words have become a rallying cry for right-wing extremists who believe that white dominance in the United States is being overwhelmed by changing demographics due to immigration and politically correct culture.

Endangered Souls RC/Crew 519 claims that it is not an "MC" (motorcycle club). They claim to possess no territory (as motorcycle clubs tend to do), nor do they care about claiming territory. Rather, "our race is our territory" (Endangered Souls RC/Crew 519). The group ends its introduction with "#WHITELIVES-MATTER" AND "#F—YOURFEELINGS" (Endangered Souls RC/Crew 519).

The Endangered Souls RC/Crew 519 group participated in two White Lives Matter neo-Nazi rallies in Tennessee in late 2017 (Restoring the Honor). The group "can be easily spotted by their emblem, a black and orange crest featuring the numbers '519' at the top and an Odal and Algiz or 'life rune ' separated by an axe. Runic symbols are generally fetishized by Nazis due to the Third Reich's historical appropriation of these ancient symbols" (Restoring the Honor).

See also: Neo-Nazis; The Order; White Supremacist Movement

FURTHER READING

Berry, Harrison. February 15, 2017. "SPLC Reports Idaho Anti-Muslim Groups." *Boise Weekly*. https://www.boiseweekly.com/boise/splc-report-counts-idaho-anti-muslim-groups/Content?oid=3982974. (Accessed June 12, 2018.)

Endangered Souls/Crew 519. https://www.endangerdsouls519.com/. (Accessed June 12, 2018.)

Poppino, Nate. April 22, 2018. "Idaho Groups Listed on the SPLC Hate Map—and Why." *Idaho Statesman*. http://www.idahostatesman.com/news/local/article209584429.html. (Accessed June 12, 2018.)

Restoring the Honor. October 24, 2017. "Endangered Souls Racial Club/Crew 519 Set to Join in Shelbyville and Murfreesboro 'White Lives Matter' Nazi Rallies on Saturday." Restoring the Honor. http://restoringthehonor.blogspot.com/2017/10/endangered-souls-racial-clubcrew-519.html. (Accessed June 12, 2018.)

Southern Poverty Law Center. "Neo-Nazi." Southern Poverty Law Center. https://www.splcenter.org/fighting-hate/extremist-files/ideology/neo-nazi. (Accessed June 12, 2018.)

Viets, Sarah. February 11, 2016. "American and International Racists Create 'United Aryan Front' Coalition." Southern Poverty Law Center: Hatewatch. https://www.splcenter.org/hatewatch/2016/02/11/american-and-international-racists-create-united-aryan-front-coalition. (Accessed June 12, 2018.)

Williams, James. May 23, 2017. "Florida Is Home to Many Neo Nazi Groups and Grow-ing." News Talk Florida. https://www.newstalkflorida.com/featured/florida-home -many-neo-nazi-groups-growing/. (Accessed June 12, 2018.)

EURO (European-American Unity and Rights Organization)

The European-American Unity and Rights Organization (EURO) "is an Ameri-can organization led by David Duke, former Grand Wizard of the Knights of the Ku Klux Klan (KKKK). Founded in January 2000, the group has been described by the Southern Poverty Law Center as a white nationalist and white supremacist organization" (Southern Poverty Law Center, EURO). EURO "claims to fight for 'white civil rights' for 'Europeans and Americans wherever they live'" (South-ern Poverty Law Center, EURO). In 2000, Duke told reporters that white people in America were facing "genocide" from nonwhite immigration and miscegena-tion. Duke originally called the organization "NOFEAR (the National Organiza-tion for European American Rights)." But after the group No Fear Inc. challenged the name, Duke renamed the organization EURO. Soon after its founding in 2000, a member of EURO wrote that the new group was not only to foster and protect the white race but to blame the Jews for the problems being confronted by whites:

> The Jewish media and Jews in general will attack us for wanting to restore White America. The Jews are the enemy of the White race, and they are largely responsi-ble for the 'browning' of America. The Jews want to rule over a multi-racial brown America that is too ignorant to ever rebel against them. (Southern Poverty Law Center, EURO)

EURO immediately got off to a rocky start. In late 2000, "federal agents carted away 22 boxes of papers, computer discs, credit card records, and other docu-ments from David Duke's home in Mandeville, Louisiana" (Southern Poverty Law Center, EURO). At the time, Duke was in Russia, but he wrote, "Make no mistake about it. This probe is nothing more than a political assassination on the part of government officials who are seeking to silence my voice on our European heritage and rights" (Southern Poverty Law Center, EURO). For two years, Duke remained abroad while his lawyers fought charges of mail fraud against their cli-ent. In December 2002, "Duke pleaded guilty to one count of mail fraud" and one count of making false statements on his 1998 income—which he had vastly under-stated. Under the terms of a plea deal, "Duke was sentenced to one-and-a-half years in federal prison" (Southern Poverty Law Center, EURO).

In Duke's absence, EURO floundered under poor interim leaders. However, in May 2004, Duke was released from prison and "was welcomed back with a well-attended racist conference in Louisiana co-sponsored by EURO, the National Alliance, the Council of Conservative Citizens, and Holocaust denial groups" (Southern Poverty Law Center, David Duke). EURO was among the original sig-natories of what became known as the New Orleans Protocol (NOP), "a set of principles pledging adherents to a pan-European outlook" (Southern Poverty Law Center, EURO). "An estimated 67,000 racists from around the world logged on to EURO's website to view the festivities" (Southern Poverty Law Center, EURO).

Though EURO remains semiactive, its activities have been largely confined to rants perpetrated by Duke himself through his website. In 2014, revelations came to light that Steve Scalise, then the number three Republican in the House, had given a speech before EURO more than 10 years before. When confronted with the fact that EURO was considered a white nationalist and white supremacist organization, Scalise feigned ignorance of EURO's goals and the criticisms of his speeches as stemming from a "manufactured blogger story" (Potok). When Scalise reiterated that he had no idea what EURO was and that he "went and spoke to any group that called," a *Washington Post* blogger asked whether he would have spoken to a KKK rally or to the American Nazi Party (Potok).

Today, EURO remains "Duke's primary organizing and fundraising vehicle, along with his books and personal website" (Southern Poverty Law Center, EURO).

See also: Council of Conservative Citizens; Holocaust Denial; National Alliance; Neo-Nazis; White Nationalism; White Supremacist Movement

FURTHER READING

Potok, Mark. December 30, 2014. "Steve Scalise's Denials Are Not Believable." Southern Poverty Law Center: Hatewatch. https://www.splcenter.org/hatewatch/2014/12/30 /steve-scalise's-denials-are-not-believable. (Accessed June 1, 2017.)

Southern Poverty Law Center. "David Duke." Southern Poverty Law Center. https://www .splcenter.org/fighting-hate/extremist-files/individual/david-duke. (June 1, 2017.)

Southern Poverty Law Center. "Euro." Southern Poverty Law Center. https://www.splcen ter.org/fighting-hate/extremist-files/group/euro. (Accessed June 1, 2017.)

Southern Poverty Law Center. July 1, 2007. "Extremist Euro-Deputy Group Formed." Southern Poverty Law Center: Intelligence Report. https://www.splcenter.org /fighting-hate/intelligence-report/2007/extremist-euro-deputy-group-formed. (Accessed June 1, 2017.)

European American Action Coalition

The European American Action Coalition (EAAC) "is an organization that is dedicated to standing up and confronting people that push an anti-white agenda" (European American Action Coalition). The group is also sometimes referred to as the European American Republican Coalition because its founder, Steve Smith, is a member of the "Republican Party's county committee in Luzerne County, Pennsylvania" (Nelson). On its Facebook page, EAAC notes that it is "a coalition of Republicans that fight for the interests of European Americans, which is the founding stock of our Constitutional Republic" (European American Republican Coalition). The Southern Poverty Law Center (SPLC) has designated EAAC as a white nationalist hate group with headquarters in Pittston, Pennsylvania (Southern Poverty Law Center). According to the SPLC:

> White nationalist groups espouse white supremacist or white separatist ideologies, often focusing on the alleged inferiority of non-whites. Groups listed in several other categories—Ku Klux Klan, neo-Confederate, neo-Nazi, racist Skinhead, and Christian Identity—could also be described as white nationalist. (Southern Poverty Law Center)

Founded in the fall of 2011, the EAAC has been referred to as "the NAACP for white people" (Lance). Its founder, Steve Smith, was "recruited into the neo-Nazi movement while he was stationed at Fort Bragg in the 1990s, [and] has been active in an extraordinary array of white nationalist, skinhead, and neo-Nazi groups" (Nelson). These groups have included the "American Third Position [also known as the American Freedom party], Keystone United (formerly Keystone State Skinheads), and the Council of Conservative Citizens" (Nelson). Smith is "a former Aryan Nations member and former leader of the Philadelphia chapter of the National Association for the Advancement of White People" (Nelson).

In January 2012, Smith published a letter in the Wilkes-Barr *Times Leader* that stated:

> Many experts predict that, if current trends continue, whites will be a minority in the United States by 2050; some predict it can happen sooner. If this prediction comes true, it will be catastrophic to our country and well-being. The European American Action Coalition is committed to reversing this anti-white trend. The coalition is an organization dedicated to educating, advancing and defending our culture, rights and heritage. (Nelson)

In June 2012, Smith won a seat as a "Republican Committeeman in Luzerne County, PA" (Philly Antifa). In April 2016, Smith was reelected to his post, winning 69 of 73 votes (Viets, 2016). After his victory, Smith posted the results on Stormfront, "the largest white supremacist online forum" (Viets, 2016). Smith has stated that he wants to "take over the Pennsylvania Republican Party." In fact, Smith stated at a Traditionalist Worker Party event, "I think we can get involved in the Republican Party on the local grassroots level . . . we can take it bit by bit. We'll take over this Republican Party in Luzerne county, maybe the whole state of Pennsylvania. We'll be pro-white republican committee members" (Viets, 2017). Smith also noted, "2016 has been a great year for nationalists. Trump wins the Presidency. The United Kingdom votes to leave the European Union. Ryan Wojtowicz [another white nationalist] and I win elections to the Luzerne County Republican Committee. Let's keep it rolling in 2017!" (Viets, 2017).

In March 2017, Smith appeared alongside Andrew Shecktor, a "Berwick city council member" who was running for a U.S. Senate seat. Though Shecktor favored "a plan to integrate undocumented immigrants who have been here and are productive citizens," Smith intended to use immigration "as a wedge issue to reshape the county's republican party" (Viets, 2017). In fact, Smith told a "room full of skinheads and white nationalists" that

> I've won a lot of people over my four years serving as committeeman . . . I can still broadcast my pro-white views [and] you find out [that] most of them agree with

you. . . . But, If you're afraid to be openly pro-white . . . just say [you're] against illegal alien immigration, the illegal alien invasion. (Viets, 2017)

See also: American Freedom Party; Aryan Nations; Council of Conservative Citizens; Keystone United; Neo-Nazis; Racist Skinheads; Stormfront; Traditionalist Worker Party; White Nationalism; White Supremacist Movement

FURTHER READING

European American Action Coalition. November 11, 2011. "European American Action Coalition." https://europeanamericanactioncoalition.wordpress.com/. (Accessed July 14, 2018.)

European American Republican Coalition. "About." https://www.facebook.com/pg/White Republican/about/. (Accessed July 14, 2018.)

Label56. "European American Action Coalition: Stand Up & Speak Out!" Label56.com. http://www.label56.com/2012/02/european-american-action-coalition-stand-up -speak-out/. (Accessed July 14, 2018.)

Lance, Stacy. August 8, 2012. "Moosic Officials: 'White Rights' Group Not Welcome." WNEP.com. https://wnep.com/2012/08/08/moosic-officials-white-rights-group-not -welcome/. (Accessed July 14, 2018.)

Nelson, Leah. May 30, 2012. "Longtime White Supremacist to Serve on Penn. County GOP Committee." Southern Poverty Law Center: Hatewatch. https://www.splcen ter.org/hatewatch/2012/05/30/longtime-white-supremacist-serve-penn-county -gop-committee. (Accessed July 14, 2018.)

Philly Antifa. August 10, 2012. "KSS/A3P Frong Group 'The European American Action Coalition's' Event Cancelled by Moosic Borough." Philly Antifa. https://phillyan tifa.org/kssa3p-front-group-the-european-american-action-coalitions-event-can celled-by-moosic-borough-23/. (Accessed July 24, 2018.)

Southern Poverty Law Center. February 17, 2016. "Active Hate Groups in the United States in 2015." Southern Poverty Law Center: Intelligence Report. https://www .splcenter.org/fighting-hate/intelligence-report/2016/active-hate-groups-united -states-2015. (Accessed July 14, 2018.)

Viets, Sarah. April 27, 2016. "Co-Founder of Pennsylvania Skinhead Group Wins Re- Election for County Committee Seat." Southern Poverty Law Center: Hatewatch. https://www.splcenter.org/hatewatch/2016/04/27/co-founder-pennsylvania-skin head-group-wins-re-election-county-committee-seat. (Accessed July 14, 2018.)

Viets, Sarah. March 9, 2017. "U.S. Senatorial Candidate Andrew Shecktor Poses for Photo with Pennsylvania Skinhead." Southern Poverty Law Center: Hatewatch. https:// www.splcenter.org/hatewatch/2017/03/09/us-senatorial-candidate-andrew-sheck tor-poses-photo-pennsylvania-skinhead. (Accessed July 14, 2018.)

F

Family Research Council

The Family Research Council (FRC) is a "non-profit charitable organization" that lobbies on behalf of American Christian conservative values. The FRC was founded in 1981 to promote traditional family values in American society by lobbying and advocating "for socially conservative policies. FRC opposes and lobbies against equal rights for LGBT people (such as same-sex marriage, same-sex civil unions, and LGBT adoption), abortion, divorce, embryonic stem-cell research, and pornography" (Hernson, et al.). In 2010, "the Southern Poverty Law Center (SPLC) classified the FRC as an anti-gay hate group" (Southern Poverty Law Center, Family Research Council). FRC's president, Tony Perkins, labeled the designation a smear by a "liberal organization" and called the SPLC an intolerant organization that simply did not agree with the organization's belief that "marriage should be between a man and a woman" (Thompson). A columnist for the *Washington Post* called the designation "reckless," as it characterized the FRC "in the same category as groups such as Aryan Nations, Knights of the Ku Klux Klan, Stormfront, and the Westboro Baptist Church" (Brydum).

To combat LGBT civil rights measures, the FRC strongly promotes the belief that gays can be "cured" of their affliction, though the American Psychological Association (APA) issued a report in 2009 stating that there are no credible studies that "provide evidence of sexual orientation change" (American Psychological Association). The SPLC contends that the FRC's strategy is to "pound home the false claim that gays and lesbians are more likely to sexually abuse children than heterosexual people" (Southern Poverty Law Center, 2016). However, the APA has concluded that "homosexual men are not more likely to sexually abuse children than heterosexual men are." FRC's president, Tony Perkins, has labeled gay men as "pedophiles."

The FRC "supports a federal conscience clause that would allow medical workers to refuse to provide certain treatments or medications to patients such as abortions, blood transfusions, or birth control" (Family Research Council). The FRC also opposes same-sex marriage, same-sex unions, and gambling and has questioned humans' responsibility for climate change (CNN).

In 2010, "the FRC paid $25,000 to lobbyists to sink a resolution" in the U.S. Congress denouncing legislation in Uganda that included the death penalty for homosexual acts (McEwen). In the same year, on Chris Matthews's *Hardball* program on NBC, a spokesperson for the FRC stated that gay behavior should be outlawed in the United States and that "criminal sanctions against homosexual behavior should be enforced." The FRC also took a public stance against the "repeal of the 'Don't Ask, Don't Tell' policy stating that the repeal of the policy would encourage molestation of heterosexual service members" (McMorris-Santoro).

In 2012, the FRC extended the range of issues with which it disagrees by attacking Islam and Muslim immigration to the United States. The FRC "enlisted the support of retired Lt. General William G. 'Jerry' Boykin as executive vice-president of the organization. Boykin had previously served as the undersecretary for defense under President George W. Bush. Boykin has stated that the United States is in a 'spiritual battle' against Satan, and intimated that Islam was the greatest evil and the war on terror was a religious battle that had to be won." According to the SPLC:

> Boykin has also claimed that Islam is evil because it calls for innocent blood. He has said that the U.S. government is infiltrated by the Muslim Brotherhood and that the continent of Europe is lost to it. He has even claimed that there is a "cabal, a group of very nefarious people, who very much want to create a global government," and that American billionaire George Soros is part of it—a prevalent conspiracy theory on the right. (Southern Poverty Law Center, Family Research Council)

In 2013, FRC president Tony Perkins accused President Barack Obama of working the "totalitarian homosexual lobby" and stated that Obama's agenda would destroy freedom of religion (Southern Poverty Law Center, Family Research Council). After the "2015 U.S. Supreme Court ruling in *Obergefell v. Hodges*, which legalized same-sex marriage throughout the United States," the FRC began to work furiously with other groups and state legislatures to support "religious liberty laws that would allow those who object to same-sex marriage to refuse goods and services to same-sex couples" (Southern Poverty Law Center, 2016).

In 2016, FRC's president, Tony Perkins, "was a delegate from Louisiana for the Republican National Convention. Perkins helped craft the most anti-LGBT platform in the party's history, a platform that affirmed the right of parents 'to determine the proper medical treatment and therapy for their minor children' as well as issuing a call for the overturning of marriage equality" (Southern Poverty Law Center, 2016).

After the election of Donald Trump, an FRC senior fellow "was on Trump's transition team as head of domestic policy" (Southern Poverty Law Center, Family Research Council). The FRC thus worked to undo progress that had been made by LGBT people by recommending that President Trump issue a list of executive orders rescinding LGBT-friendly policies that had been put in place by the Obama Administration.

See also: Alliance Defending Freedom; American College of Pediatricians; American Family Association; Family Watch International; Liberty Counsel; Pacific Justice Institute; Ruth Institute; Traditional Values Coalition; Westboro Baptist Church; World Congress of Families

FURTHER READING

American Psychological Association. August 5, 2009. "Insufficient Evidence That Sexual Orientation Change Efforts Work, Says APA." American Psychological

Association. http://www.apa.org/news/press/releases/2009/08/therapeutic.aspx. (Accessed March 24, 2018.)

Brydum, Sunnivie. August 17, 2012. "Washington Post Writers: Putting FRC in Same Club as KKK Is Unfair." *Advocate.* http://www.advocate.com/crime/2012/08/17 /washington-post-columnists-continue-blaming-hate-group-classification-frc -shooting. (Accessed March 24, 2018.)

CNN. March 14, 2007. "Global Warming Gap among Evangelicals Widens." CNN. http:// www.cnn.com/2007/POLITICS/03/14/evangelical.rift/index.html?eref=rss_poli tics. (Accessed March 24, 2018.)

Family Research Council. May 4, 2011. "FRC Action Praises Bipartisan House Majority for Approving a 'No Taxpayer Funding for Abortion Act.'" FRC Action. https:// www.frcaction.org/action/frc-action-praises-bipartisan-house-majority-for -approving-no-taxpayer-funding-for-abortion-act. (Accessed March 24, 2018.)

Hernson, Paul S., Ronald G. Shaiko, and Clyde Wilcox. 2005. *The Interest Group Connection: Electioneering, Lobbying, and Policymaking in Washington.* CQ Press.

McEwen, Alvin. June 3, 2010. "Family Research Council Accused of Undermining Support for Resolution against Uganda's Anti-Gay Bill." Huffington Post. http://www .huffingtonpost.com/alvin-mcewen/family-research-council-a_b_600171.html. (Accessed March 24, 2018.)

McMorris-Santoro, Evan. November 24, 2010. "Family Research Council Labeled 'Hate Group' by SPLC over Anti-Gay Rhetoric." Talking Points Memo. http://talking pointsmemo.com/dc/family-research-council-labeled-hate-group-by-splc-over -anti-gay-rhetoric. (Accessed March 24, 2018.)

Sanchez, Casey. January 1, 2003. "Memphis Area Love in Action Residential Program to 'Cure' Homosexuality." Southern Poverty Law Center: Intelligence Report. https://www.splcenter.org/fighting-hate/intelligence-report/2003/memphis-area -love-action-offers-residential-program-cure-homosexuality. (Accessed March 24, 2018.)

Southern Poverty Law Center. "Family Research Council." Southern Poverty Law Center. https://www.splcenter.org/fighting-hate/extremist-files/group/family-research -council. (Accessed March 24, 2018.)

Southern Poverty Law Center. February 11, 2016. "'Religious Liberty' and the Anti-LGBT Rights." Southern Poverty Law Center. https://www.splcenter.org/20160211 /religious-liberty-and-anti-lgbt-right. (Accessed March 24, 2018.)

Thompson, Krissah. November 24, 2010. "'Hate Group' Designation Angers Same-Sex Opposition Opponents." *Washington Post.* http://www.washingtonpost.com /wp-dyn/content/article/2010/11/24/AR2010112405573.html. (Accessed March 24, 2018.)

Tripodi, Paul. August 16, 2012. "Lobbying Report." Lobbying Disclosure. U.S. House of Representatives. http://disclosures.house.gov/ld/pdfform.aspx?id=300256072. (Accessed March 24, 2018.)

Family Research Institute

The Family Research Institute (FRI) "is an American non-profit organization based in Colorado-Springs Colorado" that states that it has "one overriding mission: to generate empirical research on issues that threaten the traditional family, particularly homosexuality, AIDS, sexual social policy, and drug abuse" (Family Research Institute, 2012). The FRI is often associated "with the Christian right movement in the United States," which seeks to shape and influence political debate in the United States, particularly on issues that have biblical connections (Family Research Institute, About). The FRI seeks "to restore a world where marriage is upheld and honored, where children are nurtured and protected, and where homosexuality is not taught and accepted, but instead is discouraged and rejected at every level" (Family Research Institute, About). The FRI was founded by Paul Cameron in 1982 as "the Institute for the Scientific Investigation of Sexuality. He later changed the name to the Family Research Institute" (Kranish). Cameron received "a Ph.D. in psychology from the University of Colorado at Boulder in 1966," but his methods and research into gay psychology have largely been debunked and discredited by more respected researchers (Southern Poverty Law Center, 2006).

In 1978, Cameron "made his first foray into anti-gay activism with the publication of *Sexual Gradualism*, a book in which Cameron suggested that parents should allow their children to experiment with heterosexual sex, short of intercourse, as a means of preventing homosexuality" (Southern Poverty Law Center, Paul Cameron). Cameron defended his suggestion by pointing out that "[w]hile no parent wants his child starting the process 'too young,' better too young than homosexual" (Southern Poverty Law Center, Paul Cameron). Under the auspices of the Institute for the Scientific Investigation of Sexuality, which he founded in 1982, Cameron "began to disseminate anti-gay propaganda in 'pay-to-publish' journals" (Southern Poverty Law Center, Paul Cameron). As the AIDS crisis advanced during the 1980s, Cameron "advocated establishing concentration camps for 'sexually active homosexuals'" (Southern Poverty Law Center, Paul Cameron).

In 1987, "Cameron moved to Washington, D.C. and changed the name of his organization to the Family Research Institute." In 1992, Cameron moved the group to Colorado Springs, Colorado, after supporters of an antigay amendment in Colorado (Amendment 2) succeeded in placing the amendment on the state ballot. He and the Family Research Institute gained great notoriety at the time, as supporters of the amendment "distributed 100,000 copies of his study, 'What Do Homosexuals Do?'" Among many false claims in the publication, the study claimed that "17% of LGBT people enjoy consuming human feces" (Southern Poverty Law Center, Paul Cameron). Amendment 2 was eventually passed by Colorado voters but was later overturned by the U.S. Supreme Court in *Romer v. Evans*.

Cameron and the Family Research Institute continue to publish "pseudoscientific studies" purporting to prove that "gays and lesbians are more prone than heterosexuals to commit murder, die young and molest children" (Southern Poverty Law Center, Paul Cameron). A March 2014 article by the Family Research Institute even suggested that gay parents are more apt to commit incest (Family Research Institute). Other claims supported by the Family Research Institute suggest that "children raised by homosexuals disproportionately experience emotional disturbance and sexual victimization" and that homosexuality promotes "demographic suicide," as areas where homosexuality is tolerated or legalized show declining birth rates that threaten civil society (Southern Poverty Law Center, Paul Cameron).

Cameron and the work of the Family Research Institute (FRI) remain central to anti-LGBT groups on the extreme right of the political spectrum, "even though such work has been discredited by the American Psychological Association and the American Sociological Association" (Southern Poverty Law Center, 2006). Despite repudiations of claims put forward by Cameron and the FRI, however, Cameron's "junk science" is continually cited by campaigns that work against civil rights for gays and lesbians (Southern Poverty Law Center, 2006).

See also: American College of Pediatricians; American Family Association; Family Research Institute; Liberty Counsel; Ruth Institute; Traditional Values Coalition; Westboro Baptist Church; World Congress of Families

FURTHER READING

Brooke, James. October 11, 1995. "Colorado Is Engine in Anti-Gay Uproar." *New York Times*. http://www.nytimes.com/1995/10/11/us/colorado-is-engine-in-anti-gay-uproar.html. (Accessed April 29, 2017.)

Family Research Council. January 18, 2012. "Saving Society from Demographic Suicide." Family Research Council. http://www.familyresearchinst.org/category/public-policy/. (Accessed April 29, 2017.)

Family Research Institute. "About." http://www.familyresearchinst.org/about/. (Accessed January 30, 2019.)

Family Research Institute. March 2014. "Are Gay Parents More Apt to Commit Incest?" Family Research Institute. http://www.familyresearchinst.org/2014/04/frr-mar-2014-are-gay-parents-more-apt-to-commit-incest/. (Accessed April 29, 2017.)

Kranish, Michael. July 31, 2005. "Beliefs Drive Research Agenda of New Think Tanks." *Boston Globe*. http://archive.boston.com/news/nation/articles/2005/07/31/beliefs_drive_research_agenda_of_new_think_tanks/. (Accessed April 29, 2017.)

Schlatter, Evelyn. September 20, 2012. "Anti-LGBT Propagandist Published Again in Academic Journal." Southern Poverty Law Center: Hatewatch. https://www.splcenter.org/hatewatch/2012/09/20/anti-lgbt-propagandist-published-again-academic-journal. (Accessed April 29, 2017.)

Southern Poverty Law Center. "Paul Cameron." Southern Poverty Law Center. https://www.splcenter.org/fighting-hate/extremist-files/individual/paul-cameron. (Accessed April 29, 2017.)

Southern Poverty Law Center. January 31, 2006. "UC-Davis Psychology Professor Gregory Here Aims to Debunk Anti-Gay Extremist Paul Cameron." Southern Poverty Law Center: Intelligence Report. https://www.splcenter.org/fighting-hate/intelligence-report/2006/uc-davis-psychology-professor-gregory-herek-aims-debunk-anti-gay-extremist-paul-cameron. (Accessed April 29, 2017.)

Family Security Matters

Family Security Matters (FSM) was a right-wing organization founded in the aftermath of 9/11. According to its website, it was

> borne of a need to educate the American public about the many threats to our national and family security, from what is taught in our classrooms; to the dangers of feckless national security and foreign policy; to how and why the government

executes foreign policy, in particular in relation to Israel and other allies and enemies; to the terror threats of fundamentalist Islam all over the globe; to the unwelcome influence of politics on our safety . . . and much, much more. (FSM National Security Team, March 2018)

FSM began as a "defacto extension of the anti-Muslim hate group Center for Security Policy (CSP)" (Southern Poverty Law Center). In 2005, it became an independent organization and became infamous for "espousing anti-Muslim conspiracy theories and painting Muslims as criminals" (Southern Poverty Law Center). In 2010, it took up the cause of anti-Islamists Robert Spencer and Pamela Geller—and their organization the American Freedom Defense Initiative—in decrying the proposal to build a Muslim mosque near the site of Ground Zero in lower Manhattan. Both Spencer and Geller wondered:

> Could it be that most Americans are against a Ground Zero mosque because it is a slap in the face to the memory of those who died there? Might the reason most Americans think that Obama is a Muslim stem from the fact that they see him defending, praising, justifying, and favoring this religion over all others, especially Christianity, and even over a basic respect for American patriotic values? (Southern Poverty Law Center)

For nearly 15 years, FSM perpetuated anti-Muslim stereotypes, fueled Muslim hatred, and provided a venue for anti-Muslim authors to vent their hatred and conspiracy theories of Islam and Muslims. In 2016, an article on the FSM website noted that "[f]ighting and attacking others with knives and other sharp objects appears to be in the Muslim DNA" (Southern Poverty Law Center). The next year, a longtime contributor to FSM, Paul Hollrah, wrote:

> It is estimated that, by the end of this century, in the absence of some unforeseen divine intervention, Muslims will exceed 50 percent of the world's population. But long before that time, it is reasonable to assume that most of 21st century Western civilization will have become unraveled and our descendants will find themselves facing a squalid 7th century lifestyle. (Southern Poverty Law Center)

After being added to the SPLC's "hate groups" list, the FSM urged its readers and contributors to "strike back" against dark forces that infringe upon the rights of free speech and demand political correctness and conformity in political thought (FSM National Security Team, January 2018). Borrowing a term made popular by President Donald Trump, the FSM wrote: "Many Americans are aware of how the 'deep state' works very hard to sabotage conservative issues. Many Americans also view the Southern Poverty Law Center (SPLC) as part of the 'deep state' entity" (FSM National Security Team, January 2018). A contributor to FSM, Tom DeWeese, a noted conspiracy theorist, said that the SPLC was "a powerful force operating to divide the American people and silence opposing views." DeWeese told FSM readers that the SPLC was "in many ways more dangerous than other organizations that are fueling the flames of the far left radicals who use violence and lies to stop honest political debate" (DeWeese).

In March 2018, FSM announced that after "publishing many thousands of articles, experts, videos, polls and white papers, and knowing that our site truly made a difference in people's fluency and understanding of our national security needs, we believe it is time to sit back, congratulate ourselves . . . and retire" (FSM National Security Team, March 2018). Upon the announcement, the SPLC noted that among the thousands of articles published by FSM from dozens of authors, each perpetuated an anti-Muslim platform that was used to "promote everything from conspiracy theories about Muslims in America to advocating for racial and religious profiling" (Hatewatch staff).

See also: American Freedom Defense Initiative; Center for Security Policy

FURTHER READING

DeWeese, Tom. January 18, 2018. "It's Time to Bring the Southern Poverty Law Center to Justice." Family Security Matters. http://www.familysecuritymatters.org/publica tions/detail/its-time-to-bring-the-southern-poverty-law-center-to-justice. (Accessed May 28, 2018.)

FSM National Security Team. January 2018. "Family Security Matters Added to SPLC's Hate List." Family Security Matters. http://www.familysecuritymatters.org/publi cations/detail/family-security-matters-added-to-splcs-hate-list. (Accessed May 28, 2018.)

FSM National Security Team. March 2018. "Family Security Matters Says Good-Bye." Family Security Matters. http://familysecuritymatters.org/publications/detail /family-security-matters-says-good-bye. (Accessed May 28, 2018.)

Hatewatch Staff. March 22, 2018. "Amid Its Quindecinnial Anniversary of Publishing Anti-Muslim Hate, Family Security Matters Bids Farewell." Southern Poverty Law Center: Hatewatch. https://www.splcenter.org/hatewatch/2018/03/22/amid -its-quindecinnial-anniversary-publishing-anti-muslim-hate-family-security-mat ters-bids. (Accessed May 28, 2018.)

Southern Poverty Law Center. "Family Security Matters." Southern Poverty Law Center. https://www.splcenter.org/fighting-hate/extremist-files/group/family-security -matters. (Accessed May 28, 2018.)

Family Watch International

Family Watch International (FWI) was founded in 1999 by "longtime anti-LGBT and anti-choice activist Sharon Slater" (Southern Poverty Law Center, Family Watch International). Slater claims that it was her attendance at the 1999 World Congress of Families (WCF) that prompted her to launch her campaign against LGBT causes. The FWI mission, according to its website, is to "protect and pro-mote the family as the fundamental unit of society at the international, national and local level" and "to protect the family by working to preserve and promote traditional marriage, safeguard parental rights, defend human life, uphold reli-gious liberty, and protect the health and innocence of children" (Family Watch International). FWI agitates with the United Nations and primarily African coun-tries to promote its policies "under the name Global Helping to Advance Women and Children" (Global HAWC) (Southern Poverty Law Center, 2015). FWI con-tends that the UN's push "for equal rights for LGBT people and women is part of a Western neo-imperialistic project" (Southern Poverty Law Center, 2015).

Slater's close alliance with antigay African activists, such as Ugandan pastor Martin Ssempa, who supported the country's "Kill the Gays" bill in 2014, has helped her to gain credibility in her campaigns to oppose the decriminalization of homosexuality around the world. The FWI claims that "children raised in same-sex households have 'serious problems' and support discredited and often dangerous 'ex-gay' therapy to try to make people heterosexual" (Southern Poverty Law Center, 2015). And while claiming "that the FWI does not condone violence against homosexuals and transgenders," Slater "has compared homosexuality to 'incest, sexual abuse, and rape . . . drug dealing, assaults, and other crimes'" (Southern Poverty Law Center, 2015).

FWI has used its consultative status with the United Nations "to limit the advancement of comprehensive sexuality education, reproductive health services including abortion, and basic rights and protections for LGBTQ people" (Southern Poverty Law Center, 2015). In 2011, FWI created a website entitled "100 Questions for the Girl Scouts." The purpose of the website was to

> inform parents about the many ways the youth organization was "increasingly connecting young girls to radical feminism, the promotion of sexual rights, LGBT (lesbian, gay, bisexual, transgender) issues, and the abortion rights movement." According to Slater, "radical feminism" embraced perceived evils ranging from public daycare programs and Title XI (which mandates that any program receiving federal funding cannot discriminate on the basis of sex) to "communism, Marxism, existentialism, and extreme environmentalism." (Southern Poverty Law Center, 2015)

Slater and the FWI oppose anything that is seen as being in opposition "to the heterosexual, divinely ordained, 'natural family,' including abortion, birth control, and homosexuality" (Southern Poverty Law Center, Family Watch International). In October 2017, Slater warned participants at the National Association for Research & Therapy of Homosexuality (NARTH) Training Institute:

> The crux of this presentation is to help you to understand that they are after our children. This is the target of the sexual rights movement. Because they know if they can raise up the next generation and indoctrinate them in their radical gender and sexual ideologies, they will have the culture, they will have the future, they will have the government. (Southern Poverty Law Center, Family Watch International)

See also: Family Research Council; Focus on the Family; World Congress of Families

FURTHER READING

Family Watch International. "Family Watch Mission." Family Watch International. https://familywatch.org/about-us/#.Wwxhc4oh3RY. (Accessed May 28, 2018.)

Hatewatch Staff. May 22, 2017. "Anti-LGBT Hate Group World Congress of Families to Gather This Week in Budapest." Southern Poverty Law Center. https://www.splcenter.org/hatewatch/2017/05/22/anti-lgbt-hate-group-world-congress-families-gather-week-budapest. (Accessed May 28, 2018.)

Southern Poverty Law Center. "Family Watch International." Southern Poverty Law Center. https://www.splcenter.org/fighting-hate/extremist-files/group/family-watch-international. (Accessed May 28, 2018.)

Southern Poverty Law Center. October 21, 2015. "Everything You Need to Know about the Anti-LGBTQ World Congress of Families (WCF)." Southern Poverty Law Center. https://www.splcenter.org/news/2015/10/21/everything-you-need-know-about -anti-lgbtq-world-congress-families-wcf. (Accessed May 28, 2018.)

Federation for American Immigration Reform

The Federation for American Immigration Reform (FAIR) is an organization "whose mission is to limit immigration into the United States" (Southern Poverty Law Center, FAIR). Specifically, "FAIR seeks to overturn the 1965 Immigration and Nationality Act, which ended a decades-long, racist quota system that limited immigration mostly to northern Europeans" (Southern Poverty Law Center, FAIR). Representatives from FAIR have testified before the U.S. Congress on many occasions, but many of its adherents express racist and eugenicist thought that betray its true intentions. Dan Stein, president of FAIR, has stated:

> I blame ninety-eight percent of responsibility for this country's immigration crisis on Ted Kennedy and his political allies, who decided some time back in 1958, earlier perhaps, that immigration was a great way to retaliate against Anglo-Saxon dominance and hubris, and the immigration laws from the 1920s were just this symbol of that, and it's a form of revengism, or revenge, that these forces continue to push the immigration policy that they know full well are [sic] creating chaos and will continue to create chaos down the line. (Berrier)

John Tanton founded FAIR in 1979 in Washington, D.C. Tanton was originally interested in the effects of population growth on the environment, as he had also been a member of the Sierra Club and "the president of the Zero Population Growth, a group founded by biologist and longtime FAIR advisor, Paul Ehrlich, author of the best-selling novel *The Population Bomb*." (Southern Poverty Law Center, 2002). With the founding of FAIR, Tanton became convinced that one crucial element to prevent unchecked population growth was to set immigration quotas and prevent illegal immigration.

In 1988, secret memos published by the Arizona Republic revealed Tanton's, and FAIR's, agenda. The memos revealed Tanton's warnings of a "Latin onslaught" and complained of the "low educability" of Latinos. Tanton also "expressed concerns about the role of the Catholic Church in America," and he worried that increasing Latino immigration into the United States would give the church more political influence in the country (Southern Poverty Law Center, 2002). Linda Chavez, a prominent Reagan administration official and executive director of U.S. English, one of Tanton's groups, resigned over the memos, calling them "repugnant and not excusable" and "anti-Catholic and anti-Hispanic" (Southern Poverty Law Center, 2002).

But the memos were not the extent of Tanton's extremism. Tanton also had associations with Holocaust deniers and leading white nationalist thinkers, such as Jared Taylor—founder and editor of the white nationalist magazine *American Renaissance*—and radical anti-Semitic professor Kevin MacDonald. In a 1993 memo to FAIR, Tanton stated his desire to limit nonwhite immigration into the

United States, saying, "Projections by the U.S. Census Bureau show that midway into the next century, the current European-American majority will become a minority. . . . This is unacceptable; we decline to bequeath to our children minority status in their own land" (Southern Poverty Law Center, 2002).

Between 1985 and 1994, FAIR "received some $1.2 million in grants from the Pioneer Fund, a eugenicist organization that devotes itself to 'race betterment' through promoting studies that purportedly demonstrate the racial superiority of the white race" (Southern Poverty Law Center, 2002). From 1996 to 1997, FAIR produced a television program called *Borderline* that featured a number of white nationalists, including Sam Francis, Jared Taylor, and Peter Brimelow, who founded the anti-immigrant hate site VDARE. The *Borderline* program "often advanced ideas popular in white nationalist circles; particularly popular was the idea that immigrants are destroying American culture or displacing Western civilization with degenerate, Third World ways" (Southern Poverty Law Center, FAIR).

In the late 2000s, "FAIR became very active in pushing for anti-immigrant laws at the state and local levels" (Southern Poverty Law Center, FAIR). FAIR has also been an advocate for ending the "birthright citizenship provision of the 14th Amendment, which provides that all children born on U.S. soil are automatically granted U.S. citizenship" (Concisepolitics). FAIR has also targeted organizations that attempt to aid those fleeing violence in other countries. In 2014, FAIR named locales where refugees were being resettled and the organizations that were helping them in the effort. FAIR helped organize protests against such efforts in such states as California and Michigan.

In 2015, Julie Kirchner, FAIR's executive director, left the organization to become an immigration adviser to the campaign of Donald Trump (Piggott). In February 2017, Kirchner was named the "chief of staff of U.S. Customs and Border Protection (CBP), the federal agency that oversees Border Patrol" (Vasquez). The headline announcing the appointment proclaimed, "Trump's New Immigration Official Used to Lead Hate Group" (Vasquez).

See also: American Border Patrol/American Patrol; American Renaissance; Center for Immigration Studies; Holocaust Denial; Pioneer Fund; Remembrance Project; VDARE; White Nationalism; White Supremacist Movement

FURTHER READING

Berrier, Justin. August 19, 2011. "CNN Turns to Anti-Immigrant Hate Group FAIR for Immigration Commentary." MediaMatters. https://mediamatters.org/blog/2011/08/19/cnn-turns-to-anti-immigrant-hate-group-fair-for/183858. (Accessed March 13, 2018.)

Concisepolitics. November 7, 2014. "FAIR = Federation for American Immigration Reform = An Ugly Hate Group." https://concisepolitics.com/2014/11/07/murrieta-ca-fair-federation-for-american-immigration-reform-an-ugly-hate-group/. (Accessed November 10, 2018.)

Piggott, Stephen. January 23, 2017. "Former Executive Director of Anti-Immigrant Hate Group FAIR Joins Trump Administration." Southern Poverty Law Center: Hatewatch.

https://www.splcenter.org/hatewatch/2017/01/23/former-executive-director-anti-immigrant-hate-group-fair-joins-trump-administration. (March 13, 2018.)

Smith, Laura. February 2, 2017. "Could This Anti-Immigrant Hardliner Grab a Top Border Patrol Spot?" *Mother Jones.* http://www.motherjones.com/politics/2017/01/trump-customs-border-protection-julie-kirchner. (March 13, 2018.)

Southern Poverty Law Center. "Federation for American Immigration Reform." Southern Poverty Law Center. https://www.splcenter.org/fighting-hate/extremist-files/group/federation-american-immigration-reform. (Accessed March 13, 2018.)

Southern Poverty Law Center. June 18, 2002. "John Tanton Is the Mastermind behind the Organized Anti-Immigration Movement." Southern Poverty Law Center: Intelligence Report. https://www.splcenter.org/fighting-hate/intelligence-report/2002/john-tanton-mastermind-behind-organized-anti-immigration-movement. (Accessed March 13, 2018.)

Vasquez, Tina. January 26, 2017. "Trump's New Immigration Official Used to Lead Hate Group." Rewire. https://rewire.news/article/2017/01/26/trumps-new-immigration-official-used-lead-hate-group/. (Accessed March 13, 2018.)

Fitzgerald Griffin Foundation

The Fitzgerald Griffin Foundation ("Griffin Foundation") is "designated by the Southern Poverty Law Center (SPLC) as a white nationalist hate group" (Southern Poverty Law Center, White Nationalist). White nationalist groups "espouse white supremacist or white separatist ideologies, often focusing on the alleged inferiority of nonwhites. . . . Adherents of white nationalist groups believe that white identity should be the organizing principle of the countries that make up Western civilization" (Southern Poverty Law Center, White Nationalist). The Griffin Foundation was founded in 2003 with the express purpose "to preserve the glorious traditions and culture of Western civilization and Christianity" (Fitzgerald Griffin Foundation). The Griffin Foundation spreads its message through publishing projects focusing on such issues as "religious liberty, American culture and society, war and peace, immigration, the sanctity of marriage between one man and one woman, modern American history, morality in politics, church history . . . [and] pre-born citizens' rights" (Fitzgerald Griffin Foundation).

In 2007, the Griffin Foundation made headlines when it hosted a meeting at the National Press Club in Washington, D.C. At the meeting, E. Michael, a noted "hard-line anti-Semite," caused a "ruckus" as he and others promoted the white nationalist ideals of Sam Francis, who had died two years earlier. At the meeting,

> [a] red-faced and shouting Jones devoted a full hour to denouncing the "revolutionary Jew" who, he claimed, has been fighting the Catholic Church and Christianity in general for some 2,000 years. Among other things, Jones denounced the civil rights movement as "controlled by Jews" who used blacks as "pawns." (Southern Poverty Law Center, 2007)

The 2007 meeting also highlighted that Fran Griffin, the head of the Griffin Foundation, had published a newsletter entitled *Sobran's*, by columnist Joe Sobran, "an anti-Semite who has written for a Holocaust denial journal" (Southern Poverty Law Center, 2007).

In the aftermath of the Charlottesville, Virginia, "United the Right" protests, in which white nationalists and white supremacists "protested the removal of a statue of Confederate General Robert E. Lee," the Griffin Foundation was again in the news. This time, the group's designation as a 501(c)(3) nonprofit organization— meaning the foundation operated without paying taxes while accepting tax-deductible donations—was questioned given its association with extremists and its designation by the SPLC as a "hate group." Mark Potok, a senior fellow at the SPLC, sees the tax-exempt status of groups that advocate for white supremacy as problematic. "In effect, the American taxpayer is subsidizing false propaganda defaming minority groups," Potok says. "Claims by watch-list organizations to be educational institutions are simply a facade." He added: "There's a difference between education and propaganda" (Stiffman).

See also: White Nationalism; White Supremacist Movement

FURTHER READING

Fitzgerald Griffin Foundation. "About Us." Fitzgerald Griffin Foundation. http://www .fgfbooks.com/AboutUS.html. (Accessed June 2, 2018.)

Rittiman, Brandon, and Anna Staver. August 17, 2017. "Verify: Yes, Some Hate Groups Get Tax Exempt Status." 9News.com. https://www.9news.com/article/news/local /verify/verify-yes-some-hate-groups-get-tax-exempt-status/73-465210606. (Accessed June 2, 2018.)

Southern Poverty Law Center. "White Nationalist." Southern Poverty Law Center. https:// www.splcenter.org/fighting-hate/extremist-files/ideology/white-nationalist. (Accessed June 2, 2018.)

Southern Poverty Law Center. July 6, 2007. "U.S. Navy Suspends 'Radical Traditionalist Catholic.'" Southern Poverty Law Center: Intelligence Report. https://www .splcenter.org/fighting-hate/intelligence-report/2007/us-navy-suspends-radical -traditionalist-catholic. (Accessed June 2, 2018.)

Stiffman, Eden. December 22, 2016. "Dozens of 'Hate Groups' Have Charity Status, *Chronicle* Study Finds." *Chronicle of Philanthropy*. https://www.philanthropy .com/article/Dozens-of-Hate-Groups-/238748. (Accessed June 2, 2018.)

Williamson, Jeff. August 15, 2017. "Group Finds 42 Hate Groups in Virginia." WSLS. com. https://www.wsls.com/news/virginia/group-finds-42-hate-groups-in-virginia. (Accessed June 2, 2018.)

Focus on the Family

Focus on the Family is an anti-LGBT organization based in Colorado Springs, Colorado. James Dobson founded the organization was founded in 1977 as a conservative Christian lobbying organization intent on articulating its socially conservative views on public policy. Focus on the Family's stated mission is "nurturing and defending the God-ordained institution of the family and promoting biblical truths worldwide" (Focus on the Family). Focus on the Family promotes traditional and socially conservative values consistent with staunchly evangelical Christian organizations, such as abstinence-only sexual education; creationism; adoption by married, opposite-sex parents; school prayer; and traditional gender roles (Focus on the Family). The Southern Poverty Law Center (SPLC) considers the group an anti-LGBT group because of its virulent rhetoric and opposition to such issues as LGBT rights, particularly LGBT adoption, and same-sex marriage. Founder James Dobson stated that "the battle against LGBT rights is essentially a 'second civil war' to put control of the U.S. government in the right hands, meaning those who reject LGBT rights" (Southern Poverty Law Center, Anti-LGBT). Focus on the Family has stated that homosexuality is "preventable and treatable" and has conducted programs to spread "reparative therapy," or conversion therapy, in which LGBT people are psychologically treated or spiritually counseled to change their sexual orientation from homosexual or bisexual to heterosexual. Focus on the Family has asserted that the U.S. federal government has a "gay agenda" to "sneak homosexuality lessons into [public] classrooms" (Costello).

Perhaps Focus on the Family's most controversial program has been its "Love Won Out" initiative, which focused on reparative or conversion therapies of gay individuals. The organization founded Love Won Out in 1998 and eventually sold it to Exodus International, an ex-gay Christian organization, in 2009. Love Won Out was to "provide a Christ-centered, comprehensive conference which will enlighten, empower and equip families, church and youth leaders, educators, counselors, policy-makers, and the gay community on the truth about homosexuality and its impact on culture, family, and youth" (Burack and Josephson). In 2013, Exodus International ceased activities. Its leader, John Paulk, a "former" gay man, apologized to the LGBT community, saying:

> From the bottom of my heart I wish I could take back my words and actions that caused anger, depression, guilt and hopelessness. In their place I want to extend love, hope, tenderness, joy and the truth that gay people are loved by God.
>
> Today, I see LGBT people for who they are—beloved, cherished children of God. I offer my most sincere and heartfelt apology to men, women, and especially children and teens who felt unlovable, unworthy, shamed or thrown away by God or the church.
>
> I want to offer my sincere thanks to everyone who encouraged me to take this initial step of transparency. Even while promoting "ex-gay" programs, there were those who called me on my own words and actions. I'm sure I didn't appreciate it at the time, but they have helped me to realize this truth about who I am. (Baldock)

Critics of the Love Won Out initiative believed that the program really wasn't interested in "converting" people from gay to straight. Rather, they believe that the program was actually a veiled attempt to deny gay people equal rights. As a spokesman for the National Organization of Women stated, "Their message is simple: Since gay people can 'change,' they do not deserve protection from discrimination" (Anonymous).

One month before the U.S. presidential election in 2008, Focus on the Family began distributing a 16-page letter, titled *Letter from 2012 in Obama's America*. The letter described "an imagined American future in which 'many of our freedoms have been taken away by a liberal Supreme Court of the United States and a majority of Democrats in both the House of Representatives and the Senate." According to *USA Today*, the letter "'is part of an escalation in rhetoric from

Christian right activists trying to paint Democratic Party presidential nominee Senator Barack Obama in a negative light" (White).

In 2010, an unnamed "educational analyst" for Focus on the Family suggested that antibullying efforts in public schools were meant to draw attention to LGBT students as part of a "gay agenda" being perpetrated by the federal government to "sneak homosexuality into classrooms" (Costello). According to critics, Focus on the Family's goal in this case was "to make schools less safe for LGBT students and more safe for their harassers" (Costello).

The Southern Poverty Law Center (SPLC) has described Focus on the Family as one of a "dozen major groups [that] help drive the religious right's anti-gay crusade" (Southern Poverty Law Center, 2005).

See also: Family Research Council

FURTHER READING

Anonymous. "10 Things You Should Know about Focus on the Family." Human Rights Campaign. http://www.hrc.org/resources/10-things-you-should-know-about-focus-on-the-family. (Accessed June 2, 2017.)

Baldock, Kathy. April 24, 2013. "John Paulk, Former Exodus & Love Won Out Leader Apologizes." Canyonwalker Connections. http://canyonwalkerconnections.com/john-paulk-former-exodus-love-won-out-leader-apologizes/. (Accessed June 2, 2017.)

Burack, Cynthia, and Jyl J. Josephson. September 18, 2004. "A Report from 'Love Won Out: Addressing, Understanding, and Preventing Homosexuality.'" National Gay and Lesbian Task Force Policy Institute. http://www.thetaskforce.org/static_html/downloads/reports/reports/LoveWonOut.pdf. (Accessed June 2, 2017.)

Costello, Maureen. September 3, 2010. "Focus on the Family Goes After LGBT Students." Southern Poverty Law Center. https://www.splcenter.org/news/2010/09/03/focus-family-goes-after-lgbt-students. (Accessed June 2, 2017.)

Focus on the Family. "Foundational Values." Focus on the Family. http://www.focusonthefamily.com/about/foundational-values. (Accessed June 2, 2017.)

Gryboski, Michael. September 13, 2013. "Focus on the Family Cutting 40 More Staff as Part of Restructuring." *Christian Post*. http://www.christianpost.com/news/focus-on-the-family-cutting-more-staff-as-part-of-restructuring-104516/. (Accessed June 2, 2017.)

Southern Poverty Law Center. "Anti-LGBT." Southern Poverty Law Center. https://www.splcenter.org/fighting-hate/extremist-files/ideology/anti-lgbt. (Accessed June 2, 2017.)

Southern Poverty Law Center. "Family Research Council." Southern Poverty Law Center. https://www.splcenter.org/fighting-hate/extremist-files/group/family-research-council. (Accessed June 2, 2017.)

Southern Poverty Law Center. April 28, 2005. "A Dozen Major Groups Help Drive the Religious Right's Anti-Gay Crusade." Southern Poverty Law Center: Intelligence Report. https://www.splcenter.org/fighting-hate/intelligence-report/2005/dozen-major-groups-help-drive-religious-right's-anti-gay-crusade. (Accessed June 2, 2017.)

White, Chet. October 27, 2008. "Christian Right's Mailings Depict Disastrous Future under Obama." *USA Today*. https://usatoday30.usatoday.com/news/religion/2008-10-27-christian-right-obama_N.htm. (Accessed June 2, 2017.)

Foundation for the Marketplace of Ideas

The Foundation for the Marketplace of Ideas (FMI) was founded on March 26, 2016, by several white nationalist leaders "to educate the public about the freedoms guaranteed by the United States Constitution and people who and organizations which strive to usurp said freedoms" (Tanner and Burghart). According to the American Freedom Party, an organization dedicated to returning the United States to white rule, the FMI based itself on the "successful business models of the Southern Poverty Law Center and Anti-Defamation League" and billed itself as a "racist version of the ACLU" (Eyes on the Right, 2018). The FMI "aspires to serve as the patriotic alternative to organizations which demand the imposition upon our people of the orthodoxy of political correctness at the cost of our dignity, fundamental rights, and American heritage" (American Freedom Party). In essence, the FMI was started to "become the legal arm of the racist radical right" (Lenz).

The primary inspiration behind the FMI's founding was Kyle Bristow, a young lawyer practicing in the Detroit, Michigan, area. Even before his association with the FMI, however, Bristow was well known in white nationalist and white supremacist circles. White attending Michigan State University (MSU), Bristow founded a chapter of Young Americans for Freedom (YAF), a conservative student organization founded to "diligently advance conservatism" in colleges and universities in the United States (Young Americans for Freedom). While president of the YAF at Michigan State, Bristow "organized numerous bigoted publicity stunts, including 'Catch an Illegal Immigrant Day' (cancelled), a 'straight power' rally, and a 'Koran desecration contest.' Bristow also invited notorious white nationalist leaders to MSU" (Tanner and Burghart). While at MSU, Bristow also issued a 13-point program "to govern student life that called for capturing undocumented immigrants in the area, cutting school funding for non-heterosexual student groups, and giving more representation to men and whites on the student council than others" (Lenz). After "obtaining his law degree from the University of Toledo," Bristow became a "go-to attorney for a growing cast of racists" (Lenz). He also became associated with several groups related to the alternative right (alt-right). As noted by Ryan Lenz, a writer for the Southern Poverty Law Center (SPLC):

> If it wasn't obvious that the Alt-Right is pretty much the same thing as the old white supremacist right—even if it does favor suits and ties over Klan robes or faux Nazi uniforms—that was cleared up just 11 days after [Donald] Trump's election, when an Alt-Right conference sponsored by the National Policy Institute concluded with several audience members sieg-heiling [alt-right founder Richard] Spencer during his speech. (Lenz)

After the founding of the FMI, other lawyers sympathetic to extremist causes began to network with Bristow and the FMI (Eyes on the Right, 2018). Bristow promised that FMI would "defend racist activists against social justice warriors," depicting itself as the "legal muscle behind the alt-right phenomenon " (Lenz). To this end, in the first eight months of FMI's existence, the foundation "offered pro bono legal advice to 'Alt-Right guerrilla activists' on college campuses and defended their right to distribute personal information about anti-racists" (Lenz).

In recent months, FMI

> has begun researching U.S. Supreme Court cases in the hope of explaining how "social justice warriors" and their allies have manipulated culture and public opinion to define the "zeitgeist" of civil rights. "Positions on certain issues—such as civil rights—that are accepted as absolute truths today, however, were hotly contested issues yesteryear. (Lenz)

Though FMI is registered as a 501(c)(3) nonprofit corporation, it has "an abundancy [sic] of bigotry on the board of directors list" (Eyes on the Right, 2018). Among these members are "are white nationalist William Johnson, Jason Robb (son of Knights of the Ku Klux Klan leader Thomas Robb), and anti-gay conservative activist Ryan Sorba" (Eyes on the Right, 2016). Bristow has stated that FMI is needed because "the media, big businesses, and other entities 'despise' their [alt-right adherents'] philosophy and heritage." As Bristow noted,

> Today, what is known as the alt-right no longer consists of "political lepers" who are "rejected by all." They have "established beachheads on social media," and have their own websites (Red Ice Radio, American Renaissance, etc.), philosophers (Richard Spencer, Kevin MacDonald, etc.), and even their own entertainers (such as Paul Ramsey and Milo Yiannopoulos).
>
> And some would even say that we have our own political party which is going to make America white, I mean, great again! (Eyes on the Right, 2016)

After clearing the way for alt-right founder Richard Spencer to speak on Michigan State University's campus, on March 3, 2018, Kyle Bristow abruptly resigned from FMI, cutting his ties with the group, which bills itself as the "'sword and shield' of the white nationalist, alt-right movement" (*Detroit Free Press* staff). Bristow complained that the press had "vilified" him, stating, "In recent weeks, journalists have published horrifically disparaging articles about me which contain acerbic, offensive, juvenile and regrettable statements I mostly made over a decade ago while I was in college and a prominent and staunchly conservative activist" (*Detroit Free Press* staff). Bristow continued:

> The media is not whatsoever justified in vilifying me. Just as I have stood up for the free speech rights of people on the right side of the political spectrum, I have likewise—in my capacity as an attorney—stood up for the rights of people on the left side of the political spectrum. (Ikonomova)

In the aftermath of Bristow's resignation, the website and Facebook site he created for FMI were offline, "with no indication that they will be returning anytime soon" (Barrouquere).

See also: Alt-Right Movement; American Freedom Party; White Nationalism; White Supremacist Movement

FURTHER READING

American Freedom Party. May 10, 2016. "Launch of the 'Foundation for the Marketplace of Ideas, Inc.'" American Freedom Party. http://american3rdposition.com/launch-foundation-marketplace-ideas-inc/. (Accessed June 2, 2018.)

Barrouquere, Brett. March 19, 2018. "After Kyle Bristow Walks Away, FMI's Future in Question as Online Presence Disappears." Southern Poverty Law Center: Hatewatch.

https://www.splcenter.org/hatewatch/2018/03/19/after-kyle-bristow-walks-away
-fmi%E2%80%99s-future-question-online-presence-disappears. (Accessed June 2,
2018.)

Detroit Free Press Staff. March 3, 2018. "Macomb Attorney Kyle Bristow Resigning
from Alt-Right, Blames Media." *Detroit Free Press*. https://www.freep.com/story
/news/local/michigan/macomb/2018/03/03/macomb-attorney-kyle-bristow
-resigns-alt-right/392209002/. (Accessed June 4, 2018.)

Eyes on the Right. September 11, 2016. "Kyle Bristow: The Alt-Right Has Its Own Political Party That Will 'Make America White' Again." Angry White Men. https://
angrywhitemen.org/2016/09/11/kyle-bristow-the-alt-right-has-its-own-political
-party-that-will-make-america-white-again/. (Accessed June 2, 2018.)

Eyes on the Right. January 2, 2018. "Kyle Bristow Claims He's Fighting the Left with a
Racist Version of the ACLU." Angry White Men. https://angrywhitemen
.org/2018/01/02/kyle-bristow-claims-hes-fighting-the-left-with-a-racist-version
-of-the-aclu/. (Accessed June 2, 2018.)

Ikonomova, Violet. March 3, 2018. "Richard Spencer's Metro Detroit Lawyer Disassociates from Alt-Right following Negative Press." *Metro Times*. https://www
.metrotimes.com/news-hits/archives/2018/03/03/richard-spencers-metro-detroit
-lawyer-dissociates-from-alt-right-following-negative-press. (Accessed June 4,
2018.)

Lenz, Ryan. February 15, 2017. "Attorney for Aryans." Southern Poverty Law Center:
Intelligence Report. https://www.splcenter.org/fighting-hate/intelligence-report/2017
/attorney-for%E2%80%85aryans. (Accessed June 2, 2018.)

Tanner, Chuck. March 2, 2018. "The Foundation for the Marketplace of Ideas Brings
National Socialism to Michigan State University." Institute for Research and Education on Human Rights. https://www.irehr.org/2018/03/02/foundation-market
place-ideas-brings-national-socialism-michigan-state-university/. (Accessed June 2,
2018.)

Tanner, Chuck, and Devin Burghart. March 2, 2018. "What Is the Foundation for the Marketplace of Ideas?" Institute for Research and Education on Human Rights. https://
www.irehr.org/2018/03/02/foundation-marketplace-ideas/. (Accessed June 2, 2018.)

Young Americans for Freedom. https://students.yaf.org/young-americans-for-freedom/.
(Accessed June 4, 2018.)

Fraternal Order of Alt-Knights

The Fraternal Order of Alt-Knights (FOAK) "was founded in 2017 by 'repeat-
felon' Kyle Chapman," to "protect and defend our right-wing brethren" through
"street activism, preparation, defense and confrontation" (Southern Poverty Law
Center). FOAK has been dubbed the "tactical arm" of the Proud Boys, a "far
right," "pro-Western fraternal organization for men who refuse to apologize for
creating the modern world" (Marantz). As one FOAK supporter noted, "The need
for defense has grown since recent premeditated attacks by the radical Marxist
group 'Anti-Fa' have become the norm at any cultural event politically to the right
of Jane Fonda" (Bazile). FOAK, who attend rallies "in homemade armor and
equipped with batons, hammers, daggers, tasers and pepper spray" always seem
to be spoiling for a fight. Though they claim that their presence at rallies is only in
defense of others' rights to articulate free speech from the far right, the group's
founder, Kyle Chapman, was heard to say at one rally, "Did anybody get to bash a

commie yet?" (Southern Poverty Law Center). For the Alt-Knights, "violence is the only way to eradicate what Chapman calls the 'unholy alliance' of 'globalism, radical Islam, and communism' that seeks to enslave white, Christian Americans and, in the process, destroy Western civilization" (Southern Poverty Law Center).

Kyle Chapman became a right-wing celebrity in March 2017 when,

> sporting a gas mask, ski goggles, bike helmet and homemade shield with a design inspired by a Ron Paul campaign logo—he beat a counter-protestor over the head with a wooden rod during the #March4Trump in Berkeley, California. Footage of the attack spread online, transforming Chapman into "Based Stick Man"—"based" referring to an indifference toward other's opinions, and "stick," of course, being his weapon of choice. The right quickly embraced Chapman, and images of Based Stick Man in his Berkeley armor were photo-shopped into scenes of Captain America, on the Gadsden flag, and into a painting of a charging Confederate army. (Southern Poverty Law Center)

Chapman's actions buoyed the spirits of so-called "alt-righters" who had been on their heels since a video of alt-right founder Richard Spencer being sucker punched at Donald Trump's inauguration had gone viral.

Upon founding FOAK in April 2017, Chapman partnered with the Proud Boys, a union he contended was "necessary for the progress of the movement: with violent 'neo-Marxists' stopping at nothing to destroy Western civilization, a contingent of men should be in place to defend against the ever-present threat" (Southern Poverty Law Center). Chapman has been quoted as saying that FOAK members should consider any rally they attend to be "open season on antifa" (the anti-right, leftist protesters who show up to counterprotest at alt-right rallies) and that members should "smash on sight" any antifa counterprotesters (Southern Poverty Law Center). At one rally in July 2017, Chapman tried to impress upon FOAK members "the necessity of sacrifice," saying, "You're going to have to come to the realization that you may have to bleed to keep this going . . . and you very may well have to die." He told the crowd, "I'm willing to die. Are you guys willing to die?" (Southern Poverty Law Center).

Though Chapman "claims not be a member of the Alt-Right, his beliefs and philosophies are consistent with those of the Alt-Right movement," which emphasize elements of white nationalism, white supremacy, and anti-Semitism (Southern Poverty Law Center). Chapman "hawks an anti-white guilt agenda,"

> arguing that white people "are the least racist and most generous ethnicity on the planet" and "the worst sufferers of racism in the world." He frequently cites an ongoing and intensifying war against whites, using the hashtags #WhiteGenocide and #TheWarAgainstWhitesIsReal. In August 2017 he outlined a supposed biological assault against Western men when he spoke at the "Make Men Great Again" event, warning they risk further decline due to low sperm mobility and birthrates, and implored men to stay away from BPA in plastics and to work out more in order to increase their testosterone levels. (Southern Poverty Law Center)

FOAK has "upwards of 42,000 Facebook followers, and more than 33,000 followers on Twitter" (Southern Poverty Law Center). Many of those who post on Facebook and Twitter "spout Islamophobic and anti-immigrant speech, recruit new members and mobilize followers to go to demonstrations where violence might erupt, taking advantage of the porous standards that social media companies set for offensive and violent speech" (Feuer and Peters). After the "Unite the Right" rally in Charlottesville, Virginia, in August 2017, in which Heather Heyer, an individual protesting the tenets of white supremacy being espoused at the rally, was hit and killed by a car, a meme appeared on FOAK's social media pages that showed George Washington "entering the car before it drove through counterprotestors and another that include[d] the caption 'Communism is bad for your health'" (Southern Poverty Law Center).

See also: Alt-Right; Proud Boys; White Nationalism; White Supremacist Movement

FURTHER READING

Bazile, Pawl. April 24, 2017. "The Kids Are Alt-Knights." Proud Boy Magazine. http://officialproudboys.com/news/the-kids-are-alt-knights/. (Accessed June 5, 2018.)

Buchanan, Susy. February 10, 2018. "From Memes to Marches: Why the Far Right Might Never Be 'United.'" Southern Poverty Law Center: Intelligence Report. https://www.splcenter.org/fighting-hate/intelligence-report/2018/memes-marches-why-far-right-might-never-be-%E2%80%98united%E2%80%99. (Accessed June 5, 2018.)

Feuer, Alan, and Jeremy W. Peters. June 2, 2017. "Fringe Groups Revel as Protests Turn Violent." *New York Times*. https://www.nytimes.com/2017/06/02/us/politics/white-nationalists-alt-knights-protests-colleges.html. (Accessed June 5, 2018.)

Kelly, Brendan Joel. February 16, 2018. "Turning Point USA's Blooming Romance with the Alt-Right." Southern Poverty Law Center: Hatewatch. https://www.splcenter.org/hatewatch/2018/02/16/turning-point-usas-blooming-romance-alt-right. (Accessed June 5, 2018.)

Marantz, Andrew. February 6, 2017. "Trump Supporters at the Deploraball." *New Yorker*. https://www.newyorker.com/magazine/2017/02/06/trump-supporters-at-the-deploraball. (Accessed June 5, 2018.)

Morlin, Bill. April 25, 2017. "New 'Fight Club' Ready for Street Violence." Southern Poverty Law Center: Hatewatch. https://www.splcenter.org/hatewatch/2017/04/25/new-fight-club-ready-street-violence. (Accessed June 5, 2018.)

Southern Poverty Law Center. "Fraternal Order of Alt-Knights (FOAK)." Southern Poverty Law Center. https://www.splcenter.org/fighting-hate/extremist-files/group/fraternal-order-alt-knights-foak. (Accessed June 5, 2018.)

St. John, Paige, and Veronica Rocha. April 27, 2017. "Conservative and Alt-Right Groups Gather for 'Free Speech' Rally in Berkeley." *Los Angeles Times*. http://www.latimes.com/local/california/la-live-updates-berkeley-ann-coulter-conservative-and-alt-right-groups-1493319826-htmlstory.html. (Accessed June 5, 2018.)

Fraternal Order of the Cross

The Fraternal Order of the Cross is a group based in Madison, Indiana, that "has been designated by the Southern Poverty Law Center (SPLC)" as a Ku Klux Klan (KKK) hate group. According to the SPLC, KKK groups "are the oldest and most infamous of American hate groups (Southern Poverty Law Center, March 2, 2015). Historically, black Americans have been the most frequent targets of KKK activity. Jews, gays and lesbians, and Catholics have also been the focus. In recent years, however, immigrants—particularly the issue of illegal immigration—has mobilized many KKK groups. This emphasis is attributable to the fear expressed among many KKK groups that white Americans are losing their traditional grip on power and that whites will soon be a minority in the United States.

In Indiana in September 2014, the Fraternal Order of the Cross distributed flyers targeting illegal immigrants. Ryan Lenz of the SPLC explained that the KKK has been fractured for decades "but is now hoping to capitalize on several race-themed news stories, such as the unrest in Ferguson, Missouri, in order to launch itself back into the public discourse" (Fentem). Lenz added, "They're looking to build, and they're looking to build fast." He said, "It seems we have a news background right now where they're hoping to take the news and use it to fuel their movement" (Fentem).

In 2017, the Fraternal Order of the Cross was no longer listed as active on the SPLC's Hate Group list (Southern Poverty Law Center, Ku Klux Klan).

See also: Brotherhood of Klans; Imperial Klans of America; Knights of the Ku Klux Klan; Ku Klux Klan

FURTHER READING

Fentem, Sarah. September 4, 2014. "Seymour KKK Fliers Part of National Trend." Indiana Public Media. https://indianapublicmedia.org/news/seymour-kkk-fliers-part-national-trend-71454/. (Accessed June 4, 2018.)

Southern Poverty Law Center. "Ku Klux Klan." Southern Poverty Law Center. https://www.splcenter.org/fighting-hate/extremist-files/ideology/ku-klux-klan. (Accessed June 4, 2018.)

Southern Poverty Law Center. March 2, 2015. "Active Ku Klux Klan Groups." Southern Poverty Law Center: Intelligence Report. https://www.splcenter.org/fighting-hate/intelligence-report/2015/active-ku-klux-klan-groups. (Accessed June 4, 2018.)

Southern Poverty Law Center. March 10, 2015. "Active Hate Groups in the United States in 2014." Southern Poverty Law Center: Intelligence Report. https://www.splcenter.org/fighting-hate/intelligence-report/2015/active-hate-groups-united-states-2014#kkk. (Accessed June 4, 2018.)

G

Gallows Tree Wotansvolk Alliance

Gallows Tree Wotansvolk Alliance is characterized as a neo-Volkisch hate group by the Southern Poverty Law Center (SPLC). Similar to neo-Nazis, neo-Volkisch extol the virtues of the white race over others and "argue that those of Germanic descent have always been superior" (Southern Poverty Law Center). Present-day neo-Volkisch adherents "couch their white supremacy in unfounded claims of bloodlines informing one's identity. At the cross-section of hypermasculinity and ethnocentrism, this movement seeks to defend against the baseless threats of the extermination of white people and their children" (Southern Poverty Law Center). Within the neo-Volkisch Movement:

> Hyper-masculine imagery fetishized within neo-Völkisch spheres reinforces misogyny and traditional gender roles. This degradation and disrespect of women, often couched in a cherishing of women as the keepers of the home, echoes broader trends within the so-called "alt-right" that derive from the virulently anti-woman "manosphere," the online blogosphere-turned-movement supposedly rescuing masculinity from rabid feminists and other forces of political correctness. (Southern Poverty Law Center)

The founder of Gallows Tree Wotansvolk Alliance, Michael Peters—who also goes by the name of "Ragnar Whiteson"—claims that his group has nothing to do with white nationalism or white supremacism. Rather, "[w]e consider ourselves a tribe, but basically we are a religious group that follows the religion of Wotanism" (VanGilder). Wotanism is a "neopaganist white separatist movement" founded by David Lane, a member of the neo-Nazi and white supremacist group the Order, as well as the author of the infamous 14 Words: "We must secure the existence of our people and a future for white children" (Anti-Defamation League). Peterson was convicted of arson in 1997, and he served nearly nine years in federal prison, where he claims he discovered his religion (VanGilder). On his neck is a tattoo that looks suspiciously like a swastika but that Peterson claims is "a shield from the side of a Viking ship" (VanGilder). And though he strikes a pose on his group's website with his right arm raised, Peterson claims that this "is not a salute to Hitler, but a work-out move. It's a work-out regime that I follow, and that is the symbol that they use" (VanGilder).

As a neo-Volkisch hate group, Gallows Tree Wotansvolk Alliance professes an urgency for preserving its "Folkish" ways. Though adherents "veil their ethnocentric beliefs in arguments for the necessity of separate societies, or tribes, to preserve all ethnicities," the group—like the movement—is, at its heart, racist, with one follower stating: "I will defend my race. I will fight for my race, primarily with words and ideas, but I will fight more literally if I have to" (Southern Poverty Law Center).

See also: Neo-Nazi; Neo-Volkisch; White Nationalism; White Supremacist Movement

FURTHER READING

Anti-Defamation League. "14 Words." Anti-Defamation League. https://www.adl.org
/education/references/hate-symbols/14-words. (Accessed June 6, 2018.)
CNN. August 17, 2017. "Southern Poverty Law Center Lists Active Hate Groups by
State." WMAR. https://www.wmar2news.com/news/national/southern-poverty
-law-center-lists-active-hate-groups-by-state. (Accessed June 6, 2018.)
South Side Chicago Anti-Racist Action. "Exposing Grand Rapids Nazi Michael Peterson
'Ragnar Whiteson.'" South Side Antifa. https://southsideantifa.blogspot.com
/2011/01/exposing-grand-rapids-nazi-michael.html. (Accessed June 6, 2018.)
Southern Minnesota News. August 14, 2017. "KKK to Black Separatist: 10 Hate Groups
in Minnesota." *Southern Minnesota News.* http://www.southernminnesotanews
.com/kkk-black-separatist-10-hate-groups-minnesota/. (Accessed June 6, 2018.)
Southern Poverty Law Center. "Neo-Volkisch." Southern Poverty Law Center. https://
www.splcenter.org/fighting-hate/extremist-files/ideology/neo-volkisch. (Accessed
June 6, 2018.)
VanGilder, Rachael. August 16, 2017. "Leader Denies Group Is Neo-Nazi: 'Witch Hunt.'"
WoodTV. http://www.woodtv.com/news/ottawa-county/alleged-hate-group-leader
-denies-nazi-affiliation/1003133897. (Accessed June 6, 2018.)
Wotan's Reich. "Gallows Tree." https://positivethoughtproject.blogspot.com/p/gallows
-tree.html. (Accessed June 6, 2018.)

Golden State Skinheads

The Golden State Skinheads (a.k.a. Golden State Solidarity) is a racist skinhead group based in California. According to the Southern Poverty Law Center (SPLC), racist skinheads "form a particularly violent element of the white supremacist movement, and have often been referred to as the 'shock troops' of the hoped-for revolution" (Southern Poverty Law Center). According to their website, the Golden State Skinheads are

> a crew of white nationalists that seeks to establish an all-white nation state. We regularly organize and attend state/nationwide events, protests and pro white shows. We are aggressively out spoken against those that wish to destroy our race and way of life. We oppose multiculturalism, globalization and Zionism. Our ultimate goal is to establish a state owned and inhabited exclusively by the White race where we may peacefully exist and prosper governing ourselves without alien influence. (Terrorism Research and Analysis Consortium)

In June 2016, violent confrontations took place between "various white nationalist and white supremacist groups, including the Golden State Skinheads (GSS)," and anti-fascist (antifa) protesters in Sacramento, California (Roberts). In the aftermath of the violence that took place in Sacramento, the U.S. Federal Bureau of Investigation (FBI) undertook an investigation of GSS and its members. After a year, the FBI "proceeded to start arresting members on rally related crimes whilst adding on a vast number of erroneous charges that we can only suspect as being falsified" (Golden State Skinheads, Sacramento Rally Backlash). In explaining its reasons for its members' presence at the Sacramento rally, GSS stated:

> It's no secret that the modern left-wing way of thinking is ultimately communism; this of course means that their views and motives are polar opposite of ours almost in their entirety. As members of G.S.S., we've spent many years fighting the ever-increasing tide of the communist and globalist agendas in the political arena that is destroying our nation at its core. We have made sure to carefully take every step to maintain a consistent legal and professional stance since our first day of inception. As "Skinheads" we have grown accustomed to the law not taking kindly to us and our views and in knowing this we've strived to maintain an above average standard of legality; far surpassing the degenerate left-wing opposition who seemingly oppose every active law and are openly encouraged to do so by main stream media and government officials. (Golden State Skinheads, Sacramento Rally Backlash)

In the aftermath of the charges brought against the group for its actions at Sacramento, the GSS stated, "We strongly believe we were in the right to defend ourselves and see this entire situation as obvious self defense." They also maintain that the FBI acts to "appease the public eye" and finds a "simpler avenue in 'crucifying' our members instead of addressing the real issues at hand" (Golden State Skinheads, Sacramento Rally Backlash).

See also: Racist Skinheads; White Nationalism; White Supremacist Movement

FURTHER READING

Anti-Defamation League. "Golden State Solidarity." Anti-Defamation League. https://www.adl.org/education/references/hate-symbols/golden-state-solidarity. (Accessed June 9, 2018.)

Golden State Skinheads. "About Us." Golden State Skinheads. http://goldenstateskinheads.org/us/. (Accessed June 9, 2018.)

Golden State Skinheads. "Sacramento Rally Backlash." http://goldenstateskinheads.org/. (Accessed June 12, 2018.)

Hankes, Keegan. June 27, 2016. "Violent Clashes Erupt in Sacramento between White Nationalists and Anti-Fascists." Southern Poverty Law Center: Hatewatch. https://www.splcenter.org/hatewatch/2016/06/27/violent-clashes-erupt-sacramento-between-white-nationalists-and-antifascists. (Accessed June 9, 2018.)

Roberts, Michael. February 2, 2018. "Potential Antifa v. Neo-Nazi Clash Looms Over CSU." Westword. https://www.westword.com/content/printView/9947640. (Accessed November 10, 2018.)

Sorci, Anthony. August 16, 2017. "States Listed with Most Hate Groups. Where Does California Rank?" *Sacramento Bee*. http://www.sacbee.com/news/local/article167274202.html. (Accessed June 9, 2018.)

Southern Poverty Law Center. "Racist Skinhead." Southern Poverty Law Center. https://www.splcenter.org/fighting-hate/extremist-files/ideology/racist-skinhead. (Accessed June 9, 2018.)

Southern Poverty Law Center. March 2, 2015. "Active Racist Skinhead Groups." Southern Poverty Law Center: Intelligence Report. https://www.splcenter.org/fighting-hate/intelligence-report/2015/active-racist-skinhead-groups. (Accessed June 9, 2018.)

Terrorism Research and Analysis Consortium. "Golden State Skinheads." https://www
.trackingterrorism.org/group/golden-state-skinheads. (Accessed June 9, 2018.)

Great Lakes Knights of the Ku Klux Klan

The Great Lakes Knights of the Ku Klux Klan ("Great Lakes Knights") is a Ku Klux Klan (KKK)-affiliated organization that has been designated by the Southern Poverty Law Center (SPLC) as a Ku Klux Klan hate group (Southern Poverty Law Center, 2017). According to the SPLC, "the KKK has a long history of violence in the United States" and "is the most infamous—and oldest—of American hate groups" (Southern Poverty Law Center, Ku Klux Klan). Although "black Americans have typically been the Klan's primary target, it also has attacked Jews, immigrants, gays and lesbians and, until recently, Catholics" (Southern Poverty Law Center, Ku Klux Klan).

The Great Lakes Knights continue to exist despite what the Anti-Defamation League (ADL) claims is a "continuing long-term trend of decline" in KKK ranks. The ADL notes "that there are only about 30 active KKK groups in the United States today" (Anti-Defamation League). Although most of them are "very small," the "association of Klan members with criminal activity has remained consistent" (Anti-Defamation League). According to the ADL:

> The long-term decline of Ku Klux Klan groups is due to several factors, including increasing societal rejection of what the Klan stands for; a growing perception by white supremacists that Klan groups are outdated; and competition with other white supremacist movements, from racist skinheads to white supremacist prison gangs, over the small pool of potential recruits. In recent years, one of the clearest signs of the declining state of Ku Klux Klan groups has been in their complete inability to maintain anything resembling stability. (Anti-Defamation League)

The Great Lakes Knights, formed in 2016, are among "the newer Klan groups [that] promote a traditional Klan ideology infused with neo-Nazi beliefs, continuing a trend from the early 2000s" (Anti-Defamation League). The Great Lakes Knights identify as a "Christian hate group" and "a group unlike other groups." Like some other KKK affiliates, the Great Lakes Knights "accept all Nazis and skin heads (sic) cause we have the same beliefs" (Anti-Defamation League).

The Great Lakes Knights of the Ku Klux Klan maintain a mailing address and a website based in Alpena, Michigan. On its website,

> the group describes itself as "a militant order of White Aryan patriots dedicated to living by the '14 words.'" Coined by the leader of a white supremacist terrorist group who died in prison, the "14 words" phrase is a slogan adopted by the majority of white supremacist groups around the world, which states, "We must secure the existence of our people and a future for white children." The term, according to the Anti Defamation League, reflects the white supremacist worldview in the late 20th century and early 21st centuries that unless immediate action is taken, the white race is doomed to extinction by an alleged "rising tide of color" purportedly controlled and manipulated by Jews.
> The Great Lakes group states on its website that it's a "brotherhood of politically motivated individuals" that welcomes both Christians and non-Christians and fully

subscribes to National Socialism. Membership, the group states, is open to any "White Aryan individual who is proud of their heritage and ready to fight to preserve their race." However, the site stipulates that members must be 18 or older and of "sound moral character," specifically heterosexual, against race mixing and without "any type of record of sexual assault, animal abuse or other crimes deemed inexcusable." (Elliott)

Soon after the white nationalist and white supremacist protests that occurred in Charlottesville, Virginia, in August 2017, Michigan State senator Curtis Hertel Jr. (D-East Lansing) sponsored a resolution, which was passed by the Michigan Senate, that denounced "radical hate groups, including white nationalist and neo-Nazi groups, and declare[d] them domestic terrorist organizations" (Senatedems). In referring to groups like the Great Lakes Knights of the Ku Klux Klan, Senator Hertel said, "We fought two of the deadliest wars in the history of this country against these ideologies, and we cannot allow homegrown extremists to revive such evil. The right to spew hatred is not protected when the goal is to limit the rights of others by ending their lives" (Senatedems).

See also: Ku Klux Klan; National Socialist Movement; Neo-Nazis; White Nationalism; White Supremacist Movement

FURTHER READING

Anti-Defamation League. "Tattered Robes: The State of the Ku Klux Klan in the United States." Anti-Defamation League. https://www.adl.org/education/resources/reports/state-of-the-kkk. (Accessed July 14, 2018.)

Dalbey, Beth. August 14, 2017. "28 Michigan Hate Groups, 10 Ways to Fight Them: Southern Poverty Law Center." Patch.com. https://patch.com/michigan/detroit/28-michigan-hate-groups-10-ways-fight-them-southern-poverty-law-center. (Accessed July 14, 2018.)

Elliott, Kevin. September 28, 2017. "A Catalog of Hate Groups Operating in Michigan." *Downtown News Magazine*. https://www.downtownpublications.com/single-post/2017/09/28/A-catalog-of-hate-groups-operating-in-Michigan. (Accessed July 14, 2018.)

Senatedems. September 6, 2017. "Senate Approves Sen. Hertel Resolution Declaring Neo-Nazi Groups as Terrorists." Senatedems.com. http://senatedems.com/hertel/2017/09/06/senate-approves-sen-hertel-resolution-declaring-neo-nazi-groups-as-terrorists/. (Accessed July 14, 2018.)

Southern Poverty Law Center. "Ku Klux Klan." Southern Poverty Law Center. https://www.splcenter.org/fighting-hate/extremist-files/ideology/ku-klux-klan. (Accessed July 14, 2018.)

Southern Poverty Law Center. February 15, 2017. "Active Hate Groups 2016." Southern Poverty Law Center: Intelligence Report. https://www.splcenter.org/fighting-hate/intelligence-report/2017/active-hate-groups-2016. (Accessed July 14, 2018.)

H

Hammerskin Nation

The Anti-Defamation League (ADL) has called Hammerskin Nation "the most violent and best-organized neo-Nazi skinhead group in the United States" (Anti-Defamation League). Also known as "Hammerskins," the group was formed in Dallas, Texas, in 1988 as a white supremacist group espousing the "14 Words" of former Order member David Lane: "We must secure the existence of our people and a future for White Children" (Hammerskin Nation). In their own words, Hammerskin Nation

> is a leaderless group of men and women who have adopted the White Power Skinhead lifestyle. We are blue collar workers, white collar professionals, college students, entrepreneurs, fathers and mothers. The Hammerskin brotherhood is way of achieving goals which we have all set for ourselves. These goals are many but can be summed up with one phrase consisting of 14 words. (Hammerskin Nation)

The group drew its inspiration from the 1979 rock album *The Wall* by the group Pink Floyd. The album was made into a film in 1982.

> The Wall tells the story of Pink, a rock singer who becomes a drug addict, loses his grip on reality and turns to fascism. Pink performs a song in which he expresses a desire to line all of the "queers," "Jews," and "coons" in his audience "up against the wall" and shoot them. In obvious references to the Holocaust, he sings of the "final solution" and "waiting to turn on the showers and fire the ovens." The swastika is replaced by Pink's symbol: two crossed hammers, which he boasts will "batter down" the doors behind which frightened minorities hide from his fascist supporters. (Anti-Defamation League)

Though a variety of neo-Confederate and racist skinhead groups were organized during the 1980s, there was little continuity among the groups, and even less leadership. As 1987 "drew to a close, a few skinheads got together after having become disillusioned with the state of the skinhead movement" (Hammerskin Nation). As they stated, "the White Power scene was coming into its own. Most of the skinheads in the [Dallas] area had grown up as such, educated themselves without the help of a central leader and soon realized they could create a force to be reckoned with if they formed a dynamic, focused and productive group" (Hammerskin Nation). Thus, the Hammerskin Nation was born. Since most of the founding members were from the South, the Confederate battle flag was embraced, and a logo was designed: "marching Hammers from Pink Floyd's movie, 'The Wall'" (White Prison Gangs). The logo, "depicting two claw hammers crossed to resemble goose-stepping legs," was paired with the Hammerskins' new motto: "Hammerskins Forever, Forever Hammerskins" (HFFH) (CRW Flags). Hammerskin

Nation embraced the racist message of *The Wall*, as well as its message of violence against minorities.

Hammerskin Nation soon realized that it could spread its message of hate through rock music. To this end, it organized concerts such as the "Summer of Hate" and the "Hammerfest, which became an annual event in both the United States and Europe" (CRW Flags). According to Ed Wolbank, past director of the Northern Hammerskins, "Music is number 1. It's the best way to reach people. Through music people can start getting into the scene, then you can start educating them. Politics through music" (Anti-Defamation League). Hate rock "has been both a powerful inspirational force and an effective recruiting tool for racist skinhead groups like the Hammerskins" (Anti-Defamation League).

At the height of its activities, Hammerskin Nation members committed crimes ranging from vandalism to arson to murder. Soon after its founding, "Hammerskins vandalized a synagogue and a Jewish community center by shooting out windows, smashing doors and spray painting anti-Semitic slogans and swastikas" (Anti-Defamation League). In 1991, a Hammerskin member "firebombed a residence he mistakenly thought was occupied by rival skinheads" (Anti-Defamation League). And in June 1991, three 16-year-old members of Hammerskin Nation "murdered an African American, Donald Thomas, while he sat on the back of a truck with two white friends" (Anti-Defamation League).

Throughout its violent history, Hammerskin Nation members have continued to brutalize minorities (particularly blacks), Jews, and immigrants. In 2001, a civil suit was filed against several Hammerskins, "their families, and the Hammerskin Nation." The suit alleged that Hammerskin Nation was a "street gang," as "defined by the California Penal Code, and describ[ed] the group as encouraging its members, 'to commit acts of violence and intimidation against African-Americans to promote their white supremacist goals'" (Anti-Defamation League).

Over the years, Hammerskin Nation has ebbed in its influence and membership. In 2003, racist skinheads Brien James and Eric "the Butcher" Fairburn formed the Vinlanders Social Club (VSC). Both James and Fairburn had been associated with the Outlaw Hammerskins, but they founded the VSC in order to challenge the parent organization of the Outlaws—Hammerskin Nation. By the time of the founding of VSC, Hammerskin Nation had "dominated the racist skinhead scene for more than a decade" (Southern Poverty Law Center). James had stated that the VSC "was to be something that was going to replace and surpass the old guard in the skinhead scene. Even by force if necessary" (Southern Poverty Law Center).

In 2016, Hammerskin Nation announced that a "Hammerfest" would be held in Georgia. The gathering was to feature white supremacist speakers, as well as "a prominent up-and-coming leader in the white power movement" (Atlanta Anarchist Black Cross). The gathering intended to "draw Hammerskin Nation members and supporters from across the country, as well as militants from other parts of the white power movement" (Atlanta Anarchist Black Cross). The "up-and-coming" leader turned out to be Matthew Heimbach, "head of the white nationalist and anti-Semitic Traditionalist Worker's Party," described by the Southern Poverty Law Center (SPLC) as a "movement gadfly" (Hatewatch staff).

Though Hammerskin Nation is not as prominent as it once was on the hate scene, its most committed members are fiercely loyal. Jimmy Matchette, a Hammerskin Nation member, stated:

Being a Hammerskin is the distinct feeling of being set apart from the entire planet. And of knowing we will conquer & overcome all obstacles to achieve our goals and accomplish our great work, knowing that if we fail, all is lost forever and the west will perish. Even though I am locked down in a maximum security federal penitentiary, I wouldn't [have] traded the opportunity for all the gold in the world. You my true comrades hold all the glory of victory at your fingertips. We really are the most notorious White power Skinhead group in the entire World! (Anti-Defamation League)

See also: Confederate Hammerskins; Crew 38; Eastern Hammerskins; Midland Hammerskins; Neo-Confederates; Neo-Nazis; Northern Hammerskins; Northwest Hammerskins; The Order; Traditionalist Worker Party; Vinlanders Social Club; Western Hammerskins; White Nationalism; White Supremacist Movement

FURTHER READING

Anti-Defamation League. "The Hammerskin Nation." Anti-Defamation League. https://www.adl.org/education/resources/profiles/hammerskin-nation. (Accessed June 2, 2018.)

Atlanta Anarchist Black Cross. August 24, 2016. "Neo-Nazi 'Hammerfest' Gathering Planned for Georgia, October 1st." It's Going Down. https://itsgoingdown.org/neo-nazi-hammerfest-gathering-planned-georgia-october-1st/. (Accessed June 2, 2018.)

Beirich, Heidi. November 20, 2013. "The End of Volksfront?" Southern Poverty Law Center: Intelligence Report. https://www.splcenter.org/fighting-hate/intelligence-report/2013/end-volksfront. (Accessed June 2, 2018.)

CRW Flags. "Hammerskin Nation (U.S.)." CRWFlags.com. https://www.crwflags.com/fotw/flags/us%7Dhs.html. (Accessed June 2, 2018.)

Hammerskin Nation. https://www.hammerskins.net/. (Accessed June 2, 2018.)

Hatewatch Staff. October 10, 2016. "Hate, Hypocrisy, and Head Wounds: Matthew Heimbach at Hammerfest." Southern Poverty Law Center: Hatewatch. https://www.splcenter.org/hatewatch/2016/10/10/hate-hypocrisy-and-head-wounds-matthew-heimbach-hammerfest. (Accessed June 2, 2018.)

Michaelis, Anno. June 25, 2015. "This Is How You Become a White Supremacist." *Washington Post*. https://www.washingtonpost.com/posteverything/wp/2015/06/25/this-is-how-you-become-a-white-supremacist/. (Accessed June 2, 2018.)

Reynolds, Michael. December 15, 1999. "Hammerskin Nation Emerges from Small Dallas Group." Southern Poverty Law Center: Intelligence Report. https://www.splcenter.org/fighting-hate/intelligence-report/1999/hammerskin-nation-emerges-small-dallas-group. (Accessed June 2, 2018.)

Southern Poverty Law Center. "Vinlanders Social Club." Southern Poverty Law Center. https://www.splcenter.org/fighting-hate/extremist-files/group/vinlanders-social-club. (Accessed May 29, 2018.)

White Prison Gangs. "Hammerskins." White Prison Gangs Blogspot. http://whiteprisongangs.blogspot.com/2009/05/hammerskins_02.html. (Accessed June 2, 2018.)

Holocaust Denial

Holocaust denial is an expression of anti-Semitism. Holocaust denial is intended to distort, misuse, and deny strategies meant to elicit public sympathy for the enormity of crimes committed against Jews and others during World War II, and it is meant "to undermine the legitimacy of the State of Israel—which some believe was created as compensation for Jewish suffering during the Holocaust—to plant seeds of doubt about Jews and the Holocaust, and to draw attention to particular issues or viewpoints" (United States Holocaust Memorial Museum). Through the Internet and the ease with which individuals and groups can access information, both real and fabricated, Holocaust denial can be conducted in anonymity or with seeming authoritative credentials. Key Holocaust denial assertions are

> that the murder of approximately six million Jews during World War II never occurred, that the Nazis had no official policy or intention to exterminate the Jews, and that the poison gas chambers in Auschwitz-Birkenau death camp never existed. Common distortions include, for example, assertions that the figure of six million Jewish deaths is an exaggeration and that the diary of Anne Frank is a forgery. (United States Holocaust Memorial Museum)

Scholars "use the term 'denial' to distinguish the views and methodologies of those who contend the Holocaust never happened from legitimate historical revisionists, who challenge orthodox interpretations of history using established historical methodologies" (McFee). Holocaust deniers don't usually identify themselves as deniers (just as terrorists rarely identify themselves as terrorists). Rather, they prefer to be known as revisionists, though revisionism is the reinterpretation of known and accepted facts. Holocaust deniers most likely fall into the category of "negationism," in that "Holocaust deniers attempt to rewrite history by minimizing, denying, or simply ignoring widely documented and accepted facts":

> Negationism means the denial of historical crimes against humanity. It is not a reinterpretation of known facts, but the denial of known facts. The term negationism has gained currency as the name of a movement to deny a specific crime against humanity, the Nazi genocide on the Jews in 1941–45, also known as the holocaust (Greek: complete burning) or the Shoah (Hebrew: disaster). Negationism is mostly identified with the effort at re-writing history in such a way that the fact of the Holocaust is omitted. (Elst)

Harry Elmer Barnes epitomizes Holocaust denial in the post–World War II era. Barnes, once considered a legitimate historian, "became convinced that allegations made against Germany and Japan, including the Holocaust, were fabrications used as wartime propaganda to justify U.S. involvement in World War II" (Shah). Several protégés of Barnes began to follow up on his theme and constructed elaborate theories and alternative explanations to the widely accepted facts associated with the Holocaust. The "publication of Arthur Butz's *The Hoax of the Twentieth Century: the Case Against the Presumed Extermination of European Jewry* in 1976; and David Irving's *Hitler's War* in 1977 brought other Holocaust deniers into the fold" (Lipstadt, 1994).

In 1996, "Irving filed a libel suit against Deborah Lipstadt and her publisher after the publication of her book, *Denying the Holocaust: The Growing Assault on Truth and Memory*" (Lipstadt, 2006). The trial, held in Great Britain, featured several witnesses for the defense who expertly provided compelling evidence of the reality of the Holocaust. Moreover, the witnesses were able to demonstrate that Irving had misrepresented and mischaracterized factual information in his writings, as well as knowingly "using forged documents as source material. The judge in the case ultimately delivered a verdict in favor of Lipstadt and referred to Irving as a 'Holocaust denier' and right-wing pro-Nazi polemicist" (Lipstadt, 2006).

Willis Carto, another well-known Holocaust denier, founded the Institute for Historical Review (IHR) in 1978. Though critics of the organization designate the IHR as engaged in "Holocaust denial," the IHR contends that it "does not 'deny' the Holocaust. Indeed, the IHR as such has no 'position' on any specific event or chapter of history, except to promote greater awareness and understanding, and to encourage more objective investigation" (IHR). Despite the IHR's protestations, a careful reading of its mission reveals that the IHR wished to "provide factual information" and "sound perspective" on "the Jewish-Zionist role in cultural and political life" (IHR). In 1980, "the IHR promised a $50,000 reward to anyone who could prove that Jews were gassed at Auschwitz" (Southern Poverty Law Center). When individuals came forward with definitive proof, including eyewitnesses who had lost family members in the camp, IHR refused to pay the amount. After lawsuits were instigated against IHR, a judgment against IHR was issued in the amount of $90,000 after a judge ruled that the existence of gas chambers at Auschwitz was "common knowledge" and therefore "did not require evidence that gas chambers, in fact, existed" (Nizkor Project). The judge in the case ruled that in addition to the monetary judgment, IHR had to "issue a letter of apology to the plaintiff, a survivor of Auschwitz-Birkenau and Buchenwald, and all other survivors of Auschwitz for 'pain, anguish and suffering' caused to them" (Nizkor Project).

Despite the rebuke, IHR continues to propagate Holocaust denial. In 1989, IHR published a piece by Lutheran pastor Herman Otten, in which he says:

> There is no dispute over the fact that large numbers of Jews were deported to concentration camps and ghettos, or that many Jews died or were killed during World War II. Revisionist scholars have presented evidence, which Exterminationists have not been able to refute, showing that there was no German program to exterminate Europe's Jews and that the estimate of six million Jewish wartime dead is an irresponsible exaggeration.
>
> The Holocaust, the alleged extermination of some six million Jews (most of them by gassing) is a hoax and should be recognized as such by Christians and all informed, honest and truthful men everywhere. (Otten)

Holocaust denial is not just a phenomenon among Westerners. Denials of the Holocaust "have been publicly perpetrated by various Middle Eastern figures and media" (Havardi). In 1983, Mahmoud Abbas, cofounder of Fatah and president of the Palestinian National Authority, published a book, entitled *The Other Side: The Secret Relationship between Nazism and Zionism*, based on his dissertation. Abbas denied that 6 million Jews had died in the Holocaust, "dismissing it as a 'myth' and a 'fantastic lie'" (Havardi). At most, he wrote, 890,000 Jews were killed by the Germans (Havardi). Organized Holocaust denial institutes have also been identified in Egypt, Qatar, and Saudi Arabia (Satloff). Former Iranian president Mahmoud Ahmadinejad is also a frequent Holocaust denier who formally questions the wealth of widely accepted facts related to the Holocaust. In December 2005, Ahmadinejad stated:

> They have fabricated a legend, under the name of the Massacre of the Jews, and they hold it higher than God himself, religion itself and the prophets themselves. . . . If somebody in their country questions God, nobody says anything, but if somebody denies the myth of the massacre of Jews, the Zionist loudspeakers and the governments in the pay of Zionism will start to scream. (Ahmadinejad)

Holocaust denial "is explicitly or implicitly illegal in 17 countries: Austria, Belgium, Czech Republic, France, Germany, Hungary, Israel, Liechtenstein, Lithuania, Luxembourg, Netherlands, Poland, Portugal, Romania, Russia, Slovakia, and Switzerland" (Bazyler). In January 2007, "the United Nations General Assembly condemned 'without reservation any denial of the Holocaust,' though Iran disassociated itself from the resolution" (United Nations).

As noted by author Deborah Lipstadt, "Holocaust denial is a virulent form of anti-Semitism. But it is not only that." She explains, "It is also an attack on reasoned inquiry and inconvenient history. If this history can be denied any history can be denied."

> Holocaust deniers have, thus far, been decidedly unsuccessful in convincing the broader public of their claims—although many people worry that after the last of the Holocaust survivors has died (most are now in their 80s) deniers will achieve greater success. However, historians, carefully relying on a broad array of documentary and material evidence . . . can and already have demonstrated that Holocaust denial is a tissue of lies. (Lipstadt, 2011)

See also: Barnes Review; Institute for Historical Review

FURTHER READING

Ahmadinejad. December 14, 2005. "Ahmadinejad: Holocaust a Myth." Al Jazeera. http://www.aljazeera.com/archive/2005/12/200849154418141136.html. (Accessed June 27, 2018.)

Anti-Defamation League. "The Holocaust: Global Awareness and Denial." Anti-Defamation League: Global 100. http://global100.adl.org/info/holocaust_info. (Accessed June 27, 2018.)

Bazyler, Michael J. "Holocaust Denial Law and Other Legislation Criminalizing Promotion of Nazism." *Yad Vashem*. http://www.yadvashem.org/holocaust/holocaust-antisemitism/articles/holocaust-denial-laws. (Accessed June 27, 2018.)

Elst, Koenraad. 2014. *Negationism in India: Concealing the Record of Islam*. Voice of India.

Green, Emma. May 14, 2014. "The World Is Full of Holocaust Deniers." *Atlantic*. https://www.theatlantic.com/international/archive/2014/05/the-world-is-full-of-holocaust-deniers/370870/. (Accessed June 27, 2018.)

Havardi, Jeremy. August 14, 2012. "Holocaust Denial Undermines the Palestinian Cause." *Commentator.* http://www.thecommentator.com/article/1524/holocaust_denial_un dermines_the_palestinian_cause. (Accessed June 27, 2018.)

IHR. "About the IHR: Our Mission and Record." *Institute for Historical Review.* http:// www.ihr.org/main/about.shtml. (Accessed June 27, 2018.)

Jewish Virtual Library. "Holocaust Denial: Background & Overview." Jewish Virtual Library. https://www.jewishvirtuallibrary.org/background-and-overview-of-holo caust-denial. (Accessed June 27, 2018.)

Lipstadt, Deborah. 1994. *Denying the Holocaust: The Growing Assault on Truth and Memory.* Plume.

Lipstadt, Deborah. 2006. *History on Trial: My Day in Court with a Holocaust Denier.* Harper Perennial.

Lipstadt, Deborah. February 17, 2011. "Denying the Holocaust." BBC. http://www.bbc.co .uk/history/worldwars/genocide/deniers_01.shtml. (Accessed June 27, 2018.)

McFee, Gord. "Why Revisionism Isn't." PHDN.org. http://phdn.org/archives/holocaust -history.org/revisionism-isnt/. (Accessed June 27, 2018.)

Nizkor Project. Shofar FTP Archive File: people/m/mermelstein.mel//mermelstein.order. 072285. Nizkor Project. http://www.nizkor.org/ftp.cgi/people/m/mermelstein.mel /ftp.py?people/m/mermelstein.mel//mermelstein.order.072285. (Accessed June 27, 2018.)

Otten, Herman. "Christianity, Truth and Fantasy: The Holocaust, Historical Revisionism and Christians Today." Institute for Historical Review. http://www.ihr.org/jhr/v09 /v09p321_otten.html. (Accessed June 27, 2018.)

Satloff, Robert. October 8, 2006. "The Holocaust Arab Heroes." *Washington Post.* http:// www.washingtonpost.com/wp-dyn/content/article/2006/10/06/AR20061006 01417.html. (Accessed June 27, 2018.)

Shah, Zia H. September 18, 2012. "Holocaust Denial: Limits of Free Speech?" Muslim Times. https://themuslimtimes.info/2012/09/18/holocaust-denial-limits-of-free-spe ech/. (Accessed November 10, 2018.)

Southern Poverty Law Center. "Holocaust Denial." Southern Poverty Law Center. https:// www.splcenter.org/fighting-hate/extremist-files/ideology/holocaust-denial. (Accessed June 27, 2018.)

United Nations. "UN General Assembly Condemns Holocaust Denial by Consensus; Iran Disassociates Itself." UN News Centre. http://www.un.org/apps/news/story.asp?N ewsID=21355&Cr=holocaust&Cr1#.WTGTWNylvRY. (Accessed June 27, 2018.)

United States Holocaust Memorial Museum. "Holocaust Denial and Distortion." United States Holocaust Memorial Museum. https://www.ushmm.org/confront-antisemi tism/holocaust-denial-and-distortion. (Accessed June 27, 2018.)

I

Identity Evropa

Identity Evropa (IE), pronounced "Europa," is an organization that associates itself with the "Identitarian" movement, whose stated purpose is the preservation of Western (European white) culture. The Southern Poverty Law Center (SPLC) has noted that

> Identity Evropa is at the forefront of the racist "alt-right's" effort to recruit white, college-aged men and transform them into the fashionable new face of white nationalism. Rather than denigrating people of color, the campus-based organization focuses on raising white racial consciousness, building community based on shared racial identity and intellectualizing white supremacist ideology. (Southern Poverty Law Center, Identity Evropa)

The SPLC characterizes IE as a "white nationalist hate group," while the Anti-Defamation League (ADL) labels the organization as a "white supremacist group focused on the preservation of 'white American culture' and promoting white European identity" (Anti-Defamation League). According to the ADL, IE promulgates "the idea that America was founded by white people for white people and was not intended to be a multiracial or multicultural society."

> In that vein, they [IE] adopted and popularized the white supremacist slogan "You will not replace us," which is a substitute for the better-known white supremacist motto the "14 words." Both phrases reflect the white supremacist worldview that unless immediate action is taken, the white race is doomed to extinction at the hands of an alleged "rising tide of color," which is purportedly controlled and manipulated by Jews. (Anti-Defamation League)

IE was founded in 2016 by Nathan Damigo, a veteran of the Iraq War who was raised in California. In his youth, Damigo stated that he always felt out of place in the multicultural landscape that was San Jose, his hometown. "There were all of these different neighborhoods and I noticed that many of my friends who were non-white—were perhaps Filipino or something like that—they had their own cultures and a very tight-knit kind of group thing going on," Damigo said (Southern Poverty Law Center, Identity Evropa). It wasn't until Damigo joined the Marines at age 18 that "Damigo recalls feeling more at ease in the predominantly white environment of his training class." In the Marines, Damigo recalls, he finally felt for the first time that he was surrounded "by people from similar backgrounds. . . . Damigo describes his time in the military as important to his first steps down the road toward white nationalism, describing himself at the time as 'race aware' but not 'race conscious'" (Southern Poverty Law Center, Nathan Benjamin Damigo).

In November 2007, "just a month after returning home from active service," Damigo "went out drinking following the anniversary of the death of one of his friends and fellow soldiers" (Southern Poverty Law Center, Nathan Benjamin Damigo). At the end of the night, Damigo "pulled a loaded gun on an innocent man who 'looked Iraqi,' robbing him of $43 before being arrested and convicted for armed robbery in relation to the incident" (Southern Poverty Law Center, Nathan Benjamin Damigo). Following his arrest, "Damigo was given an Other Than Honorable (OTH) discharge from the Marines," and he pleaded guilty to the armed robbery charge and received a reduced sentence of five years. While in prison, "upon the suggestion of a fellow inmate, Damigo read David Duke's *My Awakening* and became a committed ethno-nationalist" (Southern Poverty Law Center, Nathan Benjamin Damigo).

Once released from prison, Damigo looked for an organization that was "explicitly pro-white." Not find a group that satisfied the criteria for which he was looking,

> [he] found himself inspired by the growing cadre of identitarians in Europe. The youth-led movement is the ideological offspring of the French New Right, or Nouvelle Droite, a far-right faction that formed in academic circles in the late 1960s. The New Right's opposition to multiculturalism, paired with its emphasis on European identity and localism, helped inspire a new generation of European far-right activists reacting to increasing non-European immigration in the early 2000s. (Southern Poverty Law Center, Identity Evropa)

Damigo founded IE in March 2016, using "white supremacist imagery and language." IE's logo is a

> blue or white dragon's eye, an ancient European symbol that represents the choice between good and evil. For their posters and fliers, IE often uses black and white images of sculptures, including Michelangelo's statue of David and Nicolas Coustou's Julius Caesar. These classic European images are accompanied by variably subtle white supremacist messages: "Our destiny is ours," "White people do something," "Our future belongs to us," "Only we can be us," "Let's become great again," "Serve your people" and "Protect your heritage." (Anti-Defamation League)

Members of IE are "heavily vetted and must be of 'European, non-Semitic heritage" (Southern Poverty Law Center, Identity Evropa).

According to the SPLC, IE was "founded with two goals in mind: first, to occupy both figurative and literal space with their ideas and, second, to build 'European identity and solidarity'" (Southern Poverty Law Center, Identity Evropa). To this end, Damigo committed the group to eschewing the normal trappings of white nationalism and white supremacy (e.g., swastikas, skinhead looks, robes, burning crosses, and Nazi salutes) in favor of a more sophisticated and dignified look. Moreover, IE was determined to change the rhetoric of the national conversation to "make the racist label meaningless" (Southern Poverty Law Center, Identity Evropa). Thus,

> the group not only promised to recruit young people to the movement, but to lend the alt-right a veneer of respectability by counting among their followers college-aged men in khakis. And colleges, of course, stand at the frontlines of the cultural

and political battles waged by the alt-right. Damigo has stated that college campuses are IE's "number one target" because they represent "the epicenter of cultural Marxism in America." In other words, colleges—one of the institutions non-whites "are actively trying to disenfranchise us from"—are attempting to subvert real American values and spread "anti-white rhetoric." So-called race realists, he and Spencer believe, deserve a seat at the seminar table. (Southern Poverty Law Center, Identity Evropa)

IE's membership increased dramatically after the election of Donald Trump, with Damigo claiming that Trump "would be very beneficial for people of European heritage" and that, as president, Trump would be "the closest to us that we've ever had in recent memory" (Southern Poverty Law Center, Identity Evropa). When an interviewer pointed out the racist overtones in IE's message, an IE member "loyally repeated one of Damigo's talking points": "I think those slurs like 'racist,' 'white supremacist,' 'Nazi,' these are anti-white slurs'" (Southern Poverty Law Center, Identity Evropa).

Despite its claim that "Identity Evropa is an explicitly non-violent organization" (Identity Evropa, About Us), Damigo and IE helped plan the events of the "Unite the Right" rally in Charlottesville, Virginia, in August 2017 (Southern Poverty Law Center, Identity Evropa). But the negative backlash that came from the rally, particularly because of the death of a counterprotester due to the actions of an alleged white supremacist sympathizer, was unwelcome to IE and the image that it wished to cultivate. In fact, in the words of one journalist:

> For all the publicity alt-right groups receive for cross burnings and tiki-torch protests, their [IE's] ultimate goal is to become invisible, inserting themselves into the mainstream political process. Groups like I.E. adopt the business casual uniforms of polo shirts and khakis, and have strict rules against using "vulgar language" or mentioning "divisive topics" like National Socialism or the Third Reich. The rule prohibiting "vulgar language" states that "in order to foster a more positive culture for our people's future, the use of crude and unbecoming language is not permitted. This includes, without limitation, excessive cursing, and any use of vulgar racial epithets." (Argyle)

Today, IE's main objective "is to create a better world for people of European heritage—particularly in America—by peacefully effecting cultural change."

> As Identitarians, we believe that identity matters, inequality is a fact of life, and ethnic diversity, as demonstrated by substantial historical and sociological evidence, is an impediment to societal harmony. Unfortunately, the fetishization of diversity has resulted in a paradigm wherein "less White people"—in academia, employment, and countries overall—is accepted as a moral imperative. We categorically reject this "progressive" morality and instead demand that we, people of European heritage, retain demographic supermajorities in our homelands.
>
> While the SPLC and the ADL may smear us as "White supremacists", this is not the case. We are not supremacists because we do not believe that White people should rule over non-White people. Rather, we are ethno-pluralists: We believe that all ethnic and racial groups should have somewhere in the world to call home— a place wherein they can fully express themselves and enjoy self-determination. Even the Left generally agrees with this assertion, so long as people of European heritage are excluded. (Identity Evropa, About Us)

By its own accounts, "Identity Evropa had roughly 1,000 members during the first month of 2018" and aimed to have 5,000 members by the end of 2018 (Southern Poverty Law Center, Identity Evropa).

See also: Alt-Right Movement; Identity Vanguard; White Nationalism; White Supremacist Movement

FURTHER READING

Anti-Defamation League. "Identity Evropa." Anti-Defamation League. https://www.adl .org/resources/profiles/identity-evropa. (Accessed August 3, 2018.)

Argyle, Samuel. June 12, 2018. "My Weekend with White Nationalists." Outline. https:// theoutline.com/post/4907/my-weekend-with-white-nationalists-convention-iden tity-evropa. (Accessed August 3, 2018.)

Bauer, Shane. May 9, 2017. "I Met the White Nationalist Who 'Falcon Punched' a 95-Pound Female Protestor." *Mother Jones*. https://www.motherjones.com/poli tics/2017/05/nathan-damigo-punching-woman-berkeley-white-nationalism/. (Accessed August 3, 2018.)

Branson-Potts, Hailey. December 7, 2016. "In Diverse California, a Young White Supremacist Seeks to Convert Fellow College Students." *Los Angeles Times*. http://www .latimes.com/local/lanow/la-me-ln-nathan-damigo-alt-right-20161115-story.html. (Accessed August 3, 2018.)

Ellis, Emma Grey. May 22, 2017. "Your Handy Field Guide to the Many Factions of the Far Right, from the Proud Boys to Identity Evropa." Wired.com. https://www .wired.com/2017/05/field-guide-far-right/. (Accessed August 3, 2018.)

Hatewatch Staff. March 15, 2018. "Identity Evropa Holds Its First National Conference Setting Off a Dispute over Who Represents the Future of the Alt-Right." Southern Poverty Law Center: Hatewatch. https://www.splcenter.org/hatewatch/2018/03/15 /identity-evropa-holds-its-first-national-conference-setting-dispute-over-who -represents. (Accessed August 3, 2018.)

Identity Evropa. https://www.identityevropa.com/. (Accessed August 2018.)

Identity Evropa. "About Us." Identity Evropa. https://www.identityevropa.com/about-us. (Accessed August 3, 2018.)

Shukman, Harry. February 15, 2017. "Meet the Neo-Nazi Coming to Put Up White Pride Posters on Your Campus." Tab. https://thetab.com/us/2017/02/15/nathan-damigo -identity-evropa-60697. (Accessed August 3, 2018.)

Southern Poverty Law Center. "Identity Evropa." Southern Poverty Law Center. https:// www.splcenter.org/fighting-hate/extremist-files/group/identity-evropa. (Accessed August 3, 2018.)

Southern Poverty Law Center. "Nathan Benjamin Damigo." Southern Poverty Law Center. https://www.splcenter.org/fighting-hate/extremist-files/individual/nathan-ben jamin-damigo. (Accessed August 3, 2018.)

Southern Poverty Law Center. "White Nationalist." Southern Poverty Law Center. https:// www.splcenter.org/fighting-hate/extremist-files/ideology/white-nationalist. (Accessed August 3, 2018.)

Identity Vanguard

Identity Vanguard (IV), based in Grovetown, Georgia, was founded in July 2015 to fight "against a 'new tyranny' in the United States—multiculturalism and political correctness" (Hankes). The group was started by Joshua Bates, a former marine turned web developer. Bates claims that IV is a "cultural preservation organization" and that "his group is designed to take to the streets to protect white identity" (Hankes). IV is part of a larger movement known as "Identitarianism," a movement "born in France in recent years that preaches opposition to multiculturalism, often taking shape in the form of anti-Muslim xenophobia" (Hatewatch staff, 2015). While Identitarian groups

> on both sides of the Atlantic claim their opposition to multiculturalism isn't racist, their direct action tactics and end goals indicate otherwise. Put simply, identitarians want regions and nations that are different from one another—but at the same time culturally and ethnically homogenous within their borders. (Hatewatch staff, 2015)

According to the Southern Poverty Law Center (SPLC):

> The ideological roots of the Identitarian movement go back to the French "New Right," and mix elements of European chauvinism, biological determinism, fierce localism and even typically left-wing ideas like Swiss-style direct democracy and criticism of capitalism. Still, the eminent scholar of fascism, Walter Laqueur, has described it as fundamentally a doctrine closely related to fascism.
>
> Its organizational expression came, in the early 2000s, in Generation Identitaire, the youth wing of the Bloc Identitaire, a French anti-immigrant coalition that also opposes "imperialism, whether it be American or Islamic." Bloc Identitaire became known in recent years for trying to serve "identity soups" in Muslim neighborhoods. The soups, containing pork which practicing Muslims cannot eat, were a mocking publicity stunt that drew widespread accusations of racism and xenophobia. (Hatewatch staff, 2015)

Identitarianism has ideological roots with the racist skinhead movement:

> Like their skinhead forebearers, the Identitarians position themselves as "nationalist-revolutionary." They call for cultural rootedness and local economic and political independence from globalization, all the while framing far-right demands—such as their call for the "remigration" of Muslims and immigrants—as a defensive civilizational quest. When they yell out "Sainte Geneviève is with us," Identitarians attempt to show themselves as young patriots stepping up where institutions have failed, a very deliberate strategy to mainstream their hateful narrative. (Hatewatch staff, 2018)

Identity Vanguard's ideology has taken a "militaristic tone," proclaiming to be "creative, proud, insolent and rebellious youth on the frontline" (Hankes). IV's leader, Joshua Bates, has argued that "affirmative action is racist" (Hankes). According to Bates:

> Whites have much more to worry about than anti-White discrimination in the form of Affirmative Action. We as Whites need to use these cases to tear the wool from the eyes of our kin and expose the numerous and varying manners in which our detractors are attempting to steal both our country and identity away from us. (Hankes)

Though the notion of Identitarianism has been picked up by various groups, including the alt-right movement, there is at least one scholar who does not see the movement as having much staying power in the United States. Cas Mudde, "a Dutch scholar and long-time analyst of the European radical right who now teaches at the University of Georgia," has stated:

I don't see much of a future for the Identitarian movement in the U.S. The American radical right is built entirely around the idea of race, whereas the European version increasingly emphasizes local ethnic and cultural identities within a European framework—what one nationalist from the French region of Brittany calls the "Europe of 100 flags." (Hatewatch staff, 2015)

See also: Alt-Right Movement; Identity Evropa; Racist Skinheads; Traditionalist Youth Network

FURTHER READING

Hankes, Keegan. November 12, 2015. "Identifying the Vanguard: A Georgia Web Developer Is Organizing Another Identitarian-Inspired Outfit." Southern Poverty Law Center: Hatewatch. https://www.splcenter.org/hatewatch/2015/11/12/identifying-vanguard-georgia-web-developer-organizing-another-identitarian-inspired-outfit. (Accessed July 31, 2018.)

Hatewatch Staff. October 12, 2015. "American Racists Work to Spread 'Identitarian' Ideology." Southern Poverty Law Center: Hatewatch. https://www.splcenter.org/hatewatch/2015/10/12/american-racists-work-spread-%E2%80%98identitarian%E2%80%99-ideology. (Accessed July 31, 2018.)

Hatewatch Staff. February 14, 2018. "How to Write like an Identitarian." Southern Poverty Law Center: Hatewatch. https://www.splcenter.org/hatewatch/2018/02/14/how-write-history-identitarian. (Accessed August 1, 2018.)

Imperial Klans of America

The Imperial Klans of America (IKA) is a white supremacist organization modeled after the original Ku Klux Klan (KKK). The IKA targets "Jews, homosexuals, blacks, Latinos, and so-called race traitors" (Southern Poverty Law Center). The group predicts the "end of the white race by the year 2100 if white hate groups do not mobilize and unite to protect racial purity" (Terrorism Research & Analysis Consortium). The beliefs of the IKA derive from Christian Identity, whose adherents believe that white people are God's chosen people and that Jews are the result of a union between Satan and Eve. The IKA claims that "[h]istory, archaeology, and the Bible now prove that ancient Anglo-Saxon-Celtic-Scythian people are all Caucasian descendants of the House of Israel" (Terrorism Research & Analysis Consortium). Until the late 2000s, the IKA was one of the largest Klan groups in the United States, but its assets and membership were severely affected by "a $2.5 million judgment against its leader and several followers in 2008," which greatly diminished the scope and influence of the organization (Southern Poverty Law Center).

The IKA is headed by Ron Edwards and claims to be part of the sixth incarnation of the KKK and, like Klan groups of previous eras, contends that its constitutional right as an "unorganized militia" applies to the group (Southern Poverty Law Center). The group is headquartered in Dawson Springs, Kentucky, but claims to have affiliates in Australia, Canada, England, Scotland, and South Africa, as well as other countries in Europe and South America. The "Dawson Springs compound serves as the venue for an annual racist music festival" that attracts a variety of white supremacist groups, as well as "skinheads, neo-Nazis, and other Ku Klux Klan groups." At a 2006 festival, a brawl between rival skinhead groups marred the festivities, as IKA security allowed the warring racists to fight it out (Southern Poverty Law Center).

In recent years, IKA has focused on the bogeyman of illegal immigration to whip up racist sentiments among its members. In July 2006, two IKA members "attacked Jordan Gruver, a 16-year-old who was enjoying the Meade County Fair in Brandenburg, Kentucky" (Southern Poverty Law Center). The IKA members, believing Gruver to be a Latino, hurled racial slurs such as "spic" at him during their attack. Gruver "was beaten to the ground and kicked with steel-toed boots" (Southern Poverty Law Center). Gruver, who weighed 150 pounds, was brutally attacked, with one of his attackers standing six feet five inches tall and weighing 330 pounds. The IKA members "cracked Gruver's ribs, broke his arm and broke his jaw. The IKA members were later sentenced to three-year prison terms for the attack" (Southern Poverty Law Center).

The Southern Poverty Law Center (SPLC) filed a civil rights lawsuit again the IKA in July 2007, naming founder Ron Edwards and several ranking members of the IKA as defendants. During the trial, Edwards defended his racist views on the basis that they were "only words and symbols, and that no matter how offensive his views might be to others, he had the constitutional right to freedom of speech." He said, "Nobody in America should be persecuted for what they believe in" (Southern Poverty Law Center).

But the SPLC "made the case that First Amendment protections did not immunize Edwards and the IKA from violent activities" (Southern Poverty Law Center). A recitation of the criminal histories of IKA members followed, with SPLC lawyers arguing that IKA enlisted men with violent histories to seek out others with similar backgrounds as new recruits. The SPLC argued that, rather than trying to control his recruits, Edwards and the IKA sought to perpetrate violence (Southern Poverty Law Center).

The trial was held in November 2008. The jury returned a verdict against Edwards and the IKA, finding that Edward had failed to properly supervise his members "and that he had encouraged violence. The jury awarded just over $1.5 million in compensatory damages and $1 million in punitive damages to Gruver" (Southern Poverty Law Center). The judgment essentially bankrupted IKA, bringing down what was once the second largest Klan group in the United States (Southern Poverty Law Center).

A post on the racist website Stormfront in December 2014 noted that IKA was still in existence and that Ron Edwards was reportedly out of prison and would "probably" resume leadership of the group once he was no longer on home confinement (Stormfront).

See also: Christian Identity; Ku Klux Klan; Neo-Nazis; Racist Skinheads; Stormfront; White Supremacist Movement

FURTHER READING

Southern Poverty Law Center. "Imperial Klans of America." Southern Poverty Law Center. https://www.splcenter.org/fighting-hate/extremist-files/group/imperial-klans-america. (Accessed May 30, 2017.)

Stormfront. December 30, 2014. "Is the Imperial Klans of America Still Active?" Stormfront. https://www.stormfront.org/forum/t1079808/. (Accessed May 30, 2017.)

Terrorism Research & Analysis Consortium. "Imperial Klans of America, Knights of the Ku Klux Klan (IKA)." Terrorism Research & Analysis Consortium. https://www.trackingterrorism.org/group/imperial-klans-america-knights-ku-klux-klan-ika. (Accessed May 30, 2017.)

Institute for Historical Review

The Institute for Historical Review (IHR) was founded in 1978 by Willis Carto, an individual "infamous for his pro-Nazi and rabidly anti-Jewish views" (Southern Poverty Law Center, Willis Carto). According to its website, the IHR claims to "provide factual information and sound perspective on US foreign policy, World War Two, the Israel-Palestine conflict, war propaganda, Middle East history, the Jewish-Zionist role in cultural and political life, and much more" (Institute for Historical Review). The IHR is most often criticized for its position that the Holocaust was a fabrication and never, in fact, took place. This position and IHR's associations with neo-Nazi organizations cause others to view IHR as an anti-Semitic organization. Many writers who post their pieces on the IHR website state that their primary focus is to deny or reinterpret key facts related to Nazism and the genocide of the Jews. The IHR insists that its work tends toward "revisionism" of Holocaust material, opposed to denial of such material:

> The Institute does not "deny the Holocaust." Every responsible scholar of twentieth century history acknowledges the great catastrophe that befell European Jewry during World War II. All the same, the IHR has over the years published detailed books and numerous probing essays that call into question aspects of the orthodox, Holocaust-extermination story, and highlight specific Holocaust exaggerations and falsehoods. (Institute for Historical Review)

Barbara Kulaszka, a contributor to IHR, "defends the distinction between 'denial' and 'revisionism' by arguing that considerable revisions have been made over time of most historical material" and concludes: "For purposes of their own, powerful, special-interest groups desperately seek to keep substantive discussion of the Holocaust story taboo. One of the ways they do this is by purposely mischaracterizing revisionist scholars as 'deniers' " (Kulaszka).

The IHR was spun off from Willis Carto's blatantly anti-Semitic Liberty Lobby. The IHR "presented itself as a legitimate historical research group by hijacking the revisionist term that was being used by historians at the time to reinterpret the origins of World War I" (Southern Poverty Law Center, Institute for Historical Reviews). But the "revisionist" movement associated with studies of the Holocaust supported by the IHR "was made up of white supremacists and neo-Nazis, and it would draw expertise from the like-minded around the world. Its mission was to erase the Holocaust by any means at its disposal—including distortion, misquotation and outright falsification" (Southern Poverty Law Center, Institute for Historical Review).

The first annual conference of the IHR attracted Holocaust deniers from around the world in 1979. David Duke, "who was then the leader of the Knights of the Ku Klux Klan," was so enamored with the IHR's historical revisionist mission that he devoted a special issue of his publication to the question (Southern Poverty Law Center, Institute for Historical Review). Moreover, the leader of the National Socialist Party of America embraced the IHR's mission by stating, "There was no Holocaust, but they deserve one—and will get it" (Southern Poverty Law Center, Institute for Historical Review).

Though the IHR was to outside observers blatantly anti-Semitic, it attempted to soften its views by applying a pseudoacademic gloss to its reports. In the *Journal of Historical Review*, the IHR published a number of Holocaust denial claims, including ones that Anne Frank's diary was a fraud, that death camp ovens were incapable of burning the volume of bodies claimed by the allies, and that the "quality of Zyklon B gas used to kill the Jews" was not of high enough quality to exterminate in the numbers claimed. Through it all, "IHR sought to give the appearance that its writers were honest, if skeptical, students of history" (Southern Poverty Law Center, Institute for Historical Review).

In 1993, Mark Weber, who was "former news editor of the National Alliance's neo-Nazi publication, the *National Vanguard*," wrested control of the IHR from Carto (Granberry). Weber and other IHR leaders eventually sued Carto, contending that Carto had embezzled some $10 million from the IHR. In 1996, "IHR won a $6.4 million judgment against Carto" (Granberry). Carto would go on to found other publications, in which he referred to Weber as a "rat," "cockroach," and the "devil."

The fight between the IHR and Carto took a toll on the organization. By 2003, the organization's *Journal of Historical Review* ceased publication, and the annual conferences hosted by the IHR were reduced from lavish, multiday affairs with dozens of speakers to "small, one-day affairs with a couple of speakers." A major blow came in 2009 when "Weber decided to downgrade Holocaust denial in favor of criticizing Jews and Israel. Weber was viciously attacked by several important revisionists, many of whom called for his resignation from IHR" (Southern Poverty Law Center, Institute for Historical Review). Today, Weber maintains control of IHR, but the organization clearly does not have the influence among extremists that it once had.

See also: Holocaust Denial; Neo-Nazis; White Supremacist Movement

FURTHER READING

Anti-Defamation League. "Willis Carto." Anti-Defamation League. https://www.adl.org/sites/default/files/documents/assets/pdf/combating-hate/Willis-Carto-Extremism-in-America.pdf. (Accessed April 29, 2018.)

Granberry, Michael. November 16, 1996. "Jude Awards $6.4 Million to O.C. Revisionist Group." *Los Angeles Times*. http://articles.latimes.com/1996-11-16/local/me-65105_1_judge-awards. (Accessed April 29, 2018.)

Institute for Historical Review. "About the IHR: Our Mission and Record." Institute for Historical Review. http://www.ihr.org/main/about.shtml. (Accessed April 29, 2018.)

Kulaszka, Barbara. "What Is 'Holocaust Denial'?" Institute for Historical Review. http://www.ihr.org/leaflets/denial.shtml. (Accessed April 29, 2018.)

Southern Poverty Law Center. "Institute for Historical Review." Southern Poverty Law Center. https://www.splcenter.org/fighting-hate/extremist-files/group/institute-historical-review. (Accessed April 29, 2018.)

Southern Poverty Law Center. "Willis Carto." Southern Poverty Law Center. https://www.splcenter.org/fighting-hate/extremist-files/individual/willis-carto. (Accessed April 29, 2018.)

International Keystone Knights of the Ku Klux Klan

The International Keystone Knights of the Ku Klux Klan (IKKKKK) is listed by the Southern Poverty Law Center as a Ku Klux Klan (KKK) hate group with "klaverns," or chapters, in Arkansas, Georgia, and Mississippi (Southern Poverty Law Center, Ku Klux Klan). The IKKKKK's stated purpose is to bring together the various disparate klans that now dot the American political and social landscape:

> In the 1920's Col. William J. Simmons had the right idea that the klan was not to be an alliance and unified only into one klan. Years later the United Klans of America was formed under Robert Shelton with the same principle of no alliance and one klan. The leaders of several klan groups have abandoned this idea and formed several different klans and say they want unity and alliances but only practice it in public and not on private rally sites. The Black lives matter movement is one group only, the gays and lesbians are one group only do you all get the picture. The klan needs to be united again under one KLAN, one NATION, and one FLAG like it was on top of Stone Mountain and declared the 2nd era of the Klan, and the way it was under the United Klans of America (UKA) of the past, not the UKA of today. To all the leaders of various different klans in the United States are we going to stand together under ONE KLAN banner, or a DIVIDED KLAN under several banners. If you all decide that several banners are better we will never win, and the other movements that stand together as one will win [emphasis in original]. (International Keystone Knights of the Ku Klux Klan)

The IKKKKK has made headlines for some notable reasons. In 2012, the groups sued the state of Georgia "for not allowing it to participate in the state's 'Adopt-A-Highway' program" (FindLaw). In denying the group's request to have a sign posted along a stretch of highway with a 65-mile-per-hour speed limit, the commissioner of transportation for the state declared:

> The impact of erecting a sign naming an organization which has a long-rooted history of civil disturbance would cause a significant public concern. Impacts include safety of the traveling public, potential social unrest, driver distraction, or interference with the flow of traffic. These potential impacts are such that were the application granted, the goal of the program, to allow civic-minded organizations to participate in public service for the State of Georgia, would not be met. (FindLaw)

The IKKKKK filed a case against the commissioner of transportation, the Department of Transportation, and the state of Georgia claiming that their First

Amendment rights of free speech had been denied. In 2014, a trial judge declared that Georgia's refusal to allow the IKKKKK's application for the Adopt-A-Highway program amounted to "impermissible viewpoint discrimination" and explained that the IKKKKK's application "was singled-out for scrutiny not given to other applicants to the program" (FindLaw). The trial court then

> entered a declaratory judgment that a denial of an application to the [Adopt-A-Highway program] for public concern related to a group's history of civil disturbance represents an unconstitutional infringement on an applicant's right to free speech, and it enjoined the Department from denying applications to the [program] for public concern related to a group's history of civil disturbance. (FindLaw)

The State of Georgia appealed the case, which is still making its way through the courts.

In 2016, the IKKKKK secured a permit to hold a public rally in Rockmart, Georgia. Four of the five organizers of the event were "Klan or Neo-Nazi" adherents. The point of the October 2016 rally was to promote a place for "White Christians" to gather for "god, race, and nation" (Atlanta Antifascists). The theme of "god, race, and nation" is reinforced on the IKKKKK's website, which notes "One Nation, One Flag, & One Klan" (International Keystone Knights of the Ku Klux Klan).

In July 2017, the former leader of the IKKKKK from Alabama was "convicted of sexually assaulting a medicated woman and videotaping the crime" (Morlin). Steven Joshua Dinkle, who served as the Ozark chapter's "exalted cyclops" of the IKKKKK, "was arrested by the FBI in November 2013 in Mississippi on federal hate crime charges stemming from a 2009 cross burning in a predominantly black neighborhood in Ozark" (Morlin). Dinkle "was released from prison in 2015 for the cross-burning conviction, only to be arrested again for being a felon in possession of a .32 caliber pistol" (Morlin). He "pled guilty to the charge and was sentenced to 15 months in prison," only to receive an additional 10-year sentence when he was convicted of sexual assault (Morlin).

See also: Ku Klux Klan; White Nationalism; White Supremacist Movement

FURTHER READING

Atlanta Antifascists. September 20, 2016. "Speak Out against the Klan's Public Gathering in Rockmart GA, October 1st 2016." Atlanta Antifascists. https://afainatl.word press.com/tag/international-keystone-knights/. (Accessed June 30, 2018.)

FindLaw. "*State of Georgia v. International Keystone Knights of the Ku Klux Klan Inc.*" FindLaw. https://caselaw.findlaw.com/ga-supreme-court/1741603.html. (Accessed June 30, 2018.)

International Keystone Knights of the Ku Klux Klan. http://www.ikkkkk.org/. (Accessed June 30, 2018.)

Morlin, Bill. July 11, 2017. "Cross-Burning KKK 'Cyclops' Convicted of Sexual Assault on Medicated Woman." Southern Poverty Law Center: Hatewatch. https://www .splcenter.org/hatewatch/2017/07/11/cross-burning-kkk-%E2%80%98cyclops %E2%80%99-convicted-sexual-assault-medicated-woman. (Accessed June 30, 2018.)

Southern Poverty Law Center. "Ku Klux Klan." Southern Poverty Law Center. https://
www.splcenter.org/fighting-hate/extremist-files/ideology/ku-klux-klan. (Accessed
June 30, 2018.)

Southern Poverty Law Center. February 17, 2016. "Active Hate Groups in the United
States in 2015." Southern Poverty Law Center: Intelligence Report. https://www
.splcenter.org/fighting-hate/intelligence-report/2016/active-hate-groups-united
-states-2015. (Accessed June 30, 2018.)

Israel United in Christ

Israel United in Christ (IUIC) is "a black Hebrew Israelite group based in the
Bronx, New York, [that] thinks white people are 'the devil,' Jews are 'fake Jews'
and members of the LGBT community are 'sinners'" (Hatewatch staff). The
Southern Poverty Law Center (SPLC) characterizes IUIC as a "black nationalist"
hate group. According to the SPLC:

> The black nationalist movement is a reaction to centuries of institutionalized white
> supremacy in America. Black nationalists believe the answer to white racism is to
> form separate institutions—or even a separate nation—for black people. Most
> forms of black nationalism are strongly anti-white and anti-Semitic. Some religious
> versions assert that black people are the biblical "chosen people" of God. (Southern
> Poverty Law Center, Black Nationalist)

As Mark Potok of the SPLC has stated, "Black racism in America is largely, if not
entirely, a response to white racism" (Rugh). Nevertheless, IUIC has been
described as the "precise analogue of Christian Identity, whose white adherents
believe the Jews are decedents of Satan" (Rugh). Potok points out "that Neo-Nazi
leader Tom Metzger has labeled them [the IUIC] the 'black counterparts' to his
white-supremacist movement" (Rugh).

Along with "a number of other Israelite groups,"

> IUIC teaches that blacks, Latinos and Native Americans are the true genealogical
> descendants of the biblical Israelites—and that this heritage has been stolen and
> obscured over time. Modern day Jews, IUIC teaches, are imposters and usurpers of
> Hebrew Israelites's [sic] true heritage. White people, the group teaches, are descen-
> dants of the biblical Edomites. (Kestenbaum)

Edomites are the "descendants of Esau, the first born of Isaac and the twin brother
of Jacob" (Got Questions). Esau forsook his birthright and became the father of
the Edomites, while Jacob became the father of the Israelites. Members of IUIC
believe that black peoples' "disobedience to God's laws" have been the source of
all of their [blacks'] historical troubles" (Israel United in Christ, About). According to IUIC:

> Blacks and Hispanics everywhere suffer the same racial, social, economic problems
> world wide. Voting has not helped us, Christian churches have failed us. It's time for
> a change. In these last days we must give the bibles medicine to a sin sick people,
> then and only then will things begin to change. (Israel United in Christ, About)

Though IUIC claims that whites are "possessed by Satan" and that there "is a
group of secretive white people who are in touch with the Dark Lord and control

the world economy" (Rugh), in 2018 some of its members traveled to Liberia, "where they attempted to proselyte a man known as General Butt Naked in an attempt to make him a member" (Hatewatch staff). Naked, whose real name is Joshua Milton Blahyi, was recruited by IUIC's leader, Bishop Nathanyel Ben Israel. Naked, who received his name because he led an army of mostly naked children "in efforts to keep then-Libyan leader Samuel Doe in power,"

> would tell his young troops that killing was a game and have them participate in mutilation in an effort to desensitize them. He sacrificed a human, often a child, before each battle, then fed them to his adolescent army under the belief that it would purify them. He also admits to giving them cocaine, which he procured, along with weapons by trading in blood diamonds. (Hatewatch staff)

Today, the IUIC disputes the SPLC's characterization of it as a black nationalist hate group, calling the allegations against them "false" (Israel United in Christ).

See also: Black Nationalism; Black Separatists

FURTHER READING

Got Questions. "Who Were the Edomites?" Got Questions. https://www.gotquestions .org/Edomites.html. (Accessed June 12, 2018.)

Hatewatch Staff. April 11, 2018. "Courting Butt Naked: Israel United in Christ Attempts to Recruit Former Cannibal and Leader of Liberian Child Army." Southern Poverty Law Center: Hatewatch. https://www.splcenter.org/hatewatch/2018/04/11 /courting-butt-naked-israel-united-christ-attempts-recruit-former-cannibal-and -leader. (Accessed June 12, 2018.)

Israel United in Christ. https://israelunite.org/#. (Accessed June 12, 2018.)

Israel United in Christ. https://www.facebook.com/israelunited.inchrist/posts/665480 593638111. (Accessed June 12, 2018.)

Israel United in Christ. "About." Israel United in Christ. http://israelunitedinchrist.tumblr. com/. (Accessed June 12, 2018.)

Kestenbaum, Sam. October 2, 2017. "Hebrew Israelite Leader Warns Kendrick Lamar against Public Embrace." Forward. https://forward.com/news/383237/spiritual- leader-says-kendrick-lamar-shouldnt-be-tied-to-hebrew-israelites/. (Accessed June 12, 2018.)

Rugh, Peter. May 1, 2014. "The Black Israelites Think Whites Are Possessed by the Devil." Vice. https://www.vice.com/en_us/article/dpwyqz/white-people-black-jesus -will-enslave-you. (Accessed June 12, 2018.)

Southern Poverty Law Center. "Black Nationalist." Southern Poverty Law Center. https:// www.splcenter.org/fighting-hate/extremist-files/ideology/black-nationalist. (Accessed June 12, 2018.)

Southern Poverty Law Center. August 29, 2008. "Racist Black Hebrew Israelites." South- ern Poverty Law Center: Intelligence Report. https://www.splcenter.org/fighting -hate/intelligence-report/2008/racist-black-hebrew-israelites-becoming-more -militant. (Accessed June 12, 2018.)

Israelite Church of God in Jesus Christ

The Israelite Church of God in Jesus Christ (ICGJC) is an extremist fringe of the Black Hebrew Israelite (BHI) movement, which believes that blacks and other people of color (e.g., Hispanics and Native Americans) are the true descendants of the House of Israel and are, therefore, "God's chosen people" (Southern Poverty Law Center, 2008). ICGJC literature states that "[t]hose whose fathers are of Negroid and Indian descent make up the 12 tribes of the nation of Israel" and that "modern-day Jews are devilish impostors and white people are evil personified, deserving of death or slavery" (Morlin). The Southern Poverty Law Center (SPLC) has designated ICGJC as a black nationalist hate group (Southern Poverty Law Center, Black Nationalist). According to the SPLC, the black nationalist movement

> is a reaction to centuries of institutionalized white supremacy in America. Black nationalists believe the answer to white racism is to form separate institutions—or even a separate nation—for black people. Most forms of black nationalism are strongly anti-white and anti-Semitic. Some religious versions assert that black people are the biblical "chosen people" of God. (Southern Poverty Law Center, Black Nationalist)

The "About Us" section on ICGJC's website says that the church exists

> to expose and teach the truth about the historical lineage of Blacks, Hispanics and Indians scattered throughout North, Central, South America, the Caribbean Islands and the rest of the world, as well as to prepare them for their mental, spiritual and physical liberation by Jesus Christ as prophesied in the King James Version of the Holy Bible. (Israelite Church of God in Jesus Christ)

ICGJC also claims that it is time for "the great truth about our people, which is found in The Holy Bible, to be revealed that we are the Hebrew Israelites—the true chosen people of God! Jesus Christ, the true Biblical Jews and all of the Holy Prophets of The Bible are Black!!!" (Israelite Church of God in Jesus Christ). The church also claims that "Blacks, Hispanics and Indians come from a royal heritage of honor, dignity and glory. We were and still are the greatest and mightiest people in the earth" (Israelite Church of God in Jesus Christ).

According to the SPLC, congregations of ICGJC can be found in Connecticut, Florida, Maryland, Minnesota, Nebraska, New York, North Carolina, Oregon, Pennsylvania, and Washington, D.C.

For nearly two decades, the leader of ICGJC was Jermaine Grant, who was also known by his Hebrew title and name, "Chief High Priest Tazadaqyah" (Hatewatch staff). Grant is also known to his congregants as "The Comforter" (Southern Poverty Law Center, 2008). For many years, Grant preached of a coming apocalypse that would precipitate "an imminent and bloody demise for whites and other enemies at the hands of . . . a bloodthirsty black Yahweh (Christ)" (Southern Poverty Law Center, 2008). Grant believed that the coming apocalypse would also confirm "Black Hebrew Israelites as the true children of God and the true heirs to the House of Israel" (Southern Poverty Law Center, 2008). Though Grant never predicted when the apocalypse would come, "his prophecy still heightened the mood of eager anticipation for the coming doom of all enemies of the true Israelites" (Southern Poverty Law Center, 2008).

Under Grant's leadership, ICGJC members were required to submit "tithes and general offerings" to the church. In November 2016, the church was raided by the

"U.S. Federal Bureau of Investigation (FBI) and the Internal Revenue Service (IRS) in relation to an investigation into financial irregularities" (Morlin). In April 2018, Grant and ICGJC's "director, vice president and treasurer, Lincoln Warrington," were arrested on charges that the pair "diverted over $2 million from the group's coffers to other ventures, including the leaders' luxury household expenses. It is also alleged that they did not report over $5 million in income to the IRS" (Hatewatch staff). The indictment also alleged "that Grant and Warrington took money straight from ICGJC which paid for properties, luxury cars, clothing and home furnishings for the Grant family, private school for the Grant children, as well as a personal chauffeur, and a Disney vacation" (Hatewatch staff). It also alleged that "he shopped at Gucci, Louis Vuitton, and Nieman Marcus outlets" using an ICGJC debit card (Hill).

Upon the initial raid on ICGJC in 2016, Grant stated that "the persecution has begun. I want all you brothers and sisters to hold your heads up high because we are doing nothing wrong and we're being persecuted for righteousness. The Lord our God will fight for us" (Morlin).

See also: Black Hebrew Israelites; Black Muslims; Black Nationalism; Black Separatists; Sicarii 1715

FURTHER READING

Hatewatch Staff. April 30, 2018. "Leaders of Israelite Church of God in Jesus Christ Arrested for Bilking Millions from the Organization." Southern Poverty Law Center: Hatewatch. https://www.splcenter.org/hatewatch/2018/04/30/leaders-israelite-church-god-jesus-christ-arrested-bilking-millions-organization. (Accessed June 22, 2018.)

Hill, Crystal. April 26, 2018. "Pastor of Church Labeled a Hate Group Spent Its Money on Disneyland Trips and Cars, Feds Say." *Miami Herald*. http://www.miamiherald.com/news/nation-world/national/article209939089.html. (Accessed June 22, 2018.)

Israelite Church of God in Jesus Christ. "About Us." Israelite Church of God in Jesus Christ. http://www.icgjcmd.org/. (Accessed June 22, 2018.)

Morlin, Bill. November 3, 2016. "Police Raid Black Supremacist Church in New York City." Southern Poverty Law Center: Hatewatch. https://www.splcenter.org/hatewatch/2016/11/03/police-raid-black-supremacist-church-new-york-city. (Accessed June 22, 2018.)

Southern Poverty Law Center. "Black Nationalist." Southern Poverty Law Center. https://www.splcenter.org/fighting-hate/extremist-files/ideology/black-nationalist. (Accessed June 22, 2018.)

Southern Poverty Law Center. "Hate Map by State." Southern Poverty Law Center. https://www.splcenter.org/hate-map/by-state. (Accessed June 22, 2018.)

Southern Poverty Law Center. August 29, 2008. "Racist Black Hebrew Israelites Becoming More Militant." Southern Poverty Law Center: Intelligence Report. https://www.splcenter.org/fighting-hate/intelligence-report/2008/racist-black-hebrew-israelites-becoming-more-militant. (Accessed June 22, 2018.)

Terrorism Research & Analysis Consortium. "Israelite Church of God in Jesus Christ (ICGJC)." Terrorism Research & Analysis Consortium. https://www.trackingterrorism.org/group/israelite-church-god-jesus-christ-icgjc. (Accessed June 22, 2018.)

Israelite School of Universal Practical Knowledge

The Israelite School of Universal Practical Knowledge (ISUPK) is a black nationalist and black separatist hate group that can trace its roots back to the Black Judaism movement that began in the late 1800s. According to Black Judaism doctrine, "when the Kingdom of Israel was destroyed, the Israelites were first scattered across the African continent and then selectively targeted by enemy African tribes who captured and sold them to European slave traders for bondage in the New World" (Southern Poverty Law Center, History of Hebrew Israelism). According to the leader of ISUPK, "General Yahanna," "It's a common myth that slaves were randomly shackled up and carried off to slavery. Actually, Slave traders sailed for months and days to get to specific pickup points. They knew what people they were taking—specifically, the lost tribes of Israel" (Southern Poverty Law Center, History of Hebrew Israelism). Like many black nationalist and black separatist groups, the ISUPK "preaches hatred of white people, Jews and anyone else who doesn't embrace its radical black separatist ideology" (Southern Poverty Law Center, 2008). The ISUPK believes that white people are "inherently evil and hated by God" (Southern Poverty Law Center, History of Hebrew Israelism). When asked about this belief, one follower of ISUPK stated:

> We don't call white people the devil because they're white. We're basing this on a history, a well-documented history of the acts committed against us on this earth. That has to be understood: This isn't a color thing with us. The word 'devil' simply means deceiver. That's all it means. . . . This is why we refer to the white man as the devil, because of the lies. And again, because of the acts committed against us. (Schmid, A Black Separatist Leader)

According to the Cult Education Institute, members of the ISUPK "are militant, and see themselves as part of an End-Time army. They see their 'Commanding General Yahanna' as second only to Christ Himself" (Cult Education). The ISUPK uses "radical rhetoric and confrontational street theater" to preach their message. They reject "the 'Muslim' beliefs of groups like the Nation of Islam and [have] refused to join with the pork-eating secularists of groups like the Black Panthers" (Southern Poverty Law Center, History of Hebrew Israelism).

In 2008, Washington, D.C., "passed a noise ordinance intended to quiet down Yahanna and his followers' use of amplifiers" during their street presentations (Southern Poverty Law Center, 2008). Yahanna, whose real name is John Lightborne, has stated that "it's not only white people destroying black communities, but also black women, the Rev. Al Sharpton and lesbians" (Southern Poverty Law Center, 2008). Yahanna espouses "the future enslavement of white people, and condemns the actions of Barack Obama and Martin Luther King, Jr." (Southern Poverty Law Center, 2008). One ISUPK adherent stated that "with [Barack] Obama in office, what that did to our people was give them a false idea of inclusion in this society, or in this system. Then the smack in the face came, and here's Trump. The exact opposite of what Obama was. For the record, Obama is not one of our people either" (Schmid, A Black Separatist Leader).

The ISUPK is based in Upper Darby, Pennsylvania (Bradley).

See also: Black Hebrew Israelites; Black Nationalism; Black Separatists; Israel United in Christ; Israelite Church of God in Jesus Christ; Nation of Islam; Sicarii 1715

FURTHER READING

Bradley. June 30, 2012. "Israeli School of U.P.K. Black Jewish Supremacist Extremist Group." *Adventures of Bradley*. http://www.bradleyfarless.com/israeli-school-of -u-p-k-black-jewish-supremacist-extremist-group/. (Accessed July 23, 2018.)

Cult Education. June 19, 2018. "Israelite School of Universal Practical Knowledge." Cult Education Institute. https://forum.culteducation.com/read.php?12,140720. (Accessed July 23, 2018.)

Israelite School of Universal Practical Knowledge. http://www.isupk.org/. (Accessed July 23, 2018.)

Schmid, Thacher. January 24, 2018. "A Black Separatist Leader Explains Why He Wants Out of America: 'The Bullshit Has Become the Norm.'" *Willamette Week*. http:// www.wweek.com/news/2018/01/24/a-black-separatist-leader-explains-why-he -wants-out-of-america-the-bullshit-has-become-the-norm/. (Accessed July 23, 2018.)

Schmid, Thacher. January 24, 2018. "A National Watchdog Says Three of Four Hate Groups in Portland Are Black. How Is That Possible?" *Willamette Week*. http:// www.wweek.com/news/2018/01/24/a-national-watchdog-says-three-of-four-hate -groups-in-portland-are-black-how-is-that-possible/. (Accessed July 23, 2018.)

Southern Poverty Law Center. "History of Hebrew Israelism." Southern Poverty Law Center: Intelligence Report. https://www.splcenter.org/fighting-hate/intelligence -report/2015/history-hebrew-israelism. (Accessed July 23, 2018.)

Southern Poverty Law Center. August 29, 2008. "'General Yahanna' Discusses Black Supremacist Hebrew Israelites." Southern Poverty Law Center: Intelligence Report. https://www.splcenter.org/fighting-hate/intelligence-report/2008/%E2%80% 98general-yahanna%E2%80%99-discusses-black-supremacist-hebrew-israelites. (Accessed July 23, 2018.)

J

Jewish Defense League

The Jewish Defense League (JDL) "is a radical organization that preaches a violent form of anti-Arab, Jewish nationalism" (Southern Poverty Law Center). The group "was founded in 1968 by Rabbi Meir Kahane," and it preaches violence against Arabs and Palestinians while supporting extreme forms of Jewish nationalism (Anti-Defamation League). The JDL's stated political position is to deny any Palestinian claims to land in Israel, and it calls for "the removal of all Arabs from Jewish soil" (Southern Poverty Law Center). The group has been responsible for terror attacks both in the United States and abroad, and it has engaged in "intense harassment of foreign diplomats, Muslims, Jewish scholars and community leaders, and officials" (Southern Poverty Law Center). The JDL's five principles of action are:

> (1) Love of Israel and Judaism; (2) Dignity and Pride in Jewish traditions, faith, culture, land, history, and peoplehood; (3) Iron, or the need to help Jews everywhere project a strong and forceful image; (4) Discipline and Unity; and, (5) Faith in the Indestructibility of the Jewish People. (Jewish Defense League Canada Blog)

The JDL "was characterized as a right-wing extremist group by the U.S. Federal Bureau of Investigation in 2001, and is considered a hate group by the Southern Poverty Law Center" (Southern Poverty Law Center).

The JDL was founded in 1968 to protect Jews from the backlash that occurred because of a teacher's union strike in that year. The strike "brought to the surface racial tensions between the predominantly Jewish teachers unions and black residents who were seeking greater control over neighborhood schools" (Southern Poverty Law Center). The rising tensions that existed at the time because of black nationalism and black militantism caused many Jews to fear for their lives. Kahane even warned of a "second Holocaust." Kahane organized the JDL to protect Jews from violence, establishing neighborhood watches and roaming patrols of neighborhoods. The JDL's actions increased ethnic polarization in neighborhoods and contributed to many street clashes (Anti-Defamation League).

By 1970, the JDL had changed its focus from neighborhood protection to "the plight of Soviet Jews. From this point on, the JDL's main objective was to terrorize Soviet establishments in the United States to compel the Soviet Union to change its anti-Semitic policies—specifically its ban on allowing Russian Jews to emigrate to Israel" (Southern Poverty Law Center). In 1970, "the JDL committed five acts of terrorism against Soviet interests" (Southern Poverty Law Center). The violence became so intense that President Richard Nixon believed that the JDL's action would scuttle the Strategic Arms Limitation Talks (SALT) that were then under way between the United States and the Soviet Union. Though the JDL's actions did not cause any loss of life, the actions were nevertheless viewed as terroristic in nature. After every incident, "the JDL would claim responsibility by phoning in its official slogan—'Never Again'—a Jewish reference that indicated that the Jews would never again allow themselves to be slaughtered as they were during the Holocaust" (ABC News).

Though the Soviets were the primary targets of the JDL's actions, the group targeted anyone that it considered to be a threat to Jewish nationalism. This included "U.S. and foreign diplomats, domestic radical-right organizations, Arab and Muslim activists, journalists and scholars, and Jewish community members who are simply not 'Jewish enough'" (Southern Poverty Law Center). When the United Nations General Assembly "voted for a resolution equating Zionism with racism," the JDL began targeting diplomats of all countries that had voted in favor of the resolution (Southern Poverty Law Center).

JDL's founder, Rabbi Meir Kahane, emigrated to Israel in 1971. His successor in the United States "could not maintain unity in the organization in succeeding years so Kahane returned to the U.S. in 1974 and appointed Russel Kelner as the international chairman of JDL. Kelner was a former U.S. Army lieutenant and guerilla warfare expert" who was determined to use paramilitary tactics in the furtherance of JDL's goals (Southern Poverty Law Center).

In 1990, Kahane was assassinated in the United States by an Arab after he (Kahane) had delivered a speech at a Zionist conference in New York City. In 1994, a JDL member, Baruch Goldstein, "massacred 29 Palestinian Muslims worshiping at the Ibrahimi Mosque in the West Bank City of Hebron. The JDL's website justified Goldstein's mass murder by stating that Goldstein took a preventative measure against yet another Arab attack on Jews" (Southern Poverty Law Center).

The election of Donald Trump to the U.S. presidency in November 2016 emboldened JDL followers, who believed that Trump's victory would help revive the group in the United States. One JDL adherent stated, "Our movement is part of the Trump movement. . . . There is a major shift in US foreign policy. We now feel that the government, I don't want to say it's in our hands, but we are part of it and we believe it's going to help us advance our cause once January 20 comes around" (Kestler-D'Amours).

The JDL was quick to take advantage of what it believed was a change in the priorities of U.S. foreign policy under Donald Trump. In March 2017, two JDL members were arrested as they confronted protesters outside a policy conference that was conducted by the American Israel Public Affairs Committee (AIPAC). Several members of JDL attacked a Palestinian-American professor and knocked another man unconscious as they protested outside AIPAC's headquarters in Washington, D.C. "They beat him after they heard he was Palestinian," one of the victim's daughters stated. "He was not threatening at all, it's perfectly clear that my father was brutalized simply because of who he is" (Mathias). Heidi Beirich, director of the Intelligence Project at the Southern Poverty Law Center, said that the tactics are typical of JDL: "The JDL's position and activities have always been violent counter-protests. Their attitude is to take it to the streets and do in-your-face protest actions" (Altshuler).

In 2018, the leader of the JDL went on trial for allegedly "planning a pipe-bomb attack against Arab-Americans" (ABC News). The JDL—which "views America and the world at large as strongly anti-Semitic, and insists that only the most extreme forms of resistance, including violence, can protect the Jewish people—continues to utilize in its promotional material such slogans as "'For every Jew a .22' and 'Keep Jews Alive with a .45' " (ABC News).

See also: ACT for America; Family Security Matters

FURTHER READING

ABC News. March 19, 2018. "Bomb Plot Charge Only Latest JDL Controversy." ABC News. https://abcnews.go.com/US/story?id=91809&page=1. (Accessed July 23, 2018.)

Action Network. "Tell AIPAC: Condemn the Violence the Jewish Defense League (JDL) Committed on Your Doorstep." ActionNetwork.org. https://actionnetwork.org /petitions/tell-aipac-condemn-the-jdl-and-the-violence-they-committed-on-your -doorstep. (Accessed July 23, 2018.)

Altshuler, George. March 27, 2017. "Jewish Defense League Counter-Protests Turn Violent Outside AIPAC Conference." *Washington Jewish Week*. http://washington jewishweek.com/37612/jewish-defense-league-counter-protests-turn-violent-out side-aipac-conference/news/. (Accessed July 23, 2018.)

Anti-Defamation League. "The Jewish Defense League." Anti-Defamation League. https://www.adl.org/education/resources/profiles/jewish-defense-league. (Accessed July 23, 2018.)

Jewish Defense League. "About." http://www.jdl.org/about.html. (Accessed July 23, 2018.)

Jewish Defense League Canada Blog. "JDL 5 Principles." https://jdlcanada.wordpress .com/jdl-5-principles/. (Accessed November 10, 2018.)

Kestler-D'Amours, Jillian. January 9, 2017. "Jewish Defence League Wants U.S. Comeback." The New Arab. https://www.alaraby.co.uk/english/indepth/2017/1/9/jewish -defence-league-wants-us-comeback. (Accessed July 23, 2018.)

Mathias, Christopher. March 31, 2017. "Hate Group Implicated in Vicious Attack on Palestinian-American Professor." Huffpost. https://www.huffingtonpost.com/entry /jewish-defense-league-attacks-palestinian-man-aipac_us_58dd448ee4b05 eae031e0438. (Accessed July 23, 2018.)

Southern Poverty Law Center. "Jewish Defense League." Southern Poverty Law Center. https://www.splcenter.org/fighting-hate/extremist-files/group/jewish-defense -league. (Accessed July 23, 2018.)

K

Keystone United

Keystone United, "known until 2009 as the Keystone State Skinheads (KSS)," began as a single-state racist skinhead organization, but it has expanded to include associates in New Jersey, Maryland, and New York (Woodruff). The Southern Poverty Law Center (SPLC) has dubbed Keystone United as "one of the largest and most active racist skinhead groups in the country" (Southern Poverty Law Center). Keystone United attempts to portray itself as a new and more sophisticated breed of skinheads by frequently sponsoring "family-friendly" events such as white power picnics and music festivals, although the music is usually some variation of "hate rock." One member of Keystone United reiterated this "new brand" when he posted on Stormfront, a white supremacist and neo-Nazi website, that at the group's appearance at an event, "There were no [R]oman salutes, wearing of swastikas, or shouting of tired old racial slogans like 'White Power' and 'Sieg Heil.' . . . I think we are making inroads in changing people's perception of skinheads" (Southern Poverty Law Center).

The KSS was formed near Harrisburg, Pennsylvania, in 2001. The group took its name from Pennsylvania's nickname, the "Keystone State." A second chapter of KSS was soon founded in Lancaster, Pennsylvania. In 2002, World Church of the Creator leader Matt Hale was scheduled to speak at a public library in York, Pennsylvania. But the white supremacists who had assembled for Hale's speech were met by hundreds of anti-racist and anti-fascist individuals who protested Hale's appearance and the presence of various racist and skinhead groups at the event. This speech was a turning point for the group, as they stated:

> After being refused entry into a public meeting held at a local library, we found ourselves standing shoulder to shoulder on the streets of York, PA in defense of other White Nationalists. Within less then [sic] a year, we had forged chapters in virtually every major part of the state from Philadelphia and Lancaster to Pittsburgh, Altoona and the Wilkes Barre/Scranton area. (Keystone United)

Keystone United's motto is "Freedom through Nationalism" (Keystone United). And though they contend that they are committed to "being active in our communities, public awareness, contacting local politicians, or just simply showing people we are not ashamed of who we are," the group nevertheless has a history of criminal violence (Southern Poverty Law Center). Between 2002 and 2008, KSS members have been arrested for assault, ethnic intimidation, terroristic threats, attempted homicide, aggravated assault, criminal solicitation, second-degree murder, racketeering, and weapons charges (Southern Poverty Law Center).

In late 2008, "KSS changed its name to Keystone United" in order to attract more white supremacists and to emphasize a new direction (Keystone United). As stated on their website, Keystone United claimed to remain focused on our initial goals and grow in a much more progressive direction, away from the outdated elements of the movement. We now intend to focus our efforts on raising awareness among today's youth through an increase in public activism and the creation of various outreach programs. These programs have been designed in an effort to channel the frustration caused by today's hostile atmosphere and the lack of options offered to our youth. (Keystone United)

Though it posited a new direction, Keystone United continued to rail against "subversive Zionist organizations such as the A.D.L. [Anti-Defamation League] and Southern Poverty Law Center [SPLC] [that] used their influence among law enforcement agencies" (Keystone United).

In 2016, Keystone United was energized by the candidacy of Donald Trump. As noted by one Pennsylvania journalist, white supremacists and white nationalists, like those associated with Keystone United, "love Trump," as he taps into a sort of "Rust Belt racism" (Woodruff). Indeed,

Industrial decline in the state hasn't just fed the economic depression that Trump promises to magically fix; it's also fueled a white supremacist renaissance whose participants are primed to lap up the mogul's calls for anti-Muslim discrimination and xenophobic immigration policies. (Woodruff)

Trump's anti-Muslim and anti-immigration policies helped the candidate to capture Pennsylvania in November 2016, propelling him to the United States presidency. Groups like Keystone United were more than happy to "stump for Trump."

See also: Neo-Nazis; Stormfront; White Nationalism; White Supremacist Movement

FURTHER READING

Anti-Defamation League. July 2015. "With Hate in Their Hearts: The State of White Supremacy in the United States." Anti-Defamation League. https://www.adl.org /sites/default/files/documents/assets/pdf/combating-hate/state-of-white-supremacy-united-states-2015.pdf. (Accessed March 28, 2018.)

Bello, Marisol. October 21, 2008. "White Supremacists Target Middle America." USA Today. http://usatoday30.usatoday.com/news/nation/2008-10-20-hategroups_N .htm. (Accessed March 28, 2018.)

Keystone United. "About Us." Keystone United. https://keystone2001united.wordpress .com/about/. (Accessed March 28, 2018.)

Southern Poverty Law Center. "Keystone United." Southern Poverty Law Center. https:// www.splcenter.org/fighting-hate/extremist-files/group/keystone-united. (Accessed March 28, 2018.)

Woodruff, Betsy. April 26, 2016. "Skinheads Come Out in Full Force for Donald Trump in Pennsylvania." Daily Beast. http://www.thedailybeast.com/articles/2016/04/26 /skinheads-come-out-in-full-force-for-donald-trump-in-pennsylvania.html. (Accessed March 28, 2018.)

Kingdom Identity Ministries

Kingdom Identity Ministries (KIM) is an organization related to Christian Identity, a racist ideology that is white supremacist in nature, as it believes that the only true descendants of Abraham, Isaac, and Jacob are those with Germanic, Anglo-Saxon, Celtic, Nordic, or Aryan heritage. Christian Identity "generally identifies people of color as soulless sub-humans and Jews as satanic or cursed by God" (Southern Poverty Law Center). KIM functions primarily as a publishing house for Christian Identity literature, including texts from "early Identity leaders such as Wesley Swift" (Southern Poverty Law Center). KIM "teaches that Judgment Day will arrive in the form of a sanctified race war, a theory widely popular with prison-based racist gangs like the Aryan Brotherhood" (Southern Poverty Law Center). It supports the "two-seed" theory that asserts that whites are the chosen race and the true inheritors of the blessings of Abraham, Isaac, and Jacob, whereas Jews are literally the offspring of Satan (Southern Poverty Law Center). The founder of KIM, Mike Hallimore, calls the organization a "politically incorrect Christian Identity outreach ministry to God's chosen race, true Israel, the White, European peoples." In his sermons, Hallimore has made calls in support of the "death penalty for idolatry, homosexuality, blasphemy and abortion" (Southern Poverty Law Center).

KIM's position in the white nationalist and white supremacist world is bolstered by its possession of copyrighted material by prominent Christian Identity thinkers. In 1983, just one year after its founding, KIM inherited the copyrights of the "written works of Bertrand Comparet, one of the principal early thinkers of the Christian Identity" (Southern Poverty Law Center). Comparet was the "ideologue" of the two-seed theory. In 2002, KIM also "inherited the exclusive rights to publish the works of another hard-line Identity ideologue, Wesley Swift" (Southern Poverty Law Center). Thus, most of the historical teachings of two of Christian Identity's most important theorists are controlled by KIM. This control allows KIM to assert, on a Christian Identity website,

> [W]e believe that the Europeans and their descendants are the chosen people of God. We believe this, not because we think that the white race is superior, but because there is overwhelming proof in support of this belief. We do not back down from this belief, because we are certain. (Christian Identity Ministries)

Kim's founder, Mike Hallimore, had frequent correspondence with David Lane, an infamous member of the terror group the Order, who was sentenced to 190 years in prison for the "machine-gun assassination of Jewish talk show host, Alan Berg, in Denver, Colorado in 1984" (Hilliard and Keith). Hallimore praised Lane as a "race slayer." In 2001, Hallimore wondered to a British journalist, "Why, in the Bible, it's permitted to slay race mixers" (Southern Poverty Law Center). Hallimore recounted the story, "taken from the Book of Numbers, of an Israelite called Phineas who kills a fellow Israelite for taking a woman from another tribe as his lover" (Southern Poverty Law Center). Because Berg had criticized such teachings and other beliefs associated with white supremacism, Lane was justified in taking his life (at least according to Hallimore).

In 2006, KIM ventured further into the white supremacist world by publishing a pamphlet that was distributed in the Lehigh Valley region of Pennsylvania, which was 97 percent white. The pamphlet stated, "In your area, it's [our] understanding that there are a number of white Christian people and [that] there is a racial problem in terms of integrating of the races" (Southern Poverty Law Center). In 2007, KIM funded the distribution of "a white-power rock CD that was handed out by skinheads in public schools across the country" (Southern Poverty Law Center). Hallimore said:

> I hate heavy metal as a form of music, but I realize those bands attract a lot of youth and so it works as a great outreach tool. Kids can listen to this music, get the message and grow spiritually. I'd rather see these CDs being passed out in schools than condoms. (Southern Poverty Law Center)

In 2008, "Hallimore placed an advertisement on his website seeking a white Christian lady" (Southern Poverty Law Center). He expressed his desire to find a woman who is "racially pure, honest and of high moral character." Also required were "genuine sweet genteel feminine mannerisms." Hallimore made it clear, however, that "Government, Jewish, or other agents do not qualify" (Southern Poverty Law Center).

See also: Aryan Brotherhood; Christian Identity; The Order; White Nationalism; White Supremacist Movement

FURTHER READING

Christian Identity Ministries. "More About Us." Christian Identity Ministries. http://www.christianidentityministries.com/more.html. (Accessed May 29, 2018.)

Hilliard, Robert L., and Michael C. Keith. 1999. *Waves of Rancor: Turning Into the Radical Right*. Routledge.

Kingdom Identity Ministries. "Doctrinal Statement of Beliefs." Kingdom Identity Ministries. http://www.kingidentity.com/doctrine.htm. (Accessed May 29, 2018.)

Southern Poverty Law Center. "Kingdom Identity Ministries." Southern Poverty Law Center. https://www.splcenter.org/fighting-hate/extremist-files/group/kingdom-identity-ministries. (Accessed May 29, 2018.)

Kinist Institute (Kinism)

The Kinist Institute, "an organization that promotes Kinism, has called for laws against racial intermarriage, an end to non-white immigration, expelling all 'aliens' ('to include all Jews and Arabs'), and restricting the right to vote to white landholding men over the age of 21" (Hankes). The Kinist Institute embraces the principles of "Kinism," an ideology that asserts that the Bible "condones segregation" and that "God has divided humanity into 'nations' which may be properly translated as races or ethnicities" (Anti-Defamation League). Kinism "emerged in the late 1990s/early 2000s when members of a Virginia chapter of the League of the South (LOS)" publicly introduced the principles of Kinism (Anti-Defamation League). Kinism is based on a racist interpretation of Christianity in which the white race is supreme over all other races.

> While accepting many standard Christian tenets and declaring Jesus as their Savior . . . Kinists assert that whites have a "God-given right" to preserve their own kind and live separately from other races in their own communities. Kinists declare

that the social order for man is based on "tribal and ethnic" (by which they mean racial) ties. (Anti-Defamation League)

Kinists embrace the views of Robert Lewis Dabney, a 19th-century Confederate army chaplain and Southern Presbyterian minister who "defended an idealized version of the Old South at the very apex of Christian civilization. He [Dabney] didn't believe that the freed slaves should be allowed to vote and was against public education of both blacks and whites. Dabney also claimed black slaves learned to be civilized only through interaction with their white master" (Anti-Defamation League).

At present, the movement appears small, but it is attracting a growing number of younger white supremacists who feel that Kinism "offers a religious foundation for their racist and anti-Semitic beliefs" (Anti-Defamation League). Kinists "use biblical references to make the claim that God wants different races to live separately" (Anti-Defamation League). Kinists deny that they are racists, claiming that their ideology simply encourages the "belief that the love of racial or ethnic kin is similar to that of family ties" (Anti-Defamation League). Given that belief,

> Kinists often argue that the foundations of Kinism existed long before the League of the South members introduced the "Kinist Statement" in 2001. In fact, they often seek bridges with other white supremacists by claiming that all white Christians who have embraced a "racial identity" can be called Kinists, because Kinism is simply about wanting to live and worship with one's own kind. (Anti-Defamation League)

But although Kinists strongly believe that "whites should seek unity with other whites" and that "all races can achieve salvation through belief in Jesus Christ" as long as they do so in their own, separate communities, Kinists are vehemently anti-Semitic (Anti-Defamation League). Kinists "often refer to Jews as anti-Christs [and] they see Jews as plotting to destroy both Christianity and the white race" (Anti-Defamation League). Randall Jamison, one of the originators of the "Kinist Statement," which defines the beliefs of the Kinist Institute, wrote in 2010:

> Let every man, woman, and child among us shout from the rooftops that we are proud racists! This is what our Southern ancestors did with the epithet "rebel." . . . We too must choose between racism and patricide. Whether to triumph or not, we vow to stand with our race. The Bible very clearly calls Jews "anti-Christs." Yet the numerous crimes committed against our people have not instilled in us a sense of revenge. (Anti-Defamation League)

Today, "white supremacists, including racist skinheads, are increasingly adopting the language and ideology of Kinism" (Anti-Defamation League). Indeed, the ideas of Kinism echo the infamous 14 Words, the guiding principle of hardcore white supremacists as enunciated by the now-deceased David Lane, former member of the terror group the Order: "We must secure the existence of our people and a future for White Children" (Anti-Defamation League). For hardcore white supremacists, the principles of Kinism "legitimize their racism and anti-Semitism" (Anti-Defamation League).

See also: League of the South; Neo-Confederates, White Nationalism; White Supremacist Movement

FURTHER READING

Anti-Defamation League. "Kinism: A Racist and Anti-Semitic Religious Movement." Anti-Defamation League. https://www.adl.org/sites/default/files/documents/assets/pdf/combating-hate/Kinism-Racist-and-Anti-Semitic-Religionfinal2.pdf. (Accessed May 28, 2018.)

Hankes, Keegan. October 19, 2015. "Meet the New Wave of Extremists Gearing Up for the 2016 Elections." Southern Poverty Law Center: Hatewatch. https://www.splcenter.org/hatewatch/2015/10/19/meet-new-wave-extremists-gearing-2016-elections. (Accessed May 28, 2018.)

Slick, Matt. "What Is Kinism? Is It Biblical?" Christian Apologetics & Research Ministry. https://carm.org/what-is-kinism. (Accessed May 28, 2018.)

Southern Poverty Law Center. August 11, 2006. "The New Racialists." Southern Poverty Law Center: Intelligence Report. https://www.splcenter.org/fighting-hate/intelligence-report/2006/new-racialists. (Accessed May 28, 2018.)

Knights of the Ku Klux Klan

There is some confusion as to the origins of the Knights of the Ku Klux Klan (KKKK). David Duke, its supposed founder and first national director, claimed that the KKKK was founded in 1956 by Jim Lindsay, a supporter of the National Socialist White People's Party and an admirer of Adolf Hitler (Bridges). Yet there is no mention of the group until 1973, and "the KKKK was not formally incorporated in Louisiana until 1975" (Southern Poverty Law Center, Knights of the Ku Klux Klan). There are those who believe that Duke perpetrated the ruse of an earlier founding date in order "to fend off depictions of the group as an inconsequential upstart" (Southern Poverty Law Center, Knights of the Ku Klux Klan). After Lindsay was murdered, Duke dubbed himself the group's "national director," which sounded better than grand or imperial wizard.

Duke's strategy with the KKKK was to make it a more mainstream organization by reimagining its image and strategy. Duke was famous for encouraging fellow Klansmen to "get out of the cow pasture and into hotel meeting rooms" (Southern Poverty Law Center, Knights of the Ku Klux Klan). Duke eschewed the traditional trappings of the Klan—white robes and cross burnings—in favor of a new Klan that would present itself as an organization for social and racial justice. Duke was also responsible for taking the KKKK from a simple hate group that focused on racial minorities—with blacks being their favorite targets—to a group that became "Nazified," focusing on Jews and "spinning conspiracy theories about everything from Jewish control of the Federal Reserve to Jewish control of the Civil Rights movement" (Southern Poverty Law Center, Knights of the Ku Klux Klan). The KKKK aligned itself with a host of neo-Nazi figures, such as Don Black, Tom Metzger, and David Lane.

Duke built the KKKK into an organization "with an estimated 1,500 members with another 10,000 non-member supporters" (Southern Poverty Law Center, Knights of the Ku Klux Klan). But Duke's womanizing and craving for personal and political glory alienated many followers. In 1980, a breakaway group from the KKKK, "the Invisible Empire, Knights of the Ku Klux Klan, boasted more members than Duke's original KKKK" (Southern Poverty Law Center, Knights of the Ku Klux Klan). Duke left the KKKK after "being caught on camera trying to sell the Knights' membership list to other groups" (Southern Poverty Law Center, Knights of the Ku Klux Klan). During most of the 1980s, Klan membership declined, and the KKKK almost passed into oblivion. In 1989, Thomas Robb assumed control of the group and intended to follow Duke's to portray a reimagined KKK for public consumption.

Robb, whose gift for organization and oratory revitalized the KKKK for a time, continued Duke's decision to shy away from traditional KKK monikers, such as "imperial wizard," in favor of the more businesslike "national director." An adherent of Christian Identity, Robb attracted listeners with sermons on "white pride" and the idea that whites were God's chosen people. Robb's theology also was anti-Semitic, as Christian Identity taught that Jews were the spawn of Satan and Eve. Like Duke, Robb was criticized by those who claimed that he was financially mismanaging the group. There were also those who did not like the "kinder and gentler" approach that Robb advanced, favoring instead a more confrontational style.

Today, Robb bills the KKKK as "the most active white rights organization in America," though it clearly does not have the membership numbers to back up these claims. Robb eventually moved away from the KKKK name, instead calling his organization the 'Knights Party' in an attempt to garner more members (Southern Poverty Law Center, Knights of the Ku Klux Klan). Robb still follows Duke's approach in his advocacy of hate, however, as the Knights Party continues to portray itself as a softer and more political organization that only maintains an association with the KKK label because of name recognition and the traditional values that are associated with the Ku Klux Klan (Southern Poverty Law Center, Knights of the Ku Klux Klan).

See also: Ku Klux Klan; Neo-Nazis; White Supremacist Movement

FURTHER READING

Bridges, Tyler. 1995. *The Rise of David Duke*. University Press of Mississippi.
Southern Poverty Law Center. "Church of the National Knights of the Ku Klux Klan. Southern Poverty Law Center. https://www.splcenter.org/fighting-hate/extremist -files/group/church-national-knights-ku-klux-klan. (Accessed August 18, 2018.)
Southern Poverty Law Center. "Knights of the Ku Klux Klan." Southern Poverty Law Center. https://www.splcenter.org/fighting-hate/extremist-files/group/knights-ku-klux -klan. (Accessed April 1, 2018.)

The Knights Party

The Knights Party is "characterized by the Southern Poverty Law Center (SPLC) as a Ku Klux Klan (KKK) hate group" (Southern Poverty Law Center, Ku Klux Klan). According to the SPLC, KKK groups have a "long history of violence" and are the "oldest and most infamous of American hate groups" (Southern Poverty

Law Center, Ku Klux Klan). The Knights Party, begun as the Knights of the Ku Klux Klan (KKKK), was founded by David Duke in 1975 as he "attempted to put a 'kinder, gentler' face on the Klan, courting media attention and attempting to portray itself as a modern 'white civil rights' organization" (Southern Poverty Law Center, Knights of the Ku Klux Klan). In 1989, Pastor Thomas Robb, leader of an organization known as the Christian Revival Center, became the head of the organization and renamed the KKKK "the Knights Party" in "an attempt to emphasize what he [saw] as the need for a softer, more political approach along the lines of David Duke's tactics" (Southern Poverty Law Center, Knights of the Ku Klux Klan). Today, the Knights Party seeks to fulfill the 14 Words that form the mantra of nearly all white nationalist and white supremacist organizations: "We must secure the existence of our people and a future for white children" (Counter Extremism Project). The website of the Knights Party states that most white children don't understand "what it means to have white pride." White parents, the Knights Party contends,

> are still being victimized by the entertainment industry and the news industry. They are being told the wonderful world they fought for (they call this wonderful?) is in dire straights [sic] because their liberal ideas are being threatened. After all you were primed right from the get go with shows like Sesame Street telling you how great it was to go to an integrated school. But you soon learned the truth when you saw the hatred for white people in your school. It didn't just come from non-whites. It was in the text books and your teachers talked about it. It seems they would have us believe that white people are stupid, uncaring, uncool, hateful oppressors who can't dance. Is it any wonder so many young people are experimenting with interracial dating? Who wants to date a loser and if white people are the bafoons they are made out to be then it would make perfect sense to go out with the more desirable black guy or the cute little Asian girl, wouldn't it? (Knights Party, Fellow Patriots)

In defending its association with the Ku Klux Klan (KKK), the Knights Party offers its reasons: "It is a matter of principle; It is an organizational asset; and, It is a tactical asset" (Knights Party, Why the Klan?). The Knights Party states:

> We believe in the Ku Klux Klan. We believe that the founders of the Ku Klux Klan were led by divine providence and that once again just like the Klan saved the white race during "Black Reconstruction" it will arise like the great phoenix—The Knights Party—to bring our people once again back from the brink of destruction. Our people led by the hand of God will once more rule our great land. A time of prosperity and racial healing—a great White Christian revival!
>
> Furthermore, as America becomes increasingly polarized and white people begin feeling the full force of non-white hatred, they won't care about the alleged "violent" past of the Ku Klux Klan. The one thing they know for sure is that the Klan stands for white people. When they begin to realize that the alleged violence of the Klan of the past was in fact lawful executions of murderers, rapists, and child molesters, they will understand that it has been an anti-Christian force in this nation that has tarnished the once immensely popular and beloved Ku Klux Klan. They won't care what the agenda driven entertainment media has to say about this truly Christian and family oriented movement. They will only stop to consider . . . NO ONE is speaking out on behalf of my white Christian heritage and family . . . NO ONE but the Klan! (Knights Party, Why the Klan?)

The Knights Party does not view its ethos as "racist" but rather as "racialist." According to the Counter Extremist Project, "the term racialism as used by the Knights Party describes a simple preference for one race over another, rather than racism, which entails negative discrimination against other races" (Counter Extremism Project). As stated by one KKK imperial wizard (leader), "We don't hate people because of their race. . . . We want to keep our race the White race. . . . We want to stay White. It's not a hateful thing to want to maintain White Supremacy" (Counter Extremism Project).

Much of the Knights Party's recruitment material seems to be aimed at young white people, indicating that it is hard to tell parents that one is "White and proud." After all, "the Black Lives Matter groups are encouraged to talk about black pride." But white parents have accepted that they "are in the minority not the majority. Their complete generation was almost won over. So if you are White and proud your parents may be freaked out. Don't blame them. Remember they are victims of a one-world, one-color philosophy" (Knights Party, Fellow Patriots).

The Knights Party calls upon white young people to secure the future of the white race:

> The young people today have an awesome responsibility. They can look at the last generation and see the mistakes that were made and how America has ended up because of the decisions made by the baby-boomers and decide to make a positive change or they can fall dutifully in line with the one-world types. For a lot of young people it's too late. They have already fallen for the whole homosexual, race mixing, anti-white ploy. But a few will dare to say no to the establishment and will brave into a world of heritage, of love for one's people, for wholesome Christian conduct. They will be an asset to their people. They will stay in school, get to college however they can, educate themselves, surround themselves by positive thoughts and work and study hard. They will be heroes for tomorrow's generation. Perhaps a generation where you aren't sneered at by the establishment because you prefer to be around White straight people. It's tough enough to be a young person today. Can you imagine what it's going to be like for your kids someday? It won't be as far off as you think! (Knights Party, Fellow Patriots)

See also: Knights Party Veterans League; Ku Klux Klan; White Nationalism; White Supremacist Movement

FURTHER READING

Counter Extremism Project. "Ku Klux Klan (KKK)." Counter Extremism Project. https://www.counterextremism.com/threat/ku-klux-klan. (Accessed July 14, 2018.)

Knights Party. https://www.kkk.com/. (Accessed July 14, 2018.)

Knights Party. "Fellow Patriots: The Leadership Problem." Knights Party. https://kkk.bz/fellow-patriots/. (Accessed July 14, 2018.)

Knights Party. "Our Goal." Knights Party. https://kkk.bz/our-goal/. (Accessed July 14, 2018.)

Knights Party. "Why the Klan?" Knights Party. https://kkk.bz/why-the-klan/. (Accessed July 14, 2018.)

Southern Poverty Law Center. "Knights of the Ku Klux Klan." Southern Poverty Law Center. https://www.splcenter.org/fighting-hate/extremist-files/group/knights-ku-klux-klan. (Accessed July 14, 2018.)

Southern Poverty Law Center. "Ku Klux Klan." Southern Poverty Law Center. https://
        www.splcenter.org/fighting-hate/extremist-files/ideology/ku-klux-klan. (Accessed
        July 14, 2018.)
Southern Poverty Law Center. March 2, 2015. "Active Ku Klux Klan Groups." Southern
        Poverty Law Center: Intelligence Report. https://www.splcenter.org/fighting-hate
        /intelligence-report/2015/active-ku-klux-klan-groups. (Accessed July 14, 2018.)
Tep-online. "The Knights' Party Platform." Tep-online.info. http://www.tep-online.info
        /laku/usa/mino/kkk/kkkparty.htm. (Accessed July 14, 2018.)

Knights Party Veterans League

The Knights Party Veterans League (KPVL) has been "designated a Ku Klux Klan (KKK) hate group by the Southern Poverty Law Center" (SPLC) (Southern Poverty Law Center, Ku Klux Klan). According to the SPLC, KKK groups have a "long history of violence" and are "the most infamous—and oldest—of American hate groups. Although black Americans have typically been the Klan's primary target, it also has attacked Jews, immigrants, gays and lesbians and, until recently, Catholics" (Southern Poverty Law Center, Ku Klux Klan). The KPVL is "an organization within The Knights Party consisting of Knights Party associates that are military veterans, active duty, or family members of veterans or active duty associates. The KPVL is a natural extension, and active implementation of the two planks of the [Knights] party's platform" (Knights Party Veterans League, Party Info). The two planks of the Knights Party platform are, first, advocacy of a "strong defense department to safeguard American citizens," and, second, the unqualified support of all U.S. veterans—"we should find those that are missing and take care of those who have come home" (Knights Party Veterans League, Party Info). The KPVL is based in Harrison, Arkansas (Southern Poverty Law Center, 2015).

At first glance, the KPVL may seem like an innocuous veterans' organization. Yet its ideology is still that of the KKK. According to an exposé by the Counter Extremism Project, the Knights Party—the parent organization of the KPVL—was created in 1975 by David Duke, a grand wizard of the KKK. Duke launched the Knights Party "explicitly seeking to soften the Klan's image" (Counter Extremism Project). According to the Knights Party:

> [T]he KKK seeks to "secure the existence of our people and a future for white children" and advocates for white self-determination in the U.S. The Knights Party thus describes its ethos as "racialist" rather than "racist" and explicitly rejects charges of racism, claiming, "How disappointed they must be when they find out the Klan does not hate Negroes!" (Counter Extremism Project)

As used by the Knights Party, the term "racialism describes a simple preference for one race over another, rather than racism, which entails negative discrimination against other races" (Counter Extremism Project). Yet, as noted by the Counter Extremism Project, "the Oxford English Diction and most dictionaries" treat racialism and racism as "synonymous" (Counter Extremism Project).

A closer look at KPVL's website indicates its preferences and its belief that the United States has been taken over by minorities and other groups:

> The time in which we live is very exciting and any like-minded individual would be proud to be an associate or supporter of this grass-roots movement to take back

America. The Knights Party, will in the years to come, become recognized by the American people as THE WHITE RIGHTS MOVEMENT! Where ever they live, whatever their personal religious denomination may be, no matter what present political or fraternal organization they may be with, everyone should support The Knights Party as the political PARTY of the future and the Last Hope for America. The Knights Party, realizing that to achieve true security for our people we must achieve political power in the United States. [Emphasis in original] (Knights Party Veterans League, Party Info)

The Knights Party platform, embraced by KPVL, includes the following items:

The recognition that America was founded as a Christian nation.

The recognition that America was founded as a White nation.

The necessity of putting American FIRST in all foreign matters.

The immediate cessation of all foreign aid.

The abolition of ALL discriminatory affirmative action programs.

The placement of American troops on our border to STOP the flood of illegal aliens.

The abolition of all anti-gun laws.

The active promotion of America's unique European (White) culture.

Mandatory drug testing for all welfare recipients.

The abolition of abortion, except in cases of rape or incest or endangerment of mother.

The imposition of the death penalty for those convicted of molestation and rape.

A national law against the practice of homosexuality.

The placement of all persons HIV positive into national hospitals.

The restoration of individual freedom to Christian America.

The voluntary repatriation of everyone not satisfied with living under White Christian rules of conduct back to the native lands of their people. [emphasis in original] (Knights Party Veterans League).

See also: Knights Party; Ku Klux Klan; White Nationalism; White Supremacist Movement

FURTHER READING

Counter Extremism Project. "Ku Klux Klan (KKK)." Counter Extremism Project. https://www.counterextremism.com/threat/ku-klux-klan. (Accessed July 14, 2018.)

Knights Party Veterans League. "Our Platform." Knights Party Veterans League. http://www.knightspartyveteransleague.com/?page_id=4. (Accessed July 14, 2018.)

Knights Party Veterans League. "Party Info." Knights Party Veterans League. http://www.knightspartyveteransleague.com/?page_id=2. (Accessed July 14, 2018.)

Southern Poverty Law Center. "Ku Klux Klan." Southern Poverty Law Center. https://www.splcenter.org/fighting-hate/extremist-files/ideology/ku-klux-klan. (Accessed July 14, 2018.)

Southern Poverty Law Center. March 2, 2015. "Active Ku Klux Klan Groups." Southern Poverty Law Center: Intelligence Report. https://www.splcenter.org/fighting-hate/intelligence-report/2015/active-ku-klux-klan-groups. (Accessed July 14, 2018.)

Ku Klos Knights of the Ku Klux Klan

The Ku Klos Knights of the Ku Klux Klan (KKKKKK) are a Ku Klux Klan (KKK)-affiliated group that is "characterized by the Southern Poverty Law Center (SPLC) as a KKK hate group" (Southern Poverty Law Center, 2017). According to the SPLC, KKK hate groups are "the oldest and most infamous hate groups in the United States" (Southern Poverty Law Center, Ku Klux Klan). When it was formed in 1865, the KKK "was a single, unitary organization. Today, there are dozens of competing Klan groups. Although black Americans have typically been the Klan's primary target, it has also attacked Jews, immigrants, homosexuals, and Catholics" (Southern Poverty Law Center, 2017). The KKKKKK has local chapters, or "klaverns," in several U.S. states, including Alabama, Florida, Idaho, Illinois, Indiana, Kentucky, Michigan, Missouri, Mississippi, North Carolina, New York, Ohio, Pennsylvania, Tennessee, Texas, and Virginia (CNN). The organization has headquarters in Church Hill, Tennessee (Southern Poverty Law Center, 2017). In August 2017, "following the fatal violence at a rally of white nationalists in Charlottesville, Virginia," police officials in Gurnee, Illinois, requested that the SPLC remove the village from its hate map as the municipality could find no basis for the KKKKKK being listed as active in Gurnee (Newton and Abderholden).

On the KKKKKK's website, the group clearly lays out its ideology:

> We are White Christian patriots of the true Invisible Empire of the Ku Klux Klan of our great country. We are for the future of our white Christian children and for our generations to come, join a traditional white klan who believes in the teachings of Jesus and therefore we do not believe in HATE. We are against homosexuals of both genders and we believe that marriage is between one man and one woman as Jesus teaches. The ku klux klan of our country has never been more relevant than today and we stand for the protection our past history and for our future. This is a message of hope that we of the KKK believe in our country. There is now a war going on against our people, our children, our cherished way of life and our principles. We must stand true to our klan and our brothers and sisters and family and pray that we can maintain our sense of loyalty to each other. Stand up and be counted! (Ku Klos Knights of the Ku Klux Klan)

In late August 2017, "[a]n openly gay man running for office in the town of Cape Coral, Fla. allegedly received two threatening letters from the Ku Klos Knights, a division of the Ku Klux Klan" (NBC News). The candidate, who was running for a seat on the city council, indicated that his partner had found a note on the doorstep of their home that read, "We know where you live. We are going to win. Quit now. When you girls least expect it, We will be here for a nice visit" (CBS News).

See also: Ku Klux Klan; White Nationalism; White Supremacist Movement

FURTHER READING

CNN. August 17, 2017. "Southern Poverty Law Center Lists Active Hate Groups by State." WPTV.com. https://www.wptv.com/news/national/southern-poverty-law-center-lists-active-hate-groups-by-state. (Accessed July 21, 2018.)

Ku Klos Knights of the Ku Klux Klan. http://www.kuklosknights.com/. (Accessed July 21, 2018.)

NBC News. August 31, 2017. "KKK Allegedly Threatens Gay Political Candidate in Florida." NBC News. https://www.nbcnews.com/feature/nbc-out/kkk-allegedly-threatens-gay-political-candidate-florida-n797891. (Accessed July 21, 2018.)

Newton, Jim, and Frank S. Abderholden. August 17, 2017. "Gurnee Seeks Removal from National Hate Group Map." *Chicago Tribune.* http://www.chicagotribune.com/suburbs/lake-county-news-sun/news/ct-lns-hate-groups-lake-county-st-0817-20170816-story.html. (Accessed July 21, 2018.)

Southern Poverty Law Center. "Hate Map." Southern Poverty Law Center. https://www.splcenter.org/hate-map. (Accessed July 21, 2018.)

Southern Poverty Law Center. "Ku Klux Klan." Southern Poverty Law Center. https://www.splcenter.org/fighting-hate/extremist-files/ideology/ku-klux-klan. (Accessed July 21, 2018.)

Southern Poverty Law Center. February 15, 2017. "Active Hate Groups 2016." Southern Poverty Law Center: Intelligence Report. https://www.splcenter.org/fighting-hate/intelligence-report/2017/active-hate-groups-2016. (Accessed July 21, 2018.)

Ku Klux Klan (KKK)

The Ku Klux Klan, also known as the KKK or the Klan, has been associated with three distinct periods of extremist activity characterized by sentiments of "white supremacy, white nationalism, anti-immigration, and, in later iterations, anti-Catholicism, anti-Semitism, and Nordicism" (Anti-Defamation League). Historically, the KKK has resorted to terrorism against groups or individuals whom they opposed (O'Donnell and Jacobs). The KKK's penultimate goal has been the "purification" of American society in order to secure a white, Anglo-Saxon protestant nation. The KKK has traditionally been associated with right-wing extremism (Southern Poverty Law Center, Ku Klux Klan). Today's KKK is a shadow of the organization as it appeared at its zenith in the 1920s. In most cases, the KKK is perceived as old and outdated (Anti-Defamation League Report). In addition, the KKK must now compete for membership with other types of white supremacist groups that are much more technology savvy and that communicate a message that spans many issue areas, such as immigration, economics, citizens' rights, and the like. Where once the KKK could boast millions of adherents, today there are probably no more than a few thousand that are active in KKK organizations around the United States (U.S. History).

The original Ku Klux Klan "was organized by ex-Confederate elements to oppose Reconstruction policies" after the U.S. Civil War, and the group tried to maintain white supremacy by terrorizing freed slaves and their supporters (Infoplease). The first era of the Klan was organized in Pulaski, Tennessee, by former Confederate general Nathan Bedford Forrest. The first Klan sowed fear through "its strange disguises, its silent parades, its midnight rides, [and] its mysterious language and commands, all of which were found to be most effective in playing upon fears and superstitions" (Infoplease). The Klan covered their faces and wore white to portray themselves as the spirits of dead Confederates returning to exact vengeance. The Klan was "particularly effective at keeping blacks away from the polls," but measures passed by the U.S. Congress to combat the Klan took a toll, and by the end of Reconstruction, the Klan had largely disappeared (Infoplease).

The Klan enjoyed its most prolific presence in the United States during its second era, which began during World War I. Following the release of D. W. Griffith's movie *The Birth of a Nation* in 1915, interest in Klan activity surged. The movie, which glorified the Confederacy and the Ku Klux Klan, won praise from President Woodrow Wilson, who lauded the film, commenting that it was "like writing history with lightning" (Janik). In November 1915, William J. Simmons—a Georgia preacher—and several friends who had also been inspired by *The Birth of a Nation* climbed Stone Mountain outside of Atlanta and burned a cross, thereby birthing the second iteration of the Ku Klux Klan. The new Klan was not simply about white supremacy or the denial of black civil rights. Rather the second Klan's appeal was in "its militant advocacy of white supremacy, anti-Catholicism, anti-Semitism, and immigration restriction, but the organization also attracted the support of many middle-class Americans by advocating improved law enforcement, honest government, better public schools, and traditional family life" (Lay). At its peak in the mid-1920s, the membership of the Ku Klux Klan numbered between 4 and 5 million (Lay). The state governments of Alabama, Colorado, Georgia, Indiana, Louisiana, Oklahoma, Oregon, and Texas included officials who were Klan members, and those governments were profoundly influenced by the Klan during the 1920s. In many other parts of the country, the organization won electoral victories in many municipal elections. By 1924, "the perceived power of the Klan was such that neither major political party was willing to denounce it formally" (Lay).

At the height of its power, the second Klan era spiraled into a steep decline as it was racked with internal feuding, political scandals, and the "fading of the group's romantic image" (Lay). The Great Depression severely hampered membership, as new recruits could not pay dues to finance Klan activities. By 1944, the second era of the Klan had come to an end as it officially disbanded (Lay).

Samuel Green, an Atlanta physician, attempted to revive the Klan soon after its official demise, but his death in 1949 left the movement hopelessly fragmented. Most of the membership that remained was in small, fanatical groups, in contrast to the large numbers that the Klan had enjoyed during its heyday in the 1920s.

The U.S. Supreme Court ruling of *Brown v. Board of Education* in 1954 reenergized the Klan for a time as southern whites engaged in "massive resistance to federal mandates for desegregation, and the Klan emerged as a key player in this resistance. In 1955, the Knights of the Ku Klux Klan (KKKK) was formally organized in Atlanta" (Lay). Like the organizers of the second era of the Klan, the founders of the new Klan movement rallied atop Stone Mountain, the massive igneous outcrop of stone outside of Atlanta. The rally drew 3,500 attendees determined to maintain racial segregation in the South (Lay).

The third era of the Klan was particularly violent as "attacks against blacks and civil rights workers occurred throughout the South" during the early 1960s. On September 15, 1963, "a bomb exploded before Sunday morning services at the 16th Street Baptist Church in Birmingham, Alabama. The church was a known gathering place for civil rights leaders" (History.com). The bombing killed four young black girls and injured several more, precipitating violent clashes between protesters and police that drew national attention to the civil rights movement, which was then being punctuated by violent struggles in many Southern cities. Alabama's governor, George Wallace, "was a leading opponent of desegregation, and Birmingham had one of the strongest and most violent chapters of the KKK. The Birmingham city police commissioner was also notorious for his willingness to use brutal tactics against demonstrators, particularly blacks" (History.com). It wasn't until 1977 that the first prosecutions for those responsible for the bombing were conducted. In that year, a Klan member was tried and convicted for the Birmingham Baptist Church bombing. Other prosecutions would lead to convictions in 2001 and 2002 (History.com).

A third-era Klan group was also involved in the murder of three civil rights workers—two white and one black—during the Freedom Summer voter registration drive that took place in Mississippi in the summer of 1964. On June 21, 1964, three volunteers of the Freedom Summer movement—James Cheney, Andrew Goodman, and Michael Schwerner—were murdered by Klansmen after having been pulled over and jailed in Neshoba County, Mississippi. When the three young men went missing, "a massive search of the area was conducted by the Federal Bureau of Investigation" (FBI). After three days, the burned-out car of the three civil rights workers was found in a swamp. However, it would be two months before the three men's bodies "were discovered buried in an earthen dam" (Joiner). Over the course of the FBI investigation, "it emerged that members of the local White Knights of the Ku Klux Klan, as well as the Neshoba County Sheriff's office and the Philadelphia, Mississippi Police Department had been involved in the incident" (PBS). In 1967, 18 men were tried and convicted on civil rights chargers. An all-white jury convicted seven of the men for violating the civil rights of the Freedom Summer volunteers, but none of those convicted served more than six years in prison. In 2005, 41 years after the fact, Edgar Ray Killen, a Baptist preacher, was convicted of manslaughter and sentenced to 60 years in prison (Joiner). However, no investigation ever definitively revealed who killed Cheney, Goodman, and Schwerner, and in 2016 the state of Mississippi officially closed the case (Joiner).

Following the passage of the Civil Rights Act of 1964, "blacks gained a measure of political power in the South and the Klan eventually became weakened and marginalized" (U.S. History). Legal actions against the Klan in civil cases severely curtailed the scope and influence of local organizations, and several were forced to disband following legal judgments against them.

Near the middle of the 1970s, the Klan experienced a mini revival when David Duke reorganized the Knights of the Ku Klux Klan (KKK). Duke was a new leader who wanted to shed the image of the KKK as a bunch of vigilantes running around in robes. Instead, Duke wanted to replace the robes with suits and ties and get members into positions of prominence. For his part, Duke ran for various political offices for a number of years, succeeding only once, when he was elected to the Louisiana House of Representatives.

During the 1980s and 1990s, the growing militant racism and anti-Semitism of Klan members caused many to associate with more virulent white supremacist groups, such as Aryan Nations and the National Alliance, as well as other neo-Nazi factions. In 1981, the Southern Poverty Law Center (SPLC) took a Klan group led by Louis Beam to court after the Klan had "harassed and intimidated Vietnamese shrimpers in and around Galveston Bay in Texas." The Klan had burned crosses near the shrimpers, and in some cases had fired shots at them as well as burned their boats. After the SPLC brought suit against them, the Klan was "permanently enjoined against violence, threatening behavior, or any other harassment of the Vietnamese shrimpers" (Greenhaw).

In 1985, the SPLC won a civil rights suit against members of the Carolina Knights of the Ku Klux Klan for harassment and terrorist threats "against a black prison guard and members of his family" (Greenhaw). In January 1985, a federal judge issued an order against the Carolina Knights that prohibited the group's grand dragon, Frazier Glenn Miller, and his followers from "holding parades in black neighborhoods, and from harassing, threatening or harming any black person or white persons who associated with black persons" (Southern Poverty Law Center, Person).

In 1987, the "SPLC won a case against the United Klans of America for the lynching of Michael Donald, a black teenager in Mobile, Alabama" (*Los Angeles Times*). The $7 million verdict against the organization forced the United Klans into bankruptcy. In July 1998, the SPLC won a $37.8 million verdict against two KKK chapters (Christian Knights of the Ku Klux Klan and Invisible Empire Inc.) for the arson of a historic black church (Southern Poverty Law Center, Macedonia). Finally, "in November 2008, the SPLC won a case against the Imperial Klans of America (IKA), the nation's then-second largest Klan organization" (Greenhaw). A jury awarded $2.5 million to Jordan Gruver, who had been severely beaten by two members of the IKA. The award bankrupted IKA, and the organization eventually disbanded (Associated Press).

In 2016, the KKK burst back onto the American national scene when a Republican presidential nominee was endorsed by one of the KKK's "official" newspapers, the *Crusader*. Under the banner "Make American Great Again," the entire front page of an issue of the *Crusader* before the November 2016 election featured an article in which the question was asked, "What made American great in the first place?" The article continued, "The short answer to that is simple. America was great not because of what our forefathers did—but because of who our forefathers were. America was founded as a White Christian Republic. And as a White Christian Republic it became great" (Holley). Though the Trump campaign disavowed the endorsement, there was no doubt that Donald Trump's overtly nationalist, anti-immigration rhetoric attracted tens of thousands of racists, white nationalists, white supremacists, and neo-Nazis to his campaign banner (Osnos). After Trump's stunning upset of rival Hillary Clinton, former KKK grand wizard David Duke commented, "Make no mistake about it, our people have played a HUGE role in electing Trump!" [emphasis in original] (Cancryn). Though Duke was not clear as to whom "our people" referred to, it was evident to most readers that Duke was referring to extremists, like himself, who wished to see curbs on immigration, aggressive actions against Muslims, and other nationalist items pushed by white voters.

Though the Trump victory did accord a measure of prominence to the Ku Klux Klan, there is no question that the Klan is a shell of the organization that made it one of the most powerful political forces in the United States during the 1920s. Today, the KKK is a "collection of mostly small, disjointed groups with no predominant leadership or stability" (Anti-Defamation League). While many Klan groups are

> adept at exploiting the media by staging political endorsements, leafleting, and occasional rallies, most organized Klan groups suffer from a lack of cohesion and paucity of members, key factors in its long-term trend of decline. Other factors in its decline include a perception that Klan groups are old or outdated, as well as the presence of other types of white supremacist groups that compete for membership with Klan groups. (Anti-Defamation League)

Many Klan groups today "promote a traditional Klan ideology that would be recognized by Klan members of the past—i.e., white supremacy" (Anti-Defamation League Report). However, many Klan groups "updated" their ideology by infusing it with varying degrees of "neo-Nazi beliefs and affiliations" (Anti-Defamation League). For some Klan groups, "neo-Nazi tenets have resulted in symbiotic relationships with neo-Nazi groups" (Anti-Defamation League). Klan groups today still use robes and other historic symbols of the organization (e.g., cross burnings) to make their case, but they are much more likely to rally against illegal immigration, urban crime, economic dislocation, and same-sex marriage (Knickerbocker). However, a more visible target of the KKK's vitriol in recent years has been Islam. Klan supporters in recent years have been quick to distribute "anti-Muslim fliers urging readers to help the Klan in its fight to prevent the spread of radical Islam" (Anti-Defamation League).

Most of the Klan's strength remains in the Deep South, though there are several Klan groups scattered about the country (Southern Poverty Law Center, 2011). Although their rhetoric and their hate speech remain potent, the KKK has largely been replaced by more virulent white supremacists, such as neo-Nazis, and has had its message more expertly co-opted by other right-wing extremist groups that are more adept at using the new technologies associated with the distribution of hate across the Internet.

See also: Aryan Nations; Knights of the Ku Klux Klan; National Alliance; Neo-Nazis; White Nationalism; White Supremacist Movement

FURTHER READING

Anti-Defamation League. "The State of the Ku Klux Klan in the United States." Anti-Defamation League. https://www.adl.org/sites/default/files/documents/assets/pdf/combating-hate/tattered-robes-state-of-kkk-2016.pdf. (Accessed June 8, 2017.)

Anti-Defamation League Report. "ADL Report: KKK Declining in Stature and Significance." Anti-Defamation League. https://www.adl.org/news/press-releases/adl-report-kkk-declining-in-stature-and-significance. (Accessed June 8, 2017.)

Associated Press. November 15, 2008. "Klan Group Ordered to Pay $2.5 Million." NBC News. http://www.nbcnews.com/id/27728315/ns/us_news-crime_and_courts/t/klan-group-ordered-pay-million/#.WTq5oNy1vRY. (Accessed June 9, 2017.)

Balleck, Barry J. 2015. *Allegiance to Liberty: The Changing Face of Patriots, Militias, and Political Violence in America*. Praeger.

Cancryn, Adam. November 9, 2016. "David Duke: 'Trump Win a Great Victory for Our People.'" Politico. http://www.politico.com/story/2016/11/david-duke-trump-victory-2016-election-231072. (Accessed June 9, 2017.)

Editors. "Ku Klux Klan." *Encyclopedia Britannica*. https://www.britannica.com/topic/Ku-Klux-Klan. (Accessed June 8, 2017.)

Friedersdorf, Conor. March 27, 2015. "The Audacity of Talking about Race with the Ku Klux Klan." *Atlantic*. https://www.theatlantic.com/politics/archive/2015/03/the-audacity-of-talking-about-race-with-the-klu-klux-klan/388733/. (Accessed June 8, 2017.)

Greenhaw, Wanye. 2011. *Fighting the Devil in Dixie: How Civil Rights Activists Took On the Ku Klux Klan in Alabama*. Zephyr Press.

History.com. "Birmingham Church Bombing." History.com. http://www.history.com/topics/black-history/birmingham-church-bombing. (Accessed June 9, 2017.)

Holley, Peter. November 2, 2016. "KKK's Official Newspaper Supports Donald Trump for President." *Washington Post*. https://www.washingtonpost.com/news/post-politics/wp/2016/11/01/the-kkks-official-newspaper-has-endorsed-donald-trump-for-president/. (Accessed June 9, 2017.)

Infoplease. "Ku Klux Klan: The First Ku Klux Klan." Infoplease.com. https://www.infoplease.com/encyclopedia/history/united-states-canada-and-greenland/us-history/ku-klux-klan/the-first-ku-klux-klan. (Accessed June 8, 2017.)

Janik, Rachel. February 8, 2015. "'Writing History with Lightning': *The Birth of a Nation* at 100." *Time*. http://time.com/3699084/100-years-birth-of-a-nation/. (Accessed June 8, 2017.)

Joiner, Lottie L. June 21, 2016. "Mississippi Closes the Case on Freedom Summer Murders." Daily Beast. http://www.thedailybeast.com/mississippi-closes-the-case-on-freedom-summer-murders. (Accessed June 9, 2017.)

Knickerbocker, Brad. February 9, 2007. "Anti-Immigrant Sentiments Fuel Ku Klux Klan Resurgence." *Christian Science Monitor*. http://www.csmonitor.com/2007/0209/p02s02-ussc.html. (Accessed June 9, 2017.)

Lay, Shawn. July 7, 2005. "Ku Klux Klan in the Twentieth Century." *Georgia Encyclopedia*. http://www.georgiaencyclopedia.org/articles/history-archaeology/ku-klux-klan-twentieth-century. (Accessed June 8, 2017.)

Los Angeles Times. February 13, 1987. "The Nation: Klan Must Pay $7 Million." *Los Angeles Times*. http://articles.latimes.com/1987-02-13/news/mn-2157_1_klan-million-nation. (Accessed February 10, 2019.)

O'Donnell, Patrick, and David Jacobs. 2006. *Ku Klux Klan: America's First Terrorists Exposed*. Idea Men Productions.

Osnos, Evan. February 29, 2016. "Donald Trump and the Ku Klux Klan: A History." *New Yorker*. http://www.newyorker.com/news/news-desk/donald-trump-and-the-ku-klux-klan-a-history. (Accessed June 8, 2017.)

PBS. "Murder in Mississippi." *PBS: American Experience*. http://www.pbs.org/wgbh/americanexperience/features/freedomsummer-murder/. (Accessed June 9, 2017.)

Southern Poverty Law Center. "Ku Klux Klan." Southern Poverty Law Center. https://www.splcenter.org/fighting-hate/extremist-files/ideology/ku-klux-klan. (Accessed June 8, 2017.)

Southern Poverty Law Center. "*Macedonia v. Christian Knights of the Ku Klux Klan*: Case Number 96-14-217." Southern Poverty Law Center. https://web.archive.org/web/20070930152516/http://www.splcenter.org/legal/docket/files.jsp?cdrID=29. (Accessed June 9, 2017.)

Southern Poverty Law Center. "*Person v. Carolina Knights of the Ku Klux Klan*: Case Number 84-534." Southern Poverty Law Center. https://www.splcenter.org/seek ing-justice/case-docket/person-v-carolina-knights-ku-klux-klan. (Accessed June 9, 2017.)

Southern Poverty Law Center. February 28, 2011. "Ku Klux Klan: A History of Racism." Southern Poverty Law Center. https://www.splcenter.org/20110301/ku-klux-klan -history-racism. (Accessed June 8, 2017.)

U.S. History. "The Modern Ku Klux Klan." U.S. History.com. http://www.u-s-history .com/pages/h1657.html. (Accessed June 8, 2017.)

L

League of the South

The League of the South (LOS) is "a white supremacist and white nationalist organization that espouses neo-Confederate ideals" (Southern Poverty Law Center). The LOS envisions a southern region of the United States that would be a "Christian theocratic state run by Anglo-Celtic (i.e., white) people" that would politically and socially dominate blacks and other minorities (Southern Poverty Law Center). The LOS advocates for the secession of the states of the "old confederacy" and denounces the federal government and most states in the Northeast (the old Union) as part of an "empire" that is overly materialistic and anti-religious in nature. The group was founded by a group of southern intellectuals, mostly university professors, but much of the original membership left the organization as it became more overtly racist. In recent years, the LOS has railed against multiculturalism, unchecked immigration, gay marriage, and other issues that it believes are leading to the ruination of the United States. Apart from secession of states from the United States, the LOS also encourages

> individuals and families to personally secede from the corrupt and corrupting influence of post-Christian culture in America. We call this "abjuring the realm," and it's a real and dramatic first step all of us can take by simply withdrawing our support of and allegiance to a regime that has imperiled our future. . . . Once our Southern culture is re-established, then the political issues will begin to take care of themselves. Good leaders flow naturally out of a healthy culture; however, power-hungry, self-seeking politicians are all we can expect from the debased cultural climate we have today. (League of the South)

The LOS was founded in 1994 by Michael Hill, "a history professor and specialist in Celtic history at Stillman College, and other southern intellectuals" (Southern Poverty Law Center). LOS began as a "religious and social movement that advocated a return to a more traditional and conservative, Christian-oriented culture," as epitomized by the gentility of the Old South (League of the South, Core Beliefs). LOS calls for a "natural societal order of superiors and subordinates, using as an example, Christ [as] the head of His Church; husbands are the heads of their families; parents are placed over their children; employers rank above their employees; the teacher is superior to his students, etc." (League of the South, Core Beliefs).

Not long after its founding, the LOS burst onto the political scene when it orchestrated a "Dump Beasley" campaign in South Carolina. David Beasley, "then-Governor of South Carolina and a moderate Republican, supported the removal of the Confederate Battle Flag from atop the state Capitol dome in Columbia" (Southern Poverty Law Center). The racist bent of LOS quickly emerged as

Jack Kershaw, one of the group's founding members, told a reporter in 1998, "Somebody needs to say a good word [about] slavery. Where in the world are the Negroes better off today than in America?" (Southern Poverty Law Center).

By 2013, after seeing its membership dramatically rise and fall, LOS took cues from the white nationalist organization Council of Conservative Citizens and began to employ a strategy of small street demonstrations with no more than 30 members who stuck to strictly scripted messages. The LOS "jettisoned the use of the Confederate battle flag at its demonstrations in favor of a more innocuous 'Southern national flag,' a black St. Andrews cross over a white background" (Southern Poverty Law Center). In 2014, LOS began erecting billboards throughout the Southeast reading #SECEDE. In the fall of 2014, the group announced "the formation of a paramilitary unit called the 'Indomitables' to advance the cause of secession, though the group quickly fizzled" (Southern Poverty Law Center).

In February 2017, Michael Hill, president of LOS, announced "Directive 02022017," a vigilante "defense force to combat the leftist menace to our historic Christian civilization" (Hatewatch staff). As announced, the group was meant to "plan for contingencies—natural or man-made—that might affect the Southern people." The original announcement read:

> [T]he League of the South is calling for all able-bodied, traditionalist Southern men to join our organization's Southern Defense Force for the purpose of helping our State and local magistrates across Dixie combat this growing leftist menace to our historic Christian civilization. As private citizens in a private organization, we will stand ready to protect our own families and friends, our property, and our liberty from leftist chaos. Moreover, we will be ready to assist our local and State authorities in keeping the peace should they find it necessary to "deputize" private citizens for that purpose. (Hatewatch staff)

Some observers believe that Hill's announcement was prompted by President Donald Trump's promises to crack down on immigration and take a harder line against Islamic extremism. As Hill has previously stated: "[P]eople other than white Christians would be allowed to live in his South, but only if they bowed to the cultural dominance of the Anglo-Celtic people and their institutions" (Southern Poverty Law Center).

See also: Council of Conservative Citizens; Neo-Confederates; White Nationalism; White Supremacist Movement

FURTHER READING

Hatewatch Staff. February 6, 2017. "League of the South Announces Formation of 'Southern Defense Force.'" Southern Poverty Law Center: Hatewatch. https://www .splcenter.org/hatewatch/2017/02/06/league-south-announces-formation-southern -defense-force. (Accessed March 16, 2018.)

League of the South. http://leagueofthesouth.com/.

League of the South. "League of the South Core Beliefs Statement." League of the South. https://web.archive.org/web/20080615205851/http://dixienet.org/NewSite/core beliefs.shtml. (Accessed March 16, 2018.)

Smith, Janet, and Ryan Lenz. November 15, 2011. "League of the South Rhetoric Turns to Arms." Southern Poverty Law Center: Intelligence Report. https://www.splcenter .org/fighting-hate/intelligence-report/2011/league-south-rhetoric-turns-arms. (Accessed March 16, 2018.)

Southern Poverty Law Center. "League of the South." Southern Poverty Law Center. https://www.splcenter.org/fighting-hate/extremist-files/group/league-south. (Accessed March 16, 2018.)

Liberty Counsel

Liberty Counsel is an organization that instigates litigation in support of Christian values. It was founded in 1989 by husband and wife Mathew and Anita Staver, both of whom are attorneys. Liberty Counsel states that it stands in absolute solidarity with Israel and was in full support of the U.S. military's policy of "banning homosexual activity within the armed forces. Liberty Counsel defends employment discrimination against gay workers, and opposes the addition of sexual orientation, gender identity, or similar provisions to hate crimes legislation. Liberty Counsel also opposes same-sex marriage, civil unions, and adoption by gay people" (Liberty Counsel, About). The Southern Poverty Law Center (SPLC) has designated Liberty Counsel a hate group. Liberty Counsel "debunks" the designation, stating that

> the SPLC's false labeling of people or organizations would mean that every civilization and its people and every major religious denomination would be similarly labeled by the SPLC as a hater or hate group. It is SPLC that demonizes good people and organizations and spews false accusations against those with whom it disagrees. The SPLC is reckless and its false labels are dangerous. (Liberty Counsel, 2015)

Liberty Counsel is staffed by some 10 attorneys and 300 more volunteer attorneys who defend Christians who believe that their rights are being trampled upon by a secular society. With the expansion of LGBT rights, Liberty Counsel has worked "to ensure that Christians can continue to engage in anti-LGBT discrimination in places of business under the guise of 'religious liberty'" (Southern Poverty Law Center, Liberty Counsel). Founder Mat Staver "has warned about homosexuality, abortion, and the consequences for Christians who oppose homosexuality and marriage equality," stating that they "will be targeted for the views" (Southern Poverty Law Center, Liberty Counsel). Staver has cited the work of Paul Cameron, "a discredited psychologist who paints LGBT adults as threats to children." Staver has also cited discredited "science" that indicates that homosexuality is a lifestyle choice, stating, "There is no evidence that a person is born homosexual. And there is evidence that people can change" (Southern Poverty Law Center, Liberty Counsel). Staver has also said:

> We are facing the survival of western values, western civilization. . . . One of the most significant threats to our freedom is in the area of sexual anarchy with the agenda of the homosexual movement, the so-called LGBT movement. It does several things, first of all it undermines family and the very first building block of our

society, but secondly, it's a zero sum game as well and it's a direct assault on our religious freedom and freedom of speech. (Southern Poverty Law Center, Liberty Counsel)

Staver has called for a new "revolutionary war" in the wake of marriage equality and has confirmed that he would personally advocate for civil disobedience in the light of "any U.S. Supreme Court ruling favoring marriage equality," stating that, "collectively, we cannot accept that [marriage equality] as the rule of law" (Hooper; Mantyla). Staver "has also supported the criminalization of homosexuality in the United States" and has stated in an *amicus curiae* brief to the U.S. Supreme Court that anti-sodomy laws in the United States should be upheld and that "this Court again should decline to deprive states of the power to enact statutes that proscribe harmful and immoral conduct" (Southern Poverty Law Center, 2017).

Staver supports conversion, or reparative, therapy for gays, stating that "given the health risks associated with homosexual behavior, our youth deserve to know that unwanted same-sex attractions can be overcome." Many of the most "reputable American medical, psychological, psychiatric, and counseling associations in the United States have rejected conversion therapy, noting that homosexual orientation is normal and not a disorder and thus requires no attempts to change it" (Schlatter and Steinback).

In the aftermath of the U.S. Supreme Court's ruling in *Obergefell v. Hodges* (2015), which legalized gay marriage in all 50 U.S. states, Liberty Counsel took "a leading role in defending Kim Davis, the Rowan County, Kentucky clerk who refused to grant same-sex marriage licenses claiming that her religion would not allow her to sign such licenses" (Southern Poverty Law Center, 2017). Southern nationalists, white nationalists, and neo-Confederates, as well as the antigovernment Oath Keepers, pledged that they would protect Davis from further arrest after the Supreme Court refused to hear her appeal (Niewert). Legal experts on conservative Fox News slammed Liberty Counsel's Mat Staver, saying that his statement questioning whether the U.S. Supreme Court "had the Constitutional authority to issue the same-sex marriage was ridiculously stupid" (Edwards).

In 2016, Liberty Counsel was thrown into the national spotlight when it became known that the organization would defend Sandra Merritt in the wake of her indictment in Texas for tampering with a government record, a felony punishable by up to 20 years in prison. Merritt and a fellow antiabortion activist, David Daleiden, had shot undercover video in a Planned Parenthood clinic in Houston, Texas, with the intention of demonstrating that Planned Parenthood was involved in the selling of body parts of aborted fetuses. The videos shot were deceptively edited, and they "spawned numerous calls from the right to defund Planned Parenthood and investigate its practices" (Hatewatch staff). Staver, who has called Planned Parenthood a "corrupt organization," implied a conflict of interest in the case, noting that a prosecutor in the Houston office was a board member of Planned Parenthood (Ertelt). Though the prosecutor named by Staver was not involved in the Planned Parenthood case, the "conspiracy theory" suggested by Staver picked up steam in several right-wing news arenas (Hatewatch staff).

In March 2017, Liberty Counsel was again in the national news when a federal court ordered that a lawsuit against the group could proceed. The lawsuit, brought by Janet Jenkins, alleges that Liberty Counsel assisted Jenkins's lesbian partner, Lisa Miller, in kidnapping and relocating the couple's daughter. Miller, who had renounced her lesbianism, fled with the couple's child to Nicaragua. Jenkins, along with attorneys from the Southern Poverty Law Center (SPLC), were successful in convincing the federal court that Liberty Counsel, as well as Mat Staver, could be fully investigated for the organization's part in assisting in the kidnapping of Isabella, Jenkins and Miller's daughter. A spokesperson for the SPLC stated, "We are pleased the court recognized that our allegations suggested 'significant wrongdoing' by these lawyers, including Mat Staver, and we will move swiftly to learn more about their wrongdoing and to hold everyone involved in the kidnapping to account" (Southern Poverty Law Center, 2017).

See also: Alliance Defending Freedom; American College of Pediatricians; American Family Association; Family Research Council; Family Watch International; Oath Keepers; Pacific Justice Institute; Ruth Institute; Westboro Baptist Church; World Congress of Families

FURTHER READING

Edwards, David. September 7, 2015. "Fox News Panel Concludes that Kim Davis' Lawyer Is 'Ridiculously Stupid.'" RawStory.com. http://www.rawstory.com/2015/09/fox-news-panel-concludes-that-kim-davis-lawyer-is-ridiculously-stupid/. (Accessed June 3, 2017.)

Ertelt, Steven. January 26, 2016. "Planned Parenthood Board Member Works in Office of D.A. Who Indicted David Daleiden." LifeNews.com. http://www.lifenews.com/2016/01/26/planned-parenthood-board-member-works-in-office-of-d-a-who-indicted-david-daleiden/. (Accessed June 3, 2017.)

Hatewatch Staff. January 29, 2016. "Anti-LGBT Hate Group Liberty Counsel to Defend Indicted Anti-Abortion Activist." Southern Poverty Law Center. https://www.splcenter.org/hatewatch/2016/01/29/anti-lgbt-hate-group-liberty-counsel-defend-indicted-anti-abortion-activist. (Accessed June 3, 2017.)

Hooper, Jeremy. April 1, 2014. "Liberty Counsel Continues Penchant for Inciting 'Revolution.'" Good As You. http://www.goodasyou.org/good_as_you/2014/04/liberty-counsel-continues-penchant-for-inciting-revolution.html. (Accessed June 3, 2017.)

Liberty Counsel. "About Liberty Counsel." Liberty Counsel. https://www.lc.org/about. (Accessed June 3, 2017.)

Liberty Counsel. October 5, 2015. "Debunking the SPLC 'Hate Group' Myth." Liberty Counsel. https://www.lc.org/newsroom/details/debunking-the-splc-hate-group-myth-1. (Accessed June 3, 2017.)

Mantyla, Kyle. March 13, 2015. "Mat Staver Will Disobey SCOTUS Marriage Equality Ruling Just as He'd Refuse to Turn a Jew Over to the Nazis." Right Wing Watch. http://www.rightwingwatch.org/post/mat-staver-will-disobey-a-scotus-marriage-equality-ruling-just-as-hed-refuse-to-turn-a-jew-over-to-the-nazis/. (Accessed June 3, 2017.)

Niewert, David. September 10, 2015. "Oath Keepers Head to Kentucky to Repeat Bundy Ranch Tactics in Kim Davis Dispute." Southern Poverty Law Center: Hatewatch. https://www.splcenter.org/hatewatch/2015/09/10/oath-keepers-head-kentucky-repeat-bundy-ranch-tactics-kim-davis-dispute. (Accessed June 3, 2017.)

Schlatter, Evelyn, and Robert Steinback. February 27, 2011. "10 Anti-Gay Myths Debunked." Southern Poverty Law Center: Intelligence Report. https://www .splcenter.org/fighting-hate/intelligence-report/2011/10-anti-gay-myths-debunked. (Accessed June 3, 2017.)

Southern Poverty Law Center. "Liberty Counsel." Southern Poverty Law Center. https:// www.splcenter.org/fighting-hate/extremist-files/group/liberty-counsel. (Accessed June 3, 2017.)

Southern Poverty Law Center. March 20, 2017. "Federal Court Permits Vermont Lesbian to Sue Liberty Counsel, Mat Staver for Role in International Kidnapping." Southern Poverty Law Center. https://www.splcenter.org/news/2017/03/20/federal -court-permits-vermont-lesbian-sue-liberty-counsel-mat-staver-role-international. (Accessed June 3, 2017.)

Liberty Fellowship

Liberty Fellowship is a ministry founded in 2011 by Chuck Baldwin, former pastor of Crossroad Baptist Church in Pensacola, Florida. Liberty Fellowship was formed after Baldwin moved to Montana in 2010 with his entire family in support of the "Pioneer Little Europe (PLE) Movement, which seeks to establish a whites-only homeland in northwest Montana" (Holthouse). Among the known congregants of the Liberty Fellowship are Randy Weaver, who was involved in a standoff with government officials in 1992 at his compound in Ruby Ridge, Idaho, and April Gaede, an avowed neo-Nazi, who has stated that Baldwin's sermons have "moved her to tears." The congregation, located in Kalispell, Montana, counts among its adherents many individuals known to have anti-government sentiments and to be followers of the patriot movement. The Southern Poverty Law Center (SPLC) describes such people as those "who generally believe that the federal government is an evil entity that is engaged in a secret conspiracy to impose martial law, herd those who resist into concentration camps, and force the United States into a socialistic 'New World Order'" (Potok).

Liberty Fellowship remains as a bastion for patriot sympathizers and members of the PLE movement. Adherents believe "in a strict interpretation of the U.S. Constitution and the Declaration of Independence." Organizers call "for targeting communities that will be attractive to 'restless whites' who are conscious of the threats around them" (Holthouse).

Though Baldwin and Liberty Fellowship remain as the epitome of a desire for a whites-only homeland, the organization itself claims that there is no racial bias or segregation within the congregation. The official website of Liberty Fellowship states:

> Any charge of "anti-government extremism" against LF [Liberty Fellowship] from people and organizations such as the Southern Poverty Law Center (SPLC) is completely unfounded and untruthful. Such accusations can only come from people who hold an extreme anti-Christian bias of their own.
>
> LF is one of the most racially-diverse Christian fellowships in the entire State of Montana. In fact, the racial diversity of Liberty Fellowship FAR EXCEEDS [emphasis in original] the racial diversity of the State in general. The congregation of our fellowship is happily comprised of Asians, Indians, Hispanics, Blacks, and Caucasians,

including several mixed-raced families. Any accusations of racism against Chuck Baldwin and Liberty Fellowship is complete balderdash. (Liberty Fellowship)

See also: White Nationalism

FURTHER READING

Holthouse, David. November 16, 2011. "High Country Extremism: Patriot Games." Media Matters for America. http://mediamatters.org/blog/2011/11/16/high-country -extremism-patriot-games/181612. (Accessed January 4, 2018.)

Liberty Fellowship. "Liberty Fellowship Statement of Belief and Practice." Liberty Fellowship. http://libertyfellowshipmt.com/AboutUs/StatementofFaith.aspx. (Accessed January 4, 2018.)

Potok, Mark. March 2, 2012. "The 'Patriot' Movement Explodes." Southern Poverty Law Center: Intelligence Report. https://www.splcenter.org/fighting-hate/intelligence -report/2012/patriot-movement-explodes. (Accessed January 4, 2018.)

Liberty Lobby

The Liberty Lobby was a right-wing group founded as a patriotic lobby group dedicated to the preservation of the U.S. Constitution and the advancement of conservative principles. It became known, however, for its advocacy of white supremacism and anti-Semitism (Southern Poverty Law Center, Willis Carto). The organization was founded by Willis Carto in 1955. Carto "was known for his promotion of anti-Semitic conspiracy theories and Holocaust denial" (Southern Poverty Law Center, Willis Carto). The Liberty Lobby went defunct in 2001 after Carto was sued for fraud and mismanagement over another one of his ventures, the *Institute of Historical Review*, a pseudoacademic journal that publishes pieces defending Nazism and the perpetuation of Holocaust denial. The publishing arm of the Liberty Lobby, the *Spotlight*, also folded in 2001. Today, however, a website still exists that uses both the Liberty Lobby and the *Spotlight* monikers and claims its roots in Carto's original organization.

The Liberty Lobby was organized at a time when Americans feared communism as "a threat to the American way of life." For that reason, its dedication to the Constitution and conservative principles attracted many high-powered adherents. During the 1960s, the Liberty Lobby's newsletter boasted a circulation greater than that of older and better-known conservative publications, such as the *National Review*. National politicians "and big name conservatives appeared and spoke at Liberty Lobby meetings, including Christian Right hardliner Phyllis Schlafly in 1965. Even some Hollywood types backed him, including Gloria Swanson and Eddie Albert" (Beirich). The association of mainstream conservatives was troubling given that the Liberty Lobby's board was reportedly populated with anti-Semites and racists, including individuals who had openly opposed school desegregation in the South (Beirich).

By the 1970s, most of the Liberty Lobby's acceptable conservative advocates had fallen away. Carto, no longer feeling bound to placate the right, established the *Institute for Historical Review*, a journal known for publishing articles related to Holocaust denial and supporting racist and white supremacist causes. In 1988, ultraconservative Judge Robert Bork, one-time Supreme Court nominee and "then on the Court of Appeals for the District of Columbia, ruled that the Liberty Lobby was 'anti-Semitic,' effectively certifying Carto from that moment on as an extremist" (Beirich).

Liberty Lobby is perhaps most well known for the Supreme Court case known as *Anderson v. Liberty Lobby, Inc.* (477 U.S. 242 [1986]). In the case, Liberty Lobby claimed that Jack Anderson, a conservative columnist, had libeled the organization by publishing false and derogatory statements about its operations. A district court ruled in favor of Anderson, but an appellate court reversed the ruling, and Anderson appealed to the U.S. Supreme Court. The Supreme Court reversed the appellate court decision, thereby articulating the standard to grant summary judgment—the standard that allows a judgment to be "entered by a court for one party against another party summarily; i.e, without a full trial." *Anderson v. Liberty Lobby, Inc.* is one of the most recited Supreme Court cases (Most Cited Cases).

In 1993, Mark Weber, a member of the board of the *Institute for Historical Review* (IHR), wrested control of the IHR from Carto. The entire board of IHR later sued Carto for fraud and mismanagement of money that was left in a bequest for IHR. After protracted legal battles, Carto was ordered to pay millions of dollars to IHR (Southern Poverty Law Center, Willis Carto). As a result of the judgments, Liberty Lobby folded up in 2001, as did the organization's publication, the *Spotlight*.

After the loss of the Liberty Lobby, Carto formed the *American Free Press*, which continued to publish anti-Semitic articles, secret "New World Order" conspiracy theories, racist rants against Jews and Israel, and Holocaust denial stories. Carto also included pieces on Christian Identity, a theology that claims that Jews are the biological descendants of Eve and Satan (Southern Poverty Law Center, Carto).

Carto died in 2015. The Liberty Lobby name continues today with a website that claims to have its origins in the founding of Carto's original organization.

See also: Holocaust Denial; Institute for Historical Review; White Supremacist Movement

FURTHER READING

Beirich, Heidi. November 30, 2008. "Willis Carto: The First Major Biography." Southern Poverty Law Center: Intelligence Report. https://www.splcenter.org/fighting-hate /intelligence-report/2008/willis-carto-first-major-biography. (Accessed May 4, 2018.)

Kaplan, Jeffrey, editor. 2000. *Encyclopedia of White Power: A Sourcebook on the Radical Racist Right*. Alta Mira Press.

Liberty Lobby. http://www.libertylobby.org/index.html. (Accessed May 3, 2018.)

Most Cited Cases. https://web.archive.org/web/20091121082359/http://listproc.ucdavis.edu / archives/law-lib/law-lib.log9909/0171.html. (Accessed May 3, 2018.)

Nizkor Project. "Liberty Lobby and *The Spotlight*." Nizkor Project. http://www.nizkor .org/hweb/orgs/american/adl/paranoia-as-patriotism/liberty-lobby.html/. (Accessed May 4, 2018.)

Southern Poverty Law Center. "Willis Carto." Southern Poverty Law Center. https://
www.splcenter.org/fighting-hate/extremist-files/individual/willis-carto.
(Accessed May 4, 2018.)

Southern Poverty Law Center. August 29, 2001. "The Spotlight, Extinguished." Southern
Poverty Law Center: Intelligence Report. https://www.splcenter.org/fighting-hate
/intelligence-report/2001/spotlight-extinguished. (Accessed May 4, 2018.)

Loyal White Knights of the Ku Klux Klan

The Loyal White Knights of the Ku Klux Klan (LWKKKK) is a Ku Klux Klan
(KKK)-affiliated group that is characterized by the Southern Poverty Law Center
(SPLC) as a KKK hate group. According to the SPLC, KKK hate groups "are the
oldest and most infamous hate groups in the United States" (Southern Poverty
Law Center, Ku Klux Klan). When it was formed in 1865, the KKK "was a single,
unitary organization. Today, there are dozens of competing Klan groups. Although
black Americans have typically been the Klan's primary target, it has also attacked
Jews, immigrants, homosexuals, and Catholics" (Southern Poverty Law Center,
2017). The LWKKKK has local chapters, or "klaverns," in several U.S. states,
including Alabama, California, Florida, Georgia, Illinois, Louisiana, Michigan,
Mississippi, North Carolina, New York, Ohio, South Carolina, Texas, and Virginia (CNN).

Formed in 2012, the LWKKKK has its headquarters in Pelham, North Carolina
(Southern Poverty Law Center, 2017). According to the Terrorism Research &
Analysis Consortium:

> The Loyal White Knights of the Ku Klux Klan is a legal, purportedly law-abiding,
> "Christian" organization which main goal is to "protect our family, race and nation"
> and "restore America to a White, Christian nation founded on God's word." The
> Loyal White Knights maintain the Ku Klux Klan's traditions and rituals, ceremo-
> nies, costumes, and hierarchy of offices [that] closely imitate those of the original
> and the second KKK. Members of the organization meet at rally events and occa-
> sionally wear traditional robes and hoods decorated with symbols associated with
> the previous Klans. Moreover, the organization cultivate[s] typical Ku Klux Klan's
> traditions such as ritualistic gatherings or cross lightings [sic]. White supremacy is
> the belief that is shared by all members of the organization. According to the web-
> site, only "a native- born white American Citizen, (. . .) of Christian Faith" who
> "believe in White Supremacy and an American Citizen are allowed to join." (Ter-
> rorism Research & Analysis Consortium)

In November 2016, a "grand klaliff," or "second in command," of the "California
realm" LWKKKK commented on the election of Donald Trump, saying he "hoped
and believed that Trump would do great things for white nationalists." The
LWKKKK member, James Zarth, stated:

> "I noticed something was going wrong in America decades ago." He mentioned the
> TV shows "Father Knows Best," "Andy Griffith," "The Brady Bunch," and "Little
> House on the Prairie." "Usually, those shows had a Christian moral," he said. "But
> now that the Jews own the majority of the media stations, they're showing things
> that are against God's law, like race-mixing and homosexuality." He pointed to

America's diverse population as its primary source of violence and conflict. "We advocate for living separately within America. We are a benevolent, fraternal, Christian, white-civil-rights organization," he claimed. "We are for family and for God. We see our race and our heritage going away and being harmed by intermixing with these mongrel races. It has to stop."

He added, "I think we now have a President [Trump] with some of the same ideals." He insisted that the Loyal White Knights had been growing since Trump's victory. When I asked him for specifics, he replied, "I can't give out exact numbers—that's why we're called 'the invisible empire.' But I can tell you this: since Trump has been elected, people have been calling us left and right wanting to join, from all walks of life." (Bethea)

In August 2017, after various right-wing extremist groups protested the Charlottesville (Virginia) City Council's announcement that it would remove a statue of Confederate hero Robert E. Lee, another LWKKKK member made news when he celebrated the death of a counterprotester, Heather Heyer. Heyer was killed when a right-wing protester "allegedly drove a car into a crowd of protesters at high speed, then fled the scene by backing up. Nineteen other people were injured" (Crump). Justin Moore, "Grand Dragon for the Loyal White Knights of the Ku Klux Klan," said "he was glad Heyer died in the attack." Moore stated:

I'm sorta glad that them people got hit and I'm glad that girl died. They were a bunch of Communists out there protesting against somebody's freedom of speech, so it doesn't bother me that they got hurt at all. I think we're going to see more stuff like this happening at white nationalist events. (Crump)

Moore went on to state:

We were out there and I seen [sic] a lot of Communist flags and anti-fascists and we're going to see more stuff like this. White people are getting fed up with the double standard setup in America today by the controlled press. We should have been able to go out there and have our protest and it should have been peaceful but it's the anti-fascists and the communists . . . continuing to try and stop us. So I think there will be more violence like this in the future to come. (Crump)

According to a CBS News report, the LWKKKK claims that it is a "non-violent pro-white civil rights movement" (CBS News).

See also: Ku Klux Klan; White Nationalism; White Supremacist Movement

FURTHER READING

Bethea, Charles. August 17, 2017. "What a White Supremacist Told Me after Donald Trump Was Elected." *New Yorker.* https://www.newyorker.com/news/news -desk/what-a-white-supremacist-told-me-after-donald-trump-was-elected. (Accessed July 21, 2018.)

CBS News. "Loyal White Knights of the Ku Klux Klan." CBS News. https://www .cbsnews.com/pictures/hate-groups-in-america/3/. (Accessed July 21, 2018.)

CNN. August 17, 2017. "Southern Poverty Law Center Lists Active Hate Groups by State." WPTV.com. https://www.wptv.com/news/national/southern-poverty-law -center-lists-active-hate-groups-by-state. (Accessed July 21, 2018.)

Crump, Steve. August 15, 2017. "'I'm Glad That Girl Died' during Virginia Protest, Says NC KKK Leader." *Charlotte Observer.* https://www.charlotteobserver.com/news /local/article167303682.html. (Accessed July 21, 2018.)

Southern Poverty Law Center. "Hate Map." Southern Poverty Law Center. https://www .splcenter.org/hate-map. (Accessed July 21, 2018.)

Southern Poverty Law Center. "Ku Klux Klan." Southern Poverty Law Center. https:// www.splcenter.org/fighting-hate/extremist-files/ideology/ku-klux-klan. (Accessed July 21, 2018.)

Southern Poverty Law Center. February 15, 2017. "Active Hate Groups 2016." Southern Poverty Law Center: Intelligence Report. https://www.splcenter.org/fighting-hate /intelligence-report/2017/active-hate-groups-2016. (Accessed July 21, 2018.)

Terrorism Research & Analysis Consortium. "Loyal White Knights of the Ku Klux Klan (LWK)." Terrorism Research & Analysis Consortium. https://www.tracking terrorism.org/group/loyal-white-knights-ku-klux-klan-lwk. (Accessed July 21, 2018.)

M

Mary Noel Kershaw Foundation

The Mary Noel Kershaw Foundation ("Kershaw Foundation") is a 501(c)(3) entity, which "can receive tax deductible contributions for artistic and educational purposes carried on within the Southern States" (Hill). The foundation was established by John Karl "Jack" Kershaw, "who was best known as the lawyer who defended James Earl Ray, the killer of Martin Luther King, Jr." (Southern Poverty Law Center). Kershaw also helped found the League of the South, a neo-Confederate, white nationalist, and white supremacist organization whose goal is "a free and independent Southern Republic" (League of the South). Upon his death, the Southern Poverty Law Center (SPLC) called Jack Kershaw "one of the most iconic American white segregationists of the 20th century" (Steinback). Jack Kershaw founded the Mary Noel Kershaw Foundation in honor of his wife, Mary Noel, who preceded him in death in 1989. The SPLC has designated the Kershaw Foundation a neo-Confederate hate group because one of its primary functions is to provide funds for self-defense training for LOS members (Rubino).

The Kershaw Foundation gained notoriety in the aftermath of the Charlottesville, Virginia, white nationalist protests that erupted in August 2017. Before the "Unite the Right" protests, "LOS president Michael Hill, a board member of the Kershaw Foundation, told attendees to 'prepare for violence'" (Reicher). As LOS members and other white nationalists clashed with counterprotesters, a white nationalist protester "rammed his car into a crowd of anti-white supremacist protestors, leaving one woman dead." Two police officers on their way to the protests died when their police helicopter crashed.

Soon after the protests ended, it was made public that Robert L. Echols, a former federal judge of the U.S. District Court for Middle Tennessee and "prominent Nashville, Tennessee attorney, had contributed nearly $3,000 to the Kershaw Foundation" (Reicher). After Charlottesville, Echols issued a statement saying that he was "horrified by the actions of hate groups in Charlottesville, including the League of the South" (Reicher). Echols said he learned of the Kershaw Foundation's hate associations "when he was contacted by members of the media." Echols had been led to believe by his Bible study leader that he was "making donations to a Christian school and that my financial support would help families" (Reicher). Tax filings indicate that the Kershaw Foundation did provide grants to the Heritage Covenant Schools to teach a course entitled "A History of the Southern People" (Reicher).

David O. Jones, "a minister and Christian home schooling advocate," was the president of the Kershaw Foundation prior to the Charlottesville protests. His organization, Heritage Covenant Schools, "provides resources for families who homeschool their children using a conservative Christian curriculum" (Janik). He resigned as the president of the Kershaw Foundation after its associations with the League of the South became public. Jones did not initially see a conflict with funneling money meant for home schooling through the Kershaw Foundation, even though he knew of its associations with the League of the South. In fact, the Kershaw Foundation does not have its own website, but it distributes its information through the LOS website. In retrospect, Jones stated, "I don't want to taint my school or my ministry by an association that I never really thought through" (Janik).

See also: League of the South; Neo-Confederates; White Nationalism; White Supremacist Movement

FURTHER READING

Hill, Michael. February 13, 2015. "The Mary Noel Kershaw Foundation." League of the South. http://leagueofthesouth.com/the-mary-noel-kershaw-foundation/. (Accessed May 29, 2018.)

Janik, Rachel. August 28, 2017. "Tennessee Minister Funneled Christian School Donations Through Neo-Confederate Hate Group." Southern Poverty Law Center: Hatewatch. https://www.splcenter.org/hatewatch/2017/08/28/tennessee-minister-funneled-christian-school-donations-through-neo-confederate-hate-group. (Accessed May 29, 2018.)

League of the South. "What Is the League of the South?" League of the South. http://leagueofthesouth.com/what-is-ls/. (Accessed May 29, 2018.)

Reicher, Mike. August 16, 2017. "Former Nashville Federal Judge Donated to Hate Group Tied to Charlottesville Protests." *Tennessean*. https://www.tennessean.com/story/news/2017/08/16/former-nashville-federal-judge-donated-group-tied-charlottesville-protests/573025001/. (Accessed May 29, 2018.)

Rubino, Kathryn. August 17, 2017. "Former Federal Judge Donated to White Supremacist Cause." Above the Law. https://abovethelaw.com/2017/08/former-federal-judge-donated-to-white-supremacist-cause/. (Accessed May 29, 2018.)

Southern Poverty Law Center. "League of the South." Southern Poverty Law Center. https://www.splcenter.org/fighting-hate/extremist-files/group/league-south. (Accessed May 29, 2018.)

Steinback, Robert. September 24, 2010. "Jack Kershaw, Stalwart of White Nationalism, Dies." Southern Poverty Law Center: Hatewatch. https://www.splcenter.org/hatewatch/2010/09/24/jack-kershaw-stalwart-white-nationalism-dies. (Accessed May 29, 2018.)

Maryland State Skinheads

The Maryland State Skinheads (MSS) are classified by the Southern Poverty Law Center (SPLC) as a racist skinhead hate group. According to the SPLC, "Racist Skinheads form a particularly violent element of the white supremacist movement, and have often been referred to as the 'shock troops' of the hoped-for revolution. The classic Skinhead look is a shaved head, black Doc Martens boots, jeans with suspenders and an array of typically racist tattoos" (Southern Poverty Law Center). The SPLC notes that skinheads are particularly violent and that "criminal attacks by shaved-head, boot wearing white youths" show "no sign of fading" (Southern Poverty Law Center). Indeed, in recent years, skinheads have beaten victims to death with a baseball bat, crushed the skull of a victim with concrete, and "strangled a 62-year-old gay man in Oklahoma City as a rite of passage in his gang" (Southern Poverty Law Center). The MSS, which are part of this violent culture, are based in Baltimore, Maryland (Rentz).

The Southern Poverty Law Center "has reported that the number of hate groups has been rising in Maryland," as well as around the country, in recent years (Renz). Most of the growth, according to the SPLC, has occurred in neo-Nazi groups (such as the Maryland State Skinheads), as well as in anti-Muslim and black nationalist groups (Rentz). The SPLC has "attributed the growth to white supremacists energized by the presidency of Donald Trump and black nationalist groups rising in response" (Rentz). A spokesperson for the SPLC has stated, "The world allows you to spread propaganda like never before, and Trump has heightened the hate" (Rentz).

In March 2017, a Veterans of Foreign Wars (VFW) post in Joppatowne, Maryland, canceled a rental agreement they had with the Maryland State Skinheads after realizing that the organization was a white supremacist organization. The VFW post commander stated that he did not realize that the skinheads were a white supremacist group. It was only after being tipped off by the Mid-Atlantic General Defense Committee Local 21 that the VFW realized that it was renting to a white supremacist organization. The Mid-Atlantic General Defense Committee Local 21 describes itself as an "anti-racist, anti-sexist and anti-capitalist organization" (Hendricks).

See also: Neo-Nazis; Racist Skinheads; White Nationalism; White Supremacist Movement

FURTHER READING

Hendricks, Ted. March 23, 2017. "Joppatowne VFW Post Cancels Contract after Learning Renters Are White Supremacists." *Baltimore Sun.* http://www.baltimoresun.com /news/maryland/harford/aegis/ph-ag-vfw-rental-0324-20170323-story.html#. (Accessed July 21, 2018.)

Rentz, Catherine. February 23, 2018. "Southern Poverty Law Center: Hate Groups on the Rise in Maryland, Nationwide." *Baltimore Sun.* http://www.baltimoresun.com /news/maryland/bs-md-hate-groups-20180222-story.html. (Accessed July 21, 2018.)

Southern Poverty Law Center. "Racist Skinhead." Southern Poverty Law Center. https:// www.splcenter.org/fighting-hate/extremist-files/ideology/racist-skinhead. (Accessed July 21, 2018.)

Viets, Sarah. April 27, 2016. "Co-Founder of Pennsylvania Skinhead Group Wins Re-Election for County Committee Seat." Southern Poverty Law Center: Hatewatch. https://www.splcenter.org/hatewatch/2016/04/27/co-founder-pennsylvania-skin head-group-wins-re-election-county-committee-seat. (Accessed July 21, 2018.)

Midland Hammerskins

The Midland Hammerskins (MHS) are a regional chapter, or "crew," of the larger Hammerskin Nations, which the Anti-Defamation League labels as "the most violent and best-organized neo-Nazi skinhead group in the United States" (Anti-Defamation League). The Southern Poverty Law Center (SPLC) characterizes the Midland Hammerskins and Hammerskin Nations as racist skinhead hate groups that "form a particularly violent element of the white supremacist movement, and have often been referred to as the 'shock troops' of the hoped-for revolution" (Southern Poverty Law Center, Racist Skinheads). According to the website for Hammerskin Nation:

> The Hammerskin Nation is a leaderless group of men and women who have adopted the White Power Skinhead lifestyle. We are blue collar workers, white collar professionals, college students, entrepreneurs, fathers and mothers.
>
> The Hammerskin brotherhood is way of achieving goals which we have all set for ourselves. These goals are many but can be summed up with one phrase consisting of 14 words.
>
> "We must secure the existence of our people and a future for White Children." (Hammerskin Nation, Who We Are)

Hammerskin Nation was created in the late 1980s in Dallas, Texas. "This in turn resulted in alliances between skinhead crews from across the U.S. giving way to the now infamous regions of CHS [Confederate Hammerskins], NHS [Northern Hammerskins], EHS (Eastern Hammerskins], and WHS [Western Hammerskins]" (Midland Hammerskins). The name and symbol of the Hammerskin Nation

> came from The Wall, a 1979 album by the rock group Pink Floyd that was made into a film in 1982. The Wall tells the story of Pink, a rock singer who becomes a drug addict, loses his grip on reality and turns to fascism. Pink performs a song in which he expresses a desire to line all of the "queers," "Jews," and "coons" in his audience "up against the wall" and shoot them. In obvious references to the Holocaust, he sings of the "final solution" and "waiting to turn on the showers and fire the ovens." The swastika is replaced by Pink's symbol: two crossed hammers, which he boasts will "batter down" the doors behind which frightened minorities hide from his fascist supporters. (Atha)

According to the Midland Hammerskins website:

> In the year 2000 it was time to recognize there was a need for proper representation of a somewhat older and partially new region that was to be known as the Midland Hammerskins. Members from Kansas and Missouri who had been active within the region since the early 1990's founded MHS. The intention of the newly constructed region was and is to help promote and represent the current uprise [sic] in the central United States. We in MHS feel this region to be necessary to ensure the quality of skinheads in the Midwest and south-central U.S. We will continue to be relevant for some many decades to come. The states included in this region are Kansas, Missouri, Colorado, Iowa, Nebraska, South Dakota, Wyoming and Texas. (Midland Hammerskins)

As noted by the Anti-Defamation League, the Midland Hammerskins—like their parent organization, Hammerskin Nation—are extremely violent and are often drawn together by white power music. Indeed, "hate rock has been both a powerful inspirational force and an effective recruiting tool for racist skinhead groups like the Hammerskins" (Anti-Defamation League). As noted by one author:

> Violence is a large part of the skinhead subculture, among racist and nonracist skinheads alike. Racist skinheads have committed a large number of violent hate crimes across the United States during the past two decades, ranging from brutal beatings to outright murder. As one of the most prominent white power skinhead groups in the country, the Hammerskins have frequently shocked the communities in which they are active with the violence of some of their activities. (Atha)

Many Hammerskins members, including those from Midland Hammerskins, have found themselves in prison, where their racism spreads among other inmates. Many members of the Midland Hammerskins have "been charged with murder, attempted murder, conspiracy to commit murder, violation of civil rights and hate crimes" (White Prison Gangs). As a whole, the Hammerskins "remain the most dangerous skinhead gang in the US" (White Prison Gangs).

See also: Confederate Hammerskins; Crew 38; Eastern Hammerskins; Hammerskin Nation; Neo-Nazis; Northern Hammerskins; The Order; Racist Skinheads; Western Hammerskins; White Nationalism; White Supremacist Movement

FURTHER READING

Anti-Defamation League. "The Hammerskin Nation." Anti-Defamation League. https://www .adl.org/education/resources/profiles/hammerskin-nation. (Accessed July 18, 2018.)

Atha, Randi. September 15, 2014. "Midland Hammerskins." Prezi.com. https://prezi.com /afvfaamg3wsl/midland-hammerskins/. (Accessed July 18, 2018.)

Hammerskin Nation. "Our History." Hammerskin Nation. https://www.hammerskins .net/. (Accessed July 18, 2018.)

Hammerskin Nation. "Who We Are." Hammerskin Nation. https://www.hammerskins .net/. (Accessed July 18, 2018.)

Holthouse, David. October 19, 2006. "Motley Crews: With Decline of Hammerskins, Independent Skinhead Groups Grow." Southern Poverty Law Center: Intelligence Report. https://www.splcenter.org/fighting-hate/intelligence-report/2006/motley -crews-decline-hammerskins-independent-skinhead-groups-grow. (Accessed July 18, 2018.)

Michaelis, Arno. June 25, 2015. "This Is How You Become a White Supremacist." *Washington Post*. https://www.washingtonpost.com/posteverything/wp/2015/06/25 /this-is-how-you-become-a-white-supremacist/. (Accessed July 18, 2018.)

Midland Hammerskins. http://www.hammerskins.net/mhs/. (Accessed July 18, 2018.)

Reynolds, Michael. December 15, 1999. "Hammerskin Nation Emerges from Small Dallas Group." Southern Poverty Law Center: Intelligence Report. https://www .splcenter.org/fighting-hate/intelligence-report/1999/hammerskin-nation -emerges-small-dallas-group. (Accessed July 18, 2018.)

Southern Poverty Law Center. "Racist Skinhead." Southern Poverty Law Center. https:// www.splcenter.org/fighting-hate/extremist-files/ideology/racist-skinhead. (Accessed July 18, 2018.)

Southern Poverty Law Center. February 15, 2017. "Active Hate Groups 2016." Southern Poverty Law Center: Intelligence Report. https://www.splcenter.org/fighting-hate /intelligence-report/2017/active-hate-groups-2016. (Accessed July 18, 2018.)

Terrorism Research & Analysis Consortium. "Hammerskin Nation." Terrorism Research & Analysis Consortium. https://www.trackingterrorism.org/group/hammerskin -nation. (Accessed July 18, 2018.)
White Prison Gangs. "Hammerskins." White Prison Gangs. http://whiteprisongangs .blogspot.com/2009/05/hammerskins_02.html. (Accessed July 18, 2018.)

Militant Knights of the Ku Klux Klan

The Militant Knights of the Ku Klux Klan (MKKKK) are a Ku Klux Klan (KKK)-affiliated group that "is characterized by the Southern Poverty Law Center (SPLC) as a KKK hate group" (Southern Poverty Law Center, Ku Klux Klan). According to the SPLC, "KKK hate groups are the oldest and most infamous hate groups in the United States." When it was formed in 1865, the KKK "was a single, unitary organization. Today, there are dozens of competing Klan groups. Although black Americans have typically been the Klan's primary target, it has also attacked Jews, immigrants, homosexuals, and Catholics" (Southern Poverty Law Center, 2017). The MKKKK has local chapters, or "klaverns," in several U.S. states, including Alabama, Maine, Michigan, Minnesota, Missouri, Mississippi, New Jersey, New York, Ohio, Pennsylvania, Tennessee, and Texas (CNN).

See also: Ku Klux Klan; White Nationalism; White Supremacist Movement

FURTHER READING

CNN. August 17, 2017. "Southern Poverty Law Center Lists Active Hate Groups by State." WPTV.com. https://www.wptv.com/news/national/southern-poverty-law -center-lists-active-hate-groups-by-state. (Accessed July 20, 2018.)
Southern Poverty Law Center. "Hate Map." Southern Poverty Law Center. https://www .splcenter.org/hate-map. (Accessed July 20, 2018.)
Southern Poverty Law Center. "Ku Klux Klan." Southern Poverty Law Center. https:// www.splcenter.org/fighting-hate/extremist-files/ideology/ku-klux-klan. (Accessed July 20, 2018.)
Southern Poverty Law Center. February 15, 2017. "Active Hate Groups 2016." Southern Poverty Law Center: Intelligence Report. https://www.splcenter.org/fighting-hate /intelligence-report/2017/active-hate-groups-2016. (Accessed July 20, 2018.)

N

Nation of Islam

The Nation of Islam (NOI) was founded in 1930 to improve the "spiritual, mental, social, and economic condition of African Americans in the United States and all of humanity" (Nation of Islam, Brief History). During its first two decades of existence, it gathered few members and was mostly known for some of its strange mix of doctrines and creeds that were not always consistent with the more traditional practice of Islam. NOI's growth exploded during the 1950s and 1960s when the civil rights movement, and the violent reactions it provoked among whites, reinforced the "white devil" idea perpetrated by NOI doctrine. Between 1952 and 1964, membership in NOI grew from around 400 to between 100,000 and 300,000 (Southern Poverty Law Center). But NOI's bitter and abusive rhetoric "and its advocacy for self-defense and violence in place of nonviolence alienated it from the bulk of other civil rights groups of the day." Today, the NOI "has grown into one of the wealthiest and best-known organizations in black America. However, its theology of the superiority of blacks over whites is deeply racist. Moreover, NOI spews anti-Semitic and anti-gay rhetoric that has caused the Southern Poverty Law Center (SPLC) to designate the Nation of Islam as a hate group" (Southern Poverty Law Center).

The Nation of Islam was founded by Wallace D. Fard (Farad Muhammad) and "his messenger and successor, Elijah Muhammad" (Southern Poverty Law Center). As the civil rights movement accelerated in the 1950s, along with the violent backlash it produced from white America, thousands of African Americans in the United States flocked to NOI, swelling its ranks. Among the new adherents to the organization at this time were Malcolm X, who had joined NOI in prison, and Muhammad Ali (previously Cassius Clay), the heavyweight champion of professional boxing. Malcolm X, who became NOI's primary spokesperson, exhorted black Americans to throw off the "shackles of racism by any means necessary," including violence (Biography.com). By 1959, Martin Luther King Jr. "was warning of a hate group arising in our midst that would preach the doctrine of black supremacy" (Southern Poverty Law Center).

In 1964, Malcolm X split with NOI and denounced the "sickness and madness" of NOI's racist views. In 1965, Malcolm X was assassinated by three members of NOI. His successor was Louis Farrakhan, who had joined NOI in 1955. Viewed as a charismatic speaker and a powerful organizer, Farrakhan filled the void left by Malcolm X's death and became the NOI's national spokesperson in 1967. When "Elijah Muhammad died in 1975, Farrakhan initially remained loyal to Elijah Muhammad's son, Wallace Deen Muhammad" (Southern Poverty Law Center). But when the younger Muhammad attempted to align NOI more with mainstream

Islam, Farrakhan broke from the group and proclaimed a "resurrected" Nation of Islam (Southern Poverty Law Center).

NOI's historical "characterization of whites as devils" was exacerbated under Farrakhan. Farrakhan, too, ramped up the anti-Semitic view espoused by NOI by continually denouncing Jewish influence in politics, business, and entertainment. During Jesse Jackson's 1984 presidential bid, Farrakhan made remarks "calling Adolf Hitler 'a very great man' and Judaism a 'dirty religion'" (Southern Poverty Law Center). NOI's anti-Semitism is a long-standing trope of the group. In 1962, American Nazi Party leader George Lincoln Rockwell had dubbed Elijah Muhammad the "Hitler of the Blacks." Similarly, "American neo-Nazi and White Aryan Resistance founder Tom Metzger has praised NOI's anti-Semitic rhetoric and has even donated a symbolic amount of money to the Nation" (Southern Poverty Law Center).

Farrakhan is also "well-known for bashing gays and lesbians, Catholics, and white devils," whom Farrakhan refers to as "potential humans . . . [who] haven't evolved yet" (Southern Poverty Law Center). During the 1990s, Farrakhan attempted to moderate his message. But an attempt to reach out "to the Congressional Black Caucus failed after the Anti-Defamation League (ADL) published an article detailing a speech by a top NOI official in which he bashed Jews, Catholics, LGBT people, and whites" (Southern Poverty Law Center). The NAACP, though it "endorsed the Million Man March"—the mass gathering of African American men in Washington, D.C., in 1995—where Farrakhan was a keynote speaker, "refused to participate in any other way" (Southern Poverty Law Center).

In 2010, Farrakhan publicly announced that NOI was embracing Dianetics, the "ideas and practices regarding the metaphysical relationship between mind and body developed by Church of Scientology founder L. Ron Hubbard." Farrakhan urged NOI members to participate in auditing sessions and to become trained as auditors (Gray). Today, membership in the NOI is much less than at its height in the 1960s, but the organization still claims numbers upward of 50,000 (MacFarquhar).

See also: Israel United in Christ; Israelite Church of God in Jesus Christ; New Black Panther Party; Nuwaubian Nation of Moors

FURTHER READING

Biography.com. "Malcolm X Biography." Biography.com. http://www.biography.com /people/malcolm-x-9396195. (Accessed March 17, 2018.)

Gray, Eliza. October 5, 2012. "Thetans and Bowties: The Mothership of All Alliances: Scientology and the Nation of Islam." New Republic. https://newrepublic.com /article/108205/scientology-joins-forces-with-nation-of-islam. (Accessed March 18, 2018.)

MacFarquhar. Neil. February 26, 2007. "Nation of Islam at a Crossroad as Leader Exits." *New York Times*. http://www.nytimes.com/2007/02/26/us/26farrakhan.html. (Accessed March 18, 2018.)

Nation of Islam. "Brief History on Origin of Nation of Islam." https://www.noi.org/noi -history/. (Accessed March 17, 2018.)

Nation of Islam. "Nation of Islam in America: A Nation of Beauty & Peace." Nation of Islam. https://www.noi.org/noi-history/. (Accessed March 17, 2018.)

Southern Poverty Law Center. "Nation of Islam." Southern Poverty Law Center. https://www.splcenter.org/fighting-hate/extremist-files/group/nation-islam. (Accessed March 18, 2018.)

National Alliance

The National Alliance was "for over three decades the most dangerous and best organized neo-Nazi formation in the United States" (Southern Poverty Law Center, National Alliance). Its ideology was totally dedicated to the extermination of Jews and other nonwhite races, the execution of white sympathizers of such groups, and the establishment of an all-white homeland in the United States (Southern Poverty Law Center, National Alliance). The founder of the National Alliance, William Pierce, published a novel in 1975, entitled *The Turner Diaries*, that served as an inspiration for domestic terrorists and terrorist groups alike, including the Order and Timothy McVeigh, who in 1995 killed nearly 170 people in the bombing of the Alfred P. Murrah Federal Building in Oklahoma City. Before the unexpected death of William Pierce in 2002, the U.S. Federal Bureau of Investigation (FBI) "considered the National Alliance the best-financed and best-organized white nationalist organization of its kind in the country." In 2002, membership in the National Alliance was estimated at over 2,500, with an annual income of $1 million (Southern Poverty Law Center, National Alliance).

The National Alliance "developed out of the National Youth Alliance (NYA) which had been founded from the ashes of Youth for Wallace," an organization that had supported the pro-segregationist presidential campaign of Alabama governor George Wallace in 1968 (Southern Poverty Law Center, William Pierce). When factional infighting tore the organization apart after Wallace's failed campaign, William Pierce gained control of the largest faction and renamed the group the National Alliance in 1974. From his hilltop compound near Mill Point, West Virginia, Pierce honed the message of the National Alliance to attract a disparate cross section of anti-Semites, neo-Nazis, white supremacists, and anti-government sympathizers from across the United States and the world. Though Pierce was relatively unknown to most of the country in the early 1970s, "he had been an associate of the leader of the American Nazi Party, George Lincoln Rockwell" (Southern Poverty Law Center, William Pierce).

At the time of Pierce's death in 2002, the National Alliance had forged relationships with neo-Nazis and white supremacist groups in both the United States and Europe. The group's annual income topped $1 million, mostly from income from the group's magazine, *Resistance*, as well as Resistance Records, "a racist white power music label started years before by skinheads that had been acquired by Pierce" (Southern Poverty Law Center, William Pierce).

Upon Pierce's death, a power struggle ensued among his successors that significantly weakened the organization. Several high-profile scandals that involved the leadership disillusioned the rank-and-file members, and the National Alliance lost many of its leaders and key activists. Today, the National Alliance, once the most "ideological and criminal powerhouse of the American radical right," has become moribund and almost irrelevant (Southern Poverty Law Center, National Alliance).

See also: Creativity Movement; National Alliance; National Socialist Movement; Neo-Nazis; The Order; Traditionalist Worker Party; White Nationalism; White Supremacist Movement

FURTHER READING

MacDonald, Andrew (a.k.a. William Pierce). 1978. *The Turner Diaries: A Novel.* Barricade Books.
Southern Poverty Law Center. "Creativity Movement." Southern Poverty Law Center. https://www.splcenter.org/fighting-hate/extremist-files/group/creativity-movement-0. (Accessed January 4, 2018.)
Southern Poverty Law Center. "National Alliance." Southern Poverty Law Center. https://www.splcenter.org/fighting-hate/extremist-files/group/national-alliance. (Accessed January 4, 2018.)
Southern Poverty Law Center. "Neo-Nazi." Southern Poverty Law Center. https://www.splcenter.org/fighting-hate/extremist-files/ideology/neo-nazi. (Accessed January 4, 2018.)
Southern Poverty Law Center. "William Pierce." Southern Poverty Law Center. https://www.splcenter.org/fighting-hate/extremist-files/individual/william-pierce. (Accessed January 4, 2018.)

National Association for the Advancement of White People

The National Association for the Advancement of White People (NAAWP) "was a group founded in 1980 by former Ku Klux Klan (KKK) imperial wizard David Duke" (Southern Poverty Law Center, Knights of the Ku Klux Klan). Duke founded the NAAWP after being forced out of his position as leader of the Knights of the Ku Klux Klan (KKKK) for trying to steal the Knights' membership list. Many of the Knights' members "followed Duke to his new, non-Klan group, the National Association for the Advancement of White People, and the KKKK almost entirely collapsed several years later" (Southern Poverty Law Center, Knights of the Ku Klux Klan). Duke took the NAAWP's name "from the National Association for the Advancement of Colored People (NAACP), the black organization which for decades had been advocating for the rights of African Americans and people of color" (Southern Poverty Law Center, Knights of the Ku Klux Klan). The group maintains that its goal "is not to hate others but rather to build 'a new, better society. A homogeneous community where everyone contributes, everyone benefits, and all share a common set of values and moral beliefs, without the continual attacks on culture'" (Encyclopedia.com).

In August 2000, the NAAWP kicked off an initiative known as "Operation Appalachian," which was meant to "deliver the basic staples of life to . . . the deserving folks of Appalachia . . . particularly among Whites of European extraction" (Southern Poverty Law Center, 2000). As noted by the Southern Poverty

Law Center, "The racists gave away book bags, notebooks, calculators, pencils—and their own hateful propaganda" (Southern Poverty Law Center, 2000). Members of the Loudendale, West Virginia, Church of the Nazarene, where the giveaway was held, were unaware of the NAAWP's background, thinking instead "that they were just the lucky beneficiaries of free school supplies from a charitable group." By the time church leaders discovered the true motives behind the giveaway, "it was too late to stop the event. However, church leaders determined that the NAAWP would not be invited back." The decision by the NAAWP

> to target lower-income whites in the Appalachian region was made by NAAWP leaders in Florida and Louisiana. This "charity" is a new tactic by the NAAWP—a white supremacist group that focuses obsessively on black crime and, in particular, black rape of white women—in its effort to portray itself as a mainstream civil rights organization devoted to the welfare of whites. (Southern Poverty Law Center, 2000)

The SPLC noted, however, that "the NAAWP wasn't so progressive when it came to civil rights for black people." At the time, the group's website defended "the American slave system and argue[d] that the white southerners suffered during the Civil War as much as blacks did under slavery" (Southern Poverty Law Center, 2000).

In early 2000, David Duke created another organization "to protect the rights and heritage of European Americans. The group was named the National Organization for European American Rights (NOFEAR)" and was intended to "fight against what Duke argued was widespread discrimination against whites by minorities" (Southern Poverty Law Center, EURO). In 2001, "a lawsuit was filed against Duke for trademark infringement by No Fear Inc., a sportswear company. To avoid legal action, Duke changed the name of his organization to EURO" (Southern Poverty Law Center, EURO).

In 2018, the group remains active in name, and an associated website still bears the acronym NAAWP. David Duke, however, appears to no longer be affiliated with the NAAWP, though he has spoken in support of organizations such as "White Lives Matter (WLM), which has been branded a hate group by the SPLC" (Stack).

See also: EURO; Knights of the Ku Klux Klan; White Lives Matter; White Nationalism; White Supremacist Movement

FURTHER READING

Barrouquere, Brett. April 9, 2018. "On a Rainy Day, Neo-Confederates Celebrate the Career of Aging Racist and Neo-Nazi David Duke." Southern Poverty Law Center: Hatewatch. https://www.splcenter.org/hatewatch/2018/04/09/rainy-day-neo -confederates-celebrate-career-aging-racist-and-neo-nazi-david-duke. (Accessed July 20, 2018.)

Encyclopedia.com. "National Association for the Advancement of White People." Encyclopedia.com. https://www.encyclopedia.com/politics/legal-and-political-magazines /national-association-advancement-white-people. (Accessed July 20, 2018.)

National Association for the Advancement of White People. http://naawp.org.tripod.com/. (Accessed July 20, 2018.)

Southern Poverty Law Center. "EURO." Southern Poverty Law Center. https://www
.splcenter.org/fighting-hate/extremist-files/group/euro. (Accessed July 20, 2018.)
Southern Poverty Law Center. "Knights of the Ku Klux Klan." Southern Poverty Law
Center. https://www.splcenter.org/fighting-hate/extremist-files/group/knights-ku
-klux-klan. (Accessed July 20, 2018.)
Southern Poverty Law Center. December 6, 2000. "Racists Offer Poor Whites School
Supplies and Hate." Southern Poverty Law Center: Intelligence Report. https://
www.splcenter.org/fighting-hate/intelligence-report/2000/racists-offer-poor
-whites-school-supplies-and-hate. (Accessed July 20, 2018.)
Stack, Liam. August 30, 2016. "White Lives Matter Has Been Declared a Hate Group."
New York Times. https://www.nytimes.com/2016/08/31/us/white-lives-matter-has
-been-declared-a-hate-group.html (Accessed July 20, 2018.)

National Black Foot Soldiers Network

The National Black Foot Soldiers Network (NBFSN) is a shadowy organization "that may include the remnants of a black supremacist religious cult" whose goal is to kill white people, particularly white police officers (Nelson). The most infamous act associated with the NBFSN occurred on November 29, 2009. On that date, Maurice Clemmons "walked into a Lakewood, Wash., coffee shop and shot four police officers to death execution-style." Clemmons "was himself shot to death by a Seattle police officer two days later" (Nelson). The "day after Clemmons died, two blogs"—

> The Last Crusade and Black Male Felon—announced that the Seattle chapter of a little-known organization called the National Black Foot Soldiers Network (NBFSN) would hold a rally to celebrate Clemmons as a "Crowned BOW (Black on White) martyr" who did his part to destroy the "white terror racist police regime." (Nelson)

Though the NBFSN "has been characterized by the Southern Poverty Law Center (SPLC) as a black separatist hate group, open source information on the group is very limited and it is unknown at this time how many individuals are active within this network" (WikiLeaks). However, the SPLC believes the NBFSN to be active in the following states: Alaska, Arkansas, California, District of Columbia, Florida, Georgia, Illinois, Indiana, Kentucky, Louisiana, Massachusetts, Maryland, Michigan, Missouri, North Carolina, Nebraska, New Jersey, New York, Ohio, Oklahoma, Oregon, South Carolina, Tennessee, Virginia, and Washington (WikiLeaks). The NBFSN seems to adhere to belief systems

> stemming from various extremists groups such as the Black Hebrew Israelites and the Nation of Islam. The dominant theme in their propaganda is anti-White and anti-Jewish rhetoric, along with a strong hatred of "white Police" and the U.S. military. Their websites display disclaimers stating that the NBFSN does not advocate black on white crime or violence against white police; however, all of the individuals honored or memorialized on their website have successfully carried out or planned to carry out acts of violence against military personnel or law enforcement officers. (WikiLeaks)

The SPLC has noted that critics of NBFSN have discovered "a sprawling network of viciously anti-white black nationalist bloggers whose forte is celebrating the deaths of white people and police officers" (Nelson). The anonymous blogger— Black Male Felon—used in the Maurice Clemmons case writes one of at least 18 blogs in the National Black Foot Soldiers Network bearing such names as S—tycop, Amerikkka the Beautiful, Ultraviolet Holocaust and Mass Media Killers. The authors use pseudonyms such as "Slaughter Lightfoot," "Creaux Steele" and "Antioch Hades." Even the network itself goes by multiple names: National Black Foot Soldiers Network, the New Day Nigrescent Hebrew Pagans, Black Hebrew Pagans, the Yacub (or Yakub) Muslims, the Yacub 7 Ali Sun Worshipers and The Yacub 13 X Sun Worship Movement, among others.

By all appearances, the bloggers in the network are mainly involved in E-talk—but it's racially charged trash talk of the highest caliber. Their writings, usually styled as journalistic reporting or press releases, refer to a set of institutions, holy men, experts, and individuals that only rarely appear on the Internet. The ideology, such as it is, is a mish-mash of ideas drawn from the religious doctrines of various black nationalist groups of the past century. It is those ideas that provide a key clue as to the identity of those behind the NBFSN. They are likely the remnants of a group with a violent history. (Nelson)

According to the SPLC, NBFSN's message "can be distilled into four themes":

Whites owe reparations for centuries of oppressing blacks. Blacks who commit crimes against whites are sometimes referred to as "slave avengers" or "reparations protestors."

White police are "state commissioned racial terrorists." Black officers are viewed as race traitors.

The people who call themselves Jews today are actually impostors and "birthright thieves." Black people are the "real" descendants of the Hebrews of the Bible, the true chosen people. (This idea, commonly known as Black Hebrew Israelism, is widespread among black nationalist groups and is one of many that give the lie to the network's self-description as a "non religious movement.")

God hates white people and, in a 2012 cataclysm that the bloggers call the "Ultraviolet Holocaust," all whites will die. They declare that ultraviolet light—because of its link to skin cancer—"is the Fire of the 2nd Rapture of God." "The Sun of God," they say, "hates white people." (Nelson)

Though there are many theories as to who the members of NBFSN are, they are likely "people drawn from other black supremacist cults like the Nation of Yahweh, or freelancers who have created an entirely new concept" (Nelson). In any case, members of this group have brought an "apocalyptic hatred of whites into the 21st century" (Nelson).

See also: Black Muslims; Black Nationalism; Black Separatists; Israel United in Christ; Nation of Islam; Nuwaubian Nation of Moors

FURTHER READING

Nelson, Leah. June 17, 2011. "'Black Foot Soldiers' Blog Network Cheers Murders of Police Officers." Southern Poverty Law Center: Intelligence Report. https://www .splcenter.org/fighting-hate/intelligence-report/2011/black-foot-soldiers-blog -network-cheers-murders-police-officers. (Accessed July 20, 2018.)

Southern Poverty Law Center. "Black Nationalist." Southern Poverty Law Center. https:// www.splcenter.org/fighting-hate/extremist-files/ideology/black-nationalist. (Accessed July 20, 2018.)

Southern Poverty Law Center. March 2, 2015. "Active Black Separatist Groups." Southern Poverty Law Center: Intelligence Report. https://www.splcenter.org/fighting

-hate/intelligence-report/2015/active-black-separatist-groups. (Accessed July 20, 2018.)

Thefourthangelsbowl. https://thefourthangelsbowl.wordpress.com/category/national-black-foot-soldier-network/. (Accessed July 20, 2018.)

WikiLeaks. "National Black Foot Soldier Network: Is November 29th a New Global Allahu Akbar Day?" Wikileaks.org. https://wikileaks.org/gifiles/attach/124/124230 __NBFSN-%20Is%20Nov.pdf. (Accessed July 20, 2018.)

You Have to Ask Why? May 8, 2013. "National Black Foot Soldier Network." Youhave-toaskwhy.blogspot.com. http://youhavetoaskwhy.blogspot.com/2013/05/national-bl ack-foot-soldier-network.html. (Accessed July 20, 2018.)

National Coalition for Issue Reform

Founded by Barbara Coe as the California Coalition for Immigration Reform (CCIR), the organization changed its name to the National Coalition for Issue Reform (NCIR) after Coe's death in 2013. Coe was infamous for her rants against illegal immigration and her racist rhetoric, often calling Mexicans "savages" and "invaders" who were out to reconquer and destroy the United States. Coe also perpetuated myths of a "New World Order" that was being forced upon the United States and "globalists" intent on subjugating the country and destroying its independence and freedom. Later in life, Coe admitted to "being a member of the Council of Conservative Citizens (CCC)," a far-right political organization dedicated to white nationalism and white separatism. Coe helped write and push through California's Proposition 187, a piece of legislation that intended to "cut off undocumented immigrants from social services like public school and hospital care" (Southern Poverty Law Center, Barbara Coe). Coe often referred to President Barack Obama as a "lying Muslim" (Southern Poverty Law Center, Barbara Coe).

Coe did not demonstrate her prejudices throughout her life. When she was in her fifties, she began to become concerned about the number of illegal immigrants that were making their way to California. Coe said that everything changed for her in 1991 when she and "an elderly friend walked into an Orange County social services center":

> I walked into this monstrous room full of people, babies and little children all over the place, and I realized nobody was speaking English. . . . I was overwhelmed with this feeling: "Where am I? What's happened here?" (Woo)

After her experience, Coe helped craft legislation that would become California Proposition 187 (Prop. 187). Prop. 187 would appear on the November 1994 ballot in California and eventually would be passed by California voters, 59 percent to 41 percent. The initiative prohibited "illegal aliens from using non-emergency health care services," barred them from public education, and blocked their access to other public services in the state of California. The law was challenged "and found unconstitutional by a federal district court in 1999. Governor Gray Davis eventually halted all state appeals of the ruling," prompting Coe to label Davis as a "communist" and to organize efforts to recall him from the governorship (Southern Poverty Law Center, Barbara Coe).

In 2003, Coe "responded to an Immigrant Workers Freedom Ride—which sought a path to citizenship for all immigrant workers—by urging members of CCIR to flood Congress and the White House with calls to arrest the riders." Coe stated:

> These people are criminals. . . . As such, they have NO 'RIGHTS' other than emergency medical care and humane treatment as they are being DEPORTED! We can only wonder how many in this group of foreign invaders have robbed, raped and possibly murdered law-abiding American citizens and legal residents. [Emphasis in original] (Southern Poverty Law Center, Barbara Coe)

In May 2005, Coe and the CCIR claim to have exposed a Mexican plan to reconquer the American Southwest. In 2007, she jumped on the "globalist conspiracy" bandwagon and claimed that illegal immigration was an effort being imposed by the New World Order on the United States (Southern Poverty Law Center, National Coalition for Issue Reform). Coe declared that "illegal aliens are the ground troops needed by Bush Jr. [President George W. Bush] and his globalist buddies for the ultimate death of America" (Southern Poverty Law Center, Barbara Coe). She went on to charge "that globalists have a plan to take control of America by encouraging illegal immigration and then exploiting their herd mentality to win elected offices" (Southern Poverty Law Center, Barbara Coe).

Though the focus of the National Council for Issue Reform has long been immigration, the group has also been associated with charges of racism. Coe and her organization have been associated with white nationalist and white supremacist groups such as the Council of Conservative Citizens (CCC) and the American Freedom Party, both of which advocate for policies that would return the Unite States to white rule.

See also: American Freedom Party; Council of Conservative Citizens; White Nationalism; White Supremacist Movement

FURTHER READING

Southern Poverty Law Center. "Barbara Coe." Southern Poverty Law Center. https://www.splcenter.org/fighting-hate/extremist-files/individual/barbara-coe. (Accessed July 24, 2018.)

Southern Poverty Law Center. "National Coalition for Issue Reform." Southern Poverty Law Center. https://www.splcenter.org/fighting-hate/extremist-files/group/national-coalition-issue-reform. (Accessed July 24, 2018.)

Woo, Elaine. September 4, 2013. "Barbara Coe Dies at 79; Foe of Services for Those in U.S. Illegally." *Los Angeles Times.* http://articles.latimes.com/2013/sep/04/local/la-me-barbara-coe-20130905. (Accessed July 24, 2018.)

National Knights of the Ku Klux Klan

The National Knights of the Ku Klux Klan ("National Knights"), sometimes called "the Church of the National Knights of the Ku Klux Klan (KKK), was once one of the largest and most active Klan groups in the United States" (Southern

Poverty Law Center). The National Knights "were formed in 1960 as a reaction to the growing Civil Rights Movement in the United States" (Southern Poverty Law Center). Originally, the group was organized in order to combine splintered Klan groups into one organization. By 1963, the group had come under the leadership of James Venable, who "served as the group's Imperial Wizard, or national leader," from 1963 until his death in 1993 (Southern Poverty Law Center). Venable was a powerful symbolic leader, as his ancestors had once owned the legendary Stone Mountain near Atlanta, Georgia. Stone Mountain "was the site of the 1915 rally that inaugurated the so-called 'second era' of the Klan—arguably the beginning of the KKK's greatest power in the United States" (Southern Poverty Law Center). Venable "used the mountaintop and nearby family land for annual rallies that drew not only members of the National Knights to the hallowed spot, but also other Klan factions as well" (Southern Poverty Law Center). At its height, the National Knights claimed between 10,000 and 15,000 members and conducted more than 1,000 cross burnings (Southern Poverty Law Center). In 2016, the Anti-Defamation League "observed that the National Knights are a 'shadow' of their former selves" (Anti-Defamation League).

On its website, the National Knights articulate their beliefs, which they define as follows:

1. The White Race: The irreplaceable hub of our nation, our Christian Faith, and the high levels of Western Culture and Technology.
2. The Constitution: As originally written and intended the finest system of government ever conceived by man.
3. Free Enterprize [sic]: Private property and ownership of business, but an end to high finance exploitation.
4. Positive Christianity: The right of the American people to practice their faith, including prayers in schools. (Church of the National Knights of the Ku Klux Klan)

After Venable died in 1993, his successor, Ray Larsen, moved the group to its new headquarters just outside of South Bend, Indiana. In 2000, the National Knights became known as the Church of the National Knights of the Ku Klux Klan. As explained by the organization:

Reverend Ray Larsen, Imperial Wizard of the NKKKK Inc. was able to get us a Church status. Does this mean we only allow religious people? NO! The reasons we became a Church are many. One of them is so we would be able to get our materials into places that we were not previously allowed, such as jails, and also we would be more securely protected under the First Amendment. It has also helped us in court cases, where being Klan would have not carried weight. Our becoming a Church has. (Church of the National Knights of the Ku Klux Klan)

By becoming a church, the National Knights can, with impunity, spout their racist beliefs:

We believe in the Bible before liberals translated it. We of the White Race came from Adam and Eve, not monkeys. The Bible clearly shows we are of one lineage, and makes reference to Beasts who walked on two legs. It also spoke of the wrongs of sleeping with these beasts. So we believe that blacks are not our Brothers and Sisters, but are beasts of burden. To accept evolution fully, is to say that we are equal with these animals, which history shows that we are not equal to, and in fact are superior to. While the Supreme Court has accepted animals to Vote and Marry with our race, we have not and never will accept this. (Church of the National Knights of the Ku Klux Klan)

Since Venable's death in 1993, the National Knights have gained somewhat of a reputation as being "Keystone Kops" (Southern Poverty Law Center). One example occurred in 2002 when members of the National Knights hosted a "Christmas unity rally." The organizers hoped to bring various KKK factions together at the rally. Close to 50 people "showed up for the rally and the cross burning" (Southern Poverty Law Center). But as the lunch was served, the National Knights organizers had forgotten that a large number of the attendees were followers of Christian Identity, "a racist and anti-Semitic theology that holds that Jews are biologically Satanic and whites are the true Israelites—meaning, according to Identity adherents' reading of the Bible, that whites can't eat pork" (Southern Poverty Law Center). When guest Klansmen entered the shed for lunch, they recoiled in disgust when they "were confronted with a dead pig, that by all accounts was barely cooked." The bumbling of the National Knights was punctuated further by the burning of a swastika, which fell over and burned on the ground, and a cross that had to be shortened by 12 feet in order to remain erect (Southern Poverty Law Center).

In 2006, "two members of the National Knights pleaded guilty to charges in connection with a plot to blow up the Johnston County, North Carolina courthouse" (Southern Poverty Law Center). Since that time, the National Knights have receded from national prominence, as have most KKK groups. In fact, in 2017 the Southern Poverty Law Center (SPLC) reported that the KKK "had shrunk by 32 percent, which the SPLC said was due in part to the so-called 'Alt-Right' movement which are a recent rebranding of white supremacy for public relations purposes, albeit one that de-emphasizes Klan robes and Nazi symbols in favor of a more 'intellectual' approach" (Begley).

See also: Alt-Right Movement; Christian Identity; Ku Klux Klan; White Nationalism; White Supremacist Movement

FURTHER READING

Anti-Defamation League. 2016. "Tattered Robes: The State of the Ku Klux Klan in the United States." Anti-Defamation League. https://www.adl.org/sites/default/files /documents/assets/pdf/combating-hate/tattered-robes-state-of-kkk-2016.pdf. (Accessed May 23, 2017.)

Begley, Sarah. February 15, 2017. "Read the List of the 917 Hate Groups Identified by the Southern Poverty Law Center." *Time*. http://time.com/4671800/hate-groups-on -the-rise/. (Accessed May 23, 2017.)

Church of the National Knights of the Ku Klux Klan. http://cnkkkk.net/. (Accessed May 23, 2017.)

Southern Poverty Law Center. "Church of the National Knights of the Ku Klux Klan." Southern Poverty Law Center. https://www.splcenter.org/fighting-hate/extremist -files/group/church-national-knights-ku-klux-klan. (Accessed May 23, 2017.)

National Policy Institute

The National Policy Institute (NPI) is "a white nationalist and white supremacist think tank based in Alexandria, Virginia" (Wines and Saul). The NPI is "dedicated to the heritage, identity, and future of people of European descent in the United States, and around the world" (National Policy Institute). It was founded in 2005 by William Regnery and Samuel T. Francis, in conjunction with Louis R. Andrews. The NPI claims to publish books, journals, essays, and blogs—as well as electronic media—"all dedicated to the revival and flourishing of *our* people" [emphasis added] (National Policy Institute). Louis R. Andrews, who became the NPI's chairperson when the group was founded, stated that he had supported Barack Obama for the U.S. presidency in 2008 because "I want to see the Republican Party destroyed, so it can be reborn as a party representing the interests of white people, and not entrenched corporate elites" (Washington). After Andrews's death in 2010, the new chairman, and new face of the NPI, became Richard Bertrand Spencer. Spencer has honed the NPI's message, communicating that it aims "to elevate the consciousness of whites, ensure our biological and cultural continuity, and protect our civil rights. The institute . . . will study the consequences of the ongoing influx that non-Western populations pose to our national identity" (Southern Poverty Law Center, Richard Bertrand Spencer). The NPI's senior fellows include Wayne Lutton, an extreme right writer; Jared Taylor, editor of *American Renaissance*, which promotes pseudoscientific studies and research that purports to show the inferiority of blacks to whites; and Kevin Lamb, a noted racist (Southern Poverty Law Center, Groups). The NPI burst onto the scene of American political consciousness when the organization, as well as the alt-right movement, became a talking point during the 2016 presidential campaign of Donald Trump. Speaking for NPI, Spencer warned white Americans that they "are increasingly under siege in their own country" and are "doomed to be a hated minority as people of color grow ever more numerous and politically powerful" (Marans). Spencer praised Trump's nationalistic fervor and his disdain for "political correctness." As Spencer noted, one must have a "starting point" when attempting to change attitudes and policies. For Spencer and the NPI, that "starting point" is Trump: "The starting point he [Trump] has in mind is getting white people to openly embrace their 'white' identity, and to organize as a group with common interests." Spencer and his peers "maintain that creating an intellectual community of white activists is an essential step toward making America white again" (Marans).

NPI has stated that "the dispossession of White Americans will have catastrophic effects for the entire world, not just for our people" (National Policy Institute). NPI has been classified as a white supremacist organization by the Southern Poverty Law Center (SPLC), and the Anti-Defamation League (ADL) has stated that the group was "founded to be kind of a white supremacist think tank" (Anti-Defamation League). Though the NPI is characterized as a white supremacist organization, it does not fall into the category that many Americans may associate with robes, tattoos, or skinheads. Rather, NPI tries "to take a more highbrow approach" to white supremacism, "couching white nationalist arguments as academic commentary on black inferiority, the immigration threat to whites and other racial issues" (Wines and Saul). NPI's approach to white supremacy recalls David Duke's admonition to the KKK to "get out of the cow pasture and into the hotel meeting room" (Ellis).

The SPLC has stated that it sees NPI's brand of white supremacy as an attempt to make racism "respectable." The steps to respectable racism are: (1) get a like-able, accessible front man; (2) clad yourself in the trappings of academia; and (3) make the web work for you (Ellis). Richard Spencer satisfies the first requirement, as he is seen as "polite and square-jawed, with a neat high-and-tight haircut. He doesn't sneer or curse, and he pitches big ideas about the future—like NPI becoming the alt-right equivalent of the Heritage Foundation, a lynchpin of mainstream conservative thought" (Ellis). The second step—the trappings of academia—has been used by NPI with great effectiveness. NPI couches most of its most controversial ideas in "pseudo-academic arguments, using ornate, polysyllabic, racial-slur free language. It makes people more willing to hear it" (Ellis). Finally, Spencer "is very internet savvy. He knows that most of his target audience isn't going to sit down with a tome on the 'biological reality of race.' That's why he has a Twitter account and runs sites like AlternativeRight.com to deliver his ideology in bite-sized chunks" (Ellis).

Spencer has stated that "NPI isn't only for building a movement; it's for sustaining and legitimizing one that already exists. Having our own institutions is going to take us beyond just being trolls or Trump fans," he says. "We need to destroy traditional conservatism. We're going to displace them, and we are going to be the right" (Ellis).

In March 2017, the Internal Revue Service (IRS) stripped NPI of its tax-exempt status for failing to file tax returns. The NPI's lack of tax-exempt status does not mute its message. The NPI realizes that whether it is due to "economic stagnation, a culture of xenophobia and fear, growing distrust for the government and traditional institutions, or a myriad of other causes, people's loyalties are up for grabs" (Ellis). Spencer has reinforced this notion by stating:

> America as it is currently constituted—and I don't just mean the government; I mean America as constituted spiritually and ideologically—is the fundamental problem. I don't support and agree with much of anything America is doing in the world. (Wines and Saul)

See also: Alt-Right Movement; *American Renaissance*

FURTHER READING

Anti-Defamation League. "Alt-Right: A Primer about the New White Supremacy." Anti-Defamation League. https://www.adl.org/education/resources/backgrounders/alt-right-a-primer-about-the-new-white-supremacy. (Accessed June 6, 2017.)

Ellis, Emma Grey. October 9, 2016. "How the Alt-Right Grew from an Obscure Racist Cabal." *Wired*. https://www.wired.com/2016/10/alt-right-grew-obscure-racist-cabal/. (Accessed June 6, 2017.)

Link, Taylor. March 14, 2017. "Richard Spencer's Nonprofit, Pro-Hate National Policy Institute Lost Its Tax-Exempt Status." Salon. http://www.salon.com/2017/03/14

/richard-spencers-nonprofit-pro-hate-national-policy-institute-lost-its-tax
-exempt-status/. (Accessed June 6, 2017.)

Marans, Daniel. March 7, 2016. "How Trump Is Inspiring a New Generation of White
    Nationalists." Huffington Post. http://www.huffingtonpost.com/entry/trump
    -white-nationalists_us_56dd99c2e4b0ffe6f8e9ee7c. (Accessed June 6, 2017.)

National Policy Institute. "Who Are We?" National Policy Institute. http://www.npiamerica
    .org/. (Accessed June 6, 2017.)

Southern Poverty Law Center. "The Groups." Southern Poverty Law Center: Intelligence
    Report. https://www.splcenter.org/fighting-hate/intelligence-report/2015/groups.
    (Accessed June 6, 2017.)

Southern Poverty Law Center. "Richard Bertrand Spencer." Southern Poverty Law
    Center. https://www.splcenter.org/fighting-hate/extremist-files/individual/richard
    -bertrand-spencer-0. (Accessed June 6, 2017.)

Washington, Jesse. June 11, 2009. "Gunman May Reflect Growing Racial Turmoil." NBC
    News. http://www.nbcnews.com/id/31271698/ns/us_news-crime_and_courts/t/gun
    man-may-reflect-growing-racial-turmoil#.WTbMyty1vRY. (Accessed June 6,
    2017.)

Wines, Michael, and Stephanie Saul. July 5, 2015. "White Supremacists Extend Their
    Reach through Websites." *New York Times.* https://www.nytimes.com/2015/
    07/06/us/white-supremacists-extend-their-reach-through-websites.html. (Accessed
    June 6, 2017.)

National Prayer Network

The National Prayer Network (also known as TruthTellers.org) is an Oregon-based Christian organization that disseminates New World Order conspiracy theories and criticizes Judaism and what it considers Jewish supremacism in American media and television programming. The group is led by Ted Pike, who bills himself as "the primary national opponent to federal hate crimes legislation" (National Prayer Network). Pike is best known for "pushing out anti-Semitic propaganda and for warning that there is a tendency in the United States toward Jewish domination of society" (Right Wing Watch). Pike criticizes Jews for supporting liberal policies and claims "that liberalism has striven to substitute secular, immoral, globalist values that will eventually make America amenable to participation in a Zionist-controlled new world order" (Anti-Defamation League). Pike has also warned that "Jewish international bankers were behind the Bolshevik Revolution, and that the state of Israel was the first stage in Satan's plan to take this world from Christ and give it to the Antichrist" (Right Wing Watch). Pike singles out the Anti-Defamation League (ADL) "for attacks and alleges that the ADL has created programs and influenced legislation 'that makes it illegal for Christians to criticize homosexuality'" (Anti-Defamation League). Pike has described "secular Jews as the wreckers of our civilization" and "urges Christians to stop giving aid and comfort to them" (Anti-Defamation League).

Pike has decried the "moral erosion" in America, criticizing a CBS program that presented a fictional portrayal of wife-swapping couples, and he continues to blame what he dubs the "Jewish media." According to one source, Ted Pike "is a notorious anti-Semite who uses Christianity as his front to promote hatred and suspicion and polarize and divide people who MAY [emphasis in original] otherwise receive a true Biblical message" (Maugans).

The National Prayer Network under Pike's direction has accused critics of his group, such as the Southern Poverty Law Center (SPLC) and Anti-Defamation League (ADL), as being "Christian haters" and "Jewish supremacists who 'want to actually outlaw Christian political activity and evangelism. The ADL created hate crime laws that will particularly outlaw reproof of sodomy and evangelism of non-Christians, especially Jews'" (Right Wing Watch).

As spokesperson of the National Prayer Network, Pike has lamented that "patriots" have not done enough to defeat the "homosexual lobby" and its drive to enact its agenda of wide-ranging hate crimes legislation in the United States. If true patriots do not act to stem the tide of moral degeneracy in the United States, Pike warns:

> Let me remind you how infinitely more wearying it will be to exist night and day, year after year, shivering and starving in the gulags of the New World Order. If we allow [hate crimes bills] to first take away our free speech, then all other freedoms are going down the drain. Once that happens, there will be nothing to restrain mass arrest, imprisonment, deportation, and murder of probably millions. (Scherr)

The National Prayer Network has also intoned that hate crimes legislation will protect pedophiles because "especially within the homosexual community [they] are an increasingly powerful political force" (Scherr). Pike continually blames the "Jewish supremacists" who are trying to "corrupt Christian nations so they can rule the world from Jerusalem" (Scherr).

After the hate crimes bill passed, white supremacist groups spoke out and stated that passage of the legislation implied that "it's ok to rob, rape and murder as long as one declares the criminal act had nothing to do with race, etc." (Scherr).

See also: Christian Identity; White Supremacist Movement

FURTHER READING

Anti-Defamation League. June 7, 2012. "'Christian News' Promotes Anti-Semitic Writers." Anti-Defamation League. https://www.adl.org/blog/christian-news-promotes-anti-semitic-writers. (Accessed May 31, 2018.)

Maugans, Randy. "Ted Pike & the National Prayer Network." Christian Media Research. http://www.christianmediaresearch.com/tedpike.html. (Accessed May 31, 2018.)

National Prayer Network. http://www.truthtellers.org/. (Accessed May 31, 2018.)

National Prayer Network. "Rev. Ted Pike: Biography." TruthTellers.org. https://www.truthtellers.org/tedpikebiography.html. (Accessed May 31, 2018.)

Right Wing Watch. May 5, 2008. "The Nazi Thing." Right Wing Watch. http://www.rightwingwatch.org/post/the-nazi-thing/. (Accessed May 31, 2018.)

Scherr, Sonia. July 17, 2009. "Religious Right Promotes Falsehoods in Last-Ditch Attempt to Stall Federal Hate Crimes Bill." Southern Poverty Law Center: Hatewatch. https://www.splcenter.org/hatewatch/2009/07/17/religious-right-promotes-falsehoods-last-ditch-attempt-stall-federal-hate-crimes-bill. (Accessed May 31, 2018.)

National Socialist German Workers Party

The National Socialist German Workers Party (NSDAP) is "characterized as a neo-Nazi hate group by the Southern Poverty Law Center" (SPLC) (Southern Poverty Law Center, Neo-Nazi). According to the SPLC, neo-Nazi hate groups "share a hatred for Jews and a love for Adolf Hitler and Nazi Germany. While they also hate other minorities, gays and lesbians and even sometimes Christians, they perceive 'the Jew' as their cardinal enemy" (Southern Poverty Law Center, Neo-Nazi). The NSDAP is the brainchild of Gary "Gerhard" Lauck, an American-born neo-Nazi who has been "nicknamed the 'Farm Belt Fuhrer' because of his rural origins" (Southern Poverty Law Center, Lauck). Lauck grew up in Milwaukee, Wisconsin, which once hosted the "largest German-born population in the United States outside of Chicago and New York City" (Vaughan). At age 11, Lauck moved with his family to Lincoln, Nebraska, where his father was a professor of engineering at the University of Nebraska (Atkins). From his Nebraska home, "he founded the NSDAP/AO, the German language acronym for the National Socialist German Workers Party/Overseas Organization, the translated name of the original Nazi party's overseas unit" (Southern Poverty Law Center, Lauck). Lauck reportedly "exported or smuggled millions of pieces of neo-Nazi propaganda in to at least 30 countries from the 1980s to the 1990s" (Lee). In 1995, Lauck was arrested in Denmark and was extradited to Germany for violating German law regarding the distribution of neo-Nazi propaganda (Lee). He was tried and found guilty and "sentenced to four years in prison." Lauck was released in 1999 and was extradited back to the United States. However, by that time the advent of the Internet had passed by Lauck and his printed-material propaganda. Today, Lauck disseminates his neo-Nazi material via his website, NSDAP.info.

Lauck spent his early years "as a member of the neo-Nazi National Socialist White People's Party (the successor to George Lincoln Rockwell's American Nazi Party), and the National Socialist Party of America," which later imploded because of the revelation that its leader was of Jewish descent and was also a child molester (Southern Poverty Law Center, Neo-Nazi). In 1974, Lauck founded the NSDAP/AO with the intent to promote "a worldwide National Socialist-led White Revolution for the restoration of White Power in all White nations" (NSDAP.info). He gained the moniker the "Farm Belt Fuhrer" because of the "Hitlerite" mustache he sported as well as his put-on German accent. Lauck would sometimes march "through the streets of Lincoln, Nebraska in Nazi uniforms, but he largely assumed a low profile in his community" (Southern Poverty Law Center, Lauck).

Lauck's greatest successes were overseas, where he was able to disseminate Nazi paraphernalia and propaganda at a time when several European countries maintained strict bans on the publication or distribution of such material. During the 1980s and 1990s, "Lauck produced, translated, and helped smuggle enormous amounts of German-language propaganda into Europe, as much as eight million pieces per year" (Southern Poverty Law Center, Lauck). Overall, Lauck was able to place hate material in as many as 30 countries in 10 different languages. A prominent neo-Nazi leader, "who eventually renounced his racist ways," wrote that Lauck "was the publisher and distributor of the bulk of neo-Nazi propaganda pasted up on the walls and windows from Berlin to Sao Paulo [Brazil], and was also the center of a worldwide umbrella organization with which practically every neo-Nazi had contact" (Southern Poverty Law Center, Lauck).

After several run-ins and arrests during the 1970s for his public Nazi glorification activities, Lauck was arrested in 1995 in Denmark "on international warrants stemming from his importation of illegal propaganda into Germany" (Southern Poverty Law Center, Lauck). He was extradited to Germany, where he "served four years in prison for his activities. By the time of his release from prison in 1999, internet-based hate literature had supplanted Lauck and rendered moot the illegal smuggling of neo-Nazi literature into Europe" (Southern Poverty Law Center, Lauck).

After his release from prison, Lauck "built his own website and wrote primarily in German" (Southern Poverty Law Center, Lauck). In 2001, he set up a web-hosting company and encouraged European clients to move their websites to the United States to prevent the political repression that Lauck contended was sweeping across Europe. Today, Lauck's website NSDAP.info claims to be the "largest supplier of National Socialist propaganda material in the world" (NSDAP.info). The website is published in nearly 30 languages.

See also: American Nazi Party; Neo-Nazis

FURTHER READING

Atkins, Stephen E. 2011. *Encyclopedia of Right-Wing Extremism in Modern American History*. ABC-CLIO.

Duggan, Joe. August 20, 2017. "While Not Hotbeds for Extremist Groups, Nebraska and Iowa Are Home to Some." *Omaha World-Herald*. https://www.omaha.com/news /nebraska/while-not-hotbeds-for-extremist-groups-nebraska-and-iowa-are /article_8141ace0-42b7-587e-8560-64862da89ac8.html. (Accessed July 23, 2018.)

Lee, Martin A. 1999. *The Beast Reawakens: Fascism's Resurgence from Hitler's Spymasters to Today's Neo-Nazi Groups and Right-Wing Extremists*. Routledge.

NSDAP.info. http://www.nsdap.info/. (Accessed July 23, 2018.)

Southern Poverty Law Center. "Garry 'Gerhard' Lauck." Southern Poverty Law Center. https://www.splcenter.org/fighting-hate/extremist-files/individual/gary-gerhard -lauck. (Accessed July 23, 2018.)

Southern Poverty Law Center. "Neo-Nazi." Southern Poverty Law Center. https://www .splcenter.org/fighting-hate/extremist-files/ideology/neo-nazi. (Accessed July 24, 2018.)

Southern Poverty Law Center. June 15, 1999. "Return of the (Nebraska) Fuhrer." Southern Poverty Law Center: Intelligence Report. https://www.splcenter.org/fighting -hate/intelligence-report/1999/return-nebraska-f%C3%BChrer. (Accessed July 23, 2018.)

Vaughan, Carson. July 6, 2017. "The Farm Belt Fuhrer: The Making of a Neo-Nazi." *Guardian*. https://www.theguardian.com/world/2017/jul/06/neo-nazi-gerhard -lauck-nebraska-antisemitism. (Accessed July 23, 2018.)

National Socialist Legion

The National Socialist Legion (NSL) is a "neo-Nazi splinter group from Vanguard America" (VA), a "white supremacist group that opposes multiculturalism and believes America should be an exclusively white nation" (Anti-Defamation League).

According to the Anti-Defamation League (ADL), NSL was founded in January 2018 by former members of VA who had become disillusioned with VA after the unwanted attention the organization received as a result of its participation in the "Unite the Right" rally in Charlottesville, Virginia, in August 2017. After the rally—in which a "Unite the Right" protester, who was photographed holding VA logos and who later allegedly "drove his car into a crowd of counter-protesters, killing one—VA was rocked with defections as Texas chapter members split to form the Patriot Front" (PF), taking many of VA's most active members with it. NSL's message is more explicitly National Socialist than was VA's, and its "strategy . . . is to set up homesteading cells around the country for future white migration and eventual white revolt and secession'" (Anti-Defamation League). In its brief history, NSL has targeted college campuses with its propaganda, "which ranges from veiled white supremacist language to explicitly racist images and words, often includes a recruitment element, and frequently attacks minority groups including Jews, blacks, Muslims, non-white immigrants and the LGBT community" (Sharon).

On its website, NSL articulates its mission:

> National Socialist League (NSL) is a Revolutionary National Socialist organization dedicated to protecting the White European Race, the Traditional Western Nuclear Family, destroying degeneracy and its mother ideology Cultural Marxism, and the disillusion of the Democratic process in favor of a Fascist system of governance. As a group of National Socialists dedicated to a Fascist world view, we perform both activism and readiness for the coming Racial Holy War. NSL's ultimate goal is the unification of all National Socialist groups, as NSL believes this is the only way to transform the corrupt Democratic system we live under into a Fascist Ethnostate dedicated to the protection of the White Race. NSL truly believes this route is the only way to protect our people from the "Browning" of America. Joining the National Socialist Legion means you are dedicated to NSL, its members, and its leadership. Joining NSL means you are dedicated to protecting your race and the National Socialist cause. Finally, only join NSL if you are willing to carry out your duties in the physical world. (National Socialist Legion)

In April 2018, anti-Semitic posters were found on the campus of Duke University in the city of Durham, North Carolina. One poster "depicted a figure pointing a gun at a stereotypical Jewish man with a beard, long nose and yarmulke who had tentacles wrapped around the earth." The poster read "Right of revolution" and "Your ancestors threw off foreign oppression, time for you as well" (Pink). Another poster read "Greedy Jews" and "End Zionist Oppression," while "a sticker posted at a local bus station said 'Master Race or Disgrace' and 'Kill'" (Pink).

The ADL noted that similar NSL fliers were posted in California, Colorado, Tennessee, and Florida. According to an ADL regional director, "This is an increasingly common tool used by the group [NSL] to create intimidation. The tactic is meant to draw attention . . . and create an appearance that they are more prevalent than their numbers would support" (Pink). Another ADL spokesperson stated, "We're concerned to see that white supremacists are accelerating their efforts to target schools with propaganda in hopes of recruiting young people to support their bigoted world view" (Sharon).

The NSL's actions obviously had an effect, as a Jewish Duke professor said, "I'm Jewish and these vile anti-Semitic threats, including the image of a gun pointing to a Jew, really rattled me" (Pink).

See also: National Socialist Movement; Neo-Nazis; Vanguard America; White Nationalism; White Supremacist Movement

FURTHER READING

Anti-Defamation League. "Vanguard America." Anti-Defamation League. https://www.adl.org/resources/backgrounders/vanguard-america. (Accessed August 2, 2018.)

BitChute. "National Socialist Legion." BitChute. https://www.bitchute.com/channel/NS_Legion/. (Accessed August 2, 2018.)

Gab. "National Socialist Legion." https://gab.ai/NSLegion. (Accessed August 2, 2018.)

National Socialist Legion. "Our Mission." National Socialist Legion. https://nslegion.org/. (Accessed August 2, 2018.)

Pink, Aiden. May 1, 2018. "Anti-Semitic Flyers Posted at Duke University." FastForward.com. https://forward.com/fast-forward/400182/anti-semitic-flyers-posted-at-duke-university/. (Accessed August 2, 2018.)

Sharon, Jeremy. July 5, 2018. "ADL: Rise in White Supremacist Hate Incidents on U.S. College Campuses." https://www.jpost.com/Diaspora/ADL-rise-in-White-Supremacist-hate-incidents-on-US-college-campuses-561635. (Accessed August 2, 2018.)

YouTube. "National Socialist Legion." YouTube. https://www.youtube.com/channel/UCOxNa-oR8WVECnu0QY2lHgg/featured. (Accessed August 2, 2018.)

National Socialist Liberation Front

The National Socialist Liberation Front (NSLF) is a neo-Nazi hate group with active chapters in Alabama, California, and Pennsylvania (Southern Poverty Law Center, Neo-Nazi). According to the Southern Poverty Law Center (SPLC), neo-Nazi groups "share a hatred for Jews and a love for Adolf Hitler and Nazi Germany. While they also hate other minorities, gays and lesbians and even sometimes Christians, they perceive 'the Jew' as their cardinal enemy" (Southern Poverty Law Center, Neo-Nazi). The NSLF "was originally established as a youth wing of the American Nazi Party aka National Socialist White People's Party (NSWPP) in 1969" (Terrorism Research & Analysis Consortium). However, the group "was reconstituted [in 1974] as a separate National Socialist organization after its leader Joseph Tommasi had been expelled by NSWPP leader Matt Koehl" (Terrorism Research & Analysis Consortium). Tommasi and the NSLF "broke with established National Socialist tradition by eschewing brownshirt uniforms and abandoning attempts to raise a 'mass movement' of supporters to win power through legal means." Instead, Tommasi argued that it was best "for small bands of 'National Socialist revolutionaries' to arm themselves and conduct guerrilla warfare" (Revolvy). Tommasi believed that "mass movement oriented neo-Nazism was useless" and intended that the NSLF model itself on the "aesthetics, personality and doctrine on radical leftist groups, like the terrorist Weather Underground"

(Hatewatch staff, 2018). To this end, the NSLF announced itself as being "above ground through its actions only, while existing otherwise as an underground, revolutionary terrorist cell, the first of its kind in American neo-Nazism" (Hatewatch staff, 2018). The SPLC has stated that the NSLF "fetishizes violence as the only vehicle for apocalyptic, racial cleansing and the imposition of order over its dystopian perception of the modern world" (Southern Poverty Law Center, Atomwaffen Division).

Like its neo-Nazi counterparts, NSLF espouses "tenets of racism, genetic superiority and purity, authoritarian socialism and antisemitism" (Victorious by Terror). As noted by the group:

> NSLF is not taken lightly by the Reds, the Blacks, or the System. . . . A White Man can take pride in being part of the NSLF. It is the ONLY place for a White Revolutionary to be found!
> To bring off a revolution means literally to turn the tables upside-down. It does not mean quibbling inches and degrees; turning back the hands of time; arguing two sides of the same coin. It doesn't mean patching up a rotten, sagging framework either. It means DEATH to the old order and the BIRTH of the New Order! Anything other than this is no more than a variation on a single theme: Jewish-controlled State Capitalism. [Emphasis in original] (Victorious by Terror)

According to NSLF, "The primary purpose of the N.S.L.F. is to fill in this void by educating a select group of white persons already committed to the National Socialist World View in the hopes that they will gain a better understanding of Adolf Hitler's National Socialism in relation to today's contemporary political situation" (Mason). Thus,

> [n]ot being a part of a mass Movement organization and not attempting to build a mass movement will allow us to pug [sic]forth our efforts only to those we feel will benefit from our teachings. This is necessary in so much as it will glue [sic]us a higher quality of person with which to work with. It will be from those people from which we will choose who we wish go [sic] join us in taking up arms in a guerilla war that will surely have to be waged against the system and certain other enemies of the National Socialist Revolution, We will choose those who will associate with us. This organization is NOT open to 'anyone.' We are clandestine National Socialist guerillas. We realize what is wrong in America and we realize what has to be done. But first we must learn all there is to learn about ourselves and our enemies. Without this knowledge all attempts at waging war shall end in our defeat. (Mason)

Though not as well known as other National Socialist groups, the NSLF is viewed by one commentator as among the more violent and dangerous neo-Nazi organizations. Indeed, the main points to understand and consider about the NSLF are as follows:

> The NSLF are:
>   Anti-government. National Socialist. Racial Nationalist.
>   White separatist. White supremacist.
>   Terroristic. Revolutionary.
>   Racist. Antisemitic.
>   Antidemocratic. Antidrug.
>   Anticapitalist.

The NSLF goals are to:

Move National Socialists and sympathisers towards violent political action. They do this by promoting armed revolution over political action.

Re-awaken white people, rallying the "white masses" and mobilizing them towards violent political action. They do this through stirring up racial tensions and politicizing key events.

Eliminate racial and revolutionary enemies; including blacks, Commies, Jews and uncooperative whites. This shouldn't be anything new to you! In other words, it wishes to "purify" the New State.

Implement some form of a National Socialist government, with it any of the economic, social and other changes it brings.

The NSLF promotes:

Political violence. Terrorism, revolution.

Racial violence. Religious violence.

"One-man" revolution. In other words, lone wolf terrorism.

Why does this matter now?

NSLF material, such as the writings of Jason Mason in Siege, are being widely distributed around social media and within neo-Nazi circles. (Victorious by Terror)

See also: American Nazi Party; Atomwaffen Division; National Socialist Movement; Neo-Nazis; White Nationalism; White Supremacist Movement

FURTHER READING

Hatewatch Staff. August 12, 2017. "Flags and Other Symbols Used by Far-Right Groups in Charlottesville." Southern Poverty Law Center: Hatewatch. https://www.splcenter.org/hatewatch/2017/08/12/flags-and-other-symbols-used-far-right-groups-charlottesville. (Accessed July 24, 2018.)

Hatewatch Staff. February 22, 2018. "Atomwaffen and the SIEGE Parallax: How One Neo-Nazi's Life's Work Is Fueling a Younger Generation." Southern Poverty Law Center: Hatewatch. https://www.splcenter.org/hatewatch/2018/02/22/atomwaffen-and-siege-parallax-how-one-neo-nazi%E2%80%99s-life%E2%80%99s-work-fueling-younger-generation. (Accessed July 24, 2018.)

Mason, James. "The National Socialist Liberation Front." Siege. http://67.225.133.110/~gbpprorg/obama/siege/0902.htm. (Accessed July 24, 2018.)

Revolvy. "National Socialist Liberation Front." Revolvy. https://www.revolvy.com/page/National-Socialist-Liberation-Front. (Accessed July 24, 2018.)

Southern Poverty Law Center. "Atomwaffen Division." Southern Poverty Law Center. https://www.splcenter.org/fighting-hate/extremist-files/group/atomwaffen-division. (Accessed July 24, 2018.)

Southern Poverty Law Center. "Neo-Nazi." Southern Poverty Law Center. https://www.splcenter.org/fighting-hate/extremist-files/ideology/neo-nazi. (Accessed July 24, 2018.)

Terrorism Research & Analysis Consortium. "National Socialist Liberation Front (NSLF)." Terrorism Research & Analysis Consortium. https://www.trackingterrorism.org/group/national-socialist-liberation-front-nslf. (Accessed July 24, 2018.)

Victorious by Terror. November 3, 2017. "The National Socialist Liberation Front." Victorious by Terror. https://victoriousbyterror.wordpress.com/2017/11/03/the-national-socialist-liberation-front/. (Accessed July 24, 2018.)

National Socialist Movement

The National Socialist Movement (NSM) is currently the "largest neo-Nazi group in the United States" (Anti-Defamation League). As noted by the Anti-Defamation League (ADL), however, "This is due primarily to setbacks experienced by other major neo-Nazi groups in the country between 2002 and 2007" (Anti-Defamation League). The group is currently led by Jeff Schoep, who has directed it since 1994. Despite the stability provided by Schoep, the NSM has not attracted the large numbers that its predecessors did in the late 1990s and early 2000s. Today its membership consists of only several hundred members (Anti-Defamation League). The group is known for its virulent "anti-Jewish rhetoric, its racist views, and its wearing of Nazi uniforms" (Southern Poverty Law Center). In 2007, however, NSM traded in its "brown shirts" for black "Battle Dress Uniforms" (Southern Poverty Law Center). On its website, nsm88.org, NSM puts forth its "25 Points of American National Socialism" (National Socialist Movement). Among the 25 points is the imperative that "[a]ll non-White immigration must be prevented. We demand that all non-Whites currently residing in America be required to leave the nation forthwith and return to their land of origin: peacefully or by force." The NSM states that "[t]he leaders of the movement promise to work ruthlessly—if need be to sacrifice their very lives—to translate this program into action" (National Socialist Movement, About Us).

NSM "has its roots in the original American Nazi Party founded by George Lincoln Rockwell in 1959" (Southern Poverty Law Center). After Rockwell was assassinated in 1967, two of his followers formed the National Socialist American Workers Freedom Movement in St. Paul, Minnesota. In 1994, the leadership of this group passed to Jeff Schoep, who, at 21, sought to reinvigorate the ranks of the neo-Nazi movement by attracting younger followers, many of whom had drifted away from older Ku Klux Klan (KKK) or skinhead groups. The biggest gains in NSM's membership came when a major power vacuum in neo-Nazi leadership emerged with the deaths of William Pierce, leader of the National Alliance, and Richard Butler, leader of the Aryan Nations, in 2002 and 2004, respectively. The neo-Nazi leadership ranks were further reduced in 2004 when Matt Hale, leader of the World Church of the Creator (later renamed the Creativity Movement), "was sentenced to 40 years in prison for soliciting the murder of a federal judge" (Southern Poverty Law Center).

NSM generally overshadowed other neo-Nazi groups of its era, including Kevin Strom's National Vanguard, with its theatrical street tactics undertaken in traditional Nazi uniforms. NSM was also unique among other groups in that it allowed members to join its ranks while still maintaining membership in other extremist groups. NSM mirrors the ideology expressed by the original American Nazi Party in almost every way. The group idolizes and reveres Adolf Hitler, referring to him as "Our Fuhrer, the beloved Holy Father of our age . . . a visionary in every respect" (National Socialist Movement, Frequently Asked Questions). In addition, the group maintains that its core beliefs

> include defending the rights of white people everywhere, preservation of our European culture and heritage, strengthening family values, economic self-sufficiency, reform of illegal immigration policies, immediate withdrawal of our national

military from an illegal Middle Eastern occupation, and promotion of white separation. (National Socialist Movement, About Us)

NSM is perhaps best known for instigating the 2005 Toledo riot. In December of that year, NSM made a public statement that it would march in Toledo, Ohio, through a predominantly black neighborhood to protest gang activity in the city. The march sparked rioting by counterprotesters and neighborhood residents, costing the city more than $336,000 in additional police expenses and prompting a citywide 48-hour curfew. NSM leader Jeff Schoep said of the destruction, "The Negro beasts have proved our point for us" (Southern Poverty Law Center). The group threatened a similar march in the aftermath of the shooting of Trayvon Martin, "an unarmed African-American teenager who was shot and killed by a neighborhood watchman" in Sanford, Florida, in February 2012 (Southern Poverty Law Center). However, the march never materialized.

In November 2016, following the election of Donald Trump, NSM changed its logo, replacing the swastika with "an Odai rune (a symbol from a pre-Roman alphabet that was also adopted by the Nazis) in an attempt to become more integrated and more mainstream" (Kovaleski, et al.).

See also: American Nazi Party; Aryan Nations; Creativity Movement; Ku Klux Klan; National Alliance; National Vanguard; Neo-Nazis; White Nationalism; White Supremacist Movement

FURTHER READING

Anti-Defamation League. "The National Socialist Movement." Anti-Defamation League: Extremism, Terrorism & Bigotry. https://www.adl.org/education/resources/profiles/national-socialist-movement. (Accessed March 13, 2018.)

Kovaleski, Serge F., Julie Turkewitz, Joseph Goldstein, and Dan Barry. December 10, 2016. "An Alt-Right Makeover Shrouds the Swastikas." *New York Times*. https://www.nytimes.com/2016/12/10/us/alt-right-national-socialist-movement-white-supremacy.html. (Accessed March 13, 2018.)

National Socialist Movement. "25 Points of American National Socialism." National Socialist Movement. http://www.nsm88.org/25points/25pointsengl.html. (Accessed March 13, 2018.)

National Socialist Movement. "About Us." National Socialist Movement. http://www.nsm88.org/aboutus.html. (Accessed March 13, 2018.)

National Socialist Movement. "Frequently Asked Questions about National Socialism (Nazism) and the National Socialist Movement." National Socialist Movement. http://www.nsm88.org/faqs/frequently asked questions about national socialism.pdf. (Access March 13, 2018.)

Southern Poverty Law Center. "National Socialist Movement." Southern Poverty Law Center. https://www.splcenter.org/fighting-hate/extremist-files/group/national-socialist-movement. (Accessed March 13, 2018.)

National Vanguard

National Vanguard is a white supremacist, white nationalist, and anti-Semitic organization based in Charlottesville, Virginia. It was founded in 2005 by Kevin

Strom, a former protégé of National Alliance founder William Pierce. When Pierce died in 2002, Strom was slated to become the new leader of National Alliance (NA). Strom had created NA's weekly radio show, *American Dissident Voices*; had been editor of NA's publication, *National Vanguard*, and had "convinced Pierce to venture into the white power music business" (Southern Poverty Law Center, National Vanguard). However, after Pierce's death, a power struggle ensued in NA that led to the appointment of Erich Gliebe over Strom. Gliebe orchestrated the expulsion of Strom and other disgruntled NA members. In retaliation, Strom took hundreds of NA members with him and formed the National Vanguard, having taken the name of the NA's publication with him. He had transferred the rights to the name to his wife before the split between the two groups. In a few short months, the membership rolls of the National Vanguard soared, until Strom was arrested, and eventually convicted, on child pornography charges.

When Strom left the National Alliance in 2005, he gained the support of other prominent white supremacists, including David Duke and Don Black, founder of the neo-Nazi Internet forum Stormfront. Many members of NA, "angry over Gliebe's perceived failures as chairman of the organization," defected to National Vanguard, increasing Strom's influence within white supremacist circles (Southern Poverty Law Center, National Vanguard). Strom's foray into white power music also attracted the attention of April Gaede, a former high-profile member of the National Alliance who had been a strong supporter of William Pierce. For several years in the 2000s, Gaede's twin daughters, Lynx and Lamb, performed white supremacist music under the name "Prussian Blue."

National Vanguard quickly overshadowed the more famous National Alliance until early January 2007, when Strom was arrested near his home in Stanardsville, Virginia, "for possessing and receiving child pornography, as well as enticing a minor to perform sex acts" (Southern Poverty Law Center, National Vanguard). Because of the backlash from his supporters as a result of the charges, Strom disbanded National Vanguard in March 2007. Strom subsequently faced two trials on charges of child pornography. In the first, he prevailed. However, in January 2008, "Strom faced a second trial on the charge of possessing child pornography." Strom struck a plea deal wherein "he pled guilty to possessing child pornography and prosecutors dropped several counts of receiving child pornography" (Southern Poverty Law Center, Strom). Strom was sentenced to 23 months in jail. With time served, he was released from prison in September 2008 (Southern Poverty Law Center, Strom).

Upon his release, Strom dabbled in movement politics and ran two racist websites. After Erich Gliebe resigned his position at the National Alliance in 2014, NA's new leader, William Williams, invited Strom back to be the organization's communication director. However, white supremacists continued to view Strom with contempt because of his child pornography conviction.

National Vanguard does not currently exist as an organization, but Strom continues to use the National Vanguard name as a website in support of white supremacist causes. In an "About Us" section on the website, National Vanguard states:

Without racial divergence, the evolution of life itself could never have taken place.

But powerful forces are attempting to obliterate all racial, ethnic and cultural differences worldwide, with the goal of "uniting humanity" into one global, anonymous mass. Open borders, "outsourcing," and the growth of corporate and governmental globalism are all elements in the systematic destruction of human biological and cultural diversity.

The European race is uniquely beautiful and creative. It is imperative that we survive and progress. (National Vanguard)

See also: National Alliance; Neo-Nazi; Stormfront; White Nationalism; White Supremacist Movement

FURTHER READING

National Vanguard. "About Us." National Vanguard. http://nationalvanguard.org/about/. (Accessed March 13, 2018.)

Southern Poverty Law Center. "Kevin Strom." Southern Poverty Law Center. https://www.splcenter.org/fighting-hate/extremist-files/individual/kevin-strom. (Accessed March 13, 2018.)

Southern Poverty Law Center. "National Vanguard." Southern Poverty Law Center. https://www.splcenter.org/fighting-hate/extremist-files/group/national-vanguard. (Accessed March 13, 2018.)

National Youth Front

The National Youth Front (NYF) "was the official youth wing of the white nationalist party, American Freedom Party (AFP)," before going defunct in 2017 (Hankes, October 2015). The official tagline of the NYF was, "To promote and preserve Western Civilization, to create continuity for youth, and for the development of further leadership" (National Youth Front). The NYF focused on recruiting young adults, aged 18–35, into white national groups and white nationalism causes. When members turned 36, they were automatically enrolled in the AFP. During the height of its activity, NYF became known for targeting immigrant and Muslim communities and trumpeting the dangers these communities posed to American society. A former chairperson of NYF, Caleb Shumaker, stated that NYF "march[es] to take back our streets not by words but with action" (Hankes, February 2015). The NYF stated that its goal "is to take power from those who have weaponized our institutions against us. To put an end to the invasions of our nations. To stop the ongoing defamation of our people. . . . To eliminate the endless ideological subversion of our nation's most precious gift. Its youth. . . . This is a declaration of war" (Hankes, February 2015).

In 2015, the reins of power of the NYF were passed from Caleb Shumaker to Angelo John Gage, a two-tour veteran of the Iraq War. Shumaker was forced out of NYF "because of his interracial marriage," which caused a great deal of backlash among white nationalist supporters (Hankes, February 2015). Less than a year later, Gage resigned from NYF amid fund-raising issues and a lawsuit that threatened to change the name of the organization (Hankes, October 2015). Gage was succeeded by Nathan Damigo, another Iraq War veteran, who garnered a lot of press "for aggressively targeting college professors at Arizona State University and Boston University who taught courses that the organization deemed 'anti-white'" (Hankes, October 2015). Damigo had "discovered his inner white nationalist by reading the work of Holocaust-denying ex-Klansman David Duke" (Southern Poverty Law Center).

Amid its growing troubles, Damigo folded NYF in March 2016 and founded Identity Evropa, a group that promoted "European identity and solidarity." Damigo self-identified as an "identitarian," a term popularized by various European racist movements, "and rejected terms like 'racist' and 'supremacist' as 'anti-white hate speech'" (Southern Poverty Law Center). Members of Damigo's new Identity Evropa must be of "European, non-Semitic heritage" (Southern Poverty Law Center).

Identity Evropa now has ties to several white nationalist movements, such as the alternative-right (Alt-Right), *American Renaissance*, and American Vanguard (also known as the National Vanguard). The tactics of these groups tend to focus on college campuses, where young people are the most frequent targets of recruitment. Flyers that these groups scatter around college campuses urge white men to "take a stand against globalist traitors who are destroying your race and heritage through open borders, affirmative action, and Marxist political correctness" (Southern Poverty Law Center).

See also: Alt-Right Movement; American Freedom Party; *American Renaissance*; Identity Evropa

FURTHER READING

Hankes, Keegan. February 6, 2015. "Meet the National Youth Front: The New Racists on Campus." Southern Poverty Law Center: Hatewatch. https://www.splcenter.org/hatewatch/2015/02/06/meet-national-youth-front-new-racists-campus. (Accessed May 23, 2018.)

Hankes, Keegan. October 15, 2015. "Group Formerly Known as the National Youth Front in Disarray." Southern Poverty Law Center: Hatewatch. https://www.splcenter.org/hatewatch/2015/10/15/group-formerly-known-national-youth-front-disarray. (Accessed May 23, 2018.)

National Youth Front. "About." https://squareup.com/store/national-youth-front. (Accessed May 23, 2018.)

Southern Poverty Law Center. February 15, 2017. "White Nationalists Work to Make Inroads at U.S. Colleges." Southern Poverty Law Center: Intelligence Report. https://www.splcenter.org/fighting-hate/intelligence-report/2017/white-nationalists-work-make-inroads-us-colleges. (Accessed May 23, 2018.)

Nationalist Front

The Nationalist Front (NF) was formed in 2016 "to unite various facets of the white supremacist movement. Its ultimate goal is to create a white ethno-state in America" (Anti-Defamation League, National Socialist Movement). NF is part of the larger National Socialist Movement (NSM). Originally named the "Aryan

Nationalist Alliance (ANA)," the group changed its name in November 2016 to the Nationalist Front. At its founding, the organization consisted of "Klan groups, racist skinheads, and neo-Nazis and held small, mostly localized events that rarely drew more than 25 individuals" (Anti-Defamation League, National Socialist Movement). Today, NF is "a collective of far-right organizations including the League of the South [LOS] and neo-Nazis in the Traditionalist Worker Party (TWP), Vanguard America (VA), and National Socialist Movement (NSM)" (Hatewatch staff). All of these organizations "have been designated hate groups by the Southern Poverty Law Center" (SPLC) (Southern Poverty Law Center, February 2017). The Nationalist Front

> has been one of the most prominent and visible groups clamoring for the spotlight in the Trump-era political arena. Its members were integrally involved with the most sustained violence on the ground in Charlottesville, Virginia, during last year's [2017] Unite the Right Rally, with the NF member organizations leading the charge. (Hatewatch staff)

According to the Anti-Defamation League (ADL):

> The Nationalist Front promotes a virulent form of anti-Semitism, blaming many of the country's problems on Jews. The organization believes that the dissolution of the U.S. government is the only way to build their ethno-state, which would be devoid of Jews and other minorities.
>
> The group's mission statement proclaims, "We too in America can end the Federal tyranny and have a positive future for our people by establishing on the North American an ethnostate for our people. Each racial group in America can and should establish for themselves a nationalist community where they can be independent and govern themselves according to their culture and ethnic self interest [sic]." (Anti-Defamation League, National Socialist Movement)

NF's logo consists of "NF" surrounded "by a circle of stars, with the words 'Iunctus Stamus' ('United We Stand'). The Nationalist Front's color palette remains the red, black and white traditionally associated with National Socialism" (Anti-Defamation League, National Socialist Movement).

Though the individual groups that compose NF were present at the "Unite the Right" rally in Charlottesville, Virginia, in August 2017, they did not march under the NF banner. However, the groups did unite in October 2017 to hold a series of White Lives Matter protests in Tennessee. According to NF leaders, the protests were "meant to call attention to the ongoing problem of refugee resettlement in Middle Tennessee, with a special emphasis on the Emanuel Samson church shooting [Emanuel Samson was a black gunman who fatally shot a white woman and injured seven others after a Sunday church service in Nashville, Tennessee, in September 2017. The gunman's apparent motive was revenge for the 2015 fatal shooting of nine black parishioners at a historic black church in Charleston, South Carolina]" (Anti-Defamation League, From Alt Right to Alt Lite). NF organizers also planned to "protest the Trump administration's decision to remove Sudan from the list of countries included in the travel ban, its failure to build a border wall with Mexico and for its apparent willingness to work with Nancy Pelosi and Chuck Schumer on a new version of the DREAM Act" (Anti-Defamation League, From Alt Right to Alt Lite).

When members of NF gathered on October 28, 2017, they were joined by Ku Klux Klan (KKK) members and neo-Nazis "extending their arms in Nazi salutes. Some bore swastika tattoos and others wore 'SS' bolt patches" (Allison). The scene caused elements of the alt-right movement to criticize the rally, and NF, inasmuch as "the white nationalists' symbols and tactics that offend the general public are hurting the overall cause" (Allison). Nathan Damigo, "founder of the alt-right white nationalist group Identity Evropa," tweeted "Today's #WhiteLivesMatter protest was cringe. Self indulgent extremism is pure anti-propaganda. It's unmarketable and a serious dead end" (Allison). Damigo's sentiments "were echoed by other leaders in the white nationalist alt-right movement seeking to appeal more to the masses—people who would be turned off by the Ku Klux Klan and Nazi imagery—and trying to target a more sophisticated demographic" (Allison).

For its part, NF responded to Damigo, "referring to him as an insecure, preening, back-stabbing weasel who is overly concerned with his group's haircuts. Damigo's Twitter display name is 'Fashy Haircut,' a reference to the side-fade male hairstyle associated with Nazi Germany and now popular among members of the alt-right" (Allison).

Such sniping between groups promoting white nationalism has become the norm as each group jockeys to attract recruits. For NF, such infighting does little to promote their ultimate goal, which is to "achieve unity within the white supremacist movement" and build a white ethno-state in America (Anti-Defamation League, National Socialist Movement).

See also: Alt-Right Movement; Identity Evropa; Ku Klux Klan; League of the South; National Socialist Movement; Neo-Confederates; Neo-Nazis; Racist Skinheads; Traditionalist Worker Party; Vanguard America; White Lives Matter; White Nationalism; White Supremacist Movement

FURTHER READING

Allison, Natalie. October 30, 2017. "Alt-Right, White Nationalists Are Fighting among Themselves after White Lives Matter Rally." *Tennessean*. https://www.tennessean.com/story/news/2017/10/30/white-lives-matter-rally-alt-right-infighting-white-nationalism-ridicule/815435001/. (Accessed August 2, 2018.)

Anti-Defamation League. "From Alt Right to Alt Lite: Naming the Hate." Anti-Defamation League. https://www.adl.org/resources/backgrounders/from-alt-right-to-alt-lite-naming-the-hate. (Accessed August 2, 2018.)

Anti-Defamation League. "National Socialist Movement/Nationalist Front." Anti-Defamation League. https://www.adl.org/resources/backgrounders/national-socialist-movementnationalist-front. (Accessed August 2, 2018.)

Anti-Defamation League. October 24, 2017. "White Supremacist Nationalist Front Plans Rallies in Tennessee." Anti-Defamation League. https://www.adl.org/blog/white-supremacist-nationalist-front-plans-rallies-in-tennessee. (Accessed August 2, 2018.)

Hatewatch Staff. January 10, 2018. "The Ties That Bind: Hypocrisy at the Foundations of the Nationalist Front." Southern Poverty Law Center: Hatewatch. https://www.splcenter.org/hatewatch/2018/01/10/ties-bind-hypocrisy-foundations-nationalist-front. (Accessed August 2, 2018.)

Southern Poverty Law Center. February 15, 2017. "Active Hate Groups 2016." Southern Poverty Law Center: Intelligence Report. https://www.splcenter.org/fighting-hate /intelligence-report/2017/active-hate-groups-2016. (Accessed August 2, 2018.)

Southern Poverty Law Center. August 8, 2017. "The Nationalist Front Limps into 2017." Southern Poverty Law Center: Intelligence Report. https://www.splcenter.org /fighting-hate/intelligence-report/2017/nationalist-front-limps-2017. (Accessed August 2, 2018.)

Viets, Sarah. May 30, 2017. "Nationalist Front Chumming Up to Klan Members Once Again." Southern Poverty Law Center: Hatewatch. https://www.splcenter.org /hatewatch/2017/05/30/nationalist-front-chumming-klan-members-once-again. (Accessed August 2, 2018.)

Neo-Confederates

"Neo-Confederates" and "neo-Confederacy" are terms "used to describe 20th and 21st century revivals of pro-Confederate sentiment in the United States." Neo-confederates "are strongly nativist and support measures to end immigration that they claim have turned the United States into a multicultural empire that fundamentally contradicts the meaning of America" (Southern Poverty Law Center). Neo-confederates claim that Christianity and white heritage are cultural values that have been abandoned in modern America. Neo-Confederates also incorporate into their thinking the advocacy of traditional gender roles and strong opposition to homosexuality, and they exhibit an "understanding of race that favors segregation and suggests white supremacy" (Hague). In many cases, "neo-Confederates are openly secessionist and look to the antebellum South and the Confederate States of America (CSA)" for "lessons on leadership, values, morality and behavior" (Hague). The notions associated with neo-Confederate ideas can be found in their modern incarnations in organizations such as the League of the South and the Council of Conservative Citizens. According to the Southern Poverty Law Center (SPLC), neo-Confederatism is "a reactionary conservative ideology that has made inroads into the Republican Party from the political right, and overlaps with the views of white nationalists and other more radical extremist groups" (Southern Poverty Law Center).

Neo-Confederates are accused of historical revisionism and "are openly critical of the presidency of Abraham Lincoln and the history of Reconstruction" (Southern Poverty Law Center). Neo-Confederates view the U.S. Civil War, "often termed the war of Northern Aggression," as an "unconstitutional invasion of the Southern states by the Union forces that were perceived as the aggressor in the conflict" (Southern Poverty Law Center). Most neo-Confederates view President Lincoln as a war criminal, and they generally believe that key amendments to the U.S. Constitution—particularly the so-called Civil War Amendments, i.e., the 13th, 14th, and 15th amendments—"are illegal and their implementation is therefore illegitimate" (Hague). Neo-Confederates object to these amendments because, in addition to abolishing slavery, they grant blacks citizenship and voting rights.

As a result of these 19th-century actions, neo-Confederates today believe that the current federal government is illegitimate and has abandoned the principles set forth by the Founding Fathers. Most importantly, they believe that the United States has strayed from the social, cultural, and political foundations upon which American society was built. Federal authority

> is asserted to be an unconstitutional infringement on states' rights and U.S. culture is considered to be "profane" and incompatible with traditional American society, given its promotion of equal rights for women, ethnic minorities, homosexuals, and non-Christian religions. Because the U.S. has become a "multicultural empire," neo-Confederate ideologues argue that it is doomed to dissolution into smaller, self-governing nation-states. This is because, in neo-Confederate belief, the idea that a state can be multi-ethnic is a contradiction in terms. Often drawing on eighteenth and nineteenth century political philosophers for justification, neo-Confederates contend that the ideal unit for governance is a small, ethnically homogeneous republic. Some advocates have gone so far as to propose a return to independent city-states and local fiefdoms. Thus, neo-Confederacy is closely intertwined with nationalist and secessionist sentiment. (Hague)

Neo-Confederates are unabashedly Christian. They support public displays of Christianity, such as the Ten Commandments, and displays of the Christian cross (Religious Tolerance). Neo-Confederates are highly distrustful of the actions of the U.S. federal government and are ardent supporters of the Second Amendment's provision of the right accorded to Americans to keep and bear arms. Many neo-Confederates see a conflict between the Christian South and secular North in the United States (Sebesta and Hague). Many neo-Confederates identify with an Anglo-Celtic and Christian Identity view, believing that whites are God's "chosen race." Many neo-Confederates identify themselves as "Southern Nationalists" (League of the South).

Consistent with their views that the South was an aggrieved party during the U.S. Civil War, and that the War was fought for "Southern independence," the Confederate battle flag ("Stars and Bars") is viewed with great pride and reverence among neo-Confederates. Neo-confederates believe that the flag is not a symbol of hate but a symbol of resistance against tyranny and of southern independence. In 2015, Dylann Roof's prominent display of the Confederate flag in the aftermath of his "murder of nine black parishioners at Charleston's (South Carolina) Mother Emmanuel AME church" thrust the Confederate battle flag back into the national spotlight (Hatewatch staff). After the Charleston church shooting, a spike in neo-Confederate rallies and "flaggings" (prominent displays of the Confederate flag) were conducted in order to show "rebel pride" and a fealty to "southern heritage." In one such public display, a convoy of pickup trucks driven by neo-Confederates "drove by a young African American child's birthday party hurling racial epithets and pointing firearms." On February 27, 2017, several "flaggers" who participated in the event "were sentenced to length prison terms for aggravated assault, making terroristic threats, and violating the state of Georgia's gang act" (Bruner).

Violence perpetrated by groups that espouse neo-Confederate views, such as the League of the South (LOS) and the Council of Conservative Citizens (CCC), often elicits in the minds of the public the idea that neo-Confederatism is a movement with historically racist overtones. For their part, neo-Confederates reject this association, instead preferring to identify themselves simply as individuals who are proud of their Confederate heritage (Confederate American Pride).

Nevertheless, there are those who believe that neo-Confederates advance an ideology that justifies positions that are "anti-democratic, racist, sexist, elitist, religiously intolerant, and homophobic." According to one commentator, "It is considerably more than just support for the Confederate battle flag or nostalgia for the Old South. Neo-Confederacy is an active and ongoing attempt to reshape the United States in the Old South's image" (Hague).

See also: Council of Conservative Citizens; League of the South; White Nationalism; White Supremacist Movement

FURTHER READING

Bruner, Portia. February 27, 2017. "Judge Sentences 2 People Convicted in Confederate Flag Confrontation." *Fox 5 News*. http://www.fox5atlanta.com/news/238410026 -story. (Accessed June 5, 2017.)

Confederate American Pride. http://www.confederateamericanpride.com/. (Accessed June 5, 2017.)

Gallagher, Gary W. 1999. *The Confederate War*. Harvard University Press.

Hague, Evan. January 25, 2010. "The Neo-Confederate Movement." Southern Poverty Law Center: Hatewatch. https://www.splcenter.org/hatewatch/2010/01/26/neo -confederate-movement. (Accessed June 5, 2017.)

Hatewatch Staff. March 2, 2017. "Racial Divisions along the Neo-Confederate Spectrum." Southern Poverty Law Center: Hatewatch. https://www.splcenter.org/hate watch/2017/03/02/racial-division-along-neo-confederate-spectrum. (Accessed June 5, 2017.)

League of the South. http://www.dixienet.org/. (Accessed June 5, 2017).

Religious Tolerance. "The Ten Commandments." Religious Tolerance. http://www.religious tolerance.org/chr_10cc.htm. (Accessed June 5, 2017.)

Sebesta, Edward H., and Evan Hague. 2002. "The US Civil War as a Theological War: Confederate Christian Nationalism and the League of the South." *Canadian Review of American Studies* 32 (3). http://www.theocracywatch.org/civil_war _canadian_review.htm. (Accessed June 5, 2017.)

Southern Poverty Law Center. "Neo-Confederate." Southern Poverty Law Center. https:// www.splcenter.org/fighting-hate/extremist-files/ideology/neo-confederate. (Accessed June 5, 2017.)

Neo-Nazis

"Neo-Nazism" is a general term related to organizations that profess "fascist, white nationalist, white supremacist, or anti-Semitic beliefs" (Southern Poverty Law Center, Neo-Nazi). Such groups' political goals tend to include the restoration of a Nazi order that will establish a new social and political system based on doctrines similar to those of Nazi Germany. Neo-Nazis are most prominently characterized by a belief in white racial superiority, their shared hatred for Jews, and a love of Adolf Hitler. While they "may hate other minorities, gays and lesbians, and even sometimes Christians," neo-Nazis perceive "the Jew as their cardinal enemy, and trace social problems to a Jewish conspiracy that supposedly controls governments, financial institutions and the media" (Southern Poverty Law Center, Neo-Nazi). In the United States, the neo-Nazi movement ostensibly began with George Lincoln Rockwell, who founded the American Nazi Party in 1959. Rockwell "instructed his members to dress in imitation of SA-style brown shirts"—who were the original paramilitary wing of the Nazi Party—while flying the swastika of the Third Reich (Southern Poverty Law Center, Neo-Nazi). Later leaders of American neo-Nazism would include David Duke and William Luther Pierce, the founder of the National Alliance—"the one-time largest and most influential neo-Nazi organization in the United States" (Southern Poverty Law Center, William Pierce). Today, neo-Nazis may manifest themselves in suits and ties, as racist skinheads, or as aggressively tattooed individuals who spout anti-immigrant rhetoric while perpetuating myths of worldwide Jewish conspiracies to control the world. Members of the new alt-right movement, "a mixed group of racists, nationalists, anti-Semites, and misogynists," understand the underlying tensions in the United States today and aggressively exploit citizens' fears about the future of America (Beckett). These neo-Nazis believe that they have found a safe haven in the administration of Donald Trump (Beckett).

Neo-Nazis are extremists on the far right. Some of the major factors that have accompanied a surge in neo-Nazism are the unstable economic, political, cultural, and social conditions that individuals have experienced in the post–World War II world, including

> the simultaneous inflation and recession caused in great part by dependence on Arab oil; the disruptions of globalization and the collapse of the Soviet empire; waves of nonwhite immigration into Europe (from places formerly ruled or dominated by Europeans) and the United States; the constant threat of war, especially in the Middle East and the Persian Gulf; and the continued sense among white men that they were losing power and prestige in areas ranging from world affairs to their living rooms to their relations with women. In the United States, racial issues, not resolved in the 1960s, took the form of conflict over school desegregation, affirmative action, social welfare provision, and government social spending in general. Moreover, the failure of the Vietnam War, based on untenable Cold War premises, produced an atmosphere of political and cultural resentment on the right that became increasingly strong over time. (Jewish Virtual Library)

Neo-Nazis were among the first to understand the impact of emerging technologies and the use of the Internet to indoctrinate members. And while most "neo-Nazi frames and narratives are based on myths, demonization, and scapegoating, this does not make them less effective in building a functional identity for individuals" (Jewish Virtual Library). Neo-Nazis were among the first to perpetuate the Zionist Occupation Government (ZOG) conspiracy theory, which purports that a secret cabal of Jews controls the governments of most Western countries and works behind the scenes to establish a one-world government through their use and manipulation of political leaders as well as the global economic system.

Neo-Nazis, including such traditional racist groups as the Ku Klux Klan (KKK) and the Council of Conservative Citizens, have a strongly Christian character to them. A particularly virulent form of Christianity—known as Christian

Identity—preaches that the white race is God's "chosen people" and that Jews are the spawn of Satan and Eve. Some neo-Nazis, however, reject Christianity (as it is "Jew-based") and embrace various forms of mysticism and neo-paganism. "Wotanism" ("Will of the Aryan Nation") is a neo-Nazi, white separatist movement begun by David Lane—a member of the infamous neo-Nazi group the Order—that preaches that the Norse gods are the true representatives of the white race and should be accorded the honor of worship as opposed to Christ, who was a Jew (Southern Poverty Law Center, David Lane).

Holocaust denial is another facet of neo-Nazism, as many neo-Nazis "attempt to prove that the Holocaust was fiction and that the Nazis never engaged in a systematic campaign to exterminate the Jews" (Southern Poverty Law Center, Neo-Nazi). The Institute for Historical Review (IHR) was among the first to serve as the "international clearinghouse" of Holocaust denial, or as advocates like to fancy themselves, Holocaust revisionists (Jewish Virtual Library). The IHR was founded in 1979 by Willis Carto, founder of the Liberty Lobby, a political lobby group that was formed to "promote patriotism." Carto was noted for his projects associated with extreme-right causes and involving neo-Nazi themes, an admiration for Adolf Hitler, and perpetuation of anti-Semitic conspiracy theories (Jewish Virtual Library).

Postwar neo-Nazism began in the United States in 1959 when George Lincoln Rockwell organized the American Nazi Party. The organization gained a great deal of publicity due to its advocacy of neo-Nazi principles and its prominent display of Nazi symbols, including the swastika. But the organization never gathered many members. After Rockwell's assassination by a disgruntled member in 1967, the neo-Nazi movement drifted aimlessly for a time, though many of the anti-Semitic themes of neo-Nazism were expressed by the anti-government movement known as Posse Comitatus.

During the 1970s, a rising star in the neo-Nazi ranks was David Duke, who professed his neo-Nazi sentiments at an early age (Southern Poverty Law Center, David Duke). While at Louisiana State University (LSU), Duke would build an "international reputation as the American face of white nationalism and pseudo-academic anti-Semitism" (Southern Poverty Law Center, David Duke). Duke would unsuccessfully run for political office several times, though he would be elected for a brief stint to the Louisiana State Legislature in the early 1990s.

In the late 1970s, Richard Butler founded Aryan Nations and preached his particular brand of Christian Identity from his compound in Hayden Lake, Idaho. Aryan Nations preached that the white race was pure and that other races were "mud people." Many former KKK members would join Aryan Nations, as they believed that the group was the future of white supremacy. One of Butler's acolytes, Bob Mathews, wanted more direct action, as opposed to the speeches and demonstrations for which Aryan Nations became infamous (Balleck). In 1983, Mathews formed the Order, perhaps the most terrorist-minded of all neo-Nazi organizations. Under Mathews's direction, the Order perpetrated robberies, murder, and other crimes that landed the Order and its members on the FBI's Ten Most Wanted List (Balleck). Aside from pulling off the most lucrative armored car heist in U.S. history ($3.6 million), the Order was responsible for the assassination of

Jewish talk show host Alan Berg in Denver, Colorado, in 1984. David Lane, a prominent member of the Order, was the author of the famous 14 Words—"We must secure the existence of our people and a future for white children"—and the promoter of Wotanism, the religious belief held by many neo-Nazis (Southern Poverty Law Center, David Lane). The 14 Words have become the unofficial motto of the neo-Nazi and white supremacist movements.

Also during the 1970s, William Luther Pierce founded the National Alliance (NA). NA would become "the largest and most active neo-Nazi organization in the United States for more than two decades" (Southern Poverty Law Center, Pierce). To bolster its numbers and increase its influence, NA tapped into the emerging racist skinhead movement and hate-rock music that emerged in the 1990s. In 1999, NA purchased Resistance Record, a struggling hate-rock business, which Pierce and his minions turned into a profitable enterprise (Balleck). Aside from his persona as the face of neo-Nazism, Pierce was the author (under the pseudonym Andrew MacDonald) of the infamous dystopian novel *The Turner Diaries*. The novel became the inspiration for Bob Mathews's group, the Order, which used the name of the novel's organization that waged war against a corrupt and Jewish-laden American government. In the novel, the Order kills all Jews and "race traitors" and establishes a pure white state in the United States, inasmuch as all other races have been exterminated. *The Turner Diaries* was also the inspiration for Timothy McVeigh's bombing of the Alfred P. Murrah Federal Building in Oklahoma City, Oklahoma, in April 1995. During the attack, 168 people, including 20 children, were killed (Balleck). As in the novel, McVeigh drove a rented truck full of fuel oil and ammonium nitrate fertilizer and detonated it in front of a federal building just after 9:00 a.m. McVeigh was convinced that Jews controlled the U.S. government and that the government had become illegitimate by its actions at Ruby Ridge and Waco (Balleck).

From the 1990s onward, a number of neo-Nazi elements have aligned themselves with the causes of extreme right-wing groups like those associated with the patriot and militia movement. The rise of these groups "prompted neo-Nazi leader Louis Beam to call for 'leaderless resistance' against the government" (Jewish Virtual Library). With the demise of many mainstream neo-Nazi groups such as Aryan Nations and the National Alliance, many displaced neo-Nazis have found their way into patriot and militia groups, where their white supremacist and anti-Semitic attitudes find an audience among those who believe that the government is under Jewish control and that the United Nations is conspiring to bring the United States under a one-world government, wherein its sovereignty will be destroyed and all citizen malcontents—especially those who own guns—will be interred in special camps (Cobb).

The Council of Conservative Citizens (CCC), founded in 1988 in Atlanta, Georgia, is the successor to the segregationist Citizen's Councils of America, which was prominent in the United States during the 1950s and 1960s. The CCC is a far-right extremist organization that pushes causes that promote white nationalism and white separatism. Much of the CCC's message is anti-Semitic and anti-black, but the group also embraces the tropes of neo-Nazism. In 2015, Dylann Roof—who murdered nine black parishioners in a Charleston, South Carolina, church—drew much of his inspiration from what he read on the CCC's website (Conservative Headlines). After the massacre, Roof's penchant for white supremacism and neo-Nazi symbols became national news.

In 2017, a new dapper, buttoned-down crowd of neo-Nazis arose in the form of the alt-right movement. Alt-right "has been described as having a bent toward white nationalism, racism, and neo-Nazism, as well as anti-Semitism, nativism, Islamaphobia, anti-feminism, and homophobia" (Krieg). Alt-right's leader, Richard Spencer, is a white supremacist who advocates for an Aryan homeland in North America, necessitating a "peaceful ethnic cleansing" to halt the "deconstruction" of European culture that has been the hallmark of American life for more than 300 years (Lambroso and Appelbaum). Spencer runs the National Policy Institute, a "white supremacist think tank in Alexandria, Virginia" (Gray). After Donald Trump's surprise victory in the 2016 U.S. presidential election, Spencer was caught on tape shouting, "Hail Trump, hail our people, hail victory, and the audience responded with Nazi salutes" (Buncombe). Though Spencer protests the label of "neo-Nazi," his rhetoric and actions inescapably lead to this conclusion (Krieg).

With the election of Donald Trump to the U.S. presidency, neo-Nazis feel as though they have found a kindred spirit. According to one observer, Trump's rise to power

> has encouraged the extremists to try to bridge their divides. Neo-Nazis and Ku Klux Klan leaders were jubilant over an openly xenophobic, politically incorrect presidential candidate who promised to stop illegal immigration and enact a Muslim ban—and they have pursued news coverage, attracting headlines and staging dramatic photos. (Beckett)

It appears as though neo-Nazis and neo-Nazism are now permanent fixtures on the global scene. Despite national laws in many European countries that punish Nazi speech or displays, neo-Nazism has been emboldened by the xenophobic nationalism that has arisen in the last few years because of conflict in the Middle East and the continuing threat of Islamic fundamentalism. It is possible "that if militant religious fundamentalism, especially within Islam, continues to expand, there will more intersections with fascist and Nazi ideas, a process that is already producing lethal threats to societies around the world" (Jewish Virtual Library).

See also: Alt-Right Movement; American Nazi Party; Aryan Nations; Christian Identity; Council of Conservative Citizens; Creativity Movement; Holocaust Denial; Institute for Historical Review; Ku Klux Klan; National Alliance; The Order; Racist Skinheads; White Nationalism; White Supremacist Movement

FURTHER READING

Anti-Defamation League. "Neo-Nazis." Anti-Defamation League. https://www.adl.org/education/resources/glossary-terms/neo-nazis. (Accessed June 8, 2017.)

Anti-Defamation League. December 20, 2016. "Richard Spencer Is Making Common Cause with Neo-Nazis." Anti-Defamation League. https://www.adl.org/blog/richard-spencer-is-making-common-cause-with-neo-nazis. (Accessed June 8, 2017.)

Balleck, Barry J. 2015. *Allegiance to Liberty: The Changing Face of Patriots, Militias, and Political Violence in America*. Praeger.

Beckett, Lois. June 4, 2017. "Is There a Neo-Nazi Storm Brewing in Trump Country?" *Guardian*. https://www.theguardian.com/world/2017/jun/04/national-socialism -neo-nazis-america-donald-trump. (Accessed June 8, 2017.)

Buncombe, Andrew. May 22, 2017. "Richard Spencer Has Gym Membership Revoked after Woman Confronts Him for Being 'Neo-Nazi.'" *Independent*. http://www .independent.co.uk/news/world/americas/richard-spencer-neo-nazi-alt-right -christine-fair-a7750186.html. (Accessed June 8, 2017.)

Cobb, Don. February 19, 2013. "The New America: Agenda 21 and the U.N. One World Government Plan." RenewAmerica.com. http://www.renewamerica.com/columns /cobb/130219. (Accessed June 8, 2017.)

Conservative Headlines. http://conservative-headlines.com/. (Accessed June 8, 2017.)

Gray, Rosie. December 27, 2015. "How 2015 Fueled the Rise of the Freewheeling, White Nationalist Alt Right Movement." BuzzFeed News. https://www.buzzfeed.com /rosiegray/how-2015-fueled-the-rise-of-the-freewheeling-white-nationali. (Accessed June 8, 2017.)

Jewish Virtual Library. "Anti-Semitism: Neo-Nazism." Jewish Virtual Library. http:// www.jewishvirtuallibrary.org/neo-nazism-2. (Accessed June 8, 2017.)

Krieg, Gregory. August 25, 2016. "Clinton Is Attacking the 'Alt-Right'—What Is It?" CNN. http://www.cnn.com/2016/08/25/politics/alt-right-explained-hillary-clinton -donald-trump/. (Accessed June 8, 2017.)

Lambroso, Daniel, and Yoni Appelbaum. November 21, 2016. "'Hail Trump!': White Nationalists Salute the President-Elect." *Atlantic*. http://www.theatlantic.com/politics /archive/2016/11/richard-spencer-speech-npi/508379/. (Accessed June 8, 2017.)

Southern Poverty Law Center. "David Duke." Southern Poverty Law Center. https:// www.splcenter.org/fighting-hate/extremist-files/individual/david-duke. (Accessed June 8, 2017.)

Southern Poverty Law Center. "David Lane." Southern Poverty Law Center. https://www .splcenter.org/fighting-hate/extremist-files/individual/david-lane. (Accessed June 8, 2017.)

Southern Poverty Law Center. "Neo-Nazi." Southern Poverty Law Center. https://www .splcenter.org/fighting-hate/extremist-files/ideology/neo-nazi. (Accessed June 8, 2017.)

Southern Poverty Law Center. "William Pierce." Southern Poverty Law Center. https:// www.splcenter.org/fighting-hate/extremist-files/individual/william-pierce. (Accessed June 8, 2017.)

Neo-Volkisch

Neo-Volkisch adherents are "organized around ethnocentricity and archaic notions of gender" (Southern Poverty Law Center). They "generally identify themselves as 'Folkish' or 'Folk'-rooted, designations that signal their cherishing of ethnocentrism in a manner that promotes ethnic exclusivity, at the very least, and can even promote racial supremacy" (Southern Poverty Law Center). Though not all groups associated with the neo-Volkisch movement are racist or bigoted, the movement itself can be "understood as a movement of ethnocentric tribalism" (Southern Poverty Law Center). David Lane, a member of the white supremacist group the Order, "infamously coined the '14 Words' slogan and authored 'The 88 Precepts,' a series of tenets that many white supremacists use to guide their life choices" (Southern Poverty Law Center). Lane, a follower of Wotanism, which, like the neo-Volkisch movement, worships the Norse and Germanic gods, believed that Aryans could not "share Gods with other races and that the tribal, ethnocentric, Wotanist society he envisioned was only attainable after a period of oppressive dictatorship" (Southern Poverty Law Center). According to the Southern Poverty Law Center (SPLC):

> In line with the defensive rhetoric adopted by the "alt-right," neo-Volkisch devotees veil their ethnocentric beliefs in arguments for the necessity of separate societies, or tribes, to preserve all ethnicities. Despite their paradoxical rebuke of modernity, leaders have embraced various social media platforms to increase the palatability of the neo-Völkisch ideology. (Southern Poverty Law Center)

The Asatru Folk Assembly (AFA) has been labeled by the SPLC as "perhaps the country's largest neo-Volkisch hate group" (Southern Poverty Law Center). The group has raised money for what it has stated are the oppressed and "persecuted whites in South Africa."

> For those of you that may not know, white farmers are being savagely abused and impoverished. This abuse is racially motivated and, because they are sons and daughters of Europe, the victims are being largely ignored by the world. This is a tragedy, but take heart! There are tangible ways that your contributions can help these folk and, so far, the generosity of AFA members towards this has been overwhelming! (Asatru Folk Assembly)

Echoing the line from many white nationalist groups today, the AFA states that "it is okay to be white" while defending notions of masculinity and femininity:

> Today we are bombarded with confusion and messages contrary to the values of our ancestors and our folk. The AFA would like to make it clear that we believe gender is not a social construct, it is a beautiful gift from the holy powers of our ancestors. The AFA celebrates our feminine ladies, our masculine gentlemen, and, above all, our beautiful white children. The children of the folk are our shining future and the legacy of all those men and women of our people back to the beginning. Hail the AFA families, now and always! (Xander)

The Southern Poverty Law Center has noted:

> While violence rarely erupts from the neo-Völkisch movement, the ethnically or racially charged warrior ethos that the movement is largely premised on further entrenches belief systems that form the bedrock of contemporary notions of the relationship between volatile masculinity and nurturing femininity. Hypermasculine imagery fetishized within neo-Völkisch spheres reinforces misogyny and traditional gender roles. This degradation and disrespect of women, often couched in a cherishing of women as the keepers of the home, echoes broader trends within the so-called "alt-right" that derive from the virulently anti-woman "manosphere," the online blogosphere-turned-movement supposedly rescuing masculinity from rabid feminists and other forces of political correctness. (Southern Poverty Law Center)

Critics of the neo-Volkisch movement have noted that adherents have been heartened by the racially charged political environment in the United States in recent years. As one critic of the AFA has stated:

> It would seem the AFA is also planning to take advantage of this, appealing to a more extreme demographic by playing to feelings of ostracization in a segment of

the population that hasn't had political favor since the Brown v. Board of Education ruling in 1954. It doesn't matter that the hetero-normative 'traditional family' model they're promoting is the Christian model, or that (historically) the Norse peoples they're claiming to represent had no concept of a 'white race' and regularly interbred with people from around the world. Emotional appeals don't require logical backing, and with the nation becoming more comfortable with extremist views on race and religion, this is a stance that the AFA knows it can use to attract and maintain its membership numbers. (Xander)

See also: Alt-Right Movement; Gallows Tree Wotansvolk Alliance; The Order; White Nationalism; White Supremacist Movement; Wolves of Vinland

FURTHER READING

Asatru Folk Assembly. http://www.runestone.org/. (Accessed July 23, 2018.)

Goodrick-Clarke, Nicholas. 1993. *The Occult Roots of Nazism: Secret Aryan Cults and Their Influence on Nazi Ideology*. New York University Press.

Goodrick-Clarke, Nicholas. 2003. *Black Sun: Aryan Cults, Esoteric Nazism, and the Politics of Identity*. New York University Press.

Southern Poverty Law Center. "Neo-Volkisch." Southern Poverty Law Center. https://www.splcenter.org/fighting-hate/extremist-files/ideology/neo-volkisch. (Accessed July 21, 2018.)

Transatlantic Intelligencer. April 22, 2005. "The Ummah and Das Volk: On the Islamist and Volkisch Ideologies." Transatlantic Intelligencer. http://trans-int.blogspot.com/2005/04/ummah-and-das-volk-on-islamist-and.html. (Accessed July 21, 2018.)

Wyrdsisters. "Understanding Neo-Volkisch Satanism." Wyrdsisters. https://wyrdsister.wordpress.com/2018/05/08/understanding-neo-volkisch-satanism/. (Accessed July 21, 2018.)

Xander. August 22, 2016. "New Leadership Takes A.F.A. in More Bigoted Direction." Huginn's Heathen Hof. http://www.heathenhof.com/new-leadership-takes-a-f-a-in-more-racist-direction/. (Accessed July 23, 2018.)

Zaitchik, Alexander. October 19, 2006. "The National Socialist Movement Implodes." Southern Poverty Law Center: Intelligence Report. https://www.splcenter.org/fighting-hate/intelligence-report/2006/national-socialist-movement-implodes. (Accessed July 21, 2018.)

New Black Panther Party

The New Black Panther Party (NBPP) is a black separatist and black nationalist organization founded in Dallas, Texas, in 1989. Despite its name, it has no official affiliation with the original Black Panther Party, which was active in the United States in the 1960s and 1970s. In fact, "former members of the original Black Panthers have insisted that the NBPP is illegitimate and have firmly declared, 'There is no new Black Panther Party'" (Huey P. Newton Foundation). Former Black Panther Party member Bobby Seale has labeled the NBPP "a black racist hate group" (Southern Poverty Law Center). The NBPP "portrays itself as a modern-day expression of the black power movement," complete with militantism, but it makes no apologies for its virulently racist attitude toward whites, Jews, and law enforcement officers (Southern Poverty Law Center).

As a black separatist group, the NBPP "believes that black Americans should have their own nation." NBPP's "10 Point Platform," which is a variation of the original Black Panther Party's 10-point platform, "demands that blacks be given a country, or state, of their own within which they can make their own laws." The NBPP demands that "all black prisoners in the United States be released to "lawful authorities of the Black Nation," and "they claim that the blacks are entitled to reparations from slavery from the United States, all European countries, and the Jews" (New Black Panther Party).

The NBPP "is notable for its anti-white and anti-Semitic hatred." Its leaders have blamed the Jews for 9/11 and have insisted that Jews are to blame for the slave trade that shipped hundreds of thousands of Africans to the United States. The former party chairperson of NBPP, Khalid Abdul Muhammad, has said, "There are no good crackers, and if you find one, kill him before he changes" (Southern Poverty Law Center). NBPP members "hold black supremacist beliefs, thinking that blacks are God's chosen people" and that blacks are morally superior to all other races (Southern Poverty Law Center). This ideology is remarkably similar to Christian Identity, a quasi-religious philosophy that teaches that whites, not Jews, are God's chosen people and that the white race is morally and intellectually superior to all other races.

NBPP has co-opted virtually every symbol of the original Black Panther Party, including their name, their logo, their 10-point program, and their style of dress. Like the Panthers of the 1960s and 1970s, NBPP members "often wear coordinated, military-style uniforms when they march—black boots, black pants, black shirts with NBPP patches, and black berets" (Southern Poverty Law Center). In 1997, two original Black Panthers "won an injunction against the NBPP disallowing them from using either the Panther name or its logo. However, the injunction was never enforced and the NBPP continues to use the Panther name and logo today" (Southern Poverty Law Center).

In 1994, Khalid Abdul Muhammed, a former personal assistant to Nation of Islam (NOI) leader Louis Farrakhan, joined the NBPP. He accused Jews of "being responsible for the slave trade" and called them "bloodsuckers." Like the Million Man March that NOI had organized two years earlier, Muhammad organized the Million Youth March in 1998 in New York City. At the event, Muhammad encouraged those assembled "to attack police officers with chairs and bottles and even take the officers' guns if attacked" (Southern Poverty Law Center). Soon after the event, Muhammad assumed control of the NBPP and became the group's national chairperson.

Muhammad died in February 2001 and was replaced by Malik Zulu Shabazz, a Washington, D.C., attorney who had previously run unsuccessfully for D.C.'s City Council. In a conference held on October 31, 2001, Shabazz would say: "Zionism is racism, Zionism is terrorism, Zionism is colonialism, Zionism is imperialism, and support for Zionism is the root of why so many were killed on September 11" (Southern Poverty Law Center). During his time as national chairperson, Shabazz worked to improve relations with the NOI, where many NBPP members had their roots. Shabazz stepped down from the NBPP in 2013 to become the president of the Black Lawyers for Justice Association.

Local chapters of NBPP have made headlines for their menacing remarks and behaviors. In November 2008, "two NBPP members showed up wearing military-style fatigues and berets, at a Philadelphia, Pennsylvania polling station ostensibly to protect black voters from having their voting rights violated" (Southern Poverty Law Center). The Justice Department filed civil charges of voter intimidation against the two, plus NBPP leader Malik Zulu Shabazz, and won the case when the defendants failed to appear in court. The Obama administration dropped the charges. In 2012, an NBPP member in Sanford, Florida, offered a $10,000 "bounty" on the "Hispanic man who shot an unarmed black teen as he was walking through a gated community" (Southern Poverty Law Center). When asked whether he was inciting violence, the NBPP member replied, "An eye for an eye, a tooth for a tooth" (Southern Poverty Law Center). In July 2016, an Afghan War army veteran, Micah Xavier Johnson, shot and killed five white police officers at a protest in Dallas, Texas. Johnson had expressed sympathies for NBPP and the black separatist cause.

See also: Black Nationalism; Christian Identity; Nation of Islam

FURTHER READING

Huey P. Newton Foundation. "There Is No New Black Panther Party: An Open Letter from the Huey P. Newton Foundation." Huey P. Newton Foundation. http://web .archive.org/web/20140907064728/http://www.blackpanther.org/newsalert.htm. (Accessed March 18, 2017.)

New Black Panther Party. http://www.nbpp.org/home.html. (Accessed March 18, 2017.)

New Black Panther Party. "New Black Panther Party for Self Defense: Freedom or Death." New Black Panther Party. http://www.nbpp.org/10-point-platform.html. (Accessed March 18, 2017.)

Southern Poverty Law Center. "New Black Panther Party." Southern Poverty Law Center. https://www.splcenter.org/fighting-hate/extremist-files/group/new-black-panther -party. (Accessed March 18, 2017.)

New Black Panther Party for Self Defense

The New Black Panther Party for Self Defense (NBPP-SD) "is the largest organized anti-Semitic and racist Black militant group in America" (Anti-Defamation League). The NBPP was formed in 2013 after an internal struggle "within the New Black Panther Party. Since October 2013, Hashim Nzinga, who previously served as the group's Chief of Staff, has led the group" (Anti-Defamation League). The NBPP-SD is characterized "as a 'black nationalist' hate group by the Southern Poverty Law Center (SPLC), with chapters in Texas, Florida, Kentucky, Missouri, Georgia, and Oklahoma" (Southern Poverty Law Center). In general,

> Black Nationalist hate groups espouse hatred toward whites, the LGBT community, and Jews. Black Nationalists have also advocated for a separate territory for African Americans within the country (similar to white nationalists who argue for a white homeland in the Pacific Northwest). According to their propaganda, Black Nationalists would like a portion of the Southeast United States reserved for a black nation.

Further, they are known for their antigovernment and anti-police sentiments due to their long-held views on government corruption and police brutality. . . .

Black Nationalism's worldview is shaped by conspiracy theories, including the idea that white people were created in a test tube. Among other things, they believe wrongly that Jews ran the slave trade. Some are Holocaust deniers. Similar to other hate groups, some Black Nationalist groups conduct prison outreach programs to recruit inmates into their extremist cause. Some have also been known to recruit street gang members. (Johnson)

The current leader of NBPP-SD is Hashim Nzinga, an individual who has contempt for white people, but particularly Jews. Nzinga believes that American Jews exploited their alliances with black leaders "during the Civil Rights era of the 1960s as a means of 'infiltrat[ing]' American institutions and creating an 'international Zionist machine' that now possesses a disproportionate level of power over U.S. media outlets and record labels" (Discover the Networks). This influence, according to Nzinga, "has enabled Jews: (a) to 'own what we look at and what our kids look at every day, which means they [Jews] control our mind by remote controls in our living room;' and (b) to 'show us [blacks] before the world looking like damn fools' and 'buffoons'" (Discover the Networks). In April 2015, Nzinga stated that the U.S. government had declared war upon blacks. He added: "We pay taxes. They [the white power structure] have declared war on us and it's nothing but state racism" (Discover the Networks). Nzinga praised those "willing to die or kill to save our babies and to save a black nation that is dying before our eyes" (Discover the Networks).

In May 2017, NBPP-SD member Derick Lamont Brown, chairperson of the Dallas chapter of the group, shot and killed his "godfather, a paramedic, and an innocent bystander" (Hatewatch staff). Brown "later turned the gun on himself and died from a self-inflicted gunshot wound" (Hatewatch staff). Prior to his death, Brown had stated that he desired to unite every Black Panther in "one common struggle." He said, "As the vanguard in the community, we are here to stand to say it's our power to the people that we're willing to defend by any cause and every cause. And as a last resort If that takes fighting back, Lord have mercy for me on what should happen on the streets, but I'm willing" (Hatewatch staff).

See also: Black Nationalism; Black Separatists; New Black Panther Party

FURTHER READING

Anti-Defamation League. "Report: New Black Panther for Self Defense (NBPP)." Anti-Defamation League. https://www.adl.org/resources/reports/report-new-black-panther-party-for-self-defense-nbpp. (Accessed June 9, 2018.)

Discover the Networks. "Hashim Nzinga." DiscovertheNetworks.org. http://www.discoverthenetworks.org/individualProfile.asp?indid=2704. (Accessed June 9, 2018.)

Hatewatch Staff. May 3, 2017. "New Black Panther for Self Defense Member Committed Suicide after Shooting Three People and Killing One." Southern Poverty Law Center: Hatewatch. https://www.splcenter.org/hatewatch/2017/05/03/new-black-panther-self-defense-member-committed-suicide-after-shooting-three-people-and. (Accessed June 9, 2018.)

Johnson, Daryl. August 8, 2017. "Return of the Violent Black Nationalist." Southern Poverty Law Center: Intelligence Report. https://www.splcenter.org/fighting-hate/intelligence-report/2017/return-violent-black-nationalist. (Accessed June 9, 2018.)

Southern Poverty Law Center. "Black Nationalist." Southern Poverty Law Center. https://www.splcenter.org/fighting-hate/extremist-files/ideology/black-nationalist. (Accessed June 9, 2018.)

New Century Foundation

The New Century Foundation (NCF) was founded in 1990 by Jared Taylor, an American white nationalist, and it is the parent organization for *American Renaissance*, a white supremacist publication. NCF, under the direction of Taylor, advocates for racial separation, intoning that such views are a natural expression of racial solidarity, as opposed to white supremacism. Taylor believes that racial homogeneity is a natural human expression of individuals' innate desires to be with their own kind and believes that homogeneity is the key to peaceful coexistence between races. Taylor holds up Japan as "an exemplar of a racially homogenous society, and views Asians generally as genetically superior in intelligence to whites. He also view whites as genetically superior in intelligence to blacks" (Anti-Defamation League). The Anti-Defamation League (ADL) notes that "Taylor eschews anti-Semitism, seeing Jews as white, greatly influential, and the 'conscience of society'" (Anti-Defamation League). The Southern Poverty Law Center (SPLC) has stated that NCF is a "self-styled think tank that promotes pseudo-scientific studies and research that purport to show the inferiority of blacks to whites—although in hifalutin language that avoids open racial slurs and attempts to portray itself as serious scholarship" (Southern Poverty Law Center).

The main vehicle for the ideas advocated by the New Century Foundation (NCF) is *American Renaissance*, the publication edited by Taylor, which presents itself as a "forum for open-minded thinkers not afraid to take on the racial taboos of the time without stooping to racial epithets and the like" (Southern Poverty Law Center). *American Renaissance* serves as the front porch for the racist views of Taylor and the New Century Foundation. NCF's mission statement veils its racism by suggesting that it represents the views of the "majority" whose interests are being ignored in the current political environment:

> NCF's purpose is to encourage sensible public policy on race and immigration. We believe accurate knowledge and the willingness to face potentially unpleasant truths—both of which are conspicuously absent in the public arena—are essential to this task. We also believe the European-American majority has legitimate group interests now being ignored. (NCF)

NCF conferences have included members of the Council of Conservative Citizens—a white nationalist and white supremacist organization that condemns "racial mixing," decries the evil "of illegal immigration, and laments the decline of American civilization"—such as Don Black, the white supremacist operator of *Stormfront*—a white nationalist and neo-Nazi internet forum—and National Alliance leader Kevin Strom.

Like many organizations on the extremist right, NCF bemoans the loss of the power of the white majority in the United States. With increasing multiculturalism and the perceived loss of American exceptionalism, NCF attracts members and adherents who wish to return the United States to an idealized time in the past when all people in society knew their place. NCF's focus on "race and immigration" is simply a smokescreen to conceal a racist agenda. The pseudoscientific nature of *American Renaissance* also attempts to make NCF's racist agenda more palatable by publishing articles from "race scientists" who can, they claim, lay bare the demonstrable differences between the races.

See also: *American Renaissance*; Council of Conservative Citizens; National Alliance: Neo-Nazis; White Nationalism; White Supremacist Movement

FURTHER READING

Anti-Defamation League. "Jared Taylor/American Renaissance." Anti-Defamation League. https://www.adl.org/sites/default/files/documents/assets/pdf/combating -hate/jared-taylor-extremism-in-america.pdf. (Accessed May 9, 2017.)

New Century Foundation. "Mission Statement." New Century Foundation. https://www .guidestar.org/profile/61-6212159. (Accessed May 9, 2017.)

Southern Poverty Law Center. "American Renaissance." Southern Poverty Law Center. https://www.splcenter.org/fighting-hate/extremist-files/group/american-renaissance. (Accessed May 9, 2017.)

New Order

The New Order, a neo-Nazi, white supremacist organization "patterned after The Order," which was "a band of underground revolutionaries that murdered a Jewish radio host in 1984 and robbed armored cars to the tune of $4 million," was founded by one-time grand dragon of the Ku Klux Klan (KKK) Michael McGiffen in the mid-1990s (Jackson). McGiffen's New Order meant to take up where the old Order had left off, by planning bold acts of domestic terrorism, such as "assassinations, bombings, even poisoning a public water supply—which would again be financed by bank robberies and armored-car heists" (Jackson). When federal investigators broke up the New Order, they also discovered that the group had a hit list of prominent institutions and individuals that the New Order had targeted for assassination. The list "included Morris Dees, co-founder of the Southern Poverty Law Center"; then–Federal Reserve Chairman Alan Greenspan; filmmaker Steven Spielberg (Morlin); "the Simon Wiesenthal Center in Los Angeles; the Anti-Defamation League; and a Federal judge whose name was not disclosed" (New York Times).

According to Camille Jackson, an investigator for the Southern Poverty Law Center (SPLC), "The New Order didn't get nearly as far as the old Order; its plans were foiled when a government informant told authorities the group was stockpiling automatic weapons, even a 'light anti-tank rocket system,' to ignite a race war against blacks and Jews" (Jackson). McGiffen "claimed that his murderous plans were nothing more than drunken ramblings he never intended to carry out. If getting drunk and running your mouth can get you guilty of conspiracy, it's a sad day for America," he said (Jackson).

McGiffen pleaded guilty to weapons charges in September 1998 and spent the next six years in prison. After emerging from prison, McGiffen founded the Sadistic Souls Motorcycle Club (SS-MC), which later merged with a faction of Aryan Nations. After the arrest and imprisonment of all of its members, the New Order ceased to exist.

See also: Aryan Nations; Neo-Nazis; Sadistic Souls Motorcycle Club; White Supremacist Movement

FURTHER READING

Anti-Defamation League. September 20, 2012. "One-Time Domestic Terrorist Now Leads White Supremacist Biker Gang." https://www.adl.org/blog/one-time-domestic -terrorist-now-leads-white-supremacist-biker-gang. (Accessed June 8, 2018.)

Jackson, Camille. December 20, 2004. "Extremist Ex-Cons Back on the Street." Southern Poverty Law Center: Intelligence Report. https://www.splcenter.org/fighting-hate /intelligence-report/2004/extremist-ex-cons-back-street. (Accessed June 9, 2018.)

Morlin, Bill. January 27, 2014. "Squabbling Aryan Nations Factions Descend into Vicious Name Calling." Southern Poverty Law Center: Hatewatch. https://www.splcenter .org/hatewatch/2014/01/27/squabbling-aryan-nations-factions-descend-vicious -name-calling. (Accessed June 8, 2018.)

New York Times. March 7, 1998. "Supremacists Had Hit List, F.B.I. Agent Says." *New York Times*. https://www.nytimes.com/1998/03/07/us/supremacists-had-hit-list-fbi -agent-says.html. (Accessed June 9, 2018.)

North Mississippi White Knights of the Ku Klux Klan

The North Mississippi White Knights of the Ku Klux Klan are a Ku Klux Klan (KKK)-affiliated group located in Bruce, Mississippi (Southern Poverty Law Center, Hate Map by State). According to "the Southern Poverty Law Center (SPLC), KKK hate groups were started during Reconstruction at the end of the Civil War," and they quickly mobilized into a "vigilante group to intimidate Southern blacks—and any whites who would help them—and to prevent them from enjoying basic civil rights" (Southern Poverty Law Center, Ku Klux Klan). The SPLC notes that the KKK was and is characterized by

> outlandish titles (like imperial wizard and exalted cyclops), hooded costumes, violent "night rides," and the notion that the group comprised an "invisible empire" [that] conferred a mystique that only added to the Klan's popularity. Lynchings, tar-and-featherings, rapes and other violent attacks on those challenging white supremacy became a hallmark of the Klan. (Southern Poverty Law Center, Ku Klux Klan)

According to the SPLC, "the KKK has a long history of violence in the United States" and "is the most infamous—and oldest—of American hate groups. Although black Americans have typically been the Klan's primary target, it also has attacked Jews, immigrants, gays and lesbians and, until recently, Catholics" (Southern Poverty Law Center, Ku Klux Klan).

The North Mississippi White Knights of the Ku Klux Klan are one of around 40 active KKK groups in the United States, but their activities have been sporadic in recent years. The Anti-Defamation League (ADL) reported that the North Mississippi White Knights "promised a March 2017 demonstration at the Douglas County courthouse in Douglasville, Georgia, meant to protest lengthy sentences given to a Georgia couple following their conviction for threatening an African-American family during a child's birthday party in July 2015" (Anti-Defamation League-1). However, the Klan group never showed. Nevertheless, the ADL noted that Mississippi had more incidents of KKK activity in 2017 than any other state had (Anti-Defamation League-1).

See also: Ku Klux Klan; White Nationalism; White Supremacist Movement

FURTHER READING

Anti-Defamation League-1. "Despite Internal Turmoil, Klan Groups Persist." Anti-Defamation League. https://www.adl.org/sites/default/files/documents/CR_5173 _Klan%20Report_vFFF2.pdf. (Accessed July 20, 2018.)

Anti-Defamation League-2. "Despite Internal Turmoil, Klan Groups Persist." Anti-Defamation League. https://www.adl.org/resources/reports/despite-internal -turmoil-klan-groups-persist. (Accessed July 20, 2018.)

Southern Poverty Law Center. "Hate Map by State." Southern Poverty Law Center. https://www.splcenter.org/hate-map/by-state. (Accessed July 20, 2018.)

Southern Poverty Law Center. "Ku Klux Klan." Southern Poverty Law Center. https:// www.splcenter.org/fighting-hate/extremist-files/ideology/ku-klux-klan. (Accessed July 20, 2018.)

Northern Hammerskins

The Northern Hammerskins are a racist skinhead hate group based in Chicago, Illinois, and Detroit, Michigan (Southern Poverty Law Center, Racist Skinhead). According to the Southern Poverty Law Center, racist skinheads "form a particularly violent element of the white supremacist movement and have often been referred to as the 'shock troops' of the hoped-for revolution. The archetypal skinhead look is a shaved head, black boots with red laces, jeans with suspenders, and an array of typically racist tattoos. Skinheads are migratory and often not affiliated with groups" (Southern Poverty Law Center, 2017). The Northern Hammerskins are an upper Midwest chapter of Hammerskin Nation. The Anti-Defamation League "calls Hammerskin Nation the most violent and best-organized neo-Nazi skinhead group in the United States" (Anti-Defamation League). The Northern Hammerskins have been associated with a particularly brutal "cycle of bloodshed, retaliation, and dissent that continues to shape the level and nature of skinhead criminal activity in this country and abroad" (Holthouse).

One of the founding members of the Northern Hammerskins—Arno Michaelis—stated as a leader of the hate group that "perpetrating wanton violence against innocent people and twisting the minds of other white kids" was what the group did. According to Michaelis:

> We would comb the city, looking for the "anti-racist skinheads" and beating up whoever we could find. Though we did attack people because of skin color or suspected sexual orientation, we most often attacked random white people, claiming after the fact that they were race-traitors. Aside from trips to Chicago and Minneapolis to brawl with their anti-racists, the bulk of the violence we committed was relatively spontaneous. We had a tendency to start assaulting each other if we didn't go on a manhunt.
>
> At our most organized point, the group had weekly meetings at which the many threats we faced were lamented and our dedication to eliminating our enemies was sworn. By enemies, I mean everyone except violent, racist white people. Jews were seen as the masterminds of an ongoing genocide against the white race. "Non-white" people were seen as lazy, stupid savages that the Jews kept integrating into white society to destroy it. White people who weren't violent racists were seen as the greatest enemies of all: race-traitors complicit in our destruction. . . .
>
> When everything is going wrong in your life, it's much easier to blame Jews/Muslims/blacks/Mexicans/gays/anyone-but-yourself than it is to face your flaws and begin the hard work to account for them. The teenage outcast kid is told that it's the Jews' fault he doesn't have a girlfriend—the media they control tells white girls to be attracted to black boys. The middle-aged guy who lost his job has "illegal" immigrants to blame, and take a wild guess who the racist narrative says brings them into our country. (Michaelis)

Hammerskin Nation emerged "from the first Hammerskin group, the Confederate Hammerskins, formed in Dallas, Texas in the late 1980s" (Anti-Defamation League). After its founding, "dozens of local and regional Hammerskin groups emerged, including the Northern Hammerskins, the Eastern Hammerskins, and the Western Hammerskins" (Anti-Defamation League). According to Hammerskin Nation's website, "The Hammerskin Nation is a leaderless group of men and women who have adopted the White Power Skinhead lifestyle. We are blue collar workers, white collar professionals, college students, entrepreneurs, fathers and mothers" (Hammerskin Nation, Who We Are). The goals of the Northern Hammerskins, like all groups associated with Hammerskin Nation, are summed up in the 14 Words, the neo-Nazi ethos coined by David Lane, a member of the infamous group the Order. This ethos illustrates the foundational concept by which Northern Hammerskins and others live their lives: "We must secure the existence of our people and a future for White Children" (Hammerskin Nation, Who We Are).

See also: Eastern Hammerskins; Hammerskin Nation; Neo-Nazis; The Order; Racist Skinheads; Western Hammerskins; White Nationalism; White Supremacist Movement

FURTHER READING

Anti-Defamation League. "The Hammerskin Nation." Anti-Defamation League. https://www.adl.org/education/resources/profiles/hammerskin-nation. (Accessed July 18, 2018.)

Atlanta Anarchist Black Cross. August 24, 2016. "Neo-Nazi 'Hammerfest' Gathering Planned for Georgia, October 1st." It's Going Down. https://itsgoingdown.org

/neo-nazi-hammerfest-gathering-planned-georgia-october-1st/. (Accessed July 18, 2018.)

Hammerskin Nation. "Our History." Hammerskin Nation. https://www.hammerskins .net/. (Accessed July 18, 2018.)

Hammerskin Nation. "Who We Are." Hammerskin Nation. https://www.hammerskins .net/. (Accessed July 18, 2018.)

Holthouse, David. October 19, 2006. "Motley Crews: With Decline of Hammerskins, Independent Skinhead Groups Grow." Southern Poverty Law Center: Intelligence Report. https://www.splcenter.org/fighting-hate/intelligence-report/2006/motley -crews-decline-hammerskins-independent-skinhead-groups-grow. (Accessed July 18, 2018.)

Michaelis, Arno. June 25, 2015. "This Is How You Become a White Supremacist." *Washington Post.* https://www.washingtonpost.com/posteverything/wp/2015/06/25 /this-is-how-you-become-a-white-supremacist/. (Accessed July 18, 2018.)

Northern Hammerskins. http://www.hammerskins.net/nhs/. (Accessed July 18, 2018.)

Reynolds, Michael. December 15, 1999. "Hammerskin Nation Emerges from Small Dallas Group." Southern Poverty Law Center: Intelligence Report. https://www.splcenter .org/fighting-hate/intelligence-report/1999/hammerskin-nation-emerges-small -dallas-group. (Accessed July 18, 2018.)

Southern Poverty Law Center. "Racist Skinhead." Southern Poverty Law Center. https:// www.splcenter.org/fighting-hate/extremist-files/ideology/racist-skinhead. (Accessed July 18, 2018.)

Southern Poverty Law Center. February 15, 2017. "Active Hate Groups 2016." Southern Poverty Law Center: Intelligence Report. https://www.splcenter.org/fighting-hate /intelligence-report/2017/active-hate-groups-2016. (Accessed July 18, 2018.)

Northwest Front

By its own admission, the Northwest Front "is a political organization of Aryan men and women who recognize that an independent and sovereign White nation in the Pacific Northwest is the only possibility for the survival of the White race on this continent" (Northwest Front). The group has been dubbed a "white nationalist hate group by the Southern Poverty Law Center" (SPLC). According to the SPLC:

Adherents of white nationalist groups believe that white identity should be the orga- nizing principle of the countries that make up Western civilization. White national- ists advocate for policies to reverse changing demographics and the loss of an absolute, white majority. Ending non-white immigration, both legal and illegal, is an urgent priority—frequently elevated over other racist projects, such as ending multiculturalism and miscegenation—for white nationalists seeking to preserve white, racial hegemony. (Southern Poverty Law Center, White Nationalist)

The Northwest Front was founded by Harold Covington, a neo-Nazi who "dreams of creating a whites-only country in the Pacific Northwest" (Murphy). After Dylann Roof murdered nine black parishioners at a historically black church in South Carolina in June 2015, Covington stated that "there will be more of this kind of thing in the future as our [white] people finally begin to respond, slug- gishly and spasmodically and incorrectly, to the ongoing genocide" (Murphy).

On its website, the Northwest Front does not shy away from its unabashed position of the need to support and protect white society. Billing themselves as "American as apple pie," the group states:

> The founding fathers of the United States would be far closer to being White Nationalists than to any of the other political groups of today. The men who drafted the Declaration of Independence, the Bill of Rights, and the Constitution were all White. They shared a common cultural background, and none of them wanted racial mixing. (Northwest Front)

And in the "About" section of the Northwest Front is a portion entitled "Dear White America":

> We're going to let you in on a secret. It shouldn't be a secret, but few people dare to talk about it in today's politically correct world. White people created modern civilization and modern science.
>
> We as a people have forgotten our greatness and our courage. We've been told our beliefs are "cultural imperialism" and have been chided to accept other cultures' standards for behavior. . . .
>
> It is now fairly clear that at some point in the future, the United States of America will cease to exist as a viable political, economic, and social entity. It is a historical truth that nothing lasts forever, and the USA will not last forever either.
>
> When that collapse occurs, the many races and vested interest groups that inhabit the North American continent will begin to rip and tear at whatever's left of the United States, like vultures on a carcass. Bluntly put, we need to make sure that Whites get their piece of the carcass.
>
> We need to create a country for White people alone. Considerations of history, economics, and logistics dictate that the best place for such a country is here in the Pacific Northwest.
>
> We call this country the Northwest American Republic, and we call the fighting revolutionary Party of Northwest independence the Northwest Front (NF). (Northwest Front, About)

But the Northwest Front does not see itself as hating any other group. Indeed, they state that the "politically correct system we live under stigmatizes any kind of White racial pride or racial awareness as 'hate.' We need to learn to ignore this and not let ourselves be frightened away by a meaningless word" (Northwest Front, About). The Northwest Front claims that it stands for "freeing people—our people—from a yoke of tyranny and oppression that has become impossible for us to live with. We stand for preserving our race from biological and cultural extinction" (American Front, About).

An individual who was once part of the Northwest Front—Corinna Burt—stated that its founder, Harold Covington, often said that "he [Covington] needs to get a thousand alpha Aryan males to move to his neighborhood and then basically just start shooting everyone who isn't white" (Potok and Wood). In articulating her reasons for leaving the Northwest Front, Burt said:

> I guess I just got disillusioned with white nationalism in general. I realized, okay, no, people of other races have never done anything to me or my children in the way white nationalists have. This is the real enemy.
>
> I realized much too late that this entire movement is a huge waste of life, and people who dedicate their lives to such a cause end up with nothing to show for it

but their ruined families, destroyed careers and often a loss of personal freedom. I'm glad I got out when I did and I know there are others who want out. Look at the stories of people who have left and who have renounced their beliefs; consider that maybe they had compelling reasons for doing so, when to do so often means putting yourself at great personal risk. I decided that risk was worth it if it meant escape from a life of absolute blind hatred with no end in sight. (Potok and Wood)

See also: Neo-Nazis; White Nationalism; White Supremacist Movement

FURTHER READING

Murphy, Dan. June 18, 2015. "Why Would an American White Supremacist Be Fond of Rhodesia?" *Christian Science Monitor*. https://www.csmonitor.com/World/Security -Watch/Backchannels/2015/0618/Why-would-an-American-white-supremacist -be-fond-of-Rhodesia. (Accessed June 23, 2018.)

Northwest Front. http://northwestfront.org/. (Accessed June 23, 2018.)

Northwest Front. "About." Northwest Front. http://northwestfront.org/about/dear-white -american/. (Accessed June 23, 2018.)

Potok, Mark, and Laurie Wood. August 21, 2013. "Leaving White Nationalism." Southern Poverty Law Center: Intelligence Report. https://www.splcenter.org/fighting-hate /intelligence-report/2013/leaving-white-nationalism. (Accessed June 23, 2018.)

Southern Poverty Law Center. "White Nationalist." Southern Poverty Law Center. https:// www.splcenter.org/fighting-hate/extremist-files/ideology/white-nationalist. (Accessed June 23, 2018.)

Southern Poverty Law Center. March 2, 2015. "Active White Nationalist Groups." Southern Poverty Law Center: Intelligence Report. https://www.splcenter.org/fighting -hate/intelligence-report/2015/active-white-nationalist-groups. (Accessed June 23, 2018.)

Northwest Hammerskins

The Northwest Hammerskins are part of what is known as Hammerskin Nation. The Anti-Defamation League (ADL) has called Hammerskin Nation "the most violent and best-organized neo-Nazi skinhead group in the United States" (Anti-Defamation League). The Northwest Hammerskins are located in Idaho, Montana, North Dakota, Oregon, and Washington (Deeds). According to the Southern Poverty Law Center (SPLC), the Northwest Hammerskins are a racist skinhead hate group. Racist skinheads "form a particularly violent element of the white supremacist movement, and have often been referred to as the 'shock troops' of the hoped-for revolution. The classic Skinhead look is a shaved head, black Doc Martens boots, jeans with suspenders and an array of typically racist tattoos" (Southern Poverty Law Center, Racist Skinhead).

Hammerskin Nation, also known as "Hammerskins," was formed in Dallas, Texas, in 1988 as a white supremacist group espousing the "14 Words" of former Order member David Lane: "We must secure the existence of our people and a future for White Children" (Hammerskin Nation). In their own words, Hammerskin Nation

is a leaderless group of men and women who have adopted the White Power Skinhead lifestyle. We are blue collar workers, white collar professionals, college students, entrepreneurs, fathers and mothers. The Hammerskin brotherhood is way of achieving goals which we have all set for ourselves. These goals are many but can be summed up with one phrase consisting of 14 words. (Hammerskin Nation)

The Northwest Hammerskins are "best known for their 2015 affiliations with the racists who attacked Black Lives Matter protesters in Olympia [Washington] and for attempting to hold a march on Seattle's Capitol Hill later that year as part of their 'Martyrs Day' celebrations, which celebrate the white power guerilla group, The Order" (Puget Sound Anarchists). In recent years,

> the NorthWest Hammerskins have each December held a memorial event on Whidbey Island, Washington for neo-Nazi terrorist Robert Jay Mathews of The Silent Brotherhood/The Order. The Silent Brotherhood was a white supremacist terrorist group responsible for bank robberies and murder during the 1980s. Robert Matthews died in a confrontation with federal law enforcement on the island on December 8, 1984, and is considered to be a martyr by many within the white supremacist movement. (Anonaminita)

Though the Northwest Hammerskins have not always been as vocal or publicly demonstrative as other Hammerskin groups, "they have worked to grow their numbers underground while eagerly taking on a new tactic to spread Nazi propaganda" (Puget Sound Anarchists). The Northwest Hammerskins have been particularly active in recent years, perpetrating what is known as "overpass rallies." "Each event has a similar M.O.: find a busy overpass, often I-5, show up with a few people and provocative Nazi banners, and display them just long enough to ensure that they get viral attention on social media or even local news" (Puget Sound Anarchists).

In 2017, the Northwest Hammerskins distributed flyers advertising "Hammerfest," an "annual neo-Nazi skinhead rock concert" (Morlin). The concerts typically feature white power rock bands and are attended by a variety of extremists, including neo-Nazis, KKK members, white separatists, white supremacists, and racist skinhead groups.

See also: Hammerskin Nation; Ku Klux Klan; Neo-Nazis; The Order; Racist Skinheads; White Nationalism; White Supremacist Movement

FURTHER READING

Anonaminita. August 17, 2012. "Rose City Antifa: Hammerskins and Pacific Northwest Neo-Nazis." Grey Coast Anarchist News. https://greycoast.wordpress.com/2012/08/17/rose-city-antifa-expose-on-hammerskins-pacific-northwest-neo-nazis/. (Accessed June 23, 2018.)

Anti-Defamation League. "The Hammerskin Nation." Anti-Defamation League. https://www.adl.org/education/resources/profiles/hammerskin-nation. (Accessed June 23, 2018.)

Associated Press. August 22, 2017. "Oregon's Hate Groups: A Rundown of the State's White Supremacist, Other Bias-Driven Outfits." Oregon Live. https://www.oregonlive.com/trending/2017/08/oregons_hate_groups_a_rundown.html. (Accessed June 23, 2018.)

Deeds, Michael. August 21, 2017. "White Supremacist Skinhead Organization Plans Boise Music Festival, Says Online Flyer." *Idaho Statesman*. http://www.idaho

statesman.com/entertainment/ent-columns-blogs/words-deeds/article167774787. html. (Accessed June 23, 2018.)

Hammerskin Nation. https://www.hammerskins.net/. (Accessed June 23, 2018.)

Morlin, Bill. October 1, 2012. "Hammerfest Racist Rock Festival Planned for Boise on Saturday." Southern Poverty Law Center: Hatewatch. https://www.splcenter.org /hatewatch/2012/10/01/hammerfest-racist-rock-festival-planned-boise-Saturday. (Accessed June 23, 2018.)

Puget Sound Anarchists. February 16, 2018. "Think before You Ink: Revealing Tacoma's Nazi Skinhead Tattoo Shop." It's Going Down. https://itsgoingdown.org/think -ink-revealing-tacomas-nazi-skinhead-tattoo-shop/. (Accessed June 23, 2018.)

Southern Poverty Law Center. "Racist Skinhead." Southern Poverty Law Center. https:// www.splcenter.org/fighting-hate/extremist-files/ideology/racist-skinhead. (Accessed June 23, 2018.)

Southern Poverty Law Center. March 2, 2015. "Active Racist Skinhead Groups." Southern Poverty Law Center: Intelligence Report. https://www.splcenter.org/fighting -hate/intelligence-report/2015/active-racist-skinhead-groups. (Accessed June 23, 2018.)

Nuwaubian Nation of Moors

The Nuwaubian Nation of Moors is an offshoot group of the Nation of Islam that contends that "white people are devils" and that white settlers coming to America from Europe "spread their way of life, their filth, and religion" (Southern Poverty Law Center). The group was founded by Dwight York in Brooklyn, New York, where it was originally called the "Ansaru Allah Community" (Southern Poverty Law Center). In 1993, the group moved to Putnam County, Georgia, as it began to move away from Nation of Islam teachings. In Georgia, the Nuwaubians' theology became a "disorienting" mix of

> UFO theories, talk about the significance of Egypt and the pyramids, references to Atlantis, and retellings of stories from the Bible and other religious texts. A common claim is that the original humans were black and that blacks are genetically superior to other races. White people are called "devils," a concept derived from the Nation of Islam's beliefs, but Nuwaubians allege that their lighter skin color is the result of leprosy and the fact that their ancestors mated with dogs and jackals. (Southern Poverty Law Center)

The Nuwaubians founder, Dwight York, has stated that "Christianity is a tool of the devil to keep you, the Nubian (Black) man, woman and child blind to your true heritage and perfect way of life. It [Christianity] is another means of slavery" (Southern Poverty Law Center). In 2004, York went further in castigating the white race:

> The Caucasian has not been chosen to lead the world. They lack true emotions in their creation. We never intended them to be peaceful. They were bred to be killers, with low reproduction levels and a short life span. What you call Negroid was to live 1,000 years each and the other humans 120 years. But the warrior seed of Caucasians is only 60 years old. They were only created to fight other invading races, to protect the God race Negroids. But they went insane, lost control when they were left unattended. They were never to taste blood. They did, and their true nature

came out. . . . Because their reproduction levels were cut short, their sexual organs were made the smallest so that the female of their race will want to breed with Negroids to breed themselves out of existence after 6,000 years. It took 600 years to breed them, part man and part beast. (Southern Poverty Law Center)

After the Nuwaubians set themselves up in Georgia, they declared themselves a "sovereign country." After "a four-year investigation by the Putnam County Sheriff's Office and the FBI, reports surfaced that York was preying on the group's children" (Scott). York was eventually "convicted of child molestation and racketeering" and is "currently serving 135 years" (Scott).

See also: Black Nationalism; Black Separatists; Nation of Islam

FURTHER READING

Scott, Anderson. October 4, 2016. "The United Nuwaubian Nation of Moors." Oxford American. https://www.oxfordamerican.org/magazine/item/970-the-united -nuwaubian-nation-of-moors. (Accessed June 18, 2018.)

Southern Poverty Law Center. "Nuwaubian Nation of Moors." Southern Poverty Law Center. https://www.splcenter.org/fighting-hate/extremist-files/group/nuwaubian -nation-moors. (Accessed June 18, 2018.)

United Nuwaubian Nation of Moors Government. http://www.unnm.org/. (Accessed June 18, 2018.)

Oath Keepers

Founded in 2009 by Elmer Stewart Rhodes, Oath Keepers is an association of "former members of the American military, police, and first responders who have pledged to fulfill the oaths that they took to defend the Constitution" against all enemies, "foreign and domestic" (Oath Keepers, About). The Oath Keepers are viewed as a right-wing, anti-government organization that is associated with the patriot and militia movements in the United States (Southern Poverty Law Center). The Oath Keepers are highly suspicious of the government, perpetuating and postulating imagined threats that the U.S. government intends to enslave the population and force the country into a one-world socialist government, akin to the "New World Order" (Southern Poverty Law Center).

Since its founding, members of the Oath Keepers have been involved in several high-profile anti-government events, such as the Bundy Ranch standoff, the Sugar Pine Mine incident, and the Malheur National Wildlife Refuge standoff. Oath Keepers have also provided "protection" in the case of the Ferguson, Missouri, riots, and they were present in Rowan County, Kentucky, when "County Clerk Kim Davis was jailed for refusing to issue gay marriage licenses." After the election of Donald Trump in 2016, members of the Oath Keepers issued a national pledge via Twitter that they would "protect electors from terrorist death threats" (Oath Keepers, Official Twitter).

The Oath Keepers is one of many right-wing, anti-government organizations that were organized, or found new life, with the election of Barack Obama, the first African American president of the United States. During Obama's eight years in office, the number of such organizations increased dramatically, fueled by racism and hatred, but also by the belief that Obama would use executive powers to dramatically decrease the freedoms of the American people. As one Oath Keeper stated during President Obama's first term, "[I]t might not be long . . . before President Obama finds some pretext—a pandemic, a natural disaster, a terror attack—to impose martial law, ban interstate travel, and begin detain citizens en masse" (Sharrock).

In 2016, the Oath Keepers claimed more than 30,000 members who were sworn to defend the Constitution but who had also taken oaths to *not* obey orders they deemed unconstitutional, including "any orders to disarm the American people, orders to conduct warrantless searches of the American people, or orders to detain American citizens as 'unlawful enemy combatants,' or to subject them to military tribunals" (Oath Keepers).

See also: Three Percenters

FURTHER READING

Oath Keepers. "About Oath Keepers." https://www.oathkeepers.org/about/. (Accessed November 22, 2017.)

Oath Keepers. "Official Twitter of Oath Keepers." https://twitter.com/Oathkeepers. (Accessed November 22, 2017.)

Sharrock, Justine. March/April 2010. "Oath Keepers and the Age of Treason." *Mother Jones.* http://www.motherjones.com/politics/2010/03/oath-keepers. (Accessed November 22, 2017.)

Southern Poverty Law Center. "Oath Keepers." Southern Poverty Law Center. https://www.splcenter.org/fighting-hate/extremist-files/group/oath-keepers. (Accessed November 22, 2017.)

Occidental Dissent

Occidental Dissent is a web "blog devoted to white nationalism and other right-wing extremist views" (Southern Poverty Law Center). On Occidental Dissent's website, it is possible to find a calendar of events devoted to the activities of various extremist groups, as well as a prominently featured section entitled "American Racial History Timeline" (Occidental Dissent). The founder of Occidental Dissent, Bradley Dean Griffin, is a member of the neo-Confederate and white supremacist organization the League of the South (LOS) (Hatewatch staff). Griffin has stated: "Personally, I want to create a Jew-free, White ethnostate in North America. That's why I call myself a White Nationalist" (Southern Poverty Law Center).

Occidental Dissent was founded by Bradley Dean Griffin in 2008. The blog "houses all of Griffin's musings on white nationalism and its competing cast of contrarians" (Southern Poverty Law Center). In 2010, Griffin joined the Council of Conservative Citizens (CCC). The CCC is a far-right extremist organization that opposes "race mixing" and the "immigration of non-European and non-Western peoples into the United States." Upon joining the CCC, Griffin stated:

> I've been involved in pro-White discussion groups for almost ten years now. This is the major reason why I stayed on the sidelines for so long. My impression of the movement was that it was full of individualists who cared more about parading around in white sheets or flaunting their swastikas than making a serious effort to preserve our racial and cultural heritage. Now that I am meeting people in real life, I have discovered that the loudmouth types who I see all the time on the internet, who I mentally associated with White Nationalism, are usually keyboard commandos. (Southern Poverty Law Center)

Occidental Dissent labels itself as a site that promotes U.S. nationalism and populism. However, a quick scan of some of its posts—such as "Jews Uncensored: Israeli Politician Proclaims Supremacy of the Jewish Race"; "The End of Days Is Officially upon Us"; and "Tucker Carlson Last Honest Man Left on TV"—reveals its white nationalist and alt-right tendencies. In 2014, Griffin posted an article on Occidental Dissent entitled, "The Logic of Street Demonstrations." In the article, Griffin argued:

> By taking to the streets on a regular basis, we are demonstrating that we are no longer going to observe these taboos ["to be explicitly pro-White, pro-South, and

pro-Christian"] or acknowledge their legitimacy in the South. . . . Just as in the days of Jim Crow, the reigning taboos will only crumble under pressure when a sufficient number of White Southerners are willing to publicly rise up and stand together against them. (Southern Poverty Law Center)

Bradley Dean Griffin's "current prominence in the far-right is in large part due to his vocal role in defining the fledgling Alt-Right." He and Occidental Dissent have come to be "both a gatekeeper for the Alt-Right and the chief exporter of its most effective tactics to his ideological passion project, southern nationalism" (Southern Poverty Law Center).

See also: Alt-Right Movement; Council of Conservative Citizens; League of the South; White Nationalism; White Supremacist Movement

FURTHER READING

Hatewatch Staff. October 14, 2016. "Forget the South, Occidental Dissent's Brad Griffin Stumps for Trump." Southern Poverty Law Center: Hatewatch. https://www .splcenter.org/hatewatch/2016/10/14/forget-south-occidental-dissents-brad-griffin -stumps-trump. (Accessed June 16, 2018.)

Occidental Dissent. http://www.occidentaldissent.com/. (Accessed June 16, 2018.)

Occidental Dissent. November 23, 2016. "Alt-Right vs. Alt-Lite." Occidental Dissent. http://www.occidentaldissent.com/2016/11/23/alt-right-vs-alt-lite/. (Accessed June 18, 2018.)

Southern Poverty Law Center. "Bradley Dean Griffin." Southern Poverty Law Center. https://www.splcenter.org/fighting-hate/extremist-files/individual/bradley-dean -griffin. (Accessed June 16, 2018.)

Occidental Observer

The *Occidental Observer* is "a far-right wing online magazine that covers politics and society from a white nationalist and anti-Semitic perspective" (Southern Poverty Law Center). Its mission statement, as articulated by its founder and editor Kevin MacDonald, is to "present original content touching on the themes of white identity, white interests, and the culture of the West" (MacDonald, Mission Statement). MacDonald started the *Occidental Observer* in 2009 as an online companion to the *Occidental Quarterly*, a quarterly print journal that was founded in 2001 as a racist journal "devoted to the idea that as whites become a minority the civilization and free governments that whites have created will be jeopardized" (Southern Poverty Law Center). The *Occidental Quarterly* is described by the Anti-Defamation League (ADL) as the "primary voice for anti-Semitism from far-right intellectuals" (Anti-Defamation League, 2013). The *Occidental Observer* "seeks to distinguish itself from the *Occidental Quarterly* by printing shorter and more obviously opinionated articles" (Anti-Defamation League, 2013). Both publications feature a "wide array of writers who demonize Jews and non-whites for a variety of social ills" (Anti-Defamation League, 2013). As of 2017, MacDonald retains editorship of both the *Occidental Observer* and the *Occidental Quarterly* (Occidental Quarterly).

MacDonald is best known for his premise that Jews engage in an "evolutionary strategy" that "enhances their ability to out-compete others for resources." According to MacDonald, "like viruses, Jews destabilize their host societies to their own benefit" (Southern Poverty Law Center). MacDonald has regularly argued that Jews are a "hostile elite" in American society that have sought to undermine the traditional European roots of American society by fostering measures that have led to increased nonwhite immigration into the United States. According to the Anti-Defamation League's interpretation of MacDonald's thesis, "Jews maintain their elite position by fostering non-white immigration into America to alter the country's 'racial hierarchy'" (Anti-Defamation League).

In a July 2015 *New York Times* article, the authors pointed out that publications like the *Occidental Observer* "try to take a more highbrow approach, couching white nationalist arguments as academic commentary on black inferiority, the immigration threat to whites and other racial issues" (Wines and Saul). MacDonald replied to the *Times* article by quoting a portion of the mission statement he had articulated some years earlier in the *Occidental Observer*:

> We reject labels such as "white supremacist" or "racist" that are routinely bestowed on assertions of white identity and interests as a means of muzzling their expression. All peoples have ethnic interests and all peoples have a legitimate right to assert their interests, to construct societies that reflect their culture, and to define the borders of their kinship group. (MacDonald)

In March 2017, MacDonald vocally supported Rep. Steve King (R-Iowa), who had tweeted positively about anti-Islamic and far right-wing Dutch politician Geert Wilders and had repeated Wilders's comment that "[w]e can't restore civilization with somebody else's babies" (MacDonald, 2017). In his defense of King, MacDonald stated that King

> is opposed to allowing people into the US (or Europe) who hate Western civilization, and he complains that the left is out to destroy Western civilization and "replace it with something entirely different." He is unabashedly pro-Western civilization (Western civilization is a superior civilization and we want to share it with everybody), noting that the spread of Western civilization via the English language has been associated with increased personal freedom and higher standards of living. (MacDonald, 2017)

See also: Neo-Nazis; White Nationalism; White Supremacist Movement

FURTHER READING

Anti-Defamation League. "Kevin MacDonald." Anti-Defamation League: Extremism in America. http://archive.adl.org/learn/ext_us/kevin_macdonald/. (Accessed January 6, 2018.)

Anti-Defamation League. November 2013. "Kevin MacDonald." Anti-Defamation League. https://www.adl.org/sites/default/files/documents/assets/pdf/combating-hate/kevin-macdonald-backgrounder-november-2013rev.pdf. (Accessed March 15, 2018.)

MacDonald, Kevin. "Mission Statement: The Occidental Observer." *Occidental Observer*. http://www.theoccidentalobserver.net/mission/. (Accessed March 15, 2018.)

MacDonald, Kevin. March 14, 2017. "Rep. Steve King Gets Shamelessly Racist—Or Not." *Occidental Observer.* https://www.theoccidentalobserver.net/2017/03/14 /rep-steve-king-gets-shamelessly-racist-or-not/http://www.theoccidentalobserver .net/. (Accessed March 15, 2018.)

Occidental Quarterly. "About TOQ." *Occidental Quarterly.* http://www.toqonline.com /about/. (Accessed March 15, 2018.)

Southern Poverty Law Center. "Occidental Quarterly." Southern Poverty Law Center. https://www.splcenter.org/fighting-hate/extremist-files/group/occidental -quarterly. (Accessed March 15, 2018.)

Wines, Michael, and Stephanie Saul. July 15, 2015. "White Supremacists Extend Their Reach through Websites." *New York Times.* https://www.nytimes.com/2015/07 /06/us/white-supremacists-extend-their-reach-through-websites.html. (Accessed March 15, 2018.)

Operation Rescue

Operation Rescue (OR) is an American "anti-abortion direct action organization." It "describes itself on its website as one of the leading pro-life Christian activist organizations in the nation" (Operation Rescue, Who We Are). The Southern Poverty Law Center (SPLC) describes the organization as a "hard-line anti-abortion group" that has demanded criminal prosecution of Planned Parenthood officials (Potok). Operation Rescue claims to engage in activities that are "on the cutting edge of the abortion issue, taking direct action to restore legal personhood to the pre-born and stop abortion in obedience to biblical mandates" (Operation Rescue, Who We Are). Operation Rescue's tactics involve sit-in demonstrations to block the doors at abortion clinics and large demonstrations at national events that will garner significant media attention. At the 1988 Democratic National Convention in Atlanta, Georgia, for example, over 1,200 OR members and supporters were arrested. Operation Rescue also "offers a $25,000 reward for reports of any criminal activity at abortion clinics that leads to a criminal conviction" (Operation Rescue, 2010). Recently, Operation Rescue has been linked to the Center for Medical Progress (CMP), a group that has accused Planned Parenthood "of illegally selling body parts from aborted fetuses," allegations that were subsequently blamed for a spike in abortion clinic violence (Morlin).

Operation Rescue was founded by Jeff White, but he stepped aside in 1999 after the organization was assessed an $880,000 judgment "for harassment and intimidation of Planned Parenthood" doctors and staff. White turned the organization over to "Troy Newman who moved the group's headquarters to Kansas in 2002," ostensibly to focus on a number of allegedly "botched abortions performed at Tiller's Women's Health Care Services, the practice of Dr. George Tiller, in Wichita, Kansas" (Anonymous). Dr. Tiller was "one of few doctors in the United States at the time" who performed late-term abortions. Over the course of several years, Operation Rescue harassed Dr. Tiller and his practice, even mobilizing "support in the Kansas State Legislature to order the state's Attorney General to reinstate misdemeanor charges that had been dismissed against Dr. Tiller." In September 2006, Operation Rescue had its tax-exempt status "revoked by the Internal Revenue Service (IRS) following charges of improper contributions, and illegal endorsements of political candidates" (Internal Revenue Service).

On May 31, 2009, Dr. Tiller was murdered by Scott Roeder while Dr. Tiller served as an usher at his church, the Reformation Lutheran Church of Wichita, Kansas (Stumpe and Davey). Roeder "had been a member of the anti-government group, the Montana Freemen, and had been stopped in Topeka, Kansas" in 1996 for displaying a "Sovereign Citizen" plate "in lieu of a state-issued license plate." He had no driver's license, proof of insurance, or vehicle registration. While searching his car, police "found explosive charges, a fuse cord, a pound of gunpowder and nine-volt batters in his trunk" (Associated Press, 1996). Roeder was sentenced to probation, but "his probation was revoked a year later for failure to pay taxes and provide a social security number to his employer." It was later determined that Roeder was a member of the Sovereign Citizens Movement (Anti-Defamation League).

Operation Rescue denounced Tiller's murder as "cowardly" and "antithetical to what we believe" (Stumpe and Davey). OR's president, Troy Newman, categorically stated that Roeder had "never been a member, contributor, or volunteer with Operation Rescue" (Operation Rescue, 2009). Roeder responded to Newman's claim by stating, "Well, my gosh. I've got probably a thousand dollars' worth of receipts, at least, from the money I've donated to him" (Thomas). Roeder also reportedly wrote a letter to Newman in which he said: "You better get your story straight, because my lawyer said it'd be good for me to show that I was supporting a pro-life organization" (Thomas). In January 2010, Roeder was convicted of premeditated first-degree murder and was sentenced to 50 years in prison. This sentence was later reduced to 25 years (Associated Press, 2016).

In 2015, the Center for Medical Progress (CMP), which describes itself as a "group of citizen journalists," produced videos in which it accused Planned Parenthood "of illegally selling body parts from aborted fetuses" (Potok). The videos were criticized for deceptive editing, and the individuals associated with the production of the videos were charged with felony counts of eavesdropping and secretly recording conversations with Planned Parenthood representatives and other abortion providers (Morlin). CMP has ties "to some of the hardest-line abortion extremists and groups associated with abortion clinic and provider violence" (Morlin). Troy Newman, president of Operation Rescue, is a CMP board member. A whole array of fact-checking organizations could find no evidence that Planned Parenthood had done anything wrong. Rather, CMP had "created a fake biomedical company for the sole purpose of trying to trap Planned Parenthood officials into selling body parts for profit, [and] had taken hours of undercover video and edited it down to eight- and nine-minute videos" (Potok). As an author of a book on antiabortion extremism stated, "There's a direct connection between [Operation Rescue], the Center for Medical Progress and some of the worst characters in the anti-abortion extremist movement" (Potok).

See also: Family Research Council

FURTHER READING

Anonymous. "Christin Alysabeth Gilbert Died from a Third-Trimester Abortion." Justice for Christin. http://www.justiceforchristin.com/. (Accessed May 26, 2018.)

Anti-Defamation League. September 4, 2012. "Anti-Abortion Violence: America's Forgotten Terrorism." Anti-Defamation League. https://www.adl.org/news/article /anti-abortion-violence-americas-forgotten-terrorism. (Accessed May 26, 2018.)

Associated Press. April 17, 1996. "Suspected Freeman Arrested with Bomb Fuse." *Seattle Times.* http://community.seattletimes.nwsource.com/archive/?date=19960417&s lug=2324642. (Accessed May 26, 2018.)

Associated Press. November 23, 2016. "The Man Who Killed a Kansas Abortion Provider Has His Sentence Reduced." *Los Angeles Times.* http://www.latimes.com/nation /nationnow/la-na-kansas-trial-20161123-story.html. (Accessed May 26, 2018.)

Clarkson, Frederick. September 15, 1998. "Anti-Abortion Bombings Related." Southern Poverty Law Center: Intelligence Report. https://www.splcenter.org/fighting-hate /intelligence-report/1998/anti-abortion-bombings-related. (Accessed May 26, 2018.)

Internal Revenue Service. "Recent Revocations of 501(c)(3) Determinations." Internal Revenue Service. https://web.archive.org/web/20070519024628/http://www.irs .gov/charities/charitable/article/0,,id=141466,00.html. (Accessed May 26, 2018.)

Morlin, Bill. April 3, 2017. "New Criminal Charges Filed Against Anti-Abortion Activists." Southern Poverty Law Center: Hatewatch. https://www.splcenter.org/hate watch/2017/04/03/new-criminal-charges-filed-against-anti-abortion-activists. (Accessed May 26, 2018.)

Operation Rescue. http://www.operationrescue.org/. (Accessed May 26, 2018.)

Operation Rescue. "Who We Are." Operation Rescue. http://www.operationrescue.org /about-us/who-we-are/. (Accessed May 26, 2018.)

Operation Rescue. June 1, 2009. "Operation Rescue Statement regarding Suspect in Tiller Killing." Operation Rescue. http://www.operationrescue.org/archives/operation -rescue-statement-regarding-suspect-in-tiller-killing/. (Accessed May 26, 2018.)

Operation Rescue. January 14, 2010. "Abortion Whistleblowers—Earn a $25,000 Reward." Operation Rescue. http://www.operationrescue.org/archives/abortion -whistleblowers-earn-a-10000-reward/. (Accessed May 26, 2018.)

Potok, Mark. August 31, 2015. "Group Attacking Planned Parenthood Linked to Extremists." Southern Poverty Law Center: Hatewatch. https://www.splcenter.org/hate watch/2015/08/31/group-attacking-planned-parenthood-linked-extremists. (Accessed May 26, 2018.)

Stumpe, Joe, and Monica Davey. May 31, 2009. "Abortion Doctor Shot to Death in Kansas Church." *New York Times.* http://www.nytimes.com/2009/06/01/us/01tiller .html. (Accessed May 26, 2018.)

Thomas, Judy L. July 26, 2009. "Roeder Upset at Operation Rescue." *Wichita Eagle.* http://www.kansas.com/news/special-reports/article1009125.html. (Accessed May 26, 2018.)

The Order

The Order, "also known as Bruder Schweigen (German for 'Brothers Keep Silent') or the Silent Brotherhood," was "one the most violent and notorious domestic terror groups in the United States during 1983 and 1984" (Anti-Defamation League). The group took its name from the infamous neo-Nazi novel *The Turner Diaries*, written by William Luther Pierce, founder of America's then-largest neo-Nazi organization, the National Alliance. The Order's founder, Robert (Bob) Jay Mathews, was a tax protester in the 1970s who cultivated his white supremacist ties through his associations in Aryan Nations and the National Alliance. In late

September 1983, "Mathews and eight other men—some neo-Nazis and other participants in the racist Christian Identity movement—took an oath to protect the white race and work toward an all-white homeland in the Pacific Northwest of the United States" (Anti-Defamation League). Over the course of 15 months, from October 1983 to December 1984, the Order engaged in "counterfeiting, bank robbery, and armored car heists, netting the group some $4 million." The Order is most infamous for the "assassination of Jewish radio talk show host Alan Berg," who was brutally gunned down by members of the group in his driveway in Denver, Colorado, in June 1984 (Anti-Defamation League). The Order would effectively disappear after a member of the organization was arrested for counterfeiting and turned FBI informant. The situation led to a confrontation with several members of the group and the eventual death in December 1984 of founder Bob Mathews, when he confronted FBI agents in a standoff on Whidbey Island in Washington State. A year after Mathews's death, "nine men and one woman—all members of the group—were convicted of racketeering and other charges and sentenced to terms of 40–100 years in prison" (Nizkor Project). The group continues to inspire right-wing and anti-government extremists, and the racist, whites-only message of the Order lives on in many contemporary extremist groups.

In late September 1983, Bob Mathews and eight other men met at Mathews's home in Metaline Falls, Washington, and swore an oath to each other to wage war against the American government. To demonstrate the solemnity of the oath, they placed one of the men's six-week-old baby in the middle of a circle that they formed as a symbol of what was at stake: the white race. The assembled individuals took their name—the Order—from a novel, in which a group known as the Order determines "to use violence and crime in order to destabilize the U.S. government and establish a whites-only society" (History Commons). The Order was determined to bring about the downfall of the government, as it believed that the government had fallen under the control of a cabal of prominent Jews and that this organization controlled the political and economic workings of the country, as well as all media. Order members referred to the federal government as the Zionist Occupation Government (ZOG), and they swore to use crime and violence to destabilize the government, to assassinate race traitors, and to wage a guerilla war of sabotage against the government until their goal of a whites-only homeland could be realized. Much of what Mathews envisioned for the group had already been suggested in *The Turner Diaries*.

To finance the group, "members of The Order turned to crime. They initially targeted pimps, drug dealers, and anybody else that they judged had no morals" (Egan). Although they made off with tens of thousands of dollars, the funds were insufficient to bankroll the revolution they envisioned. The group later turned to counterfeiting, but they also experienced limited success in that area.

Frustrated that the group seemed to not be making any progress, Mathews robbed a bank north of Seattle, Washington, in December 1983 and made off with over $26,000 (History Commons). In March 1984, the group perpetrated a robbery on an armored car, which netted them $43,000. A month later, the Order hijacked another armored car, this time securing $536,000, though $500,000 of the money was in checks and was therefore useless to the group (History Commons).

On May 27, 1984, members of the Order—on the directive of Bob Mathews—murdered Aryan Nations member Walter West after Mathews learned that a drunken West had been bragging about the Order's exploits "in and around Hayden Lake, Idaho, the location of Aryan Nations' compound." Less than a month later, the Order would commit their most notorious murder when members of the group machine-gunned Jewish talk show host Alan Berg to death in the driveway of his Denver, Colorado, home. The group targeted Berg because of his confrontational style with anti-Semites and right-wing extremists who frequently called into his radio show to verbally spar with him. Berg's Jewish heritage, and his vitriol toward white supremacists and extremism, earned him a spot on the Order's hit list, which also included "Southern Poverty Law Center (SPLC) founder Morris Dees, television producer Norman Lear, and a Kansas federal judge" (Balleck). Berg was killed on the evening of June 14, 1984, as he exited his car in his driveway. Order member Bruce Pierce pumped 12 to 13 shots into Berg's face and body from his .45 caliber MAC-10 submachine gun, before jumping into a getaway car and speeding away with three other accomplices.

The next day—June 19, 1984—other members of the Order committed another armored-car robbery near Ukiah, California. The group stopped the armored car and took over $3.6 million in the heist. In the confusion of the robbery, however, Mathews dropped a registered gun that quickly led the FBI to determine who they were looking for. Within a week, a member of the Order, Tom Martinez, would be arrested in Pennsylvania for passing counterfeit bills printed by the group. Upon questioning by federal authorities, Martinez cut a deal to inform on the group in exchange for a more lenient sentence. As the federal government built its case against Mathews and other members of the Order, three FBI agents engaged Order member Gary Yarborough outside of his home on his wooded Idaho property. Yarborough escaped, but the agents found in Yarborough's home a large collection of material related to the Order's crimes, including a cache of weapons that contained "explosives, gas grenades, cases of ammunition, pistols, shotguns, rifles, two Ingram MAC-10 submachine guns with silencers, gas masks, knives, crossbows, assault vests, radio frequency scanners, and other equipment. Among the cache of weapons [was] the MAC-10 used to kill Denver radio host Alan Berg" (History Commons).

FBI informant Tom Martinez agreed to draw Mathews out, and he met with Mathews and other members of the Order in a motel room near Portland, Oregon, in November 1984. Mathews, sensing a trap, engaged in a gun battle with the FBI but escaped. Gary Yarborough, who had been with Mathews, was captured. Mathews fled to a home he had on Whidbey Island in Oregon. There he penned a four-page "Declaration of War" against the United States, which read in part:

> It is now a dark and dismal time in the history of our Race. All about us lie the green graves of our sires, yet, in a land once ours we have become a people dispossessed. Our heroes and culture have been insulted and degraded. The mongrel hordes clamor to sever us from our inheritance. Yet our people do not care.
>
> Throughout this land our children are being coerced into accepting nonwhites for their idols, their companions, and worst of all for their mates. A course which has taken us straight to oblivion. Yet our people do not see. Not by accident but by design these terrible things have come to pass. It is self-evident to all who have eyes to see

that an evil shadow has fallen across our once fair land. Evidence abounds that a certain, vile, alien people have taken control of our country. How is it that a parasite has gained dominion over its host? Instead of being vigilant our fathers have slept.

What are we to do? How bleak these aliens have made our children's future. All about us the land is dying. Our cities swarm with dusky hordes. The water is rancid and the air is rank. Our farms are being seized by usurious leeches and our people are being forced off the land. The capitalists and communists pick gleefully at our bones while the vile, hook-nosed masters of usury orchestrate our destruction.

We hereby declare ourselves a free and sovereign people. We claim a territorial imperative that will consist of the entire North American continent north of Mexico. As soldiers of the Aryan Resistance Movement (ARM) we will conduct ourselves in accordance with the Geneva Convention.

We now close this Declaration with an open letter to congress and our signatures confirming our intent to do battle. Let friend and foe alike be made aware: This Is War! We the following of sound body and mind under no duress, do hereby sign this document of our own free will, stating forthrightfully and without fear that we declare ourselves to be in a full and unrelenting state of war with those forces seeking and consciously promoting the destruction of our Faith and our Race. Therefore, for Blood, Soil and Honor, and for the future of our children, we commit ourselves to battle. Amen. (The Order)

On December 7, 1984, FBI agents cornered Mathews in his home on Whidbey Island. Mathews, who was heavily armed, barricaded himself inside his home and engaged in sporadic gunfire with the 150 agents who had him surrounded. After 35 hours of fruitless negotiation, the FBI fired "three M-79 Starburst illumination flares into the home, hoping that the house [would] catch fire and drive Mathews out. Instead, Mathews either [chose] to remain inside the house, or [was] unable to leave. He [died] in the flames" (History Commons). A year later, most of the members of the Order were in jail or awaiting trial.

The Order's brief but destructive reign of terror galvanized an emerging anti-government movement, and the group's belief in ZOG and its rhetoric encouraging whites to purge the United States of immigrants and nonwhite peoples was taken up with renewed zeal by groups such as Aryan Nations and the National Alliance. Order member David Lane would articulate the essence of the Order's racist mantra by pronouncing the 14 Words, the motto of the racist, extremist right: "We must secure the existence of our people and a future for white children" (Southern Poverty Law Center). Lane would die in prison after being sentenced to 190 years for the crimes he committed while a member of the Order. But Lane's influence, and that of the Order, would be felt for years to come in the world of anti-government extremists, inspiring the likes of Timothy McVeigh, the Oklahoma City bomber (Anti-Defamation League).

See also: Aryan Nations; Christian Identity; National Alliance; Neo-Nazis; White Nationalism; White Supremacist Movement

FURTHER READING

Anti-Defamation League. "The Order." Anti-Defamation League. https://www.adl.org /education/references/hate-symbols/the-order. (Accessed June 6, 2017.)

Balleck, Barry J. 2015. *Allegiance to Liberty: The Changing Face of Patriots, Militias, and Political Violence in America.* Praeger.

Egan, Nancy. "The Order: American White Supremacist Group." *Encyclopedia Britannica.* https://www.britannica.com/topic/The-Order. (Accessed June 6, 2017.)

History Commons. "U.S. Domestic Terrorism: The Order." History Commons. http://www.historycommons.org/timeline.jsp?timeline=us_domestic_terrorism_tmln&haitian_elite_2021_organizations=us_domestic_terrorism_tmln_the_order. (Accessed June 6, 2017.)

Nizkor Project. "Paranoia as Patriotism: Far Right Influences on the Militia Movement." Nizkor Project. http://www.nizkor.org/hweb/orgs/american/adl/paranoia-as-patriotism/the-order.html. (Accessed June 6, 2017.)

The Order. "Declaration of War." MourningtheAncient.com. http://www.mourningtheancient.com/mathews2.htm. (Accessed June 6, 2017.)

Southern Poverty Law Center. "David Lane." Southern Poverty Law Center. https://www.splcenter.org/fighting-hate/extremist-files/individual/david-lane. (Accessed June 6, 2017.)

P

Pacific Justice Institute

The Pacific Justice Institute (PJI) was founded in 1997 by Brad Dacus. It is characterized as an "anti-LGBT hate group by the Southern Poverty Law Center" (SPLC). According to the SPLC, Dacus and the PJI have

> compared legalized gay marriage to Hitler and the Nazis' ascent in Germany; endorsed so-called "reparative" or sexual orientation conversion therapy; claimed marriage equality would lead to legal polygamy and incest; fought against protections for trans children and fabricated a story of harassment by a trans student; and said that LGBT History Month promotes gay pornography to children. (Southern Poverty Law Center, Pacific Justice Institute)

PJI bills itself as "being at the forefront of attorneys who recognize the need to preserve religious liberty in America" (Pacific Justice Institute). According to its website, PJI addresses cases involving

> religious freedom including church and private school rights issues, curtailments to evangelism by the government, harassment because of their religious faith, employers attacked for their religious-based policies, students and teachers rights to share their faith at public schools. PJI also works hard to defend the rights of parents including their right to homeschool, review and have notice of public school curriculum and presentations, and opt out their children from objectionable material. (Pacific Justice Institute)

PJI was founded in 1997 after Brad Dacus sued to have a "lesbian fifth and sixth-grade teacher fired" after the teacher showed "a seven-minute, student-initiated classroom discussion about the episode of the sitcom 'Ellen' where the lead character, played by Ellen DeGeneres, comes out as gay" (Southern Poverty Law Center, Pacific Justice Institute). The teacher was eventually cleared of any wrongdoing in the case "by the school board and the state Commission on Teacher Credentialing" (Herscher). In 2007, Brad Dacus testified against federal legislation that would eventually become the "Matthew Shepard and James Byrd Jr. Hate Crimes Prevention Act" (Southern Poverty Law Center, Pacific Justice Institute). In making his argument, Dacus appealed to the First Amendment:

> The rationale behind hate crimes laws and similar efforts to provide greater protections to one group over another is undermining basic constitutional protections, including free expression and freedom of religion. A decision by Congress to inject the federal government into the culture wars and fundamental theological disputes can only engender further divisiveness and limitations on free speech. (Southern Poverty Law Center, Pacific Justice Institute)

In 2012, the PJI filed a lawsuit against a California bill that banned so-called "'reparative' therapy, or sexual orientation conversion therapy, for minors in the state, and make 'therapeutic deception' by practitioners of conversion therapy an actionable offense" (Southern Poverty Law Center, Pacific Justice Institute). Though conversion therapy has been confirmed to be "junk science" (Potok), Dacus and the PJI continued to defend its use:

> There's overwhelming evidence that reparative therapy actually works . . . I know it's at least over 80 percent, I believe it's 80 to 85 percent success rate. These are people who leave the lifestyle, get married to people, have children, and enter heterosexual relationships. It's a big mass of deception that they are trying to carry out at the expense of many hundreds of thousands or millions of youths who will be led down a path of death and destruction, unfortunately, if they get away with this . . . Parents know that the homosexual lifestyle gives for boys an average lifespan of the age of 40. It's worse than being a chain cigarette smoker. (Southern Poverty Law Center, Pacific Justice Institute)

PJI's challenge against the California conversion therapy ban was eventually dismissed, and its contention that a U.S. Supreme Court rejection of the Defense of Marriage Act (DOMA) would lead to the legalization of polygamous and incestuous marriages never was realized. In 2013, PJI fabricated a story about a transgender teen "entering girls bathrooms at a Colorado high school and even making sexually harassing comments toward girls he [sic] was encountering" (Southern Poverty Law Center, Pacific Justice Institute). The assertion was proved false, but PJI "was less than contrite, stating "the central issue in this case—a high school's decision to give a biological teenage boy full access to teenage girls' bathrooms is both disturbing and not seriously disputed" (Southern Poverty Law Center, Pacific Justice Institute).

In 2015, PJI pushed "another false narrative" of harassment by LGBT youth (Media Matters). The story "alleged that students at a Lafayette, California high school were bullied by the school's Queer Straight Alliance during a presentation" (Southern Poverty Law Center, Pacific Justice Institute). The school superintendent, however, stated unequivocally that no such incident ever happened (Media Matters).

See also: Alliance Defending Freedom; American College of Pediatricians; American Family Association; Family Research Council; Family Watch International; Ruth Institute; Traditional Values Coalition; Westboro Baptist Church

FURTHER READING

Hatewatch Staff. April 3, 2017. "Anti-LGBT Activities." Southern Poverty Law Center: Hatewatch. https://www.splcenter.org/hatewatch/2017/04/03/anti-lgbt-activities. (Accessed June 18, 2018.)

Herscher, Elaine. March 11, 1998. "Coming Out at School: Even in the Bay Area, Gay Teachers Are Taking a Risk." SFGate. https://www.sfgate.com/bayarea/article /Coming-Out-at-School-Even-in-the-Bay-Area-gay-3011228.php. (Accessed June 18, 2018.)

Media Matters. "Fox News Gets Duped by Another Bogus Anti-Gay Horror Story." Media Matters. https://www.mediamatters.org/print/659334. (Accessed June 18, 2018.)

Pacific Justice Institute. "Questions and Answers." Pacific Justice Institute. https://www
.pacificjustice.org/questions-and-answers.html. (Accessed June 18, 2018.)

Potok, Mark. May 25, 2016. "QUACKS: 'Conversion Therapists,' the Anti-LGBT Right,
and the Demonization of Homosexuality." Southern Poverty Law Center. https://
www.splcenter.org/20160525/quacks-conversion-therapists-anti-lgbt-right-and
-demonization-homosexuality. (Accessed June 18, 2018.)

Southern Poverty Law Center. "Anti-LGBT." Southern Poverty Law Center. https://www
.splcenter.org/fighting-hate/extremist-files/ideology/anti-lgbt. (Accessed June 18,
2018.)

Southern Poverty Law Center. "Pacific Justice Institute." Southern Poverty Law Center.
https://www.splcenter.org/fighting-hate/extremist-files/group/pacific-justice-institute.
(Accessed June 18, 2018.)

Patriot Front

Patriot Front (PF) is a "Texas-based alt right group" founded by Thomas Ryan Rousseau. The Anti-Defamation League (ADL) states that PF "is a white supremacist group whose members maintain that their ancestors conquered America and bequeathed it to them alone. They define themselves as American fascists or American nationalists who are focused on preserving America's identity as a European-American identity" (Anti-Defamation League, Patriot Front). PF split from Vanguard America (VA)—of which Rousseau was a member—after the Charlottesville, Virginia, "Unite the Right" rally in August 2017. The split occurred

> several months after VA participated in a white supremacist rally on the capitol steps in Austin, Texas. Both Rousseau, as the Texas leader, and Dillon Hopper (aka Dillon Irizarry), as the group's national leader, spoke during the event. Hopper later complained that Rousseau had led event organizers to believe that Rousseau, rather than Hopper, was VA's leader, and that Rousseau's lengthy speech during the rally further confused people about the group's true leader. (Anti-Defamation League, Patriot Front)

Two days after the Austin rally, Rousseau set the stage for PF's formation by taking over VA's "group's servers and its 'bloodandsoil.org' website" (Anti-Defamation League, Patriot Front). Though Rousseau was present at the "Unite the Right" rally in Charlottesville in August 2017 as a member of VA—and was infamously photographed beside James Fields Jr., who allegedly rammed his car into a group of counterprotesters, killing one—it was Hopper who took the heat for Fields's alleged association with VA. Just a few days after Charlottesville, while "Hopper isolated himself from the fallout from Unite the Right," Rousseau acted:

> Rather than take over the troubled Vanguard America, he opted to rebrand VA's "bloodandsoil.org" as the Patriot Front website. The move allowed those associated with Patriot Front to distance themselves from both Vanguard America and any association with James Field [sic]. Ironically, the bulk of those who defected to Rousseau's Patriot Front were those who attended "Unite the Right" under the Vanguard America umbrella. (Anti-Defamation League, Patriot Front)

The Southern Poverty Law Center (SPLC) remarks that "Patriot Front is notable for its utterly undisguised and unrepentant fascism. It's also utterly lacking in the often juvenile transgressive humor, and use of pop culture and irony, that are core to much of the appeal of the alt-right online. Instead, its dead-serious advocacy of white-supremacist ideology is intended to appeal to a more militant mindset" (Hatewatch staff). As the "manifesto" on its website explains:

> An African may have lived, worked, and even been classed as a citizen in America for centuries, yet he is not American. He is, as he likely prefers to be labelled, an African in America. The same rule applies to others who are not of the founding stock of our people, or do not share the common unconscious that permeates throughout our greater civilization, and the European diaspora. The American identity was something uniquely forged in the struggle that our ancestors waged to survive in this new continent. America is truly unique in this pan-European identity which forms the roots of our nationhood. To be an American is to realize this identity and take up the national struggle upon one's shoulders. Not simply by birth is one granted this title, but by the degree to which he works and fulfills the potential of his birth. No man is complete simply to live, but to do more than that, to strive to create a path onward for his people, and to connect with the heritage he is undeniably a part of. That is what completes a man. Only then is he truly deserving of the title and a place among his people. (Hatewatch staff)

According to Unicorn Riot—"a non-profit media organization of artists and journalists . . . dedicated to exposing root causes of dynamic social and environmental issues through amplifying stories and exploring sustainable alternatives in today's globalized world" (Unicorn Riot, 2015)—PF's admittedly "American fascist" leanings expose a dark and violent ideology. In March 2018, Unicorn Riot reported that an "anonymous source" from "inside Patriot Front said they represented 'a group of concerned individuals' and told us [Unicorn Riot] why they decided to take steps to expose the group's internal workings":

> We chose to obtain and pass on information about Patriot Front to ensure that anyone considering joining this group or others like it understands what type of organization they are committing to. This is a group that presents itself as a bulwark for the future of white people in public, while behind closed doors they speak openly of violent ethnic cleansing, the rape of white women, the forcible abortion of female people of color and death for members of the LGBTQIA+ community. We have seen what those like them are capable of in Charlottesville and Orange County. (Unicorn Riot, 2018)

The SPLC notes that, to date, "Patriot Front appears mainly to be comprised of small clusters of dedicated neo-Nazis intent on spreading their fascist gospel to other right-wing extremists, especially 'fence-sitting' alt-righters potentially attracted to violent street action" (Hatewatch staff).

Such violent street action was demonstrated in July 2018 when about a dozen masked PF members "invaded and briefly vandalized an 'Occupy ICE [Immigrations and Customs Enforcement]' protest encampment in San Antonio, Texas" (Neiwert). Chanting "Strong borders! Strong nation!" the PF members "attacked a corner of the encampment, kicking over banners and coolers before walking away while continuing to chant. Some of them carried a flag featuring a fasces, the symbol of Mussolini's Italian fascist movement" (Neiwert). Afterward, a post on PF's website read:

> Activists confronted assorted enemies of the nation which had created a makeshift campsite outside of an ICE detention facility to impede the efforts of officers seeking to process and deport criminal aliens from the country.

It is no surprise that one of the few wings of government left that provide tangible benefit to the nation would be under such direct assault by those who would see America turn into a continent-spanning slum. The crass calls for freedom by these would-be revolutionaries amount to nothing more than a desire to be free from order and civilization, and to be given to vice and corruption.

Patriots nationwide stand testament to the fact that the time has passed where chaos will stand unopposed. (Patriot Front, 2018)

See also: Alt-Right Movement; National Socialist Legion; Nationalist Front; Neo-Nazis; Vanguard America; White Nationalism; White Supremacist Movement

FURTHER READING

Anti-Defamation League. "Patriot Front." Anti-Defamation League. https://www.adl.org /resources/backgrounders/patriot-front. (Accessed August 2, 2018.)

Anti-Defamation League. "Vanguard America." Anti-Defamation League. https://www .adl.org/resources/backgrounders/vanguard-america. (Accessed August 2, 2018.)

Hatewatch Staff. December 11, 2017. "Meet 'Patriot Front': Neo-Nazi Network Aims to Blur Lines with Militiamen, Then Alt-Right." Southern Poverty Law Center: Hatewatch. https://www.splcenter.org/hatewatch/2017/12/11/meet-patriot-front-neo -nazi-network-aims-blur-lines-militiamen-alt-right. (Accessed August 2, 2018.)

Institute for Research and Education on Human Rights (IREHR). "Vanguard America: National Socialism American Style." IREHR.org. https://www.irehr.org/2018 /02/24/vanguard-america-national-socialism-american-style/. (Accessed August 2, 2018.)

Neiwert, David. August 1, 2018. "Masked Fascists of Patriot Front Attack San Antonio ICE Protest Camp." Southern Poverty Law Center: Hatewatch. https://www .splcenter.org/hatewatch/2018/08/01/masked-fascists-patriot-front-attack-san -antonio-ice-protest-camp. (Accessed August 2, 2018.)

Patriot Front. https://www.bloodandsoil.org/. (Accessed August 2, 2018.)

Patriot Front. "The Future That Must Be." Patriot Front. https://www.bloodandsoil.org /manifesto/. (Accessed August 2, 2018.)

Patriot Front. July 28, 2018. "Occupying the Occupants." Patriot Front. https://www .bloodandsoil.org/occupying-the-occupants/. (Accessed August 2, 2018.)

Unicorn Riot. February 19, 2015. "About." Unicorn Riot. https://www.unicornriot.ninja /about-unicorn-riot/. (Accessed August 2, 2018.)

Unicorn Riot. November 9, 2017. "'Southern Front' Logs Expose Neo-Nazi Extremist Cell." Unicorn Riot. https://www.unicornriot.ninja/2017/southern-front-logs -expose-neo-nazi-extremist-cell/. (Accessed August 2, 2018.)

Unicorn Riot. March 5, 2018. "'We're Americas, and We're Fascists': Inside Patriot Front." Unicorn Riot. https://www.unicornriot.ninja/2018/americans-fascists-inside-patriot -front/. (Accessed August 2, 2018.)

Pioneer Fund

The Pioneer Fund "was established in 1937 by Wickliffe Draper," a Massachusetts-born descendant of a long line of prominent Americans. Draper was an ardent eugenicist who formed the Pioneer Fund "to support research into the issues of heredity and eugenics." Draper provided the Pioneer Fund's "original mandate which was to pursue 'race betterment' by promoting the genetic stock of those deemed to be descended predominantly from white persons who settled in the original thirteen states prior to the adoption of the Constitution" (Southern Poverty Law Center). Today, the Pioneer Fund provides grants that support "studies of race and intelligence, as well as eugenics." The money provided by the Pioneer Fund largely goes to Anglo-American scientists searching for clues to the breeding and betterment of "perfect human beings" (Southern Poverty Law Center).

Many of the individuals involved with the Pioneer Fund in its early days had contacts with Nazi scientists who provided the template for Hitler's notion of racial purification. In the 1960s, many of the Pioneer Fund's supporters were active in their opposition to the American civil rights movement. A major recipient of Pioneer Fund grants was Arthur Jensen, the University of California–Berkeley educational psychologist who stated that black children would never be helped by Head Start—the government program designed to provide children of low income families with early educational intervention—because black children were inherently less intelligent because of their race. As Jensen noted, "no amount of social engineering would improve the performance of black children, adding that only 'eugenic foresight' would provide a solution" (Southern Poverty Law Center).

Between 1975 and 1996, the Pioneer Fund provided more than $1 million to Roger Pearson, a British eugenics activist and director of the Institute for the Study of Man. Pearson, who came to the United States in the mid-1960s, teamed up with Willis Carto, a promoter of anti-Semitic conspiracy theories and a Holocaust denier, to publish a magazine known as the *New Patriot*, which published articles with such titles as "Zionists and the Plot against South Africa," "Early Jews and the Rise of Jewish Money Power," and "Swindlers of the Crematoria" (Southern Poverty Law Center). In the mid-1990s, the Pioneer Fund began supporting the work of contributors to *The Bell Curve*, a 1994 book that "claimed that differences in intelligence among different racial groups" could be explained, at least in part, by genetic makeup (Southern Poverty Law Center).

From 2002 until his death in October 2012, the Pioneer Fund was headed by psychology professor J. Philippe Rushton, a Canadian researcher who contended that the larger sexual characteristics of blacks—in other words, genitals, breasts, and buttocks—"have an inverse relationship with brain size and, thus, intelligence" (Southern Poverty Law Center). During his time as the president of the Pioneer Fund, Rushton received nearly half a million dollars in funds, while Jared Taylor, Rushton's friend and publisher of *American Renaissance*, a white supremacist publication, received large donations to perpetuate his contention that "blacks are incapable of sustaining any kind of civilization" (Southern Poverty Law Center).

In 2013, Richard Lynn became the president of the Pioneer Fund. Lynd is an English emeritus professor of psychology at the University of Ulster and an assistant editor of *Mankind Quarterly*. Lynn is known for his belief that racial differences account for differences in intelligence.

See also: *American Renaissance*; White Nationalism; White Supremacist Movement

FURTHER READING

Falk, Avner. 2008. *Anti-Semitism: A History and Psychoanalysis of Contemporary Hatred*. ABC-CLIO.

Southern Poverty Law Center. "Pioneer Fund." Southern Poverty Law Center. https://www.splcenter.org/fighting-hate/extremist-files/group/pioneer-fund. (Accessed February 11, 2018.)

Tucker, William. 2002. *The Funding of Scientific Racism: Wickliffe Draper and the Pioneer Fund*. University of Illinois Press.

Pioneer Little Europe

Pioneer Little Europe (PLE) is a "white supremacist operation welcoming Nazis, members of the Creativity Movement, Ku Klux Klan, militants, white nationalists, and racialists to build 'arks of survival' or Aryan enclaves" (Hagen). According to Mark Potok of the Southern Poverty Law Center (SPLC), the PLE concept

> was developed primarily by Hamilton Michael Barrett and Mark Cotterill, two white supremacists with both British and American connections, in the late 1990s and early 2000s. Essentially, PLEs recognize that grandiose plans such as the Northwest Territorial Imperative are doomed to failure, because white supremacists exist in too few numbers. The PLE concept argues instead for white supremacists to gather in already existing communities and form communities within a community so that "racially conscious" whites can survive (Barrett once called them "arks of survival"). Non-whites would theoretically depart, leaving white supremacist enclaves whose members would aid and assist each other. (Potok)

Perhaps the best-known individual in the PLE movement today is Craig Cobb. Cobb is a white nationalist and neo-Nazi who also expresses anti-Semitic views in denying the reality of the Holocaust. Cobb has also expressed affinity for white separatist causes. In 2003, he opened a store in Frost, West Virginia, "not far from the headquarters of the National Alliance," called "Gray's Store, Aryan Autographs and 14 Words, LLC." The "14 words" were "coined by the late supremacist David Lane, a member of the infamous terror group The Order," who stated the famous catchphrase as a clarion call to the radical right: "We must secure the existence of our people and a future for White children" (Southern Poverty Law Center).

Cobb is best known "for his attempt to dominate the city of Leith, North Dakota and turn it in to a bastion of white supremacy." In 2012, Cobb and other white supremacists moved to Leith and displayed neo-Nazi and other white power paraphernalia on their properties. Cobb's attempt to take over the town "made the front page of the *New York Times* in 2013" (Eligon). Local residents and anti-racist organizations rallied against Cobb's attempts. In an effort to galvanize his legitimacy within the white supremacist movement, Cobb agreed to a DNA test. On a live episode of an NBC talk show, the results demonstrated that Cobb's "genes were 14 percent sub-Saharan African; i.e., black" (Hagen). Humiliated, Cobb and some of his confederates began roaming the streets of Leith, armed and conducting "patrols." Because of confrontations with local residents, Cobb was eventually arrested and charged with several counts of terrorizing (Southern Poverty Law Center).

Cobb eventually left Leith in 2014 and announced that he was "retired" from white nationalism. However, subsequent attempts to purchase properties in other Midwestern states, and Cobb's own posts on racist websites, indicate that he is still active in the white supremacy cause. In 2015, Cobb told the *Grand Forks Herald* that he wished to purchase land in Antler, South Dakota, a town with a population of only 20 (Thompson). To promote his effort, Cobb set up a web page called "Antler PLE," or Antler Pioneer Little Europe (Thompson).

See also: Christian Identity; Ku Klux Klan; Neo-Nazis; White Nationalism; White Supremacist Movement

FURTHER READING

Eligon, John. August 29, 2013. "New Neighbor's Agenda: White Power Takeover." *New York Times*. http://www.nytimes.com/2013/08/30/us/white-supremacists-plan -angers-a-north-dakota-town.html. (Accessed June 12, 2018.)

Hagen, C. S. March 23, 2017. "White Supremacist's Church Burns in Nome." C.S. News. http://www.cshagen.com/tag/pioneer-little-europe/. (Accessed June 12, 2018.)

Lenz, Ryan. November 15, 2011. "A Gathering of Eagles: Extremists Look to Montana." Southern Poverty Law Center: Intelligence Report. https://www.splcenter.org /fighting-hate/intelligence-report/2011/gathering-eagles-extremists-look-montana. (Accessed June 12, 2018.)

Lenz, Ryan. August 22, 2013. "White Supremacists Making Bid to Take Over North Dakota Town." Southern Poverty Law Center: Hatewatch. https://www.splcenter .org/hatewatch/2013/08/22/white-supremacists-making-bid-take-over-north -dakota-town. (Accessed June 12, 2018.)

Lenz, Ryan. October 7, 2015. "Elsewhere on the Plains: Craig Cobb Is Trying Once Again to Build a Home for Racists." Southern Poverty Law Center: Hatewatch. https:// www.splcenter.org/hatewatch/2015/10/07/elsewhere-plains-craig-cobb-trying -once-again-build-home-racists. (Accessed June 12, 2018.)

Potok, Mark. November 20, 2013. "Closed Circuit." Southern Poverty Law Center: Intelligence Report. https://www.splcenter.org/fighting-hate/intelligence-report/2013 /closed-circuit. (Accessed June 12, 2018.)

Siegler, Kirk. November 29, 2016. "In Montana, an Unease over Extremist Views Moving Out of the Woods." NPR. https://www.npr.org/2016/11/29/503620409/in-montana -an-unease-over-extremist-views-moving-out-of-the-woods. (Accessed June 12, 2018.)

Southern Poverty Law Center. "Craig Cobb." Southern Poverty Law Center. https://www .splcenter.org/fighting-hate/extremist-files/individual/craig-cobb. (Accessed June 12, 2018.)

Thompson, Catherine. June 15, 2015. "Try, Try Again: White Supremacist Plans to Build 'Little Europe' in North Dakota." Talking Points Memo. https://talkingpointsmemo .com/muckraker/craig-cobb-antler-nd-white-enclave. (Accessed June 12, 2018.)

Wallace, Hunter. March 16, 2015. "Pioneer Little Europe and the Perils of Cyberracialism." Occidental Dissent. http://www.occidentaldissent.com/2015/03/16/pioneer -little-europe-and-the-perils-of-cyberracialism/. (Accessed June 12, 2018.)

Proud Boys

The Proud Boys "are a self-described group of 'western chauvinists' who deny any connection with the alt-right," instead insisting that they are "simply a fraternal group spreading an 'anti-political correctness' and 'anti-white guilt' agenda" (Southern Poverty Law Center). The group was "founded at the height of the 2016 U.S. presidential campaign by Gavin McInnes, a former New York–based conservative online talk show host" (Southern Poverty Law Center). The campaign of Donald Trump resonated with McInnes, who believed that Trump's "Make America Great Again" motto and opposition to immigration into the United States were key to reviving white culture in the country. For McInnes and his followers, "there are ten ways to 'save America': Abolish prisons, give each American a gun, legalize drugs, end welfare, close borders to illegal immigrants, outlaw censorship, venerate the housewife, glorify the entrepreneur, shut down the government and declare the West is the best" (Hall). Though the Proud Boys disavow that they are bigoted or racist, "rank-and-file Proud Boys and leaders regularly spout white nationalist memes and maintain affiliations with known extremists. They are known for anti-Muslim and misogynistic rhetoric. [And] Proud Boys have appeared alongside other hate groups at extremist gatherings like the 'Unite the Right' rally in Charlottesville" (Southern Poverty Law Center). Indeed, a former member of the Proud Boys, Jason Kessler, organized the "Unite the Right" rally in Charlottesville, Virginia, that contributed to the death of three individuals. Kessler was not excised from the group until after the rally. Though the Southern Poverty Law Center (SPLC) at one point characterized the Proud Boys as just a "fraternal organization" and not a hate group, the group's continued extremist activities landed it on the SPLC's "Hate Groups" list in its Spring 2018 edition (Eyes on the Right).

The Proud Boys take their name from a song in the Disney movie *Aladdin*, entitled "Proud of Your Boy" (Southern Poverty Law Center). The group claims to be nothing more than a self-professed "drinking club" (Hall), and "they tell themselves it's like the Elks Lodge or the Knights of Columbus, but there's this political element, and the prankishness has allowed them to say they're just kidding around . . . There is a violent aspect to it, though they say it's all in self-defense" (Kacala). Though the Proud Boys profess libertarian ideals, they are fiercely chauvinistic, rejecting every aspect of feminism and venerating the role of the American housewife. Indeed, the Proud Boys believe that feminism "is about de-masculinizing men" (Southern Poverty Law Center). In September 2017, a female subject arranging an interview about the group "was asked by the potential interview subject whether he should bring condoms" (Hall). In a later interview, Proud Boy founder Gavin McInnes told the reporter that "she should give up her career, that 'you need to find a man,' and that she would run out of eggs if she did not get pregnant soon" (Hall).

The Proud Boys claim not be purveyors of hate, "but they refer to transgender people as 'gender n—' and 'stupid lunatics'" (Southern Poverty Law Center). They also hold that "western culture is superior to all others, racism is a myth created by guilty white liberals, [and] Islam is a culture of violence" (Southern

Poverty Law Center). And as further evidence of their misogyny, McInnes has written that "women want to be abused" and that "every guy I've ever known to be involved in a 'domestic' was the result of some c— trying to ruin his life" (Southern Poverty Law Center).

In order to become a Proud Boy, every potential member must pass through an initiation process. The process requires four degrees. The first degree in joining the "pro-West fraternal organization" necessitates that a prospective member declare:

> I am a western chauvinist, and I refuse to apologize for creating the modern world."
> To enter the second degree, a Proud Boy has to endure a beating until they can yell out the names of five breakfast cereals (in order to demonstrate "adrenaline control") and give up masturbation because, in theory, it will leave them more inclined to go out and meet women. Those who enter the third degree have demonstrated their commitment by getting a Proud Boys tattoo. Any man—no matter his race or sexual-orientation—can join the fraternal organization as long as they "recognize that white men are not the problem." (Southern Poverty Law Center)

The fourth degree of initiation "is a new one." It involves "enduring a major conflict related to the struggle, popularly interpreted as beating up a member of antifa at a protest or rally. (Antifa is shorthand for an antifascist; someone who might engage in so-called 'black bloc' tactics at protests and rallies, brawling with police and right-wingers alike)" (Sundaresh). It's the fourth degree that "concerns left-wing activists. If I book a tattoo with you, will there be a chance the artist or receptionist will later try to attack me and/or my leftist friends in order to become a fourth degree Proud Boy? Because that's how this group works" (Sundaresh).

Though the Proud Boys "have often been associated with the Alt-Right movement," members are quick to disavow such an association because "they are not white supremacists" but "Western-supremacists who will not apologize for creating the modern world" (Sundaresh). The alt-right

> is a segment of the white supremacist movement consisting of a loose network of racists and anti-Semites who reject mainstream conservatism in favor of politics that embrace implicit or explicit racist, anti-Semitic and white supremacist ideology. Many seek to re-inject such bigoted ideas into the conservative movement in the United States. (Anti-Defamation League)

The alt-lite, on the other hand,

> was created by the alt right to differentiate itself from right-wing activists who refused to publicly embrace white supremacist ideology. Today, the alt lite, sometimes referred to as the New Right, is [sic] loosely-connected movement whose adherents generally shun white supremacist thinking, but who are in step with the alt right in their hatred of feminists and immigrants, among others. Many within the alt lite sphere are virulently anti-Muslim; the group abhors everyone on "the left" and traffics in conspiracy theories. (Anti-Defamation League)

Proud Boys' founder McInnes has mocked the SPLC's definition of his group as a "hate group," stating that the SPLC is ignoring "real-life threats right before [their] eyes in favor of shutting down the new Elk's Lodge based on some random fear of a men's club morphing into an evil army that murders everyone who isn't like them" (Eyes on the Right).

See also: Alt-Right Movement; Fraternal Order of Alt-Knights; White Nationalism; White Supremacist Movement

FURTHER READING

Anti-Defamation League. "From Alt Right to Alt Lite: Name the Hate." Anti-Defamation League. https://www.adl.org/resources/backgrounders/from-alt-right-to-alt-lite -naming-the-hate. (Accessed June 5, 2018.)

Eyes on the Right. February 26, 2018. "The SPLC Officially Classifies the Proud Boys as a Hate Group." Angry White Men. https://angrywhitemen.org/2018/02/26/the -splc-officially-classifies-the-proud-boys-as-a-hate-group/. (Accessed June 5, 2018.)

Feuer, Alan, and Jeremy W. Peters. June 2, 2017. "Fringe Groups Revel as Protests Turn Violent." *New York Times*. https://www.nytimes.com/2017/06/02/us/politics /white-nationalists-alt-knights-protests-colleges.html. (Accessed June 5, 2018.)

Gilmour, David. September 7, 2017. "Meet the Proud Boys, the Pro-Men, Anti-Masturbation Enemy of 'Antifa.'" Daily Dot. https://www.dailydot.com/layer8/proud-boys/. (Accessed June 5, 2018.)

Hall, Alexandra. "The Proud Boys: Drinking Club or Misogynist Movement?" To the Best of Our Knowledge. https://www.ttbook.org/interview/proud-boys-drinking -club-or-misogynist-movement. (Accessed June 5, 2018.)

Hatewatch Staff. August 10, 2017. "Do You Want Bigots, Gavini? Because This Is How You Get Bigots." Southern Poverty Law Center: Hatewatch. https://www.splcenter .org/hatewatch/2017/08/10/do-you-want-bigots-gavin-because-how-you-get-bigots. (Accessed June 5, 2018.)

Hatewatch Staff. April 19, 2018. "McInnes, Molyneux, and 4chan: Investigating Pathways to the Alt-Right." Southern Poverty Law Center. https://www.splcente r.org/20180419/mcinnes-molyneux-and-4chan-investigating-pathways-alt-right. (Accessed June 5, 2018.)

Kacala, Alexander. September 7, 2017. "Meet the Pro-Gay, Anti-Masturbation Enemy of Antifa Named After an 'Aladdin' Song." https://hornet.com/stories/proud-boys -gavin-mcinnes-videos/. (Accessed June 5, 2018.)

Morlin, Bill. April 25, 2017. "New 'Fight Club' Ready for Street Violence." Southern Poverty Law Center: Hatewatch. https://www.splcenter.org/hatewatch/2017/04/25 /new-fight-club-ready-street-violence. (Accessed June 5, 2018.)

Southern Poverty Law Center. "Proud Boys." Southern Poverty Law Center. https://www .splcenter.org/fighting-hate/extremist-files/group/proud-boys. (Accessed June 5, 2018.)

Sundaresh, Jaya. July 19, 2017. "Are Proud Boys a Hate Group? Experts Weigh In." *Alt*. http://thealt.com/2017/07/19/proud-boys-hate-group-experts-say-not-yet/. (Accessed June 5, 2018.)

R

Racial Nationalist Party of America

The Racial Nationalist Party of America (RNPA), located in Lockport, New York, is characterized as a "white nationalist hate group by the Southern Poverty Law Center" (SPLC). According to the SPLC, "white nationalist groups espouse white supremacist or white separatist ideologies, often focusing on the alleged inferiority of nonwhites" (Southern Poverty Law Center). The RNPA "was founded in 1998 by Karl Hand, a long-time political activist in the pro-white movement." The RNPA claims to be "composed of white men and women of all ethnic backgrounds and religious beliefs who have united together to fight for the interests of their race" (Racial Nationalist Party of America). The main purpose of RNPA is

> to secure a future for White children. We do not believe that this is attainable without racial separation. White people make up just 8% of the world's population. White women of child bearing age make up just 2%. We are an endangered species. This is not hatred, but fact. We are below zero population, which translated, means we are a dying race. (Buffalo Record)

And RNPA's mission is

> to further promote the interests of our organization and our members to the White community. We strive to make a difference by educating the public and expanding our reach. Our most sacred mission is to inspire our folk to greatness. For this reason, we stand against all the evil influences that serve to bring us down to the lowest common denominator, whether it be in the field of politics or in art. Materialism is an attack upon our racial soul whether it be in the form of capitalism or dialectic materialism, aka communism. (Buffalo Record)

RNPA's leader, Karl Hand, is a "Holocaust denier, hates black people, and a virulent anti-Semite" (Buffalo Record). Hand rose to prominence as a member of the Ku Klux Klan, "even at one point being quite close to David Duke" (Buffalo Record). Hand has stated that "[t]he Jewish religion is not a religion at all, but rather a conspiracy against all of humanity" (Buffalo Record).

In January 2017, residents of Lockport, New York, attending a celebration of Martin Luther King Jr.'s birthday found pamphlets from the RNPA on their windshields. The slogan on the pamphlet read, "Where the White community comes together" (WKBW). And in November 2017, RNPA mailed local residents applications that asked recipients to certify that they were white Americans 18 years old or older and were "in basic agreement with the racial separatist views and objectives of the RNPA" (Pressey). The applications went on to ask recipients "to swear under penalty of perjury that he isn't—or hasn't ever been—a member of a law enforcement agency intent upon entrapment of RNPA members or its affiliates" (Pressey).

RNPA's "proclamation" to the world reads:

Let Friend And Foe Be Advised:

We shall never accept the leadership of the Status Woe or their two party swindle, as they have betrayed our folk.

We shall never accept their morality as the only thing immoral in the face of racial extinction is defeat.

We shall never accept their version of history, with their distortions and self-defeating propaganda.

We shall never accept their education system as it has proven to be a system of indoctrination bent against our folk, its values, and its traditions.

We shall never accept their clergy who have chosen to become willing tools of our racial enemies by undermining our racial will-to-resist.

We shall never accept their judicial system which is bent against all who oppose the tyranny of the majority.

We shall never accept their media, the wormtongues who work insidiously against our folk, always working with our foes, protecting them from scrutiny, while attacking our honor.

We reject all of these, and we shall never stand with them, but always against them. We reject them as they have rejected, imprisoned, tortured, murdered and scorned us.

We remember and honor our heroes and heroines, as we honor our ancestors and our history.

For all of these reasons, we are an entity unto ourselves, a community within a community, a nation within a nation. Our Race Is Our Nation—O.R.I.O.N.. [sic] Come what may!! (Buffalo Record)

See also: Ku Klux Klan; Neo-Nazis; White Nationalism; White Supremacist Movement

FURTHER READING

Anderson, Todd. August 3, 2016. "What Would You Ask a White Supremacist if You Could Ask Any Question?" WBLK. http://wblk.com/what-would-you-ask-a-white-supremacist-if-you-could-ask-any-question/. (Accessed June 18, 2018.)

Buffalo Record. "Who Is Karl Hand?" Buffalo Record. https://buffalorecord.wordpress.com/2010/07/05/who-is-karl-hand/. (Accessed June 18, 2018.)

Pressey, Debra. November 29, 2017. "Philo Man Appalled by White-Supremacist Application in His Mailbox." *News-Gazette*. http://www.news-gazette.com/news/local/2017-11-29/philo-man-appalled-white-supremacist-application-his-mailbox.html. (Accessed June 18, 2018.)

Racial Nationalist Party of America. "About the RNPA." Racial Nationalist Party of America. https://www.rnpaheadquarters.org/about-us/. (Accessed June 18, 2018.)

Southern Poverty Law Center. "White Nationalist." Southern Poverty Law Center. https://www.splcenter.org/fighting-hate/extremist-files/ideology/white-nationalist. (Accessed June 18, 2018.)

WKBW Staff. January 16, 2017. "Local White Supremacist Group Tries Spreading Its Message." WKBW. https://www.wkbw.com/news/local-white-supremacist-group-tries-speading-its-message. (Accessed June 18, 2018.)

Racist Skinheads

According to the Southern Poverty Law Center (SPLC), racist skinheads "are among the most dangerous radical-right threats facing law enforcement today" (Southern Poverty Law Center, 2012). Generally "the products of a violent and criminal subculture," racist skinheads typically consist of men and women who have been "imbued with neo-Nazi beliefs about Jews, blacks, LGBT people and others, while notoriously being difficult to track" because of their often unorganized and unaffiliated status with mainstream extremist groups (Southern Poverty Law Center, 2012). Organized into "small, mobile 'crews' or acting individually, skinheads tend to move around frequently and often without warning, even as they network and organize across regions. For law enforcement, this poses a particular problem in responding to crimes and conspiracies crossing multiple jurisdictions" (Southern Poverty Law Center, 2012).

Unlike the Ku Klux Klan (KKK), racist skinheads are not a native manifestation of the United States. The skinhead movement "actually was started in the 1960s by working class youths in England." Instead of "opting for the flamboyant and 'fancy-dress' escapism of the 'long-hairs,' the skinheads embraced working-class fashion: cropped hair, meant-to-last shoes and boots, white T-shirts and worn Levis" (Abbots). Racism among skinheads first appeared in the 1970s, "when poor economic conditions in England encouraged neo-Nazi groups to recruit skinheads into their ranks, most of whom were in low paying jobs or on welfare. Playing on the traditional nationalistic ideas of the working class, the fascist groups did their best to turn the skinheads against their immigrant neighbors" (Abbots). The nonviolent skinhead movement experienced a revival in the early 1980s with the advent of the punk rock movement.

The nativist sentiments urged by neo-Nazis in Europe spread quickly to the United States in the 1980s. At the time, the United States was experiencing its own economic downturn, and many citizens were out of work. Skinhead activity was "first reported in Texas and in the Midwest." Skinheads became immediately recognizable for their trademark style: "shaved head, combat boots, bomber jacket, neo-Nazi and white power tattoos" (Southern Poverty Law Center, 2012). A major force behind the national growth of racist skinheads in the United States was Tom Metzger, "a former Klansman and former leader of the neo-Nazi group White Aryan Resistance (WAR)." Around 1986, "Metzger founded and organized a skinhead outreach campaign." Together with his son, John, Metzger "sought to ground the dispersed movement in ideology and direct its wild and chaotic youthful energy into building smart, well-trained, and obedient street cells around the country" (Southern Poverty Law Center, 2012). In 1988, "Metzger organized the first major hate rock festival in the United States at the annual Aryan Fest Conference in Oklahoma" (Southern Poverty Law Center, 2012).

Racist skinheads burst onto the scene in 1988 when two of Metzger's acolytes attacked a group of Ethiopian immigrants in the middle of the street in Portland, Oregon, killing one of the students. The Southern Poverty Law Center (SPLC) and the Anti-Defamation League (ADL) would bring a civil rights lawsuit against Metzger and WAR, and the resulting $12.5 million judgment bankrupted Metzger and effectively ended WAR as an effective organization.

Other racist skinhead attacks during the late 1980s and early 1990s resulted in the murders of blacks in Birmingham, Alabama, and Arlington, Texas. Those responsible for the murders were part of what became known as the "Confederate Hammerskins," a confederation of skinheads that had been founded in Dallas in 1987.

In 1994, the Hammerskin Nation (HN) was formed with the idea to "unite all of the regional Hammerskin groups into a national and even international force, with affiliated chapters in Europe" (Southern Poverty Law Center, 2012). For a while, the plan worked, and HN became "the most powerful skinhead organization in the country by the end of the 1990s" (Southern Poverty Law Center, 2012). Throughout this period of time, "the skinhead movement continued to grow and was responsible for hundreds of racially motivated crimes around the country" (Southern Poverty Law Center, Racist Skinhead).

Much of the credit for the growth of the racist skinhead movement during this time goes to the end of the Cold War and the uncertainty that surrounded this period of time in American history. Gone was the looming menace of the Soviet Union and communist takeover. What was left was surging immigration into the United States from countries in Eastern Europe, the Middle East, and Latin America. These immigrant movements challenged the accepted notion of white supremacy in the country, a phenomenon that racist skinheads and other extremists resented.

By the mid-2000s, the influence of the Hammerskins had been replaced by that of the Vinlanders. The group, which was "incredibly violent, full of swagger, and loathe to take orders from anyone," attempted to revitalize the racist skinhead movement. However, the Vinlanders' founder, Brien James, informed the extremist world in 2007 that the Vinlanders were separating themselves from the racist movement. The announcement explained:

> We do not see anything positive being accomplished, for our nation or our people, by participating in the white racialist movement as it stands. We have attempted to change this movement from within and have not succeeded. It is our opinion that a large number of the people involved in the greater movement are paid informants, social outcasts, and general losers in life. (Southern Poverty Law Center, 2012)

In addition to their social and cultural influence, racist skinheads influence the music scene, as the phenomenon of "hate rock exploded alongside the punk rock movement, spreading lyrics that were anti-immigrant, anti-black, and anti-Semitic" (Southern Poverty Law Center, 2012). William Pierce, founder of the neo-Nazi National Alliance, understood the potential of hate-rock music. He stated, "Music speaks to us at a deeper level than books or political rhetoric: music speaks directly to the soul" (Southern Poverty Law Center, 2012). In 1999, Pierce purchased the hate-rock label "Resistance Records" and "built the company into a major force in the racist skinhead movement." By the early 2000s, skinhead culture was defined by "loud hate-rock, cases of cheap beer, bloody 'boot parties' directed against immigrants and others, and the flagrant display of neo-Nazi iconography and paraphernalia" (Southern Poverty Law Center, 2012).

Today, the racist skinhead culture is still prominent in the United States. Racist skinheads "have been a regular element in American prisons and juvenile correction facilities. The U.S. military has also had to contend to racist skinheads in its ranks" (Southern Poverty Law Center, Racist Skinhead). Hate rock from racist skinheads "has bled into the flow of rebellious teen music. And skinheads have taken their 'boot parties' from the street to the Internet, targeting young people for recruitment into their supposed movement" (Southern Poverty Law Center, Racist Skinhead).

Dylann Roof's massacre of "nine black parishioners at a Charleston, South Carolina church in June 2015" won him some "cred" among some racist skinheads when he declared before the shooting, "You [black people] are raping our women and taking over the country" (Ferranti). Roof's crime is exactly the kind celebrated in America's prisons among white nationalists and white supremacists. A skinhead doing time in federal prison stated, "Dylann will be my next tattoo" (Ferranti).

See also: Aryan Nations; National Alliance; Neo-Nazis; White Nationalism; White Supremacist Movement

FURTHER READING

Abbots, Jennifer. April 19, 1994. "True 'Skinheads' Are Not the Racist Thugs of Media Fame." *New York Times*. http://www.nytimes.com/1994/04/19/opinion/l-true-skinheads-are-not-the-racist-thugs-of-media-fame-829412.html. (Accessed June 5, 2017.)

Ferranti, Seth. June 19, 2015. "What Racist Skinheads in Prison Think about Dylann Roof." Vice. https://www.vice.com/en_us/article/what-racist-skinhead-prisoners-think-about-dylann-roof-619. (Accessed June 5, 2017.)

Pollard, John. 2016. "Skinhead Culture: The Ideologies, Mythologies, Religions, and Conspiracy Theories of Racist Skinheads." *Patterns of Prejudice* 50 (4–5).

Southern Poverty Law Center. "Racist Skinhead." Southern Poverty Law Center. https://www.splcenter.org/fighting-hate/extremist-files/ideology/racist-skinhead. (Accessed June 5, 2017.)

Southern Poverty Law Center. June 25, 2012. "Racist Skinheads: Understanding the Threat." Southern Poverty Law Center. https://www.splcenter.org/20100126/racist-skinheads-understanding-threat. (Accessed June 5, 2017.)

Rebel Brigade Knights of the True Invisible Empire

The Rebel Brigade Knights of the True Invisible Empire ("Rebel Brigade") is an organization that has been designated as a Ku Klux Klan (KKK) hate group by the Southern Poverty Law Center (SPLC). Where KKK members once numbered in the millions, there are now perhaps only 3,000 or so scattered among about 40 active groups (Anti-Defamation League). The Rebel Brigade is an active KKK group of about 75 members spread over 7 states, though that number is down from 300 just since 2013 (Casey). According to the Rebel Brigade's website:

> We do wish to preserve the White Christian ways. (The same way other races wish to preserve their race and beliefs!) Those once considered, minority races, are flourishing, more opportunities than the Caucasian Race! We wish to take back only the right of free speech, and right to say that WE are White and Proud! We see people of all

races walking with their heads held high, proud to be of whatever race or religion never to be persecuted or questioned as to their motives. Except for the White!!! How long will the White Race have to continue persecution? We the Rebel Brigade Knights True Invisible Empire will not let this continue! Maybe there are those who agree but do not wish to stand up for your rights, the rights of your children and grandchildren and the future for those to come. If you do not stand for what you believe in you will fall for everything. (Rebel Brigade Knights of the True Invisible Empire, About)

The imperial wizard of the Rebel Brigade, Billy Snuffer Sr., was at the August 2017 "Unite the Right" rally in Charlottesville, Virginia, that led to the deaths of three people. Snuffer, who says he was "armed with a pistol and a semi-automatic rifle," was at the rally "to protest the removal of a statue of Confederate General Robert E. Lee because it was important" (Casey). Snuffer is quick to "draw a distinction between the Rebel Brigade Knights, which he called 'traditional Klan,' and other members of the alt-right who showed up in Charlottesville for a rally that turned violent":

> He divided the white nationalist movement into three basic categories. One is neo-Nazis. Snuffer called them "idiots." Another is white supremacists. They believe other races are inferior and want a racially pure nation. Then there are white separatists, the category in which he puts the Rebel Brigade Knights. (Casey)

According to Snuffer, white separatists draw some lines. "The principal one is 'no dating [and] not mating' between the races" (Casey).

In 2015, Snuffer and other leaders of the Rebel Brigade made recruiting videos that "declared their absolute antipathy for former President Barack Obama" (Casey). And what about Donald Trump? "I love Donald Trump," Snuffer declared. "I love the man. He's not a politician and he's got the backbone to stand up and say what he believes in" (Casey).

See also: Ku Klux Klan; Neo-Nazis; White Nationalism; White Supremacist Movement

FURTHER READING

Anti-Defamation League. "Despite Internal Turmoil, Klan Groups Persist." Anti-Defamation League. https://www.adl.org/sites/default/files/documents/CR_5173 _Klan%20Report_vFFF2.pdf. (Accessed June 16, 2018.)

Casey, Dan. August 20, 2017. "Casey: KKK Leader Counsels Kinder, Gentler & 'Christian' White Nationalism." *Roanoke Times*. http://www.roanoke.com/news/dan _casey/casey-kkk-leader-counsels-kinder-gentler-christian-white-nationalism /article_91754ecf-7bdb-5890-8972-dca8b37845b3.html. (Accessed June 16, 2018.)

Rebel Brigade Knights of the True Invisible Empire. http://rebelbrigade.blogspot.com/. (Accessed June 16, 2018.)

Rebel Brigade Knights of the True Invisible Empire. "About." Rebel Brigade Knights of the True Invisible Empire. http://rebelbrigadeknightstrueinvisibleempire.yolasite. com/. (Accessed June 16, 2018.)

Southern Poverty Law Center. "Hate Map by State." Southern Poverty Law Center. https://www.splcenter.org/hate-map/by-state. (Accessed June 16, 2018.)

Southern Poverty Law Center. February 15, 2017. "Active Hate Groups 2016." Southern Poverty Law Center: Intelligence Report. https://www.splcenter.org/fighting-hate /intelligence-report/2017/active-hate-groups-2016. (Accessed June 16, 2018.)

Remembrance Project

The Remembrance Project is a nonprofit organization focused on stemming illegal immigration into the United States. It is based in Houston, Texas. The Southern Poverty Law Center (SPLC) characterizes the Remembrance Project as an "anti-immigrant hate group" (Southern Poverty Law Center, Anti-Immigrant). According to the SPLC, anti-immigrant hate groups go beyond nativism or xenophobia to promote "racist propaganda" against immigrant groups. Groups that focus on Latin American immigration tend to

> subscribe to one of two conspiracy theories that have no basis in fact: the idea that Mexico has a secret "Plan de Aztlán" to "reconquer" the American Southwest, and another theory alleging that the leaders of Mexico, Canada and the United States are secretly planning to merge into a European Union-like entity that will be known as the "North American Union." (Southern Poverty Law Center, Anti-Immigrant)

The Remembrance Project "claims to advocate on behalf of families of victims of violence and tragedy" and "misrepresents the level of crime committed by immigrants," while routinely demonizing immigrants as "invaders." The Remembrance Project also has a "record of working with white nationalism" (Southern Poverty Law Center, Remembrance Project). The founder of the Remembrance Project, Maria Espinoza, "has routinely embellished on crimes committed by undocumented immigrants":

> We have uncovered the fact that Americans are under assault, a fact under-reported by the press, and unconnected by our elected leaders at all levels of government. Sanctuary cities, unsecured communities, human trafficking, molestations of our children, are all part of the vernacular of this disease that illegal immigration speaks, and must be addressed now!
> Child molestation and rape are very numerous in this illegal alien demographic! (Southern Poverty Law Center, Remembrance Project)

Espinoza memorializes what the Remembrance Project calls "stolen lives," showing the names and pictures of those killed by undocumented immigrants portrayed on a "quilt" that is "brought to nativist events around the country in an attempt to drum up support for anti-immigrant stances and policies" (Piggott, 2016). Espinoza is no stranger to anti-immigrant and nativist tropes, stating, "No one is immune to the illegal who drives wildly drunk, or the wanna-be gang-banger who needs to machete innocent citizens to gain entry and respect into the Latino or other gangs" (Southern Poverty Law Center, Remembrance Project).

Though the Remembrance Project is a nonprofit group and, as such, cannot contribute to political campaigns, most of the group's members are firmly behind the policies of President Donald Trump. A cursory viewing of the Remembrance Project's website produces several articles with such headlines as "Soros-Funded Group Launches App to Help Illegal Aliens Avoid Feds" and "BETRAYED: Gorsuch Rules Criminal Immigrant Can Stay, No Deportation" (Remembrance Project). George Soros is the business magnate and philanthropist most often linked to liberal causes, while "Neil Gorsuch was President Trump's first appointment to the U.S. Supreme Court." In supporting President Trump's recision of the Deferred Action for Childhood Arrivals (DACA) program—the policy that allows some children of undocumented immigrants to receive deferred action from deportation—the Remembrance Project stated:

> The Remembrance Project commends the Trump administration's decision to rescind Obama's unconstitutional and unlawful program known as DACA. President Trump has met an important milestone in keeping his campaign promise to us, to our 'stolen lives' families, and to all Americans.
>
> The previous administration's unilateral circumvention and disregard for laws and procedures in place to safeguard our communities resulted in:
>
> - uptick in MS-13 gangs
> - human trafficking
> - the explosion of opioid drugs in schools
> - job loss, and
> - the most egregious of all—the loss of lives like the recent killings of Cathy Dolan, Domonick Ceceri and Artem Ziberov who were all killed by DACA-age illegal aliens.
>
> We thank and support President Trump and his administration for their commitment to restoring the rule of law.
>
> The Remembrance Project has always maintained that the best and only immigration reform needed is for legislators to finally secure our borders and strictly enforce our interior laws. Ending DACA is one critical step in the process of restoring law and order to America. (Espinoza)

In 2017, Maria Espinoza and the Remembrance Project (TRP) were rocked when a "piece on TRP published by *Politico*" reported that "a number of victims' families left the organization, claiming Espinoza was only using them to boost her public profile" (Piggott, 2017). According to the Politico piece, the money raised from a $10,000 per table fee for an event where then-candidate Donald Trump appeared never "made its way into the hands of the victims' families (Piggott, 2017). A former TRP member—whose son "was killed by an undocumented Ecuadorean man, who had been driving while intoxicated and later was convicted of manslaughter"—stated: "The more involved I got [with TRP], once I got past my son's trial and could focus more on the organization, it just seemed like my values and my goals were different than what Maria's were." She explained that "[i]t started to feel like this might be a steppingstone for her" (Piggott, 2017).

See also: American Border Patrol/American Patrol; Center for Immigration Studies; Federation for American Immigration Reform; White Nationalism

FURTHER READING

Espinoza, Maria. September 6, 2017. "The Remembrance Project's Statement on President Trump Rescinding DACA." Remembrance Project. https://theremembr anceproject.org/the-remembrance-projects-statement-on-president-trump -rescinding-daca/. (Accessed June 18, 2018.)

Piggot, Stephen. September 15, 2016. "Donald Trump to Address Anti-Immigrant Remembrance Project This Weekend." Southern Poverty Law Center: Hatewatch. https://www.splcenter.org/hatewatch/2016/09/15/donald-trump-address-anti -immigrant-remembrance-project-weekend. (Accessed June 18, 2018.)

Piggot, Stephen. July 14, 2017. "Maria Espinoza and the Remembrance Project in Hot Water after Rival Group Emerges." Southern Poverty Law Center: Hatewatch. https://www.splcenter.org/hatewatch/2017/07/14/maria-espinoza-and -remembrance-project-hot-water-after-rival-group-emerges. (Accessed June 18, 2018.)

Remembrance Project. https://theremembranceproject.org/. (Accessed June 18, 2018.)

Southern Poverty Law Center. "Anti-Immigrant." Southern Poverty Law Center. https://www.splcenter.org/fighting-hate/extremist-files/ideology/anti-immigrant. (Accessed June 18, 2018.)

Southern Poverty Law Center. "The Remembrance Project." Southern Poverty Law Center. https://www.splcenter.org/fighting-hate/extremist-files/group/remembrance -project. (Accessed June 18, 2018.)

Renegade Broadcasting

Renegade Broadcasting, located in Whitefish, Montana, is characterized "as a white nationalist hate group by the Southern Poverty Law Center" (SPLC). According to the SPLC, "white nationalist groups espouse white supremacist or white separatist ideologies, often focusing on the alleged inferiority of nonwhites" (Southern Poverty Law Center). Renegade Broadcasting was founded in 2012 by Kyle Hunt, a former Google employee, who devotes his broadcasting "to covering the destruction of the white race" (Neiwert). In 2014, Hunt organized the "White Man's March," which was an event planned for New York City "with satellite marches occurring in various other cities around the country" (Neiwert). Hunt claims that the "White Man's March" was "a response to fears that white people are being 'mocked, displaced and violently attacked' through an insidious liberal idea known as 'diversity'" (Neiwert). Hunt argues that the "diversity agenda is being directed at white countries (and only at white countries) with various programs to ensure that there are less white people at schools and in the work force, which is unfair and discriminatory. It is taking away money and opportunities from the White citizens" (Neiwert).

In addition to Renegade Broadcasting, Hunt founded the *Renegade Tribune* as the print companion to Renegade Broadcasting. On both venues, Hunt pushes his belief that the white race is being maligned by political and social forces at work in the United States. In one piece on the *Renegade Tribune*, for instance, Hunt claimed that the "DOJ" (Department of Justice) was teaming up with the SPLC "to attack White Americans" (Hunt, 2015). Hunt stated:

> Clearly the whole focus of this new initiative is geared toward suppressing pro-Whites, which is made obvious by the crucial role being played by the SPLC, an organization that determines what "hate" is and who is doing it.
>
> The SPLC's fat jewess [sic] Heidi Beirich was on hand to demand that more be done about White folks who are angry about the genocide being inflicted upon them, especially the ones who have taken to Twitter to speak their minds. (Hunt, 2015)

Hunt also stated that the "teaming up" of the federal government and the SPLC was a calculated move:

> This move by the federal government and the anti-White jewish [sic] extremists at the SPLC follows on the heels of some very big announcements. At the end of

September major US cities fell under the control to the United Nations, which wants to take away our right to self-defense. A few days after that, the secretive TPP [Trans Pacific Partnership] was finalized, with leaked documents showing its intention to eliminate free speech on the internet, amongst many other things. And this past summer the State Department worked with jewish [sic] terrorist George Soros to produce a report that labels White Americans as the biggest terror threat in the United States, which provided the basis for the arguments used by Carlin in his recent speech. Clearly the jewish [sic] elite and their anti-White Shabbos goy are worried that Whites are getting a little too uppity. (Hunt, 2015)

In September 2015, Hunt and Renegade Broadcasting were roundly criticized in *American Renaissance*, a monthly white supremacist journal, for having Nick Spero, an open transsexual, on the program. *American Renaissance* stated that "Nick Spero's public statement during his Renegade scandal revealed him to be a very pathetic homosexual and sexual degenerate who has all the attributes of a gross homosexual" (*American Renaissance*). The journal went on to give a tongue-in-cheek congratulatory nod to Renegade Broadcasting for "being Caitlin Jenner before Bruce" (*American Renaissance*).

In June 2018, after the suicide of celebrity chef Anthony Bourdain, Hunt wrote in the *Renegade Tribune*: "He [Bourdain] was a genocidal jew (on his mother's side) who celebrated the extermination of White people. Good riddance!" (Hunt, 2018). Hunt went on to say:

We must make the perpetrators of White genocide pay for their crimes against us. Never forgive. Never forget. These people want to see our people extinct. We must do everything in our power to awaken our people, neutralize our enemies, and secure a lasting future for our folk.

That's the only way. It's the only solution. It's our only hope. (Hunt, 2018)

See also: White Nationalism; White Supremacist Movement

FURTHER READING

American Renaissance. September 26, 2015. "Renegade Broadcasting—A Prime Example of White Nationalist Degeneracy." *American Renaissance*. https://anaannblog .wordpress.com/2015/09/26/renegade-broadcasting-a-prime-example-of-white -nationalist-degeneracy/. (Accessed June 18, 2018.)

Hunt, Kyle. October 19, 2015. "DOJ Teams Up with SPLC to Attack White Americans." *Renegade Tribune*. http://www.renegadetribune.com/doj-teams-up-with-splc-to -attack-white-americans/. (Accessed June 18, 2018.)

Hunt, Kyle. June 11, 2018. "Hebraic Hatred: Anthony Bourdain Wanted to See a World without White People." *Renegade Tribune*. http://www.renegadetribune.com /hebraic-hatred-anthony-bourdain-wanted-to-see-a-world-without-white-people/. (Accessed June 19, 2018.)

Neiwert, David. March 17, 2014. "'White Man's March' Events Draw Smattering of Participants, Loads of Derision." Southern Poverty Law Center: Hatewatch. https:// www.splcenter.org/hatewatch/2014/03/17/white-mans-march-events-draw -smattering-participants-loads-derision. (Accessed June 18, 2018.)

Renegade Broadcasting. http://www.renegadebroadcasting.com/. (Accessed June 18, 2018.)

Renegade Tribune. February 3, 2018. "SPLC Secretly Admits White Genocide Is Real and Has Been 'Planned for a While.' " *Renegade Tribune.* http://www.renegadetribune .com/splc-secretly-admits-white-genocide-real/. (Accessed June 18, 2018.)

Southern Poverty Law Center. "White Nationalist." Southern Poverty Law Center. https:// www.splcenter.org/fighting-hate/extremist-files/ideology/white-nationalist. (Accessed June 18, 2018.)

The Right Stuff

According to the Anti-Defamation League (ADL), the Right Stuff (TRS)

> is a racist and anti-Semitic blog that was launched in December 2012. It identifies itself as an alt right site. TRS says that is wants to reinvigorate "dialogue among a disparate and edgy right-wing." It focuses on various political issues and includes articles about alleged Jewish power and control of the media and government. (Anti-Defamation League)

TRS was founded in 2012 by Mike Peinovich, who called himself "Mike Enoch" on TRS. Peinovich quickly became a darling of the alt-right movement, acting as a "propagandist indoctrinating the young and naïve with white nationalistic bluster" (Southern Poverty Law Center). Peinovich often spoke of "his desire for TRS to become a 'media body' for the Alt-Right" (Hatewatch staff). Peinovich often appeared with Richard Spencer, founder of the alt-right movement, or had him as a guest on his podcast, the *Daily Shoah.* Peinovich is credited

> with creating the anti-Semitic (((echo))) meme that originates from the reverb effect applied when hosts of the Daily Shoah mention Jewish individuals or institutions. Members of the Alt-Right began to affix three sets of parentheses around names to denote Jewish influence—most commonly on social media platforms. (Southern Poverty Law Center)

A neo-Nazi ally of Peinovich, Mike Anglin, stated that the (((echoes))) meme "was one of the biggest propaganda coups since the death of Adolf Hitler" (Hankes). He went on to say, "Mike and TRS have been at the forefront of exposing the Jewish problem. They are, along with this website, and some older figures such as David Duke, the only people really going on hard on the Jews" (Hankes).

Peinovich's association with the world of white nationalism took a significant hit in January 2017 when he became the victim of a doxxing attack. Internet doxxers are "people who publish someone's personal information online" (Hatewatch staff). The doxxers revealed that Peinovich "had been married to a Jewish woman for the past decade" (Southern Poverty Law Center). When confronted with the reality that his secret was out, Peinovich confessed:

> As I am sure you all know, I was doxxed and an ill-advised attempt to fool the media about my identity led me to not talk to you people and try to simply ride it out by being silent. Yes my wife is who they say she is. I won't even bother denying it. . . . Don't lie for me. Don't try to defend me to those attacking me. Don't jeopardize your own reputation by defending things that you don't think you can. . . . I am just a guy that puts ideas out there on the internet. I want to save Europe, America and the white race. We are going to continue and not let this thing die. (Southern Poverty Law Center)

Richard Spencer stated that, far from losing support because of the revelation, Peinovich would "continue to be a force on the Alt Right in the future." And Peinovich's neo-Nazi ally, Mike Anglin, stated:

> He was obviously dishonest on some level, but if we look at his contribution, and ask ourselves "Did this forward the 14 words?" we will see that it did and the weirdness in his personal life doesn't change that. Tens of thousands—maybe even hundreds of thousands—of men have been brought into the movement through TRS and Mike's work, and nothing can or will change that. (Southern Poverty Law Center)

Peinovich continues to run TRS and is still an "outspoken figure for the Alt-Right" (Southern Poverty Law Center). In May 2018, Peinovich was faced with the possibility of having to reveal the names of anonymous fans of TRS in response to a federal lawsuit brought by "clergy and local Charlottesville residents who seek damages related to the violence that they believe was instigated by men like Peinovich" (Hayden). Indeed, prior to the "Unite the Right" rally in Charlottesville, Virginia, in August 2017, Peinovich stated:

> Bring whatever you need [to Charlottesville], that you feel you need for your self-defense. Do what you need to do for security of your own person, at this point. . . . We don't want [counterprotesters] to have the impression—that we are going to be showing up there, unarmed . . . that is not the case." (Hayden)

See also: Alt-Right Movement; Neo-Confederates; White Nationalism

FURTHER READING

Anti-Defamation League. December 7, 2016. "Alt Right Groups Target Campuses with Fliers." Anti-Defamation League. http://lasvegas.adl.org/alt-right-groups-target-campuses-with-fliers/. (Accessed June 16, 2018.)

Eyes on the Right. May 6, 2018. "Even White Nationalists Know Mike Peinovich Is a Bumbling Ignoramus." Angry White Men. https://angrywhitemen.org/2018/05/06/even-white-nationalists-know-mike-peinovich-is-a-bumbling-ignoramus/#more-45610. (Accessed June 16, 2018.)

Hankes, Keegan. January 17, 2017. "Beyond the Pale: Andrew Anglin's Newest Case for 'Purity Tests.'" Southern Poverty Law Center: Hatewatch. https://www.splcenter.org/hatewatch/2017/01/17/beyond-pale-andrew-anglins-newest-case-purity-tests. (Accessed June 16, 2018.)

Hatewatch Staff. January 26, 2017. "Neo-Confederates Breaking from the Right Stuff after Doxxing Scandal." Southern Poverty Law Center: Hatewatch. https://www.splcenter.org/hatewatch/2017/01/26/neo-confederates-breaking-right-stuff-after-doxxing-scandal. (Accessed June 16, 2018.)

Hayden, Michael Edison. May 1, 2018. "Anonymous White Nationalists May Have Their Identities Exposed in Lawsuit over Charlottesville, Virginia, Violence." *News week*. http://www.newsweek.com/anonymous-white-nationalists-may-have-their-identities-exposed-result-903026. (Accessed June 16, 2018.)

Right Stuff Blog. https://blog.therightstuff.biz/. (Accessed June 16, 2018.)

Southern Poverty Law Center. "Michael 'Enoch' Peinovich." Southern Poverty Law Center. https://www.splcenter.org/fighting-hate/extremist-files/individual/michael-enoch-peinovich. (Accessed June 16, 2018.)

Right Wing Resistance North America

Right Wing Resistance (RWR) North America "has been characterized as a white nationalist hate group by the Southern Poverty Law Center" (SPLC). According to the SPLC, white nationalist hate groups "espouse white supremacist or white separatist ideologies, often focusing on the alleged inferiority of non-whites" (Southern Poverty Law Center, 2016). Adherents of white nationalist groups

> believe that white identity should be the organizing principle of the countries that make up Western civilization. White nationalists advocate for policies to reverse changing demographics and the loss of an absolute, white majority. Ending non-white immigration, both legal and illegal, is an urgent priority—frequently elevated over other racist projects, such as ending multiculturalism and miscegenation—for white nationalists seeking to preserve white, racial hegemony. (Southern Poverty Law Center, White Nationalist)

According to the website of the RWR:

> The Right Wing Resistance was founded in New Zealand in 2009 as an organization of Anglo-Saxon men and women, who came together in Unity to form an action based group, that would be prepared for the impending danger that lies ahead of Europeans, and European heritage. The Right Wing Resistance spread to many countries within a short period of time following its birth. It was realized that the white races [sic] existence was clearly threatened with extinction internationally, and soon organizations began planning, growing and expanding all through-out the world, including North America. (Right Wing Resistance)

As the RWR's ideas spread, new groups were formed throughout the world. In the same year as its parent organization was established, RWR North America was founded by Americans and Canadians who "realized the severe threat their race faced" (Right Wing Resistance North America). On its "About" page, RWR North America states:

> We are an organized unified resistance movement against mass immigration, the dilution of our european [sic] culture and pride, and the current multicultural agenda created by the current government networks designed to destroy our colonial rights and identity. We stand with an active structure that rewards those who work hard for the movement. Our primary purpose is to recruit like minded [sic] individuals and groups into an organization of active men and women. (Right Wing Resistance North America)

RWR North America ends its "About" section with an admonition for its readers: "Remember, you are White today because your ancestors believed in White nationalism yesterday" (Right Wing Resistance North America).

According to the SPLC, RWR North America is headquartered in Florida.

See also: White Nationalism; White Supremacist Movement

FURTHER READING

Right Wing Resistance. http://rwrnz.blogspot.com/. (Accessed June 18, 2018.)

Right Wing Resistance North America. "About RWR North America." Right Wing Resistance North America. https://rwrusa.weebly.com/about-rwr-north-america.html. (Accessed June 18, 2018.)

Southern Poverty Law Center. "White Nationalist." Southern Poverty Law Center. https://
    www.splcenter.org/fighting-hate/extremist-files/ideology/white-nationalist.
    (Accessed June 18, 2018.)
Southern Poverty Law Center. February 17, 2016. "Active Hate Groups in the United
    States in 2015." Southern Poverty Law Center: Intelligence Report. https://www
    .splcenter.org/fighting-hate/intelligence-report/2016/active-hate-groups-united
    -states-2015#whitenationalist. (Accessed June 18, 2018.)

Ruth Institute

The Ruth Institute (RI) has been designated by the Southern Poverty Law Center
(SPLC) as an "anti-LGBT hate group." According to the SPLC, "a central theme
of anti-LGBT organizing and ideology is the opposition to LGBT rights, often
couched in rhetoric and harmful pseudoscience that demonizes LGBT people as
threats to children, society and often public health" (Southern Poverty Law Center, Anti-LGBT). Anti-LGBT groups

> often link homosexuality to pedophilia, claim that same-sex marriage and LGBT
> people, in general, are dangers to children, that homosexuality itself is dangerous,
> support the criminalization of homosexuality and transgender identity, and that
> there is a conspiracy called the "homosexual agenda" at work that seeks to destroy
> Christianity and the whole of society. (Southern Poverty Law Center, Anti-LGBT)

The Ruth Institute is considered a right-wing Catholic group created to "conduct
youth outreach, and to warn young people about the dangers of divorce, sexual
promiscuity, and, especially, to recruit them in the fight to block the legalization of
gay marriage" (Southern Poverty Law Center, Ruth Institute). RI was founded in
2008 by Jennifer Roback Morse, "a former professor of economics at George
Mason University," who left her position to start a family. Roback Morse believed
that "without strong families, you can't have free markets or limited government"
(Southern Poverty Law Center, Ruth Institute). And so, "Roback Morse focused
her effort on strengthening the family, which in practice meant adopting an especially uncompromising version of the Catholic faith of her youth" (Southern Poverty Law Center, Ruth Institute). The core beliefs of the Ruth Institute are stated
on its website:

- Every person has the right to know his or her cultural heritage and genetic
  identity.
- Every child has a right to a relationship with their natural mother and father
  except for an unavoidable tragedy.
- The Ruth Institute rejects the idea that a child is a problem to solve if you
  don't want one and an object to purchase if you do want one. (Ruth Institute,
  About Us)

As the head of RI, Roback Morse "worked to warn young women about the
careerist trap" while undertaking the mission to "make marriage cool among high-
school and college-age men and women" (Southern Poverty Law Center, Ruth
Institute). As the legalization of same-sex marriage heated up, the Ruth Institute
created talking points to make its case: "marriage is based on procreation,

same-sex marriages are unstable, and children raised by same-sex couples are more likely to be promiscuous, suffer from depression, and engage in criminal behavior, among other negative outcomes" (Southern Poverty Law Center, Ruth Institute). And even though Roback Morse "continually asserts that her organization feels only compassion for those who 'suffer from same-sex attraction,' " RI has consistently "reprinted anti-LGBT columns over the years that denounced the decriminalization of homosexuality, claimed the most loathsome people in the world are gay activists and that gay couples would use marriage equality to acquire and sexually abuse children" (Southern Poverty Law Center, Ruth Institute).

In 2018, RI formed a book club with a focus on "What you need to know about gender identity politics: Bathroom Bullies to Pronoun Police" (Southern Poverty Law Center, Ruth Institute).

See also: Traditional Values Coalition; Westboro Baptist Church

FURTHER READING

Hatewatch Staff. December 4, 2013. "The Ruth Institute's 'Circle of Experts" on Homosexuality." Southern Poverty Law Center: Hatewatch. https://www.splcenter.org /hatewatch/2013/12/04/ruth-institute%E2%80%99s-%E2%80%98circle-experts% E2%80%99-homosexuality. (Accessed June 15, 2018.)

Ruth Institute. "About Us." Ruth Institute. http://www.ruthinstitute.org/about/about-the -ruth-institute. (Accessed June 15, 2018.)

Ruth Institute. August 23, 2017. "The Ruth Institute's Statement on Being Included on the SPLC 'Hate Map.' " Ruth Institute. http://www.ruthinstitute.org/press/the-ruth -institute-s-statement-on-being-included-on-the-splc-hate-map. (Accessed June 15, 2018.)

Southern Poverty Law Center. "Anti-LGBT." Southern Poverty Law Center. https://www .splcenter.org/fighting-hate/extremist-files/ideology/anti-lgbt. (Accessed June 15, 2018.)

Southern Poverty Law Center. "Ruth Institute." Southern Poverty Law Center. https:// www.splcenter.org/fighting-hate/extremist-files/group/ruth-institute. (Accessed June 15, 2018.)

S

Sadistic Souls Motorcycle Club

The Sadistic Souls Motorcycle Club (SS-MC), also sometimes known as the "Aryan Nations Sadistic Souls Motorcycle Club," is a "white supremacist biker gang that started in 2010" (Anti-Defamation League). The group was founded by Michael McGiffen, a former "grand dragon in the Ku Klux Klan" who left the group, calling it "wimpy" (Morlin). After spending seven years in prison on federal weapons charges, McGiffen emerged to found the SS-MC. In July 2012, "the SS-MC formally merged with the neo-Nazi group Aryan Nations, with which McGiffen [had] had past ties' (Anti-Defamation League). McGiffen had joined his group with the self-proclaimed leader of Aryan Nations, Morris Gulett. Gullet's group, Aryan Nations (Louisiana), claimed that it was the successor to the original Aryan Nations founded by Richard Butler. In 2014, Gulett split with McGiffen and SS-MC, accusing the motorcycle club of being full of "drunks and race mixers" (Morlin). Currently, the SS-MC carries on the ideology of Aryan Nations in their rhetoric:

> Since the reconstruction of the Aryan Nations Sadistic Souls MC, there have been many Changes [sic] to accommodate an ever increasing changing world. As the original order of the Church of Jesus Christ Christian Aryan Nations was to be the political arm of the CJCC, the Aryan Nation Sadistic Souls MC has taken the position of being the militant arm of our beloved Aryan Nation. Our men consist of dedicated , loyal comrades who , when called to action, unwaveringly join in and do what is necessary to insure our tactics & strategies success. Our brothers come from different theological backgrounds but all share the vision of total Aryan Victory. Anyone interested , groups or individuals, on becoming a member or in an auxiliary unit will now be considered into our ranks regardless of their religious beliefs. We expect nothing less than 100% loyalty to our Nation and when called to action , represent the Aryan Nation and roll with the mc regardless of affiliations. . . .
>
> The noble Aryan Nations Ssmc, like the phoenix, has risen out of the ash of blood, honor and victory of our forefathers, not in the same fashion, but in the ideological sense. Something the traditional mc's and white power world do not practice today. . . .
>
> The agenda of the Aryan Nations Sadistic Souls mc is to use its updated tactics and strategies to further our goal "Total Aryan Victory"! (Sadistic Souls MC)

Sadistic Souls MC founder Michael McGiffen has a long history with white supremacism. After leaving the Ku Klux Klan, McGiffen formed "the New Order," "an infamous white supremacist domestic terrorist group that was destroyed by law enforcement in 1984" (Morlin). In 1998, McGiffen and five others were arrested on federal weapons charges when it was discovered that the New Order intended to "blow up buildings, poison the water supply of major cities, murder a federal judge and other people, and rob banks and armored cars" (Morlin). Among those individuals found on the New Order hit list were "film-maker Steven Spielberg, then-Federal Reserve Chairman Alan Greenspan, and Southern Poverty Law Center co-founder Morris Dees" (Morlin).

Sadistic Souls MC broke its brief alliance with Aryan Nations (AN) after Morris Gulett, AN's leader, chastised SS-MC bikers who did not conform to the "military-style dress code of Aryan Nations" (Morlin). Rather, Gulett asserted:

> The guys from the motorcycle club wanted to just wear their vests and jeans as their uniform, plus they seemed to want to spend a lot of time drinking beer, posting photos of themselves on social networks such as Facebook wearing the Aryan Nations standard on their vests, flipping the bird and using four letter words that are unsuitable for any Aryan's conversation. (Morlin)

The "final straw for Gulett came when he found" that "McGiffen's daughter has African Americans as 'friends' on her Facebook page and that his son, Sadistic Souls member Damien M. McGiffen, is the father of a multiracial son" (Morlin). McGiffen did not refute the claim that he had a mixed race grandson, saying only that his son "does pay child support because the courts make him, but I ain't never f—ed with that kid" (Lenz and Wood).

Recent concerns expressed by white supremacists focus on SS-MC's tendency to admit members who do not conform to Aryan Nations' original notion of Christian adherents. As noted by SS-MC:

> There are multiple groups that claim status of the original AN which could not be further from the truth. We believe that religion cannot control the destiny of our folk and to be part of the Aryan Nations SSMC you may be Identity, Christian separatist, Creator, Odinist, or plain NS [National Socialist]. We will not turn good brothers down in our order due to theological issues. (Lenz and Wood)

See also: Aryan Nations; Ku Klux Klan; Neo-Nazis; New Order; White Supremacist Movement

FURTHER READING

Anti-Defamation League. September 20, 2012. "One-Time Domestic Terrorist Now Leads White Supremacist Biker Gang." https://www.adl.org/blog/one-time-domestic-terrorist-now-leads-white-supremacist-biker-gang. (Accessed June 8, 2018.)

Kramp, Kayleigh. September 4, 2015. "Sadistic Souls Motorcycle Club: Neo-Nazi Organization." Prezi. https://prezi.com/1crbiwassiyf/sadistic-souls-motorcycle-club/. (Accessed June 8, 2018.)

Lenz, Ryan, and Laurie Wood. October 12, 2016. "Ahead of Black & Silver Solution Fall Conference, Questions Linger about Leadership." Southern Poverty Law Center: Hatewatch. https://www.splcenter.org/hatewatch/2016/10/12/ahead-black-silver-solution-fall-conference-questions-linger-about-leadership. (Accessed June 8, 2018.)

Morlin, Bill. January 27, 2014. "Squabbling Aryan Nations Factions Descend into Vicious Name Calling." Southern Poverty Law Center: Hatewatch. https://www.splcenter.org/hatewatch/2014/01/27/squabbling-aryan-nations-factions-descend-vicious-name-calling. (Accessed June 8, 2018.)

Sadistic Souls MC. "About." Sadistic Souls MC. https://www.sadisticsoulsmc.org/about.html. (Accessed June 8, 2018.)

Sicarii 1715

Sicarii 1715 is a "racist fringe religious group of a larger movement known as the Black Hebrew Israelites" (Anti-Defamation League). Like the Black Hebrew Israelites, Sicarii 1715 believes that "African Americans, Hispanics, Latinos, and Native Americans are the Hebrew Israelites of the Bible" (Exodus 1715). The group maintains "that white people are agents of Satan, Jews are liars and false worshipers of God, and blacks are the true 'chosen people'" (Anti-Defamation League). The Southern Poverty Law Center (SPLC) has designated Sicarii 1715 as "a black nationalist hate group" (Southern Poverty Law Center, 2017). According to the SPLC, the black nationalist movement

> is a reaction to centuries of institutionalized white supremacy in America. Black nationalists believe the answer to white racism is to form separate institutions—or even a separate nation—for black people. Most forms of black nationalism are strongly anti-white and anti-Semitic. Some religious versions assert that black people are the biblical "chosen people" of God. (Southern Poverty Law Center, Black Nationalist)

Sicarii takes its name from an extremist breakaway sect of the Jewish Zealots, "who engaged in extremist activities to resist the Roman Empire during the First Century" (Anti-Defamation League). The group is predominantly based in San Diego, California, but can also be found in the state of Washington as well as in inland areas of California (Southern Poverty Law Center, 2017). As with that of the Black Hebrew Israelites, "the Sicarii symbol features the Star of David, and members often wear costume-like garb resembling that worn by the Jewish High Priest (the chief religious official) in the ancient Holy Temple during the Roman times" (Anti-Defamation League). According to the Anti-Defamation League (ADL), the Sicarii "justify their hateful rhetoric with an alternative interpretation of the Old and New Testaments. They twist various biblical verses to fit their worldview through a Hebrew Israelite lens" (Anti-Defamation League). A range of groups have been targeted by the Sicarii's offensive beliefs:

Women

> The Sicarii believe women should assume a subservient role to men. Married women must ask for permission from their husbands before participating in Sicarii activities or asking questions during Sicarii events.

Jews

> The Sicarii promote a number of anti-Semitic views, including the belief that Jews "stole" the Hebrew Israelites' identity as the "chosen people" and are part of a master conspiracy to control the world. In one YouTube video the Sicarii note, "You're damn right that there's an international Jewish conspiracy. You're the richest goddamn devils on the earth."
>
> They are also Holocaust deniers, arguing that the Jewish people "staged the Holocaust and did it just to steal the land [of Israel]."

Caucasians

> The Sicarii believe Bible references to the "wicked" are actually allusions to white people, whom they refer to as "the devil."

Muslims

Despite borrowing some elements from observant Muslim practice, including the dress code for female members, the Sicarii are Islamaphobic, believe that "Mohammed was a false prophet" and promote conspiracy theories that the Quran endorses pedophilia. One meme on their social media pages includes this call to arms: "All-out war on Islam has been declared. Qam yasharahla [arise Israel]."

LGBT

The Sicarii condemned the U.S. legalization of same-sex marriage in 2015, citing traditional Bible verses which frown upon homosexuality. Sicarii consider homosexuality a "wicked" act.

"You're the vile of the earth. You're sick; you promote all types of sexual deviance and debauchery . . . you're a vile creature."

America

The Sicarii harbor extreme anti-American sentiments, and blame the U.S. for slavery and white supremacist ideology. They frequently refer to America as a modern-day Babylon (possibly conflating that city with the morally corrupt Sodom and Gomorrah). One of their videos includes the line, "The Russians are going to destroy America . . . we rejoice at this fact." (Anti-Defamation League)

Sicarii 1715 hosts a public radio show with the tagline "We are the Revolution." On one particular episode, the group spoke of "Guerilla Warfare" and bringing "an offering of Black power and an array of other topics from an Israelite perspective" (Sicarii 1715). According to the Anti-Defamation League, Sicarii 1715 "spread their message of hate online, and maintain several active YouTube pages where they post lectures and footage from their demonstrations" (Anti-Defamation League).

See also: Black Hebrew Israelites; Black Muslims; Black Nationalism; Black Separatists; Israelite Church of God in Jesus Christ

FURTHER READING

Anti-Defamation League. August 3, 2017. "Sicarii Black Hebrew Israelites: Spouting Hate in Southern California." Anti-Defamation League. https://www.adl.org/blog /sicarii-black-hebrew-israelites-spouting-hate-in-southern-california. (Accessed June 21, 2018.)

Exodus 1715. "The Truth." Exodus 1715. https://www.exodus1715.org/the-truth. (Accessed June 21, 2018.)

Sicarii 1715. "Sicarii 1715—We Are the Revolution." Sicarii 1715. https://www.facebook .com/events/1903941059892832/. (Accessed June 21, 2018.) http://www.blogtalkradio .com/dothaknowledgeradio/2017/04/03/sicarii-1715-we-are-the-revolution. (Accessed June 21, 2018.)

SistaBrutha. January 21, 2018. "Black Separatists Lead the Nation in the Number of Hate Groups." SistaBrutha. https://sistabrutha.com/southern-poverty-law-center-black -separatist-groups-hate-groups/. (Accessed June 18, 2018.)

Southern Poverty Law Center. "Black Nationalist." Southern Poverty Law Center. https:// www.splcenter.org/fighting-hate/extremist-files/ideology/black-nationalist. (Accessed June 21, 2018.)

Southern Poverty Law Center. February 15, 2017. "Active Hate Groups 2016." Southern Poverty Law Center: Intelligence Report. https://www.splcenter.org/fighting-hate /intelligence-report/2017/active-hate-groups-2016. (Accessed June 21, 2018.)

Social Contract Press

The Social Contract Press (TSCP) "routinely publishes race-baiting articles penned by white nationalists" (Southern Poverty Law Center, Social Contract Press). TSCP has

> propagated the myth that Latino activists want to occupy and "reclaim" the American Southwest, argued that no Muslim immigrants should be allowed into the U.S., and claimed that multiculturalists are trying to replace "successful Euro-American culture" with "dysfunctional Third World cultures." (Southern Poverty Law Center, Social Contract Press)

TSCP was founded in 1990 by John Tanton, "the racist founder and principal ideologue of the modern nativist movement. TSCP puts an academic veneer of legitimacy over what are essentially racist arguments about the inferiority of today's immigrants" (Southern Poverty Law Center, Social Contract Press). The Southern Poverty Law Center (SPLC) has called Tanton the "racist architect of the modern anti-immigrant movement" (Southern Poverty Law Center, John Tanton). Tanton is best known "as the founder of the Federation for American Immigration Reform (FAIR)," which has been called "the most influential organization in the country on immigration" (Southern Poverty Law Center, John Tanton). The SPLC points out that the "organized anti-immigration movement is almost entirely the handiwork" of Tanton. Besides FAIR, Tanton has either funded or founded a dozen other groups devoted to anti-immigration policies (Southern Poverty Law Center, John Tanton). Among these are the "American Immigration Control Foundation, the American Patrol/Voices of Citizens Together, the California Coalition for Immigration Reform, Californians for Population Stabilization, the Center for Immigration Studies, NumbersUSA, Population-Environment Balance, Pro English, ProjectUSA, The Social Contract Press, U.S. English, and U.S. Inc." (Southern Poverty Law Center, John Tanton's Network). Many of Tanton's organizations, including FAIR, have received funds from the "Pioneer Fund, a white supremacist organization dedicated to perpetuating 'race betterment' through the support of quasi-scientific studies regarding race and eugenics" (Beirich, 2009). Tanton has also been linked to neo-Nazi causes and has stated that "for European-American society and culture to persist requires a European-American majority, and a clear one at that" (Beirich, 2009).

Tanton's white nationalist views first came to light in 1988 "when a series of memos he wrote to FAIR were leaked to the press." In these, Tanton complained of the "Latin onslaught" of American society. Tanton's group, U.S. English, was already active at that time, and it "opposed bilingualism in public schools and government agencies." However, his writings also bring to light his associations "with Holocaust deniers, former Ku Klux Klan (KKK) lawyers, and leading members of the white nationalist movement" (Southern Poverty Law Center, John Tanton).

Over the years, TSCP has published several journal articles that have praised Euro-American culture and decried the "unwarranted hatred and fear of white and white culture" that Tanton blames on an "emphasis on multiculturalism in the United States," particularly as it has been pressed by immigrant groups (Southern Poverty Law Center, John Tanton).

In 1994, TSCP became infamous for its republication of the racist novel *The Camp of Saints*, which describes

> "swarthy hordes" of Indian immigrants who take over France, send white women to "a whorehouse for Hindus" and engage in a grotesque orgy of men, women and children. The immigrants are described as "monsters," "grotesque little beggars from the streets of Calcutta" and worse. (Southern Poverty Law Center, 2001)

Despite its subject matter, Tanton claims that he was "honored" to publish such an important text. The novel has been likened to *The Turner Diaries*, a key polemic of the American white supremacist and white nationalist movements.

TSCP publishes articles by white nationalists and propagates the "Aztlán conspiracy theory that holds that immigrants come to the United States not to work, but to colonize" (Southern Poverty Law Center, Social Contract Press). In 1998, TSCP "released a particularly racist special issue entitled 'Europhobia: The Hostility toward European-Descended Americans'" (Southern Poverty Law Center, Social Contract Press). The lead article "argued that 'multiculturalism' was replacing 'successful Euro-American culture' with 'dysfunctional Third World cultures'" (Southern Poverty Law Center, Social Contract Press). In 2010, TSCP's fall issue was entitled "The Menace of Islam." The issue warned against "a conspiracy to enact Islamic law in the United States" and intimated that "Muslim immigrants should be seen as a 'Trojan horse,' a group of people who are stealthily attempting to infiltrate and destroy the United States" (Southern Poverty Law Center, Social Contract Press).

See also: Federation for American Immigration Reform; Holocaust Denial; Neo-Nazis; Pioneer Fund; White Nationalism; White Supremacist Movement

FURTHER READING

Beirich, Heidi. November 30, 2008. "John Tanton's Private Papers Expose More Than 20 Years of Hate." Southern Poverty Law Center: Intelligence Report. https://www.splcenter.org/fighting-hate/intelligence-report/2008/john-tanton's-private-papers-expose-more-20-years-hate. (Accessed June 15, 2018.)

Beirich, Heidi. January 31, 2009. "The Nativist Lobby: Three Faces of Intolerance." Southern Poverty Law Center. https://www.splcenter.org/20090201/nativist-lobby-three-faces-intolerance. (Accessed June 15, 2018.)

Hatewatch Staff. November 4, 2015. "The Social Contract Press, Defended by Kris Kobach, Has a Decades-Old History of Hate." Southern Poverty Law Center: Hatewatch. https://www.splcenter.org/hatewatch/2015/11/04/social-contract-press-defended-kris-kobach-has-decades-old-history-hate. (Accessed June 15, 2018.)

Social Contract Press. "About the Social Contract." Social Contract Press. http://www.thesocialcontract.com/info/about_the_social_contract.html. (Accessed June 15, 2018.)

Southern Poverty Law Center. "John Tanton." Southern Poverty Law Center. https://www.splcenter.org/fighting-hate/extremist-files/individual/john-tanton. (Accessed June 15, 2018.)

Southern Poverty Law Center. "John Tanton's Network." Southern Poverty Law Center. https://www.splcenter.org/fighting-hate/intelligence-report/2015/john-tantons-network. (Accessed June 15, 2018.)

Southern Poverty Law Center. "The Social Contract Press." Southern Poverty Law Center. https://www.splcenter.org/fighting-hate/extremist-files/group/social-contract-press. (Accessed June 15, 2018.)

Southern Poverty Law Center. March 21, 2001. "Racist Book, Camp of the Saints, Gains in Popularity." Southern Poverty Law Center: Intelligence Report. https://www.splcenter.org/fighting-hate/intelligence-report/2001/racist-book-camp-saints-gains-popularity. (Accessed June 15, 2018.)

Soldiers of the Cross Training Institute

The Soldiers of the Cross (SOTC) Training Institute is designated by the Southern Poverty Law Center (SPLC) as a Ku Klux Klan (KKK) hate group. According to the SPLC, the Ku Klux Klan is the "oldest and most infamous of American hate groups. Although black Americans have typically been the Klan's primary target, it also has attacked Jews, immigrants, gays and lesbians and, until recently, Catholics" (Southern Poverty Law Center, Ku Klux Klan). The SOTC Training Institute was founded in 2013 by Thomas Robb, a Christian Identity pastor based in Arkansas who is also the "head of the Knights of the Ku Klux Klan (KKKK), a group he took over after the departure of David Duke" (Southern Poverty Law Center, Thomas Robb). Robb espouses racist and anti-Semitic ideals as an adherent of Christian Identity, a pseudoreligious theology that teaches that Jews are the offspring of Eve and Satan. Robb's ministry is clear in its belief that whites are the chosen people. The mission statement of Robb's ministry reads:

> We believe that the Anglo-Saxon, Germanic, Scandinavian, and kindred people are THE people of the Bible—God's separated and anointed Israel. We do not hold that this implies the white race is especially holy or perfect, without fault or blame. However, it does mean that we have a great responsibility for imparting Christianity throughout the world, to assist in ushering in the Kingdom (government) of God (here on earth as it is in Heaven) and for following all of the Biblical guidelines in both the Old and New Testaments thereby providing an example to those not of our racial heritage to follow and enabling them to prosper.
>
> For the mission God has bestowed upon His chosen people, the white race, he requires their separation. They must honor their heritage—not despise it. Other races must honor their heritage as well. In a well ordered world—this is God's way. (Thomas Robb Ministries)

In the aftermath of Barack Obama's election in 2008, Robb predicted a "race war . . . between our people, who I see as the rightful owners and leaders of this great country, and their people, the blacks" (Southern Poverty Law Center, Thomas Robb). In the summer of 2013, Robb founded the SOTC Training Institute, "dedicated to instilling the tools to become actively involved in the 'struggle for our racial redemption' in both young and old campers" (Brantley). The camp was dubbed "Klan Kamp" by the SPLC, as its "faculty" included notable white supremacists, white nationalists, and neo-Nazis (Hatewatch staff). On the SOTC Training Institute website's "Vision" section, the group states:

> [D]eath . . . is what we can expect as the non white floods into our country. It is estimated that 100 million non whites will land on the welcome mat of America's front door over the next 30 years.
>
> And they are hungry!
>
> Is dinner ready?
>
> Most white people, still don't get it! It is difficult for them to wrap their brain around the concept and what it will mean for their children or their grandchildren. Their sensitivity has been made numb by television, schools and the church which has convinced them that it really doesn't matter. This mass deception has thoroughly penetrated and corrupted the ability for critical thinking causing people to repeat inane nonsense as if it were the Wisdom of Solomon.
>
> "Diversity is our Strength"
>
> "Guns cause violence"
>
> "There is no such thing as race." (SOTC Training Institute)

But the SOTC offers hope:

> Demographers have shown us that there is a migration of white people moving into the heartland of America. Do you understand that we are seeing the rebirth of our nation. This is going to continue over the next 20 or 30 years. We are seeing this current corrupt system steadily decay. Morally, politically and financially it is not sustainable. That is the reason why I am so excited about the opportunities this school [the SOTC Training Institute] is going to provide, allowing us to grasp the challenge which has been given us. (SOTC Training Institute)

See also: Christian Identity; Knights of the Ku Klux Klan; Ku Klux Klan; Neo-Nazis; White Nationalism; White Supremacist Movement

FURTHER READING

Brantley, Max. June 21, 2013. "'Klan Kamp': Thomas Robb's Training Program for White Supremacists in the Arkansas Ozarks." *Arkansas Times*. https://www.arktimes .com/ArkansasBlog/archives/2013/06/21/klan-kamp-thomas-robbs-training -program-for-white-supremacists-in-the-arkansas-ozarks. (Accessed June 15, 2018.)

Hatewatch Staff. June 17, 2013. "Teaching Intolerance: 'Klan Kamp' to Open in Ozarks." Southern Poverty Law Center: Hatewatch. https://www.splcenter.org/hatewatch /2013/06/17/teaching-intolerance-%E2%80%98klan-kamp%E2%80%99-open -ozarks. (Accessed June 15, 2018.)

Johnson, Daryl. September 25, 2017. "Hate in God's Name." https://www.splcenter .org/20170925/hate-god%E2%80%99s-name. (Accessed June 15, 2018.)

SOTC Training Institute. "Vision." SOTC Training Institute. https://sotctraininginstitute .com/vision/. (Accessed June 15, 2018.)

Southern Poverty Law Center. "Ku Klux Klan." Southern Poverty Law Center. https:// www.splcenter.org/fighting-hate/extremist-files/ideology/ku-klux-klan. (Accessed June 15, 2018.)

Southern Poverty Law Center. "Thomas Robb." https://www.splcenter.org/fighting-hate /extremist-files/individual/thomas-robb. (Accessed June 15, 2018.)

Southern Poverty Law Center. March 2, 2015. "Active Ku Klux Klan Groups." Southern Poverty Law Center: Intelligence Report. https://www.splcenter.org/fighting-hate/intelligence-report/2015/active-ku-klux-klan-groups. (Accessed June 15, 2018.)

Thomas Robb Ministries. "Our Mission." Thomas Robb Ministries. http://www.christian identitychurch.net/our_mission.htm. (Accessed April 1, 2017.)

Southern European Aryans League Army

The Southern European Aryans League (SEAL) Army was a short-lived hate group that emerged in Muncie, Indiana, in 2012–2013. The group was characterized by the Southern Poverty Law Center (SPLC) as a white nationalist hate group in 2013. According to the SPLC:

> Adherents of white nationalist groups believe that white identity should be the organizing principle of the countries that make up Western civilization. White nationalists advocate for policies to reverse changing demographics and the loss of an absolute, white majority. Ending non-white immigration, both legal and illegal, is an urgent priority—frequently elevated over other racist projects, such as ending multiculturalism and miscegenation—for white nationalists seeking to preserve white, racial hegemony. (Southern Poverty Law Center, White Nationalist)

The SEAL Army was the brainchild of Dustin Victory, the self-proclaimed "Don" of what he envisioned as a white supremacist street gang that would roam the streets of Muncie, Indiana. It is unclear whether the SEAL Army ever had any members other than Victory. On his personal blog, Victory stated his intentions in founding the SEAL Army (all grammar and spelling mistakes are maintained from the original post):

> I am the founder of the Southern European Aryans League Army in Muncie Indiana. I'm a White Nationalist, I stand for white pride and white right's. I don't stand for Gay Marrage, Abortions, Interracial dating nor race mixing. I believe in white separation from Black's, Jew's, Gay's, Mexican's, Interracial's cause they are inferior to the white race. I do not stand for violence but how ever I do support self defense. I support freedom of speech and expression and don't care if your offended by what I have to say, if you don't like what I say then don't read it or read it and be offended your choice. (Victory)

From a short-lived website of the SEAL Army, Victory posted another, more explicit, racist rant (again, all grammar and spelling mistakes are maintained from the original):

> Fighting The Liberal Jew propaganda
> The main enemy to the S.E.A.L. Army is the liberal's. they are in the school system and in the media. they teach our kid's Tolerance. what is Tolerance. Tolerance is a program that focuses on minority interest, meaning n—, k—, f— & etc. they teach it in schools and in the communitys. what they are doing is preaching white guild. no wonder why our white youth of today are a shamed of being proud of there white heritage and all the achievements that our race have's accomplished. to the mission to the moon and into space and back again not to mention the people behind the apolo missions where all white. tolerance don't want you to be proud of who you are. they want you to kiss the minority's a— for slavery and the holocaust

witch none of us had no part in. they lower our young womens self esteem by all the intellectual lies that seem real. they show a n— kid in Africa that's starving to death and want you to feel sorry for them when they can stop it them self by not breeding inless they can support them. we show no pity for homless or the starving people, there are jobs that you can get to make it in this jew controled economy. at the end who makes the profit? the jew b—. if you fall into there lie's then be prepared to have all your money sucked out of you and your pride and honor that you once had will be demolished. ya we are racist because we are proud to be white and face reverse racism every day by brain washed whites, n—,jews etc. they make us hate them more and more every day!

WE DON'T LIKE S— FORCED ON US!!!!!!!! (Anti-Racist Action)

The SEAL Army does not appear to be active after 2013 and has disappeared from the SPLC's annual Hatewatch lists.

See also: White Nationalism; White Supremacist Movement

FURTHER READING

Anti-Racist Action. "Dustin Victory and the Southern European Aryan League Army." Anti-Racist Action. https://antiracistaction.org/dustin-victory-and-the-southern-european-aryan-league-army/. (Accessed July 24, 2018.)

Southern Poverty Law Center. "The Groups." https://www.splcenter.org/sites/default/files/the_groups_2013.pdf. (Accessed July 24, 2018.)

Southern Poverty Law Center. "White Nationalist." Southern Poverty Law Center. https://www.splcenter.org/fighting-hate/extremist-files/ideology/white-nationalist. (Accessed July 24, 2018.)

Victory, Dustin. April 24, 2013. "Who I Am." Dustin Victory. https://dustinvictory.word press.com/. (Accessed July 24, 2018.)

Zehner, Aaron. March 24,2013. "DotTeeVee: Southern European Aryans League Army." Paperback Hero. http://paperbackheroaaron.blogspot.com/2013/03/dotteevee-southern-european-aryans.html. (Accessed July 24, 2018.)

Southern National Congress

The Southern National Congress (SNC) is designated by the Southern Poverty Law Center (SPLC) as "a neo-Confederate hate group." According to the SPLC:

"Neo-Confederacy" refers to a reactionary, revisionist predilection for symbols of the Confederate States of America (CSA), typically paired with a strong belief in the validity of the failed doctrines of nullification and secession—in the specific context of the antebellum South—which rose to prominence in the late 20th and early 21st centuries.

Neo-Confederacy also incorporates advocacy of traditional gender roles, is hostile toward democracy, strongly opposes homosexuality and exhibits an understanding of race that favors segregation and suggests white supremacy. (Southern Poverty Law Center, Neo-Confederate)

The SNC was founded in McDonough, Georgia, on March 5, 2005. The participants in the 2005 SNC Committee adopted the following resolution, which formally established the SNC:

Whereas no legitimate voice exists for the Southern people in politics, economics, culture, nor society;

Whereas the Southern people have lost control of our lives and our futures, as well as those of our children, and no institution exists to restore our independence and liberty;

Whereas we deplore that race has been used, and is used today, to divide the Southern people and to prevent us from working together to decide our own destiny;

Whereas the Southern people have a God-given right to preserve our unique and valuable way of life, which stands in danger of extinction;

Be it resolved, therefore, that we, citizens of the several Southern States here assembled, in order to convene and support a Southern National Congress as the legitimate, representative voice for Southern interests and grievances, do hereby constitute the Southern National Congress Committee, so help us God. (Dixie Outfitters)

The SNC has chapters in Alabama, Arkansas, Florida, Georgia, Kentucky, Louisiana, Maryland, Missouri, Mississippi, North Carolina, South Carolina, Tennessee, Texas, and Virginia. These states represent all of the original 11 members of the Confederacy, plus the border states of Kentucky, Missouri, and Maryland. According to its website, the Southern National Congress

is a deliberative body designed to provide Southerners with a forum to voice their authentic concerns regarding the South's continued cultural life, prosperity, and distinctive existence. The Southern National Congress provides a means of expressing Southern goals, grievances, and solutions, in an open manner not presently existing anywhere else in the public sphere. This is being accomplished within a framework conducive to the complete independence for our southern States. (Southern National Congress)

In 2008, Thomas Moore, chairperson of the Southern National Congress, explained:

It's abundantly clear to anyone not sunk deep in denial or who is not a shill for the Washington regime that today's political system does not represent the American people or the national interests. It doesn't obey the Constitution, the law, decency, or common sense. The regime has riveted the attention of the people on the raucous Presidential contest between Republicans and Democrats. But this race is a charade, and the supposed two-party system is an illusion. In reality, there is only one party—the party of the lawless, corrupt, centralized state. The GOP and Democrats don't represent real alternatives, they are merely rivals for power fighting over who gets the spoils. Both major parties and their principal candidates have prostituted themselves to Big Government, special interests, the money cartel, and corporate oligarchs. Whichever candidate wins will not even slow, much less halt, America's steady decline into an empire that is 'aggressive abroad and despotic at home,' in the prophetic words of Robert E. Lee. None of the leading candidates or parties respects the South and our particular culture, values, and interests. They only use us as cannon fodder for their endless wars and as political fodder for their cynical campaigns. We Southerners need to begin to take responsibility for our own welfare, and that's the purpose of the SNC. (Dixie Outfitters)

In the past, the SNC has been closely aligned with the League of the South (LOS), another neo-Confederate hate group that "has been obsessively driven to glorify Southern history and culture, pining for the independence denied the region by federal troops 150 years ago" (Smith and Lenz). According to the SPLC, "The League of the South is a neo-Confederate group that advocates for a second Southern secession and a society dominated by 'European Americans.' The league believes the 'godly' nation it wants to form should be run by an 'Anglo-Celtic' (read: white) elite" (Southern Poverty Law Center, League of the South). LOS has supported SNC's goal of "advancing a new [path to] secession to political means" (Smith and Lenz).

In 2013, two Tennessee Republican state legislators were scheduled to speak at an SNC annual conference. State Rep. Judd Matheny, R-Tullahoma, was scheduled to speak at the SNC event but withdrew after investigating SNC's goals. Matheny wrote in the *Nashville Post*, "I found out they were the wrong kind of freedom group and cancelled when I researched them further" (Zelinski). Upon hearing of Matheny's withdrawal, Occidental Dissent, a blog devoted to white nationalism and other right-wing extremist views, stated that "the moral of the story is don't waste your time supporting Republican politicians. They only diminish us and weaken us. They are not going to do anything for us. They are just going to reinforce our marginalization" (Wallace).

See also: League of the South; Neo-Confederates; White Nationalism; White Supremacist Movement

FURTHER READING

Confederate Wave. "The Southern National Congress." Confederate Wave. http://confederatewave.org/wave/2005/southern.nationl.congress.php. (Accessed July 26, 2018.)

Dixie Outfitters. December 5, 2008. "Southern National Congress Committee Announces Plan to Convene First Southern National Congress in December 2008." Dixie Outfitters. https://dixieoutfitters.com/2015/04/04/1st-southern-national-congress/. (Accessed July 26, 2018.)

Smith, Janet, and Ryan Lenz. November 15, 2011. "League of the South Rhetoric Turns to Arms." Southern Poverty Law Center: Intelligence Report. https://www.splcenter.org/fighting-hate/intelligence-report/2011/league-south-rhetoric-turns-arms. (Accessed July 26, 2018.)

Southern National Congress. "What Is the Southern National Congress?" Southern National Congress. http://www.thesnc.org/www.thesnc.org/WHAT_-_a_Southern_voice/index.html. (Accessed July 26, 2018.)

Southern Poverty Law Center. "League of the South." Southern Poverty Law Center. https://www.splcenter.org/fighting-hate/extremist-files/group/league-south. (Accessed July 26, 2018.)

Southern Poverty Law Center. "Neo-Confederate." Southern Poverty Law Center. https://www.splcenter.org/fighting-hate/extremist-files/ideology/neo-confederate. (Accessed July 26, 2018.)

Southern Poverty Law Center. March 2, 2015. "Active Neo-Confederate Groups." Southern Poverty Law Center: Intelligence Report. https://www.splcenter.org/fighting-hate/intelligence-report/2015/active-neo-confederate-groups. (Accessed July 26, 2018.)

Southern Poverty Law Center. February 15, 2017. "Active Hate Groups 2016." Southern Poverty Law Center: Intelligence Report. https://www.splcenter.org/fighting-hate/intelligence-report/2017/active-hate-groups-2016. (Accessed July 26, 2018.)

Wallace, Hunter. October 31, 2013. "Southern National Congress Fiasco." Occidental Dissent.   http://www.occidentaldissent.com/2013/10/31/southern-national-congress
-fiasco/. (Accessed July 26, 2018.)
Zelinski, Andrea. "Matheny Bails from Speaking to Alleged Hate Group." *Nashville Post*.
https://www.nashvillepost.com/politics/blog/20472835/matheny-bails-from
-speaking-to-alleged-hate-group-niceley-still-in. (Accessed July 26, 2018.)

Southern Nationalist Network

The Southern Nationalist Network (SNN) is a defunct white nationalist organization that was active in the United States for a few years during the mid-2010s but
apparently ceased to exist around 2015. In May 2015, the blog Anti-Neo-Confederate announced that the SNN's website, www.southernnationalist.com, had shut
down. The individual who posted the news regarding the website's demise stated:

> Over these past 5 years demonstrations have been held to rally folks to the idea of
> independence for Dixie. Many people have become serious Southern nationalists.
> Due to this rise in activity SNN will be shutting down; in order to begin a new
> phase that will inspire even more folks to get involved in the movement.
> (Anti-Neo-Confederate)

The Anti-Neo-Confederate group questioned why a "rise in activity" would neces-
sitate the shutting down of a website. An alternative explanation was that "the SNN
wasn't going anywhere," as photos of SNN demonstrations showed that "there
aren't a lot of people at the demonstrations" (Anti-Neo-Confederate).

To date, no comparable website or group has stepped in to fill the gap left by the
dissolution of SNN. In 2013, Michael Cushman, one of SNN's primary spokes-
people during the time of its existence, granted an interview to *ZeroGov* on the
issue of "Defending Dixie." When asked "What is SNN?" Cushman replied:

> Southern Nationalist Network is a website and multi-media effort which promotes
> Southern identity and independence. We have made hundreds of videos (which
> have nearly a million views on YouTube) and a couple dozen podcast interviews
> (this is a project we started fairly recently). We've organized and recorded perhaps
> a dozen or so secession demonstrations and marches in South Carolina and Geor-
> gia. We have a community of several hundred people on Facebook that we started
> about a year ago. And we also sell stickers, wristbands and T-shirts which promote
> our message. . . .
> This effort is made relatively easy for us as Southern nationalists given the the-
> ory and influence of Southern decentralists like Thomas Jefferson and proto-Aus-
> trian Southerners like John C Calhoun. (ZeroGov)

Later, Cushman was asked, "What does the culture and history of the South and
the Confederacy have to do with today?" Cushman responded:

> Some people refer to SNN as a 'neo-Confederate' site. I don't see it that way. We do
> publish many stories which relate in one way or another to the 1860s (especially
> given that this part of our heritage is constantly under attack), but our goal is not to
> bring back the government of the Confederate States of America. As Southern
> nationalists we look at the full scope of Southern history over the four centuries of
> our existence. We even trace it back beyond this, exploring the Anglo-Celtic origins

of Southern culture. The heritage side of things is just one aspect of the site and by no means all we do. The bulk of what we do is try to de-legitimize the US Empire and make our message relevant to people today. But we are inspired by our heritage and the great heroes of our past. It's impossible not to be inspired by such men of virtue and natural nobility as Robert E Lee, Thomas Jackson and Jefferson Davis. These were men who would have been exceptional in any time and place. Their character and resistance to outside domination will hopefully continue to inspire future generations of Southerners far into the distant future. (ZeroGov)

Finally, when asked about the element of racism associated with any group that longs to resurrect the Confederacy and promote the secession of Southern states from the United States, Cushman replied:

> The attempt to make the traditional Southerner into a Nazi-like symbol is a relatively new thing. Until the 1960s there was still some respect in American culture for the South despite our history of opposition. . . .
>
> My most typical reaction these days to this question is to point out that 'racist' is simply a slur the Left uses for anyone who disagrees with them. Sadly, even the Establishment Right has embraced this sort of language, often making the charge that 'The liberals are the real racists!' I think it has lost much of its power due to attempts to label practically everyone with this term. I look forward to the day when this word no longer holds any power to silence discussion or cause people to cower in fear. . . .
>
> My view is that radical de-centralisation is the best answer to the race issue as it is the best answer to most political issues. It is my hope that in a future free South the various historic cultural and ethnic communities can live in harmony by controlling their affairs independently from outside interference or centralised rule. (ZeroGov)

Currently, the Southern Nationalist Network does not appear on any of the Southern Poverty Law Center's (SPLC) active hate group lists.

See also: League of the South; Neo-Confederates; White Nationalism; White Supremacist Movement

FURTHER READING

Anti-Neo-Confederate. May 8, 2015. "Southern Nationalist Network Website Is Supposedly Shut Down Because It Is Claimed That It Has Been a Big Success." Anti-Neo-Confederate. http://newtknight.blogspot.com/2015/05/southern-nationalist-network-website-is.html#.W1tgN8InbRZ. (Accessed July 27, 2018.)

Atlanta Antifascists. January 18, 2017. "Updates on January 28th White Nationalist 'Atlanta Forum.'" Atlanta Antifascists. https://afainatl.wordpress.com/tag/southern-nationalist-network/. (Accessed July 27, 2018.)

Beirich, Heidi. August 21, 2013. "League of the South to Protest 'Southern Demographic Displacement.'" Southern Poverty Law Center: Hatewatch. https://www.splcenter.org/hatewatch/2013/08/21/league-south-protest-%E2%80%9Csouthern-demographic-displacement%E2%80%9D. (Accessed July 27, 2018.)

Confederate Catholics. https://catholicconservatives.wordpress.com/tag/southern-nationalist-network/. (Accessed July 27, 2018.)

League of the South. http://leagueofthesouth.com/. (Accessed July 27, 2018.)

Southern Nationalist Network. "Southern Nationalist Network's Podcast." https://www.podomatic.com/podcasts/snn. (Accessed July 27, 2018.)

Southern Poverty Law Center. "White Nationalist." Southern Poverty Law Center. https://
www.splcenter.org/fighting-hate/extremist-files/ideology/white-nationalist.
(Accessed July 27, 2018.)

ZeroGov. February 28, 2013. "Ten Questions for Michael Cushman of Southern Nationalist Network." ZeroGov. https://zerogov.com/ten-questions-for-michael-cushman
-of-southern-nationalist-network/. (Accessed July 27, 2018.)

Stormfront

Stormfront is the Internet website founded by white supremacist Don Black in 1995. Black, a former grand wizard of the Knights of the Ku Klux Klan, established the site just one month before the Oklahoma City bombing in April 1995. Black had learned computer coding in prison while serving a three-year sentence for plotting to overthrow the Caribbean island government of Dominica in 1981. When he emerged from prison, Black realized the potential for the Internet to be a perfect conduit and purveyor of white supremacist thought and speech. Black believed that white supremacists, and other racist elements, needed a platform free from the mainstream media's "monopoly" on thought and speech, which filtered out the elements of hate sought by Black and other white supremacists. In March 2015, Stormfront celebrated its 20th year of existence and could count over 300,000 registered members in its ranks. As it was from the beginning, Stormfront remains one of the most popular Internet sites where white supremacists and other extremists congregate to share their messages of hate.

From its founding, Don Black envisioned Stormfront to be a "safe place" where extremist thought could be expressed without the stigma that was attached to such sentiments by the mainstream media. Black believed it was important that those with racist beliefs should be free to express themselves and draw hope and inspiration from others with similar feelings. In 1995, the Internet provided the perfect platform where people could express their vitriol from home, free from the backlash that might come if such sentiments were expressed through the general media or in public settings. At first, Stormfront attracted the vilest of individuals, who used every known racial epithet and stereotype to express themselves. However, Don Black, who was friends with and a protégé of David Duke, the former grand imperial wizard of the Knights of the Ku Klux Klan, realized, as did Duke, that such speech very often turned off individuals who might harbor such thoughts but who believed that their public expression weakened their message. Like Duke, Black believed that white supremacy thought must "get out of the cow pasture and into hotel meeting rooms" (Southern Poverty Law Center, Don Black).

Stormfront has grown into "one of the most popular forums for white nationalists and other racial extremists to post articles, engage in discussions, and share news of upcoming racist events" (Southern Poverty Law Center, Stormfront). Since 2008, it has censored explicitly hate-filled posts in an attempt to be more inclusive. It has generally tried to maintain "a relatively nonsectarian stance, making people from different sectors of the radical right feel welcome to join in" (Southern Poverty Law Center, Stormfront). With white nationalism and extremist thought on the rise, it seems certain that Stormfront will continue to gain in popularity as a place on the Internet where extreme racial sentiments will be expressed.

See also: Knights of the Ku Klux Klan; Ku Klux Klan

FURTHER READING

Anti-Defamation League. "Don Black/Stormfront." Anti-Defamation League: Extremism in America. http://archive.adl.org/learn/ext_us/don-black/. (Accessed January 5, 2017.)

Southern Poverty Law Center. "Don Black." Southern Poverty Law Center. https://www.splcenter.org/fighting-hate/extremist-files/individual/don-black. (Accessed January 5, 2017.)

Southern Poverty Law Center. "Stormfront." Southern Poverty Law Center. https://www.splcenter.org/fighting-hate/extremist-files/group/stormfront. (Accessed January 5, 2017.)

Southern Poverty Law Center. March 27, 2015. "Don Black's Stormfront Turns 20." Southern Poverty Law Center: Hatewatch. https://www.splcenter.org/hatewatch/2015/03/27/don-blacks-stormfront-turns-20. (Accessed January 5, 2017.)

Supreme White Alliance

The Supreme White Alliance (SWA) is a virulently "racist skinhead group" based in several Midwestern states. The group was founded in 2007 by racist skinheads from around the United States who were trying to unite the white supremacist movement in the face of changing cultural, social, and political conditions in the United States. In late 2008, two members of SWA were arrested after federal agents uncovered "a plot to go on a multi-state 'killing spree'" (Potok). The pair also planned to assassinate then-candidate Barack Obama, who would later become the first African American president in U.S. history. Members of SWA can often be identified when they hold up "four fingers from one hand and three fingers from the other hand [that] are used to represent the number 43. The gang uses 43 as a numeric symbol because the alphanumeric equivalents of the gang's initials (19 for S, 23 for W, and 1 for A), when added together, equal 43" (Anti-Defamation League, Hand Sign). The SWA makes no apologies for its white supremacist ideology. The group claims to exist "for the Defense of our beloved White Race," wholeheartedly adopting the famous 14-word phrase of former Order member David Lane, who proclaimed, "We must preserve the existence of our people and a future for white children" (Anti-Defamation League, 2008). As evidenced by their fealty to the 14 Words, the SWA is particularly interested in attracting and "saving" young people, as they articulate on their website:

> The youth of today is falling into the hands of the enemy. Not by the enemy that we see each day, but the enemy behind the scenes, the enemy's that sit behind the media and the hidden "One World Order." They pollute our youths minds with corrupt, lies of multicultural, diversity, turning our own kind against us and making the White race out to be America's enemy when in all reality it is they who run America. They are the real enemy. When will our youth wake up and realize this? Today's

youth is our only hope for the future of the white race. Our founding fathers would be sick if they could look at what America has become. Wake up White America. Seek the truth and fight for what is right. (Combat 18)

SWA was formed to bring together "racist skinheads, neo-Nazis, neo-Confederates and other white supremacists under one banner" (Anti-Defamation League, 2008). Josh Steever, a prominent leader of the Aryan Terror Brigade—a group affiliated with SWA—described the organization as an attempt to unite the disparate groups that compose the white supremacist movement. "We have battled with many," reads one SWA statement, "and are tired of the fighting within. So we have decided to build a Club that will no longer be part of others [sic] infighting" (Anti-Defamation League, 2008).

SWA perceive their enemies as consisting mainly of "African-Americans, Hispanics and Jews." One SWA leader declared, "I despise treachery, tyrants and treason in government, and hope we are ALL collectively WAKING UP to the Jewish global White genocidal Conspiracy, while also recognizing the Gentile . . . traitors who Aid and Abet them" [emphasis in original] (Anti-Defamation League, 2008).

In October 2008, two SWA members, Daniel Cowart and Paul Schlesselman, "were arrested after federal agents uncovered a plot" that the two had constructed to go on a "multi-state killing spree" (Potok). According to federal agents, the two "got together and allegedly decided to kill 88 people, followed by beheading another 14 African Americans" (Potok). These numbers—88 and 14—have great significance in white supremacist circles, as 88 stands for HH, or "Heil Hitler," with H being the eighth letter in the alphabet. And 14 represents the 14 Words of convicted Order killer David Lane. In the criminal complaint against Cowart and Schlesselman:

> Officials said they also intended to target a predominantly black high school, a gun store, and individuals who they planned to rob to raise money. The final act, according to the affidavit, was to come when both men dressed in white tuxedoes and top hats and attempted to shoot Obama as they drove toward him while shooting through the windows, agents said. Both men fully expected to die in their final attack. (Potok)

Though SWA members exhibit many of the trappings of traditional skinheads (e.g., prominent tattoos), they understand that these do not always necessarily appeal to younger white supremacists. As they articulate as their strategy to attract followers:

> We of the S.W.A. are modernist (if you will). We respect and believe in the old ways, yet we realize that we live in a new age. As time changes, people change. We recognize that the change of today is for the worst. An age of destruction. Not only for our people but for all races. The world is committing Genocide. Our Western Civilization is falling into the hands of extinction. The White Race is 8% of the world's population. Plain and Clear, we are a dying breed. As children of this modern world, we must adapt to change. If we approach a person who has never encountered a White Separatist, we must approach him as a modern day individual. Not as an 80's Skinhead would have approached a young working class individual. In the 80's the Skinhead scene flourished. The reason being is because they dressed

accordingly and knew the feel of their times. Now as modern day Separatist, we must start a new era of the working class White youth. That is exactly what we plan on doing. (Combat 18)

See also: Aryan Terror Brigade; Neo-Confederates; Neo-Nazis; White Nationalism; White Supremacist Movement

FURTHER READING

Anti-Defamation League. "Supreme White Alliance." Anti-Defamation League. https://www.adl.org/education/references/hate-symbols/supreme-white-alliance. (Accessed May 31, 2018.)

Anti-Defamation League. "Supreme White Alliance (Hand Sign)." Anti-Defamation League. https://www.adl.org/education/references/hate-symbols/supreme-white-alliance-hand-sign. (Accessed May 31, 2018.)

Anti-Defamation League. October 28, 2008. "Supreme White Alliance: An ADL Backgrounder." Anti-Defamation League: Combating Hate. http://adlnational.pub30.convio.net/combating-hate/domestic-extremism-terrorism/c/supreme-white-alliance-an.html#.WxAwTooh3RY. (Accessed May 31, 2018.)

Combat 18. December 23, 2009. "Supreme White Alliance Florida." Combat18florida.blogspot.com. http://combat18florida.blogspot.com/2009/12/supreme-white-alliance-florida.html. (Accessed May 31, 2018.)

Potok, Mark. October 28, 2008. "Alleged Plotter against Obama Was Member of Supreme White Alliance." Southern Poverty Law Center: Hatewatch. https://www.splcenter.org/hatewatch/2008/10/28/alleged-plotter-against-obama-was-member-supreme-white-alliance. (Accessed May 31, 2018.)

T

Three Percenters

The Three Percenters (also styled as 3 Percenters, 3%ers, III%ers, the Three Percenters Club, and the 3 Percenters Movement) is a patriot movement that was created after the election of Barack Obama as president of the United States in 2008. The Three Percenters believed that Obama's elections signaled an ominous shift in American politics that would lead to increasing government interference in individual affairs and, more ominously, a greater push for stricter gun control legislation. The various groups associated with the "3 Percent" movement claim to take their designation from the 3 percent of the total population that "took up arms against the British Empire" during the American Revolution.

The official website of the Three Percenters states:

> The Three Percenter movement started shortly after the attack on the world trade centers. The movement has continued to gain momentum as our federal government grows more powerful. The states are losing control, federal judges are overruling the people, liberals and democrats are determined to disarm citizens, and the political climate is aggressive and leaning towards socialism. Our founding fathers warned us about this with their intentional laws written into the constitution and the bill of rights. Three Percenters are ex and current military, police, and trained civilians that will stand up and fight if our rights are infringed in any way. (Three Percenters Club)

The Three Percenters are a loose coalition of individuals who identify closely with many elements of the patriot and militia movements. Their belief that the government continues to overreach its constitutional limits and that average citizens must take a stand against continued government abuses is a hallmark of this philosophy. As indicated by the Three Percenters, many of their members tend to be former and current military members, as well as police and other law enforcement personnel. Many Three Percenters tend to also be members of the Oath Keepers as well as other anti-government groups. The Three Percenters believe that the "solution" to the current problems in the United States can be found in standing up for and protecting the U.S. Constitution (Three Percenters Club). If the government fails to represent the people, the Three Percenters vow to take action, though they are purposely vague about what such action might be (Three Percenters Club).

See also: Oath Keepers

FURTHER READING

Sunshine, Spencer. January 5, 2016. "Profiles on the Right Three Percenters." Political Research Associates. http://www.politicalresearch.org/2016/01/05/profiles-on-the-right-three-percenters/#sthash.PNMawnEH.dpbs. (Accessed December 13, 2017.)

Three Percenters Club. "About Us." Threepercentersclub.org. http://threepercentersclub
.org/index.php/pages/about-us. (Accessed December 13, 2017.)

Traditional Knights of the Ku Klux Klan

The Traditional Knights of the Ku Klux Klan (TKKKK) are a Ku Klux Klan (KKK)-affiliated hate group based in Braddock Heights, Maryland, with additional chapters located in Youngstown, Ohio, and Philadelphia, Pennsylvania (Southern Poverty Law Center, 2016). According to the Southern Poverty Law Center (SPLC), KKK groups are "the most infamous—and oldest—of American hate groups. Although black Americans have typically been the Klan's primary target, it also has attacked Jews, immigrants, gays and lesbians and, until recently, Catholics" (Southern Poverty Law Center, Ku Klux Klan). The TKKKK made headlines in 2014 and 2015 with protests at the Gettysburg National Military Park and with cross and swastika lightings. By 2016, the TKKKK no longer appeared on the SPLC's Hate Groups list. Apparently, the TKKKK "was another victim of the revolving door which is the state of the modern KKK" in the United States (Anti-Defamation League). According to the Anti-Defamation League (ADL), "More than half of the currently active Klan groups were formed only in the last five years. This is not, as it may first seem, a sign of growth, but rather illustrates how short-lived today's Ku Klux Klan groups actually tend to be" (Anti-Defamation League). While the TKKKK appeared very active during 2014 and 2015, the groups seemingly disappeared very quickly as members drifted away to other extremist groups or quit altogether (Monroe).

The TKKKK's most notable demonstration took place on June 28, 2014, at the Gettysburg National Military Park in Pennsylvania. On that day, about ten members of the TKKKK spent "about a half hour at Gettysburg, protesting President Barack Obama, minorities, gays, Jews, Democrats, Republicans and others" (Yeah Stub). At this demonstration, one reporter took note of the "vile reality" of the TKKKK's message. "I heard this," the reporter noted, "yelled by a Klan member to a group of about 30 to 50 onlookers":

> I, myself, will have a [sic] ethnic cleansing . . . you haven't seen nothing. You think Hitler put them in the ovens? We're gonna put them in the ground. . . . I hope your daughter does die at the hands of a savage Negro. . . . We hate n—, we hate the s—, we hate the Jew, we hate the f— and if you support them or sympathize with them, well, then we hate you too. White power. (Dougherty)

TKKKK members, using a megaphone, were also heard to say, "The only solution is an all-white revolution," and "We are taking back this land," and "Anyone who stands in our way, they're going in the ground" (OneFrederickManyVoices). When observers questioned why the TKKKK was able to spout its hateful message, law enforcement officials stated that the group, like every American, has the right to free speech, sometimes regardless of the message (OneFrederickManyVoices).

Immediately after leaving the Gettysburg demonstration, the same ten members of the TKKKK showed up at a gay pride festival in Frederick County, Maryland. One Klan member was heard to say during the demonstration: "How can gay bashing be a crime? I love to do it" (Dougherty). The TKKKK also made its feeling known about immigrants from other countries: "Put 'em back on the bus. If they come back, send 'em home in a pine box. As they cross this border, put a bullet in their head. . . . Immigration can be fixed in 30 days. You just gotta have some guts to do it" (Dougherty).

After the TKKKK's activities on June 28, the SPLC noted that the group is "small, but guttural. This is a tiny Klan group full of big, bad talk, but they have not been able to produce more than 10 people in their existence" (Loos). The SPLC noted that "[w]hile many Klan groups cast themselves as peaceful defenders of the rights of white people, the Traditional Rebel Knights' website features outright slurs against black and Jewish people, as well as images of violence" (Loos).

Following its activities in 2014, the TKKKK planned to hold a "triple cross and swastika lighting" in "honor of Columbus Day" near its headquarters in Braddock Heights, Maryland (Loos). On its website, the TKKKK distinguished between a "cross lighting and a cross burning":

> The lighting of a cross is a religious ceremony, performed in reverence to the Lord Jesus Christ, in recognition of His sacrifice. The burning of a cross is an illegal act of violence against a person or a person's home, while invading their privacy with the intent to harass or intimidate. (Loos)

The proposed cross and swastika lightings were protested by hundreds of individuals from Braddock Heights, with leaders of the Middletown ministerium, "an organization of Christian leaders of various denominations," stating that the type of Klan activity represented by the TKKKK was "the kind of hatred [that] is anathema to the community at large and . . . any kind of faith community. . . . Jesus was all about breaking down barriers between people. . . . We are called to do the same" (Loos).

By 2016, the TKKKK had been disbanded and no longer appeared on the SPLC's list of hate groups (Southern Poverty Law Center, 2017).

See also: Ku Klux Klan; Neo-Nazis; White Nationalism; White Supremacist Movement

FURTHER READING

Anti-Defamation League. "Tattered Robes: The State of the Ku Klux Klan in the United States." Anti-Defamation League. https://www.adl.org/education/resources /reports/state-of-the-kkk. (Accessed July 27, 2018.)

Dougherty, Allison. July 3, 2014. "Vile Reality of KKK Hatred Was on Display in Gettysburg: Allison Dougherty." Penn Live. https://www.pennlive.com/opinion /2014/07/vile_reality_of_kkk_hatred_was.html. (Accessed July 27, 2018.)

Loos, Kelsi. October 7, 2015. "Community Plans Candlelight Walk to Counter Braddock Heights KKK Rally." *Frederick News-Post*. https://www.fredericknewspost.com /news/social_issues/community-plans-candlelight-walk-to-counter-braddock -heights-kkk-rally/article_44872386-f6fb-57d1-a0bb-5b3b3cf669ac.html. (Accessed July 27, 2018.)

Monroe, Rachel. August 24, 2017. "The Ku Klux Klan Is Apparently Still Alive and Well in Maryland." Baltimore Fishbowl. https://baltimorefishbowl.com/stories/ku-klux -klan-apparently-still-alive-well-maryland/. (Accessed July 27, 2018.)

OneFrederickManyVoices. "Frederick County KKK 'Great Titan' Albert Fike & Klansmen Repeatedly Threaten Violence against Our Citizens. Why Aren't Law Enforcement Officials Acting?" OneFrederickManyVoices. http://onefrederick manyvoices.blogspot.com/2014/07/frederick-county-kkk-dragon-albert-fike.html. (Accessed July 27, 2018.)

Southern Poverty Law Center. "Hate Map by State." Southern Poverty Law Center. https://www.splcenter.org/hate-map/by-state. (Accessed July 27, 2018.)

Southern Poverty Law Center. "Ku Klux Klan." Southern Poverty Law Center. https://www.splcenter.org/fighting-hate/extremist-files/ideology/ku-klux-klan. (Accessed July 27, 2018.)

Southern Poverty Law Center. February 17, 2016. "Active Hate Groups in the United States in 2015." Southern Poverty Law Center: Intelligence Report. https://www.splcenter.org/fighting-hate/intelligence-report/2016/active-hate-groups-united-states-2015. (Accessed July 27, 2018.)

Southern Poverty Law Center. February 15, 2017. "Active Hate Groups 2016." Southern Poverty Law Center: Intelligence Report. https://www.splcenter.org/fighting-hate/intelligence-report/2017/active-hate-groups-2016. (Accessed July 27, 2018.)

Yeah Stub. June 29, 2014. "Traditional Rebel Knights of the Ku Klux Klan Protest Frederick, Md. (Gay) Pride." Yeah Stub. https://yeahstub.com/traditional-rebel-knights-of-the-ku-klux-klan-protest-frederick-md-gay-pride/. (Accessed July 27, 2018.)

Traditional Values Coalition

The Traditional Values Coalition (TVC) has been labeled by the Southern Poverty Law Center (SPLC) as "an anti-LGBT hate group." According to the SPLC:

> Anti-LGBT groups on the SPLC hate list often link homosexuality to pedophilia, claim that same-sex marriage and LGBT people, in general, are dangers to children, that homosexuality itself is dangerous, support the criminalization of homosexuality and transgender identity, and that there is a conspiracy called the "homosexual agenda" at work that seeks to destroy Christianity and the whole of society. (Southern Poverty Law Center, Anti-LGBT)

TVC was founded by "Presbyterian minister Lou Sheldon in 1980 to spread a 'moral code and behavior based upon the Old and New Testaments' and to warn Americans of the rising 'gay threat'" (Southern Poverty Law Center, Traditional Values Coalition). Soon after TVC's founding, Sheldon claimed that "homosexuality is a 'deathstyle' and that child molestation is the real 'homosexual agenda'" (Kelley). In 1985, Sheldon "suggested forcibly rounding up AIDS victims into 'cities of refuge,' like leper colonies, to protect the general population" (Southern Poverty Law Center, Traditional Values Coalition). Sheldon also claimed that "homosexuals are dangerous. They proselytize. They come to the door, and if your son answers and nobody is there to stop it, they grab the son and run off with him. They steal him. They take him away and turn him into a homosexual" (Southern Poverty Law Center, Traditional Values Coalition). In a TVC report entitled "Pro-homosexual Hate Crime Legislation Is Back," Sheldon claimed:

> Homosexuality is a behavior, not a fixed identity. It is similar to smoking or drug use, not an immutable characteristic like race or ethnicity. There are no "former" Blacks, but there are ex-homosexuals. The existence of ex-homosexuals is clear

evidence that homosexuality is behavior-based, not an unchangeable characteristic. It should not receive special minority rights protections in federal law. (Southern Poverty Law Center, Traditional Values Coalition)

In 2013, Andrea Lafferty, Sheldon's daughter, succeeded her aged father as president of TVC. When the House of Representatives "held hearings on transgender discrimination," Lafferty referred to the hearings as a "freak show" and "insisted transgendered individuals were 'deeply disturbed individuals who need therapy not coddling and affirmation by a liberal majority in the House of Representatives'" (Southern Poverty Law Center, Traditional Values Coalition). After Congress "introduced the Employment Non-Discrimination Act (ENDA) in 2013," TVC

> released a slew of anti-transgender press releases attacking ENDA with allegations that the bill would force every school district to hire transgender teachers and bring "gender confusion" into schools. One such press release likened school-aged children to "human shields" who were being used in the attempt to "force the acceptance of transgenders and transsexuals into mainstream culture." (Southern Poverty Law Center, Traditional Values Coalition)

TVC did not limit its attacks to LGBT issues, however. TVC has claimed that "Islamists want to destroy America and western civilization by 'conquering nation after nation' and imposing Shariah religious law upon them" (Southern Poverty Law Center, Traditional Values Coalition). Andrea Lafferty has stated that "Islam is not just a religion. Islam is a geo-political military system wrapped in a cloak of religious belief that penalizes conversion with death" (Kelley).

TVC's website—www.traditionalvalues.org—disappeared in August 2017, and the phone number for the group was disconnected (Kelley).

See also: Ruth Institute; Westboro Baptist Church

FURTHER READING

Kelley, Brendan Joel. March 30, 2018. "The Rise and Fall of the Traditional Values Coalition." Southern Poverty Law Center: Hatewatch. https://www.splcenter.org/hatewatch/2018/03/30/rise-and-fall-traditional-values-coalition. (Accessed June 16, 2018.)

Southern Poverty Law Center. "Anti-LGBT." Southern Poverty Law Center. https://www.splcenter.org/fighting-hate/extremist-files/ideology/anti-lgbt. (Accessed June 16, 2018.)

Southern Poverty Law Center. "Traditional Values Coalition." Southern Poverty Law Center. https://www.splcenter.org/fighting-hate/extremist-files/group/traditional-values-coalition. (Accessed June 16, 2018.)

Traditionalist American Knights of the Ku Klux Klan

The Traditionalist American Knights of the Ku Klux Klan (TAK) is a Ku Klux Klan (KKK)-affiliated hate group with chapters located in Alabama, Florida, Idaho, Indiana, Maine, North Carolina, Ohio, Pennsylvania, Rhode Island, South

Dakota, Tennessee, Texas, and Virginia (Southern Poverty Law Center, Hate Map by State). Its headquarters are in Park Hills, Missouri (Southern Poverty Law Center, 2017). The Southern Poverty Law Center (SPLC) characterizes the KKK, and its associated groups, as engendering a "long history of violence" and notes that the KKK "is the most infamous—and oldest—of American hate groups. Although black Americans have typically been the Klan's primary target, it also has attacked Jews, immigrants, gays and lesbians and, until recently, Catholics" (Southern Poverty Law Center, Ku Klux Klan). The TAK claims to be "a White Patriotic Christian organization that bases its roots back to the Ku Klux Klan of the early 20th century. We are a non-violent organization that believes in the preservation of the White race and the United States Constitution as it was originally written and will stand to protect those rights against all foreign invaders" (Traditionalist American Knights). The TAK has maintained that they

> must keep this [the United States] a white man's country, as it is the sole option to be "faithful to the foundations laid by our forefathers." Thus, the leaders of the organization state that "[t]his Republic was established by and for White Men [sic]", and, as such, should never "fall into the hands of an inferior race." Such statements of Traditionalist American Knights, along with overt declarations of "standing for supremacy of the White Race [which] must be maintained, or be overwhelmed by the rising tide of color," restricting membership to native-born American citizens only, obviously line up with the first Klan's beliefs and the second Klan's opinions on African Americans. Interestingly, the leaders of the group do not perceive such claims and reaffirmations that they "would not rob the colored population of their rights, but (. . .) demand that they respect the rights of the White Race in whose country they are permitted to reside" as contradictory. (Traditionalist American Knights)

From its founding in 2009, the TAK was led by Frank Ancona, who, at the time of the group's founding, had been a member of the KKK for more than 30 years (Stack). As noted by Mark Potok, a researcher at SPLC, "There are at least 29 separate, rival Klan groups currently active in the United States, and they compete with one another for members, dues, news media attention and the title of being the true heir to the Ku Klux Klan" (Stack). The TAK "was not considered the largest or the most influential iteration of the Klan, but he was skilled at attracting the spotlight" (Stack). Two incidents in particularly stand out.

First, in 2013, the TAK intended to distribute leaflets in Desloge, Missouri, but they were forbidden by the city's new traffic ordinance that prevented individuals from stepping into a street to distribute flyers or leaflets. On April 29, 2013, "Ancona and the Klan, represented by the American Civil Liberties Union, filed the present action against [Desloge] to enjoin enforcement of the April 2013 ordinance on the grounds that it violated their First Amendment rights" (FindLaw). The "district court determined"

> that Ancona and the Klan had standing to challenge the distribution provisions of the Desloge ordinance, but none related to solicitation since the Klan had not undertaken any efforts to solicit in Desloge. The court subsequently decided that the distribution provisions were not narrowly tailored and that the Klan was likely to prevail on the merits of its First Amendment challenge. Concluding that the other requirements for a preliminary injunction had been met, the district court granted the Klan's motion. (FindLaw)

On appeal, the appellate court ruled that "the district court abused its discretion in granting a preliminary injunction against enforcement of the August 2013 ordinance of the city of Desloge." The "judgment of the district court was therefore 'reversed and vacated' " (FindLaw).

Second, in November 2014, the TAK claimed it would use "'lethal force' against protesters" in Ferguson, Missouri, in a flyer that read: "There will be consequences for your actions against the peaceful, law abiding citizens of Missouri" (Counter Extremism Project). The TAK was counterprotesting, alongside other extremist groups, against those who were protesting the "killing of an unarmed black teenager—Michael Brown—by a white policeman of the Ferguson Police Department" (FindLaw).

The TAK has also regularly distributed leaflets in "neighborhoods in cities around the country in an effort to recruit more members" (Thomas). Three TAK members "were charged in Florida in 2015 with plotting to kill a black man" (Thomas).

In February 2017, Frank Ancona, who acted as the imperial wizard for TAK, was found shot to death with a "gunshot wound to the head." His "wife and stepson were later charged with murder, abandonment of a corpse and tampering with physical evidence" (Associated Press). It was believed that the killing was the result of "a marital dispute and was not connected to Mr. Ancona's membership in the K.K.K." (Stack).

After Ancona's death, the TAK website disappeared from the Internet. When an individual on the white nationalist and white supremacist website Stormfront asked in November 2017, "Traditionalist American Knights Site Down?," a respondent replied: "The Traditionalist American Knights of the Ku Klux Klan did not go anywhere. Our site was taken down by the Jews who controlled our web browser after Charlottesville. We are currently in the process working on a brand new web page. Thank you" (Stormfront).

See also: Ku Klux Klan; Neo-Nazis; White Nationalism; White Supremacist Movement

FURTHER READING

Associated Press. February 13, 2017. "Wife and Stepson Charged in Murder of Ku Klux Klan Leader in Missouri." *Guardian*. https://www.theguardian.com/us-news/2017/feb/13/kkk-leader-murdered-frank-ancona-missouri. (Accessed July 27, 2018.)

Counter Extremism Project. "Ku Klux Klan (KKK)." Counter Extremism Project. https://www.counterextremism.com/threat/ku-klux-klan. (Accessed July 27, 2018).

Cowen, Trace William. March 9, 2017. "New Details Emerge in Alleged Murder of KKK Imperial Wizard Who 'Smelled Like Cat Piss.'" Complex.com. https://www.complex.com/life/2017/03/new-details-kkk-imperial-wizard-murder. (Accessed July 27, 2018.)

FindLaw. *Traditionalist American Knights of the Ku Klux Klan v. City of Desloge Missouri*. FindLaw. https://caselaw.findlaw.com/us-8th-circuit/1688077.html. (Accessed July 27, 2018.)

Southern Poverty Law Center. "Hate Map by State." Southern Poverty Law Center. https://www.splcenter.org/hate-map/by-state. (Accessed July 27, 2018.)

Southern Poverty Law Center. "Ku Klux Klan." Southern Poverty Law Center. https://www.splcenter.org/fighting-hate/extremist-files/ideology/ku-klux-klan. (Accessed July 27, 2018.)

Southern Poverty Law Center. February 15, 2017. "Active Hate Groups 2016." Southern Poverty Law Center: Intelligence Report. https://www.splcenter.org/fighting-hate/intelligence-report/2017/active-hate-groups-2016. (Accessed July 27, 2018.)

Stack, Liam. February 13, 2017. "Leader of a Ku Klux Klan Group Is Found Dead in Missouri." *New York Times.* https://www.nytimes.com/2017/02/13/us/kkk-leader-death-frank-ancona.html. (Accessed July 27, 2018.)

Stormfront. November 6, 2017. "Traditionalist American Knights Site Down?" Stormfront. https://www.stormfront.org/forum/t1226473/. (Accessed July 27, 2018.)

Thomas, Judy L. February 12, 2017. "KKK Imperial Wizard Frank Ancona Is Found Dead in Missouri." *Kansas City Star.* https://www.kansascity.com/news/state/missouri/article132273414.html. (Accessed July 27, 2018.)

Traditionalist American Knights of the Ku Klux Klan. https://sites.google.com/site/thekukluxklannowandthen/3-4. (Accessed July 27, 2018.)

Traditionalist Worker Party

The Traditionalist Worker Party (TWP) has been designated "a neo-Nazi hate group by the Southern Poverty Law Center" (SPLC). According to the SPLC, "Neo-Nazi groups share a hatred for Jews and a love for Adolf Hitler and Nazi Germany. While they also hate other minorities, gays and lesbians and even sometimes Christians, they perceive 'the Jew' as their cardinal enemy" (Southern Poverty Law Center, Neo-Nazi). In 2015, Matthew Heimbach and Matthew Parrott founded TWP as the political wing of the Traditionalist Youth Network, which the pair cofounded in 2013 (Southern Poverty Law Center, Traditionalist Worker Party). Both Heimbach and Parrott have long been associated with white nationalist and white supremacist causes, but it is Heimbach who is perhaps the most famous, having been "frequently cited as one of the most dynamic young leaders of the white nationalist movement in the US, often being compared to David Duke in his earlier years" (Atlanta Antifascists). TWP has chapters in Alabama, Indiana, North Carolina, Ohio, Rhode Island, Tennessee, Texas, and Virginia (Southern Poverty Law Center, Neo-Nazi). The SPLC identifies its headquarters as being located in Cincinnati, Ohio (Southern Poverty Law Center, Traditionalist Worker Party).

While at Towson University in Maryland, Heimbach founded the White Student Union (WSU) "to create an avenue for people to participate in political, cultural, educational, and social events to celebrate European heritage" (Towson's White Student Union). His efforts "provided a template for occasional other efforts on US campuses" (Atlanta Antifascists). Heimbach is "media savvy and attempts to rebrand white nationalist politics as something other than hateful," and he "would challenge our use of the term 'supremacist'" (Atlanta Antifascists). In recent years, he "has been involved in organizing white separatist, supremacist and nationalist events around the country. Heimbach, who is in his mid-20s, is the affable, youthful face of hate in America" (Eltagouri and Selk).

Heimbach and Parrott founded TWP to serve as the political arm of the Traditionalist Youth Network, which they founded in 2013. According to its now-defunct website, TWP's goals were largely political in nature:

While we have candidates for political office and will run campaigns, that work is secondary to our first priority, which is local organizing and advocacy for real-life working families who share our identitarian and traditionalist vision. (Identitarianism is a closely related ideology that emerged in recent years in Europe.) (Southern Poverty Law Center, Traditionalist Worker Party)

The group uses the slogan "'Local solutions to the globalist problem,' a reference to the idea that globalization, the knitting together of nations and national economies throughout the developed world, is destroying racially homogenous communities and nations" (Southern Poverty Law Center, Traditionalist Worker Party). According to the SPLC, the Traditionalist Youth Network and the Traditionalist Worker Party are "part and parcel of the American 'Alternative Right,' an umbrella term for a racist ideology that scorns mainstream conservatism and argues that white people and white culture in America are under threat from the forces of political correctness and multiculturalism. It is also 'traditionalist' and 'identitarian'" (Southern Poverty Law Center, Traditionalist Worker Party).

TWP's version of "traditionalism"

has its roots in the "radical traditionalism" espoused by mid-20th century Italian "philosopher" Julius Evola, a fascist thinker who believed that Jews were to blame for the modern materialism and democracy that he thought subverted the natural order of the world. The TWP website includes the group's definition of traditionalism: "Traditionalism, properly applied, makes us as autonomous and self-governing as possible in relation to the modernist societies that we live in." It defines traditions as "positive cultural interactions that have existed over a long period of time" and says "those traditions have existed for a long time, because they work. They have formed European-American mores." The traditionalist ideology sees adherence to those "mores" as the best way to organize society, and argues that a traditionalist lifestyle can successfully supplant the state, since "the family is the natural enemy of the state." (Southern Poverty Law Center, Traditionalist Worker Party)

TWP's emphasis on "identitarianism," on the other hand,

refers to a movement that emerged in recent years in France that advocates for culturally and ethnically homogenous communities and blames liberals for selling out their country. Generation Identitaire, the youth wing of the anti-immigrant Bloc Identitaire movement in France, is known for its racist and xenophobic anti-Muslim stunts, like serving soups containing pork in Muslim neighborhoods. The ideology has its roots in the European New Right, or Nouvelle Droite, founded by French academic Alain de Benoist, who advocated against melting-pot societies and immigration while claiming to oppose biological racism. (Southern Poverty Law Center, Traditionalist Worker Party)

The TWP positions espouse what is known as "ethnopluralism," which argues that "liberal multiculturalism is false, as it promotes a melting pot which leads to the disappearance of ethnicities, cultures or races through miscegenation and therefore is in fact monoculturalism" (Southern Poverty Law Center, Traditionalist Worker Party). It is no surprise, then, that TWP is against racial intermarriage and government overreach in areas of social construction, stating that "communities should be able to determine their own 'religious and ethnic character' without government interference" (Southern Poverty Law Center, Traditionalist Worker Party).

Like its founders, Heimbach and Parrott, the TWP is "blatantly anti-Semitic." The group has claimed that Jews in the United States exercise "dual loyalty: The State of Israel has a large and powerful Jewish population in America, many of whom are more loyal to Israel than they are to America" (Southern Poverty Law Center, Traditionalist Worker Party). While Matthew Heimbach has claimed that "he is not against all Jews," he "blames Jews"

> for killing Christ and asserts that many Jews "have a burning hatred for [Europeans] and will stop at nothing to attempt to drive us into submission." He argues that Europeans should not hate Jews, simply distance ourselves from them as we have done for centuries. Heimbach believes that Jews should live separately from whites in America. (Anti-Defamation League)

Heimbach has stated that "[t]he Jews and capitalists cannot forever stop the flood of revival that is coming, no matter how many fingers they put in the holes of the dam" (Anti-Defamation League). In an article on the Traditionalist Youth Network (TYN) website, he also claimed: "As the rising tide of ethnonationalism continues to wash away at the collective American identity, working with other ethnonationalists should be a key component of the future for our movement" (Anti-Defamation League).

TWP's cofounder, Matthew Parrott, has also made known his disdain for Jews:

> Now is not the time for unity. It's not the time for love. It's a time for disunity and for hate. It's time to hate the migrant communities harboring this lethal threat. It's time to hate the ((((oligarchs)))) who create those communities. And if there's any hate in your heart remaining, invest it in the fools who are smiling and clapping along with the need for more 'unity,' 'inclusion,' and 'love' in the face of this existential threat to our nations, our peoples, and our future generations." (Southern Poverty Law Center, Traditionalist Worker Party)

Parrott's use of the triple parentheses, or "echoes" is a favorite trope of anti-Semites when referring to Jews (Southern Poverty Law Center, Traditionalist Worker Party).

In keeping with its goal to make TWP the political arm of the Traditionalist Youth Network, in June 2016 TWP teamed up with the Barnes Review (TBR), "the premier journal specializing in Holocaust denial" (Southern Poverty Law Center, Traditionalist Worker Party). Shortly afterward, in July 2016, TWP joined the Aryan Nationalist Alliance (ANA), "a coalition of white nationalist organizations" (Southern Poverty Law Center, Traditionalist Worker Party). About the same time, TWP endorsed Rick Tyler, "a candidate for congressman in Tennessee . . . known for putting up billboards that say 'Make America White Again' " (Southern Poverty Law Center, Traditionalist Worker Party). The TWP also "warmly praised the candidacy of GOP presidential nominee Donald Trump":

> Donald Trump is blowing the dog whistle for White racial interests harder than any other candidate, and louder than the Republic elites would ever dream a candidate would do in our politically correct age. While Donald Trump is neither a Traditionalist nor a White nationalist, he is a threat to the economic and social powers of the international Jew. Heimbach called Trump a "gateway drug" for white nationalism. "We can then move [Trump supporters] from civic nationalism and populism to nationalism for us." (Southern Poverty Law Center, Traditionalist Worker Party)

At "a Trump rally in Louisville, Kentucky in March 2016," Heimbach, while wearing a red "Make America Great Again" hat, was filmed shoving Kashiya Nwanguma, "a University of Louisville student, who was protesting Trump at the event." Heimbach and others were filmed "violently shoving and screaming what appeared to be racial epithets" at Nwanguma (Lenz). Four months later, he pleaded guilty to "disorderly conduct at the rally," with jail time "suspended on the condition that he not be charged with another crime for two years" (Eltagouri and Selk). Heimbach acknowledged that "he pushed [Nwanguma] and later wrote online: 'White Americans are getting fed up and they're learning that they must either push back or be pushed down'" (Eltagouri and Selk). Nwanguma and other protesters at the rally sued Trump, "alleging he incited a riot. Heimbach was also named in the suit" (Eltagouri and Selk).

Though he was supposed to remain out of trouble for two years, Heimbach was arrested in March 2018 for hitting his wife and choking his father-in-law, Matthew Parrott, unconscious "after the two confronted Heimbach about having an affair with Parrott's wife" (Heimbach's mother-in-law). Matthew Parrott, who was Heimbach's wife's step-father, was also cofounder with Heimbach of TWP and TYN. After the incident, both parties filed for divorce from one another, and Parrott announced that he was leaving TWP: "Matt Parrott is out of the game. Y'all have a nice life" (Barrouquere, March 27, 2018).

After Heimbach's arrest on battery charges, the TWP's "website has vanished from the internet and TWP's future remains unclear" (Barrouquere, May 3, 2018). The "federal civil lawsuit against Trump, Heimbach and multiple others stemming from the violence at the Louisville rally is [still] pending in federal court" (Barrouquere, May 3, 2018).

See also: Alt-Right Movement; Aryan Nationalist Alliance; Barnes Review; Neo-Nazis; Traditionalist Youth Network; White Nationalism; White Supremacist Movement; Youth for Western Civilization

FURTHER READING

Anti-Defamation League. "Traditionalist Youth Network." Anti-Defamation League. https://www.adl.org/resources/backgrounders/traditionalist-youth-network. (Accessed July 28, 2018.)

Atlanta Antifascists. "Exposing Joshua Bates (AKA 'Brandon Hitt'), Georgia Participant in the 'The Base'." Atlanta Antifascists. https://atlantaantifa.org/tag/traditionalist -worker-party/. (Accessed July 28, 2018.)

Barrouquere, Brett. March 27, 2018. "Lawyer: Traditionalist Worker Party Membership Roll Still Exists, Despite Mark Parrott's Vow to Destroy Database." Southern Poverty Law Center: Hatewatch. https://www.splcenter.org/hatewatch/2018/03/27 /lawyer-traditionalist-worker-party-membership-roll-still-exists-despite-matt -parrott%E2%80%99s-vow. (Accessed July 28, 2018.)

Barrouquere, Brett. May 3, 2018. "After Family Fiasco, TWP's Matthew Heimbach May Spend Summer in Jail." Southern Poverty Law Center: Hatewatch. https://www .splcenter.org/hatewatch/2018/05/03/after-family-fiasco-twps-matthew-heimbach -may-spend-summer-jail-0. (Accessed July 28, 2018.)

CBS News. "Hate Groups in America: White Nationalist Traditionalist Workers Party." CBS News. https://www.cbsnews.com/pictures/hate-groups-in-america/12/. (Accessed July 28, 2018.)

Eltagouri, Marwa, and Avi Selk. March 14, 2018. "How a White Nationalist Family Came to Blows over a Trailer Tryst." *Washington Post.* https://www.washingtonpost.com/news/post-nation/wp/2018/03/13/white-nationalist-leader-matthew-heimbach-arrested-for-domestic-battery/. (Accessed July 28, 2018.)

Lenz, Ryan. July 21, 2016. "White Nationalist Filmed Shoving Protesters at Trump Rally Faces Charges." Southern Poverty Law Center: Hatewatch. https://www.splcenter.org/hatewatch/2016/07/21/white-nationalist-filmed-shoving-protesters-trump-rally-faces-charges. (Accessed July 28, 2018.)

Southern Poverty Law Center. "Neo-Nazi." Southern Poverty Law Center. https://www.splcenter.org/fighting-hate/extremist-files/ideology/neo-nazi. (Accessed July 28, 2018.)

Southern Poverty Law Center. "Traditionalist Worker Party." Southern Poverty Law Center. https://www.splcenter.org/fighting-hate/extremist-files/group/traditionalist-worker-party. (Accessed July 28, 2018.)

Towson's White Student Union. "About the WSU." Towson's White Student Union. https://towsonwsu.blogspot.com/p/about-wsu.html. (Accessed July 28, 2018.)

Traditionalist Youth Network

The Traditionalist Youth Network (TYN) "was founded in May 2013 by Matthew Heimbach and Matt Parrott" (Terrorism Research & Analysis Consortium). The creation of the group was meant to

> provide resources and support to independent groups of high school and college students throughout North America who are learning about the Traditionalist School of thought, helping one another apply the principles and spirit of Tradition in their lives, and organizing in defense of Tradition on their campuses and in their communities. While members and supporters are encouraged to embrace a particular Tribe and Tradition, the TYN empowers them to unite and speak as one voice against the united voices of decadence, individualism, Marxism, and Modernity. (Traditionalist Youth Network)

According to the Anti-Defamation League (ADL), TYN "is against modernism, individualism, globalism and Marxism. It models itself after the European Identitaire movement, which focuses on preserving white European culture and identity in Western countries" (Anti-Defamation League). TYN members "often speak out against multiculturalism and are anti-Semitic. TYN claims to be for 'diversity' but defines diversity as each ethnic group promoting its own heritage and traditions while living apart from each other" (Anti-Defamation League).

One of TYN's two founders, Matt Heimbach, is no stranger to white supremacism and extreme right causes. While at Towson University in Maryland, he founded "the now-defunct organization, Youth for Western Civilization (YWC)," in 2011, "a group that straddled the line between mainstream and extreme views" (Anti-Defamation League). The YWC chapter at Towson "disbanded after members of the group scrawled 'white pride' around campus" (Anti-Defamation

League). The next year, in September 2012, "Heimbach founded the White Student Union (WSU) at the school, and became more openly racist and anti-Semitic" (Anti-Defamation League). In May 2013, Heimbach announced the formation of TYN:

> Working side by side we have drafted an organization that will take the message of the WSU far beyond the confines of Towson. This will be an avenue to organize a wide coalition of Kinists, social conservatives, Traditionalist Christians, believers in Right-Wing political ideologies, and other factions of the pro-white movement. (Towson's White Student Union)

In 2015, Heimbach and Parrott went on "to create the Traditionalist Worker Party (TWP) as the political wing of the TYN" (Southern Poverty Law Center, Traditionalist Worker Party).

While Heimbach claims "he is not against all Jews," he "blames Jews"

> for killing Christ and asserts that many Jews have a burning hatred for [Europeans] and will stop at nothing to attempt to drive us into submission. He argues that "Europeans should not hate Jews, simply distance ourselves from them as we have done for centuries." Heimbach believes that Jews should live separately from whites in America. (Anti-Defamation League)

Heimbach has stated that "[t]he Jews and capitalists cannot forever stop the flood of revival that is coming, no matter how many fingers they put in the holes of the dam" (Anti-Defamation League). In an article on the TYN website, he also claimed: "As the rising tide of ethnonationalism continues to wash away at the collective American identity, working with other ethnonationalists should be a key component of the future for our movement" (Anti-Defamation League).

TYN's cofounder, Matthew Parrott, has made it clear that TYN's goal is to appeal to youth in order to enlist their support in white nationalist causes. Parrott has written:

> We must be the hipsters of White identity, with an unimpeachable record of fighting and sacrificing for White families and communities before it was cool. . . . I've concluded that what's unrealistic is attempting to build a movement in favor of heritage, faith and tradition on a foundation of individualism, mercantile morality, moral relativism, and universal egalitarianism. (Anti-Defamation League)

In 2016, both the TWP and TYN partnered with the Barnes Review (TBR), "a journal dedicated to historical revisionism and Holocaust denial. In a post on TYN's website announcing this partnership, the group called the publication known for its vile take on history 'an esteemed revisionist publication'" (Viets and Lenz). TBR "practices an extremist form of revisionist history that includes defending the Nazi regime, denying the Holocaust, discounting the evils of slavery and promoting white nationalism." Its founder, Willis Carto, stated that "[w]ithout a means of confronting the onrushing third world, white civilization is doomed" (Viets and Lenz). TBR has published articles entitled "Treblinka Was No Death Camp," "Is There a Negro Race?," "'Reconquist': The Mexican Plan to Take the Southwest," and "David Duke: An Awakening" (Viets and Lenz).

Heimbach wasn't always a rabid anti-Semite. When he headed the YWC at Towson, "he promoted a pro-Israel event and reached out to Jewish students"

(Anti-Defamation League). He attended "evangelical church services when he was younger and used to describe himself as an 'ardent Zionist'" (Viets and Lenz). Heimbach credits the writings of British historian David Irving, "a holocaust denier who once claimed that Adolf Hitler 'was probably not at all anti-Semitic,'" for "changing his perspective on National Socialism" (Viets and Lenz).

According to the Anti-Defamation League, Heimbach, Parrott, and other members of TYN continue to "express their thoughts on various movements associated with white supremacy and other extreme-right ideologies" (Anti-Defamation League).

See also: Alt-Right Movement; Aryan Nationalist Alliance; Barnes Review; Kinist Institute; Neo-Nazis; Traditionalist Worker Party; White Nationalism; White Supremacist Movement; Youth for Western Civilization

FURTHER READING

Anti-Defamation League. "Traditionalist Youth Network." Anti-Defamation League. https://www.adl.org/resources/backgrounders/traditionalist-youth-network. (Accessed July 28, 2018.)

Atlanta Antifascists. August 24, 2016. "Neo-Nazi 'Hammerfest' Gathering Planned for Georgia, October 1st." Atlanta Antifascists. https://afainatl.wordpress.com/tag/traditionalist-youth-network/. (Accessed July 28, 2018.)

Eyes on the Right. September 13, 2016. "Matt Heimbach Praises North Korea as a 'Great Model' for White Nationalists." Angry White Men. https://angrywhitemen.org/2016/09/13/matt-heimbach-praises-north-korea-as-a-great-model-for-white-nationalists/#more-16339. (Accessed July 28, 2018.)

Southern Poverty Law Center. "Neo-Nazi." Southern Poverty Law Center. https://www.splcenter.org/fighting-hate/extremist-files/ideology/neo-nazi. (Accessed July 28, 2018.)

Terrorism Research & Analysis Consortium. "Traditionalist Youth Network & Traditionalist Worker Party (TYN/TWP)." Terrorism Research & Analysis Consortium. https://www.trackingterrorism.org/group/traditionalist-youth-network-traditionalist-worker-party-tyntwp. (Accessed July 28, 2018.)

Towson's White Student Union. May 22, 2013. "WSU Is Going National: Creation of the Traditionalist Youth Network." Towson's White Student Union. https://towsonwsu.blogspot.com/2013/05/wsu-is-going-national-creation-of.html. (Accessed July 28, 2018.)

Traditionalist Youth Network. "About." Traditionalist Youth Network. http://www.tradyouth.org/about/. (Accessed July 29, 2016.) (Site now appears defunct.)

Viets, Sarah, and Ryan Lenz. July 11, 2016. "Matt Heimbach's Traditionalist Youth Network Is Cutting Deals with Holocaust Deniers." Southern Poverty Law Center: Hatewatch. https://www.splcenter.org/hatewatch/2016/07/11/matt-heimbach%E2%80%99s-traditionalist-youth-network-cutting-deals-holocaust-deniers. (Accessed July 28, 2018.)

Trinity White Knights of the Ku Klux Klan

The Trinity White Knights (TWK) of the Ku Klux Klan (KKK) are a KKK-affiliated group that "has been designated as a hate group by the Southern Poverty

Law Center" (SPLC). According to the SPLC, the KKK has a "long history of violence" in the United States and is "the most infamous—and oldest—of American hate groups. Although black Americans have typically been the Klan's primary target, it also has attacked Jews, immigrants, gays and lesbians and, until recently, Catholics" (Southern Poverty Law Center, Ku Klux Klan). The TWK has its headquarters in Georgetown, Kentucky (Southern Poverty Law Center, 2015), and the imperial wizard (leader) of the organization is William Bader of Maysville, Kentucky (LinkedIn). According to its website:

> Trinity White Knights of the Ku Klux Klan openly stands and speaks out against Illegal immigration, Homosexuality same-sex marriage, race mixing, anything against Christianity and anything that's against our people and furtherance of our cause. We are a dedicated group of Klansmen and Klanswomen here to give the White People an open loud voice and backbone to stand. We will at all cost do what it takes for the protection, advancement, and well being of our people. If your [sic] interested in openly stand with and become part of TRINITY WHITE KNIGHTS then contact us today. This will be a busy spring and summer ahead with many planned events and gatherings to rally for and against..[sic] Don't miss out and let your voice be heard.. [sic] We have chapters across Kentucky and now in Indiana, Ohio, and Alabama. Contact us today and ride with the glorious TWK. [Emphasis in original] (Trinity White Knights, About Us)

According to the Anti-Defamation League, TWK is one of only a handful of KKK groups that currently exist in the United States:

> In recent years, one of the clearest signs of the declining state of Ku Klux Klan groups has been in their complete inability to maintain anything resembling stability. More than half of the currently active Klan groups were formed only in the last five years. This is not, as it may first seem, a sign of growth, but rather illustrates how short-lived today's Ku Klux Klan groups actually tend to be. (Anti-Defamation League)

In May 2016, author Craig Malisow noted that TWK appeared "to consist of four dudes hanging out in a backyard" (Malisow). In discussing the application procedures to become a member of TWK, Malisow stated:

> Based on the questions, the Trinity gang seems to just be itching for a fight: "The TWK is a private club, we reserve the right to refuse petitions to anyone for any reason. Do you agree? Answer yes or no." Another question is simply, "Do you swear that all your answers are correct?" But we'd really, really like to know the story behind this doozy: "Have you ever been judged Insane by anyone, be it a Judge, Jury or Court?"
>
> Suggesting the Trinity Klan fears plaintiffs' lawyers as much as miscegenation, the gang requires prospective members to relinquish their rights to sue and to relieve the group of liability for auto accidents. And based on the fact that one of the probably-four members likes to drive around while draped in his gigantic satiny purple regalia, it's no wonder they're concerned about insurance claims. (Malisow)

Malisow points out that to join the TWK, "[t]he newly initiated are also required to purchase 'a Robe and Vest from an outside approved independent Source within 3 months of your swear in.'" There is also a "year-long probation period" wherein newbies "can be striped [sic] of membership" (Malisow).

TWK's most notable activities of the past several years were the protests the group participated in over "the removal of the Confederate flag from the grounds of the South Carolina capitol in Columbia." TWK was protesting the removal of the Confederate flag "amid national outrage over the murder of nine black church-goers by an alleged white supremacist in Charleston in June [2015]" (Irish Times). According to the account provided by the *Irish Times*, TWK's participation in the protest outside the capitol building "was the first Klan rally outside the State House in nearly 30 years" (Irish Times). Though TWK members did not "don the Klan's traditional white hoods and robes," their presence was a message of "relentless white supremacy" (Irish Times). TWK members shouted, "This is my country," and "My ancestors founded this country" (Irish Times). William Bader, who identified himself "as a Kentucky resident and the imperial wizard of the Trinity White Knights of the Ku Klux Klan," shouted "There is no peace" (Blinder). When asked what Bader wanted to see happen as a result of the protest, his response was, "White revolution is the only solution" (Blinder).

See also: Ku Klux Klan; White Nationalism; White Supremacist Movement

FURTHER READING

Anti-Defamation League. "Tattered Robes: The State of the Ku Klux Klan in the United States." Anti-Defamation League. https://www.adl.org/sites/default/files/documents/assets/pdf/combating-hate/tattered-robes-state-of-kkk-2016.pdf. (Accessed July 28, 2018.)

Blinder, Alan. July 18, 2015. "Ku Klux Klan and New Black Panther Party Protest at South Carolina Capitol." *New York Times*. https://www.nytimes.com/2015/07/19/us/ku-klux-klanprotests-at-south-carolina-capitol.html. (Accessed July 28, 2018.)

Irish Times. July 19, 2015. "Ku Klux Klan Stages Rally at South Carolina State House." *Irish Times*. https://www.irishtimes.com/news/world/us/ku-klux-klan-stages-rally-at-south-carolina-state-house-1.2290017. (Accessed July 28, 2018.)

LinkedIn. "William Bader: Imperial Wizard at Trinity White Knights Ku Klux Klan." LinkedIn. https://www.linkedin.com/in/william-bader-a73a8712b. (Accessed July 28, 2018.)

Malisow, Craig. May 31, 2016. "Which KKK Chapter Is Right for You?" *Houston Press*. https://www.houstonpress.com/news/which-kkk-chapter-is-right-for-you-8436366. (Accessed July 28, 2018.)

Southern Poverty Law Center. "Ku Klux Klan." Southern Poverty Law Center. https://www.splcenter.org/fighting-hate/extremist-files/ideology/ku-klux-klan. (Accessed July 28, 2018.)

Southern Poverty Law Center. March 2, 2015. "Active Ku Klux Klan Groups." Southern Poverty Law Center: Intelligence Report. https://www.splcenter.org/fighting-hate/intelligence-report/2015/active-ku-klux-klan-groups. (Accessed July 28, 2018.)

Trinity White Knights of the Ku Klux Klan. "About." Trinity White Knights of the Ku Klux Klan. https://sites.google.com/site/twkofficialnationalsite/home. (Accessed July 28, 2018.)

Trinity White Knights of the Ku Klux Klan. "Who We Are." Trinity White Knights of the Ku Klux Klan. https://sites.google.com/site/twkofficialnationalsite/home/who-we-are. (Accessed July 28, 2018.)

U

United Aryan Front

The United Aryan Front (UAF), a coalition of various racist hate groups, was formed in late 2015 "with one objective in mind: to create an 'internationally-oriented network of dedicated White Separatists diligently striving to impart a New Racial Consciousness to Aryankind'" (Viets). UAF consists of a "hodgepodge" of white supremacist hate groups, such as "racist skinheads, neo-Nazis, Christian Identity adherents, and Ku Klux Klan members" (Viets). The coalition of groups that makes up UAF "was built on an ideological foundation of pan-Aryanism, a white supremacist philosophy that emphasizes the idea that white revolutionaries must adopt a global strategy to create an all-white, separate nation" (Viets). UAF was started as much out of desperation for survival as out of belief in the ideology. Since the diminishment of the once-powerful National Alliance—at one time "the largest and most active neo-Nazi organization [in the United States] with thousands of members"—there has not been a unified organization that claims to speak for the majority of white supremacists (Viets). To that end,

> UAF encourages all white nationalists to join and even openly accepts Christian Identity adherents, who claim—as DTM [Divine Truth Ministries] notes—that "White people of European ancestry are the descendants of the Biblical Israelites," and racists who identify Anglo-Saxons as the most supreme human beings in the natural order. "The different cultures of the Aryan peoples are what make us unique." (Viets)

Soon after its founding in 2015, UAF warned its followers that "'the wolves are closing in . . . and we are the sheepdog' and followed with a call for recruits: 'If you are not a part of an organization but would like to join us . . . you can!! White Lives Matter is the largest organization of whites in the world'" (Khazan). But UAF wasn't making its call through a U.S. social media site. Instead, it was doing so on VK, "also known as VKontakte—otherwise known as Russia's version of Facebook," where scores of other American extremist groups post their information (Khazan). The VK social network "has become a home for white-power groups who were pushed off of Facebook for hate speech, or who want to connect with fellow racists in other countries" (Khazan).

Almost as quickly as it appeared, UAF collapsed in 2017 after one of its leaders, "Rebecca Barnette, from Tennessee, defected to work with the Aryan National Alliance (ANA), a rival coalition rising in prominence at the time" (Hatewatch staff). But Barnette was soon shunned by the ANA, deactivating "her social media accounts for a time to escape the onslaught of criticism" (Hatewatch staff).

To date, the American white supremacist movement is still hoping to create an organization that will unify the disparate white supremacist hate groups that dot the American political landscape.

See also: Aryan National Alliance; Christian Identity; Ku Klux Klan; National Alliance; Neo-Nazis; Racist Skinheads; White Nationalism; White Supremacist Movement

FURTHER READING

Blumenfeld, Warren. July 20, 2106. "'White Lives Matter' so Whites Can Live without Fear." Good Men Project. https://goodmenproject.com/featured-content/white -lives-matter-so-whites-can-live-without-fear-wcz/. (Accessed June 25, 2018.)

Hatewatch Staff. February 1, 2017. "Neo-Nazi Factions Pinning Hopes for Racist Coalition on 2017 but Haunted by Failures." Southern Poverty Law Center: Hatewatch. https://www.splcenter.org/hatewatch/2017/02/01/neo-nazi-factions-pinning -hopes-racist-coalition-2017-haunted-failures. (Accessed June 25, 2018.)

Khazan, Olga. May 20, 2016. "American Neo-Nazis Are on Russia's Facebook." *Atlantic*. https://www.theatlantic.com/technology/archive/2016/05/extremist-groups -vkontakte/483426/. (Accessed June 25, 2018.)

Viets, Sarah. February 11, 2016. "American and International Racists Create 'United Aryan Front' Coalition." Southern Poverty Law Center: Hatewatch. https://www .splcenter.org/hatewatch/2016/02/11/american-and-international-racists-create -united-aryan-front-coalition. (Accessed June 25, 2018.)

United Dixie White Knights of the Ku Klux Klan

The United Dixie White Knights (UDWK) of the Ku Klux Klan (KKK) is a KKK-affiliated group primarily located in Mississippi, but with "klaverns," or local groups, located in Alabama, Illinois, Indiana, and North Carolina (Begley). According to the Southern Poverty Law Center (SPLC), the UDWK are a KKK hate group that targets black Americans but that in the past has also "attacked Jews, immigrants, gays and lesbians and, until recently, Catholics" (Southern Poverty Law Center, Ku Klux Klan). The SPLC states that the KKK has a "long history of violence" and is the "most infamous—and oldest—of American hate groups" (Southern Poverty Law Center, Ku Klux Klan). Though the Anti-Defamation League (ADL) claims that the UDWK is one of a number of "disbanded Klan groups," the UDWK has apparently remained active through March 2018 (WLOX staff). Its website, however, is not publicly accessible but requires permission from the site owner for access (UDWK). Mississippi Rising Coalition, a group "committed to protecting and advancing the human & civil rights of ALL MS [Mississippi] citizens via voter education and advocacy and has been active in its advocacy of removing the Confederate symbol from the Mississippi state flag," notes that UDWK is "legally registered as an LLC [Limited Liability Corporation] with the state of MS [Mississippi] since 2015" (Mississippi Rising Coalition).

The UDWK made headlines in February 2015 when its imperial wizard (local leader), Brent Waller, issued a "call to arms in Alabama in response to federal courts ruling that an amendment to the state constitution banning same-sex marriage was unconstitutional" (Hankes). The post, which appeared on a now-disabled website for the UDWK and was reposted on the online white supremacist forum Stormfront, stated:

The Mississippi Klan salutes Alabama's chief justice Roy Moore, for refusing to bow to the yoke of Federal tyranny. The Feds have no authority over individual States marriage laws. The fudgepackers from Hollywood and all major news networks are in shock that the good people from the heart of Dixie are resisting their Imperialist, Communist Homosexual agenda!

Alabama has a Constitutional amendment, that clearly says marriage is defined as being between a man and a woman.

But much as they have since the 2nd war for independence was lost in 1865, the Federal Government by way of it's foreign masters seems set to push this abomination, on the God fearing people of Alabama. Will they send Jack Booted thugs to enforce it? Remains to be seen, but a simple study of history will show they once burned, destroyed and looted the state of Alabama. Georgia was burned almost to the ground, and in our state, Meridian Mississippi was destroyed by blue bellied sledgehammers in one day.

We call upon all Klansman and White Southern Nationalist to help in the massive protest's coming, Not by wearing your colors, but by joining in with the Christian community's protests that are surly coming against tyranical Federal judges. We have made the decision that we don't want to distract attention away from the issue, as anytime the Klan rides, we are made the issue by the zionist controlled media. Members are encouraged to lend a hand, make signs, recruit etc., but leave any insignia, colors, shirts etc at the house. We want to infiltrate these protests and make sure they are kept running in military fashion and not bullied by the outside agitators.'

Let today be the day, that the outside forces that have ruled this nation since the end of the War of Northern Aggression be given notice, The God fearing White man will no longer stand for your immorality, your Illegal unjust judges and laws. Your attempts to turn us into a third world cesspool must be defeated. Unlike the 1950's and 60's we see you clearly for the enemy you are. Until we drive the spear of God and truth through your lying cold black hearts, the Klan will leave the light on for you. (Stormfront)

Waller's call to his fellow Klansmen to wear plain clothes was simple. . . . He did not want the Klan's traditional displays of robes, hoods, and symbols to become the story of the "Zionist [i.e., Jewish] controlled media." "Not that wearing robes and hoods has been a consideration before" (Hankes). Waller ended his call to the Klan with the phrase "Death Before Dishonor" (Stormfront).

UDWK's imperial wizard, Waller, sent another lengthy statement to the press in March 2018 when his group posted a YouTube video warning the group known as Mississippi Rising Coalition (MRC). MRC is known for its advocacy that "the Mississippi state flag be changed to a flag without the Confederate emblem" (Stidhum). In response to MRC's efforts, Waller stated:

Yes, we put out the video and whether the Communist anti first amendment folks at You Tube like it or not, more are coming. We opened multiple accounts way back to defeat their censorship to open up when we feel the need speak. A massive flier campaign will begin this spring in Florida, Alabama and Mississippi. As those areas are UDWK country. Any scoundrel of a politician who feels like going against the voters of Mississippi in regards to our State flag, Well we welcome them to step up to the plate so we can shine a bright spotlight upon their heads.

Phillip Gunn [R-Speaker of the Mississippi House of Representatives] is high upon our list of turncoats who chose to stab Mississippi voters in the back because he lusts for National politics. He will soon regret this decision. Our Jackson, Ms Klavern is one of the largest Ku Klux Klaverns in this country and I have given them orders to blanket Gunn's district with fliers meant to awaken the White sheep to his actions.

The Mississippi Rising Coalition is nothing more than a Ponzi scheme set up to bilk the mentally ill Homosexual crowd of it's money. Lea and that bunch and it's out of state financing are nothing but puppets for the likes of George Soros and Hollywood. A year long investigation into this bunch has brought many interesting things to light. They will have the spotlight of truth shined upon them when we are done.

White Mississippians believe in God and will never ever piss upon our ancestors graves in regards to our State flag. Now as we all can see the New World Order plan to take away our Second Amendment so they can put the final nail in America's coffin is being started. We will never give up our guns as history shows us Genocide soon follows.

These sheep who are marching do not understand the consequences of their actions. Their actions will lead to revolution and our rivers will flow with the blood of tyrants, puppets and fools as White Mississippians have never bowed down to those who seek to destroy us and by God we are not starting now.

We will fight to the bitter end and if anyone doubts that the real Ku Klux Klan are not fighters they better examine our history. Don't let these imposters the false Jews train on TV fool you, we are alive and well and are larger than we have been in years. We have learned from past mistakes and have learned the way our enemies operate. We work silently now as we were intended to be. We are working behind the scenes on many political fronts and have eyes and ears everywhere. The MRC is a wealth of info and were easily infiltrated. We see clearly who are pulling these degenerates strings.

I strongly warn our politicians not to bow down to outside political powers and the New World Order agenda especially in regards to our Second Amendment, as if they do, we are coming for their "political" heads. A war is on for our very way of life and possibly the soil under our feet. It will be stained red with blood before we ever surrender or retreat.

Waller ended his tirade by stating, "Non Silba Sed Anthar" ("Not Self, But Others"), a common phrase used by the Klan (Anti-Defamation League). The man speaking on the YouTube video, who identified himself as "Reverend Smith," stated, "Y'all aren't going to take down our flag. We gonna fight. This ain't no threat, nothing physical but we gonna fight through the court system. We gonna fight through the legal way, the proper way" (WLOX staff).

Though the UDWK made a point to indicate that the video was not a threat to the MRC, one MRC board member stated:

> By saying this is not a threat after the language they used in the video, it would be absurd to think they are not threatening—they are the United Dixie White Knights of the Ku Klux Klan. Take a moment to look at the 581 individuals that have been lynched in this state since the existence of the Klan and what they support.
>
> So, yes, we see this as a threat, but we are not our grandparents—we will not lie idly by while the Klan runs over us. (Stidhum)

Another MRC member said, "We believe you sent this to us with the intent, not only to intimidate but in the hopes that we would react publicly. You get your wish. We are eager to confront you, your hateful bigotry, white supremacy and your allies publicly" (WLOX staff).

See also: Ku Klux Klan; White Nationalism; White Supremacist Movement

FURTHER READING

Anti-Defamation League. "Tattered Robes: The State of the Ku Klux Klan in the United States." Anti-Defamation League. https://www.adl.org/sites/default/files/documents /assets/pdf/combating-hate/tattered-robes-state-of-kkk-2016.pdf. (Accessed July 30, 2018.)

Begley, Sarah. February 15, 2017. "Read the List of the 917 Hate Groups Identified by the Southern Poverty Law Center." *Time*. http://time.com/4671800/hate-groups-on -the-rise/. (Accessed July 30, 2018.)

Hankes, Keegan. February 10, 2015. "Klan Group Issues 'Call to Arms' over Alabama Same-Sex Marriage Ruling." Southern Poverty Law Center: Hatewatch. https:// www.splcenter.org/hatewatch/2015/02/10/klan-group-issues-call-arms-over -alabama-same-sex-marriage-ruling. (Accessed July 30, 2018.)

Mississippi Rising Coalition. https://www.facebook.com/mississippirising/photos/united -dixie-white-knights-of/624807937683828/. (Accessed July 30, 2018.)

Southern Poverty Law Center. "Ku Klux Klan." Southern Poverty Law Center. https:// www.splcenter.org/fighting-hate/extremist-files/ideology/ku-klux-klan. (Accessed July 30, 2018.)

Southern Poverty Law Center. March 2, 2015. "Active Ku Klux Klan Groups." Southern Poverty Law Center: Intelligence Report. https://www.splcenter.org/fighting-hate /intelligence-report/2015/active-ku-klux-klan-groups. (Accessed July 30, 2018.)

Stidhum, Tonja Renee. March 2018. "KKK to Mississippi Activists Working to Remove Confederate Emblem from State Flag: 'We Gonna Fight.'" Blavity.com. https:// blavity.com/kkk-to-mississippi-activists-working-to-remove-confederate -emblem-from-the-state-flag-we-gonna-fight. (Accessed July 30, 2018.)

Stormfront. February 10, 2015. "Call to Arms in Alabama." Stormfront. https://www .stormfront.org/forum/t1087840/. (Accessed July 30, 2018.)

United Dixie White Knights of the Ku Klux Klan (UDWK). https://kkkuniteddixiewhitek nights.com/. (Accessed July 30, 2018—Site is marked private by owner and can only be visited with permission from site owner.)

WLOX Staff. March 28, 2018. "United Dixie White Knights Admit to Sending Video to MS Rising Coalition." WTOC.com. http://www.wtoc.com/story/37829782/united -dixie-white-knights-admit-to-sending-video-to-ms-rising-coalition. (Accessed July 30, 2018.)

United Klans of America

The United Klans of America (UKA) is one of the oldest continuous Ku Klux Klan (KKK) organizations in the United States. The UKA that exists today is "the same group that had beaten the Freedom Riders in 1961, murdered civil rights worker Viola Liuzzo in 1965, and bombed Birmingham's 16th Street Baptist Church in 1963" (Southern Poverty Law Center, Donald v. United Klans of America). According to the Southern Poverty Law Center, UKA is a KKK hate group that has groups, or "klaverns," in Alabama, Tennessee, and Pennsylvania (Southern Poverty Law Center, Ku Klux Klan). Though the UKA has gone through many iterations, its basic beliefs have remained consistent; it desires to promote the white race and to disassociate itself from blacks, Jews, immigrants, and gays and lesbians (Southern Poverty Law Center, Ku Klux Klan). A recruiting pamphlet from the UKA states:

> The Knights of the Ku Klux Klan [a.k.a. the United Klans of America] . . . is not now making and does not intend to make any fight on the Roman Catholic Church as a religious institutions, but it will unalterably and unequivocally oppose any move of the Catholic Church or of any other church, individual or organization which attempts to bring about a combination of church and state in these United States.
>
> The Knights of the Ku Klux Klan is not the enemy of the negro. It opposes and will continue to oppose, the efforts of certain negro organizations and periodicals which are sowing the seeds of discontent and racial hatred among the negros of this country by preaching and teaching social equality and mongrelization of the races. . . . we hold it is obligatory upon the negro race, and upon all other colored races in America to recognize that they are living in the land of the white race by courtesy of the white race; and the white race cannot be expected to surrender to any other race, either in whole or in part, the control of its vital and fundamental governmental affairs.
>
> No Jew can obtain citizenship in the Knights of the Ku Klux Klan. . . . The constitution and regulations of the Order set forth that the living Christ is the Klansman's criterion of character. Therefore, it would be unjust to allow the Jew to enter into the fellowship with the Klavern by appealing to his patriotism, and then have him cease to attend because every meeting would be out of harmony with his religious convictions.
>
> Be it known, that the Knights of the Ku Klux Klan was YESTERDAY, is TODAY and will FOREVER be opposed to Communism in any form and to its fellow-travelor organizations. The Knights of the Ku Klux Klan will fight to our last breath, using every means at our disposal to rid our country of this insidious plague of mankind. (Social Welfare History Project)

According to its website, the UKA follows the "88 Precepts" of David Lane, a member of the infamous neo-Nazi and white supremacist organization known as the Order. Lane articulated both the 88 Precepts and the 14 Words: "We must secure the existence of our people and a future for white children." Lane later added the following reason to this statement: "Because the beauty of the White Aryan woman must not perish from the earth" (United Klans of America). To these ends, the 88 Precepts provide a "source from which we [the white race] can ascertain lasting truths" (United Klans of America). Among the 88 Precepts pertaining to the necessity of preserving the white race are these:

> 20. The White race has suffered invasions and brutality from Africa and Asia for thousands of years. . . . So, the attempted guilt- trip placed on the White race by civilizations executioners is invalid under both historical circumstance and the Natural Law which denies inter-species compassion. The fact is, all races have benefitted immeasurably from the creative genius of the Aryan People.

> 21. People who allow others not of their race to live among them will perish, because the inevitable result of a racial integration is racial inter-breeding which destroys the characteristics and existence of a race. Forced integration is deliberate and malicious genocide, particularly for a People like the White race, who are now a small minority in the world.

> 33. Inter-species compassion is contrary to the Laws of Nature and is, therefore, suicidal. If a wolf were to intercede to save a lamb from a lion, he would be killed.

Today, we see the White man taxed so heavily that he cannot afford children. The taxes raised are then used to support the breeding of tens of millions of non-whites, many of whom then demand the last White females for breeding partners. As you can see, man is subject to all the Laws of Nature. This has nothing to do with morality, hatred, good or evil. Nature does not recognize the concepts of good and evil in inter-species relationships. If the lion eats the lamb, it is good for the lion and evil for the lamb. If the lamb escapes and the lion starves, it is good for the lamb and evil for the lion. So, we see the same incident is labeled both good and evil. This cannot be, for there are no contradictions within Nature's Laws.

37. That race whose males will not fight to death to keep and mate with their females will perish. Any White man with healthy instincts feels disgust and revulsion when he sees a woman of his race with a man of another race. Those, who today control the media and affairs of the Western World, teach that this is wrong and shameful. They label it "racism." As any "ism," for instance the word "nationalism," means to promote one's own nation; "racism" merely means to promote and protect the life of one's own race. It is, perhaps, the proudest word in existence. Any man who disobeys these instincts is anti-Nature. (United Klans of America)

The UKA almost disappeared after the SPLC sued the organization and "won an historic $7 million verdict" against the group in 1987. The case, *Donald v. United Klans of America*, stemmed from the killing of 19-year-old Michael Donald, who "was on his way to the store in 1981 when two members of the United Klans of America abducted him, beat him, cut his throat and hung his body from a tree on a residential street in Mobile, Alabama" (Southern Poverty Law Center, Donald v. United Klans of America). The SPLC filed a civil suit against the UKA "on behalf of Donald's mother, Beulah Mae Donald." The $7 million verdict against UKA bankrupted the organization and sent the UKA into virtual seclusion for many years.

Nevertheless, the UKA retained several committed members. In June 2014 in Calhoun, Alabama, the UKA distributed flyers that announced, "We are working to rebuild our collapsing society on the basis of the principles: Honor, Honesty, Duty, Courage, Brotherhood and Patriotism. We are the generation of tomorrow, TODAY. . . . The United Klans of America are here to stay and by the way we are not just in Calhoun County, Alabama" [emphasis in original] (Thornton). Though the UKA and other Klan iterations preach nonviolence, "this is silliness," according to the SPLC. "The ideology [of the UKA] is exactly the same" as that which drove KKK groups of the past to commit acts of violence in the name of racial purity (Thornton).

See also: Ku Klux Klan; The Order; White Nationalism; White Supremacist Movement

FURTHER READING

Anti-Defamation League. "Tattered Robes: The State of the Ku Klux Klan in the United States." Anti-Defamation League. https://www.adl.org/sites/default/files/documents/assets/pdf/combating-hate/tattered-robes-state-of-kkk-2016.pdf. (Accessed July 30, 2018.)

Begley, Sarah. February 15, 2017. "Read the List of the 917 Hate Groups Identified by the Southern Poverty Law Center." *Time.* http://time.com/4671800/hate-groups-on-the-rise/. (Accessed July 30, 2018.)

Counter Extremism Project. "Ku Klux Klan (KKK)." Counter Extremism Project. https://www.counterextremism.com/threat/ku-klux-klan. (Accessed July 30, 2018.)

Jones, Katherine. April 24, 2018. "These Churches Are 'Hate Groups,' a Watchdog Says. But What's Really behind the Label?" *Idaho Statesman*. https://www.idahostatesman.com/news/northwest/idaho/article209568694.html. (Accessed July 30, 2018.)

Social Welfare History Project. "An Introduction to the Knights of the Ku Klux Klan [United Klans of America Pamphlet]." Social Welfare History Project. https://images.socialwelfare.library.vcu.edu/items/show/275. (Accessed July 30, 2018.)

Southern Poverty Law Center. "*Donald v. United Klans of America*. Case Number: 84-0725." Southern Poverty Law Center. https://www.splcenter.org/seeking-justice/case-docket/donald-v-united-klans-america. (Accessed July 30, 2018.)

Southern Poverty Law Center. "Ku Klux Klan." Southern Poverty Law Center. https://www.splcenter.org/fighting-hate/extremist-files/ideology/ku-klux-klan. (Accessed July 30, 2018.)

Southern Poverty Law Center. March 2, 2015. "Active Ku Klux Klan Groups. Southern Poverty Law Center: Intelligence Report. https://www.splcenter.org/fighting-hate/intelligence-report/2015/active-ku-klux-klan-groups. (Accessed July 30, 2018.)

Thornton, William. June 23, 2014. "United Klans of America 'Here to Stay' following Calhoun County Fliers, Says 'You May Already Know A UKA Member.'" AL.com. https://www.al.com/news/anniston-gadsden/index.ssf/2014/06/united_klans_of_america_says_i.html. (Accessed July 30, 2018.)

United Klans of America. "88 Precepts." United Klans of America. http://www.theuka.us/the-seven-symbols-of-the-klan.html. (Accessed July 30, 2018.)

United Northern and Southern Knights of the Ku Klux Klan

The United Northern and Southern Knights (UNSK) of the Ku Klux Klan (KKK) is a KKK-affiliated "group that has been designated by the Southern Poverty Law Center (SPLC) as a hate group" (Southern Poverty Law Center, Ku Klux Klan). According to the SPLC, KKK groups have a "long history of violence and are among the oldest, and most infamous of American hate groups" (Southern Poverty Law Center, Ku Klux Klan). Although black Americans have typically been the Klan's primary target, it also has attacked Jews, immigrants, gays and lesbians and, until recently, Catholics" (Southern Poverty Law Center, Ku Klux Klan). The SPLC notes that members of the UNSK are primarily located in Georgia but that there may also be individuals who claim affiliation with the group in California (Begley). According to the "Preamble" of the UNSK Constitution, the UNSK solemnly declares:

> To all that our original predecessors used as the governing laws of the Ku Klux Klan, during its former times and all official titles, mannerisms and rituals have not been abandoned by us. All banners, emblems, symbols, or other insignia and things proscribed or previously used by the Ku Klux Klan are held sacred to our tradition and heritage as Klansmen. We shall, in turn, preserve this heritage and valiantly protect it from profanation. It is to be known by all that we are a non-violent group that will not tolerate any sort of violent acts by our members, except in the preservation of ones [sic] personal self, ones [sic] family or the defense of another Klansman. (UNSK Constitution)

The "Objects and Purposes" of the UNSK

> shall be primarily to unite all white persons, native born Gentile citizens of the United States of America, who own no allegiance of any nature or degree to any foreign government, nation, institution, sect, ruler person or people; whose morals are good; whose reputations and vocations are respectable; whose habits are exemplary; who are of sound minds and eighteen years or more of age, under a common oath into a brotherhood of strict regulations; to cultivate and promote patriotism toward our civil government; to practice an honorable clannishness toward each other; to exemplify a practical benevolence; to shield the sanctity of the home and the chastity of womanhood; to maintain forever white supremacy; to teach and faithfully inculcate a high spiritual philosophy through an exalted ritualism, and by a practical devotion to conserver [sic], protect and maintain the distinctive institutions, rights privileges, principles traditions and ideals of a pure Americanism. (UNSK Constitution)

The UNSK made headlines in 2013 when Glendon Scott Crawford, who claimed affiliation with UNSK, was involved in a "bizarre plot to procure and use a radiation-emitting weapon" (Anti-Defamation League). According to a federal complaint, Crawford was accused "of developing a radiation emitting device that could be placed in the back of a van to covertly emit ionizing radiation strong enough to bring about radiation sickness or death against Crawford's enemies" (Terrorism Research & Analysis Consortium). According to the U.S. Federal Bureau of Investigation (FBI), Crawford "spent months designing and constructing an X-ray system that would emit deadly amounts of radiation and could be detonated remotely" (Terrorism Research & Analysis Consortium). To "help fund the construction of his weapon, Crawford inexplicably approached two synagogues in New York . . . trying to get them to give him money for the purported device" (Anti-Defamation League). "Although a member of the Ku Klux Klan, not a group usually friendly to Jews, Crawford told a group of American Jews that his weapon could 'be used by Israel to defeat its enemies, specifically, by killing Israel's enemies while they slept' " (Terrorism Research & Analysis Consortium). In August 2015, Crawford was found guilty of "conspiring to use a weapon of mass destruction and distributing information relating to weapons of mass destruction" (Anti-Defamation League).

In July 2016, residents of Fishers, Indiana, found pieces of paper in plastic bags weighted down with rocks containing "anti-immigrant words and a message promoting the Ku Klux Klan" (Lange). The messages had been distributed by UNSK, and they began, "What will you tell your children?" The message then went on to rail against homosexuality, the overreach of American government, and the flood of "drugs, weapons, disease, prostitution & crime" being "brought into the country by illegal immigrants." As the note warned its readers: "Illegal immigration is out of control, and terrorists are coming into our nation [who] are plotting to destroy America from within" (Lange).

The SPLC identifies members of the UNSK as being located in Ellijay, Georgia, and Connersville, Indiana (Southern Poverty Law Center, Ku Klux Klan).

See also: Ku Klux Klan; White Nationalism; White Supremacist Movement

FURTHER READING

Anti-Defamation League. "Tattered Robes: The State of the Ku Klux Klan in the United States." Anti-Defamation League. https://www.adl.org/sites/default/files/documents /assets/pdf/combating-hate/tattered-robes-state-of-kkk-2016.pdf. (Accessed July 28, 2018.)

Anti-Racist Action. "Everything You Wanted to Know about the United Northern and Southern Knights of the Ku Klux Klan (UNSKKKK)." Anti-Racist Action. https:// antiracistaction.org/everything-you-wanted-to-know-about-the-united-northern -and-southern-knights-of-the-ku-klux-klanunskkkk/. (Accessed July 28, 2018.)

Begley, Sarah. February 15, 2017. "Read the List of the 917 Hate Groups Identified by the Southern Poverty Law Center." *Time*. http://time.com/4671800/hate-groups-on -the-rise/. (Accessed July 28, 2018.)

Lange, Kaitlin. July 25, 2016. "KKK Notes of Fear Blanket Indiana Lawns." *USA Today*. https://www.usatoday.com/story/news/nation-now/2016/07/25/kkk-notes-fear -blanket-indiana-lawns/87532992/. (Accessed July 28, 2018.)

Southern Poverty Law Center. "Ku Klux Klan." Southern Poverty Law Center. https:// www.splcenter.org/fighting-hate/extremist-files/ideology/ku-klux-klan. (Accessed July 28, 2018.)

Southern Poverty Law Center. March 2, 2015. "Active Ku Klux Klan Groups." Southern Poverty Law Center: Intelligence Report. https://www.splcenter.org/fighting-hate /intelligence-report/2015/active-ku-klux-klan-groups. (Accessed July 28, 2018.)

Stormfront. August 30, 2009. "United Northern and Southern Knights of the Ku Klux Klan." Stormfront. https://www.stormfront.org/forum/t634971/. (Accessed July 28, 2018.)

Terrorism Research & Analysis Consortium. "United Northern and Southern Knights of the Ku Klux Klan: Ray Gun Conspirators." Terrorism Research & Analysis Consortium. https://www.trackingterrorism.org/group/united-northern-and-southern -knights-ku-klux-klan-ray-gun-conspirators. (Accessed July 28, 2018.)

United Northern and Southern Knights of the Ku Klux Klan. https://www.unskkkk.com/. (Site appears defunct, July 28, 2018).

United Northern and Southern Knights of the Ku Klux Klan Constitution (UNSK Constitution). https://www.scribd.com/document/95870309/UNSK-Constitution. (Accessed July 30, 2018.)

United Society of Aryan Skinheads

The United Society of Aryan Skinheads (USAS) is a racist skinhead hate group located primarily in San Diego, California (Southern Poverty Law Center, 2015). According to the Southern Poverty Law Center (SPLC), racist skinhead groups "form a particularly violent element of the white supremacist movement, and have often been referred to as the 'shock troops' of the hoped-for revolution. The classic Skinhead look is a shaved head, black Doc Martens boots, jeans with suspenders and an array of typically racist tattoos" (Southern Poverty Law Center, Racist Skinhead). The USAS originated in Oregon in 1987 in "prisons and on the streets" (Anti-Defamation League, USAS). In the early 1990s, "the group relocated to Riverside County, California, and the group reorganized itself in 1993 to combat infighting and drug abuse that were present in the California skinhead community" (Federal Bureau of Investigation). According to a 2005 USAS handbook:

> [T]he purpose of USAS is to "unite all members of the White race who can see the threat facing our people (White people who have the quality of character so that they are willing to stand up and do something about it) into a united fighting force of Skinheads who are ready to battle our enemies, on all fronts, and with every possible means, until we are victorious in fulfilling the 14 words." (NOTE: 14 Words refers to the statement "We must secure the existence of our people and a future for white children." This phrase was coined by wellknown [sic] and recently deceased white supremacist David Lane.) (Federal Bureau of Investigation)

Most of USAS is populated by "ex-cons," but unlike "most prison-based white supremacist groups, [USAS] actually maintains a powerful racist identity and rarely compromises principles in favor of criminal profits" (None). Members of USAS can usually be identified by "one or more of three symbols: the white power fist, the Valknot, and a specific bindrune" (Anti-Defamation League). The Valknot consists of three interlocking triangles and is used by USAS members to identify their attachment to the Norse god Odin (Anti-Defamation League, Valknot). Bindrunes "are essentially 'combination' runic symbols, in which one or more runes are joined together to make a more complex runic symbol" (Anti-Defamation League, USAS).

In 2016, USAS joined dozens of white supremacist groups to achieve "an age-old idea: unify the unruly and questionable characters that populate the ranks of the white supremacist world under a new banner" (Viets). The new group, known as the Aryan Nationalist Alliance (ANA), included "racist skinheads, Klansmen and avowed white nationalist groups" (Viets). The group's mission is to "create an 'ethnostate' where 'each racial group' could 'govern themselves according to their culture and ethnic self interest.' People of color, 'Jews and other groups who have light skin . . . should have their own homes, separate from ours'" (Viets).

USAS continues to "espouse white-power skinhead ideology" and grows every time prison members are paroled (None).

See also: Aryan Nationalist Alliance; Neo-Nazis; White Supremacist Movement

FURTHER READING

Anti-Defamation League. "USAS." Anti-Defamation League. https://www.adl.org/education/references/hate-symbols/usas. (Accessed June 25, 2018.)

Anti-Defamation League. "Valknot." Anti-Defamation League. https://www.adl.org/education/references/hate-symbols/valknot. (Accessed June 25, 2018.)

Federal Bureau of Investigation. January 5, 2010. "FBI United Society of Aryan Skinheads Activity in San Diego, California." Federal Bureau of Investigation. https://publicintelligence.net/fbi-united-society-of-aryan-skinheads-activity-in-san-diego/. (Accessed June 25, 2018.)

None. March 18, 2009. "Hate Rises." *SF Reporter*. https://www.sfreporter.com/news/coverstories/2009/03/18/hate-rises/. (Accessed June 25, 2018.)

Rubio-Sheffrey. March 8, 2012. "Hate & Extremists Groups Continue to Grow." *San Diego Reader*. https://www.sandiegoreader.com/weblogs/news-ticker/2012/mar/08/hate-extremists-groups-continue-to-grow/#. (Accessed June 25, 2018.)

Southern Poverty Law Center. "Racist Skinhead." Southern Poverty Law Center. https://www.splcenter.org/fighting-hate/extremist-files/ideology/racist-skinhead. (Accessed June 25, 2018.)

Southern Poverty Law Center. March 2, 2015. "Active Racist Skinhead Groups." Southern Poverty Law Center: Intelligence Report. https://www.splcenter.org/fighting-hate/intelligence-report/2015/active-racist-skinhead-groups. (Accessed June 25, 2018.)

Viets, Sarah. July 21, 2016. "Meet the Aryan Nationalist Alliance—A Racist Hodgepodge Doomed to Fail." Southern Poverty Law Center: Hatewatch. https://www.splcenter.org/hatewatch/2016/07/21/meet-aryan-nationalist-alliance-%E2%80%93-racist-hodgepodge-doomed-fail. (Accessed June 25, 2018.)

Vanguard America

Vanguard America (VA) is a white nationalist and neo-Nazi organization "which promotes the creation of a whites-only nation-state in the United States" (Institute for Research and Education on Human Rights). According to the Institute for Research and Education on Human Rights (IREHR), "The group espouses a vicious brand of anti-Semitism, endorsing revolution against a fantasized international Jewish conspiracy. Vanguard America's affinity for fascism (of which national socialism is a variant) is seen in its logo, which contains the fasces—a bundle of sticks surrounding an axe—also used by Benito Mussolini's National Fascist Party" (Institute for Research and Education on Human Rights). VA burst into the American consciousness because members of the group were prominent participants in the "Unite the Right" rally in Charlottesville, Virginia, in August 2017, during which a counterprotester was killed by an individual who was associated with VA (Hatewatch staff, August 12, 2017). According to the Anti-Defamation League (ADL), VA is a "white supremacist group that opposes multiculturalism and believes that America should be an exclusively white nation" (Anti-Defamation League). Their "right-wing nationalist slogan, Blood and Soil," which was featured prominently during the Charlottesville rally, "romanticizes the notion that people with 'white blood' have a special bond with 'American soil.' This philosophy originated in Germany (as Blut und Boden) and was popularized by Hitler's regime" (Anti-Defamation League). An alternate slogan used by VA is "For Race and Nation." Along these lines, VA's national platform declares:

> The racial stock of this nation was created for white Christian Anglo/Europeans by white Christian Anglo/Europeans. All other ethnicities, races, religions and demographics are absolutely not compatible with this nation's original culture. With such being stated, a mass exodus, isolation, apartheid, segregation and/or separation must be implemented to retain the good order and longevity of the country. (Institute for Research and Education on Human Rights)

VA was founded in California in 2015 by "Dillon Ulysses Hopper (previously known as Dillon Irizarry)," a "Marine Corps veteran from New Mexico" (Anti-Defamation League). Hopper changed his name from Irizarry in 2006 "and served in the military using that name" (Moyer and Bever). Hopper has said that "the 'future is about the youth' and (for that reason) his group base is 18 to 24 years old." Hopper has claimed that VA has "approximately 200 members in 20 states" (Anti-Defamation League).

Originally, VA was known as American Vanguard and "was firmly in the alt-right hemisphere, and focused on white identity" (Anti-Defamation League). Over time, however,

VA has increasingly embraced a neo-Nazi ideology. In one iteration of their manifesto, posted in February 2017, the VA explained that America was built on the foundation of White European culture and that the "glory of the Aryan nation must be recaptured." VA has also warned against the influence of "the international Jew," tweeting in July 2017, "Those behind the subversive elements eroding our culture often have something in common. Jewish influence is prevalent, invasive, dangerous." This theme is echoed in their 2018 manifesto, which states that "Islam, Judaism and all other non-European or foreign religions" should not have the freedom to practice in the United States. (Anti-Defamation League)

According to the IREHR:

Vanguard America supports policies such as English Only, curtailing immigration, and ending affirmative action and the 1964 Civil Rights Act as steps toward removing non-whites from the "national" territory. Its policy goals include the "repatriation of all African peoples back to their African nation of choice."

Vanguard America promotes eugenics policies, including that "Abortion of a physically and genetically healthy white fetus should be illegal, with a mandatory sentence of first degree murder with no less than 20 years confinement." The group also holds that "The 'freedom of religion' passage [in the U.S. Constitution] . . . was intentionally used to only describe the several separate entities of the Christian faith." In keeping with its Christianized brand of national socialism, the group calls for . . . "The reinstatement of all non-normal or abnormal mental conditions as psychological malformations and mental health issues to include but not limited to the entirety of the LGBTQ will be reinstated. These disorders and mental health issues will be studied extensively and either genetic or physical cures for these mental afflictions will be found and implemented. The current LGBTQ cult in its entirety shall be disbanded and declared a threat to the fabric of United States culture and society." (Institute for Research and Education on Human Rights)

IREHR also contends that "Vanguard America's views on women generally conform to those of national socialism—emphasizing women's role in the family and reproduction while relegating them to a subordinate position to men" (Institute for Research and Education on Human Rights).

In mid-2017, VA birthed a "new configuration of itself, the Patriot Front, in an apparent attempt to distance the group from open Nazism and re-brand fascism as American" (Institute for Research and Education on Human Rights).

In August 2017, VA members participated in the "Unite the Right" rally in Charlottesville, Virginia, "protesting the removal of a statue of Confederate general and hero, Robert E. Lee" (Moyer and Bever). Shouting their signature phrase, "Blood and Soil," VA members were prominently featured in many clashes between "Unite the Right" protesters and counterprotesters. An individual who had been photographed protesting with VA and holding its logos—James Alex Fields Jr.—later "allegedly drove a car into a crowd of counterprotesters, killing a 32-year-old woman and injuring at least 19 people." VA "was quick to say Fields was not a member of the group and had nothing to do with the contingent at the rally. He had simply walked up and grabbed a shield—which he displayed upside down, as shown in photos—and stood a post with Vanguard" (Moyer and Bever).

After Charlottesville, VA leader Dillon Hopper stated that he was "personally disgusted" with the violence that occurred at the rally. "We obviously do not condone violence. We don't tell our members to do this kind of stuff. We are a political movement . . . nothing more" (Moyer and Bever). However, as noted by IREHR, "[t]he line between supporting violence and white revolution, while masquerading as non-violent" is apparent in a speech given by Hopper:

> Soon enough our people, our race will have to set our humanity aside for a short time. We will have to subdue our empathy and compassion and do exactly what is necessary to preserve our people. . . . Those who currently have control over our systems will kill each and every one of us to maintain it. After all, we are only goyim [Jewish name for non-Jews] to them. I look back at a quote of one of our nation's founders, 'The tree of liberty must be refreshed from time to time with the blood of patriots & tyrants. It's natural manure . . .'. I will say that a human body does make excellent fertilizer, but in no way am I advocating violence. This is why we were granted the right of the second amendment, though. That is the ultimate system of checks and balances. I now say to you all, it's been 152 years since the last rebellion in this nation. Our trees are now ripe with the rot and decay of a century and a half. We have the means and the way of preserving these mighty oaks, these sturdy Ash and unyielding hickory. Will you help us clear the brush and waste from our crop to yield the spoils of our labor? Victory or Death. Conquer or Die. Capitulate, Never. We shall fight and we shall win because to lose now, is to lose our entire people. Do not lose hope. The love of our forefathers shall guide us through these dark times. I love you all. Dillon R. Hopper, Vanguard America, Commanding. (Institute for Research and Education on Human Rights)

After Charlottesville, "WordPress terminated Vanguard America's website, forcing it to create a new website. Vanguard America had helped organize the event [the "Unite the Right" rally]. Twitter also banned Vanguard America and other white nationalists from their service in late 2017" (Institute for Research and Education on Human Rights). Though Hopper had not been present at Charlottesville, the leader of VA's Texas chapter—Thomas Rousseau—was. It was Hopper, however, who took the heat and "isolated himself from the fallout from Unite the Right" (Anti-Defamation League). As noted by the Anti-Defamation League, Hopper's public absence prompted Rousseau

> to rebrand VA's "bloodandsoil.org" as the Patriot Front website. The move allowed Rousseau's followers to distance themselves from both Vanguard America and any association with James Fields. Ironically, many of those who defected to Rousseau's Patriot Front also attended "Unite the Right" under the Vanguard America umbrella. (Anti-Defamation League)

VA was further eviscerated in January 2018, "when more infighting and accusations of ineffective leadership led to the formation of a second splinter group, National Socialist Legion (NSL)" (Anti-Defamation League). NSL "is a neo-Nazi group whose strategy . . . is to set up homesteading cells around the country 'for future white migration and eventual white revolt and secession'" (Anti-Defamation League).

See also: Alt-Right Movement; National Socialist Legion; Nationalist Front; Neo-Nazis; Patriot Front; White Nationalism; White Supremacist Movement

FURTHER READING

Anti-Defamation League. "Vanguard America." Anti-Defamation League. https://www
.adl.org/resources/backgrounders/vanguard-america. (Accessed August 1, 2018.)

Cullen, Terence. August 13, 2017. "Vanguard America, Group Charlottesville Driver
James Fields Jr. Marched With, Has Increasingly Become a Neo-Nazi Voice." *NY
Daily News*. http://www.nydailynews.com/amp/news/national/vanguard-america
-increasingly-neo-nazi-voice-article-1.3408117. (Accessed August 2, 2018.)

Hatewatch Staff. August 12, 2017. "Alleged Charlottesville Driver Who Killed One Rallied with Alt-Right Vanguard America Group." Southern Poverty Law Center:
Hatewatch. https://www.splcenter.org/hatewatch/2017/08/12/alleged-charlottesville
-driver-who-killed-one-rallied-alt-right-vanguard-america-group. (Accessed
August 1, 2018.)

Hatewatch Staff. December 11, 2017. "Meet 'Patriot Front': Neo-Nazi Network Aims to
Blur Lines with Militiamen, Then Alt-Right." Southern Poverty Law Center:
Hatewatch.https://www.splcenter.org/hatewatch/2017/12/11/meet-patriot-front
-neo-nazi-network-aims-blur-lines-militiamen-alt-right. (Accessed August 1,
2018.)

Institute for Research and Education on Human Rights (IREHR). "Vanguard America:
National Socialism American Style." IREHR.org. https://www.irehr.org/2018
/02/24/vanguard-america-national-socialism-american-style/. (Accessed August
1, 2018.)

Moyer, Justin Wm., and Lindsey Bever. August 15, 2017. "Vanguard America, a White
Supremacist Group, Denies Charlottesville Ramming Suspect Was a Member."
Washington Post. https://www.washingtonpost.com/local/vanguard-america-a
-white-supremacist-group-denies-charlottesville-attacker-was-a-member/2017/08
/15/2ec897c6-810e-11e7-8072-73e1718c524d_story.html. (Accessed August 1,
2018.)

Piggott, Stephen. August 18, 2017. "Will ACT for America Provide an Outlet for the 'Alt-
Right' Post-Charlottesville?" Southern Poverty Law Center: Hatewatch. https://
www.splcenter.org/hatewatch/2017/08/18/will-act-america-provide-outlet-alt
-right-post-charlottesville. (Accessed August 1, 2018.)

Southern Poverty Law Center. February 15, 2017. "White Nationalists Work to Make
Inroads at U.S. Colleges." Southern Poverty Law Center: Intelligence Report.
https://www.splcenter.org/fighting-hate/intelligence-report/2017/white-nationalists
-work-make-inroads-us-colleges. (Accessed August 1, 2018.)

Unicorn Riot. "Vanguard America." https://www.unicornriot.ninja/tag/vanguard-america/.
(Accessed August 1, 2018.)

Unicorn Riot. November 9, 2017. "'Southern Front' Logs Expose Neo-Nazi Extremist
Cell." Unicorn Riot. https://www.unicornriot.ninja/2017/southern-front-logs
-expose-neo-nazi-extremist-cell/. (Accessed August 1, 2018.)

Vanguard News Network

The Vanguard News Network (VNN) is "an anti-Semitic, white nationalist, white supremacist, and neo-Nazi website founded by neo-Nazi Alex Linder in 2000" (Southern Poverty Law Center). A former member of the most active and important neo-Nazi organization in the United States—the National Alliance—Linder split with the group and spun off his own hate organization in the form of VNN. Linder had hopes that VNN would grow into a "White Viacom" composed of "an integrated global media and services company getting out the White message and serving the White market in a thousand forms" (Southern Poverty Law Center). VNN has proved relatively popular in neo-Nazi circles, but it never attained the market viability that Linder desired. The Southern Poverty Law Center (SPLC) has called VNN "remarkably vulgar, offending even many of the most extreme racists and anti-Semites with Linder's potty humor, untrammeled misogyny" (Linder says women should "make everything happy and smooth running by providing offspring and sex and cookies and iced tea") "and swaggering self-importance" (Southern Poverty Law Center). In 2014, VNN was at the center of a national controversy when it became known that neo-Nazi gunman Frazier Glenn Miller—who perpetrated a shooting at two Kansas City, Missouri, Jewish community centers "that left three people dead, including a 14-year-old boy and his grandfather"—had posted to VNN more than 12,000 times over the years (Terry).

VNN's motto is "No Jews, Just Right" (VNN). The site has been called a "swamp" by one white nationalist critic, who noted that multiple murderers have been linked to VNN. But perhaps the most infamous VNN-linked killer was Frazier Glenn Miller, who killed a 14-year-old boy and his grandfather outside a Kansas City Jewish community center, believing them to be Jews when, in fact, they were not. Miller had swallowed Alex Linder's propaganda of a "principled solution to exterminating the Jews." In killing Jews, Miller believed that "he would win admiration of his peers at the VNN forum" (Terry).

In 2007, white supremacists and neo-Nazis "praised former U.S. President Jimmy Carter's book, *Palestine: Peace Not Apartheid*," for its "anti-Israel, conspiratorial and anti-Semitic propaganda value" (Anti-Defamation League). For its part, VNN "praised Carter for standing up to the 'Zionist lobby' and reaffirming what VNN contributors firmly believed—i.e., that Jews are inherently evil" (VNN). After the publication of Carter's book, in addition to praise from VNN, he received accolades from the neo-Nazi website Stormfront, as well as members of the Aryan Nations. VNN posts praising Carter's book included the following:

> If anyone knows the truth about the Middle East, it's Carter. He was dealing with this same "peace process" BS 30 years ago. Israel is the problem and does not want any semblance of peace. The more wars, the better. Always has been the case, always will be. (VNN, 1/5/2007)
>
> How about everything else the Jews have corrupted through their pernicious influence, like our government, our financial institutions, and the economic future of our children and grandchildren. Maybe Carter has thought this through and truly believes the best way to bring down the power of the Jewish monopoly is through the exposing of the atrocities of the Nation of Israel itself. (VNN, 1/5/2007)
>
> "Because of powerful political, economic, and religious forces in the United States, Israeli government decisions are rarely questioned or condemned," the former president writes. Translation: "The United States has a Zionist Occupied Government." Amen. (VNN, 10/20/2006)

VNN continues to be the destination of many "swamp" dwellers. A recent post to VNN included the headline "Texas: Increasing the F— Propaganda, or, the God of Equality Strikes Again." The post, by an individual using the name "Socrates," stated in part:

> Human equality: a sick idea that isn't even possible, since humans vary greatly, even within the same race and within the same family. Anyway, some high-schoolers are only 14 years old, for hell's sake (i.e., freshmen) and already they're getting "queered up"! The absolute worst thing a parent can do is send their children to a public school. Homeschool your kids. The queer lobby is going to push homosexuality until every person in America views f— as "normal" (instead of viewing it as the disease-ridden lifestyle that it is). (VNN, 5/29/2017)

Today, VNN is still a premier site for vitriolic speech. As one critic has noted, "Just remember, if VNN did not exist, White people would be forced to invent them because VNN is racism White supremacy with a 'face,' the only face that counts, a White person's face" (Wickett).

See also: Aryan Nations; Holocaust Denial; National Alliance; Neo-Nazis; Stormfront; White Nationalism; White Supremacist Movement

FURTHER READING

Anti-Defamation League. January 12, 2007. "Anti-Semitic Reactions to Jimmy Carter's Book: White Supremacists." Anti-Defamation League. https://www.adl.org/news /article/anti-semitic-reactions-to-jimmy-carters-book-white-supremacists. (Accessed June 1, 2018.)

Southern Poverty Law Center. "Alex Linder." Southern Poverty Law Center. https://www .splcenter.org/fighting-hate/extremist-files/individual/alex-linder. (Accessed June 1, 2018.)

Terry, Don. April 14, 2014. "Vanguard News Network: A Track Record of Violence." Southern Poverty Law Center: Hatewatch. https://www.splcenter.org/hate watch/2014/04/14/vanguard-news-network-track-record-violence. (Accessed June 1, 2018.)

VNN. Vanguard News Network. http://www.vanguardnewsnetwork.com/. (Accessed June 1, 2018.)

Wickett, Josh. "VNN: Vanguard News Network." Counter-Racism. http://www.counter -racism.com/articles/internet/vnn.html. (Accessed June 1, 2018.)

VDARE

VDARE.com was a website established in 1999 by English immigrant Peter Brimelow, a former editor of *Forbes* magazine and a contributor to such conservative publications as the *Financial Post* and the *National Review*. VDARE is named for Virginia Dare, "the first white child born to English settlers in the New World in 1587. Contributors to the website have included prominent white nationalists, race scientists, and anti-Semites" (Southern Poverty Law Center, VDARE). For this reason, the Southern Poverty Law Center (SPLC) and other groups have labeled VDARE a hate site, to which its founder retorts that it is being labeled guilty only through association (Brimelow). VDARE is supported by the VDARE Foundation, also established by Brimelow, to support the work of the site. Also known as the Lexington Research Institute Limited, the VDARE Foundation is designated as a 501(c)(3) charity.

VDARE has dubbed itself as being "dedicated to preserving our historical unity as Americans into the 21st Century" (Southern Poverty Law Center). The site is markedly anti-immigrant in tone, as is its founder, Peter Brimelow. Ironically, Brimelow himself is an immigrant to the United States from England. Yet Brimelow's, and VDARE's, message is that the greatest threat to the United States is not immigration per se but immigration from nonwhite countries. Brimelow has stated that the growing number of minorities in the United States threatens the very fabric of the country. In 2006, he wrote on the VDARE website:

> The mass immigration so thoughtlessly triggered in 1965 risks making America an alien nation—not merely in the sense that the numbers of aliens in the nation are rising to levels last seen in the 19th century; not merely in the sense that America will become a freak among the world's nations because of the unprecedented demographic mutation it is inflicting on itself; [and] not merely in the sense that Americans themselves will become alien to each other, requiring an increasingly strained government to arbitrate between them. (VDARE.com)

Though these words are strong, charges of racism and white nationalism among VDARE's contributors come from the likes of Kevin MacDonald and Jared Taylor. MacDonald, a California State University at Long Beach retired professor of psychology, has advanced a notion of evolutionary theory in which he argues that "group evolutionary strategy," such as that exhibited by Jews, has given that people notable advantages that allow Jews to outcompete non-Jews for resources. MacDonald has written on VDARE that

> Jewish activity collectively, throughout history, is best understood as an elaborate and highly successful group competitive strategy directed against neighboring peoples and host societies. The objective has been control of economic resources and political power. One example: overwhelming Jewish support for non-traditional immigration, which has the effect of weakening America's historic white majority. (VDARE.com)

In like manner, Jared Taylor, an avowed white nationalist, is the founder and editor of *American Renaissance*, a magazine noted for its decidedly white supremacist contributors. Taylor, and the organizations with which he associates, has been regularly described as promoting racist ideologies (Sussman).

In 2017, VDARE.com announced the creation of a print journal featuring the "best" material from its webzine, entitled *VDARE Quarterly*. Donald Trump, the president-elect of the United States at that time, was a featured individual on the cover.

See also: White Nationalism

FURTHER READING

Brimelow, Peter. July 24, 2006. "Is VDARE.COM 'White Nationalist'? " VDARE.com. http://www.vdare.com/articles/is-vdarecom-white-nationalist. (Accessed January 5, 2018.)

Pareene, Alex. February 9, 2012. "CPAC Welcomes White Nationalists." Salon. http://www.salon.com/2012/02/09/cpac_welcomes_white_nationalists/. (Accessed January 5, 2018.)

Southern Poverty Law Center. "Peter Brimelow." Southern Poverty Law Center. https://
    www.splcenter.org/fighting-hate/extremist-files/group/vdare. (Accessed January
    5, 2018.)
Southern Poverty Law Center. "VDARE." Southern Poverty Law Center. https://www
    .splcenter.org/fighting-hate/extremist-files/group/vdare. (Accessed January 5, 2018.)
Sussman, Robert W. 2014. *The Myth of Race: The Troubling Persistence of an Unscientific
    Idea.* Harvard University Press.
VDARE.com. http://www.vdare.com/. (Accessed January 5, 2018).

Vinlanders Social Club

The Vinlanders Social Club (VSC) "was formed in 2003 by racist skinheads Brien
James and Eric, 'the Butcher,' Fairburn" (Southern Poverty Law Center, Vinlanders Social Club). Both James and Fairburn had been associated with another skinhead group known as the Outlaw Hammerskins, but they founded the VSC in
order to challenge the parent organization of the Outlaws—Hammerskin Nation.
At the time of the founding of VSC, Hammerskin Nation had "dominated the racist skinhead scene for more than a decade" (Southern Poverty Law Center, Vinlanders Social Club). James had stated that the VSC "was to be something that
was going to replace and surpass the old guard in the skinhead scene. Even by
force if necessary" (Southern Poverty Law Center, Vinlanders Social Club). The
VSC came to relish its reputation among skinhead groups for "drinking, brawling
and following a racist version of Odinism, a form of ancient paganism once practiced by Vikings" (Southern Poverty Law Center, Vinlanders Social Club).

Before founding the Vinlanders, James had been a member of the Outlaw Hammerskins, a group that directly challenged the authority of Hammerskin Nation,
the largest and best-organized skinhead group in the United States. In 2000, James
"allegedly punched and stomped a man to the point of death at a party in Indianapolis, Indiana when the party-goer refused to 'seig heil.'" James would later
brag that his "JTTF (Joint Terrorism Task Force) file is a mile long" (Southern
Poverty Law Center, Brien James). James was often described by contemporaries
as "nuts and violent" (Southern Poverty Law Center, Brien James).

James "began his gang career young when he and childhood friends formed a
gang called the Knightstown Boys in Knightstown, Indiana. In his late teens, James
became involved with the Ku Klux Klan before helping to found the Outlaw Hammerskins" (Southern Poverty Law Center, Brien James). In 2002, "James left the
Outlaw Hammerskins to found the Hoosier State Skinheads" (Southern Poverty Law
Center, Brien James). Then, in 2003, he and Fairburn, together with others, "formed
the Vinlanders Social Club, a coalition of regional skinhead groups—including those
in Indiana, Ohio, and Pennsylvania—that did not recognize the authority of Hammerskin Nation" (Southern Poverty Law Center, Brien James) In 2005, in a further
challenge to Hammerskin Nation, James helped convene several white supremacist
groups in order to assert dominance over the larger skinhead group.

VSC cofounder Fairburn, nicknamed "the Butcher," was a particularly violent
skinhead who served time in prison "for beating a homeless black man in Indianapolis, Indiana." He was unmistakable in the skinhead movement for having the

word "murder" tattooed "in large letters across the front of his neck. He was also the rhythm guitarist for the hate-rock group RAHOWA (RAcial HOly WAr)" (Southern Poverty Law Center, Eric Fairburn).

In 2000, Fairburn joined the Outlaw Hammerskins. In 2002, "he joined another group known as the Hoosier State Skinheads." After seeing the movie *Gangs of New York*, "Fairburn renamed himself the 'Butcher' after the character in the film, William 'Bill the Butcher' Cutting, a crime lord and sadist who hated all non-whites and Irish immigrants" (Southern Poverty Law Center, Eric Fairburn). To cultivate his image, Fairburn began to carry "a large sledgehammer and became known for his unpredictable and abusive conduct, especially toward women. In one instance, he tossed a female friend's dog out of a car window during heavy traffic" while the car was traveling in excess of 70 miles per hour. Fairburn would later comment that a truck hit the dog and it "exploded," to which Fairburn exclaimed, "Great stuff" (Southern Poverty Law Center, Eric Fairburn).

In May 2006, "tensions between the Vinlanders and other neo-Nazi groups exploded at a hate-rock festival known as Nordic Fest," which was held in Dawson Springs, Kentucky (Southern Poverty Law Center, Vinlanders Social Club). After a National Socialist Movement (NSM) member made a speech touting NSM's accomplishments and apparently disparaging those of the Vinlanders, the individual was beaten in front of his wife and young daughter. In the fall of 2007, James declared a truce with all Hammerskin groups and proclaimed a "New Era," announcing that "after nearly a decade of conflict and division, the Vinlanders and the Hammerskin Nation have . . . decided to declare peace" (Southern Poverty Law Center, Vinlanders Social Club).

In March 2007, "Fairburn and two other Vinlanders beat a homeless black man in Indianapolis, Indiana" (Southern Poverty Law Center, Eric Fairburn). Fairburn served two years of a five-year sentence and vowed upon his release that he would no longer associate himself with the skinhead movement, stating, "I'm 34 years old and I've got too much going on in my life to waste any more of it" (Southern Poverty Law Center, Fairburn). In September 2010, Fairburn walked into a police station in Indianapolis, Indiana, and confessed to the 2004 murder of William McDaniel, an individual who was charged in a car/motorcycle accident that had claimed the life of one of Fairburn's friends (Baird). After his extradition to Springfield, Missouri, the site of the crime, Fairburn was sentenced to life in prison (OzarksFirst.com).

By the end of 2008, the VSC was in decline (Holthouse and Wood). By 2013, with Fairburn in jail, James organized yet another skinhead group—the American Vikings—which chose as its logo the hammer of the Norse god Thor. James stated that American Vikings would be "dedicated to creating entertaining and meaningful discussion about issues affecting patriotic, constitutional libertarian leaning, working class Americans" (Morlin). James touted the new group as a project "created by long-time former members of the American White Nationalist movement in the hopes that we can create a realistic and constructive dialog amongst several different types of patriots" (Morlin).

See also: American Vikings; Hammerskin Nation; National Socialist Movement; Racist Skinheads

FURTHER READING

Anti-Defamation League. "Vinlanders Social Club." Anti-Defamation League. https://www.adl.org/education/references/hate-symbols/vinlanders-social-club. (Accessed May 29, 2018.)

Baird, Kathee. September 2009. "Skinhead Confesses to 2004 Springfield Murder." Crime Scene. http://crimesceneinvestigations.blogspot.com/2010/09/skinhead-confesses-to-2004-murder-in.html. (Accessed April 19, 2017.)

Holthouse, David, and Laurie Wood. November 30, 2008. "Racist Skinhead Group Vinlanders Social Club on the Decline." Southern Poverty Law Center: Intelligence Report. https://www.splcenter.org/fighting-hate/intelligence-report/2008/racist-skinhead-group-vinlanders-social-club-decline. (Accessed May 29, 2018.)

Morlin, Bill. May 17, 2013. "Veteran Skinhead Forms New Racist Club, Peddles T-Shirts on Internet." Southern Poverty Law Center: Hatewatch. https://www.splcenter.org/hatewatch/2013/05/17/veteran-skinhead-forms-new-racist-club-peddles-t-shirts-internet. (Accessed April 19, 2017.)

OzarksFirst.com. "Admitted Killer Sentenced to Life in Prison." *OzarksFirst.com*. http://www.ozarksfirst.com/news/admitted-killer-sentenced-to-life-in-prison/69924058. (Accessed April 19, 2017.)

Southern Poverty Law Center. "Brien James." Southern Poverty Law Center. https://www.splcenter.org/fighting-hate/extremist-files/individual/brien-james. (Accessed May 29, 2018.)

Southern Poverty Law Center. "Eric 'The Butcher' Fairburn." Southern Poverty Law Center. https://www.splcenter.org/fighting-hate/extremist-files/individual/eric-butcher-fairburn. (Accessed May 29, 2017.)

Southern Poverty Law Center. "Vinlanders Social Club." Southern Poverty Law Center. https://www.splcenter.org/fighting-hate/extremist-files/group/vinlanders-social-club. (Accessed May 29, 2018.)

Volksfront

Volksfront "was a virulently racist and anti-Semitic group" that existed in the United States from its founding in 1994 until 2012, when its 17 U.S.-based chapters were dissolved (Beirich, The End of Volksfront). For a time, the group was "the most active neo-Nazi group on the American West Coast," and its influence spread from its founding in Portland, Oregon, to include chapters "in Germany, the Netherlands, the United Kingdom, Canada, Australia, and Spain" (Beirich, The End of Volksfront). Much of the membership of Volksfront consisted of neo-Nazi skinheads and other "white power" extremists, and "a number of Volksfront members were linked with the Hammerskins, a white supremacist group formed in Texas, and Blood & Honor, a group founded in the United Kingdom" (Beirich, The End of Volksfront). As noted by the Anti-Defamation League (ADL), Volksfront was unlike other white supremacist groups in that it was "ideologically and theologically flexible, allowing its followers considerable leeway in their beliefs as long as they share a commitment to white supremacy and a 'folkish' lifestyle" (Anti-Defamation League). Volksfront in the United States disbanded in August 2012, saying that illegal harassment and investigations from the federal government forced it to cease operations. Though the group was officially disbanded, the Southern Poverty Law Center noted that "its leadership will probably live on in some form in the white supremacist world" (Beirich, Volksfront: The Leadership).

Volksfront was formed in prison in 1994 while founder Randal Krager was serving a 27-month prison term for assaulting an African American man, who had been put into a coma from Krager's single punch. After Krager's release from prison in 1995, Volksfront remained visible in the Portland, Oregon, area until harassment by law enforcement officials forced the group to move underground from 1999 to 2001. Engaging a variety of extremist activities, Volksfront began to reach out to racist skinheads and other extremists overseas. Volksfront's "white supremacist ideology and hatred of Jews, blacks, and other minorities appeared to have attracted many followers both in the United States and abroad" (Anti-Defamation League). In April 2007, "a Volksfront member received an 11-year sentence for throwing rocks engraved with swastikas at a Eugene, Oregon synagogue. Other Volksfront members engaged in similar activities" (Beirich, The End of Volksfront).

Volksfront was "heavily involved in the white power music scene." In addition "to hosting a number of white power music events, Volksfront also worked closely with several white power bands" (Anti-Defamation League). In 2002, Volksfront created a CD label—Upfront Records. Some of the groups with which Volksfront associated had names befitting the ideology that was espoused in their songs. Among these were "Jew Slaughter," "Aggressive Force," "Cut Throat," "Max Resist," "Rebel Hell," and "Down Right Hateful" (Anti-Defamation League).

Sometimes, members of Volksfront showed up at events spoiling for a fight with other neo-Nazi groups or with protesters. In December 2009, members of Volksfront and members of the Hammerskins, a rival group, showed up at a Pensacola, Florida, event known as Martyr's Day—an event that commemorated the death of Bob Mathews, founder of the terrorist group the Order, who died in a shootout with FBI agents in December 1984. Though both sides were ready for a fight, the leader of the racist American Front skinhead group was also in attendance, and he prevented the two sides from fighting with one another (Beirich).

The end of Volksfront in the United States began on August 5, 2012. On that day, a neo-Nazi strode into a Sikh temple in Oak Creek, Wisconsin, "shot six people to death," and wounded a police officer (Beirich). When the gunman was identified, it was wrongly reported that he was a member of Volksfront. Though the report was untrue, it turned out that his girlfriend was a Volksfront member. As pressure from the police and anti-racist activists mounted, Volksfront's founder—Randal Krager, now almost 40 with several children—came to a decision to end the group. In September 2012, all of Volksfront's presences on the web—from Twitter to Facebook, its website, and its Wikipedia page—were shut down.

See also: Neo-Nazis; White Supremacist Movement

FURTHER READING

Anti-Defamation League. "Volksfront." Anti-Defamation League. https://www.adl.org /education/resources/profiles/volksfront. (Accessed March 15, 2017.)

Beirich, Heidi. November 20, 2013a. "The End of Volksfront?" Southern Poverty Law Center: Intelligence Report. https://www.splcenter.org/fighting-hate/intelligence -report/2013/end-volksfront. (Accessed March 15, 2017.)

Beirich, Heidi. November 20, 2013b. "Volksfront: The Leadership." Southern Poverty Law Center: Intelligence Report. https://www.splcenter.org/fighting-hate/intelligence -report/2013/volksfront-leadership-0. (Accessed March 15, 2017.)

Stormfront. "Volksfront." Stormfront. https://www.stormfront.org/forum/t381225/. (Accessed March 15, 2017.)

War on the Horizon

War on the Horizon (WOH) is a website devoted to "the mass murder of whites and the 'ethnic cleansing' of 'black-skinned Uncle Tom race traitors'" (Terry, August 21, 2013). WOH was founded by Ayo Kimathi, a former official at the U.S. Department of Homeland Security, who was responsible for buying such items as "handcuffs, ammunition, and guns" (Terry, August 21, 2013). When he was not working at his day job, Kimathi, who called himself the "Irritated Genie of Soufeese," made it known that "warfare is eminent" and that "in order for Black people to survive the 21st century, we are going to have to kill a lot of whites—more than our Christian hearts can possibly count" (Terry, August 21, 2013).

Kimani's position at DHS was with the Immigration and Customs Enforcement (ICE) division of Homeland Security. Though federal employees must obtain written permission to engage in ventures outside of their federal jobs, Kimathi misrepresented his association with WOH by telling management that it "was an entertainment website selling videos of concerts and lectures" (Terry, August 21, 2013). On the WOH website, Kimathi spread his message "of pending race war and genocide and his disgust with 'the smallhates (white so-called "jews") and the white homos like Gay Edgar Hoover' in a series of videos and speeches he gives around the country" (Terry, August 21, 2013). WOH maintained an "enemies" list that included

> Rev. Al Sharpton, Lil Wayne, Oprah Winfrey, Whoopi Goldberg, Condoleezza Rice, Colin Powell, who he calls "Colon," and even President Obama, "a treasonous mulatto scum dweller . . . who will fight against reparations for Black people in amerikkka, but in favor of f— rights for freaks in amerikkka and Afrika." (Terry, August 21, 2013)

Though the WOH website in 2018 does not express the same vitriol it once did, in 2013 it stated that WOH

> was created for the purpose of preparing Black people worldwide for an unavoidable, inevitable clash with the white race. whites [sic] around the world are absolutely determined to exterminate Afrikan [sic] people in all corners of the Earth. As a result of this reality, WOH has dedicated our time and expertise to properly educating Black people to prepare for Racial Warfare. This includes intellectual, spiritual, psychological, and physical preparation for a global clash that will mean the end of white rule on this planet or the end of the Black Race as we know it. (Terry, August 21, 2013)

As in 2013, the WOH website today ends with the following:

> The information and perspective shared on this website are designed to enlighten the Black mind and prepare our people for Racial independence and survival. We

trust that you will find the information on our site informative and useful to you and your family. . . .

   We'll See You on the Battlefield! (War on the Horizon).

See also: Black Nationalism; Black Separatists

FURTHER READING

Southern Poverty Law Center. November 20, 2013. "Secret Extremist Life of Homeland Security Employee Exposed." Southern Poverty Law Center: Intelligence Report. https://www.splcenter.org/fighting-hate/intelligence-report/2013/secret-extremist -life-homeland-security-employee-exposed. (Accessed June 16, 2018.)

Southern Poverty Law Center. February 25, 2014. "'Irritated Genie,' Race-War Enthusiast, Finally Leaves DHS." Southern Poverty Law Center: Intelligence Report. https://www.splcenter.org/fighting-hate/intelligence-report/2014/irritated-genie -race-war-enthusiast-finally-leaves-dhs. (Accessed June 16, 2018.)

Terry, Don. August 21, 2013. "DHS Employee Promotes Race War in Spare Time, Advocates Mass Murder of Whites." Southern Poverty Law Center: Hatewatch. https:// www.splcenter.org/hatewatch/2013/08/21/dhs-employee-promotes-race-war -spare-time-advocates-mass-murder-whites. (Accessed June 16, 2018.)

Terry, Don. December 11, 2013. "Black 'Race Warrior' Leaves DHS." Southern Poverty Law Center: Hatewatch. https://www.splcenter.org/hatewatch/2013/12/11/black -race-warrior-leaves-dhs. (Accessed June 16, 2018.)

War on the Horizon. http://waronthehorizon.com/site/. (Accessed June 16, 2018.)

Washington Summit Publishers

Washington Summit Publishers (WSP) produces and sells books "on race and intelligence and related topics" (Washington Summit Publishers). WSP is located in Whitefish, Montana, and has been designated a white nationalist hate group by the Southern Poverty Law Center (SPLC). According to the SPLC:

> White nationalist groups espouse white supremacist or white separatist ideologies, often focusing on the alleged inferiority of nonwhites. Groups listed in a variety of other categories—Ku Klux Klan, neo-Confederate, neo-Nazi, racist skinhead, and Christian Identity—could also be fairly described as white nationalist. (Southern Poverty Law Center, White Nationalist)

WSP "reprints a range of classical and modern racist tracts, along with books on eugenics, the discredited 'science' of breeding better humans" (Southern Poverty Law Center, 2006). Among the authors published by WSP are Kevin MacDonald, a former professor at the University of California, Long Beach, who asserted that Jews are genetically driven to "destroy" Western societies; and Richard Lynn, who considers himself an "ethnic nationalist" who argues that only those countries that remain "racially homogenous" will flourish in the future, noting that the greatest achievements and advances in world civilization have begun in countries with homogeneous populations.

   WSP is currently run by white supremacist Richard Spencer, the founder of the alt-right movement as well as the director of the National Policy Institute. WSP also publishes *Radix Journal*, a publication that features articles from white nationalists, white supremacists, and anti-Semites.

The Institute for Research & Education on Human Rights (IREHR), whose website features the tagline "We Fight the Right," has noted the influence of publishing houses such as WSP that focus on white nationalism and other issues that appeal to issues of white dispossession:

> The white nationalist movement consists of an ever-shifting array of organizations, publishing houses, think tanks, websites and individuals with an interlocking leadership and cross-pollinating memberships. Two relatively distinct trends exist in the movement: a mainstreaming wing that hopes to build a political majority among white people, and a vanguardist wing comprised of hard-core cadres with a more violence-prone tendency. Both movement wings aim at establishing a whites-only political, cultural, and social dominance over the United States. The long-term goal of the most significant sector of the movement is the creation of an Aryans-only nation-state, separate from the rest of the country.
>
> The influence of the white nationalist movement has far exceeded its size. In the post-Jim Crow years, it has re-articulated racism and white supremacy in American life, and turned them into an ideology of white dispossession. The expected loss of majority status by white people, projected by the Census Bureau to occur around mid-century, has animated this idea. One immediate outcome has been that the public discourse about affirmative action has been dominated by notions that white people are the new "victims." Talk of discrimination quickly turns to charges of "reverse racism" and "special rights" for "minorities." More, white nationalists years ago cut the turf for the anti-immigrant sentiment that has swelled behind it. In the United States, anti-Semitism exists in its most congealed form in the Jewish conspiracy theories that white nationalists have propagated; and the notion of Holocaust denial would barely exist at all if white nationalists had not turned it into their movement's calling card. (Zeskind)

See also: Alt-Right Movement; Christian Identity; Ku Klux Klan; National Policy Institute; Neo-Confederates; Racist Skinheads; White Nationalism; White Supremacist Movement

FURTHER READING

Burghart, Devin. October 23, 2013. "White Nationalists Descend on D.C. for National Policy Institute Conference." Institute for Research & Education on Human Rights. http://www.irehr.org/2013/10/23/npi-conference-2013/. (Accessed June 16, 2018.)

Institute for Research & Education on Human Rights. https://www.irehr.org/. (Accessed June 16, 2018.)

Southern Poverty Law Center. "White Nationalist." Southern Poverty Law Center. https://www.splcenter.org/fighting-hate/extremist-files/ideology/white-nationalist. (Accessed June 16, 2018.)

Southern Poverty Law Center. August 11, 2006. "The New Racialists." https://www.splcenter.org/fighting-hate/intelligence-report/2006/new-racialists. (Accessed June 16, 2018.)

Southern Poverty Law Center. March 2, 2015. "Active White Nationalist Groups." Southern Poverty Law Center: Intelligence Report. https://www.splcenter.org/fighting-hate/intelligence-report/2015/active-white-nationalist-groups. (Accessed June 16, 2018.)

Washington Summit Publishers. "About." Washington Summit Publishers. https://wash
    summit.com/about/. (Accessed June 16, 2018.)
Zeskind, Leonard. September 18, 2009. "A New Statement by a Renewed Organization
    for New Times." Institute for Research & Education on Human Rights. https://
    www.irehr.org/2009/09/18/a-new-statement-by-a-renewed-organization-for
    -new-times/. (Accessed June 16, 2018.)

We Are Change

We Are Change is an unaffiliated media organization composed of groups and
individuals that claim to be working to "expose worldwide corruption and hold
authoritative figures to account for their actions and crimes in which their involvement has been covered up or hidden from public knowledge" (We Are Change,
About Us). The Southern Poverty Law Center (SPLC) has characterized We Are
Change as part of the conspiracy-obsessed anti-government "patriot" movement,
thus lumping the group in with other "hate" organizations such as the Ku Klux
Klan (KKK) and neo-Nazis. Though the leader of We Are Change, Luke Rudkowski, has vehemently protested the group's designation by the SPLC, he does
not apologize for its intent. According to the organization's website, We Are
Change seeks to

> expose the lies of governments and the corporate elite who constantly trash our
> humanity. By asking the hard questions the mainstream media refuses to ask, we
> shine a little more light on truth. Furthermore, we seek to connect, educate, and
> motivate those who are interested in alerting the public to the pertinent issues that
> are affecting our lives each and every day. Our goal is to create a community of
> truth-seekers and peacemakers who share a commitment to nonviolent action. (We
> Are Change, About Us)

Luke Rudkowski founded We Are Change in 2006 to hold the federal government
to account. The organization began by disseminating 9/11 conspiracy theories but
has since branched out into theories more closely associated with the radical right.
The group's website "frets about a looming one world order" and states that it
seeks "to uncover the truth behind the private banking cartel of the military industrial complex" that wants to "eliminate national sovereignty" (Beirich). Rudkowski seems "particularly concerned about the alleged role in the New World
Order" of organizations "such as the Bilderberg group and the Trilateral Commission. These institutions have been targeted for decades as major global evildoers
by Patriot groups and other far-right organizations, including several that are racist and virulently anti-Semitic" (Beirich).

   In 2011, the leader of the Los Angeles chapter of We Are Change, Bruno Ernst
Bruhwiler, was an adherent of the Sovereign Citizens Movement—a radical right-
wing movement that is virulently anti-government and that "believes that the federal government has no authority to impose law or regulation" on most
Americans—as well as a member of the Oath Keepers, a conspiracy-minded
patriot group. Bruhwiler was a participant in "redemption practices," which are
inherent to those who consider themselves sovereign citizens. Redemption is an

"ideology that claims that when the U.S. quit the gold standard in 1933, it pledged its citizens as collateral in order to borrow money based on their future earnings" (Beirich). Then, the theory goes, "the government funded a secret 'Treasury Direct Account' for each individual that it stocks with millions of dollars. Redemptionists have come up with a series of bizarre maneuvers that are meant to liberate this money from the government and have it paid to them personally" (Beirich).

Today, We Are Change has "tapped into a deep vein of suspicion among Americans who see dark conspiracies being hatched inside the federal government" (Southern Poverty Law Center). The group's emphasis on conspiracy theories fuels the suspicion of mistrust of extremists on the right-wing who believe that government is engaged in one covert operation after another in order to subvert the liberties and freedoms of American citizens. Such actions, according to the SPLC, contribute to a rise in "hate." But according to We Are Change, "the increased exposure of rampant government corruption and its blatant disregard for the American people has resulted in more social dissatisfaction and the growth of more political protest groups." And while the group agrees with the SPLC that "real extremist groups" may be growing in number, "it is clearly grossly misleading to suggest that We Are Change, a peaceful citizen journalism activist group, is on a par with cross burning racists" (We Are Change, 2011).

It probably does not help We Are Change's cause that Alex Jones, a far-right radio show host and avid conspiracy theorist whose website InfoWars.com has been labeled a fake news website, has come to We Are Change's defense (Blake). Upon learning of We Are Change's designation as a hate group, Jones protested:

> All of this makes up a sophisticated smear campaign of propaganda, which influences the minds of the ordinary public to associate anti-New World Order and 9/11 Truth organizations with racist groups. It is extremely unjust to equate patriotic activists with racism. (Jones)

See also: Oath Keepers

FURTHER READING

Beirich, Heidi. February 27, 2011. "We Are Change's L.A. Leader Belies Group's Moderate Image." Southern Poverty Law Center: Intelligence Report. https://www.splcenter.org/fighting-hate/intelligence-report/2015/we-are-changes-la-leader-belies-groups-moderate-image. (Accessed May 18, 2018.)

Blake, Andrew. December 9, 2016. "Infowars' Alex Jones Appeals to Trump for Aid over Fears of 'Fake News' Crackdown." *Washington Times*. http://www.washingtontimes.com/news/2016/dec/9/alex-jones-conspiracy-theorist-appeals-trump-aid-o/. (Accessed May 18, 2018.)

Jones, Alex. March 5, 2010. "The Southern Poverty Law Center Lumps in WeAreChange with 'Hate' Groups." InfoWars.com. https://www.infowars.com/the-southern-poverty-law-center-lumps-in-wearechange-with-hate-groups/. (Accessed May 18, 2018.)

Southern Poverty Law Center. "Meet the 'Patriots.'" Southern Poverty Law Center: Intelligence Report. https://www.splcenter.org/fighting-hate/intelligence-report/2010/meet-patriots. (Accessed May 18, 2018.)

We Are Change. "About Us." WeAreChange.org. https://wearechange.org/about/. (Accessed May 18, 2018.)

We Are Change. February 24, 2011. "SPLC Report Lumps In We Are Change with Neo-Nazis, KKK." WeAreChange.org. https://wearechange.org/splc-report-lumps-in-we-are-change-with-neo-nazis-kkk/. (Accessed May 18, 2018.)

Werewolf 88

Werewolf 88 is a neo-Nazi hate group based in Pennsylvania. The Southern Poverty Law Center (SPLC) has characterized Werewolf 88 as a hate group because of its ideals and philosophies, "which are largely anti-Semitic and in support of neo-Nazi" values (Southern Poverty Law Center). Members of Werewolf 88 believe in the supremacy of the white race over all other races. The number 88 is "a white supremacist numerical code for 'Heil Hitler' " (Anti-Defamation League). "H is the eighth letter of the alphabet, so 88 = HH = Heil Hitler" (Anti-Defamation League). The Anti-Defamation League (ADL) notes that 88 "is used throughout the entire white supremacist movement, not just neo-Nazis." (Anti-Defamation League). The ADL notes that 88 is often used in tattoos sported by neo-Nazis, in particularly members of Werewolf 88; "as part of the name of a group, publication or website; or as part of a screenname or e-mail address" (Anti-Defamation League).

The number 88 is "also frequently combined with another significant number in white supremacist and neo-Nazi circles—14" (Anti-Defamation League). This number references the so-called 14 Words slogan enunciated by David Lane, former member of the Order who was found guilty of the assassination of Jewish talk show host Alan Berg in Denver, Colorado, in 1984. The 14 Words slogan reads: "We must secure the existence of our people and a future for white children" (Anti-Defamation League).

See also: Neo-Nazis; The Order; White Supremacist Movement

FURTHER READING

Anti-Defamation League. "88" Anti-Defamation League. https://www.adl.org/education/references/hate-symbols/88. (Accessed May 30, 2018.)

Hall, Peter. August 14, 2017. "Pennsylvania Fifth in Nation for Hate Groups." *Morning Call*. http://www.mcall.com/news/police/mc-nws-pennsylvania-hate-groups-2017 0814-story.html. (Accessed May 30, 2018.)

Southern Poverty Law Center. February 15, 2017. "Active Hate Groups 2016." Southern Poverty Law Center: Intelligence Report. https://www.splcenter.org/fighting-hate/intelligence-report/2017/active-hate-groups-2016. (Accessed May 30, 2018.)

Westboro Baptist Church

Westboro Baptist Church (WBC) has been characterized as perhaps one of the most "rabid" hate groups in America (Southern Poverty Law Center, Westboro Baptist Church). The church consists of its pastor, Fred Phelps, and "nine of his 13 children (four are estranged), their children and spouses, and a small number of close family friends of the Phelps" (Southern Poverty Law Center, 2001). The WBC is small and virulently homophobic and anti-Semitic. Though it bears the moniker of a Baptist church, WBC is not associated with any mainstream Baptist organization, rather considering itself a "primitive" Baptist church. The hallmark of the organization is its propensity for staging protests at events it believes support homosexuality or otherwise subvert what its believers hold as God's laws. WBC specializes in "anti-gay vitriol, entitling its main website 'God Hates F—' " (Southern Poverty Law Center, 2001). In recent years, WBC has targeted Jewish organizations, as well as Catholic, Lutheran, and other Christian organizations, all of which WBC considers heretical (Anti-Defamation League). WBC members say that "God's hatred is one of His holy attributes and that their picketing is a form of preaching to a doomed country unable to hear their message in any other way" (Anti-Defamation League).

The WBC came into the public spotlight by utilizing its tactic of a "picketing ministry," or raising awareness of the church and ministry by conducting controversial protests. The protests are not meant to win followers but to inform individuals that they are "doomed" if they have not been predestined as one of God's chosen people (as members of WBC believe they are). The church began picketing in 1991 and since then has reportedly picketed more than 40,000 times (Southern Poverty Law Center, Westboro Baptist Church). Aside from its picketing of those it believes support homosexuality, in 2005 WBC "began picketing the funerals of American soldiers killed in the wars in Iraq and Afghanistan" (Southern Poverty Law Center, Westboro Baptist Church). The group maintains that God is "punishing the United States" in a variety of ways for condoning the sin of homosexuality. For example, when two sets of twin girls drowned in separate incidents in July and August 2010, the WBC attributed their deaths to Massachusetts's legalization of same-sex marriage in 2004 (Southern Poverty Law Center, Westboro Baptist Church). The terrorist attacks of 9/11 were also the result of America's tolerance of homosexuality. As stated by WBC founder Fred Phelps:

> We told you, right after it happened five years ago, that the deadly events of 9/11 were direct outpourings of divine retribution, the immediate visitation of God's wrath and vengeance and punishment for America's horrendous sodomite sins, that worse and more of it was on the way. We further told you that any politician, any political official, any preacher telling you differently as to the cause and interpretation of 9/11 is a dastardly lying false prophet, cowardly and mean, and headed for hell. And taking you with him! God is no longer with America, but is now America's enemy. God himself is now America's terrorist. (Southern Poverty Law Center, Westboro Baptist Church)

The WBC's tactics have earned it the reputation from the Southern Poverty Law Center as being "arguably the most obnoxious and rabid hate group in America." On March 19, 2014, WBC founder Fred Phelps died of natural causes at age 84.

See also: Alliance Defending Freedom; American College of Pediatricians; American Family Association; Family Research Council; Family Watch International; Liberty Counsel; Pacific Justice Institute; Ruth Institute; Traditional Values Coalition; World Congress of Families

FURTHER READING

Anti-Defamation League. "Westboro Baptist Church." Anti-Defamation League: Extremism in America. http://archive.adl.org/learn/ext_us/wbc/. (Accessed January 5, 2018.)

Southern Poverty Law Center. "Westboro Baptist Church." Southern Poverty Law Center. https://www.splcenter.org/fighting-hate/extremist-files/group/westboro-baptist -church. (Accessed January 5, 2018.)

Southern Poverty Law Center. March 21, 2001. "Inside the Westboro Baptist Church." Southern Poverty Law Center: Intelligence Report. https://www.splcenter.org /fighting-hate/intelligence-report/2001/inside-westboro-baptist-church. (Accessed January 5, 2018.)

Westboro Baptist Church. http://www.godhatesfags.com/. (Accessed January 5, 2018.)

Western Hammerskins

The Western Hammerskins have been designated as a "racist skinhead group" by the Southern Poverty Law Center (SPLC). According to the SPLC, "racist skinheads form a particularly violent element of the white supremacist movement, and have often been referred to as the 'shock troops' of the hoped-for revolution. The classic Skinhead look is a shaved head, black Doc Martens boots, jeans with suspenders and an array of typically racist tattoos" (Southern Poverty Law Center, Racist Skinhead). The Western Hammerskins are a regional variation of "Hammerskin Nation," which the Anti-Defamation League (ADL) has dubbed as "the most violent and best-organized neo-Nazi skinhead group in the United States" (Anti-Defamation League, Hammerskin Nation). The primary symbol and logo of the Hammerskins,

> appropriated from Pink Floyd's 'The Wall,' consists of two crossed hammers, usually superimposed over a cogwheel. The symbol typically appears in red, white, and black, the colors of the Nazi flag. In some cases the hammers and cogwheel appear over a red, black and white-colored shield. In the United States, the Hammerskins differentiate themselves regionally, such as the Confederate Hammerskins and Western Hammerskins and can sport regional variations of this logo, such as a version incorporating the Confederate flag. (Anti-Defamation League, Hammerskins)

The Western Hammerskins are found primarily in California. Like the parent group, Hammerskin Nation, Western Hammerskins "desire to have 'their own state,' which consists of only white people," and "believe they are in a race war and list any of their members who are in jail or prison as POWs" (Hall). Western Hammerskins, like others in Hammerskin Nation, ascribe great significance to the numbers 14 and 88. The number 14, which stands for the "14 Words" penned by now-deceased white supremacist David Lane, refers to the ideology of Western Hammerskins and other white supremacist groups: "We must secure the existence of our people and a future for white children" (Hall). The number 88 refers to "Heil Hitler because H is the eighth letter in the alphabet" (Hall).

Though the Western Hammerskins are often viewed as a street gang, the Hammerskins point out that they have "chapter guidelines" that most street gangs do not have. These guidelines "for how members are expected to behave" include "having strong family values, paying monthly dues to the group, not abusing alcohol and holding either a full-time job or attending school full time" (Hall).

See also: Confederate Hammerskins; Hammerskin Nation; Neo-Nazis; Racist Skinheads; White Nationalism; White Supremacist Movement

FURTHER READING

Anti-Defamation League. "The Hammerskin Nation." Anti-Defamation League. https://www.adl.org/education/resources/profiles/hammerskin-nation. (Accessed June 26, 2018.)

Anti-Defamation League. "Hammerskins." Anti-Defamation League. https://www.adl.org/education/references/hate-symbols/hammerskins?_ga=2.52790881.876358664.1529636601-1649684779.1529636601. (Accessed June 26, 2018.)

Hall, John. October 26, 2001. "Suspects Linked to Gang." *San Diego Union-Tribune.* http://www.sandiegouniontribune.com/sdut-suspects-linked-to-gang-2001oct26-story.html. (Accessed June 26, 2018.)

Hammerskin Nation. http://www.hammerskins.net/. (Accessed June 26, 2018.)

Reynolds, Michael. December 15, 1999. "Hammerskin Nation Emerges from Small Dallas Group." Southern Poverty Law Center: Intelligence Report. https://www.splcenter.org/fighting-hate/intelligence-report/1999/hammerskin-nation-emerges-small-dallas-group. (Accessed June 26, 2018.)

Southern Poverty Law Center. "Racist Skinhead." Southern Poverty Law Center. https://www.splcenter.org/fighting-hate/extremist-files/ideology/racist-skinhead. (Accessed June 26, 2018.)

Southern Poverty Law Center. March 2, 2015. "Active Racist Skinhead Groups." Southern Poverty Law Center: Intelligence Report. https://www.splcenter.org/fighting-hate/intelligence-report/2015/active-racist-skinhead-groups. (Accessed June 26, 2018.)

White Prison Gangs. "Hammerskins." White Prison Gangs. http://whiteprisongangs.blogspot.com/2009/05/hammerskins_02.html. (Accessed June 26, 2018.)

White Aryan Resistance

White Aryan Resistance (WAR) is an "American neo-Nazi and white supremacist organization founded by former Ku Klux Klan Grand Dragon Tom Metzger" (Southern Poverty Law Center). WAR does not veil its racist propensities but openly "preaches racial discrimination and solidarity among the white, Anglo-Saxon segment of the American population, especially among white blue-collar workers" (Encyclopedia.com). WAR believes that the survival of the white race is under threat in the United States, and it promotes an anti-capitalistic, anti-government stance. WAR claims to fight against the Zionist Occupation Government (ZOG), a worldwide conspiracy of Jews that purportedly controls countries around the world, including the United States. In its heyday, WAR openly courted racist skinheads and attracted such individuals to the organization through the use of hate-rock festivals known as "Aryan Fest." In 1988, three WAR skinhead members beat an Ethiopian graduate student to death in Portland, Oregon. The Southern Poverty Law Center (SPLC) brought a civil rights suit against Tom Metzger,

WAR, and the three skinheads. A jury found Metzger "liable for intentionally inciting the skinheads to engage in violent confrontations with minorities," and a subsequent lawsuit brought by the Southern Poverty Law Center (SPLC) in behalf of the victims would effectively bankrupt the organization (Southern Poverty Law Center). The judgment bankrupted Metzger and WAR, though WAR continues to have an online presence, advocating "the benefits of racial separation, [while] highlighting the dangers of multiculturalism and promoting racial identity and a territorial imperative" (White Aryan Resistance).

During the 1970s, Metzger was a member of David Duke's organization, the Knights of the Ku Klux Klan (KKKK). Metzger rose to grand dragon of the KKKK in California but left the group to form his own organization. In the early 1980s, Metzger courted racist skinhead groups in California and formed the White Aryan Resistance (WAR). Metzger hosted *Race and Reason*, "a public-accessed cable television show that aired WAR propaganda and featured neo-Nazis as guests" (Turner). The show generated great controversy because of the topics that Metzger and his guests discussed, such as holocaust denial, forced racial segregation, and anti-government activism (Turner).

In 1988, Metzger established the "WAR hotline," where people were encouraged to call in and vent their frustrations. The recorded message on the hotline stated;

> You have reached WAR Hotline. White Aryan Resistance. You ask: What is WAR? We are an openly white-racist movement—Skinheads, we welcome you into our ranks. The federal government is the number one enemy of our race. When was the last time you heard a politician speaking out in favor of white people? . . . You say the government is too big; we can't organize. Well, by God, the SS did it in Germany, and if they did it in Germany in the thirties, we can do it right here in the streets of America. We need to cleanse this nation of all nonwhite mud-races for the survival of our own people and the generations of our children. (Atkins)

On November 13, 1988, three racist skinheads associated with WAR "beat to death Mulugeta Seraw, an Ethiopian man who had moved to the United States to attend graduate school" (Southern Poverty Law Center). In October 1990, the Southern Poverty Law Center (SPLC) won a $12.5 million judgment against Metzger, WAR, and the skinheads. Neither WAR nor Metzger had the assets to satisfy the judgment, so Seraw's family only received about $150,000 (Associated Press). Metzger declared bankruptcy, but WAR continued to operate (Southern Poverty Law Center) and today operates a website that continues to promote white nationalist, white supremacist, and neo-Nazi ideals (White Aryan Resistance). Metzger encourages "white supremacists to adopt a 'lone wolf' or 'leaderless resistance' strategy"—"that is, that they engage in criminal actions only individually or in small cells to avoid detection by law enforcement" (Southern Poverty Law Center).

Metzger continues to proclaim that WAR "serves the idea that what's good for the White European Race is the highest virtue. Whatever is bad for the White European Race is the ultimate Evil" (Southern Poverty Law Center).

See also: Holocaust Denial; Knights of the Ku Klux Klan; Ku Klux Klan; Neo-Nazis; Racist Skinheads; White Nationalism; White Supremacist Movement

FURTHER READING

Anti-Defamation League. "White Aryan Resistance." Anti-Defamation League. https://
www.adl.org/education/references/hate-symbols/white-aryan-resistance.
(Accessed May 20, 2018.)

Associated Press. December 25, 1990. "Assets of White Supremacist Are Target of Legal
Maneuver." *New York Times.* http://www.nytimes.com/1990/12/25/us/assets-of
-white-supremacist-are-target-of-legal-maneuver.html. (Accessed May 20, 2018.)

Atkins, Stephen E. 2011. *Encyclopedia of Right-Wing Extremism in Modern American
History.* ABC-CLIO.

Encyclopedia.com. "White Aryan Resistance (WAR)." Encyclopedia.com. http://www
.encyclopedia.com/politics/legal-and-political-magazines/white-aryan-resistance
-war. (Accessed May 20, 2018.)

Southern Poverty Law Center. "Tom Metzger." Southern Poverty Law Center. https://
www.splcenter.org/fighting-hate/extremist-files/individual/tom-metzger.
(Accessed May 20, 2018.)

Turner, Wallace. October 7, 1986. "Extremist Finds Cable TV Is Forum for Right-Wing
Views." *New York Times.* http://www.nytimes.com/1986/10/07/us/extremist-finds
-cable-tv-is-forum-for-right-wing-views.html. (Accessed May 20, 2018.)

White Aryan Resistance. "About." White Aryan Resistance. http://www.resist.com
/About/index.html. (Accessed May 20, 2018.)

White Camelia Knights of the Ku Klux Klan

The White Camelia Knights of the Ku Klux Klan (WCKKKK) are "a group of men
and women (families) that share a common belief in religion and race" (White Camelia Knights of the Ku Klux Klan, Who We Are). The group is based in Texas, but it
claims that members reside in other states as well. The WCKKKK believe that
"White Christian ideals are under attack by anti-white and anti-Christ forces. We
believe our race, country and our Christian way of life is being systematically
destroyed" (White Camelia Knights of the Ku Klux Klan, Who We Are). The WCK-
KKK asserts that the U.S. "constitution and its bill of rights were written for and by
White Christians. Christians that, yes, owned slaves." Moreover, "[n]on-whites have
no constitutional rights. Christianity is the one and only recognized religion according to the Founding Fathers and this is also the belief of the White Camelia Knights
of the Ku Klux Klan" (White Camelia Knights of the Ku Klux Klan, Who We Are).

In 2005, the leader of the WCKKKK, Charles Lee, stated:

> We see more and more All-Black TV programs that pollute the airwaves. Where are
> the White people in these Black Sitcoms? You can be sure to find a majority of the
> credits for these Black Sitcoms belonging to the Jews. In a Country where the
> Majority rules, you would think that the White Man would be in control and there-
> fore rid this land of the evil that plagues it. But instead you have the parasitic Jew at
> the Head of Government. (Counter Extremism Project)

Charles Lee's expressions of hate are oft-repeated on the WCKKKK's website.
For instance, as pertaining to homosexuality, "The White Camelia Knights of the
Ku Klux Klan has a very clear and simple understanding on the subject of homo-
sexuality. Homosexuality is a perversion of nature and a filthy, diseased and

perverted lifestyle" (White Camelia Knights of the Ku Klux Klan, Nature's Law). As to race mixing:

> The Klan has always taken a strong stance against interracial marriage. What most people don't understand is it's against our Heavenly Father's law. White's have practiced segregation throughout our history for a couple of basic reasons. If White's had never kept themselves separate from the other peoples of the world the White race would be extinct. (White Camelia Knights of the Ku Klux Klan, Nature's Law)

Members of the WCKKKK believe that a race war is inevitable:

> We're often asked if there will be a race war in America's future. Our answer to this question is "yes." What most people don't realize is there are racial battles breaking out all across America right now. These racial battles are going to lead us into an all out race war. As the non-white race population is growing the White population is decreasing. (White Camelia Knights of the Ku Klux Klan, Nature's Law)

Finally, the WCKKKK holds fast to KKK ideology when it comes to the notion of equality among races. Whereas KKK ideology has always held that the white race is superior to all others, the WCKKKK states this sentiment very explicitly:

> Racial suicide all in the name of equality is insane. In the Klan's opinion, it shows a lack of love and caring for the White Race. The Klan believes Whites are superior to the Non-Whites. When someone comes to a Klansman and makes the comment, 'we are all God's creation and the only difference in the Race's is the color of the skin', we tell them that they are partially correct. God is the creator, and he did create us all, but there is a world of difference between the races besides skin color.
>   Why are so many people bent on promoting race-mixing and racial equality? Because, it is Satan's goal to have us violate our Heavenly Father's law on mixing our seed with the other people of the world. What use to be wrong is now right. What use to be bad is now good. Our world has been turned upside down and we have only ourselves to blame for being so gullible. (White Camelia Knights of the Ku Klux Klan, Racial Equality)

See also: Ku Klux Klan; White Supremacist Movement

FURTHER READING

Counter Extremism Project. February 29, 2016. "Charles Lee, Leader of the White Camelia Knights, 2005." Counter Extremism Project. https://www.counterextremism.com /content/charles-lee-leader-white-camelia-knights-2005. (Accessed June 9, 2018.)

White Camelia Knights of the Ku Klux Klan. "Nature's Law." White Camelia Knights of the Ku Klux Klan. http://www.wckkkk.org/nature.html. (Accessed June 9, 2018.)

White Camelia Knights of the Ku Klux Klan. "Racial Equality." White Camelia Knights of the Ku Klux Klan. http://www.wckkkk.org/eql.html. (Accessed June 9, 2018.)

White Camelia Knights of the Ku Klux Klan. "Who We Are." White Camelia Knights of the Ku Klux Klan. http://www.wckkkk.org/who.html. (Accessed June 9, 2018.)

White Lives Matter

White Lives Matter is a "racist movement formed in response to the Black Lives Matter (BLM) movement" that came into being in 2014 "after George Zimmerman was acquitted in the shooting death of Trayvon Martin in Florida" (Southern Poverty Law Center). The Black Lives Matter movement "surfaced as a trending social media hashtag, and then grew in to a nationwide political movement" as more and more incidents of the killing of blacks, very often by law enforcement, were picked up by the national media (Southern Poverty Law Center). White Lives Matter (WLM) was founded as a response to Black Lives Matter but also to the "All Lives Matter" tagline that many whites wished to use to put across the point that it was not just blacks who were the victims of out-of-control law enforcement agencies. Republican presidential candidate and New Jersey Chris Christie stated that BLM was a movement that advocated "the murder of police officers" (Viets). WLM describes itself as "dedicated to promotion of the white race and taking positive action as a united voice against issues facing our race." The group's website declares:

> The fiber and integrity our nation was founded on is being unraveled . . . [by] homosexuality and [racially] mix[ed] relationships. Illegal immigration, healthcare, housing, welfare, employment, education, social security, our children, our veterans and active military and their rights . . . are the issues we face as white Americans. The laws and immoral orders the current [Obama] administration are passing are drastically . . . targeting everything the white way of life holds dear. (White Lives Matter)

Since its founding in 2015, WLM has appeared to be populated by white supremacists and neo-Nazi adherents (Southern Poverty Law Center). Rebecca Barnette has claimed to be one of WLM's founders and has dedicated herself to spreading its message. Barnette has been involved in "several neo-Nazi groups and holds the post of the director of the Women's Division of the National Socialist Movement, the largest neo-Nazi organization in the United States" (Viets). Barnette sounds the warning that "Jews and Muslims have formed an alliance 'to commit genocide of epic proportions' of the white race" (Viets). "Now is the time," Barnette has stated, for "the blood of our enemies [to] soak our soil to form new mortar to rebuild our landmasses" (Viets). In reference to the Black Lives Matter movement, Barnette has stated that there is "a small army ready to blow their little party out of the water . . . in the proper way . . . the white" (Viets). In February 2016, a car containing six members of the Ku Klux Klan (KKK) with "White Lives Matter" signs arrived at a park in Anaheim, California, to protest "illegal immigration and Muslims." A confrontation with counterprotesters ensued, and the KKK members stabbed three people, with one person being critically injured. Five Klan members were arrested, though they were later released after claiming that the stabbings occurred in self-defense (Viets).

Several racist groups have joined the WLM movement, most likely in response to WLM flyers that have been posted in public places from Utah to Connecticut. Reading "It's Not Racist to Love Your People," the flyers have urged "supporters to find like-minded people and organize to confront issues affecting white communities," such as crime, illegal immigration, and health care (Southern Poverty Law Center).

The murder of eight Dallas, Texas, and Baton Rouge, Louisiana, police officers during the summer of 2016 prompted WLM members and conservative commentators to enjoin the Southern Poverty Law Center (SPLC), the civil rights organization that tracks "hate groups" in the United States, to designate the Black Lives Matter movement a hate group. In both the Dallas and Baton Rouge cases, police officers were killed by black men expressing sympathies for the Black Lives Matter movement. The killing of the Dallas police officers took place during a Black Lives Matter march.

Though the SPLC lists several black organizations, such as the New Black Panther Party (NBPP), as hate groups, it has declined to affix this label to the Black Lives Matter movement. Richard Cohen, president of SPLC, has stated that "hate groups are, by our definition, those that vilify entire groups of people based on immutable characteristics such as race or ethnicity. Federal law takes a similar approach" (Cohen). Cohen noted:

> There's no doubt that some protesters who claim the mantle of Black Lives Matter have said offensive things, like the chant "pigs in a blanket, fry 'em like bacon" that was heard at one rally. But before we condemn the entire movement for the words of a few, we should ask ourselves whether we would also condemn the entire Republican Party for the racist words of its presumptive nominee—or for the racist rhetoric of many other politicians in the party over the course of years.
>
> Many of its harshest critics claim that Black Lives Matter's very name is anti-white, hence the oft-repeated rejoinder "all lives matter." This notion misses the point entirely. Black lives matter because they have been marginalized throughout our country's history and because white lives have always mattered more in our society. As BLM puts it, the movement stands for "the simple proposition that 'black lives also matter.'" (Cohen)

Noting the rise of Donald Trump's intonation to "Make America Great Again," and noting that most of Trump's most ardent followers tended to be whites who felt themselves threatened in the changing social and political landscape of the United States, Cohen pointed out:

> The backlash to BLM, in some ways, reflects a broad sense of unease among white people who worry about the cultural changes in the country and feel they are falling behind in a country that is rapidly growing more diverse in a globalizing world. We consistently see this phenomenon in surveys showing that large numbers of white people believe racial discrimination against them is as pervasive, or more so, than it is against African Americans. (Cohen)

The WLM has stated that the movement is

> really about recognizing the contributions that people of European descent have made to civilization, and that we as a people and culture are worth preserving. We reject the notion that it is morally wrong for people of European descent to love and support their own race. We value Western civilization and believe that at the very least, immigrants should not make us dumber or poorer. (Mettler)

After the Dallas murders, when law enforcement attempted to push forward a movement that "Blue Lives Matter," Kevin Harris, "one of WLM's co-founders," seemed less supportive, posting "a photo of himself in front of a police car with his middle finger extended" (Southern Poverty Law Center). Rebecca Barnette echoed this sentiment, stating that "[w]hile White Lives Matter supports law and order and feels the terroristic attacks on law enforcement officers is a tragedy, we are not proponents for blue lives matter" (Southern Poverty Law Center).

See also: Neo-Nazis; New Black Panther Party; White Nationalism; White Supremacist Movement

FURTHER READING

Black Lives Matter. http://blacklivesmatter.com/. (Accessed May 13, 2018.)
Cohen, Richard. July 19, 2016. "Black Lives Matter Is Not a Hate Group." Southern Poverty Law Center: News. https://www.splcenter.org/news/2016/07/19/black-lives-matter-not-hate-group. (Accessed May 13, 2018.)
Mettler, Katie. August 31, 2016. "Why SPLC Says White Lives Matter Is a Hate Group but Black Lives Matter Is Not." *Washington Post*. https://www.washingtonpost.com/news/morning-mix/wp/2016/08/31/splc-the-much-cited-designator-of-hate-groups-explains-why-white-lives-matter-is-one/. (Accessed May 13, 2018.)
Southern Poverty Law Center. "White Lives Matter." Southern Poverty Law Center. https://www.splcenter.org/fighting-hate/extremist-files/group/white-lives-matter. (Accessed May 13, 2018.)
Viets, Sarah. August 3, 2016. "White Lives Matter." Southern Poverty Law Center: Intelligence Report. https://www.splcenter.org/fighting-hate/intelligence-report/2016/white-lives-matter. (Accessed May 13, 2018.)
White Lives Matter. http://www.whitelivesmatter.com/. (Accessed May 13, 2018.)

White Nationalism

White nationalism is a "belief that white people are a distinct race" and, as such, should maintain a separate and distinct identity from other racial groups (Southern Poverty Law Center). White nationalists "seek to ensure the survival of the white race" and protect the cultural, political, and economic systems of historical white states (Southern Poverty Law Center). Many white nationalists "believe that miscegenation (mixed-race relations), multiculturalism, immigration of non-whites, and low birth rates among white populations are threatening the white race" (Federal Bureau of Investigation). Some argue that these factors are contributing to a systematic extermination of a purely white race (Federal Bureau of Investigation). In the United States, the overt expression of white nationalism first manifested itself in the presence and activities of the Ku Klux Klan (KKK) in the aftermath of the U.S. Civil War. Starting in the 1950s, white nationalism grew out of a conservative reaction to liberal politics and policies and became the organizing principle of many right-wing extremist groups in the post–World War II era. Harvard political scientist Samuel Huntington argues that "white nationalism developed as a reaction to a perceived decline in the essence of American identity as European, Anglo-Protestant and English-speaking" (Huntington). White nationalism may include tenets related to white supremacy and white separatism, though these are sometimes thought of as distinct and separate phenomenon

(Anti-Defamation League; Taub). Since World War II, several extremist groups in the United States have arisen that embrace the ideals of white nationalism, including Posse Comitatus, Aryan Nations, the National Alliance, the Order, and neo-Nazis. More recently, the alt-right movement, "a broad term covering many different far-right ideologies and groups in the United States, some of which endorse white nationalism, has gained traction as an alternative to mainstream conservatism in its national politics" (Welton).

Following the defeat of the Confederacy in the U.S. Civil War, former Confederates founded the Ku Klux Klan (KKK) as an insurgent group to maintain white supremacy in states that were subject to federal Reconstruction policies. Over time, the KKK has gone through several incarnations, but all the while the group has emphasized white nationalism and American nativism in the face of changing social conditions.

Starting in the 1950s in the United States, a new social and cultural milieu was being created that emphasized the inclusion of groups that had traditionally been left out of the power structure (e.g., blacks). The civil rights movement emphasized the displacement of social, cultural, economic, and political structures that had been in place for decades, most of which had greatly benefitted the white majority in all parts of the country. At the time, a new conservatism arose in reaction to the perceived threat of communism, but the rising power of blacks in American society spawned the formation of groups that opposed the rapid changes that were taking place in society. In the 1960s, Posse Comitatus was formed as an anti-government organization that preached a message that white Christians were losing their social and political rights in the face of changing conditions in the United States. Though the 1960s and early 1970s tended to be dominated by extremist groups from the radical left, by the end of the 1970s, worsening economic conditions gave rise to extremist right-wing groups that viewed government actions in support of great social inclusion, support for minority groups, and support for heretofore cultural taboos (e.g., gay rights) as justification for anti-government attitudes and actions.

In 1974, William Pierce founded the National Alliance as a white nationalist, anti-Semitic, and white supremacist political organization. In 1977, Richard Butler founded Aryans Nations as the political arms of his Church of Jesus Christ Christian. An adherent of Christian Identity, Butler taught his followers that the "white race was God's chosen people" and that Jews were the result of a sexual union between Eve and Satan (Southern Poverty Law Center). Both Butler's and Pierce's teachings would spawn spinoff groups, even more virulent and disposed to hate than their parent organizations. The Order, for instance, preached that Aryans (whites) were the purest race. David Lane, a member of the Order, enunciated the slogan known as the "14 Words," which became the creed of the white supremacist and white nationalist cause: "We must secure the existence of our people and a future for white children" (Palmer).

The farm crisis of the 1980s convinced many in the American heartland that the U.S. federal government no longer cared for white people as one family farm after another fell to worsening economic conditions and government indifference

(Balleck). Membership in groups that preached anti-government extremism swelled during that time and exploded after the federal government killed anti-government activists at Ruby Ridge in Idaho in 1992 and Waco in 1993. Present-day patriot and militia movements can trace their beginnings to this period of time, and though their numbers have waxed and waned over the years, they continue to be potent voices in the cause of white nationalism.

With the election of the first African American president in U.S. history in 2008, white nationalism was provided with "renewed clarity and focus" (Smithers). Coupled with renewed anti-black, anti-immigrant, anti-Semitic, and emerging anti-Islamic sentiments among white nationalists, Barack Obama's election in 2008—and his reelection in 2012—ignited a "counterrevolution" among whites that fanned the "flames of bigotry and intolerance" and reinvigorated old hate groups and gave rise to new ones (e.g., alt-right). As noted by one commentator:

> This disparate collection of bigots, racist, and conspiracy theorists have found common cause in opposing Obama's presidency and leveling racist barbs at First Lady Michelle Obama—referred to by one West Virginia official as an "ape in heels."
>
> Racial prejudice is not a relic of American history; it's alive and thriving in twenty-first century America. Amid the smokescreens of anti-government, anti-tax, and pro-gun rights America, the racial animus that fuels the current white nationalist counterrevolution gains strength from the white supremacist traditions of the past as it is re-encoded in American political culture in new and subtle ways. (Smithers)

Today, white nationalism "is the belief that national identity should be built around white ethnicity, and that white people should therefore maintain both a demographic majority and dominance of the nation's culture and public life" (Taub). Like white supremacy, "white nationalism emphasizes placing the interests of white people over those of any other racial group or minority. White supremacists and white nationalists both believe that racial discrimination should be incorporated into law and policy" (Taub). But while there may seem to be little difference between white nationalism and white supremacism, there are those who believe that the terms are not synonymous. Eric Kaufmann, a professor of politics at Birkbeck University in London, says that "[w]hite supremacy is based on a racist belief that white people are innately superior to people of other races; white nationalism is about maintaining political and economic dominance, not just a numerical majority or cultural hegemony" (Taub).

Thus, for a long time "white nationalism was less about an ideology as it was the presumptive belief about American life" (Taub). Americans saw in their nation—in its laws, institutions, political system, culture, and social structures—"an extension of their own ethnic group. But the country's changing demographics, the civil rights movement and a push for multiculturalism in many quarters mean that white Americans are now confronting the prospect of a nation that is no longer built solely around their own identity" (Taub).

Richard Spencer, founder of the alt-right movement, states that adherents to alt-right principles believe in protecting "the heritage, identity, and future of people of European descent in the United States, and around the world" (Taub).

White nationalism can be epitomized in the remarks of a middle-aged white male from the U.S. state of Georgia who in 2016 proclaimed, "I believe our nation is ruined and has been for several decades and the election of Obama [was] merely the culmination of the change" (Smithers). As noted by one commentator:

> This sense of loss is galling to Americans who share this gentleman's perspective. What makes this sense of loss all the more difficult to stomach is the belief that a generation of intellectual and political elites have force-fed "political correctness" to unwilling citizens. Such Americans have had enough. Indeed, Obama's presidency did not usher in an era of post-racialism as millions hoped; it provided the hateful platform from which Donald Trump could rise to the presidency. (Smithers)

See also: Alt-Right Movement; American Freedom Party; *American Renaissance*; Aryan Nations; Christian Identity; Council of Conservative Citizens; Identity Evropa; Ku Klux Klan; National Alliance; Neo-Nazis; *Occidental Observer*; The Order; Social Contract Press; Stormfront; VDARE; White Supremacist Movement

FURTHER READING

Anti-Defamation League. "White Nationalism." Anti-Defamation League. https://www.adl.org/education/resources/glossary-terms/white-nationalism. (Accessed May 20, 2017.)

Balleck, Barry J. 2015. *Allegiance to Liberty: The Changing Face of Patriots, Militias, and Political Violence in America*. Praeger.

Federal Bureau of Investigation. "FOIA: FBI Monograph State of Domestic White Nationalist Extremist Movement in the U.S." Federal Bureau of Investigation. https://archive.org/stream/foia_FBI_Monograph-State_of_Domestic_White_Nationalist_Extremist_Movement_in_the_U.S./FBI_Monograph-State_of_Domestic_White_Nationalist_Extremist_Movement_in_the_U.S._djvu.txt. (Accessed May 20, 2017.)

Huntington, Samuel P. 2005. *Who Are We?: The Challenges to America's National Identity*. Simon & Schuster.

Palmer, Brian. October 29, 2008. "White Supremacists by the Numbers." Slate. http://www.slate.com/articles/news_and_politics/explainer/2008/10/white_supremacists_by_the_numbers.html. (Accessed May 20, 2017.)

Smithers, Gregory D. December 23, 2016. "A White Nationalist Counterrevolution?" *CounterPunch*. http://www.counterpunch.org/2016/12/23/a-white-nationalist-counterrevolution/. (Accessed May 20, 2017.)

Southern Poverty Law Center. "White Nationalist." Southern Poverty Law Center. https://www.splcenter.org/fighting-hate/extremist-files/ideology/white-nationalist. (Accessed May 20, 2017.)

Sterling, Joe. November 17, 2016. "White Nationalism, a Term Once on the Fringes, Now Front and Center." CNN. http://www.cnn.com/2016/11/16/politics/what-is-white-nationalism-trnd/. (Accessed May 20, 2017.)

Taub, Amanda. November 21, 2016. "'White Nationalism' Explained." *New York Times*. https://www.nytimes.com/2016/11/22/world/americas/white-nationalism-explained.html. (Accessed May 20, 2017.)

Welton, Benjamin. December 15, 2015. "What, Exactly, Is the 'Alternative Right'? " *Weekly Standard*. http://www.weeklystandard.com/what-exactly-is-the-alternative-right/article/2000310. (Accessed May 20, 2017.)

White Patriot Party

The White Patriot Party (WPP) was a "paramilitary, Christian Identity faction of the Ku Klux Klan founded by former Green Beret Frazier Glenn Miller in 1980" (Southern Poverty Law Center). At its height, the group boasted some 3,000 members. Many believe that hard economic time in the 1980s attracted many followers to the group, whose message blamed Jewish bankers and the worldwide Jewish conspiracy for the poor economic conditions of white Americans. Miller, the group's founder, stated that the goal of WPP was "Southern independence—an all-white nation within the one million square miles of mother Dixie" (Terrorism Knowledge Base). Miller's focus on a white homeland in the South was based on his view of the rest of the country and its dominance by Jewish and other interests. As Miller stated:

> We have no hope for Jew York City or San Fran-sissy-co and other areas that are dominated by Jews, perverts, and communists and non-white minorities and rectum-loving queers. (Ridgeway)

During the height of its activities, the WPP was a paramilitary organization that stockpiled guns and ammunition, conducted paramilitary activities, and marched and demonstrated against what it considered the "mongrelization" of the white race in the United States. During the early- to mid-1980s, it was one of dozens of militia groups that formed around the country in protest of the activities of the U.S. federal government. Like other groups of its ilk (e.g., white supremacist, white separatist, neo-Nazi, and anti-Semitic), WPP believed in conspiracy theories of different kinds. Preeminent among these, however, was the notion of the Zionist Occupation Government (ZOG). For many in the militia movements of the 1980s, the worldwide Jewish conspiracy to control the world manifested itself in ZOG, a shadowy group of Jews who controlled economic systems, media outlets, popular culture, and even governments. Miller and the WPP believed that ZOG had taken control of the U.S. government. In 1987, while out on bond after being convicted of criminal contempt for his activities with WPP, Miller disappeared and went underground. While hiding, he issued a "Declaration of War" and exhorted "Aryan warriors of The Order" to kill its enemies. In the declaration, Miller established a "point system" for each target that he was encouraging his followers to attack: "N— (1), White race traitors (10), Jews (10), Judges (50), Morris Seligman Dees (888)" (Southern Poverty Law Center). Morris Dees, founder of the Southern Poverty Law Center (SPLC), had brought suit against the WPP and forced Miller to publicly disband and disassociate himself from the WPP. The SPLC had found evidence that Miller and his confederates had planned to assassinate Dees, after which a "federal judge issued an injunction forbidding Miller and the WPP from engaging in any paramilitary activity" (Terrorism Knowledge Base).

When authorities caught up with Miller, they found him with "hand grenades, automatic weapons, thousands of rounds of ammunition, C-4 explosives, and $14,000 in cash" (Southern Poverty Law Center). The cash, it was later learned, had been given to Miller by Bob Mathews, the infamous leader of the Order, who had purloined the money from a series of robberies that the Order had perpetrated in order to fund white supremacist causes. When Miller cut a plea deal to lessen his sentence and testified against other white supremacists, his reputation within the community was effectively destroyed, and the WPP quietly faded away.

See also: Neo-Nazis; The Order; White Supremacist Movement

FURTHER READING

Ridgeway, James. 1995. *Blood in the Face: The Ku Klux Klan, Aryan Nations, Nazi Skin-heads and the Rise of a New White Culture*. Thunder's Mouth Press.

Southern Poverty Law Center. "Frazier Glenn Miller." Southern Poverty Law Center. https://www.splcenter.org/fighting-hate/extremist-files/individual/frazier-glenn -miller. (Accessed January 16, 2017.)

Terrorism Knowledge Base. "White Patriot Party." Terrorism Knowledge Base. http://web.archive.org/web/20070930013115/http://www.tkb.org/Group.jsp?groupID =127. (Accessed January 16, 2017.)

Terrorist Research and Analysis Consortium. "White Patriot Party." Terrorist Research and Analysis Consortium. https://www.trackingterrorism.org/group/white -patriot-party-wpp. (Accessed January 16, 2017.)

White Rabbit Radio

White Rabbit Radio (WRR) is an online radio website that perpetuates the notion that white genocide is occurring in the United States and around the world. The Southern Poverty Law Center (SPLC) characterizes WRR as a white nationalist hate group, explaining that "White nationalist groups espouse white supremacist or white separatist ideologies, often focusing on the alleged inferiority of non-whites" (Begley). WRR began in 2010 as a platform to push the beliefs and ideals of Robert Whitaker, a "curmudgeonly segregationist with a history of drug abuse" who "largely blames immigration for a 'genocide' facing white people'" (Lenz, August 2013). Whitaker was the author of the 221-word "Mantra that became a rallying cry for racists the world over" (Lenz, 2017). The "Mantra" was a "blunt attack on multiculturalism that blames immigration for a 'genocide' facing white people" (Lenz, 2017). In full, Whitaker's "Mantra" states:

> Everybody says there is this RACE problem. Everybody says this RACE problem will be solved when the third world pours into EVERY white country and ONLY into white countries.
>
> The Netherlands and Belgium are just as crowded as Japan or Taiwan, but nobody says Japan or Taiwan will solve this RACE problem by bringing in millions of third worlders and quote assimilating unquote with them.
>
> Everybody says the final solution to this RACE problem is for EVERY white country and ONLY white countries to "assimilate," i.e., intermarry, with all those non-whites.
>
> What if I said there was this RACE problem and this RACE problem would be solved only if hundreds of millions of non-blacks were brought into EVERY black country and ONLY into black countries?

How long would it take anyone to realize I'm not talking about a RACE problem. I am talking about the final solution to the BLACK problem?

And how long would it take any sane black man to notice this and what kind of psycho black man wouldn't object to this?

But if I tell that obvious truth about the ongoing program of genocide against my race, the white race, Liberals and respectable conservatives agree that I am a naziwhowantstokillsixmillionjews.

They say they are anti-racist. What they are is anti-white.

Anti-racist is a code word for anti-white. (Whitaker Online)

For three years, White Rabbit Radio operated under the voice of a figure who called himself "Horus the Avenger." In June 2013, an investigation by SPLC's Hatewatch identified Horus the Avenger as Timothy Gallaher Murdock, age 43, "an avowed anti-Semite and one-time day trader, who, at the time of his unmasking, lived in the basement of his parents' home" (Lenz, July 2013). Murdock had used White Rabbit Radio as "an online allegory designed to expose 'white genocide' and patterned after Lewis Carroll's *Alice's Adventures in Wonderland*" (Lenz, July 2013). His belief in "white genocide," as expressed in the "Mantra," is the crux of the majority of messages found on White Rabbit Radio. In fact, White Rabbit Radio's website explains:

Maybe you just heard someone say "Diversity" is a code word for White Genocide or "Anti-Racism" is just a code word for Anti-White. Or perhaps you just finished watching one of our Animations and listening to the "War on Whites." When it comes to bringing awareness to White Genocide. There are only a couple websites that started the fire. And you are currently surfing one of them. Welcome to White Rabbit Radio! (White Rabbit Radio)

The basic idea of "white genocide" as expressed in the "Mantra" is that white people, "far from ruling most of the developed world, are actually being subjected to a genocide that will ultimately wipe out their race" (Lenz, August 2013). But, as Ryan Lenz of the SPLC reported, such thinking is "not new":

It has been developing since the racist right essentially lost the civil rights battles of the 1960s, and racist writers like Wilmot Robertson began adopting the language of the civil rights movement to depict whites as increasingly "dispossessed." In the last 20 years, the idea that the white race is facing mortal attack has become the norm on the extreme right, with the neo-Nazi National Alliance, for instance, repeatedly describing whites as "Earth's Most Endangered Species." Such fears have picked up speed in recent years thanks in large part to the U.S. Census Bureau, which has predicted that non-Hispanic whites in this country will lose their majority by about 2043. (Lenz, August 2013)

Though White Rabbit Radio is alive and well—hosting a weekly program entitled "This Week in #WhiteGenocide"—Robert Whitaker died in June 2017. His lasting legacy, according to the obituary posted on his own website—Whitaker Online—was that he gave "the world the tools we need to expose this anti-White system and it's [sic] program of white genocide" (Lenz, 2017).

See also: Neo-Nazis; White Nationalism; White Supremacist Movement

FURTHER READING

Begley, Sarah. February 15, 2017. "Read the List of the 917 Hate Groups Identified by the Southern Poverty Law Center." *Time.* http://time.com/4671800/hate-groups-on -the-rise/. (Accessed June 6, 2018.)

Eyes on the Right. January 11, 2018. "Tim Murdock: White Genocide Memes Will Move the Overton Window." Angry White Men. https://angrywhitemen.org/2018/01/11 /tim-murdock-white-genocide-memes-will-move-the-overton-window/# more-45189. (Accessed June 6, 2018.)

Lenz, Ryan. July 2, 2013. "White Rabbit Radio, Font of Racist Genocide Claims, Run by Michigander." Southern Poverty Law Center: Hatewatch. https://www.splcenter .org/hatewatch/2013/07/02/white-rabbit-radio-font-racist-genocide-claims-run -michigander. (Accessed June, 2018.)

Lenz, Ryan. August 21, 2013. "Following the White Rabbit." Southern Poverty Law Center: Intelligence Report. https://www.splcenter.org/fighting-hate/intelligence-report /2013/following-white-rabbit. (Accessed June 6, 2018.)

Lenz, Ryan. June 7, 2017. "Bob Whitaker, Author of the Racist 'Mantra' on White Genocide, Has Died." Southern Poverty Law Center: Hatewatch. https://www.splcenter .org/hatewatch/2017/06/07/bob-whitaker-author-racist-mantra-white-genocide -has-died. (Accessed June 6, 2018.)

Systems and Symbols. July 3, 2013. "The Anti-White SPLC 'Reports' on Bob Whitaker and the White Rabbit." Systems and Symbols. https://systemssymbols.wordpress .com/2013/07/03/the-anti-white-splc-reports-on-bob-whitaker-and-the-white -rabbit/. (Accessed June 6, 2018.)

Whitaker Online. "The Mantra." Whitaker Online. http://www.whitakeronline.org/blog /the-white-mantra/. (Accessed June 6, 2018.)

White Rabbit Radio. "The Endgame: Full White Genocide Documentary." White Rabbit Radio. https://whiterabbitradio.net/. (Accessed June 6, 2018.)

White Revolution

White Revolution is a white supremacist, neo-Nazi group that attempted to bring together "some of the most virulent leaders and groups in the world of white supremacy" (Southern Poverty Law Center). When it was founded in 2002, White Revolution was unique among white supremacist groups in that the organization encouraged nonexclusive membership. That is, members who joined White Revolution could also be members of other extremist groups. White Revolution's leaders believed that the white supremacist movement was better served by allowing members to be part of many groups, as opposed to being devoted to only one group. Though White Revolution's membership spanned several U.S. states, its headquarters and most of its membership were located in Arkansas. White Revolution became defunct in 2011, and its members scattered to other extremist organizations.

White Revolution was founded by Billy Roper, a native of Arkansas, in 2002. Born in 1972, Roper became a skinhead as a teenager, and he "claimed that three generations of his family had members of the Ku Klux Klan" (Encyclopedia.com). Roper received a "master's degree in history and became a high school teacher" (Encyclopedia.com). In 2000, Roper was employed by "William Pierce's National Alliance (NA), at the time the most powerful neo-Nazi group in the United States"

(Encyclopedia.com). Roper rose quickly in the ranks of NA, becoming deputy membership coordinator. Roper was described as "gregarious, articulate, dedicated, and hard-working," and his organizing skills helped the National Alliance become the largest and most popular neo-Nazi group in the United States. Roper sometimes found himself at odds with NA's leadership, however. Roper believed that the NA could rapidly expand if it reached out to skinheads and other extremist groups. William Pierce and his eventual successor, Erich Gliebe, despised the idea of admitting skinheads to NA and rejected Roper's ideas.

When Pierce unexpectedly died in 2002, Gliebe became the leader of the National Alliance. Within days, Roper was pushed out, and he took dozens of NA members with him. On September 18, 2002, Roper started White Revolution "with about 100 activists (among them nearly 30 former National Alliance members), thousands of supporters, and endorsements from many white supremacist leaders" (Encyclopedia.com). Roper encouraged members to belong to multiple groups, but requirements for membership in White Revolution included "being age eighteen or above, drug-free, and heterosexual, having no non-white dependents, and being totally of white European ancestry" (Encyclopedia.com). At its height, White Revolution had about 1,200 members (Encyclopedia of Arkansas History & Culture).

Roper formed White Revolution to be "the most radical legal pro-White organization involved in public activism" (Southern Poverty Law Center). The group celebrated violence against nonwhites, but its membership became frustrated with the fact that the violence was being perpetrated by other extremist groups and not White Revolution. Roper explained:

> I understand as well as anyone how frustrating it is to delay action and to remain legal while our people's situation continues to grow increasingly desperate. When some people think of revolution, they think of guns and bombs and hand grenades. But for us, at this stage of the revolution, our weapons of choice are the pen, the leaflet, the keyboard. . . . The time may well come when we will communicate to our enemies in a manner which they will find unambiguous, but "for now we must lay the foundation and create the support networks which will be necessary for any future endeavors." (Southern Poverty Law Center)

Through most of its early history, White Revolution staged rallies and protests over a variety of issues, including a "protest of the 2004 Olympic Games in Athens, Greece, because it combined athletes of different races competing against each other" (Encyclopedia.com). In 2005, White Revolution held joint events with groups such as "Aryan Nations, the Creativity Movement, the National Socialist Movement, factions of the Ku Klux Klan, and White Aryan Resistance" (Southern Poverty Law Center). Roper's ultimate goal was to "combine all white supremacist organizations under one umbrella, thereby strengthening the cause for white America" (Southern Poverty Law Center).

Roper and White Revolution were adamantly anti-immigration, stating that "the white race is growing smaller both in the United States and throughout the world." Roper believed that, given demographic trends in the United States, whites would be a minority in the country by 2025. In order to regain control of their fate, therefore, "members of White Revolution hope to establish a government within the United States whose priority is the preservation of the white race" (Encyclopedia.com).

White Revolution "created the White Caucus, a group that specifically endorsed white nationalist candidates for public office" (Encyclopedia of Arkansas History & Culture). Roper himself ran "as a write-in candidate for Arkansas governor in 2010." The "long-term goal of the White Caucus was to establish a coalition with the Nationalist Party of America . . . [and promote initiatives to] combine campaign strategies such as ballot access, petition initiatives, and fundraising efforts in order to get as many white nationalist candidates on the ballot in as many states as possible for the 2012 elections" (Encyclopedia of Arkansas History & Culture). Unable to secure funds for his efforts, Roper disbanded the White Caucus soon after his failed gubernatorial bid.

In September 2011, Roper shuttered White Revolution, stating, "As the leader of the organization, I am solely responsible and accept full responsibility for White Revolution's lack of success as a membership organization" (Southern Poverty Law Center). Roper announced that he was not leaving the white supremacist movement but that he was joining forces with longtime Klan leader Thomas Robb.

Though White Revolution was short-lived, for a short time it did bring very disparate groups together in the cause of white supremacy.

See also: Aryan Nations; Creativity Movement; National Alliance; Neo-Nazis; White Nationalism; White Supremacist Movement

FURTHER READING

Encyclopedia.com. "White Revolution." Encyclopedia.com. http://www.encyclopedia
     .com/politics/legal-and-political-magazines/white-revolution. (Accessed May 2,
     2017.)
Encyclopedia of Arkansas History & Culture. "White Revolution." Encyclopedia of
     Arkansas History & Culture. http://www.encyclopediaofarkansas.net/encyclopedia
     /entry-detail.aspx?entryID=6893. (Accessed May 2, 2017.)
Southern Poverty Law Center. "White Revolution." Southern Poverty Law Center. https://
     www.splcenter.org/fighting-hate/extremist-files/group/white-revolution.
     (Accessed May 2, 2017.)

White Supremacist Movement

White supremacy has been the default reality in the United States since its founding. The millions of black African slaves kept by white slave owners made white supremacy both a de facto ("in fact") and de jure ("in law") reality, as evidenced by the social, cultural, economic, and political institutions that were created to perpetuate white dominance. White supremacy is at its core a racist ideology that promotes the "belief that the white race is superior to other races" in the basic characteristics, traits, and attributes that distinguish one race from another (Southern Poverty Law Center). White supremacists believe that white people should dominate every society politically, economically, socially, and culturally, inasmuch as the white race is the most morally evolved, socially just, and politically enlightened of all races. During the 1800s, Europeans spoke of the "white man's burden" as they colonized societies less "civilized" than themselves. In the United States, Americans believed in "Manifest Destiny," the idea that the superior attributes of white society must be spread from east to west and north to south in the Western Hemisphere. Thus, "white supremacists of any sort exhibit at least one of the following beliefs: (1) whites should be dominant over people of other backgrounds; (2) whites should live by themselves in a whites-only society; (3) white people have their own 'culture' that is superior to other cultures; and, (4) white people are genetically superior to other people. Anti-Semitism is also important for the majority of white supremacists, most of whom actually believe that Jews constitute a race of their own—a race with parasitic and evil roots" (Anti-Defamation League, With Hate in their Hearts). The "white supremacist movement in the United States today" is punctuated by a variety of extremist hate groups, but, as noted by the Anti-Defamation League (ADL), "[m]ost white supremacists do not belong to organized hate groups, but rather participate in the white supremacist movement as unaffiliated individuals. Thus the size of the white supremacist movement is considerably greater than just the members of hate groups" (Anti-Defamation League, With Hate in their Hearts). Because of the perception among right-wing individuals that American society is being threatened by a variety of forces beyond their control, the white supremacist movement is probably more active today than it has ever been in the past.

White supremacy in the United States is not confined to any one geographic region. Though there is the belief that the American South, with its connections to the legacies of the Civil War, has a monopoly on white supremacist groups and individuals, white supremacists:

> come from America's heartland—small towns, rural cities, swelling suburban sprawl outside larger Sunbelt cities. These aren't the prosperous towns, but the single-story working-class exurbs that stretch for what feels like forever in the corridor between Long Beach and San Diego (not the San Fernando Valley), or along the southern tier of Pennsylvania, or spread all through the Upper Peninsula of Michigan, across the vast high plains of eastern Washington and Oregon, through Idaho and Montana. There are plenty in the declining cities of the Rust Belt, in Dearborn and Flint, Buffalo and Milwaukee, in the bars that remain in the shadows of the hulking deserted factories that once were America's manufacturing centers. (Kimmel)

Though the white supremacist may be somewhat indistinguishable from a white nationalist, this was not always the case. White supremacism was institutionalized by the Founding Fathers, who, by and large, believed that the white race was unambiguously superior. The abolitionist movement of the 19th century galvanized white supremacist thought that was reinforced by laws that perpetuated the dominance of the white majority. As blacks gained more political rights in the aftermath of the Civil War, white supremacist groups such as the Ku Klux Klan (KKK) attempted to prevent the rise of an equal class of political contenders. White supremacy was reinforced as different groups entered the United States, particularly those that did not come from predominantly white countries. Over time, however, white supremacism "evolved to reflect the new social and political realities that were found in the country" (Anti-Defamation League, Alt Right). Many white supremacists today have changed their rhetoric and tactics and moved away from a fight "to maintain white dominance to a fight to prevent white extinction" (Anti-Defamation League, With Hate in their Hearts). This belief in possible white extinction began to emerge in the 1970s and 1980s as white supremacists noted that miscegenation, immigration from nonwhite countries, and lower birth rates among whites threatened the majority status that whites have always enjoyed. This sentiment was captured in what became known as the "14 Words," enunciated by white supremacist and neo-Nazi David Lane: "We must secure the existence of our people and a future for white children" (Anti-Defamation League, With Hate in their Hearts).

In the United States, though the white supremacist movement is characterized by hate groups that are well-known on the American political landscape (e.g., Posse Comitatus, National Alliance, Aryan Nations, the KKK, racist skinheads, and neo-Nazis) the influence of these groups has been replaced by that of new, more virulent groups spewing hatred toward immigrants, Muslims, gays, and conservative politicians ("cuckservatives") who have "sold out" and embraced key premises of the left and who secretly sympathize with liberal values (Potok). Among domestic extremist movements, "white supremacists are the most violent of all groups, committing about 83 percent of the extremist-related murders in the United States over the past 10 years and being involved in about 52 percent of the shootouts between extremists and police" (Anti-Defamation League, With Hate in their Hearts). White supremacists also have a high degree of involvement in traditional forms of crime. Thus, a great deal of gang activity is associated with white supremacism, and the prisons are now one of the fast-growing venues for the formulation and dissemination of white supremacist thought (Anti-Defamation League, With Hate in their Hearts).

White supremacists in the United States tend to be Christian, but not just any form of Christian. White supremacists tend to be evangelical Protestants, Pentecostals, and members of radical sects that preach the word of Christ from a perspective of racial purity. Christian Identity, which was the founding belief of the white supremacist and anti-Semite group Aryan Nations, provided a theological justification for the superiority of whites over other racial groups, particularly Jews. It is "from Christian Identity that white supremacists get the theological claim" that

> Adam is the ancestor of the Caucasian race, whereas non-whites are pre-Adamic "mud people," without souls, and Jews are the children of Satan. According to this doctrine, Jesus was not Jewish and not from the Middle East; actually, he was northern European, his Second Coming is close at hand, and followers can hasten the apocalypse. It is the birthright of Anglo-Saxons to establish God's kingdom on earth; America's and Britain's "birthright is to be the wealthiest, most powerful nations on earth . . . able, by divine right, to dominate and colonize the world." (Kimmel)

When U.S. president George H. W. Bush pronounced the arrival of the New World Order in 1991, he ignited among white supremacists a belief that a shadowy conspiracy was afoot to enslave the American people and destroy their freedoms. The "unbridled actions of the federal government at Ruby Ridge, Idaho, and Waco, Texas" kick-started both the patriot and militia movements that rose in reaction to a post–Cold War environment in which the "enemy" was no longer a political ideology, such as communism, or its embodiment in the Soviet Union. Rather, for patriots and militia groups, the U.S. government became the enemy. Aside from its trampling of rights, the government was the catalyst for seismic cultural and social changes on the American landscape—from unchecked illegal immigration to tolerance for radical Muslims to promotion of LGBT rights and gay marriage.

One of the most prominent purveyors of white supremacist thought today is found in the alt-right movement. The founder of alt-right, Richard Spencer, ran online journals that acted as forums for racists, anti-Semites, and others (Anti-Defamation League, Alt-Right). White identity is at the core of the alt-right movement, and many "alt-righters" want the preservation of white identity—the cultural and genetic heritage that makes whites the dominant race. The alt-right movement wants to preserve what they claim are traditional Christian values, but from a uniquely white supremacist perspective (Anti-Defamation League, Alt-Right). Alt-righters see threats to traditional American values in issues such as LGBT rights and gay marriage, and they view multiculturalism (evinced by unchecked immigration) and pluralism of any kind as diluting the dominance of whites in the political realm. In the aftermath of Donald Trump's surprise victory in the U.S. presidential election in November 2016, Richard Spencer stood before the annual conference of the National Policy Institute and shouted, "Hail Trump, hail our people, hail victory!" (Lambroso and Appelbaum). The gesture, a Nazi salute reminiscent of the kind offered to Adolf Hitler, was in exaltation of Trump's victory, which Spencer and others saw as a boon for the cause of white America. As Spencer stated, "America was until this past generation a white country designed for ourselves and our posterity. It is our creation, it is our inheritance, and it belongs to us" (Lambroso and Appelbaum).

Though there is some debate as to whether white supremacism is waning or waxing in the United States (Shivani; Kimmel), there is no doubt that white supremacy movements and attitudes will continue inasmuch as "white supremacy as a type of group power is how individual white people in American society can still passively benefit from white racism and the psychological, material and political advantages it brings to their group" (DeVega).

See also: Alt-Right Movement; American Freedom Party; *American Renaissance*; Aryan Nations; Christian Identity; Council of Conservative Citizens; Identity Evropa; Ku Klux Klan; National Alliance; Neo-Nazis; *Occidental Observer*; The Order; Social Contract Press; Stormfront; VDARE; White Nationalism

FURTHER READING

Anti-Defamation League. "Alt-Right: A Primer about the New White Supremacy." Anti-Defamation League. https://www.adl.org/education/resources/backgrounders/alt-right-a-primer-about-the-new-white-supremacy. (Accessed May 20, 2017.)

Anti-Defamation League. "With Hate in Their Hearts: The State of White Supremacy in the United States." Anti-Defamation League. https://www.adl.org/education

/resources/reports/state-of-white-supremacy#white-supremacist-ideology. (Accessed January 30, 2019.)

DeVega, Chauncey. April 23, 2014. "10 Things Everyone Should Know about White Supremacy." Alternet.org. http://www.alternet.org/civil-liberties/10-things-everyone -should-know-about-white-supremacy. (Accessed May 20, 2017.)

Kimmel, Michael. November 17, 2013. "America's Angriest White Men: Up Close with Racism, Rage and Southern Supremacy." Salon. http://www.salon.com/2013/11/17 /americas_angriest_white_men_up_close_with_racism_rage_and_southern _supremacy/. (Accessed May 20, 2017.)

Lambroso, Daniel, and Yoni Appelbaum. November 21, 2016. "'Hail Trump!': White Nationalists Salute the President-Elect." *Atlantic.* http://www.theatlantic.com /politics/archive/2016/11/richard-spencer-speech-npi/508379/. (Accessed May 19, 2017.)

Potok, Mark. February 15, 2017. "The Year in Hate and Extremism." Southern Poverty Law Center: Intelligence Report. https://www.splcenter.org/fighting-hate/intelligence -report/2017/year-hate-and-extremism. (Accessed May 20, 2017.)

Shivani, Anis. April 23, 2017. "What Is 'White Supremacy?' A Brief History of a Term, and a Movement, That Continues to Haunt America." Salon. http://www.salon .com/2017/04/23/what-is-white-supremacy-a-brief-history-of-a-term-and-a -movement-that-continues-to-haunt-america/. (Accessed May 20, 2017.)

Southern Poverty Law Center. "White Nationalist." Southern Poverty Law Center. https:// www.splcenter.org/fighting-hate/extremist-files/ideology/white-nationalist. (Accessed August 18, 2018.)

Wolves of Vinland

The Wolves of Vinland (WoV) has been alternately described as a "white supremacist cult" (Woodruff, November 11, 2015), a tool of the alt-right movement to attract gay men into its ranks (Minkowitz), and a white separatist, neo-Volkisch movement that is intended to promote "ethnocentric beliefs in arguments for the necessity of separate societies, or tribes, to preserve all ethnicities" (Southern Poverty Law Center, Neo-Volkisch). WoV claims chapters in Colorado, Oregon, Tennessee, Washington, and Virginia (Southern Poverty Law Center, Hate Map). WoV has been described as

> a tribe of heathens, who worship a particularly Germanic strain of Wotanism, despise the modern world, and are invested in an anti-equality worldview. The Wolves eschew Christianity for what they recognize as the indigenous religion of those descended from true Europeans; heathenism or paganism. Myriad supremacists claim membership among them. (Hatewatch staff)

While the Southern Poverty Law Center (SPLC) characterizes WoV as a "neo-Volkisch" group, it notes that "violence rarely erupts from the neo-Volkisch movement" (Southern Poverty Law Center, Neo-Volkisch). Nevertheless, as noted by one commentator, "They are by no means pacifistic. They practice Germanic shamanism and MMA-style fisticuffing. They are, in fact, more-or-less a biker gang" (Wallace). In 2015, "two neo-pagan white supremacists" who fostered beliefs similar to WoV "allegedly conspired to bomb black churches" in order to start a race war (Woodruff, November 12, 2015).

The WoV was started roughly in 2006 by "white supremacist Paul Waggener along with his brother Mattias" (Rose City Antifa). The two brothers, "drawing from Nazi era Norse imagery, total misreadings of Germanic and Scandinavian paganism, Men's Rights Activist ideology, and drawing on the power lifting and black metal subcultures . . . cobbled together a 'tribalist' Evolian cadre organization" (Rose City Antifa). The theories of Julius Evola "are a primary influence on WoV":

> Evola's thought can be considered one of the most radically and consistently anti egalitarian, anti liberal, anti democratic, and anti popular systems in the twentieth century. . . . The esotericist Evola believed that the world, specifically the West, has been and is going through a decline rooted in materialism, a lack of spiritual awareness, and opposition to "masculine" principles. This final phase of decay and collapse is called the "Kali Yuga" (Evola borrows the concept from the Hindu cycle of Yugas.) This phase would be ended by willing individuals (called "aristocrats of the soul") bringing about a rebirth by implementing a "Traditional society"—basically a return to some imagined Golden Age. Evola wrote about Roman society with regard to this theory, but Evola's claims been applied to other western cultures as well. (Rose City Antifa)

As noted by one commentator:

> Evola's ideas have also been useful to more recent neofascist movements. These ideas are best known in Europe but dovetail neatly with American notions of the tough, heroic individual as well as anti-state sentiment among disaffected whites who feel their power in society slipping. Nothing is more astutely "American" than calls for cleansing violence without a party mechanism and a "dictator" in charge. (Rose City Antifa)

The members of WoV are "surprisingly candid about their practices, beliefs, and goals," and they have many "admirers within the white supremacist Internet sphere" (Woodruff, November 12, 2015). Perhaps most disturbing of WoV's practices is that of animal sacrifice. As noted by cofounder Matthias Waggener:

> [Animal sacrifice] is a tool that can heighten the function of the human mind to a state where it can open doors that appear closed or non-existent to the normal state of observation. . . . In this type of ritual you are "sacrificing" the life of the animal to achieve this state in order to gain the wisdom beyond those doors. With this wisdom we increase the effectiveness and potential of our actions that will in turn bring glory to ourselves and our Gods. This reconciles the practice back to one of Odinic sacrifice of Blood, and life for the attainment of knowledge to increase the life of those sacrificing. (Woodruff, November 11, 2015)

One practitioner of WoV, Jack Donovan—an openly gay white man—has extolled the virtues of violence in the pursuit of political and social goals. "The ability to use violence effectively is the highest value of masters," Donovan said before a fascist think tank in Germany. "It is the primary value of those who create order, who create worlds. Violence is a golden value. Violence rules. Violence is not evil—it is elemental" (Minkowitz). At a 2015 National Policy Institute conference, Donovan told a largely neo-Nazi crowd "to leave the world the way you entered it, kicking and screaming and covered in somebody else's blood" (Minkowitz). Donovan "calls women 'whores' and 'bitches,' and, when a questioner on Reddit asked him his views of the Holocaust, responded, 'What is this Holocaust thing? I'm drawing a blank'" (Minkowitz). Donovan has also stated that "real men want to 'control our borders,' decried the 'black-on-white crime rate,' denounced 'the deeply entrenched anti-white bias' of our culture, and said, 'I support White Nationalists,' who 'I call . . . The Mighty Whites'" (Minkowitz).

Donovan's attitudes are typical of the Wolves of Vinland group and the neo-Volkisch movement:

> [T]he ethnically or racially charged warrior ethos that the movement [neo-Volkisch] is largely premised on further entrenches belief systems that form the bedrock of contemporary notions of the relationship between volatile masculinity and nurturing femininity. Hyper-masculine imagery fetishized within neo-Völkisch spheres reinforces misogyny and traditional gender roles. This degradation and disrespect of women, often couched in a cherishing of women as the keepers of the home, echoes broader trends within the so-called "alt-right" that derive from the virulently anti-woman "manosphere," the online blogosphere-turned-movement supposedly rescuing masculinity from rabid feminists and other forces of political correctness. (Southern Poverty Law Center, Neo-Volkisch)

Though the membership in the Wolves of Vinland remains small, it is typical of white nationalist and white supremacist groups, being "comprised predominantly of working class, blue collar, once-upon-a-time criminal miscreants" (Wallace).

See also: Alt-Right Movement; National Policy Institute; Neo-Volkisch; White Supremacist Movement

FURTHER READING

Donovan, Jack. December 3, 2016. "The Only Way Forward Is Upward. Wolves of Vinland Announce Space Program." Jack Donovan.com. https://www.jack-donovan.com/axis/2016/12/wolves-of-vinland-announce-space-program/. (Accessed June 9, 2018.)

Hatewatch Staff. March 27, 2017. "A Chorus of Violence: Jack Donovan and the Organizing Power of Male Supremacy." Southern Poverty Law Center: Hatewatch. https://www.splcenter.org/hatewatch/2017/03/27/chorus-violence-jack-donovan-and-organizing-power-male-supremacy. (Accessed June 9, 2018.)

Minkowitz, Donna. June 5, 2017. "How the Alt-Right Is Using Sex and Camp to Attract Gay Men to Fascism." Slate. http://www.slate.com/blogs/outward/2017/06/05/how_alt_right_leaders_jack_donovan_and_james_o_meara_attract_gay_men_to.html. (Accessed June 9, 2018.)

Perry, David. May 31, 2017. "White Supremacists Love Vikings, but They've Got History All Wrong." *Washington Post*. https://www.washingtonpost.com/posteverything/wp/2017/05/31/white-supremacists-love-vikings-but-theyve-got-history-all-wrong/. (Accessed June 9, 2018.)

Rose City Antifa. November 7, 2016. "The Wolves of Vinland: A Fascist Countercultural 'Tribe' in the Pacific Northwest." Rose City Antifa. https://rosecityantifa.org/articles/the-wolves-of-vinland-a-fascist-countercultural-tribe-in-the-pacific-northwest/. (Accessed June 9, 2018.)

Ross, Alexander Reid. March 29, 2017. "The Left-Overs: How Fascists Court the Post-Left." Anti-Fascist News. https://antifascistnews.net/tag/wolves-of-vinland/. (Accessed June 9, 2018.)

Southern Poverty Law Center. "Hate Map by State." Southern Poverty Law Center. https://www.splcenter.org/hate-map/by-state. (Accessed June 9, 2018.)

Southern Poverty Law Center. "Neo-Volkisch." Southern Poverty Law Center. https://www.splcenter.org/fighting-hate/extremist-files/ideology/neo-volkisch. (Accessed June 9, 2018.)

Wallace, Eric. May 5, 2015. "Eco Punks: The Wolves of Vinland Badasses Dare You to Re-Wild Yourself." Blue Ridge Outdoors. https://web.archive.org/web/20151119022642/http://www.blueridgeoutdoors.com/go-outside/eco-punks-the-wolves-of-vinland-badasses-dare-you-to-re-wild-yourself/. (Accessed June 9, 2018.)

Woodruff, Betsy. November 11, 2015. "Inside Virginia's Church-Burning Werewolf White Supremacist Cult." Daily Beast. https://www.thedailybeast.com/inside-virginias-church-burning-werewolf-white-supremacist-cult. (Accessed June 9, 2018.)

Woodruff, Betsy. November 12, 2015. "Inside Virginia's Creepy White-Power Wolf Cult." Daily Beast. https://www.thedailybeast.com/inside-virginias-creepy-white-power-wolf-cult. (Accessed June 9, 2018.)

World Congress of Families

According to its website, "the World Congress of Families (WCF) convenes major international public events to unite and equip leaders, organizations, and families to affirm, celebrate, and defend the natural family as the only fundamental and sustainable unit of society" (International Organization for the Family). The WCF also supports publications that inform and inspire "leaders to promote the natural family as the fundamental group unit of society and to protect the sanctity and dignity of all human life" (International Organization for the Family). According to the Southern Poverty Law Center (SPLC), WCF is an anti-LGBT hate group, as it uses the guise of the "natural family" to "curtail LGBT and reproductive rights across the world" (Southern Poverty Law Center). The Human Rights Campaign (HRC), an organization dedicated to LGBT equality, notes that the WCF "fosters homophobia and transphobia" and "is connected to some mainstream conservative organizations and to the very highest levels of government in the countries where it operates" (Human Rights Campaign). Because of its political connections, WCF "has had an outsized influence on anti-LGBTQ (lesbian, gay, bisexual, transgender, queer) sentiment and legislation in many places" (Human Rights Campaign).

WCF was founded in 1997 as part of the International Organization for the Family (IOF), which "functions predominantly as an international organizer of fellow Christian Right individuals and organizations" (Southern Poverty Law Center). According to the SPLC:

> Through its ideology of the so-called "natural family," WCF promotes a strict view of family, one based exclusively on the marriage of one heterosexual man to one heterosexual woman and their biological children, to the exclusion of many different types of families. Closely tied to this ideology is an adherence to strict binary gender roles, in which men serve as the heads of households and women as their helpmates and the bearer of children. Only this type of family, they contend, can quell the "demographic winter," the idea that European populations, especially, are

in decline because of homosexuality, abortion, feminism, women in the workplace, and a variety of other things that deviate from the "natural family." (Southern Poverty Law Center)

WCF was founded, in part, as a reaction to concerns about the drop in European population that became acute after the end of the Cold War. Some theorists believed that demographic decline was the result of "sexual and feminist liberation" (Southern Poverty Law Center). The "natural family—one man married to one woman and their biological children—later emerged as the WCF's unifying doctrine, with anti-LGBT sentiment eventually gaining a bigger place in WCF congresses to help paper over cultural differences" (Southern Poverty Law Center). The natural family, according to the SPLC,

> has since become shorthand for the American Christian Right's global political program, one opposed to marriage equality and to reproductive rights, which still embraced free-market liberalism, believed in small government and in the family as the basic economic unit of society.
> Retrograde in its outlook, the doctrine of WCF's natural family embraces a world of villages and towns where the heterosexual family reigns supreme. By promoting one definition of the family, it simultaneously seeks to deny rights to other types of families, including LGBT people, single and divorced parents, and parents raising children of other family members. (Southern Poverty Law Center)

WCF's emphasis on "demographic winter"—the belief that Europe and other white societies are losing demographic ground to "hundreds of thousands of illegal immigrants"—is the result of "fewer marriages . . . producing fewer children and the population is aging and therefore declining" (Southern Poverty Law Center). Allan Carlson, president of WCF, has published several books on demographic shifts, colloquially known by the WCF and its adherents as "demographic winter." However, according to the organization known as Political Research Associates:

> Carlson argues that declining birth rates threaten the decline of civilization—Western civilization. As researcher and journalist Kathryn Joyce puts it, "The concern is not a general lack of babies, but the cultural shifts that come when some populations, particularly immigrant communities, are feared to be out-procreating others." Put another way, the demographic winter thesis cultivates racism and xenophobia in support of exclusionary "natural family" policies. A main objective of the WCF's demographic scare tactics is to convert nationalism into natalism, and thereby mobilize a larger anti-abortion, "natural family" base. (Natalism prioritizes human procreation, including public policies that reward birthing children.) (Parke)

Given the nativist movements that have seen a resurgence in Europe in recent years, enthusiasm for the "demographic winter" thesis and the emphasis on the "natural family" have found fertile ground, particularly in Eastern Europe, where the "WCF currently appears to be focusing major organizational efforts" (Southern Poverty Law Center).

See also: Alliance Defending Freedom; American College of Pediatricians; American Family Association; Family Research Council; Family Watch International; Pacific Justice Institute; Ruth Institute; Traditional Values Coalition; Westboro Baptist Church

FURTHER READING

Human Rights Campaign. "Exposed: The World Congress of Families." Human Rights Campaign. https://www.hrc.org/resources/exposed-the-world-congress-of-families. (Accessed June 23, 2018.)

International Organization for the Family. "Mission." International Organization for the Family. http://profam.org/mission/. (Accessed June 23, 2018.)

Parke, Cole. January 21, 2015. "Natural Deception: Conned by the World Congress of Families." Political Research Associates. http://www.politicalresearch.org/2015 /01/21/natural-deception-conned-by-the-world-congress-of-families/#sthash .Em2cJr0V.n5zXMPmj.dpbs. (Accessed June 23, 2018.)

Right Wing Watch. "World Congress of Families." Right Wing Watch. http://www.right wingwatch.org/organizations/world-congress-of-families/. (Accessed June 23, 2018.)

Southern Poverty Law Center. "World Congress of Families." Southern Poverty Law Center. https://www.splcenter.org/fighting-hate/extremist-files/group/world-congress -families. (Accessed June 23, 2018.)

World Congress of Families. http://www.worldcongressoffamilies.org/. (Accessed June 23, 2018.)

WorldNetDaily

WorldNetDaily (WND), founded in 1997 by Joseph and Elizabeth Farah, considers itself "an independent news company dedicated to uncompromising journalism, seeking truth and justice and revitalizing the role of the free press as a guardian of liberty" (WorldNetDaily, About WND). The Southern Poverty Law Center (SPLC), however, categorizes WND as an organization whose "pages are devoted to manipulative fear-mongering and outright fabrications designed to further the paranoid, gay-hating, conspiratorial and apocalyptic visions of Farah and his hand-picked contributors from the fringes of the far-right and fundamentalist worlds" (Southern Poverty Law Center). The organization Media Bias/Fact Check, which is an "independent online media outlet . . . dedicated to educating the public on media bias and deceptive news practices," has labeled WND a "right bias" source (Media Bias/Fact Check, WND).

WND has been characterized as an "alt-right website" (Blake) that "dabbles in right wing conspiracies such as President Obama's birth certificate. They also use misleading clickbait headlines that do not always match the content of the article" (Media Bias/Fact Check, WND). According to the SPLC:

> Fear-mongering is WorldNetDaily's specialty. It regularly publishes paranoid fantasies billed as fact, such as a baseless six-part series claiming that soybean consumption causes homosexuality. It has heavily promoted The Pink Swastika, a wretched opus by gay-basher Scott Lively that claims gay men orchestrated the Holocaust. WND also fingered Satan as the first leftist, and trumpeted a secret 20-point Muslim plan "for conquering the United States by 2020." Another secret plan WND has warned about concerns international elites' alleged intention to create a "North American Union" that merges Mexico, the United States and Canada. (Southern Poverty Law Center)

WND regularly features in its columns race baiters, homophobes, and white nationalists. It also profits from selling products online. The WND Superstore

> offers "Unique Products for Discerning Minds." Such minds apparently crave items like the NRA-endorsed Second Amendment Range Pack, designed to hold four pistols and 36 magazines in an attractive carry-all imprinted with the words of the Second Amendment. The superstore also offers 830 books on "history, theology, philosophy, political science, education, natural science, society, and family." These are "thoroughly examined" by WND's "review board" to "enlighten and empower you in your personal quest to protect your family, engage the culture, speak out against injustice, and fight for what is right." (Southern Poverty Law Center)

See also: Alt-Right Movement; White Nationalism

FURTHER READING

Blake, Aaron. December 1, 2016. "Introducing the 'Alt-Left': The GOP's Response to Its Alt-Right Problem." https://www.washingtonpost.com/news/the-fix/wp/201612/01/meet-the-alt-left-the-gops-response-to-its-alt-right-problem/. (Accessed June 23, 2018.)

Borchers, Callum. August 12, 2016. "The Highly Reliable, Definitely-Not-Crazy Places Where Donald Trump Gets His News." *Washington Post*. https://www.washingtonpost.com/news/the-fix/wp/2016/08/12/the-highly-reliable-definitely-not-crazy-places-where-donald-trump-gets-his-news/. (Accessed June 23, 2018.)

Bruno, Debra. February 21, 2016. "There's the Major Media. And Then There's the 'Other' White House Press Corps." *Washington Post*. https://www.washingtonpost.com/lifestyle/style/theres-the-major-media-and-then-theres-the-other-white-house-press-corps/2016/02/21/f69c5f92-c460-11e5-8965-0607e0e265ce_story.html. (Accessed June 23, 2018.)

Media Bias/Fact Check. "About." Media Bias/Fact Check. https://mediabiasfactcheck.com/about/. (Accessed June 23, 2018.)

Media Bias/Fact Check. "World Net Daily (WND)." Media Bias/Fact Check. https://mediabiasfactcheck.com/world-net-daily-wnd/. (Accessed June 23, 2018.)

Nelson, Leah. August 25, 2012. "WorldNet Daily Continues to Pump Out Outrageous Propaganda." Southern Poverty Law Center: Intelligence Report. https://www.splcenter.org/fighting-hate/intelligence-report/2012/worldnet-daily-continues-pump-out-outrageous-propaganda. (Accessed June 23, 2018.)

Nelson, Leah. October 23, 2012. "WorldNetDaily Now Peddling White Nationalism." Southern Poverty Law Center: Hatewatch. https://www.splcenter.org/hatewatch/2012/10/23/worldnetdaily-now-peddling-white-nationalism. (Accessed June 23, 2018.)

Southern Poverty Law Center. "WorldNetDaily." Southern Poverty Law Center. https://www.splcenter.org/fighting-hate/extremist-files/group/worldnetdaily. (Accessed June 23, 2018.)

WorldNetDaily. "About WND." http://www.wnd.com/about-wnd/. (Accessed June 23, 2018.)

WorldNetDaily. June 20, 2018. "WorldNetDaily: SPLC Apologizes, Pays Up, for 'Hate' Labeling." WorldNetDaily. http://www.irli.org/single-post/2018/06/20/WorldNetDaily-SPLC-apologizes-pays-up-for-hate-labeling. (Accessed June 23, 2018.)

Y

Youth for Western Civilization

Youth for Western Civilization (YWC) was founded in 2008 by Kevin Deanna, a white supremacist who has vowed "to defend Western culture from the perils of radical multiculturalism" (Southern Poverty Law Center). Echoing the message of other white supremacists, such as former Colorado Congressman Tom Tancredo (who, at one time, was YWC's honorary chairman) and Jared Taylor, founder and editor of the white supremacist magazine *American Renaissance*, YWC defines itself as "a campus youth movement with a mission to organize, educate and train activists dedicated to the revival of Western Civilization" (Gomez). The group declares itself to be fighting against "illegal immigration, affirmative action, radical multiculturalism, and leftist curricula" (Gomez).

Before founding YWC, Kevin Deanna became infamous running a conservative student newspaper at the College of William and Mary that became known for its derogatory and demeaning portrayals of women. Deanna was also a member of Young Americans for Freedom, which, in 2007, organized several racist events at Michigan State University, including a "Catch an Illegal Alien Day" game and a "Koran desecration contest." The Young Americans for Freedom group also "jokingly threatened to distribute small-pox infected blankets to Native American students," posted "Gays spread AIDS" flyers, and "called Latino students and faculty members 'savages' " (For Student Power). The following year, in 2008, Deanna founded YWC in concert with Marcus Epstein, who had pleaded guilty to the use of racial epithets and assault against a black woman in 2007. Both Deanna and Epstein would meet Richard Spencer, founder of the alt-right, later that year, before the founding of YWC.

In 2009, YWC made its first impact on the white nationalist community when it cosponsored the annual Conservative Political Action Conference (CPAC), "the right wing's most important annual shindig" (Southern Poverty Law Center). At 2011's annual CPAC meeting, Deanna appeared with Colorado's Tom Tancredo, also YWC's honorary chairman, who argued that immigration and multiculturalism were the "daggers pointed at the heart of Western civilization" (Southern Poverty Law Center). Deanna argued that immigration was bad "because it's about our dispossession as a people" (Southern Poverty Law Center).

After his appearance at the 2011 CPAC meeting, Deanna was interviewed by Christian Gomez of the *New American*. In explaining the views of YWC, Deanna told Gomez why multiculturalism, in the minds of YWC followers, was such an important concern:

Pat Buchanan was right—the death of the west is happening; what else matters?

Because if you cannot reverse that—if you do not have an actual United States of America that exists as a real entity any more—it's irrelevant to talk about the Constitution . . . limited government . . . national sovereignty, because the thing you are defending is already gone. And especially on a college campus this would be an important point I would make ([particularly] for older readers), that [the] sense of American identify connected with . . . a real authentic American history has been totally removed.

So when you are appealing to the Constitution or . . . to limited government, these things have no resonance with a lot of young Americans, except for . . . being a vaguely "racist" remnant of a terrible past. So if you are not going to combat that, how are you going to get back to a constitutional government—how are you going to get back to limited government? (Gomez)

On its official website, YWC states that "[t]he end goal of Youth for Western Civilization is an awakening of young Westerners that will fight for their heritage and their liberties against leftist occupation and restore sanity to American universities" (For Student Power).

See also: Alt-Right Movement; *American Renaissance*

FURTHER READING

For Student Power. "Youth for Western Civilization." Forstudenpower.org. http://www .forstudentpower.org/youth-for-western-civilization. (Accessed May 24, 2018.)

Gomez, Christian. February 16, 2011. "Youth for Western Civilization." *New American*. https://www.thenewamerican.com/culture/education/item/256-youth-for-western -civilization. (Accessed May 24, 2018.)

Potok, Mark, and Eveylyn Schlatter. August 24, 2011. "The Company They Keep." Southern Poverty Law Center: Intelligence Report. https://www.splcenter.org/fighting -hate/intelligence-report/2015/company-they-keep. (Accessed May 24, 2018.)

Southern Poverty Law Center. "Kevin Deanna." Southern Poverty Law Center. https:// www.splcenter.org/fighting-hate/extremist-files/individual/kevin-deanna. (Accessed May 24, 2018.)

Index

Note: Page numbers in **bold** indicate the location of main entries

About the Author

Barry J. Balleck, PhD, is professor and chair of the Department of Political Science and International Studies at Georgia Southern University. He received a bachelor of arts degree in political science and a master's degree in international studies from Brigham Young University. Balleck received his doctorate in political science from the University of Colorado at Boulder with emphases in international relations, American politics, and political theory, and then joined the faculty of Georgia Southern University, where he held a joint appointment in both the Department of Political Science and the Center for International Studies. For the past 20 years, he has also directed Georgia Southern University's Model United Nations (MUN) program, one of the oldest and most continuous programs of its kind in the country. Balleck's primary research and teaching interests are in the fields of international and domestic terrorism, U.S. foreign policy, the rhetoric of politics, the United Nations, and international human rights. He has dozens of conference presentations to his credit and has published in such journals as *Presidential Studies Quarterly, Politics & Policy,* and *Peace Psychology Review.* His books include *Allegiance to Liberty: The Changing Face of Patriots, Militias, and Political Violence in America* and *Modern American Extremism and Domestic Terrorism: An Encyclopedia of Extremists and Extremist Groups.*